A Critical Biography,
New and Revised Edition

Franz Schulze and
Edward Windhorst

Mies van der Rohe

The University of Chicago Press
CHICAGO AND LONDON

Franz Schulze is the Hollender Professor of Art Emeritus at Lake Forest
College. His many books include *Philip Johnson: Life and Work* and, as
coauthor, *Chicago's Famous Buildings*, the latter also published by the
University of Chicago Press.

Edward Windhorst studied architecture with Myron Goldsmith at the Illinois
Institute of Technology. He has written two books about modernism in
Chicago.

The University of Chicago Press, Chicago 60637
The University of Chicago Press, Ltd., London
© 2012 by The University of Chicago
All rights reserved. Published 2012.
Printed in the United States of America

21 20 19 18 17 16 15 14 13 12   1 2 3 4 5

ISBN-13: 978-0-226-75600-4 (cloth)
ISBN-13: 978-0-226-75602-8 (e-book)
ISBN-10: 0-226-75600-9 (cloth)
ISBN-10: 0-226-75602-5 (e-book)

Library of Congress Cataloging-in-Publication Data

Schulze, Franz, 1927–
    Mies van der Rohe : a critical biography / Franz Schulze and
  Edward Windhorst. — New and revised edition.
      pages.   cm.
    Includes bibliographical references and index.
    ISBN 978-0-226-75600-4 (hardcover : alkaline paper)—
  ISBN 0-226-75600-9 (hardcover : alkaline paper)—
  ISBN 978-0-226-75602-8 (e-book)—ISBN 0-226-75602-5 (e-book)
  1. Mies van der Rohe, Ludwig, 1886–1969.   2. Architects—Biography.
  3. Architecture, Modern—20th century.   I. Windhorst, Edward.   II. Title.
  NA1088.M65S38 2012
  720.92—dc23
  [B]

2011050382

♾ This paper meets the requirements of ANSI/NISO Z39.48-1992
(Permanence of Paper).

Contents

Illustrations

Preface

A quarter century has passed since the 1985 release of *Mies van der Rohe: A Critical Biography*, by Franz Schulze. In the intervening years, so much new material has emerged that it is time for this new and expanded edition, by co-authors Schulze and architect Edward Windhorst. Our text addresses its subject in substantially different form from other recent scholarship on Mies. Most important is our analytical and critical commentary on his built and unbuilt work. We subject Mies's buildings and projects to sometimes intensive examination, chiefly from an architect's perspective and only secondarily in the context of a broader art historical narrative. And while we believe in the excellence of Mies's building art, we offer negative assessments where called for.

In matters biographical, we have uncovered facts that significantly extend and clarify what is known of Mies's career. By our own efforts, and with the help of colleagues — and happy accident — we have identified the architect's earliest known drawings, studies for the design of his first house. And in a major find that corrects and illuminates the story of one of the architect's seminal buildings, the Farnsworth House, we have for the first time located and analyzed the transcript of the famous trial that pitted Mies against his client, Edith Farnsworth. The struggle that played out in the courtroom of a small Illinois town during the early 1950s is brought to life in this document, which discloses new information about Mies's design intentions, the history of the house, and the relationship of architect to client. The six hundred pages of Mies's transcribed testimony constitute an unequaled cache of his talk and thinking.

Our new and revised edition addresses a number of topics touched on slightly or not at all in the first: details of the relationship between Mies and the developer Herbert Greenwald; the workings of Mies's American office and the role played by significant figures in his employ, among them Bruno Conterato, Edward Duckett, Joseph Fujikawa, Myron Goldsmith, Dirk Lohan, and Gene Summers; the activity of fellow faculty in Germany and Chicago, Ludwig Hilberseimer, Walter Peterhans, and Alfred Caldwell; the character of Mies's commitment to architectural education and his effectiveness as a teacher; his understanding of the arts of painting and sculpture, with special attention to his collecting; and information, newly learned, about his family and romantic attachments. We also use significant additional material from candid interviews with Mies's American companion, Lora Marx, conducted by one of us (Schulze). We have much more to say in this edition about Mies's personal and professional relationship with his colleague Lilly Reich; about his well-known interest in philosophy; and about the intellectual background of his European years. Our closing chapter treats Mies's personality and character as perceived by his American students, colleagues, friends, and adversaries, and a major appendix examines some of the best buildings of his most important students and followers. A second appendix recounts and assesses the history of Mies's reception by scholars and in exhibitions, while finally, a brief afterword lists the most important publications with Mies as subject.

We have undertaken this project respectful of other major publications with Mies as principal subject. They include *Ludwig Mies van der Rohe: Furniture and Furniture Drawings from the Design Collection and the Mies van der Rohe Archive, the Museum of Modern Art* (1977), by Ludwig Glaeser; *Mies van der Rohe: The Villas and Country Houses* (1985), by Wolf Tegethoff; *The Mies van der Rohe Archive*, an illustrated catalog of the Mies drawings in the Museum of Modern Art, in twenty volumes, four edited by Arthur Drexler (1986) and sixteen by one of us (Schulze) and George E. Danforth (1990, 1992); and Fritz Neumeyer's *The Artless Word: Mies van der Rohe on the Building Art* (1991). We are also indebted to substantial volumes that accompanied exhibitions: *Mies in Berlin* (2001), edited by Terence Riley and Barry Bergdoll, and *Mies in America* (2001), edited by Phyllis Lambert.

Our own work occupies what we believe to be a unique place in Miesian scholarship. The above-mentioned studies have each concentrated on specific aspects of the Mies story rather than all of it. This book concerns itself in depth with the man and his architecture. Insofar as Mies can be treated in a single volume, we have attempted to be synoptic.

Prologue

The subject of this study is the most remarkable two-act career in modern architecture. By the late 1920s, still in his early forties, Ludwig Mies van der Rohe—born Maria Ludwig Michael Mies, third son of a provincial stonemason—had become the leading architectural representative of Germany's avant-garde. A combination of talent, will, and extraordinary self-education had already produced two of the architectural masterpieces of the twentieth century: the German Pavilion of the Barcelona International Exposition (1929), commonly known as the Barcelona Pavilion, and the Tugendhat House in Brno, Czechoslovakia (1930).

As it turned out, these two buildings were the last material triumphs of a European career that would last almost another decade. During that span a world economic crisis and the related rise of German National Socialism destroyed the modernist program in central Europe. By the mid-1930s, his professional future in grave doubt, Mies could no longer afford to ignore invitations tendered by academic institutions outside Germany. In 1938 he finally accepted a faculty position in Chicago. Yet sudden and unexpected pressure from the Gestapo turned an orderly move into a race for the border.

Mies the émigré could count himself lucky and luckless. Both his destination and promise of livelihood were the fruits of his international reputation. But he was fifty-two years old, and his only language was German. He had left behind, perhaps forever, family and colleagues; he was also forced to abandon an architectural practice and a hard-won professional independence of twenty years' standing. It was a difficult end to his life in Europe, and an uncertain beginning to the final chapter of his career.

It is a marvel that Mies, having put down roots in the United States, shortly emerged as a force in American architecture. As an educator at Illinois Institute of Technology and as the designer of a modern campus for that school, he was at last building on a large scale and with authentic artistic freedom. A return to Germany was unthinkable; he liked America, and America liked him.

During his second career, Mies believed that he had developed a new architectural *language*—a set of principles and methods that could be taught and passed on within the profession, reflecting the realities, values, and possibilities of what he called "the epoch." Using this language, during the 1950s and 1960s he produced a series of masterworks, beginning with the celebrated Lake Shore Drive Apartments and the Farnsworth House, continuing with

S. R. Crown Hall, the Seagram Building, and Chicago's Federal Center, and ending, in a poignant personal circle, with the New National Gallery in Berlin.

Though he insisted on the objectivity of his architecture and especially the central role of what he termed "a clear structure," it is now evident, four decades after his death, that Mies's architecture was personal and inimitable, and that his finest works were the product of his own searching solitude. The epoch of glass and steel associated with Mies would be brief; new technologies and new performance imperatives rendered his steel-and-glass tectonics obsolete even before his death. Yet his buildings, projects, professional influence, and educational and personal legacy remain. Their elucidation and celebration are the aim of this book.

Youth in Imperial Germany: 1886 – 1905 $\boxed{1}$

We made drawings the size of a whole quarter of a room ceiling, which we would then send on to the model makers. I did this every day for two years. Even now I can draw cartouches with my eyes closed.   **MIES**, recalling his on-the-job education

Go to Berlin; that's where things are happening.
ARCHITECT DÜLOW, advising his friend Ludwig Mies

Nothing about Mies's early life prefigures significant professional achievement. Aachen, Germany, where he was born and grew up, was and had been a provincial city for centuries. Until adulthood he never traveled more than a few miles beyond its borders. His forebears, stonemasons for generations, were proud of their calling, but only as ambitious as the trade required. His formal education was comparably limited. Any native intellectual or creative gift, even if evident, was unlikely to have been nurtured by those around him. Thus, he remained in Aachen until he was nineteen, living with his parents and following a predetermined path of long standing.

Though in reputation Aachen then ranked below a dozen other German cities, it looked back on an impressive history. Late in the eighth century, Charlemagne made it the center of his empire, the first great unified state in northern Europe, a domain that extended from the Pyrenees to Saxony and from the North Sea to Rome. Scholars of the Carolingian court generated the earliest major revival of the classical spirit in the West. Charlemagne's personal identification with the emperors of Rome, together with his passionate admiration of Roman culture — and the fateful alliance he forged with the pope — contributed seminally to the shape of the Middle Ages and the emergence of the Renaissance.

Aachen was the site of Charlemagne's long-vanished palace, which stood across a courtyard from the splendid ninth-century domed chapel that survives (fig. 1.1). Designed by Odo of Metz after the example of the Byzantine Church of San Vitale in Ravenna, it was the most sophisticated northern European building of its time, and served as the coronation hall for German kings for six hundred years. Mies knew the chapel as a boy and remembered it as a man. He had stood in awe of the powerful piers and the octagonal dome they support: "One could apprehend everything that went on. The whole space was

FIGURE 1.1
(*facing*).
Interior of the
Palatine Chapel,
Aachen, begun in
792 and conse-
crated by Pope Leo
III in 805. Designed
for Charlemagne
by Odo of Metz, the
octagonal domed
chapel is the most
important surviving
example of Carolin-
gian architecture.
Mies's family wor-
shipped here when
he was a child.
Photo courtesy of
M. Jeiter.

a unity, everywhere alive with the sights and sounds of the ceremony, even the smells of it."[1] Late in life he recalled accompanying his mother to morning Mass, where he sat in rapt silence, transfixed by the mighty stones that make up the piers and arches.

The cathedral proper, of which the chapel is a part, consists of a fifteenth-century Gothic choir surrounded by a veritable wall of glass surmounted by spidery vaults. It stands in the oldest part of town, a maze of narrow streets and medieval houses mostly of brick, intimately related to the building traditions of Holland and Belgium, the borders of which lie within walking distance of Aachen's city limits. Mies described these anonymous buildings with embracing affection: "Mostly simple, but very clear.... [They] did not belong to any epoch.... [They] had been there for a thousand years and were still impressive.... All the great styles passed, but they remained.... They were *really* built."[2] This is mature Miesian sentiment as we know it from published pronouncements: affirmation of clarity and simplicity in the design and construction of buildings, especially as apparent over the reach of time, balanced by the negation of individuality and "style."

Yet there was much of "style" and clamorous change in the Aachen of Mies's youth, especially in parts he would have known better than the chapel and its environs. He was born March 27, 1886, in a house at Steinkaulstrasse 29 (fig. 1.2). His family moved several times during his childhood, but remained in the same neighborhood until he was fifteen; it is therefore likely that in the 1890s he witnessed the rebuilding of the Oppenhoffallee, a kilometer to the south. The Oppenhoffallee was and remains an elegant boulevard lined by buildings characteristic of Wilhelmine architectural decoration at its most unbridled. At the time of Mies's birth, less than a generation after unification and victory over the French in 1870, Germany had taken on a new national identity bound up with military power. National pride and confidence swelled during the eighties and nineties, and along with it ambition, abetted by the explosively swift pace of German industrialization.

Aachen fully bore out the image. In 1825 its population was 35,428. By 1886, at Mies's birth, it passed 100,000, and by 1905, when he left for good, it was 145,000. While Aachen continued to enjoy the tourist trade that had been drawn to its hot sulfur springs since Roman times (Aachen means "water" in Old German), it now witnessed a flash growth of industry. Traditionally a textile center, in the years following German unification it exploited the extensive nearby coalfields. By the 1890s, the largest and best-equipped steelworks in Germany, Aachen's Rothe Erde, employed five thousand workers.

This furious activity was reflected in institutional proliferation. The Technical Institute (Rheinisch-Westfälische Technische Hochschule) was founded in 1870, eventually gaining a reputation as the most distinguished traditionally oriented architecture school in northwestern Germany. (Mies might have

FIGURE 1.2.
Steinkaulstrasse 29, Aachen, birth-
place of Mies van der Rohe. Photo by
Tim Brown (Creative Commons).

studied there had his family been inclined and able to send him.) A main post
office was completed in 1893, in neo-Romanesque style, with a portal flanked
by larger-than-life statues of Kaiser Wilhelm I and Charlemagne. Twelve years
later, the new train station opened, its Jugendstil—the German equivalent of
art nouveau—reflecting the latest in turn-of-the-century fashion. The municipal trolley system was electrified in 1892, and motion pictures were shown at
the Kurhaus as early as 1896. The fourteenth-century Town Hall, a huge edifice
built on the foundations of Charlemagne's palace and badly damaged by fire
in 1883, was redesigned three years later and rebuilt by 1903, its two towers
inflated to the grandiose scale beloved of the period (fig. 1.3).

. . .

Most of the little we know of Mies's family background is gleaned from records
in the Aachen *Stadtarchiv*. As far back as can be traced—the late eighteenth
century—his family on both sides were Catholics of German stock who lived
close to the Dreiländereck, the "three-country corner" where Holland, Belgium, Germany, and their respective cultures meet. His father, Michael Mies,
was the first of either line born in Aachen proper, in 1851. Michael's father,

6 / 7

Jakob, born in Blankenheim in the Eifel in 1814, first appears in the 1855 Aachen address book as a marble carver. Amalie Rohe, Mies's mother, was born in Monschau, a picturesque suburb of Aachen, in 1843. She was eight years older than Michael Mies, and thirty-three when they married in 1876 (fig. 1.4).

During the 1870s, Jakob Mies shared a "marble business and atelier" with his son Carl, Michael's older brother, at Adalbertstrasse 116. Michael, who joined the business later, is listed in the 1875 address book as a marble worker. His name does not appear again until the edition of 1880, and by then his marriage to Amalie had produced a male child, Ewald Philipp, born October 13, 1877, first son, heir and *Stammhalter* (preserver of the line), a familial designation of considerable importance in nineteenth-century Germany.

Michael and Amalie now lived at Steinkaulstrasse 29, where their other four children were born: Carl Michael, second oldest, born May 18, 1879 (died aged two, the cause unrecorded); Anna Maria Elisabeth, born September 16, 1881; Maria Johanna Sophie, born December 30, 1883; and the youngest, Maria Ludwig Michael, who would become Ludwig Mies van der Rohe in the early 1920s, when by his own lights he linked his father's and mother's surnames with the invented "van der."

The Steinkaulstrasse is outside and east of the limits of Aachen's ancient second wall (today replaced by streets), not far from the Adalbertsteinweg (a continuation of the Adalbertstrasse), where Michael, listed as a master mason by 1883, and Carl, identified as a sculptor, took over the family business after

FIGURE 1.3. Town Hall, Aachen, in 1903. Constructed in the Gothic manner in the fourteenth century, it was renovated a number of times, each in the style of the day. Two baroque-era flanking towers and most of the roof were lost in a fire in 1883. In 1886 a restoration was carried out to the neo-Gothic plans of Darmstadt architect Friedrich Puetzer. Photo: Stadtarchiv Aachen.

Youth in Imperial Germany

FIGURE 1.4.
Mies's parents,
Amalie, née Rohe
(1843–1928), and
Michael Mies (1851–
1927), in 1921.
Private collection.

their father's death about 1888. This was the fastest-growing part of Aachen in the 1880s and 1890s. Rents were still low, and it was close to the city's cemeteries, an important factor for a business specializing in gravestones.

Within the Mies enterprise, Michael ran the studio and Carl handled sales. There were frequent trips to Paris and occasionally even as far as North African quarries. By 1893 two new cemeteries had opened on the west side of Aachen, prompting Michael to establish a branch there in 1895. By 1901 he and his eldest, the twenty-four-year-old Ewald, now also a master mason, had moved family and studio to the Vaalserstrasse, the road to the Netherlands.

Ludwig was then fifteen. His family was middle-class—more exactly craftsman/middle-class—in the preindustrial sense of the term; Michael Mies's children were at home with objects and craft rather than ideas and commerce. Uncle Carl was the salesman during the heady 1880s, but father Michael was always happiest with the tools of his trade.

The chief source of what we know of early experiences pertinent to Mies's professional destiny is a 1968 conversation with his grandson, the architect Dirk Lohan:

> *Lohan*: When you were very young, were you obliged to help in the family atelier?
>
> *Mies*: I did it for the fun of it. And always when we had vacations. I especially remember that on All Souls Day, when so many people wanted new monuments for the graves, our whole family pitched in. I did the lettering on the stones, my brother did the carving, and my sisters put the finishing touches on them, the gold leaf, and all that. I don't think we added very much to the process, but it probably was a little better for it.[3]

Mies described his father as a craftsman reluctant to act the businessman, who collided unavoidably with changing times and values: "About the economics of capitalist speculation he understood nothing. 'To make this thing,' he would say to a customer, 'I need three weeks. And it will cost so-and-so much, to be paid when I deliver it.' That was the craftsman's way, not the merchant's. There was no room in it for flexibility, for consideration of long-term profits as opposed to short-term gains, that could carry the business over hard times." On Mies's visits home after he moved to Berlin, he listened to Ewald debate their father. "My brother would say, 'Look, we can produce such-and-such an ornament without all that fuss, especially if it is way up high on a building façade where no one can look closely at it.' My father wanted no part of that. 'You're none of you stonemasons anymore!' he would say. 'You know the finial at the top of the spire of the cathedral at Cologne? Well, you can't crawl up there and get a good look at it, but it is carved as if you could. It was made for God.'"[4]

Despite Michael's reverence for tradition, he could not afford to live in the past; Germany's industrial revolution and the kaiser's new empire saw to that. Since the passing of the guild system, training in the crafts had moved to schools, where a dash of theory had been added to the rule of thumb. Ludwig, aged ten, was sent off from the elementary to the cathedral school, which he attended from 1896 to 1899. We surmise that he was a promising student, since the cathedral school enjoyed a substantial reputation throughout the Rhineland. Yet late in life he told an interviewer that he was "not very good," implying that his abilities were more practical than intellectual.[5] At thirteen he might have been finished with schooling altogether, but his father sent him on — as he had Ewald — for two years at the Spenrathschule, the trade school, having secured a full-tuition scholarship for each, thereby indicating his faith in their schooling to the limits of the family's ambition and circumstances.

"The trade school," Mies recollected, "was not the same as a crafts school. It offered the kind of two-year course that would enable a graduate to get a job in an office or a workshop. Great stress was laid on drawing, because it was something everybody had to know. You understand, the curriculum was no theoretically contrived program. It was based on experience, on the sort of thing tradesmen really had to use." He added that Aachen had other technical schools "of a higher level," with four-year programs, like the machine construction and building construction schools. He also mentioned the *Hochschule*, which offered a theoretical curriculum. Yet his heart belonged to those practically trained: "They were flawless in their work habits. I would rather have dealt with them than with anyone from the *Hochschule*. They could draw expertly—a roof frame for example, that was perfect in detail. What you needed on a job, that is what they learned to do, masterfully."[6]

Mies was eighty-two when these words were recorded, and had long since rationalized his training. That he never matriculated at the Aachen *Hochschule* may in part explain his sympathy with architectural education grounded in the facts of building. If he had little formal learning, he earned his calluses, and he deeply valued his experience at job sites and in shops following trade school. Signing on at fifteen, he worked for a year as an apprentice at local building sites and then, for four years, as a draftsman in several Aachen ateliers. He recalled the way houses were put up in his youth:

Someone dug the foundation and laid the mortar bed, slaked the lime and let it run down there. Then came the bricks. That's where *we* started. We didn't have concrete, at least not for these house foundations, which were made of brick, first laid dry, with no binder, then covered with mortar. We had to make our own mortar and carry it on shoulder boards shaped like half-cylinders. We loaded bricks and stones in them too, using one hand to hold the board pole steady, the other to help ourselves up the ladder. Whoever could carry the most was cock of the walk.

Once you were there, on the wall, it was good. You learned to work slowly, not like some wild animal that gets tired after fifteen minutes, but quietly, for hours and hours. If you were really experienced, you learned how to do corners, which was very complicated. Mostly we laid the bricks in cross bond, and now and then we'd make mistakes. The foreman would often just let us make them and carry on. Then we'd get a wall up a way and he would say, "O.K., that's wrong. Take the whole thing down." Finally, when we were finished, the carpenters would show up and we were shifted to the vital assignment of getting the water for the workmen's coffee.

We had little pots, and we could buy boiling water for them for two Pfennige. We'd put powdered coffee into the pot, pour the water over it and deliver it to the workers. We could also get sausage for five Pfennige. Or cheese. Cheese was the staple. Bread you brought from home. The Schnaps came later. At the end of the week, when people got paid, that's when you got your Schnaps, lots of it, five Pfennige a shot.

At this point in his narrative Mies was not sixteen, and had yet to collect a day's pay. It was time to end the boy's schooling, at least as supported by the family. So Ludwig asked the supervisor of the apartment house project where he was working if he could be put on wages.

Of course the boss said no. He had had me for a year for nothing: why should he give me money now?

As it happened, I had a friend, a school chum, who knew of someone in town who needed a draftsman. I could draw. I had learned it at school. And I was good at lettering, with all that work on the tombstones behind me. So I applied to be a draftsman in a stucco factory run by a man named Max Fischer.

I got the job, though they put me in the office, not the atelier, and I had to keep the books and lick the postage stamps and get on a bicycle to take the wages to the workers at the construction sites. This I did for at least half a year.

Then the chief draftsman was called into the army and I was promoted to the drafting room. If I thought I knew how to draw before, I really learned now. We had huge drawing boards that went from floor to ceiling and stood vertically against the wall. You couldn't lean on or against them; you had to stand squarely in front of them and draw not just by turning your hand but by swinging your whole arm. We made drawings the size of a whole quarter of a room ceiling, which we would then send on to the model makers. I did this every day for two years. Even now I can draw cartouches with my eyes closed.

Lohan: You worked in all styles?

Mies: All historical styles, plus modern. All conceivable ornaments.

Lohan: Did you design any yourself?

Mies: When I was able — which is not as easy as it might sound.

Mies made a sudden departure from the stucco workshop. His boss, angry about a drawing mistake, made an abrupt, unexpectedly threatening gesture. Mies stiffened. "Don't try that again," he warned. The man backed off. Mies packed his things and left. "Mind you," he told Lohan, "the police were sent to haul me back, as if I were an apprentice and he owned me! But I was a novice draftsman. There is a difference!" Mies had his pride. "My brother knew who I

FIGURE 1.5.
Mies family tombstone, West Cemetery, Aachen (1929), designed and executed by Ewald Mies. Mies's stonemason brother was an outstanding craftsman. The clarity, directness, and economy of Ewald's work is characteristically "Miesian."

was as well as I, and when the cops arrived, he was there to tell them so, in no uncertain terms. 'Go home,' he said, and they went. Nothing more came of it. I was finished with the man and the job."

Mies had an ardent affection for his older brother, to whom he was at all times closer than to either of his parents or his sisters. Ewald was guardian and spiritual counselor. The brothers shared interests and talents, especially for what is today called graphic design. The family monument in Aachen's Westfriedhof, planned and executed by Ewald in 1929,[7] is a masterly example of modernist sans serif graphics, with the understated refinement that marks the work of his famous brother (fig. 1.5).

Ewald remained an Aachener all his life, and never married. Ludwig was ambitious, and the skill he demonstrated in the Fischer workshop made a return to the family stone yard unlikely. Between 1901 and 1905, according to his papers, he worked for two architects in Aachen, the first identified only as "Architect Goebbels," the second "Albert Schneider, Architect." The dates of these employments are not known. During the same four-year period he attended what he described as "Evening and Sunday Vocational School" while working full-time and living at home.

"I somehow made contact," he told Lohan,

with the office of an architect [presumably Schneider] in Aachen who was designing a big department store downtown, a branch of the Tietz Company. He had conceived a highly ornamental façade for the building, but his reach was greater than his grasp; he couldn't draw it. He asked me if I could. I said, "Yes." He wanted to know how long it would take. I said, "Do you want it this evening? Or do I have a little more time?" He looked at me as if I were a fraud for promising to do it so fast. "Give it to me tomorrow," he said, and I did. Then he asked me to work for him.

Meanwhile, Tietz had decided to transfer control of the department store project to the large Berlin firm of Bossler and Knorr, demoting Mies's boss Schneider to the role of associate. A battalion of architects, engineers, and clerical assistants descended on the Aachen office, and Mies found himself consorting with sophisticated invaders from the metropolis. His efforts met their standards.

Lohan: The story has it that someone in the office gave you the idea of moving to Berlin.

Mies: It was an architect named Dülow, from Königsberg, an admirer of Schopenhauer. He invited me one evening for dinner. It was Schopenhauer's birthday. The fact is I was not very educated in that sort of thing.

Enlarging on the same story in an interview with his daughter Georgia, he said: "On the day I was assigned to a drawing table at Schneider's, I was cleaning it out when I came across a copy of *Die Zukunft* [The Future], a journal published by Maximilian Harden, plus an essay on one of Laplace's theories. I read both of them and both of them went quite over my head. But I couldn't help being interested. So every week thereafter, I got hold of *Die Zukunft* and read it as carefully as I could. That's when I started paying attention to spiritual things. Philosophy. And culture."[8]

To Lohan, Mies continued:

In the course of the evening Dülow said to me, "Listen, why do you want to hang around here, in this tank town? Go to Berlin; that's where things are happening." I said, "That's easier said than done. I can't just buy a train ticket, head for Berlin and stand around the Potsdamer Bahnhof without the faintest idea of where to go."

So he pulled out an architectural journal, *Die Bauwelt*, or some such, from his desk drawer. There were two classified ads in it, both for draftsmen, one for the new town hall in Rixdorf, the other for general work at the big Berlin firm of Reinhardt and Süssenguth. Send drawings, the ad said—nothing more, no diplomas, no recommendations. So I sent them a pile of things and got an offer from both places. The Rixdorf project promised two hundred Marks a month, forty less than the other one. But Dülow said, "Take Rixdorf; I have a good friend who is in charge of the project there. His name is Martens, a fine man, from the Baltic, painstaking architect . . . above all, an artist."

It was time for the train to Berlin. With his departure, Mies effectively relinquished any claim to the family business. His brother would assume full ownership following the deaths of Michael in 1927 and Amalie five months later, in 1928. Over the years the Aachen address book regularly listed Ewald as a stonemason, though now and then he advertised himself as an architect. He had no training in the field, though in Germany as late as the 1920s "hanging out a shingle" was a legally acceptable way of identifying oneself as a professional designer of buildings.[9]

. . .

Consistent with the male domination of Wilhelmine society, the women of the Mies family appear only indistinctly. When Mies spoke of his mother, as he did in recalling visits with her to the cathedral, he was affectionate and respectful but vague. His sisters, Elise and Maria, hardly appear in recorded recollections. They were both still single when they opened a grocery store in 1911 on the Vaalserstrasse, just a few doors from the family residence. The store survived into the 1950s. Elise was past fifty at the time she married Johann Josef Blees, a widower with a teenage son. Maria never married.

In old age, Mies claimed to have little recall of family life during his childhood, which he attributed to his "early departure" from home at the age of nineteen. His father was a "strict authoritarian" whom his mother "obeyed dutifully." He said he had "little sense of the relation he had had with his parents." Nonetheless, he remembered his father's scolding: "Don't read these dumb books. Work."[10]

Whatever we make of the fragmentary record of Mies's early life, none of it points to exceptional promise. His chief source of confidence was ability as a draftsman, a gift sufficient to impress professionals he met while still a teenager. At nineteen he was unaccustomed to long-distance train travel, still less to a destination as formidable as the capital of the German Empire. Thirty miles under way he developed acute nausea, which subsided only slightly at the first stop, Cologne. "Around 8:15," Mies recalled in the Lohan interview, "the train started up again, and at 8:16, I opened the window, stuck my head out, and threw up." His distress persisted until he felt Berlin beneath his feet, though as soon as he mounted a taxi headed for Rixdorf he lost his stomach again. He deserted the cab, sat down on a curbstone, and waited for the return of equilibrium. Hoisting himself onto a trolley, he endured long enough to reach his immediate destination, the office of the municipal building department.

Apprenticeship, Marriage, and World War: 1905–18

2

But I can build a house. I just haven't done it on my own. **MIES**, to his first client

A huge stone wall with windows cut out of it. And that is that. You see with how few means you can make architecture—and what an architecture!
MIES, remembering the Palazzo Pitti in Florence

I want to love you with my hot young heart. **MIES**, courting Ada Bruhn

There was something about him that thrived on freedom, required exemption from convention. **MARY WIGMAN**, of Mies

Though within the orbit of Berlin, Rixdorf was independent and growing fast enough to require a new town hall. A "picturesque" design by the architect Reinhold Kiehl[1] was then under construction, and Mies was assigned to detail Kiehl's neo-Gothic paneling for the Council Chamber. At least for the drafting, Mies's work in the Fischer studio left him well prepared. But as he later reminisced, the details were wood, and "for all the time I had already spent with stone and brick and mortar and all such, I had never properly learned to handle wood, neither in school nor at home nor during my apprentice year in Aachen."[2] But his labors were soon interrupted by a stint, as a draftee, in the imperial German army.

"One day not long after induction . . . ," he recalled,

> we were ordered out onto the drill field for exercises. It was raining pitilessly, and the water kept rolling in torrents off our helmets—those comical old things with the spikes on them. When we heard the command "Attention!" one of the poor recruits in the first row of our unit was thoughtless enough to reach up and wipe the water from his face. At this the drill sergeant flew into a rage. It was a breach of discipline, not to be tolerated. The company captain was equally furious, since it had happened in his outfit. So we were all ordered to do calisthenics in the pouring rain, for hour after hour until eight o'clock that night. It was utterly imbecilic, the whole thing, so much soldier nonsense, and its main effect was that next morning I was unable to get out of bed. I couldn't move. I was in terrible shape—not only me, but half a dozen

others. We were all hauled off to the hospital, where it turned out I had developed a bad lung infection.

Since the army still had loads of healthy bodies and didn't really need us cripples, I was discharged as "unfit for service." I never went back to Rixdorf.[3]

In late 1905 or early 1906, Mies resumed his study of wood, and considerably more. He secured a connection, first as an employee, then as a student, with one of the most remarkable and versatile spirits in the German art world of the period, and the first figure of historic consequence in his life: Bruno Paul.

After completing his studies in Dresden in 1894, Paul had moved to Munich, then Germany's most progressive arts center. The Bavarian capital was at the heart of a gathering revolt against the imperialist-materialist values of late nineteenth-century European civilization. For Paul, the way of the 1890s was the Jugendstil. Its serpentine line and flat, abstracted patterns offered an alternative to the recycled manners of the 1880s, not just in painting and sculpture but in the utilitarian arts as well. Paul was also an accomplished illustrator. From 1894 to 1907, the social liberalism and bold, protoexpressionism of his contributions to the Munich satirical journal *Simplicissimus* epitomized the antiestablishment position.

During the first decade of the new century, Paul turned to architecture and applied arts, especially furniture. In 1904, when the German design section of the St. Louis World's Fair won worldwide praise, critics hailed him as one of the most impressive members of the group. He distinguished himself further in 1906, with several crisply geometrized interiors at the Third German Industrial and Applied Arts Exhibition in Dresden.

By 1907 Paul had moved to Berlin, then eclipsing Munich as the artistic capital of the nation. There he was appointed head of the education department of the Berlin Kunstgewerbemuseum (Museum of Applied Art), a position of considerable authority within the German academic bureaucracy. An irony attaches to this, as to other affiliations that grew out of the collision of radical and traditional forces in a time of abrupt cultural transition. The kaiser, though he professed appreciation for the arts, was aesthetically and politically archconservative. Had he known of Paul's *Simplicissimus* drawings, the appointment would surely have been blocked. Paul, as aware of this as anyone, continued to draw for *Simplicissimus* under the alias Kellermann.

Paul was one of the twelve founding members of the Deutscher Werkbund. Created in 1907, the Werkbund developed into a major progressivist force for German art, crafts, and architecture. It worked to improve the quality of all artifacts, a mission that grew out of the English Arts and Crafts movement, whose principal spirit, William Morris, deplored the dehumanizing effects of machine production on the handicrafts. While the Arts and Crafts movement took inspiration from medieval craft models, the Werkbund promoted improvements in both handmade and industrial goods, with the ultimate goal of aligning all artifacts with the cultural aspirations of German society. In further evidence of English influence on German design, Berlin architect Hermann Muthesius published the monumental *Das englische Haus* (1904–5), in which he argued that English domestic architecture excelled in comfort, informality, and economy of means, assets comparing favorably with the historicist ostentation of German residential design during the effusive 1880s.

The German vanguard of the new century also embraced stylistic restraint under the banner *Sachlichkeit*—a combination of matter-of-factness, objectivity, and sobriety. By 1905 a new language of form with its own iconography was in place. Geometric forms replaced the organic curves of Jugendstil, and a simplified neoclassicism now represented the virtues of clarity and reserve. Bruno Paul's work moved toward an understated precision that recalled early nineteenth-century Biedermeier.

.   .   .

Mies worked for Paul and also enrolled in both of Paul's Berlin schools. He took quickly and enthusiastically to furniture design, and even tried printmaking. One day in 1906, while working on a woodcut in the studio of Joseph Popp,[4] an assistant to the painter Emil Orlik, Mies observed a smartly dressed woman enter the room. She approached Popp and asked for assistance in the design of a birdbath for her lawn. Popp apparently complied to her satisfaction, for some weeks later she returned with a more ambitious request. She and her husband, Alois Riehl, professor of philosophy at Friedrich Wilhelm University in Berlin, wanted to build a house in the upper-class Berlin suburb of Neubabelsberg.[5] Not interested in an established architect, the couple hoped to advance the career of a gifted young designer. Popp nominated Mies—not yet twenty-one—and made the introductions.

Mies continued the story in his interview with Lohan. Frau Riehl asked what he had designed himself. "I said, 'nothing.' Then she answered, 'that will not do. We don't want to be guinea pigs.' But, I said, I *can* build a house. I just haven't done it on my own. What would life be like if everybody insisted you must have actually built such-and-such a thing by yourself? I'd be an old man and have nothing to show for the aging. Then she laughed, and said she wanted me to meet her husband."[6]

Frau Riehl then announced that she and her husband were hosting a formal dinner party that very evening. She invited Mies.

> I'll never forget it. First [Popp] told me I'd have to have a dinner jacket. I had no idea what a dinner jacket was. So he said, "You can buy one anywhere, or perhaps rent one."

Well, I went around Paul's office from A to Z, borrowing money until I had enough to buy a dinner jacket. Then of course I didn't know what sort of cravat to wear, and I picked up some wild thing in yellow or something else equally crazy. When the evening came I went to the Riehls' apartment in Berlin and there was a pair of people in the elevator with me. Very fancily dressed, the man in tails and covered all over with medals. I figured they must be going where I was going, so I let them get off first. Then the door opened and I felt almost dizzy. I saw how they glided, zumm zumm zumm, across the parquet like ice-skaters, and I was afraid I might break my neck. Then came the host, moving easily from one person to the next and greeting them. It was remarkable.

After dinner [Professor Riehl] invited me to the library, where he asked me all kinds of questions. Then he said, "We don't want the other guests to wait long and we'll go back to the salon." Then to his wife: "This one will build our house." This came as a shock to her. She didn't quite trust her husband, so she asked if she could meet with me the next day. I told her I was working for Bruno Paul, who wants me to build a tennis pavilion for him, a clubhouse. Why don't you ask him what he thinks of me. And he told me later that she said, "You know Mies is talented, but he is very young, and lacking in experience."

Bruno Paul suggested that I could work on the design in his own office. I said no. He asked how I found the nerve to say that. You see, he just didn't understand. Well, I got the assignment. And when the house was finished, he asked me for photographs of it that he could include in one of his student exhibitions. I was told later that he said to someone, "The house has only one thing wrong with it—that I didn't build it." He was very decent to me, in no way small-minded.

While the design of the Riehl House owes more to custom than originality, it is a remarkable accomplishment, the product of a neophyte with a few years' experience as a draftsman (figs. 2.1 and 2.2). The plan and elevations and especially the siting and landscaping disclose a fully professional achievement.

The house, at Spitzweggasse 3, is stucco over load-bearing masonry, with a steeply pitched, tiled roof above a rectangular main volume, wholly in the tradition of modest villas common to Potsdam-Neubabelsberg. It recalls specifically the treatment of the eaves and the low-relief pilasters on the façade of Paul's Westend House in Berlin, which was in design at the time. There are two principal elevations: one the entrance, block-like on the southeast overlooking a partially walled level lawn, the other, on the northwest side, a four-columned loggia capped by a gabled roof surveying a slope and a stand of trees. The loggia overlooks Lake Griebnitz, the shore of which is about five hundred feet to the east–northeast. Below and extending from both ends of the loggia elevation is a tall, broad retaining wall running almost the width of the site.

FIGURE 2.1. Alois and Sophie Riehl House, Potsdam-Neubabelsberg (1907). The Riehl house is Mies's first realized building, designed on his own when he was twenty-one. The clients were a respected Berlin philosophy professor and his wife. The Riehls developed an abiding fondness for Mies and brought him into their family and social circle. It was Mies's first encounter with high society and success.

A basement with a secondary entrance is concealed behind this wall, and is reached from a walkway running along the sloping lawn.

The siting offers attractively contrasting vistas: one at street level, to the tidy, formally planted lawn, the other to the broad slope and distant views. The plan is clear and the interior design, for the period, restrained. The great room, or *Halle*, of the first floor is similar to English domestic models celebrated by Muthesius (fig. 2.3). However, if England was the indirect antecedent of the *Halle* plan, its more immediate decorative source was the dining room that Paul had designed for the 1906 Dresden exhibition. The wooden lattice that Mies used as a wall motif, together with a blank frieze and the absence of a dado, produced a more formal, abstract (and less costly) effect than the work of his teacher. Elsewhere, Mies adopted the new vocabulary of the time: neo-Biedermeier wooden crossbars on the glazed cabinets again point to Paul, and a decorative swag over the front door is traceable to illustrations in one of the books widely discussed in Germany at the time, Paul Mebes's *Um 1800*.[7] Mebes opposed the formal excesses of recent domestic designs and called for a return to the simpler houses of the earlier nineteenth century.

For Mies, the real legacy of the Riehl commission was the relationship he developed with his formidable clients (fig. 2.4). Alois Riehl, sixty-three years old when the house was completed, was a figure of consequence in German

FIGURE 2.2.
Riehl House,
Potsdam-Neubabels-
berg (1907). View
from the garden, op-
posite and below the
street. The house is
an ingenious pairing
of two quite different
elevations, one over-
looking a garden en-
closed by a rampart,
the other (seen here)
incorporating a log-
gia surveying a broad
slope toward Lake
Griebnitz. Begin-
ning with his earliest
work, Mies strove to
unify building and
landscape.

philosophy and the wider cultural community of Berlin. He was an important neo-Kantian, a prolific author, and an early scholar and expositor of Friedrich Nietzsche. Once he and his wife, Sophie, took possession of their new house, which they named Klösterli (Little Cloister), they used it to entertain fellow elites. Mies, the young provincial, found special favor with the Riehls and was welcome in their midst ever after. While his lately developed interest in philosophy certainly appealed to Riehl, it hardly accounts for the depth of the professor's affection. Mies's evidently attractive personality surely played a role. In a gesture both paternalistic and didactic, the Riehls, at their expense, sent Mies on a six-week tour through Germany to Italy in 1908. There he was able to study landmarks he could only have dreamed of while in Aachen.

Mies was accompanied by Joseph Popp:

We headed to Munich, where there was an exhibition. . . . We were advised to visit it, since Frau Riehl liked it, and she just wanted us to observe whatever would improve our knowledge. It was a very interesting trip. For my taste Popp went too often to museums, to look at paintings. I can understand that, but I preferred myself to stay outdoors and look the city over. It was wonderful. We then went over the Brenner Pass to Bozen [Bolzano, in Italian] and from there on the way to Vicenza, where Palladio had built so much. Some of his most important buildings were in this area. Wonderful villas, not only the Rotonda, which is very formal, but others that are freer. The beautiful villa on

FIGURE 2.3.
Halle, or great
room, of the Riehl
House, Potsdam-
Neubabelsberg
(1907). The paneled
walls and square
tiles of the fireplace
reflect Mies's inter-
est in and knowl-
edge of contem-
porary English
residential archi-
tecture.

the Wannsee, by [Alfred] Messel, reminded me of a villa by Palladio near Vicenza.[8] Both Messel and Palladio detailed their buildings elegantly, but Messel did it better. That is clearly a sensitivity; some people have it.[9]

In later interviews Mies also expressed his admiration for the Palazzo Pitti in
Florence: "A huge stone wall with windows cut out of it. And that is that. You
see with how few means you can make architecture—and what an architecture!"[10]

After his return, Mies continued to visit Klösterli, where he met and mixed
with prominent people from Berlin and beyond. The Riehls' guests included
leading lights of German society, industry, and academia, including the industrialist Walther Rathenau, the philologist Werner Jaeger, the politician Hans
Delbrück, the art historian Heinrich Wölfflin, the archeologist Friedrich Sarre,
the philosopher Eduard Spranger, the African explorer Leo Frobenius, and
the psychologist Kurt Lewin, as well as foreign visitors like Chicago physician
Charles Sumner Bacon. These names are known to us because the Riehl guest
book, covering the years 1909–24 and filled with figures of historical consequence, came to light in 2000.[11]

FIGURE 2.4.
Mies at age twenty-
six in formalwear
at the Riehl House,
about 1912. Private
collection.

Recently, the Riehl House has attracted renewed attention. In an essay published in the catalog of the *Mies in Berlin* exhibition of 2001, Barry Bergdoll makes the case that Mies's design extended beyond the building proper and encompassed the surrounding garden.[12] This was evidence of Mies's engagement with Wohnreform, one of the new movements of the twentieth century's first decade, which "sought a formal and ideological reform of the everyday environment in the faith that new kinds of spaces in the verdant outskirts of the metropolis would bring with them healthful living and an ethical renewal of German culture." Mies, Bergdoll argues, was responsible for the integration of the house with the garden around it, and the individual rooms to a carefully coordinated exterior architecture. Further to this, Muthesius, in the revised edition of another of his publications, *Landhaus und Garten*, promoted the kindred concept of the "architectonic garden," citing the Riehl House, "with its interwoven interior and exterior spatial design."[13]

A significant discovery further illuminates Mies's design. After the fall of the Berlin Wall in 1989, the house was purchased by a Berlin couple.[14] A full-scale restoration followed, but only after the new owners had come across a group of pencil perspectives depicting the exterior and interior of the house (fig. 2.5). The drawings were discovered in a suitcase that had belonged to a previous owner. They are unsigned, but the hand is recognizably Mies's. The line is free and assured, with hatching close to that in countless drawings cer-

FIGURE 2.5.
During the Cold War, the Riehl
House was taken over by the
government of the German
Democratic Republic. It was
used for offices and otherwise
substantially altered, and left
in near ruins by the time the
Berlin Wall came down. The
family that acquired the house
in 1989 discovered a cache of
sketches of the exterior and
interior that are Mies's first
known drawings. These three
sketches show alternate massing schemes. Photo courtesy
of Dirk Lohan, for the estate
of Ludwig Mies van der Rohe.
Used by permission of Margit
Kleber.

tified as his. Published for the first time here, they are the earliest known drawings attributable to Mies. The bedrooms as built are identical with the images
as drawn. Yet more intriguing (albeit inconclusive) are several exterior studies
showing what appear to be successive proposed stages, the earliest showing
the loggia elevation as the single front of the building. Had this design been
realized, there would have been no room for a space as large as the one that
came to be the *Halle*. The arguments of some scholars that the loggia was
conceived after the garden elevation and later added to it, and that, as Fritz
Neumeyer has contended, "it comes in at the side door," are in conflict with
these drawings.[15]

We are again indebted to the Lohan interview for Mies's account of the next phase of his professional life: "Just about the time the [Riehl] house was finished, Paul Thiersch came by. He was Bruno Paul's office manager. Earlier he had been with [Peter] Behrens, and he told me Behrens once told him, 'Look, any time you see a talented youngster, let me know about him. Send him to me.' And Thiersch said to me, 'Now Behrens! There is a first-class man. You ought to look him up'" (fig. 2.6). Since Behrens was among the most famous architects in Germany, Mies probably knew of him, either on his own or through Paul. Behrens and Paul had met in Munich during the 1890s. They had both been trained in painting and graphics, coming to architecture as autodidacts via the decorative arts.[16]

By the turn of the century, Behrens's designs in glass, porcelain, and furniture, all in the Jugendstil, had won him a national reputation and membership in an artists' colony in Darmstadt, a city then aspiring to become the center of German applied arts. On the Mathildenhöhe, a hill overlooking the town, an exhibition of Behrens's work opened in 1899, and in 1901 he completed his own house on the grounds, executed, appropriately enough, in the Jugendstil. Within a few years he had quit both city and style, his work shifting rapidly during 1904 in the direction of severe geometric forms. By this time he had taken over directorship of the School of Arts and Crafts in Düsseldorf, on the recommendation of Muthesius.

Behrens, like Paul, was a founding member of the Deutscher Werkbund. In 1907 he accepted a position with the Berlin electrical conglomerate Allgemeine Elektricitäts-Gesellschaft, an assignment that would have immense consequences for both that firm and German industry. Though initially appointed "artistic advisor," by late 1908 he was in charge of all AEG imagery, including product design, advertising, and even its stationery, as well as its architectural embodiment, including factories, exhibition halls, and administrative and ceremonial buildings. Behrens proposed to integrate all physical reflections of the AEG into a program that would highlight the economic and cultural power of his client. In this work he contributed signally to the creation and development of what we now call corporate identity and industrial design.

AEG was one of the most spectacular phenomena of the German industrializing period.[17] Founded as late as 1883 by the engineer Emil Rathenau, by the turn of the century it had become a model for the machine industry and a key exemplar of German technology. By 1900 Rathenau and his colleagues, most notably his son Walther (who signed the Riehl guest book), had come to believe that the visual arts could add a cultural component to the firm's identity, producing a complex and commensurately profitable symbiosis. With

FIGURE 2.6.
Peter Behrens in
1913. Of the famous
dictum "Less is
more," Mies said,
"I heard it first from
Peter Behrens."

AEG's commitment to the arts, the visions of Behrens and the Rathenaus were joined. The AEG pavilion at the German Shipbuilding Exhibition of 1908 in Berlin, Behrens's first major building for the firm, represented the mighty corporation in common cause with the new culture. Behrens's worldview was confirmed: the artist had accepted the facts of the industrial age and transmuted them into culture, at the same time serving the ends of German nationalism. To a significant degree, this position had been forged by Behrens's study of Viennese art historian Alois Riegl, who argued that art is a reflection of society's social and religious preoccupations and its technological condition — its *Zeitgeist*.[18] Behrens believed that the *Zeitgeist* was most instructively revealed in the art of architecture. The architect must investigate and understand the

Zeitgeist, and work toward its expression. But paradoxically, the architect's own will was a crucial factor in the equation, independent of material fact and rising above it.[19]

This was Peter Behrens, architect and intellectual, recommended to Mies by Paul Thiersch. Despite his success with the Riehl House, Mies recognized that it was too early in his career for independent practice. He hired on with Behrens in October 1908. The connection would prove one of the most important of his life. For the next four years, he worked in one of Germany's major architectural offices, engaged in professional activity of international scope. Behrens had a large workload during this period, but he maintained a relatively small staff, housed in a studio on his estate in Neubabelsberg. Principal attention was given to the AEG. Among the first completed buildings was the aforementioned pavilion for the Shipbuilding Exhibition. It embodied the stylistic objectives Behrens set for his AEG buildings: conventionally academic forms, chiefly classical, but with strictly functional details. The octagon of the pavilion, surmounted by a low-pitched roof, called to mind the Baptistery in Florence and Charlemagne's chapel in Aachen, even as the clean, abstract surfaces were a reprise of Behrens's lately adopted geometries.

Behrens's work was inspired and confirmed by the model of Prussia's greatest nineteenth-century architect, Karl Friedrich Schinkel. A product of the exceptionally fecund period in German cultural history that followed the Napoleonic Wars, Schinkel spent most of his life in Berlin, where he realized an extraordinary array of buildings of intrinsic and urbanistic excellence. While some of his works were neo-Gothic, the most admired were neoclassical. Especially impressive is the Altes Museum of 1823–33, which, though based on classical models, is distinguished by an expansive plan fronted by an unprecedented porch of eighteen Ionic columns. From within the museum, sightlines extend to the Lustgarten, the Royal Castle, and Schinkel's own neo-Gothic Werder Church. Nearby, the Schauspielhaus of 1818–26, of comparable excellence, features an Ionic portico that leads to an interlocking mass of cubic forms illuminated by rows of simply framed lights (windows) almost on the order of modern punched windows. The symmetrical siting of the building on the Gendarmenmarkt, between the French and German cathedrals, completes one of Berlin's great urban passages.

These and other works of Schinkel were visited frequently by Behrens (figs. 2.7 and 2.8). He regarded them as splendid achievements unto themselves, and as works according in spirit with the most recent stylistic developments. Behrens's staff often accompanied him on inspections of Schinkel's work, an experience that constituted Mies's first sustained encounter with an architect and artist whom he, too, quickly came to admire. His devotion to Schinkel would figure in the work he did for Behrens after 1911, when he became the master's assistant for several projects in the classical vocabulary.

FIGURE 2.7.
The Neue Wache
(New Guard House)
by Karl Friedrich
Schinkel, Berlin
(1816). Along Un-
ter den Linden in
central Berlin, this
outstanding ex-
ample of German
neoclassicism was
beloved of Peter
Behrens and an
object of study by
Mies. In 1930, Mies
entered a compe-
tition—which he
did not win—for
a memorial to the
German dead of
World War I. It was
to be located in the
lower level of this
building.

Two years earlier, in the summer of 1909, Mies took part in a study tour to England organized by the German Garden City Society, with visits to Hampstead, Letchworth, Bourneville, and Port Sunlight. He claimed to have made another trip to London, where, in the company of German painter Heinrich Vogeler and Karl Ernst Osthaus, founder and director of the Folkwang Museum in Hagen and one of Germany's leading arts patrons, he visited the German Garden City exhibition.[20] That connection was probably made through Behrens, who was a close friend of Osthaus's. It has been contended but not proved that Mies made yet another trip to England, in 1913, again with the German Garden City Society, where he is said to have visited London, Birmingham, Liverpool, and Letchworth. It is certain that interest in gardens was very high in Germany at that time, and that England was a favorite destination for professional study.[21]

In Behrens's studio, Mies occupied a lesser position than that of Walter Gropius, who had joined the office a year ahead of Mies. Gropius and Mies were roughly the same age, but with almost opposite backgrounds. Born in 1883 into a Berlin family of solid upper-class standing, Gropius enjoyed all the benefits that wealth, status, and family tradition could bestow. After completion of the *Abitur* program, he enrolled in the *Technische Hochschule* in Munich, where he spent a term before returning to Berlin. He remained in the capital for a brief architectural apprenticeship before volunteering for a year with the famed Wandsbeck Hussar cavalry regiment in Hamburg—in contrast to Mies's brief service as a common draftee. In 1905 Gropius resumed his architectural studies, attending the *Technische Hochschule* of Berlin-Charlottenburg. Two years later he traveled to Spain, where he met Osthaus, who recommended him to Behrens.

FIGURE 2.8.
Schinkel's New Pavil-
ion at Charlottenburg
Palace, Berlin (1825).
The square plan, with
identical opposite
elevations, is based
on the Villa Reale
del Chiatamone in
Naples. The elegance
and simplicity of the
detailing are aston-
ishing for the period.

There was natural cause for Mies and Gropius, two comparably ambitious young stalwarts, to develop a wary mutual circumspection. In the course of their long lives, it sometimes became adversarial. But for the two years they were together with Behrens, Gropius was professionally senior. He was also the more advanced designer. He left Behrens in 1910 to form a partnership with another promising Behrens graduate, Adolf Meyer. The two set up in Berlin, Gropius acting on the conviction that he was by then the equal of Behrens in talent, and decidedly further along as a modernist. In 1911 he and Meyer de-signed the Faguswerk, a factory in Alfeld-an-der-Leine, a pure prism in which the floors are carried on a steel frame and the walls, of transparent glass, highlight the absence of structure at the corners. The building, testimony to Gropius's uncompromising embrace of industrial materials, is one of the most important works of early architectural modernism.

By comparison with Gropius, Mies at the end of the decade was more con-servative, closer to the mainstream progressive position in Germany. As that view was frequently rationalized, modernity was one thing, and rightly to be admired; of extremes, however, there had been enough. In 1910, just a year be-fore Gropius's Faguswerk, the critic Anton Jaumann wrote a review of Mies's Riehl House. To Jaumann the building epitomized the architecture of the younger generation, the "new growth," as he put it, which "is not motivated by an impulse to novelty or a striving to move ever ahead. On the contrary: their work, by contrast with that of the past decade [the 1890s], is reserved,

FIGURE 2.9.
The AEG Turbine
Factory by Peter
Behrens, Berlin-
Moabit (1909).
South elevation.
Mies worked on the
design as a staff ar-
chitect in Behrens's
office. Photo: AEG-
Telefunken.

even coolly critical. What do these young ones want? They seek resolution and balance, as surely as they avoid anything that smacks of radicalism. They prefer a 'golden' mean, between the old and the new."[22]

Of Mies's assignments for Behrens, we are only partly informed. In addition to a number of corroborating secondhand reports,[23] in a 1960s visit to Behrens's Turbinenhalle of 1908–9, the most renowned of his AEG buildings in Berlin, Mies stated to Dirk Lohan that he had worked on the famous long elevation, and could still remember its dimensions[24] (figs. 2.9 and 2.10). But he never claimed responsibility for its design. Stanford Anderson, a leading Behrens scholar, has reported a 1961 interview in which Mies acknowledged work on the Small Motors Factory of 1910–13 and the Large Machine Assembly Hall of 1911–12, but did not mention the Turbinenhalle.[25] Hearsay has it that Mies worked on the interiors and the furniture for the Feldmann and Schroeder Houses in Hagen.

Sometime in 1910, shortly before another young architect destined for fame, Charles Jeanneret (later Le Corbusier), spent a few months in Behrens's employ, Mies left the office and returned to Aachen. (Mies recalled Le Corbusier: "I met him briefly; just as I was entering the office, he was going out. So I really never got to know him.")[26] What prompted Mies's departure, at least in part,

FIGURE 2.10. The springing point of one of the three-hinged exoskeletal arches of Behrens's AEG Turbine Factory, Berlin-Moabit (1909). Dirk Lohan and his grandfather visited the building in the 1960s, and Mies confirmed that he had worked on this, the famous east elevation.

is recounted in a document written in 1911 by Salomon van Deventer, reporting a conversation he had just had with Mies. On August 29, van Deventer, an assistant to Dutch industrialist A. G. Kröller, for whom Behrens was then designing a residence near The Hague—with Mies as project architect—wrote a letter to Kröller's wife in which he remarked that professional animosity between Mies and an unnamed member of Behrens's staff had grown so sharp that Mies "left [the office] after a year. During the year in which he was separated from Behrens, however, he came to realize the greatness in Behrens, and he decided that Behrens was the only man who could offer him something as an architect. So he put everything else away and returned to Behrens, where he has been now for three-quarters of a year."[27]

.   .   .

In Aachen during this hiatus, Mies had the opportunity to design independently and at large scale for the first time. In his 1910 competition entry for a monument to Otto von Bismarck, he drew powerfully on his two strongest early influences—for inspiration, Schinkel, and for architectural vocabulary, Peter Behrens. The proposal, which was presented in sophisticated drawings and collages, was the first of his career to suggest a substantial talent.

In 1909, after two years of preparation, the Berlin government announced a competition for a major monument to Bismarck, the politician largely responsible for the unification of the fatherland and the creation of imperial Germany. Following his death in 1898, Bismarck had become a popular symbol of patriotism, but this commemoration was meant to be unique. The one-hundredth anniversary of the Iron Chancellor's 1815 birth was approaching, and it became the target date for a celebration of German unity. In those days the line separating national aspiration from nationalistic apprehension was easily blurred, as reflected in the competition brief, which declared that "a Bismarck monument must stand in those oft-embattled, much threatened yet faithfully defended borderlands of Germany."[28] (This meant the Rhineland.) It was a message addressed to the German people, but spoken loudly enough to be heard by the French.

The monument was to be sited atop the Elisenhöhe, a four-hundred-foot bluff commanding the west bank of the Rhine at Bingen. The brief required that the monument address the river, and in the opposite direction incorporate a festival field. Any German-speaking architect, artist, or sculptor could participate in the competition. Each aspirant received a site plan and five photographs of the existing conditions, meant for study or for inclusion in the submitted material. The competition deadline, originally July 1, 1910, was extended once, to November 30. There was enormous interest, and 379 entries

FIGURE 2.11. Bismarck Monument competition entry, for a site overlooking the Rhine at Bingen (1910). Mies's exceptional draftsmanship was demonstrated in the two large colored drawings he submitted to the competition. This is an elevation view.

FIGURE 2.12. Bismarck Monument competition entry by "L and E Mies" (1910), colored perspective view. The statue of Bismarck (*in shadow*) inside the exedra was to be designed by Ewald Mies, who had no record of creating representational sculpture. Compare the scheme here with Behrens's German Embassy in St. Petersburg (fig. 2.15), which Mies had worked on. Photo courtesy of the Mies van der Rohe Archive of the Museum of Modern Art, NY.

were received. They were to be judged blind, and therefore without reference to the social and professional status of the entrants.

Mies teamed with Ewald, who was listed as "sculptor," and together they identified themselves as "L and E Mies"—not in the order of their ages. Evocative of Schinkel in setting and form, their proposal is brooding and majestic (figs. 2.11 and 2.12). A terrace at river's edge supports a massive podium at lordly height. The podium was to carry five interlocking building masses consisting of two long, parallel colonnades perpendicular to the river and enclosing a festival field; two mighty pylons at the river end of each colonnade; and, framed by the pylons, a half-circle cylindrical wall (in classical terminology an exedra), also in the form of a colonnade, thrust out above the Rhine. In the exedra would be a huge effigy of the seated Bismarck, the only figurative element of the design, facing away from the river (but toward France) and looking over the festival field. Though traditionally the focus of a classical temple—which this was—in Mies's presentation the sculpture was barely rendered, seen only between columns, darkly.

Mies developed the building masses and disposed and detailed the colonnades and pylons in emulation of his work for Behrens. In the colonnade, pylon massing, and stonework, as well as in the simplified and abstracted cornices, Behrens's German Embassy in St. Petersburg is particularly discernible. Mies would later work on the embassy project during its construction in Russia, but in 1909 it was probably already in design in Behrens's office. Mies's model was the Behrens of classical massing and composition but of minimal classical *decoration*, with cornices reduced to one or two projecting lines and columns and pilasters in the form of pure ashlar prisms, but without the naturalistic components of standard classical detailing. Mies used all these simplifying devices, producing a geometrized classicism that pointed to the future. Nonetheless, he still depended on the classical temple as a conveyor of monumentality. (He labeled his entry "Deutschlands Dank"[Germany's Gratitude].) Late in life, Mies would grant that under Behrens "I learned the grand form."[29]

Mies knew his history well enough to select the antecedents appropriate to his goals. The elevation of temple on podium was as old as Greece. Schinkel, Mies knew, was habituated to it. Mies's entry for Bingen was essentially a prototypical classical temple honoring a demigod. It was set in an extravagantly romantic landscape, traceable to Schinkel's published Schloss Orianda project of 1838, a giant pavilion for the Prussian royal family intended for a commanding site in the Crimea. Mies's commitment to a traditional language of classicism and to Peter Behrens stands in contrast to the severely simplified masses of Walter Gropius's competition entry. Nonetheless, and again unsurprisingly, both submissions were indebted to an unbuilt Bismarck monument designed by Behrens himself in 1907–8 for a site at Bookholzberg in Oldenburg.[30]

Though Mies's scheme was stylistically conventional, his presentation was anything but. Its graphic power surely impressed the jury. The colored elevation drawing and the nearly eight-foot-wide perspective capture the scale and solemnity of the concept, with impressive shading and persuasive realism in the crucial details of stone coursing and texture. The presentation alone points to an incipient master. In a preliminary review of January 1911, the competition jury included the Mies brothers' project among twenty-six chosen for "special mention," praising it as "both very simple and very impressive." But they later eliminated it for "obviously excessive building costs."[31]

The competition turned into an imbroglio typical of the conflicts between modern and traditional ideas that racked the arts in Germany during the first years of the century. The jury consisted of two founders of the Werkbund, Muthesius and Theodor Fischer, the conservative sculptor of animals August Gaul, the aesthetician Max Dessoir, and Walther Rathenau of the AEG. The panel awarded first prize to the proposal of the architect German Bestelmeyer (a one-time student of Theodore Fischer's) and the sculptor Hermann Hahn, a remarkably restrained design of columns, trees, and a single statue of Siegfried, the dragon-slayer of the epic *Niebelungenlied*. A faction of the judges revolted, complaining that the entry lacked the necessary commanding force. The organizing committee, after much quarreling, yielded to the rebels and revised the jury's decision, selecting the design of a colossal domed edifice flanked by a pair of giant eagles—"Faust"—the work of the architect Wilhelm Kreis and the sculptor Bruno Schmitz, two established favorites of the Wilhelmines. One of the rebel jurors who favored the Kreis-Schmitz proposal was no less a champion of modernism than Muthesius—further testimony to the turmoil of taste in prewar Germany. Plans for the Bismarck monument vanished in the cataclysm of World War I.

. . .

During 1910 Mies had occasion to be in Berlin briefly, and while there he made the acquaintance of Hugo Perls, a well-to-do lawyer and collector of contemporary art. Like the Riehls, Perls had turned his home into a gathering place for intellectuals. "So it was, one evening," he wrote in his memoir, "Mies van der Rohe came."[32] Mies was probably invited by another artist, though it has been suggested that he and Perls were brought together by the Bruhns, an upper-middle-class Berlin family with their own cultural connections. Mies knew the Bruhns—whose daughter Ada he would marry—through Alois and Sophie Riehl. Profiting from the society he enjoyed at Klösterli, he had begun to seek out people of taste and influence, like Perls. Perls recalled his first evening with Mies, testimony to Mies's growing personal and professional attractiveness:

> [Mies] did not say much but the few things he did say made a deep impression on me. In building, something like a new era seemed to have begun. The better architects were concerned to keep superfluous decoration, nooks and crannies, projections and all the appurtenances of romanticism off their facades. A new classicism was coming into being, [and] people were beginning to talk about "dignity" in architecture....
> Mies van der Rohe would have nothing to do with traditional forms. But that did not prevent him from appreciating them in the architecture of the

FIGURE 2.13.
Hugo Perls House,
Berlin-Zehlendorf
(1912–13). Mies's
first built work in
the manner of Karl
Friedrich Schinkel.

past. And so we met in our delight in Schinkel. I see Schinkel as a unique phenomenon; I do not believe that any architect before or after has had his ability to design in the "Gothic" tradition one day and in the "Greek" the next without ever losing his originality.

In the Grunewald, near Krumme Lanke [in Zehlendorf], Mies van der Rohe built our house. My far too conservative ideas led to many a friendly skirmish. The house could have been better, for Mies was one of the founders of the new architecture [Neues Bauen]. . . . He was so far in advance of his time.[33]

Completed in 1912 at Hermannstrasse 14–16, the house is much different from what was first conceived (fig. 2.13). The earliest drawings, signed "F. Goebbels" (most likely Ferdinand Goebbels, a Behrens office colleague acting as what we would today term Mies's architect-of-record), show a tall pitched roof with a pediment on the garden elevation and a recessed loggia at grade. As built, the loggia is retained, but the roof is shallow and the pediment omitted. The house is two stories of stucco over brick. All four elevations are symmetrical except for an entry on the main floor that leads to a small foyer,

FIGURE 2.14.

Perls House, Berlin-Zehlendorf (1912–13). Murals for the interior by Max Pechstein were commissioned by the client, probably without Mies's involvement. They were at stylistic odds with the neoclassical architecture. Photo courtesy of Ute Frank.

thence to a dining room, with access to a partially sunken garden on the west, reached via the loggia. Both the house and the two gardens—the other is directly south of the loggia—are rectilinear in plan and of similar size.

Mies's borrowings resonate. The loggia is most likely a reference, with levels inverted, to Schinkel's pavilion at Schloss Charlottenburg, just as the crossed axes were a favorite device of the earlier master. The placement of a study and a library-music room, each adjacent to the dining room and forming a *U* in plan, plus the insertion of a fireplace in one of the short walls of the dining room follow the interior of Behrens's house of 1912, built in Berlin-Dahlem for the archeologist Theodor Wiegand. The flat exterior and the abstracted cornice are traceable to both Schinkel and Behrens. So are the gardens.

These features did not keep Perls from commissioning a set of highly idiosyncratic paintings for one of the major interior spaces. The artist was Max Pechstein, one of the early expressionists and an original member of the Dresden movement Die Brücke. The group had moved to Berlin by 1911, a year before the Perls House was completed. Perls commissioned Pechstein to adorn the dining room with a set of murals on canvas that featured thirty-eight nudes in an Arcadian landscape (fig. 2.14). They were rendered in ochre, green, and blue, in the nervous, angular manner of Pechstein's Berlin period. Perls later gave these paintings to a friend as a birthday gift. They were transferred to the Berlin Nationalgalerie, but, as Perls reported, "they disappeared soon after and I do not know what happened to them."[34] From photographs reproduced in a magazine of the 1920s, the paintings were striking, though the impression is inconsistent with Mies's muted classicism.

FIGURE 2.15.
Imperial German Embassy, St. Petersburg, Russia (1911–13), by Peter Behrens. In a major reworking of an existing building, Behrens created a monumental frontispiece of engaged Doric columns of red granite blocks. The overscaled sculpture above the entry, of Castor and Pollux, was by the German Eberhard Enke. It celebrated the united German Empire. Mies was Behrens's on-site representative during the construction.

. . .

The two Behrens projects in which Mies played his most prominent role led to his final exit from the office. The break was unfriendly, symptomatic of deepening differences with Behrens and of Mies's growing personal and artistic independence. The first of the two projects was the 1912 Imperial German Embassy in St. Petersburg, a monumental edifice executed in Behrens's soberly opulent neoclassical manner[35] (fig. 2.15). Mies supervised the interior design, and between 1911 and 1912 was his employer's representative in St. Petersburg. There he incurred Behrens's displeasure twice: once when he secured substantially lower bids than Behrens had, and again when he allowed his discussion of some of Behrens's plans for the interior to be overheard by a journalist who publicized them before German officials could be formally advised.

Mies's involvement with the second project, the Kröller-Müller House, was more significant, and the conflict with Behrens both protracted and serious. In February 1911, while Behrens was occupied with the design of the embassy, he was called on in Berlin by Mr. and Mrs. A. G. Kröller of Holland, who wished to construct a villa on a large piece of dune land they had purchased near Wassenaar, an affluent suburb of The Hague. The meeting was cordial, and it led to another conversation a month later at the Kröllers' residence in Scheveningen, where Behrens was awarded the commission.

The names of Anton G. Kröller and his wife, born Helene E. L. J. Müller, are remembered today for the formidable art collection they assembled and housed in the Kröller-Müller Museum and Sculpture Garden in Otterlo. The main building of the present-day complex was not completed until 1938, the product of a convoluted history of both villa and museum, neither in the end designed by Behrens.

Kröller was a Dutch bourgeois who married into a German fortune in 1888 and took over his father-in-law's firm a year later. He moved its headquarters from Düsseldorf to Rotterdam and later to The Hague, and turned it into an international enterprise with interests in shipping, mining, and heavy industry. A consummate entrepreneur, Kröller was content to leave cultural concerns to his wife, who in her middle years developed an intense commitment to the arts. In 1907 she met the art critic Hendricus Petrus Bremmer, under whom she began a study of art that grew into a consuming passion. Bremmer became her counselor, mentor, and intellectual pastor. In 1909, under his influence, she began buying the work of the still controversial Vincent van Gogh. Bremmer advised her in all matters of taste, including the patronage of artists and the organization, care, and housing of an ambitious collection.

In 1910 Mrs. Kröller-Müller and her daughter traveled to Florence, where she was struck by the splendor of the art and the role of the Medici in its creation. They had been patrons too, she reflected, and collectors—and commercial people, like her husband and herself. Returning to Holland, she determined to build a house at Ellenwoude, the name they gave to their new property. It would be a country place where they could take their leisure surrounded by their art. Since the collection was weighted toward contemporary painting, the villa was to be in the modern manner. "I want no decorative embellishments," she wrote Bremmer. "I prefer to build on the edge of the dunes, so that I have a backdrop of the woods behind me and great space in front of me, a large, spreading meadow," adding in later correspondence, "The house [should] be long on its front, longer than deep."[36]

For the Kröller-Müller project, Behrens made Mies his assistant. Over the course of the next several months, a concept took form. In its final stage, obedient to Mrs. Kröller-Müller's prescription, the villa would be low-lying and longer than deep, with a pair of two-story wings connected by a central block and a loggia of square-section Doric columns.[37] The connecting block was to be slightly higher than the wings, and the roofs flat. A slender cornice would be the sole exterior adornment. The massing was to be cubical and the manner abstract-classical. Judged by images in Fritz Hoeber's 1913 monograph on Behrens, the entrance, to be placed on the side of the left wing, led to a series of reception rooms intended for guests and business associates. The central element housed the family's quarters. The paintings were to be shown not simply as décor but in a special exhibition gallery illuminated by a skylight. The family wing would also contain an apartment for Mrs. Kröller-Müller, as well as a garden screened from the front by a greenhouse.

Though the reasons are unclear, Mrs. Kröller-Müller was never content with Behrens's proposal. She was uneasy as early as a few weeks after he took the job. On March 18, 1911, she wrote Salomon van Deventer: "[Behrens] loves long perspectives, and so he thinks he ought to make the house ever so much larger. But I want to see it whole against a background, so that it is contained, closed off."[38] Mr. Kröller, in an extravagant gesture meant to resolve his wife's uncertainties, arranged for a full-scale mock-up of the villa to be built on the Ellenwoude site in January 1912. It was constructed of painted sailcloth over wood framing, and set up on a system of rails so that it could be moved about. Judging from photographs, the façade, though comfortably extended, hardly suggests the excessively "long perspectives" Mrs. Kröller-Müller had opposed. It appears that the meadow would have spread away from the front of the house, with the woods as backdrop, just as she wished. Still, her sense that Behrens was not attuned to the "life concept" she had in mind—whatever that meant—hardened into certainty. Behrens's work was rejected.

Mies was still on the scene, as he had been since mid-1911. Over those months he was in frequent professional contact with Mrs. Kröller-Müller, and he had made a sufficiently deep impression on her that she entertained the possibility of turning the design over to him, even as her confidence in Behrens waned. In turn, Behrens had begun to suspect his assistant of coveting the commission.

A sense of the impression Mies made on the people involved in the project, and not Mrs. Kröller-Müller alone, can be gleaned from a letter to her from van Deventer: "[Mies] is in so many respects a man like myself, but deeper, greater, more gifted, all in all my superior. I sensed from his words great respect for you, his grasp of the issues, and although we had spent but a few hours together, I felt as if we had known each other for years."[39] Van Deventer went on to relate something of the personal tensions that rose in the ranks of the home office. In the course of work on the project, Mies had resumed the inter-office struggle with the colleague who aggrieved him before his 1910 exodus. (Van Deventer does not identify the man, save to say that he and Mies were the leading figures in Behrens's studio in 1911. This is enough to identify him as Jean Krämer, who would himself go on to an important and prolific career.)[40]

FIGURE 2.16.
Aerial view of the
model of Mies's
Kröller-Müller House
project (1912).
Though influenced
by Behrens's design
for the same project,
Mies's work was fun-
damentally his own.
A competition set up
between the twenty-
six-year-old Mies and
Dutch architect Hen-
drik Berlage—whom
Mies admired—
ended with Berlage's
triumph. Photo cour-
tesy of the Mies van
der Rohe Archive of
the Museum of Mod-
ern Art, NY.

At yet another point in the Kröller proceedings, Mies, in discussion with Behrens, expressed his growing admiration for the contemporary Dutch architect Hendrik Petrus Berlage, whose work he had come to know in Holland. Behrens remarked that he found Berlage's work passé. "Perhaps," Mies said, adding archly, "assuming you are not simply deceiving yourself." Behrens wheeled on him angrily and appeared, Mies reported, "as if he would have liked nothing better than to punch me in the face."[41]

Mies formally left Behrens's employ early in 1912, at about the time Mrs. Kröller-Müller elected to turn the design of the villa over to him. Bremmer took a dim view of the decision. He doubted that Mies could handle the project, and he also hoped that Berlage himself might be available. What amounted to an invited competition then ensued between Mies, unknown but championed by Mrs. Kröller-Müller, and Berlage, Bremmer's new favorite, a giant of European architecture whom Mies would come to revere even as he worked to defeat him. By spring, Mrs. Kröller-Müller had established Mies in a studio at the company offices in The Hague. It was a huge room, typical of the outsized appetites of the Kröllers. As Mies recalled, it was also filled with art: "About fifty van Goghs were hanging there. I became a van Gogh expert in spite of myself; there was no way of avoiding the pictures."[42]

In these circumstances he labored alone through most of the summer of 1912. Ostensibly to acquaint him with the environment, the Kröllers drove him all over the Dutch countryside. As her devotion deepened, Mrs. Kröller-Müller visited Mies in the studio daily. Berlage carried on his own work in Amsterdam, calling on the family sporadically. By September Mies's design was complete (fig. 2.16). He had retained much of the spirit of Behrens's earlier project, and the two designs are alike enough to have been confused in publications. They had the following in common: a long, low profile with a longitudinal central block that rose above flanking wings; flat-roofed masses organized axially and disposed around courts in a blend of symmetry and asymmetry that recalled Schinkel; formal basins and gardens; and axial approaching roadways. Among comparably similar details were square-sectioned Doric columns, flat walls with inset windows, and slender cornices set tight to the roofline. But Mies made the massing of the central block the dominant element. A pergola on the garden side connects the ends of the two wings, enclosing a court. Another pool, as long as the distance between the outer faces of the wings, is set to the rear. On the front elevation a portal stands at the corner of one wing, while from the far end of its counterpart a lower mass extends longitudinally, nestling a second court.

There is no known contemporaneous floor plan. Mies reconstructed one from memory twenty years later, when he was teaching at the Dessau Bauhaus.[43] According to this drawing, the wing into which the portal led—the north wing—contains an entry, a *Halle* or reception area, and a formal dining room and a gallery to the west. The two-story central block houses family quarters upstairs and a corridor on the ground floor that serves as exhibition space for porcelain. This passage leads to the south wing: first to another *Halle*, thence to additional galleries, including a windowless main exhibition space and a room for prints. Still farther to the south is a court bounded by a pergola and a conservatory.

The massing of Mies's design is interlocking and prismatic, similar to the constructivist compositions that influenced him in several of his post–World War I residential projects. He later made the observation that the Kröller villa, absent its classical detailing, would have strongly resembled the abstracted cubic forms of the 1920s modernists, himself included. And like his later projects, the villa, though more centrally compact than Behrens's version, spread farther into the landscape and met it less abruptly. Solids descended gradually from the main block, first to the flanking wings, then, on the garden side, to the pergola-colonnade and, on the front side, to the conservatory pavilion. Photographs of the model suggest a grand, stately country house, with a thrusting horizontality more pervasive than anything Mrs. Kröller-Müller had complained of in Behrens's concept.

In an assessment of Mies's design, the eminent German critic Julius Meier-Graefe wrote: "Nothing is piecemeal. All the parts hang together and are developed logically; the whole fits well the flat land for which it was meant." Meier-Graefe's words were addressed to Mies in a letter dated November 13, 1912, from Paris, where the critic then lived: "I should like to congratulate you. I see here an uncommonly felicitous solution to the design of a house in which the essential problem has been to unite liveableness with a rational display

FIGURE 2.17.
Mock-up of Mies's
Kröller-Müller House
project (1912). The
design was modeled
life size in sailcloth
over wood framing
at the proposed site,
and set up on rails
so that it could be
moved about. Photo
courtesy of the Mies
van der Rohe Archive
of the Museum of
Modern Art, NY.

of artworks. The need to preserve the gallery's integrity could easily lead to its isolation. Your design has happily avoided this. Instead, the gallery seems an essential part of the architectural whole, chiefly because of its handsome asymmetrical arrangement."[44]

Mies traveled to Paris to solicit this critique from Meier-Graefe, confident that the endorsement of so distinguished an authority would help him win the commission,[45] but Meier-Graefe's letter appears to have been written too late. The Kröllers' decision had been made in September, when drawings and models by Mies and Berlage were assembled one evening in the company office. Bremmer delivered his judgment in the form of a verdict. Van Deventer was present and reported: "Bremmer scrutinized the sketches and the maquettes long and thoughtfully. At last he motioned toward the Berlage pieces and said, 'That is art,' then to Mies's work: 'That is not.' He followed this with a torrent of argument in support of his view."[46]

Helene Kröller-Müller was crushed. Bremmer, certain of his authority and opinions, never wavered. Kröller returned to the strategy that succeeded earlier: the Mies project was translated into a full-scale, canvas-and-wood model (fig. 2.17). Trusting Bremmer, Kröller speculated that the weaknesses his own critic had seen in Mies's design — they are not recorded — would be even more apparent when magnified. The stratagem worked. Mrs. Kröller-Müller yielded. In January 1913 she wrote her husband: "Bremmer's judgment was the right one."[47]

The history of this museum-house, troubled by demons more diverse than a wealthy client's irresolute temperament, continued inconclusively. Berlage's design was never constructed. Shortly after presenting it, he was retained as Kröller's resident architect and awarded several commissions relating to both company and family affairs. A condition of the contract was that he work for no one else. For six years he devoted himself exclusively to the Kröllers, though neither his original design for Ellenwoude nor several subsequent variations were ever built. In 1919 he severed his relationship with family and firm.

Within a year, Mrs. Kröller-Müller had turned to yet another architect, whose Leuring House in The Hague had first triggered her obsession with a modern villa: the Belgian Henry van de Velde. He was invited to produce a plan for a museum, and he came up with one that had entered construction before it was abandoned in the anxieties of the 1922 international monetary crisis, which threatened the very existence of the Kröller business. The building that was finally realized in 1938, in Otterlo, after one more design by van de Velde, was said to be "temporary," though it serves as the main quarters of the museum to this day.

Mies had passionately wanted it for himself. If his visit to Meier-Graefe in Paris were not evidence enough, his letters to Mrs. Kröller-Müller early in 1913, after her decision had gone against him, tell us how much he had invested in his labors, yet how grateful he remained. "I hardly need to tell you," he wrote,

> that your decision, though I expected it and though I accept it, came as a blow. I believe I allowed too much of my heart to be put into the assignment. I do understand the necessity of your decision. My feelings of admiration and appreciation, dear lady, for both you and your family, are not at all changed by the fact that my project was turned down. Indeed, the way you handled the matter and the concern you showed me only deepened these feelings.[48]

Irrespective of his disappointment, Mies was hardly at a total loss. He had the project itself to show for his time in Holland. However much it displayed the influence of Behrens, it conveys the grand manner implicit in its program. Derivation may not end there. An exhibition of the work of Frank Lloyd Wright took place in Berlin in 1910 and 1911, and Mies visited it. One of the entries was Wright's unrealized 1907 McCormick House for Lake Forest, Illinois. It is remarkably similar in plan and scale to Mies's Kröller-Müller project. Of the Wright/Berlin show Mies later wrote: "The more we were absorbed in the study of these creations, the greater became our admiration for [Wright's] incomparable talent, the boldness of his conceptions and the independence of his thought and action. The dynamic impulse emanating from his work invigorated a whole generation. His influence was strongly felt even when it was not actually visible."[49]

. . .

By the end of 1912, Mies was back in Berlin. He opened an atelier in the suburb of Steglitz and, as it would turn out, devoted himself almost exclusively to housing the haute-bourgeoisie. Forever welcome in the home of Alois and

FIGURE 2.18.
Ludwig Mies in
1912, around the
time he opened his
own office. Private
collection.

FIGURE 2.19.
Ada Bruhn in 1903.
Private collection.

Sophie Riehl, at one of their receptions he met Ada Bruhn.[50] The Bruhns and the Riehls were close, and it was only a matter of time before Ada would encounter the young architect who had designed the Riehls' house. The introduction occurred in 1911.

It was equally likely that the two young people would find themselves more than casually attracted. Judging from photographs, Mies was ruggedly handsome (fig. 2.18), of more than medium height, and solidly built. A high forehead crowned chiseled features, pronounced among them sharp hazel eyes that were the chief agent of a commanding, if reserved, presence. Ada, born Adele Auguste Bruhn in Lübeck on January 25, 1885, was a year older than Mies, at twenty-six or twenty-seven a mature woman when they met (fig. 2.19). She cut a stately figure and was, from all accounts, beautiful, with long, straight brown hair and solemn eyes. She was also well fixed. Her father, Friedrich Wilhelm Gustav Bruhn, like the rest of her family a north German (born also in Lübeck, 1853), was a tax inspector at the time of her birth. Later he became a manufacturer of small motors, with holdings that eventually included a factory in London. He invented the taxi meter that was standard in Berlin cabs of the Wilhelmine period, and an altimeter used in early German military aircraft. As a personality he was exacting and stiff. He was remembered by Ada and Mies's daughters for treating his own children with an authoritarian hand that gave way inconsistently to spasms of guilt and the expiatory lavishing of gifts. We can only conjecture how deeply these traits affected Ada; her lifelong struggle with somatic illness and depression are a matter of record.

Though Mies had met Ada at the Riehls', he spent much of his courtship in the Dresden suburb of Hellerau, well known in the early twentieth century as a new garden city, planned between 1909 and 1914 principally by Heinrich Tessenow, a leading figure in the German Garden City movement. The back-to-nature impulse behind the creation of such communities had affected Mies's own garden design at Klösterli. It also established Hellerau as an ideal place for Swiss educator-composer Émile Jaques-Dalcroze to open his school of eurhythmics in 1910. A form of dance based on gymnastics correlated with music, eurhythmics shared with the Garden City idea the objective of a "natural," spiritually liberated society. Appropriately, it was Tessenow who, between 1910 and 1912, designed the Jaques-Dalcroze Institute, employing the abstract-classicist manner of the day. There Ada Bruhn had enrolled as a student, at about the time the school began operations.

Ada shared a small house in Hellerau with three other young women. One was Marie Wiegmann, later Mary Wigman, who became the most celebrated female exponent of modern dance during the Weimar period. Even more well off than Ada was the Swiss Erna Hoffmann, later the wife of the psychiatrist Hans Prinzhorn, whose *Bildnerei der Geisteskranken* (The art of psychotics) was a major early study of art and psychopathology. The third woman, who remained a lifelong intimate friend of both Mies's and Ada's, was Elsa Knupfer, born in Estonia to a German school principal and member of the czar's court.

Traveling by train from Berlin to Dresden, Mies was able to call on Ada frequently, and he soon got to know Wiegmann, Hoffmann, Prinzhorn, and Knupfer, as well as the painter Emil Nolde, a friend of the elder Hoffmann, who occasionally accompanied them on visits to their daughter. According to Wigman,[51] an easy cordiality developed among the whole small society. Their way of life was free, open, and self-consciously modern, the sort of lifestyle that became a norm among German liberals during the 1920s. In 1912 this environment would have been considered in advance of middle-class mores, and for that reason all the more attractive to young people with artistic and intellectual ambitions.

Mies brought to his relationship with Ada the spiritual equivalent of her material wealth: he was talented and committed to his art, which more than made up for his limited education and lack of inherited social standing. There was also an air of emotional intensity about him, another sign of the creative fires to which Ada, by her very presence at the Jaques-Dalcroze Institute, was surely drawn. Gifted and well schooled, she had been invited by the conductor Bruno Walter to study music in Vienna, and she was at the piano the day she met Mies at Klösterli.

Before she met Mies, Ada had been engaged to the renowned Heinrich Wölfflin, the reigning art historian of his generation and twenty years her senior. But he bored her, and she found the courage to reject him. Mies then came into her life and began a bold, steady pursuit that led soon enough to their engagement. In his letters to her he found the words:

"You, my beloved sweetheart!" he wrote in September 1911,

> I am especially in love with you today. It is regrettable that we cannot be with each other today. How I wish, my darling, that we may soon be in our own home, where I want to love you with my hot young heart. Then we shall become ever more friend and comrade, ever more husband and wife. Our lives will be filled with beauty and love. And our life together will be dedicated to our little son.
>
> I kiss you from the bottom of my heart,
> Your Ludwig[52]

At this stage in the relationship, these words must be taken as a measure of Mies's feelings for Ada, who brought to him devotion sufficient to his attentions, plus grace, comeliness, and, not least, wealth and social connections through which he could advance his career. The Bruhn family initially opposed the marriage, but finally accepted Mies for some of the same reasons Ada found him worthy: he looked like a man with a future. His surname, alas, was not an asset. In German *mies* means "wretched," "miserable," "out of sorts": "The weather is *mies*"; "I am feeling *mies*." A *Miesmacher* is a complainer, a grouser. To the cultivated Bruhns, "Ludwig Mies" hardly rang with the music of the spheres; "Ada Mies" probably grated even more. "Ada Wölfflin" had a finer sound.

The couple married on April 10, 1913, in a Lutheran ceremony in Berlin-Wilmersdorf. They honeymooned at Lago Maggiore in Italy and took up residence in the upper-middle-class suburb of Lichterfelde west of town, not far from Dahlem, Zehlendorf, Potsdam, and Neubabelsberg—country associated with Schinkel and Behrens.

· · ·

At the time, Mies was at work on another project of his newly independent practice, a house in Zehlendorf for the engineer Ernst Werner, completed in 1913 (fig. 2.20). Werner had inherited property adjacent to the Perls House. His daughter Renate's suspicion that Mies was retained because her father greatly admired the Perls House is itself suspect, since the Werner House seems in no way inspired by that design; it is the most schoolish piece of Mies's early work. The Werners had their own comfortable position in the Berlin cultural world, opening their home to artists and musicians much the way the Perls and Riehls did theirs. Mrs. Werner's father was an instructor of drawing in Dresden, her brother an art historian, and she a committed patroness, the

subject of several portraits by well-known contemporary painters, including one by the rising young expressionist August Macke.

The Werner family was deeply impressed by Mies—"an imposing, forceful, vital man," in Renate Werner's words—and altogether happy with the house, irrespective of its conservatism.[53] Its exterior follows Prussian eighteenth-century precedent: a four-sided gambrel roof of pan tiles takes up twice as much of the elevation as the stuccoed wall, beginning at the top of the first story with a pagoda-like lip, then rising steeply past the pedimented dormers of the second story and breaking into a gentle slope at the attic. Perpendicular to the service end of the rear façade is a roof pergola that faces inward to a formal garden accessible from the house via three French doors. While the elevations are conventional, the pergola and garden are traceable directly to Behrens and indirectly to Schinkel. The plan is almost identical with that of Behrens's Wiegand House, which likewise features a frontal projection of the service wing toward the street and an entry to the right. The main axis of the ground floor, following Behrens's example, leads through a foyer into a living room and to the garden. Mies's architect-of-record for the project was the same man who played a part in the Perls House design, Ferdinand Goebbels.

More interesting than the architecture of the Werner House is the furniture Mies designed for it (fig. 2.21). The dining room contained a round pedestal table with arm and side chairs, a sofa, and a china cabinet. The neoclassical manner common to Schinkel and Behrens was employed with notable assurance.

Shortly after the Mies-Bruhn wedding, the couple bought a large tract in Werder, a resort suburb west of Potsdam. Mies either found or put up a modest weekend house on the grounds. Sometime during World War I, he and Ada

FIGURE 2.21. Dining room of the Werner House, Berlin-Zehlendorf (1912–13), with interior by Mies, in 1913. Photo courtesy of Renate Werner.

were forced to give up this retreat, chiefly because a caretaker could not be found.[54] Until that time they made good use of it. Mies frequented the lakeside taverns of Werder by himself, finding pleasure in them and drinking it up, so Mary Wigman tells us, as if it were a nectar that leaked from the first cracks in the marriage vessel.

By agreement of all who knew him, Mies was neither a responsible husband nor, even after Ada bore him three daughters in three years, a caring father. "As a married man," Wigman recollected, "he was a caricature.... I lived through some pretty terrible times with the two of them, early in their marriage. I recall Ada, sometimes in the middle of the night, threatening to jump out of the window of their house, to get away from him, to leave him."[55] As it turned out, he left her, not permanently—not yet—but often, on regular weekend excursions to Werder, where he struck up numerous casual liaisons, with little more motive, apparently, than to have the best time possible. "Remarkably," recalled Wigman,

it was somehow all right that way with him. I could never bring myself to say to him, "Ludwig, how *could* you?!" There was something about him that thrived on freedom, required exemption from convention. It was his way, and he blossomed. And dear Ada herself, after they were married a while, would say, "I want only to be a haven to him, a place he can come back to and find peace." Is that a woman's nature, to be so yielding, so without rancor? I don't know. I do know the whole thing didn't work.[56]

For a while, though, it had to. Ada wanted it to, either in spite or because of the distress it caused her. Although she later moved out, he remained, boon or burden, locked in her heart. With affection and pride, her daughters remembered how she taught them to respect their father's need for independence. Mies was an artist, Ada would remind them, and he required disencumbrance from the demands and distractions of bourgeois life.

The birth of a daughter on March 2, 1914, led Ada to spend more time at Werder. The child, named Dorothea,[57] was lovingly welcomed, at least on the evidence of Ada's daybooks, which are full of adoring references to Mies and not a hint of the stress Wigman reported.[58]

For Mies's part, he devoted some of 1914 to a house he conceived for himself, and presumably for his family, on the Werder site. The only documentary evidence of this work consists of two drawings, now lost, published in February 1927 by the critic Paul Westheim in *Das Kunstblatt* (fig. 2.22). Each is an aerial perspective showing the building—or a pair of connected buildings—and the surrounding landscape. One drawing shows a long mass with two wings extending forward to embrace a court. The roof is flat, while the walls have an understated cornice above widely spaced, cleanly incised windows that begin at grade. The second sketch shows the house divided at right angles

into two prisms, the smaller sliding just forward of the rear plane of the larger. As with the interlocking blocks of the Kröller villa, this treatment prefigures Mies's constructivist work of the following decade. A telling asymmetry, again reminiscent of Schinkel, reappears in both designs in the garden, extending forward and away from the forecourt. A flight of steps leads to a broad walk below. A rose garden lies beyond, sited well to the left of the axis running into and through the main block. Both drawings show asymmetrical but formally composed stands of trees flanking the house, possibly the famous cherry trees of Werder. The commingling of architecture and nature, though traceable to Schinkel, in this instance takes on a characteristic twentieth-century form.

. . .

In its protomodernity, the Werder project was ahead of Mies's designs of the second decade of the century, all of which were traditional. Further evidence to this effect came to light in 2002 with the discovery, by the Berlin architectural historian Markus Jager, of one of Mies's houses, the very existence of which was long doubted.[59] Records maintained by Mies in his Chicago office listed a 1913 "House on the Heerstrasse." Nothing was known about this building until Jager found material in the Berlin Landesarchiv proving beyond question that Mies had designed a house that was built on the Heerstrasse in 1914 and demolished in 1959. The client was Johann Warnholtz, director of the German-East African Society. Photographs and record plans show an ample residence for a family of means. Standing two stories, with an attic illuminated by eyebrow windows, the house was symmetrical front and rear. The walls were stucco except for some heavy masonry ornament on the front elevation, visible in engaged columns and a flat arch at the entrance, in quoins at the ground floor corners, and in the center windows of the second floor. A pediment interrupted a mansard roof that took up more than half the height of the building. The main floor entry led through a foyer to a salon flanked by parlor and music room, then to a library, guest room, and open arched veranda, left, or to the dining room and closed veranda, right. The second story housed bedrooms, while a terrace at the rear overlooked a garden.

The Heerstrasse was and still is a major artery in the western part of Berlin, a continuation of the Charlottenburg Chaussee (today's Street of the 17th of June). In 1905 Kaiser Wilhelm II directed that sites fronting it be used solely for large villas with extensive lawns, and the Warnholtz House, among the first dwellings built there, fully conformed. Consonant with the kaiser's conservative tastes, it broke no new stylistic ground, while in antecedents it was notably less reliant on Mies's old idols Behrens and Schinkel than on the turn-of-the-nineteenth century Prussian models promoted by Paul Mebes in *Um 1800*. Indeed, it appears to have been taken almost directly from the Oppenheim House, an upscale residence designed in 1908 by the highly regarded Berlin architect Alfred Messel. The mansard roof and eyebrow windows of the Warnholtz House—devices that Mies had used in earlier houses—were consistent with Mebes's examples, while the arcaded veranda and masonry décor were nearly identical with counterparts in the Oppenheim House. The Warnholtz House was Mies's largest completed work to this time, and unlike the Perls and Werner Houses, which had involved Ferdinand Goebbels, it was his alone, for he signed the plans "Ludwig Mies."

Sometime in 1914 or early 1915, Mies made the acquaintance of the Berlin banker Franz Urbig, a connection effected once again through the Riehls, whom Urbig and his wife counted among their friends, and whose house they admired. By the summer of 1915, Mies was at work on a residence for the Urbigs that rivaled the Warnholtz House in luxury. Its final form, however, was not the first design Mies submitted. An initial proposal "provided for a one-story neo-classical villa which bore a close resemblance to the plans for [Mies's] own residence in Werder, likewise not carried out."[60] When the Urbigs elected to build fronting Lake Griebnitz, just a short walk from Klösterli, Frau Urbig hoped for a Schinkelesque design, which Mies produced. But her husband balked at the flat roof, whereupon a quite different solution was offered and accepted. Here again Mies employed an architect-of-record, Werner von Walthausen, who worked for Heinrich Tessenow and Peter Behrens before opening his own Berlin office in the 1920s.

The Urbig House has a rich exterior and lavish interior appointments (fig. 2.23). It is a two-story rectangular block, except for a one-story wing contain-

ing a dining area and an arcaded loggia adjacent to a paved terrace. The front façade is symmetrical, with seven bays, an arched entry portal under a fanlight, and, above that, a balcony. The exterior is stucco. These conventionalities recall the Warnholtz House, but differences and their likely sources are notable. The front elevation of the Urbig House is marked by shallow bays alternating with a grand order of abstract pilasters rising from grade to the eaves of a hipped roof. Windows are framed in travertine, and at ground level the French windows are surmounted by inset panels with ornamental relief carvings of swags. Framing the windows is a reveal typical of both Schinkel and Behrens.

Interior passage from the entrance hall across a transverse corridor to a reception room is bracketed by two fluted Doric columns, resembling the pair Schinkel had designed for Schloss Tegel in Berlin. The corridor leads on the left to a stair and to the dining room, on the right to the study and a bay-windowed parlor. Parlor, reception room, and dining room connect through double doors to the terrace. At the rear of the house, a broad flight of stairs leads to a formal garden, and then, as originally conceived, to two more stairs and a view of Lake Griebnitz. Karl Foerster, a major figure in the garden reform movement that had inspired Mies when he worked on the Riehl House (where Mies may have met him), played a major role in the design of the Urbig garden.

Over the years, the Urbig House has amply reflected the affluence desired by the client, especially when it served as the temporary residence of British prime minister Winston Churchill during the Potsdam Conference of 1945. During the Cold War it contained administrative offices for the German Democratic Republic. The Berlin Wall was built directly behind the garden. After the collapse of the GDR, the house returned to private hands.

. . .

Following a second conscription into the German army, in 1915, Mies served in a clerical office at his regimental headquarters in Berlin, and was able to look after the Urbig House until it was finished. He also moved his pregnant wife and their daughter to an address in the Tiergarten district of Berlin, Am Karlsbad 24. He maintained this rented residence for the remainder of his life in Germany, that is, until he immigrated to the United States in 1938. It was a gracious apartment on the third floor of a typical central Berlin town house, built between 1857 and 1858.[61] Mies covered the entire apartment with plaited Chinese mats and designed all the furniture in traditional forms akin to what he had done for the Werner House.[62]

Ada's daybooks describe the period immediately following this move as the happiest of her married life. Nineteen-month-old Dorothea, nicknamed Muck, doted on her father "now that she has moved to Berlin after a summer in which she saw so little of him." On October 25, Ada wrote that Mies "has to leave for the army, and the happy atmosphere of the family will be given up for a while. Muck looks everywhere in the apartment for her papa, and is over and over again disappointed."[63]

On November 12, 1915, Ada bore a second daughter. Mies was in Hanau, near Frankfurt, assigned to an army railroad detail. Lacking a university education or its equivalent, he would remain in noncommissioned rank for the duration of the war. In December Ada wrote: "His first greeting after my news of his second daughter was, 'I am grateful to you, and joyful over Marianne!' (it was he who gave her the name)."[64]

According to Ada, Mies was back in Berlin by the spring of 1916. She had taken the children to Werder for Easter, and upon their return to the city she found him incapacitated with appendicitis. He underwent an appendectomy and was hospitalized for two months. Convalescence was fitful and slow. His military duties, to which he returned in the summer, were interrupted by another illness in September. Packing the children off with their governess, Ada joined Mies for a fourteen-day rehabilitation leave in Eisenach, where, quite probably, their third child was conceived. "It is October," her next entry reads, "and we are all together as a family in Karlsbad. Pappi is enjoying a deep contentment."

Probably no earlier than the beginning of 1915, Mies developed another close friendship, with the sculptor Wilhelm Lehmbruck, who had moved to Berlin from Cologne the preceding November. According to Lehmbruck's son Manfred, the two men and their families saw each other frequently during 1915 and 1916, exchanging visits in Berlin and Werder. The friendship was one of the deepest of Mies's early years, and perhaps of his whole life. Like Mies, Lehmbruck was a native Rhinelander, five years older, with a working-class background (mining). They met in Paris in 1912 when Mies was soliciting Julius Maier-Graefe's endorsement of the Kröller-Müller project design. Thereafter, Lehmbruck enjoyed several sojourns in Italy, lived for four years in Paris, and made a trip to New York, where he participated in the famous 1913 Armory Show, sold a major work, and established himself as a sculptor of international repute.

Lehmbruck was the kind of aesthete whose company Mies was coming to prefer to utilitarian consorts in the architectural world. "Whenever Mies came over to our place," Manfred Lehmbruck recollected, "he could deliver the obligatory incantation without delay: 'Lehmbruck, open up the battery! [the bar].'"[65] Of course, the two of them knew each other's work, and they talked endlessly, late into the night, about philosophical issues and surely, too, about the war. Lehmbruck had resisted conscription, first by working as a medical orderly in Berlin and then by fleeing to Zurich late in 1916. He spent most of the remainder of the war in Switzerland, but suffered recurring bouts of depression. In January 1918 he wrote in despondency: "Who stayed behind after these murders? / Who survived this bloody sea? ... / You who prepared so much death / Have you no death for me?"[66] In the spring of 1919, Lehmbruck committed suicide, aged thirty-eight.

Mies saw no combat in World War I, but sometime in 1917 he was ordered to quit his regimental offices in Berlin and report to a field assignment in Romania. "That trip took fourteen days by rail," Ada reported in her daybook. "Twelve men in each barely heated fourth-class coach. With no straw to sleep on."[67] There he was attached to a company of bridge engineers and road builders. He is reported by a later associate, the architect Bodo Rasch, to have quarreled with a sergeant and ended up "in an outlying region guarding railway sidings." At that time, also in Rasch's telling, "he had a love affair with a gypsy woman, who provided him with food, of which he sent a lot to his daughters in Germany."[68]

On June 15, 1917, in Mies's absence, a third daughter was born. Her name, Waltraut, rich in overtones of Wagner and nineteenth-century German romanticism, seems as improbable as Dorothea, given the modernist tastes of her parents. Still, it should be noted that Ada spent much of her young marriage alone with her girls or in the house of her parents, who could not be expected to encourage her more progressive attitudes. During the waning months of the war, she may have found a measure of comfort in the uses of tradition. Then, on the occasion of Mies's last army leave, in mid-1917, she exulted:

> July 21: When Waltraut was five weeks old, her beloved father returned, in the midst of a wild rainstorm, fresh and cheerful, like a real soldier. He has spent twelve days in our little house in the sun.
>
> On the 27th, Waltraut's baptism. A country church procession, through a lovely old stone gate, always under sunshine. Our two big sisters there too, festively done up, dear, proud, so well-behaved. An hour or two at a café followed, then a long walk. Pride in the baptismal child. Supper and a moonlight cruise on the lake.[69]

Ada's renewed spirits survived her own appendectomy and subsequent intestinal misery in early 1918, as well as the prolonged lung infection Marianne suffered during the international influenza pandemic of that spring. On November 22, 1918, with the war over, Mies returned from Romania, and by early January 1919 he was once again with his family in Berlin. Ada offers no information about his reaction to Germany's military defeat. She herself was preoccupied with more than her own physical distress. During the spring of 1919, she wrote of "the severe illness of my mother, followed by an operation. I had to care for her until the middle of May. But then at last we all moved to Karlsbad. It is now an indescribably beautiful, harmonious time; the blossoming chestnuts fill our room with light, and in their own little corner the children are lost in their own happy little world."[70]

Though we do not know the precise timing, and Ada mentions nothing of it, according to the testimony of Lora Marx, Mies's companion in the United States, Mies told her that "right after" World War I "he had what I would call a nervous breakdown," a "spiritual crisis which revolved around his worries about what principles in architecture to follow." Lora continued: "He had bought a farm near Berlin.... When the problem hit him, he had to get out of the bustle of Berlin, into the country. There he might think in serenity. He said he solved the crisis by reasoning that architecture must be a thing of its time."[71]

Europe out of the Ashes: 1918–26

If we want our culture to rise to a higher level, we are obliged ... to change our architecture.... We can only do that by introducing glass architecture, which lets in the light of the sun, the moon, and the stars, not merely through a few windows, but through every possible wall, which will be made entirely of glass.
PAUL SCHEERBART, in *Glasarchitektur* (1914)

We refuse to recognize problems of form, but only problems of building. Form is not the aim of our work, but only the result. Form, by itself, does not exist.
MIES, in the journal *G*

You are of all people the dearest to me. But don't adopt your life to mine. Be strong enough that you no longer need me. Then we will belong to a shared freedom; then we will belong to each other. **MIES**, breaking off his marriage

Measured against the fate of the typical German, Mies's life in the aftermath of the war was a study in ease and good fortune. The military casualties sustained by his countrymen over four debilitating years—almost two million dead, more than four million wounded—were grievous enough, with the chief solace following surrender to the Allied powers the end of actual warfare. Yet adversity continued in a different form. A new republic was proclaimed on November 9, 1918, but it was immediately crippled by savage political conflict. The Socialists, who were likely to lead a new government, split into factions that contended, often violently, among themselves and with other parties. Independent Socialist Kurt Eisner, who proclaimed a republic in Bavaria, was assassinated in February 1919, one month after the murder in Berlin of the Spartacist leaders Rosa Luxemburg and Karl Liebknecht. The kaiser had been stripped of power, but generals sympathetic to him remained hostile to any form of republican government. The right wing made itself felt in March 1920 in an attempted putsch organized by the civil servant and politician Wolfgang Kapp, together with army general Walther von Lüttwitz, whose troops seized Berlin preliminary to an attempt to establish a counterrevolutionary nationalist dictatorship. The Kapp Putsch, as it is known, failed due to resistance by the city's trade unions, but only after the spilling of much blood.

The political, economic, and psychological burdens imposed on Germany by the Treaty of Versailles were staggering. They included the surrender of all colonies, the return of Alsace-Lorraine to France, occupation of the left bank of the Rhine, and reparations that would later contribute to hyperinflation. And more murders were to come. In 1922 the government's foreign minister, Walther Rathenau—former associate of Peter Behrens's and a friend of Alois and Sophie Riehl's—was killed by ultranationalist army officers. More putsches followed; one of them, in 1923, was led by the thirty-four-year-old Adolf Hitler. Only in 1924, when American banker Charles Gates Dawes negotiated loans from the United States, did the so-called Dawes Plan restore a semblance of stability to the German economy.

How did Mies pass these grim years? While in the army in both Berlin and Romania, he was hundreds of miles from the military fronts. He returned to a Berlin household still dependent on Ada's wealth, which in turn derived from her father. Although Bruhn's London factory was seized by the British for war reparations, his fortune survived the inflation, and his family—and Mies's—were still comfortable. The couple's three daughters continued to attend private schools.

Though the inert economy generated little work, Mies continued with his practice, interwoven as it was with the aforementioned "spiritual crisis." Judging from her daybooks already cited, Ada loved and believed in him, and the consistency of those sentiments suggests that she had no notion of any infidelities. In any case, we can do nothing but wonder about circumstances immediately preceding her receipt of this remarkable letter, dated February 25, 1920:

> Dear Ada,
> You are of all people the dearest to me. But don't adopt your life to mine. Be strong enough that you no longer need me. Then we will belong to a shared freedom; then we will belong to each other. Without compulsion, without consideration, bound by nothing. I love this freedom not out of selfishness, but rather because I find it worthier to live in such an atmosphere.
> In deepest love I think of you.
> Lutz[1]

Ada replied:

> My nature tends toward the internalized intensity of life together, to a certain contemplativeness or harmony that is not possible for you. Surely this springs from my childhood, while you are accustomed to a way that looks ahead, unhindered. If I cannot fly with you, then I cannot make my love your bondage, and I will not hang like lead around your feet. But let our love that has struggled greatly through the shadows remain an anchor. You shall have your free way and I will be a haven to which you can return at any time. Help me with love to realize that!
> Ada[2]

FIGURE 3.1.
Ada Mies about 1920, around the time she and Mies
separated. Private collection.

There is enough in these letters to allow us to speculate about some of the reasons for the breakup. On the surface Mies is self-serving, if not selfish, and Ada loving and charitable, even if rejected. Ada contrasts the burden of her childhood with Mies's "unhindered" confrontation of life. And Mary Wigman's testimony that the marriage was troubled shortly after the wedding may be reflected in Ada's acknowledgment of the couple's struggles "through the shadows." Ada suffered for most of her life from somatic and psychological problems more severe than anything that befell Mies (fig. 3.1). His decision to leave her was consistent with an apparent need for freedom as well as his tendency, stronger as his life went on, to steer clear of intimate involvements. The couple took separate ways, but never divorced.[3]

·   ·   ·

We are better informed about Mies's life outside the household after the war. He remained at Am Karlsbad 24, while Ada, with the children and a housekeeper, moved to an apartment in the western Berlin suburb of Bornstedt. There she followed progressive principles in schooling her daughters (fig. 3.2). In 1922 American dancer Isadora Duncan opened an academy on the grounds of the Neues Palais in Potsdam. To Ada, Duncan's freely expressive form of dance was the essence of modernity, akin to her studies in Hellerau. Accordingly, she enrolled the children, who spent two years at the school before restlessness descended on her. She quit Bornstedt, and with the girls began a journey of various residential stops that ended only in the 1930s, when her daughters were almost fully grown.

Mies occasionally visited his family in Bornstedt, but later, as they moved

FIGURE 3.2.
Marianne, Dorothea, and Waltraut working together on a construction, about 1920.

about, he saw them less. He made over the Berlin apartment—at 220 square meters a very comfortable flat—into a combination bachelor's quarters and architectural office. The rooms facing the street, including the two largest, were made into studio spaces, and a front bedroom was converted to an office. The front balcony was occasionally used to test and photograph models. Mies's staff, such as it was, came and went in these areas. The rear of the apartment remained private, with a bath (accessible from the studio spaces), two small bedrooms, and the kitchen (fig. 3.3).

. . .

Mies was now free to focus on the intellectual ferment that animated the German architectural world. At the end of the 1910s, the dominant force in the arts of central Europe was expressionism, a movement that identified the inner vision of the artist as the fount of artistic expression. Expressionism had become preeminent among avant-gardists before 1914, and by inertia alone it sustained a following after the war. A number of important German architects were drawn to its emphasis on picturesque and fantasy-driven forms "expressive" of the designer's will. Among the best-known expressionist buildings were Hans Poelzig's Grosses Schauspielhaus of 1919 in Berlin, with a ceiling imitative of stalactites, and Fritz Hoeger's Chilehaus of 1923 in Hamburg, with its strikingly jagged exterior. Such effects were evidence that expressionism was indebted to romanticism and tinged with mysticism, even as it was also related to progressive political movements that opposed the conservatism of the kaiser's discredited regime.

Entwined motives romantic and mystical point to a specific person, the writer Paul Scheerbart, whose short stories and novellas celebrated glass as the material of a new architecture and, even more, crystal, a substance his-

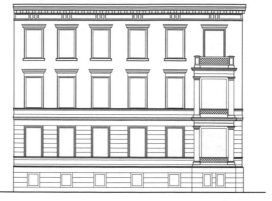

Elevation

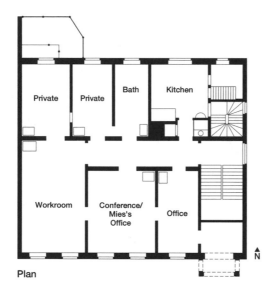

Plan

FIGURE 3.3.
Elevation and plan (top floor) of Mies's
220-square-meter Berlin atelier, Am
Karlsbad 24. Mies lived here with
Ada and the children between 1915
and 1920, and alone until 1938. After
1920 his professional offices occupied
the three large rooms and the small
space off the balcony. Constructed in
1858, the building was demolished by
the Nazis in 1939/40 to make way for
Albert Speer's unrealized North-South
Axis concourse.

torically endowed with mystical significance. "If we want our culture to rise
to a higher level," Scheerbart wrote in *Glasarchitektur*, "we are obliged, for
better or for worse, to change our architecture.... We can only do that by introducing glass architecture, which lets in the light of the sun, the moon, and
the stars, not merely through a few windows, but through every possible wall,
which will be made entirely of glass."[4] Among the architects most influenced
by Scheerbart was Bruno Taut, who developed a series of fantasy schemes for
his *Alpine Architektur: Eine Utopie* of 1919, in which he proposed the transfor-
mation of vast mountain landscapes by purpose-cut clefts filled with enormous spears of colored glass. Glaciers would be decorated with precious
stones and vitreous panes to reflect and magnify the sun's rays, and alpine
lakes would be embellished with floating crystalline elements. In their shimmering transparency and abstracted geometric form, these mountains of
glass represented the very remaking of man and the world. Especially in the

German-speaking world, crystal would become the central metaphor of expressionist architecture. It offered an ideal unity of iconography and form: a trinity of solidity, transparency, and reflectivity suggesting universal meaning and a concentration of the many into one.

The power of the expressionist worldview was exemplified by the postwar generation's zeal for utopia. Even at the old Kunstgewerbeschule (School of Arts and Crafts) Weimar, newly named the Staatliches Bauhaus and reopened in 1919 under the direction of the erstwhile functionalist Walter Gropius, the tone was more passionate than rational. The final sentence of Gropius's famous manifesto for the school reads: "Together let us will, conceive, and create the new building of the future, which will embrace architecture and sculpture and painting in one unity and will one day rise toward heaven from the hands of a million craftsmen, like the crystal symbol of a coming new faith."[5]

For all its dominance, expressionism had its adversaries. The critic and art historian Adolf Behne, who had opposed expressionist mysticism as early as 1914, now promoted the rationalism of the Russian constructivists and the Dutch movement de Stijl. In turn the Dadaists, who interpreted the war as the encompassing failure of Western civilization, disdained aesthetics altogether, most of all expressionism. George Grosz spoke contemptuously of the artist who "lives in a filthy studio and dreams of higher things."[6] But Dada, offering nothing positive, played an increasingly marginal role as the 1920s unfolded. Much of its energy was transferred to other collective endeavors that sought to affect rather than reject the world. These movements shared the conviction that the world would be neither moved nor transformed by the self-involvement of the expressionists or the negativity of Dada.

In a sense, it was 1905 again. As the Jugendstil had given way to *Sachlichkeit* in the first decade of the century, the romance of expressionism and the impudence of Dada were now challenged by what came to be called a *neue Sachlichkeit*. This "new objectivity" inspired art of widely differing tempers, ranging from the savage social criticism of Grosz and Otto Dix to a hopefully socialized architecture that began to produce mass housing for the German public by the mid-1920s. "Realism" was the point of departure common to these two strains of *neue Sachlichkeit*, just as, formally, they were both impersonally exact in the handling of their respective media. Grosz and Dix painted in a dry, linear manner stripped of the expressionist painterly gesture, while the new architects cleansed their work of ornament and historical reference.

The *neue Sachlichkeit* was destined to win the day in Germany. It was related to an impulse felt everywhere on the Continent that led to the production of cool, order-conscious endeavors in all the arts. By 1923 Igor Stravinsky was composing in an astringent neoclassical style emphasizing musical form rather than personal expression while Pablo Picasso painted figurative images in a classicizing mode. Strenuous antiromantic movements took form—de

Stijl in Holland and constructivism in the Soviet Union—while in Paris Le Corbusier was promoting a *rappel a l'ordre* in design on the pages of the journal *L'Esprit Nouveau*.

. . .

Ludwig Mies, stonecutter's son, one-time employee of Bruno Paul's and Peter Behrens's, disciple of Schinkel and admirer of Hendrik Berlage, now began to construct a series of professional relationships appropriate to the modern world he was part of. By the end of 1921, he had come to know Theo van Doesburg, the chief ambassador of de Stijl, who had moved to Berlin a year earlier. Russian-born constructivist El Lissitzky was also in the capital, and in contact with van Doesburg. Thus, the most persuasive spokesmen for two of the boldest new movements in European art converged on the German capital—if not on Mies—almost at once.

Through van Doesburg Mies met Hans Richter, an artist of varied talents and interests who personified the adventurous mood of the German arts in the aftermath of the war.[7] Richter had been part of the Dada group in Zurich before returning to his native Berlin in 1919. There he collaborated with Swedish artist Viking Eggeling in abstract "scroll pictures" that quickly evolved into abstract films. The two men joined the Novembergruppe, a society of artists, including painters, architects, and filmmakers, who sought to advance the revolutionary cause through the arts, especially in exhibitions of newly conceived work.[8] Richter's atelier became a favorite meeting place for a company of international artists, poets, and critics drawn to Berlin by an atmosphere of intellectual freedom unique in Europe.

"This circle," Richter later wrote, "included Arp, Tzara, Hilberseimer, van Doesburg, but soon also Mies van der Rohe, Lissitzky, Gabo, Pevszner [*sic*], Kiesler, Man Ray, Soupault, Benjamin, Hausmann, etc."[9] Among that company, van Doesburg and El Lissitzky were especially vigorous in promoting the doctrine of abstraction, the elimination of naturalistic references from painting and sculpture and of historical references from architecture. In their own work, the two had already carried geometric abstraction to sophisticated, rationalized extremes.

Mies found much to accept—and a good deal to learn from—in the published statements of van Doesburg, whose lecture "The Will to Style," delivered widely during 1921 and 1922, included the claim that "all that we used to designate as Magic, Spirit, and Love will now be efficiently accomplished."[10] And van Doesburg's affinity with the constructivists is reflected in Alexander Rodchenko's aphorism: "Consciousness, experiment ... function, construction, technology, mathematics—these are the brothers of the art of our age."[11] Indeed, the "age" now became a special preoccupation of nearly all modernist artists, and no one was more obsessed with it than van Doesburg.

. . .

At a time when these views were at their liveliest and most influential, Mies, in an act of will, began to work in a modernist manner. Looking back on it from the perspective of forty years, he made the following reply to the assertion that "in 1919 you seem to have broken completely with everything you had done before":

> I think the break started long before. The break started when I was in the Netherlands working on the problem of the Kröller museum. There I saw and studied carefully Berlage. I read his books and his theme that architecture should be construction, clear construction. His architecture was brick, and it may have looked medieval, but it was always clear.[12]

An alternate explanation was offered by Gene Summers, Mies's chief assistant during much of his American career, who noted that Mies "had lots of time when he was in the army to think. He had just gotten back to Berlin where so many things were happening in the arts. I am not sure that these were his exact words, but that was the meaning: he said 'I knew that I had to get on with it. I had to make this change.'"[13] It is also likely that Mies was reacting to his rejection from the 1919 Exhibition of Unknown Architects, an event, sponsored by the Arbeitsrat für Kunst (Workers' Council for Art), that sought to present the most innovative recent European art and architecture. Mies's Kröller-Müller project was turned down by the show's organizer, none other than Walter Gropius, who said: "We can't exhibit it; we are looking for something entirely different."[14] It is not certain whether Mies's purchase of a painting in the same year, 1919, was another reflection of a changed attitude, but the work, *Winter II*, by Wassily Kandinsky, was at the leading edge of European modernist painting when it was executed in 1911. Mies bought it from Herwarth Walden's Galerie der Sturm, then the gallery of choice for Berlin's avant-garde. Mies of the Riehl House years was mostly indifferent to painting, but the Kandinsky canvas, which he hung in his Berlin apartment, may be another indicator of his new commitment to modernism.

The first strictly architectural evidence of that commitment came two years later, in a competition entry for a skyscraper that is among the seminal achievements of his career. As early as 1912, the *Berliner Morgenpost* had issued an open letter asserting that tall buildings could bring a more effective concentration of business and social activities to the urban core. Despite the post-armistice economic distress, this idea was revived with enthusiasm in the early 1920s. Germans were hugely impressed with American skyscrapers, and with the United States itself—"the land of unlimited possibility," as it was commonly called—and the skyscraper was its most potent symbol. In the words of Germany's foreign minister, Walther Rathenau: "Nothing since the Middle Ages is as architecturally imposing as New York City."[15]

Late in 1921, the Berlin Turmhaus-Aktiengesellschaft (literally "tower corporation") sponsored one of the first German skyscraper competitions, for an office building on a prominent, three-sided site it controlled on the Friedrichstrasse, adjacent to Berlin's gateway railroad station of the same name. Issued with only a six-week deadline, the brief was daunting, including most notably the requirement that the already dense urban environment be enhanced, and not "brutalized," by a building up to eighty meters tall. The program called for offices, studios, shops, a café, a movie theater, and a garage. With little paying work on the boards, virtually all of Berlin's major architects responded, and 145 entries were received.

Most of the proposals featured one or multiple towers set back from shorter, flanking masses. The dominant style, though in great variety, was expressionist; acute angles, spiky forms, and massive blocks disposed against one another were legion. Yet *Sachlichkeit* was also in evidence. Adolf Behne, surveying the lot in *Wasmuths Monatshefte für Baukunst*, was gratified that "our architects knew quite precisely that antique columns do nothing for a skyscraper." Consistent with his antiexpressionist views, Behne praised Mies's entry, code-named Wabe, or "Honeycomb," because "it does nothing to conjure any particular emotion."[16] And Max Berg commended its "striv[ing] for the highest simplicity ... the broadest concept ... an enriching effort to master the fundamental problem of a tall building."[17]

There is evidence that "Honeycomb," the only Friedrichstrasse Office Building now remembered by history, was reworked after the competition and possibly substantially reconceived for inclusion in the publications that would make it famous. The competition proved to be little more than a publicity stunt; the sponsors had secretly proposed a construction on their own. That project failed, due in large part to financial problems, and nothing was ever built.[18]

Mies's entry drew no official notice. The jury, all conservative Berlin architects, no doubt felt justified in ignoring it. Mies offered a connected, nearly symmetrical bundle of three obliquely angular prismatic towers, twenty stories high, sheathed entirely in floor-height glass. The building volumes are pushed to the points of the triangular site and connected by linking corridors and stairs to a circular array of elevators. The face of each triangular unit is in turn interrupted by a semicircular notch aligned in plan—for no obvious reason—with the terminus of an interior corridor. The exterior walls on either side of this notch are canted slightly inward, enhancing the elevational play of reflection. The structure is likely of steel, though in the renderings and collages the floors and columns are impossibly thin, and the necessary shear walls entirely absent. Berg again, less affirmatively: "The plan corresponds not at all with the image of a building of manifold function. Only if it were meant as a warehouse would there be some excuse for the great depth of the rooms and the exceptional amount of light that would surely come through such large expanses of glass."[19]

Technically, Berg may have been right, but he failed to appreciate that Mies offered not a building but a manifesto. His Friedrichstrasse Office Building was exactly what Berg had called it, an attempt to "master the fundamental problem of a tall building."[20] In this, his first notable modernist project, the essential Mies van der Rohe is already in evidence, "solving" what he took to be "architectural problems," in search of a modern solution for the prototypical tall building.

However idiosyncratic it may appear, the design is remarkable — not least, as we have already witnessed, as a product of Mies's exceptional draftsmanship, but even more as the first proposal for a tall building sheathed in glass (fig. 3.4). It hardly matters than an all-glass skin was far beyond the threshold of constructability. Free of historicism as well as any of the vocabulary of the contemporaneous (American) skyscraper, the conjoined tower components reflect one another in a lively juxtaposition of acute and obtuse angles. Again, through the brilliance of the graphic presentation, these angles all but dematerialize a building of three-quarters of a million square feet, large even by twenty-first-century European standards. In plan the concept is less inspired, and even confused. There are too many angles and nooks, and none of what Mies would later make a central principle of his art: a clear, ordered structure.

Mies commented on "Honeycomb" in his first published writing, which appeared in the summer issue of *Frühlicht*, a magazine published by Bruno Taut:

> Only in the course of their construction do skyscrapers show their bold, structural character, and then the impression made by their soaring skeletal frames is overwhelming. On the other hand, when the facades are later covered with masonry this impression is destroyed and the constructive character denied, along with the very principle fundamental to artistic conceptualization. These factors become overpowered by a senseless and trivial chaos of forms. The best that can be said for such buildings is that they have great size; yet they should be more than a manifestation of our technical ability. Above all we must try not to solve new problems with traditional forms; it is far better to derive new forms from the essence, the very nature of the new problem. The structural principle of these buildings becomes clear when one uses glass to cover non-load bearing walls. The use of glass forces us to new ways.[21]

The rhetoric is recognizably Miesian—given to aphorism, selectably quotable, and sometimes at odds with itself. His antiexpressionist, antidecorative position is clear in his scorn for "a senseless and trivial chaos of forms." In search of a rational method, he called for the derivation of building from the "nature of the ... problem," setting a course he would pursue for the rest of his life. And though he emphasized "structural character" and rationalized his application of glass—which "forces us to new ways"—he was so captivated by the material itself that in his famous perspective drawing he celebrated the shimmering expanse of wall at the expense of any commitment to the building's structure.

Immediately following the Friedrichstrasse project, Mies developed a second and, as it proved, even more influential tall building proposal, now known as the Glass Skyscraper (fig. 3.5). It is associated with no client, program, or definite site. Mies probably developed the drawings and model with the goal, quickly realized, of publication and professional promotion. At thirty stories the Glass Skyscraper was to be half again taller than the Friedrichstrasse design, though Mies allowed the vanguard journal *G* to publish a twenty-one-story version to fit the cover of its issue no. 3. The Glass Skyscraper was to be freely amoeboid in plan, each identical floor an impossibly thin slab supported by a few improbably slender columns. The structural system was not described, and though it was probably conceived to be concrete, the flat slabs shown had not yet been invented and, in common with the Friedrichstrasse project, the necessary structure to resist lateral loads is absent. Like Friedrichstrasse, the envelope was to be floor-height glass, each panel about two meters wide, stunningly transparent in the model and seductively reflective in Mies's beautiful charcoal drawings. The photograph of the model became the project's chief memorial—a soaring extrusion of undulating, crystal-clear glass wrapping a dramatically attenuated structure. Both skin and structure were unbuildable at the time.

As late as 1951, in a letter to a correspondent who had requested details, Mies defended the project as wholly conceptual; "it was," he wrote, "entirely of an abstract nature[,] not to solve the specific function of each space, nor to solve the mechanical or structural problems, but, specifically, to investigate the use of glass as an exterior enclosing element and to find what the consequences would be architecturally."[22] Mies may have believed this when he wrote it, but the model, drawings, and photographs give the reasonable impression that the Glass Skyscraper was a complete building proposal, not a narrow experiment. It was the free-form plan and unprecedented structural drama, not the investigation of glass, that made the project famous.

The Friedrichstrasse Office Building and the Glass Skyscraper, in spite and because of an encompassing absence of detail, remain landmarks in tall building history. This is not simply because they are the early, inspired of-

ferings of the modern Mies van der Rohe. In these first efforts at imagining tall buildings, Mies created—apparently entirely on his own—novel, compellingly free forms, radically without reference to the planning, massing, or historicist detailing of any architecture up to that time. Other architects had advocated these goals, especially in the symbolically important category of the tall building; but none had delivered on them, even as proposals. The forms Mies imagined were (nearly) made possible by the application of a new technology: uninterrupted glazing as a building enclosure complete in itself. But here Mies was literally fifty years ahead of his time, for the technology to realize frameless, total glass enclosure was not available, and was not used to sheath whole buildings until the 1970s. It is an irony that the Mies of the 1920s, and the American Mies even more so later, had argued against the making of what others understood to be architectural *form*. The Friedrichstrasse Office Building and the Glass Skyscraper are vitreous forms par excellence—imagined buildings that vaulted their designer into the leadership of Germany's modernist phalanx.

·   ·   ·

During a twelve-month period beginning in early 1923, Mies produced designs for villas now known as the Concrete Country House and the Brick Country House. In an extended analysis, the architectural historian Wolf Tegethoff has argued from the limited evidence that Mies was very likely his own client for both projects, notwithstanding their lavish scale.[23] Each was probably conceived for the same site in Neubabelsberg—already the location of some of his built work—where Mies had been considering property and soliciting wealthy clients who were likewise seeking to build.

Of the Concrete Country House, no plan exists. Two photographs of a clay or plaster model offer the best exterior detail, though an entire elevation is undisclosed and the model is lost (figs. 3.6 and 3.7). There are perspective drawings of the exterior in various colors but of the same view. Still less survives to document the Brick Country House, which is known from just two contemporaneous photographs: one of a perspective drawing by an unidentified hand and a second, partially out of focus, of the now iconic plan. A second floor is referenced, but no plan for it exists or, insofar as we know, ever did.

In spite of the fragmentary record, these two houses are among the most famous of the twentieth century. Both are early examples of the modernist "open plan," and both embody structural and detailing strategies that Mies would soon make famous in the German Pavilion at Barcelona's International Exposition and the Tugendhat House. Debts to the flowing residential interiors of Frank Lloyd Wright are often mentioned, and legitimately, though Mies's planning is far more radical. In any event, there is much more than the open

FIGURE 3.6.
Model of the Con-
crete Country House
(1924). Note the pin-
wheel plan.

FIGURE 3.7.
Model of the Con-
crete Country House
(1924). The several
changes of grade are
a common theme in
Mies's domestic ar-
chitecture.

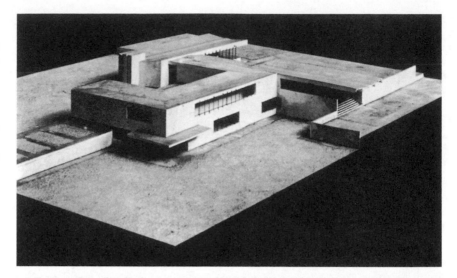

plan in both proposals, especially in the Concrete Country House, which, of the two, is conceptually richer.

Mies's own remarks about the Concrete Country House, like much of his other writing of this period, are matter-of-fact:

The chief advantage in the use of reinforced concrete as I see it is the opportunity to save a great amount of material. In order to realize this in a dwelling it is necessary to concentrate the bearing and supporting forces on only a few points in the structure. The disadvantage of reinforced concrete is its inefficiency as an insulator and its being a great conductor of sound. There-fore it is necessary to provide special insulation as a barrier against outside temperatures. The simplest method of dealing with nuisance of sound con-duction seems to me to be the elimination of everything that generates noise: I am thinking more of rubberized flooring, sliding windows and doors, and other similar precautions, but then, too, of spaciousness in the ground floor layout.[24]

To these words Mies added nothing about expressive significance, and his observations about concrete, though narrowly correct, are largely irrelevant, especially his mention of saving "a great amount of material," since in practice any such saving would have been swamped by the cost of forming, reinforc-ing, and finishing his exotic system. Structurally, the Concrete Country House was to be a group of freely disposed, interlocking concrete volumes of walls and roofs acting as prismatic shells. Each volume would be carried on at most four columnar points that were independent of the enclosure. The plane of the all-concrete roof was to be reinforced with embedded steel beams or very flat trusses (it is unclear which). Thus, Mies envisioned a potentially new ap-plication for concrete construction, one in which a building enclosure could be freely punctuated by long strips of windows, oversized doors, or even voids. Strip windows, soon to become a cliché of International Style mod-ernism, appeared here for the first time in Mies's work. The whole was em-bellished with boldly cantilevered canopies, and the possibilities for three-dimensional form-making, though only modestly exploited, are nevertheless clear. This same system would allow for optimization of views and access to light, thereby investing residential architecture with a new kind of spatial and visual communion with nature. And even though the structural system would be unaffordable, it was not a technical fantasy.

The Brick Country House of 1924, by contrast, is structurally even more of a cipher (fig. 3.8). Here we witness the modern open plan at its birth, with Mies apparently redefining domesticity (with, as speculated, himself as client) in total service to a spatial concept. Interior space and the boundary between inside and out are suggested but uncircumscribed by bearing walls or glass, or, in most cases, even by the conventional meeting of two vertical planes to form a corner. An interior program is barely suggested; the plan offers but two lettered designations, "living space" and "service space." There are no rooms as such, and doors are absent. Walls, mere opaque planes, are all the same indeterminate thickness, and presumably of brick. We cannot be sure of what we presume to be fireplaces. Even the limits of construction are indetermi-nate, with walls pinwheeling beyond the edge of the drawing.

The conceptual purity of the Brick Country House—or, alternately, its am-biguity—is partly a function of its hypothetical nature. Indeed, each of the

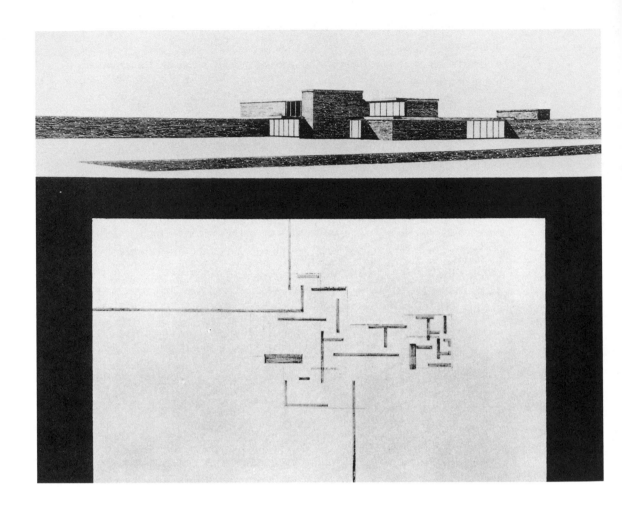

FIGURE 3.8.
Aerial perspective
(*top*) and plan of the
Brick Country House
project (1924). The
plan drawing re-
sembles images pro-
duced by the Dutch
de Stijl movement. It
has often been com-
pared with Theo van
Doesburg's painting
*Rhythm of a Russian
Dance*. But van Does-
burg's image evolved
from naturalistic fig-
uration. Mies's was
an architectural ab-
straction.

1921–24 projects thus far discussed, as well as another, the Concrete Office Building, to some degree achieved coherence and influence because of their nonreality. That Mies's reputation as a member of the avant-garde depended so much on hypothetical projects is without precedent in architecture's modern movement.

． ． ．

It was during this period and in this atmosphere that Mies assumed a new professional identity. In the fall of 1921, he began to call himself Ludwig Mies van der Rohe. On his September 13, 1921, submittal for a building permit for the Eichstaedt House, he signed his name "MRohe," and at roughly the same time he changed his stationery to read "Miës van der Rohe." (Charles Jeanneret had become Le Corbusier the previous year.) In the first of myriad subsequent misspellings, Mies became "Mis van der Rohe" in Max Berg's *Bauwelt* review (May 25, 1922) of "Honeycomb."[25]

Thus, Mies joined his surname to his mother's maiden name by the invented linkage *van der*. Coming from Aachen, he had long admired things Dutch, and Holland's reputation for orderly living and sober good sense sat well with Germans of the Weimar years. He would not have dared to assume the designation of *real* German nobility, *von*, but *van der* was permissible; in German it sounded faintly elegant, though it was common enough to the Dutch.[26] In a further effort to muffle the disagreeable connotation of *Mies*, he added an umlaut over the *e* (a form never encountered in German): *Miës*, pronounced "myess." He persisted with this invention into the 1930s—it was on his professional stationery—though with less regularity. Most people continued to address him as Herr Mies, or Herr Mies van der Rohe, or, if they were personally close or in his employ, simply as Mies. *Ludwig* and its variants, including *Lutz* or *Louis*, became vestigial for all but family and a few childhood and prewar friends. Georgia van der Rohe (also an assumed name) claimed that *Rohe* was traceable to francophone Belgium, where it was originally *Roé*, later *Roye*, and finally *Rohe*.[27]

. . .

Concurrent with Mies's shift to modernism and the parallel redefinition of his own persona, progressive artists, designers, and theoreticians continued to pursue new directions in their work. The professional literature in all fields reflected these rapidly changing values and objectives. Russian novelist Ilya Ehrenburg, arriving in Berlin late in 1921, joined forces with his countryman, the ubiquitous El Lissitzky, to found the periodical *Veshch*, which aspired to "acquaint creative workers in Russia with the latest Western art [and] inform Western Europe about Russian art and literature." It would stand for "constructive art, whose task," in Lissitzky's words, "is not to decorate our life but to organize it." Similar statements issued from the Hungarian journal *MA* in the words of László Moholy-Nagy, now also in Berlin: "Constructivism is pure substance. It is not confined to the picture frame and pedestal. It expands into industry and architecture, into objects and relationships. Constructivism is the socialism of vision."[28]

In Paris the new direction toward an architecture of serious purpose and abstract rectilinearity was evident not only in the pages of *L'Esprit nouveau* but in Le Corbusier's seminal *Vers une Architecture*. Published in 1923, the book quickly established itself as the most significant summary of the postwar position. With the momentum swinging to the constructivist/*Sachlichkeit* view across the Continent, the restless van Doesburg carried the battle to the Bauhaus in Weimar. Uninvited by Gropius and less than officially welcome at the school, he presented a series of off-campus lectures in 1921 and 1922, inveighing against the crafts-expressionist emphasis that had dominated the school since its opening in 1919. Van Doesburg also railed against the teaching and influence of the school's then dominant faculty member, the mystic Johannes Itten.

By the end of 1923 Itten was gone, replaced by Moholy-Nagy, who became the chief faculty promoter of the constructivist ideals that guided the school through much of the rest of the decade. Gropius had begun his own retreat from expressionism even before Moholy arrived, demonstrated by the constructivist design he and Adolf Meyer submitted to the 1922 Tribune Tower competition in Chicago. Bruno Taut's magic dreams began to evaporate as his appointment to the directorship of municipal building in Magdeburg forced him toward practicality and *Sachlichkeit*. Within a few years he would be talking affirmatively about the relationship of architecture to the machine and industrial production.

The swift pace of events in the early and mid-1920s in Germany may be measured by Mies's personal connections as well as by changes in his work and outlook. These were years of polemics and politics, ego and ideals, of individuals and groups jockeying for position, colliding, and conspiring. Ideology was the order of the day; there was no other route to acceptance in the world with which Mies had allied himself. Over the next decade, he would see to it that he was continuously in print.

.   .   .

According to Richter, the magazine *G* was conceived in 1920, when van Doesburg, on his first visit to Berlin, urged Richter and Eggeling to put together a journal of opinion on the arts.[29] "Beginning 1922," Richter wrote, "we finally had enough material for two numbers. But that moment the money was already gone and besides that, Eggeling and I had separated; and only towards the end of 1922 I got [a] small amount of money that allowed me at least to start.

"The title '*G*' was conceived in 1922 by Lissitzky as an abbreviation of Gestaltung ['formation,' 'forming,' or 'creative organization'].... To honor Doesburg's co-foundership," reported Richter, "we put a square behind the letter G."[30]

The first issue appeared in July 1923 under the editorship of Richter, Lissitzky, and the young Bauhaus-educated Werner Graeff.[31] It declared an uncompromising hostility toward romance and subjectivity in art. Statements on the cover page were implacably materialist, dismissive of individualized aesthetics, and advanced in the exalted and abstract terms of a café manifesto:

"The fundamental demand of elemental form creation is economy. Pure relation of power and material. That requires elemental means, total control of means. Elemental order, regularity...

"We have no need for a beauty that, as a mere flourish, is pasted onto our (precisely oriented) existence—we need an inner order for our existence."[32]

The authors of these words, which define ends and not means, are listed as Richter and Graeff. Mies contributed his own openly confrontational statement to the same issue:

"We reject every aesthetic speculation, every doctrine, and every formalism...

"Create the form from the nature of the task with the means of our time. That is our task."[33]

He was no less bold in the second issue of G, published in September 1923:

> We know no formal problems, only building problems.
>
> Form is not the goal but the result of our work.
>
> There is no form in itself [an sich].
>
> Form as goal is formalism, and we reject that....
>
> Our task is precisely to liberate building activity from the aesthetic speculation of developers and to make it once again the only thing it should be, namely building.[34]

The foregoing prose is "elementary" in the ultimate sense; in raising "problems of building" above "problems of form," it effectively does away with style.

. . .

During the period in which the first issue of G was assembled—late 1922 or early 1923—Mies developed a major speculative project, the Concrete Office Building. It was the last of what became known as the famous five projects of 1921–24,[35] and the most sachlich, the least hospitable to subjective nuance, and closest in tone to the editorializing of G (fig. 3.9). We know it from yet another example of Mies's exceptional graphics (though in this instance he directed the work of assistants), a nine-foot-wide charcoal perspective displayed at the Great Berlin Art Exhibition of 1923, and from a statement over Mies's byline in the first issue of G:[36]

> The office building is a place of work ... of organization ... of clarity ... of economy.
>
> Bright, wide working spaces, clearly laid out, undivided, subdivided only according to the organism of the firm.
>
> Maximum effect with minimum expenditure of means.
>
> The materials are concrete, iron, glass.
>
> Ferroconcrete buildings are by nature skeleton buildings. Neither baked goods nor armored towers. Supporting girder construction; a non-supporting wall. Hence: skin-and-bone buildings.[37]

FIGURE 3.9.
Concrete Office
Building project
(1923). The charcoal-
on-paper draw-
ing, rendered over
a rough plaster sur-
face, was nine feet
wide. It was first
shown at the Great
Berlin Art Exhibition
of 1923.

Mies discussed the plan, dimensions, and other specifics, describing a reductively functional office building free of blandishments and quirks. Rhetorically, the Concrete Office Building was emblematically progressive. At the
same time, as architecture, it approaches the dystopian.

Skin and bones it was, on a scale then unknown in Europe. As depicted, the
building seems of intentionally indeterminate length; but assuming the entry
is near the center of the elevation, the floor plate was around 100,000 square
feet—less the area of a barely suggested interior court—an office behemoth
even by today's standards. The reinforced-concrete slab, girder, and flared-
column structure is admirably clear and powerful, though Mies strangely concealed much of it behind the tall concrete parapet, which is *of* a structural
material but not *employed* structurally. Mies argued in *G* that the parapet
could accommodate (and screen from the outside) typical file cabinets, free-
ing space on the interior. But such a prescribed placement was surely too rigid
for the filing requirements of a typical office, and an all-glass exterior, which
Mies embraced for his skyscraper proposals, would have been rational and
structurally demonstrative.

While we have only a single drawing from which to judge, the whole effort is
hulking, cold, and disturbingly without scale. Today we would dismiss it as ur-
banistically anticontextual, a transgression that some claim modern architecture invented. And the concept was inseparable from its scale; Mies identified
the vastness of his creation with the scale of modern business organization,
and his rhetoric celebrated that identity. Still, there are subtleties: Mies very
slightly increased the end-bay cantilever from floor to floor, whether for visual

or structural reasons or both, though the change is almost too small to read. The attic floor and the partially below-grade occupancy relieve and invigorate the massing, but they were probably introduced not for visual reasons but as functional solutions to the six-story height limit then imposed in Berlin. We have no idea of the exterior wall texture, or of the jointing and detailing of the concrete parapet, and Mies may not have addressed this or even considered it important. Nevertheless, a real building of this type and scale would likely succeed or fail on these critical details.

G appeared in three more issues, and Mies went so far in his commitment to its hard line to personally finance the third issue in 1924, evidently at considerable cost, since it included the assembly of a full sans-serif font that, in Graeff's words, "was 'elemental,' for it alone reveals clearly that it is constructed, whereas the customary printing types ... imitate the character of handwriting."[38]

From among the G group, van Doesburg emerged as Mies's closest intellectual comrade, at least for a time. Never comfortable in his relationship with Gropius, Mies sided with van Doesburg when Gropius, as we have noted, shifted from an expressionist to a constructivist position in 1922/23. That so-called reform, Mies wrote van Doesburg, had led not to an "authentically constructive" approach to design but to an arty formalism, a "juggling of Constructivistic form."[39] Yet during the very time Mies was criticizing Gropius to van Doesburg, he was carrying on an altogether cordial correspondence with the director of the Bauhaus. Though Gropius had declined the Kröller-Müller project for the 1919 Arbeitsrat für Kunst exhibition, he now asked Mies to participate in a show at the Bauhaus planned as a review of the best of the new European architecture. Mies promptly accepted, and sent several postwar pieces.

Comparable ambivalence marked Mies's relationship with two other significant figures of the period. In 1921 he invited Swabian architect Hugo Häring to share working space in his office/atelier. There the two men spent hours discussing the art of building, mostly on friendly terms, although their differences were sharp enough to eventually become memorable notes in the legend of the modern movement. Häring—more theorist than builder—was a believer in a special type of "organic" architecture that, as he defined it, consisted of developing designs solely as they fit their purpose and independent of any preconceived aesthetic principle. Mies might have found little to dispute in that point of view, but the buildings Häring derived from it bore no resemblance to those of Mies. Gut Garkau, a group of buildings Häring designed in 1923–26 for a farm in Schleswig-Holstein, is notable for eccentric massing, freedom from standard geometric strategies, and novel structural solutions.

The relationship of Mies and Häring endured comradeship and contention. Both had been members of a group of progressive architects calling itself the

Zehnerring (Circle of Ten), which met during 1923 and 1924 at Am Karlsbad 24. In 1926 the group, with the two colleagues continuing as members, expanded beyond Berlin and changed its name to the Ring, which proved to be one of the most important forces for the New Architecture during the remainder of the 1920s. Häring was also an assistant in the production of Mies's early site plan for the 1927 Weissenhof housing settlement in Stuttgart. Yet sharp disagreements between the two over Weissenhof led Mies to withdraw from the Ring in 1927. The relationship came to a full stop with Mies's immigration to the United States in 1938 and Häring's decision to remain in Germany.

Mies's association with van Doesburg also ran on two tracks. In the March 1923 issue of *De Stijl*—published during the high tide of *G*, of which van Doesburg was one of the founders—van Doesburg referred to painting as "the most advanced form of art," which "indicates the path leading toward modern architecture."[40] This was probably meant as a critical reproach to the anti-aesthetic ideology of *G*. Mies rejected van Doesburg's elevation of aesthetics above constructive logic. Indeed, his statement in *G* of May 1923, "We reject all aesthetic speculation, all doctrine, all formalism," was likely intended as a rebuttal to van Doesburg.

Yet two months later, van Doesburg invited Mies to show his work in a fall exhibition at Leonce Rosenberg's L'Effort Moderne gallery in Paris, and Mies eagerly accepted. The curious composition of that show was a further sign of the mixed allegiances of the day. It was devoted to the architecture of de Stijl, though among the exhibitors only Mies was not a member of the movement. Van Doesburg specifically encouraged him to submit a model of the Glass Skyscraper, a work hardly illustrative of the principles of de Stijl. Mies also wanted a model of the Concrete Office Building included in the exhibition, so as to display the two works in relation to each other, and to underscore his elementarist belief that as building problems differ, so must the product. In the end, shipping problems made it impossible to include the models, and Mies was represented by perspectives and photographs of both projects as well as a perspective of the Concrete Country House.

Before long, Mies began to soften the edges of the constructivist materialism that had been the driving force of *G*. The time was right. During 1924 and 1925, the Weimar Republic enjoyed a hopeful reversal of political and economic fortunes. In 1924 the aforementioned Dawes Plan went into effect. Organized to help Germany ease her burden of runaway inflation, the plan also provided that the Ruhr be evacuated by Allied occupation troops, who had been there since Germany defaulted on reparations. The murderous inflationary spiral ended, and the nation began a swing toward prosperity and stability that it had not known since the Hohenzollerns.

Architecture was affected almost immediately, fueled especially by new subsidy programs enacted by national, provincial, and municipal governments. Modern architecture became buildable, on a scale destined to grow over the coming years. An acute housing shortage, combined with the activated patronage of a progressive Social-Democratic government, made for circumstances in which the New Architecture became physical fact.

But as modernism advanced, so did resistance, chiefly from conservative individuals and agencies opposed to change in traditional German architecture. Mies threw himself into the debate. Having earlier ignored progressive organizations, he now entered their councils with a will. Following the 1923 shows at L'Effort Moderne in Paris and the Bauhaus in Weimar, he was included in exhibitions in Jena, Gera, Mannheim, Düsseldorf, and Wiesbaden, even in Poland, Italy, and the Soviet Union. He restricted his entries to recent projects: the Glass Skyscraper, the Concrete Office Building, the Concrete Country House, and now and then the Brick Country House. He welcomed publication in avant-garde journals: *Die Baugilde* and *Die Form*, organs, respectively, of the Bund Deutscher Architekten and the Deutscher Werkbund, plus *Querschnitt*, *Qualität*, and *Merz* in Germany and *L'Esprit Nouveau* in France. He joined the BDA in 1923, at about the same time the Zehnerring began operations.

The Ring assumed its new name in 1926, two years after Ludwig Hoffmann stepped down as Berlin building commissioner. As the progressives saw it, Hoffmann's retirement occurred at a critical moment. The position was central to both city planning and the regulatory approval of individual buildings. A veteran architect with Wilhelmine roots, Hoffmann was conservative by 1920s standards, and the younger architects considered him a professional foe. Sensing that his departure and the promising new economic conditions added up to an opportunity to reshape municipal architectural policy, the Ring promptly issued demands for reforms in the commissioner's office: greater freedom for individual architects, elimination of politics in judging designs, quicker approvals, and better-qualified competition jurors.

A long, noisy conflict followed. Conservatives of the BDA sought to dissociate themselves from the Ring and vice versa. Mies, one of the strongest proponents of the vanguard position, finally resigned from the BDA in January 1926. Within weeks, the Ring initiated efforts to form a national organization of progressive architects, an objective reached in November, at about the time Martin Wagner, a founding member of the Ring and a confirmed progressive, was appointed building commissioner in Berlin.

The modernist cause thus leaped still further ahead, as it had in other ways throughout Germany in the months following economic stabilization. Cooperative, limited-profit building societies in several major cities, subsidized by state loans, began to produce housing projects on a significant scale, providing progressives with important commissions in the process. Most of these projects were designed in the functionalist-geometric manner that was becoming the hallmark of the New Architecture. Individual architects—Ernst May, Bruno Taut, Walter Gropius, Erich Mendelsohn, and Mies himself—drew increased public attention even as they excited hostility from their opponents. The most advanced and controversial architecture in the world was now German, encouraged by the atmosphere of experimentation and radical theorizing that had risen from the ashes of a discredited prewar tradition.

In 1925 Mies accepted an invitation to join the Deutscher Werkbund, reasoning that the organization was ready, as he put it, for a "transfusion of new blood."[41] Historically, the Werkbund had stood for quality in visual design, and to that end refused to endorse a movement or style. Now, however, with the hope of an artistic revival under the leadership of an architecture livelier than ever, the membership threw its weight behind the architects of *Sachlichkeit* with whom Mies was politically allied.

Mies himself traced this development largely to the radical sculptor Paul Rudolf Henning, who as a member of the Werkbund had been arguing that quality was attainable through elementarist construction (*elementare Gestaltung*): "In place of formal quality, the most important task for us is the design ideal of originality, self-evidence and purity of construction."[42] At the time, these words might have been Mies's. Henning and Mies lectured to the Werkbund on elementarist construction in mid-1924, with Mies thereafter exercising more and more personal sway over younger members. In 1926 he was named vice president, and though he insisted that Peter Bruckmann, honored elder statesman of the Werkbund and a symbol of organizational solidarity, occupy the presidency, Mies at forty had become the most powerful figure in the most firmly established technical society in Germany.

. . .

In later years, when Mies was enjoying fame in the United States, he was known as the silent Mies, taciturn and profound, who expressed himself in works rather than words. "Build, don't talk" was the charge his admiring students attributed to him. The image, exaggerated even then, is at odds with his active and skillful politicking within the Germany of the mid-1920s. Yet consistent with his biography, he was a long time in seeing his modern ideology translated into modern work. Among his realized designs, almost all were so traditional that by 1925 it could be said that he talked more modern architecture than he made.

We are not sure of his first post–World War I commission. It may have been nothing more auspicious than the marker he designed for the grave of Hugo Perls's mother, Laura, who died in 1919. An illustration in a magazine article of 1927 ascribed to Mies a flat-roofed Schinkelesque villa identified only as "Haus K," also dated 1919. This is the sole evidence of what may have been

FIGURE 3.10. Mosler House, Potsdam-Neubabelsberg (1926). Beginning with the Riehl House of 1907 and ending with the Mosler House of 1926, Mies designed traditional houses for nineteen years. But only six years passed between the Wolf House of 1927 and the Lemke House of 1933—the years in which he gained fame as a *modern* architect. Photo: T. Paul Young.

a preliminary stage of a house for Frau Franziska Kempner, which was completed to a different design by April 1922. The plans were submitted for approval of the Berlin building authorities in the summer of 1921, the year Mies resumed his practice in earnest. By the following November, he had also designed a house for the industrialist Cuno Feldmann, which was completed in June 1922. Stylistically close to each other, the Kempner and Feldmann Houses had austere, faintly Georgian brick exteriors: each a long, flat-faced, two-story mass flanked by wings and surmounted by a steep hipped roof. The Kempner House, in Berlin-Charlottenburg, was demolished in 1952. The Feldmann House in Berlin-Grunewald was razed following damage in World War II. The Eichstaedt House of 1923, which survives in Berlin-Nikolassee, is a hipped-roofed, square-plan villa in stucco that has been significantly altered. In 1924 Mies designed a one-story gymnasium that was added as a wing to Frau Butte's Private School, a neo-German, Renaissance-style building in Potsdam. Later additions so altered Mies's that our only reliable record is a pair of drawings discovered recently in the Potsdam Denkmalamt. One shows a plan and sections; the other, elevations. The last of Mies's traditional designs, the 1926 Mosler House in Neubabelsberg, recalls Kempner and Feldmann in its similarities with the layout of the Urbig House. The Mosler House is a long rectilinear brick mass with a steep hipped roof and dormer windows, with low annexes at its sides (fig. 3.10).

Mies did nothing to encourage critical attention to his conservative work. It was attractive and respectably executed, but it provides few hints of what was to come. Mies's cleanly incised, regularly ordered windows are apparent in the Kempner, Feldmann, and Mosler Houses, as is the origin of such concerns in Schinkel. Most intriguing is a side of Mies we rarely see: during the early 1920s, he was anything but unidirectional. In a client solicitation from 1924, he cited the Kempner, Urbig, and Mosler Houses as examples of his competence and promise. Yet in the same year, he wrote in a vanguard journal: "It is hopeless to try to use the forms of the past in our architecture. Even the strongest artistic talent must fail in this attempt. Again and again we see talented architects who fall short because their work is not in tune with their age. In the last analysis, in spite of their great gifts, they are dilettantes."[43] And even as he continued to design in traditional manners for some clients in the early 1920s, he offered modernist work to others. A perspective of the unbuilt Petermann House of 1921 features large windows set in walls free of ornament, while the plan of the Lessing House project of 1923 prefigures Mies's use of interiors linked to open courtyards. Neither project materialized, and we do not know why.

Much has been learned about the Ryder House since the publication of the first edition of this book, where it was mentioned briefly.[44] In 1923 Ada Ryder, an Englishwoman living in Wiesbaden, asked a local architect, Gerhard Severain, to design a house for a lot in the historic district of the city. Severain, who had little experience with construction, requested the assistance of Mies, with whom he had been friends since both were boys in Aachen. Mies undertook the complete design of the house, but took his time in sending the necessary drawings to Wiesbaden. Severain was aggrieved by the delay. He said so to Mies in letters harsh enough to threaten their friendship. Mies responded in kind.

The earlier bonhomie was eventually restored, but in the meantime a payment dispute developed between Severain and Ryder. Construction was stopped in 1924, and the house remained unfinished and unoccupied until it was purchased by one August Zobus, who saw to its completion in 1928. The shadow cast by these disagreements obscured the fact that Mies's design, his first with a flat roof, predated the modernism that was first fully realized in the 1926 Wolf House (finished two years before the Ryder House).

During these years, many of Mies's projects came to naught. He worked at a deliberate pace, sometimes against his interests. A 1925 project for the well-known painter Walter Dexel, director of the Jena Kunstverein, is an example, though the fault lay chiefly with his client.[45] On January 7, 1925, just four days after Mies was awarded the commission for a house in Jena, Dexel was prodding him to present concepts. Mies was soon peppered with anxious letters—to no effect. "For people whose store of patience tends to be below rather than above average," wrote Dexel, apparently without irony, "the idea of having an architect off somewhere [Mies was in Berlin] who neither keeps his promises nor answers questions is most unpleasant."[46] Dexel grew angry, and in the spring the commission was withdrawn. But before Dexel gave up on him, Mies asked for one extension, after which he produced a number of promising sketches. For a gently sloping site he proposed a two-story rectangular building with a one-story studio-office wing attached at a corner, with a veranda next to the garden doors of the main block of the house. Several variations featured an animated grouping of masses around a central chimney and attractive sightlines into the landscape.

In March 1925, Mies began work on another residential design that for reasons unknown was also never built. The client was Berlin banker Ernst Eliat. The site was in Nedlitz, a Potsdam suburb. The Eliat House, like Dexel's, was intended for a sloping site. Mies proposed a one-story elevation for the living quarters, overlooking a multiterraced sunken garden, and for services, a two-story lower level that offered a view of Lake Fahrländer. The plan is a modified pinwheel, recalling the Concrete Country House. From a core containing the entry, three wings probe the landscape, each with its own vista. The integration of architecture and landscape, which began at the Riehl House of 1907 and would continue with the Wolf House of 1926 and after, had become an abiding theme.

Mies's traditionalism ended with the Mosler House of 1926, and everything that followed was modern. But he did not go the way of the social functionalists, who began to dominate German architecture as the economy improved. Only once did he venture into low-cost, multiunit housing. His apartment complex on Berlin's Afrikanischestrasse was commissioned by the municipal authorities and constructed in 1926/27. Consisting of three U-shaped buildings with three-story façades and two-story wings at either end, and a fourth component of staggered two-story blocks, the group typified the leanly functional architecture of the *Existenzminimum*, identifiable as his chiefly by the carefully disposed, well-proportioned windows.

. . .

Commissioned in early 1925, the large house in Guben for the textile merchant and art collector Erich Wolf was Mies's first realized modern building. It survived not quite two decades; late in World War II it was bombed and burned out, its brick salvaged for other rebuilding. During that time Guben (now Gubin) became part of present-day Poland. These factors account for the house's relative obscurity prior to renewed scholarly interest in the 1990s. From the excellent photographic record (Mies's commissioned photographs are of the exterior only) and the surviving drawings, it is clear that the house offered Mies the opportunity to apply concepts recently conceived for the Brick and Concrete Country House projects for a client of progressive tastes and sufficient

means (fig. 3.11). We know that the client was satisfied, for in 1930 an adjacent parcel was acquired for an art gallery designed by Mies and intended for
Wolf's collection of nineteenth- and twentieth-century paintings and sculpture. For reasons unknown, the addition was never built.

The Wolf House enjoyed a panoramic view from a long, narrow, sloping lot
running down to the Neisse River. Mies sited it at the top of a series of existing
riprap terraces. Entry from the street was at the rear. There the vista was hidden by the interlocking cubical masses of the load-bearing, three-story brick
building, but it was visible from a suite of first-floor living and entertainment
spaces that opened onto an expansive paved terrace. In plan the living room,
music room, dining room, and study are an interlocked set, demarked here and
there by the stubs of freestanding walls. The spaces effectively flow together,
but the feeling is nevertheless far from the unbounded dynamism of the Brick
Country House. The dining room, facing south, was shaded by an ample concrete canopy continuous with the roof and supported by a single, too massive
cantilevered beam, drawn directly from the model of the Concrete Country
House. The terrace featured a sunken planting bed, in plan a rectilinear reflection of the house, framed by pinwheeled pavers, simple steps, and brick

84 / 85

retaining walls (fig. 3.12). The elevations were of Flemish-bond brick punched by asymmetrically disposed windows and doors. The fenestration was of two- and then three-light groupings. Doors were in some cases single, in others paired, but from the living room, three wide. Opening from the second-floor bedrooms—all conventionally enclosed rooms—were brick-paved terraces that exploited the views. Mies also wrapped a cantilevered balcony with ship's railings for the street-side second floor. Like almost all of Mies's European houses, before and after, the Wolf House was large and expensive.

The Wolf House preceded the German Pavilion at Barcelona by only about three years, and given what Mies would achieve in the pavilion with a similar vocabulary, it is therefore easy to criticize. The massing is ponderous; the brick is unrelenting; the plan is only tentatively open and hardly dynamic. The elevations, surprisingly for Mies, could benefit from *more* order.

Much of the furniture was designed by Mies together with the Berlin-born Lilly Reich, whom he met in 1924 and with whom he went on to establish a personal and professional relationship destined to last until her death in 1947. Of wood and upholstery, the Wolf furniture followed the conservative, austere lines of Mies's designs for his own Berlin apartment. Indeed, the house had remnants of traditional detailing Mies would soon abandon altogether—most prominently the soldier-course brick cornice and the decorative reentrant corners of the terrace chimney (themselves simplifications of an earlier concept even more decorative). As Wolf Tegethoff has pointed out, the house as seen from the Neisse below was particularly unsuccessful because

FIGURE 3.12.
Wolf House, Guben, Germany (later Gubin, Poland) (1927). The terrace, which featured a sunken planting bed, continued the geometry and materials of the house proper.

the garden retaining wall obscured the receding masses of the second and third floors. Tegethoff politely suggests that the "effect . . . was obviously not considered during the planning," but it is more likely that at this point the forty-year-old Mies—young by the standards of his profession—was still finding his way.[47] He would continue with brick houses into the 1930s, but his next major efforts, the Lange and Esters Houses, would not be load-bearing brick, and in the drive toward openness and transparency, "structural honesty" was not yet a goal. By comparison with the material splendor and radical openness of Barcelona, or even more so with the much later Farnsworth House, the Wolf House, despite its unhappy fate, remains in memory mostly a promise.

· · ·

Mies's other realized project of 1926 was no less exceptional. Indeed, it is singular within his corpus, not just because he never did anything else quite like it, but because it emerged from an unlikely mixture of capitalist wealth, Marxist-Communist ambition, the intent of the old arts, and the manner of the new. Mies may have abandoned historicism by 1926, but he retained an interest in clients of means. He learned that the Hugo Perls House, one of his early designs, had been purchased by the cultural historian, art collector, and political activist Eduard Fuchs, author of the well-known multivolumed *Sittengeschichte* (History of Morals). Knowing that Fuchs had put together an art collection, as Erich Wolf had in Guben, Mies hoped to meet Fuchs and persuade him to commission a new house similarly modern, with an exhibition space like the one he had designed for Wolf.

Fuchs had dreams of his own—not of a new house but of a new wing for his old one. And he knew of Mies, whom he already had in mind as his architect. One evening Fuchs invited Mies for dinner. We do not know when Mies joined the Gesellschaft der Freunde des neuen Russlands (Society of Friends of the New Russia),[48] but his membership card was issued in January 1926. The affiliation probably had something to do with Fuchs, who was not only a rich bourgeois but a high-ranking member of the German Communist Party. Mies may have rationalized his membership in the society by associating it with the many vanguard groups in the Berlin of the mid-1920s. There is no record of his later activity in its behalf.

Mies did produce an addition for the Fuchs-Perls House, but it had to wait two years. "After discussing his house problem" at dinner, Mies later recounted, "Mr. Fuchs then said he wanted to show us something . . . a photograph of a model for a monument to Karl Liebknecht and Rosa Luxemburg."[49] Fuchs was soliciting a design for a memorial to the martyrs of the ill-fated uprising of 1919 by the Spartacus League. Party official Wilhelm Pieck had proposed such a monument, and in July 1925 he claimed to have secured a model of it, the central feature of which was to be a sculpture by Auguste Rodin. This plan was never carried out. Mies reported that Fuchs, on the occasion of this, their first dinner together, showed him drawings of an elaborate neoclassical creation "with Doric columns and medallions of Luxemburg and Liebknecht," the two who had been slain. "When I saw it," said Mies, "I started to laugh and told [Fuchs] it would be a fine monument for a banker." Fuchs was not amused. Still, he telephoned Mies the next morning to ask what *he* would propose. "I told him I hadn't the slightest idea," Mies said he told Fuchs, ". . . but as most of these people were shot in front of a wall, a brick wall would be what I would build. . . . A few days later I showed him my sketch. . . . He was still skeptical about it and particularly when I showed him the bricks I would like to use. In fact, he had the greatest trouble to gain permission from his friends who were to build the monument."[50]

What Mies showed Fuchs and finally saw built in the Friedrichsfelde Central Cemetery in Berlin-Lichtenburg was what he had promised: a brick wall of sorts, more exactly a huge, rectilinear sculptural assembly in brick, 6 meters high, 12 long, and 4 wide (fig. 3.13). It consisted of a series of horizontal rectangular prisms in staggered layers, each vaguely like a single enormous Roman brick within a comparably outsized section of wall—"bonded," however, in the asymmetrical manner of constructivist sculpture, here extruded, there retracted.

The brick was purplish clinker, rough and burnt, scavenged by Communist workers from demolished buildings. That fact heightened the desired coarseness of what was metaphorically an executioner's wall. But the assembly was quite the opposite: the prismatic components were carefully proportioned and the laying up of the brick as refined as that in the Wolf House. At the bottom of each prism was a single header course underlining the unit, and there was even a set of brick treads in the base to facilitate climbing on. The whole had a rude, studied solemnity. Uncharacteristically for Mies, it was art meant for emotional effect. One cannot resist the posthumous irony of a remark made before World War I by Liebknecht himself to Hugo Perls: "Your architect seems a very capable man. Wait till the Independent Socialists [as opposed to the Social Democrats] are in power and we'll be able to make good use of him."[51]

By comparison with Mies's stoic masses, the symbolic star with the hammer and sickle is a superfluous literalism. Whether Mies wanted it or acceded to it is not known. The inscription ICH BIN ICH WAR ICH WERDE SEIN (I Am, I Was, I Will Be) on one of the panels to the left of the star appears in a photograph, but was removed by 1931 for reasons unknown. Mies took special pains to obtain the star, which was two meters in diameter, too large to be entrusted to a small fabricator. At first the Krupp Steelworks refused to supply what was clearly a

symbol of leftist radicalism, whereupon Mies ordered five identical diamond-shaped plates, which Krupp saw fit to provide. He had them assembled on-site to form the star that hung in place when the Communists, led by Ernst Thäl-mann and Wilhelm Pieck, unveiled the monument on June 13, 1926.

There were problems at the ceremony. The lighting of an eternal flame had not been rehearsed, and when the oil was ignited, a massive cloud of soot and ash burst forth, blackening the assembled. Afterward, Mies and several of his companions proceeded to a restaurant, where they were turned away on account of their appearance. The monument stood for seven years before it was demolished by the Nazis in 1933.[52]

. . .

Mies had been living the artist-bachelor's life for five years. Contacts with his family were confined to his own vacation trips and his daughters' visits to Berlin, with and without their mother. Convinced that a genteel martyrdom was the best she could offer a husband she loved but could not possess, Ada accepted her situation as permanent. Among those she knew from an earlier time and continued seeing socially was Karl Foerster, the renowned garden-reform theorist with whom Mies had worked most recently on the Urbig House and who maintained a large and varied garden in Bornstedt.

At the end of the 1922–23 school year, Ada and her daughters made their way to the Wallis district of French-speaking Switzerland (fig. 3.14). At a sanitarium in the resort town of Montana they visited Elsa Knupfer, a friend of both Ada's and Mies's since the Hellerau days, who was suffering from tuberculosis of the spine. Ada spent the summer close by her side, while "Knüpferlein" gave French lessons to the oldest daughter, Muck. In 1924 Ada moved with the children to Zuoz in the Swiss Engadin, where they joined another old Hellerau friend, Erna Hoffmann Prinzhorn, who had recently divorced her husband. The Mies girls were enrolled in a private German-language school. With their mother they spent most of a year in Zuoz, the four departing Switzerland in the spring of 1925, then pressing on to the South Tyrol, newly a part of Italy though steeped in its prewar Austrian heritage. There they rented a patrician town house in the village of Maria Assunta (Mariahimmelfahrt) overlooking the city of Bolzano (Bozen), halfway up the mountain to Soprabolzano (Oberbozen).

Life was materially comfortable, though Ada's health was fragile. She loved the mountains but was gradually forced to curtail her hiking as she suffered more and more from a fear of heights. When or why she first sought psychiatric help is not certain. Her daughters claimed she was not in any special distress, and that she entered psychoanalysis chiefly because in the 1920s it was the modish thing to do. But a letter dated June 15, 1925, to Mies from Hans Prinzhorn (who was himself practicing psychiatry in Frankfurt) suggests a

FIGURE 3.14.
Ada Mies with the
children, Waltraut
(*seated*), Marianne,
and Dorothea (*right*),
Montana, Switzer-
land, 1924.

more serious and enduring problem: "I hear from [Karl] Fahrenkamp [a Stuttgart heart specialist] that Ada has managed a recovery, through [Emile] Coué.
That would be wonderful, not just for the end of it, but thanks to all the sub-
terranean work of years."[53]

Ada sought additional therapy in the early 1930s from Heinrich Meng, a
Freudian analyst in Frankfurt, where she was then living. In view of this, the recovery that Fahrenkamp claimed had been achieved with the help of another
famous therapist, Emile Coué of Nancy, may be doubted. Meng's widow, born
Mathilde Köhler, who knew Ada and considered her a friend, recalled that her
psychic pain was of long standing, with origins traceable to her father.[54]

In view of Mary Wigman's recollection of Mies's need for personal and artistic freedom, it is unlikely that he would have extended sympathy or solicitude to a woman from whom he was content to be separated. Lora Marx, his
American companion, reported that he was, when she knew him, antagonis-
tic toward psychotherapy. His exchanges with Prinzhorn, whom he knew primarily as a friend, skirted the subject of psychiatry except where it touched
the arts.

This still left a lot to draw the two men together. Mies saw to the publication in *G* of an article by Prinzhorn on the latter's well-known topic, the art of psychotics. In turn Prinzhorn, who in 1925 was planning to produce an enormous "encyclopedia of living knowledge," was confident that Mies would contribute the text for an entire volume on the subject of architecture.

Prinzhorn misjudged his friend's capabilities. If Mies was professionally deliberate, he could be even slower in composing so much as a letter. Yet since Mies wrote more in the mid-1920s than at any other time in his life, Prinzhorn's error may be understood to a degree, and more so since Walter Gropius also asked Mies to write an essay for a volume in the series of *Bauhausbücher*, monographs published under the sponsorship of the Bauhaus, beginning in 1925. Mies produced nothing for either petitioner.[55]

Mies's relations with Gropius grew friendlier as the decade passed. In a private note to a colleague, Mies would sometimes repeat his misgivings about "formalism" at the Bauhaus, of which he had complained to van Doesburg in 1923/24. Yet the correspondence between Mies and Gropius grew trusting, even solicitous. Late in 1925, when Mies was approached by leading citizens of Magdeburg to make himself available for the post of city building commissioner (from which Bruno Taut had lately resigned), he received the following from Gropius:

> Of course I urgently counseled them to get you. I heard about the position several days ago, in Halle, and I was asked at that time what you had had to do earlier with Behrens. Apparently somebody in Magdeburg—I can guess who—has spoken out against you, suggesting you were dishonorably discharged by Behrens, or some such thing. I rejected that notion outright, without knowing any other details, simply because I know Behrens myself, well enough. Nevertheless, I would suggest to you confidentially that you keep your eyes open for the signs of burrowing moles.[56]

Mies's reply includes a reference to the same unnamed (and still unknown) enemy: "He has no idea how closely we work with Behrens today. In any case I thank you for your recommendation."[57]

Mies's comradeship with both Gropius and Behrens evidently counted for more than the quarrels and disagreements he had with either. His conduct toward them might further explain his ambivalent attitude toward van Doesburg, with whom he was still corresponding warmly in 1925, or with Mendelsohn, whose work he disliked for what he thought was its excessive plasticity. Mendelsohn was no fonder of Mies's work, finding it hard and angular, but Mies included him, as he did Gropius and Behrens, in several of the Novembergruppe exhibitions he organized in the mid-1920s.

In the politics of the German architectural world Mies had become a force, and he knew it. Persuaded that the Magdeburg authorities were looking for an *apparatchik* rather than someone of independent judgment, he advised the industrialist G. W. Fahrenholtz, who had earlier sought to interest him in the position, that he was not Magdeburg's man:

> If it is not possible for me to pursue the objectives I have set for myself in my own work, I have no intention of going there; Magdeburg must decide whether it wants to entrust the office to a *Routinier* or to a man of spiritual values.... It is being bruited about here that I am interested in Magdeburg because I want to be called a commissioner. The degree of my title mania is best measured by the record, namely, that I turned down the [directorship of the] Magdeburg [industrial design] school as well as professorships in Breslau and Dresden. No more words need be wasted over this.[58]

Mies resisted Magdeburg's subsequent efforts to placate him. He was, after all, well ensconced in Berlin by the end of 1925, with contacts only a cosmopolis could provide, enjoying the society that went with his art and his own expanding reputation. And he had a far more important assignment awaiting him than anything Magdeburg had to offer.

Weimar at High Tide: 1926–30

The whole thing bears more resemblance to a suburb of Jerusalem than to a group of houses in Stuttgart. **PAUL BONATZ**, disparaging the Weissenhofsiedlung, 1927

I asked, "For what purpose?" They [the government] said, "We don't know—just build a pavilion, but not too much glass!"
MIES, on the German Pavilion at the International Exhibition, Barcelona

Why shouldn't something be as good as possible? I cannot follow the train of thought where people say, that is too aristocratic, that is not democratic enough. As I've said, for me it is a question of value, and I make things as good as I can.
MIES'S opinion about the pavilion

From the first moment we met him, it was clear to us that he should be the one to build our house, so impressed were we by his personality. **GRETE TUGENDHAT**

Sponsored by the Deutscher Werkbund and completed in 1927, the Weissen-hofsiedlung (Weissenhof Settlement) was a demonstration housing colony in Stuttgart (fig. 4.1). As the project's "artistic director," Mies assembled an international company of designers of such talent, scope, and record that the buildings they designed for a hill overlooking the city certified, as nothing before, the triumph of the modernist program. His plan for the project together with the apartment block he contributed to it, and his codesign with Lilly Reich of the Plate-Glass Hall for an affiliated exhibition, embodied principles that he and others of his generation had only postulated. Weissenhof also proved to be the crucible in which Mies articulated a new understanding of architecture that was profoundly different from what he had thus far expressed in his writings. In the process, he resumed an interest in furniture design that had begun with Bruno Paul in 1907, and soon enough he took his place among the leading figures who transformed that art into modernist form.

By 1927 housing projects sponsored by German municipal governments and cooperative building societies had already been designed by some of the most important figures of the German vanguard: Otto Haesler in Celle, Ernst May in Frankfurt, Walter Gropius in Dessau, and Martin Wagner, Bruno Taut, and Hugo Häring in Berlin. The Deutscher Werkbund promoted this development. Convinced that architecture derived from machine technology, and

FIGURE 4.1.
Aerial view of the
Weissenhofsiedlung,
Stuttgart, in 1927.
View looking north-
west. Mies, Le Cor-
busier, and Gropius,
all alumni of Beh-
rens's Neubabels-
berg atelier, along
with Behrens him-
self, were among the
architects who par-
ticipated in the Stutt-
gart demonstration
project.

that machine form would revive the arts in contemporary society, the membership increasingly supported its radical leaders: Häring and Adolf Rading
were elected to the executive in 1926, and Ludwig Hilberseimer in 1927. The
association's journal, *Die Form*, became so preoccupied with the modernist
challenge that by 1927 it had become the unofficial organ of the New Architecture.

The Werkbund exhibition following the 1923 inflationary crisis was titled
Form ohne Ornament (Form without Ornament). It was organized by the Württemberg chapter and mounted in Stuttgart in 1924. In March 1925 the Werkbund proposed another exhibition for the following year, intended as its most
important since the historic 1914 exhibition in Cologne. That event was remembered for its buildings (notably Gropius's Model Factory, Bruno Taut's
Glass Pavilion, and van de Velde's Werkbund Theater), and for the famous controversy between Muthesius, who favored standardized products, and van de
Velde, who championed the individualized artwork. Stuttgart was again chosen as the site, due to the vanguardist record of the Württemberg branch and
its director, Gustav Stotz. The theme was the modern home, to be represented
by a colony of houses, including interiors and furnishings, by designers from
across Europe. "Only those architects," declared Werkbund president Peter
Bruckmann, "who work in the spirit of a progressive artistic form suited to to-

CHAPTER FOUR

day's conditions, and who are familiar with the appropriate technical equipment for house construction, will be invited."[1]

In view of Mies's record as a practitioner and polemicist, it was no surprise that the Werkbund executive selected him as the exhibition's artistic director. Just a year earlier, Mies had written in *G*: "I consider the industrialization of building methods the key problem of the day for architects and builders. Our technologists must and will succeed in inventing a material that can be industrially manufactured and processed. . . . All the parts will be made in a factory and the work at the site will consist only of assemblage, requiring extremely few man-hours. This will greatly reduce building costs. Then the new architecture will come into its own."[2]

Weissenhof seemed a promising vehicle to advance these possibilities. It was distinguished from other experimental housing projects of the day by its call for new methods in construction for a range of housing types. Economy was also central to the program. What emerged at Stuttgart followed this line, though inconsistently. Mies sought to achieve something else and something more at Weissenhof than he had affirmed in *G*. This could be inferred from his initial list of designers. Late in September 1925, Stotz, who became Mies's most trusted colleague at Stuttgart, submitted names for Mies's review: Peter Behrens, Paul Bonatz, Richard Döcker, Theo van Doesburg, Josef Frank, Walter Gropius, Hugo Häring, Richard Herre, Ludwig Hilberseimer, Hugo Keuerleber, Ferdinand Kramer, Le Corbusier, Adolf Loos, Erich Mendelsohn, Mies, J. J. P. Oud, Hans Poelzig, Adolf Schneck, Mart Stam, Bruno Taut, and Heinrich Tessenow.[3] Mies dropped Herre, Keuerleber, and Bonatz—all Stuttgarters—and Loos and Frank, adding Henry van de Velde, Hendrik Berlage, Otto Bartning, Arthur Korn, Wassily Luckhardt, Alfred Gellhorn, and Hans Scharoun.[4] He evidently preferred people he knew in Berlin, or in the Ring, to those he did not in Stuttgart. The presence of van de Velde and Berlage, both of whom were still committed to a craft tradition, indicates that Mies felt no obligation to promote a machine aesthetic exclusively.

The same independence is evident in his own site studies, photographs of which he had submitted to Stotz several weeks earlier. Mies's proposal was characteristically original, and not altogether consistent with economy or functionalism. He ignored the *Zeilenbau* system of the typical 1920s German housing project, in which units were spaced for sunlight and ventilation and disposed in straight, parallel rows at right angles to thoroughfares. Instead, he conceived a meandering assembly of interconnected, quasi-cubic forms— houses and apartments—arranged in curving terraces. Walkways free of automobile traffic were to provide access to a plaza surrounded and dominated by several large but low buildings. Like the Liebknecht-Luxemburg monument, the plan evokes the asymmetrical, interlocking massing of constructivist sculpture. As an urban plan it was unprecedented.

FIGURE 4.2.
Arab Village, a Nazi-sponsored manipulated photograph ridiculing the Weissenhofsiedlung, Stuttgart. Photo courtesy of the Mies van der Rohe Archive of the Museum of Modern Art, NY.

Mies was ostensibly generous in supporting design freedom for contributing architects. He required only that they employ flat roofs and white exteriors. Still, Mies's comments to Stotz indicate that he refused to sacrifice planning unity to individual liberties: "I have striven for an interconnected layout because I believe it *artistically desirable*, but also because we will not be so dependent on the individual collaborators. I have the presumptuous idea of inviting all the architects of the [aesthetic] left, which I believe would be an unheard-of success as an exhibition strategy."[5]

This was hardly the determinism that chilled the pages of *G*. Mies sounded not only like an artist but like an impresario alert to the plaudits of history. Although loyal to generality and unity in architecture, and opposed to individuality, he assumed his own right to define and interpret these principles. He was nonetheless accused of trespasses against *Sachlichkeit*, and attacked from both the Right and Left. The harshest critics were a pair of well-known architect-professors at the local *Hochschule*, Paul Bonatz and Paul Schmitthenner, leaders of the so-called Stuttgart school of architecture. More conservative than the new architects but heirs of a proud tradition, Bonatz and Schmitthenner published newspaper articles in Stuttgart and Munich accusing Mies of the very offenses he condemned in others. Schmitthenner called Mies's plan "formalistic" and "romantic," while Bonatz denounced it as *unsachlich* and "dilettantish ... a heap of flat cubes, arranged in manifold horizontal terraces, [which] pushes narrowly and uncomfortably up the slope; the whole thing bears more resemblance to a suburb of Jerusalem than to a group of houses in Stuttgart"[6] (fig. 4.2).

Bonatz's remarks went to the root of the opposition to the New Architecture that was growing among German conservatives. The simple massing that Mies identified with a purification of architectural form his antagonists labeled technically flawed and, worse, destructive of the "culturally German" pitched roof.[7] The New Architecture was understood by rallying antimodernists as yet another surrender, this time to presumably inferior ethnic traditions.

Mies had more than Bonatz to contend with. He answered all critics with a bluntness free of self-doubt. His own fellow modernist and confrere within the progressive circles of Stuttgart, Richard Döcker, wrote that he had intended to reproach Bonatz until he saw photographs of Mies's model. "I was taken aback, having expected something quite different," wrote Döcker, who went on to question whether Mies's plan was even reasonable: "The attempt, for example, to mix the one-, two-, and three-story blocks together as you have, is unorganic, in plan at best only partially possible, and thus *unsachlich*."[8]

Mies answered acidly:

> I must decline your good efforts to be helpful.... The model, let me make it clear, was meant to provide a representation of a general idea, not to indicate house sizes and the like.... I didn't receive the final space specifications until the middle of May [1926] anyway.... [And] do you really believe I would design rooms without light and air? ... You seem to understand a plan only in the old sense, as so many separate building parcels.... I think it necessary at Weissenhof to strike a new course. I believe that the new dwelling must have an effect beyond its four walls.[9]

Mies's planning position is consistent with his projects for the Concrete and Brick Country Houses of 1923 and 1924, and with his abiding interest in landscape. But his hopes of realizing these objectives were frustrated when the city decided that the exhibition houses, once finished, would be sold to private buyers, and that circulation internal to the compound must include automobiles. Real estate interests prevailed, and "separate parcels" became the rule.

The colony opened to the public July 23, 1927, one year late according to the original schedule (the project was canceled outright for a time in early 1926), and it is surprising that it was ready by then. To Mies's battles with local political officials, exhibition functionaries, his own presumed cohorts, and a legion of avowed enemies must be added his own trademark procrastination. Mia Seeger, who assisted Werner Graeff in the Weissenhof press department, called him "colossally slow," noting that it took him days to write a one-paragraph introduction to the exhibition catalog.[10] He approached Le Corbusier with an invitation to participate only on October 5, 1926, and as late as the following February, Max Taut, brother of Bruno—the two of them now among the Weissenhof designers—wrote Döcker: "My brother and I are shocked that the Stuttgart matter progresses no faster than it does. We find it incomprehensible that our colleagues are so far behind in their work.... Is there no way to get them moving, for that matter to press the city of Stuttgart to some conclusion about the direction it wants to take?"[11]

Construction began in March 1927, and it proceeded quickly, in many cases too much so, as technical failures proved soon enough. Inevitably, the list of architects had changed many times, with the final group of sixteen representing five countries: Mies, Behrens, Döcker, Gropius, Hilberseimer, Poelzig, Rading, Scharoun, Schneck, and the Tauts, all from Germany; Oud and Stam from the Netherlands; Frank from Austria; Le Corbusier from France; and Victor Bourgeois from Belgium. The large crowds drawn to the show during the summer and early fall (forcing a three-week extension) were significantly motivated by the contentious debate the project generated.

Yet there is no gainsaying the exhibition's historic impact. The twenty-one buildings comprising sixty dwellings proved to be remarkably unified, with their glistening white rectilinear massing, flat roofs, and ship's-railing balconies. The various strains of argument and architectural theorizing had somehow given way to an "international style"—the name by which much modernist architecture eventually came to be known. Weissenhof was the communal realization of a new art of building in concert with progressive politics. Mies's original concept was still traceable in the graceful arcs of houses lining the curved streets, and in the steady rise of the complex to a height dominated by his own austere three-story apartment block. Anchor outcroppings at both ends of his plan now took the form of a pair of houses by Le Corbusier (done with his cousin Pierre Jeanneret) at the southern end, and a twelve-unit apartment building by Peter Behrens at the northern. Gropius's two houses stood a few feet from Le Corbusier's. Behrens's Neubabelsberg atelier was reunited. That Mies took special pride in his accomplishment is suggested by his decision to invite Ada and Georgia to the opening ceremonies.[12]

Mies had reason to be satisfied. His twenty-four-unit apartment building at Am Weissenhof 14–20, the development's largest (an advantage he had granted himself, evidently without opposition), is also notable as one of the earliest examples of steel-framed multiunit housing in Europe (fig. 4.3). It was his first built work in structural steel. The steel frame allowed for large, almost continuous strips of windows and, at least theoretically, for flexible interior planning (masonry walls were limited to those between units). In crucial respects, however, Mies failed to exploit the expressive possibilities of the structural system; the broad white planar massing is indistinguishable from the stucco-clad, load-bearing block of the standard housing of the day. The elevations are composed without regard to individuating dwelling units—the signature triplet windows are sometimes shared by two apartments—but the whole is assuredly proportioned and sufficiently rational to satisfy Mies's own standards of objectivity.

FIGURE 4.3.
Weissenhof apartment building, Stuttgart (1927). The Killesberg hill was flattened to accommodate this, the largest building in the Weissenhof ensemble. Though not legible on the exterior, it was Mies's first building of skeletal steel construction. Note the elegant double-cantilevered rooftop shading.

For all those achievements, his apartment block was less experimental than his own Wolf House or Le Corbusier's entries. The principal living-dining area of Le Corbusier's single-family house was almost completely open in plan, with space circulating freely around a central hearth. It was vertically open as well, rising two stories and interrupted only by the floor slab of the boudoir, which extended into and overlooked the room below. Of all the Weissenhof interiors, it was by consensus the most compelling.

Mies was impressed by Le Corbusier's work and by the man himself, whom he met for the second time at Stuttgart in November 1926. We have no record of their conversations—there is a well-known photograph of them striding together (fig. 4.4), with Mies in spats—and are left to speculate that Mies's gathering doubts about functionalism were fed by his contact with Le Corbusier. As early as 1923, the year of *Vers une architecture*, Le Corbusier argued that functionalism was the province of the engineer, and that the architect must raise his efforts above it, to the level of art. Mies's foreword to the exhibition's catalog is nearly a paraphrase of Le Corbusier: "The problem of the modern dwelling is an architectural [*baukünstlerisches*] problem in spite of its technical and economic aspects. It is a complex problem, and so can be solved only

FIGURE 4.4.

Le Corbusier and
Mies conversing at
Stuttgart, 1926.

by creative talents, not by computation or organization. I therefore felt it necessary, despite our current slogans such as 'rationalization' and 'standardization,' to keep the tasks set for Stuttgart free from a one-sided and doctrinaire
approach."[13]

Mies expressed himself even more pointedly in a statement published in
the journal *Die Form* in 1927: "We value not the result but the starting point of
the form-giving process. This in particular reveals whether form was derived
from life or for its own sake. This is why the form-giving process appears to
me so important. Life is what matters. In its entire fullness, in its spiritual and
concrete interconnection."[14] Among other influences, this language reflects
Mies's involvement during the late 1920s with several members of the Catholic youth movement Quickborn.[15] Quickborn's meeting place was the castle

of Rothenfels in Lower Franconia. The group's leading thinker was the theologian Romano Guardini, since 1923 holder of the Chair for Philosophy of Religion and Catholic World Views at the Friedrich Wilhelm University of Berlin. In *Sacred Signs*, he argued for the imperative of spirit in a secular, industrial society, and an awareness of "the most self-understood things, the everyday actions, which contain that which is most profound."[16] In Mies's copy of Guardini's *Letters from Lake Como*, the following passage is marked: "We must, with fully justified effort, press forward with the new, in order to master it. We must become the lord of unchained forces and build them into a new order related to humanity."[17]

These words are strikingly similar to those by another member of Quickborn, an even stronger believer in the importance of spirit in architecture. In a lecture delivered at Castle Rothenfels in 1927, Rudolf Schwarz, an architect, affirmed that

> there is something called spirit.... There is not only brute force and there is not only "soul"; there is also "spirit" ... something quite ultimate ... and it is this that is in tune with nature, and in it inanimate nature discovers its worthy adversary.... This necessitates that we become free: that we stand at each moment both within time and above it. This demands an awareness that can say even today: I am the master. This demands that we commit ourselves to absolute freedom.[18]

Some three decades later Mies was still enthralled, giving unrestrained voice to his esteem for Schwarz. In 1958 he wrote a foreword for the English translation of *The Church Incarnate*, written by Schwarz in 1938. An excerpt:

> This book was written in Germany's darkest hour, but it throws light for the first time on the question of church building, and illuminates the whole problem of architecture itself....
>
> I have read it over and over again, and I know its power of clarification. I believe it should be read not only by those concerned with church building but by anyone sincerely interested in architecture. Yet it is not only a great book on architecture, indeed, it is one of the truly great books—one of those which have the power to transform our thinking.[19]

Mies's thinking, both before and after his contact with Guardini and Schwarz, was more traditional than original. His argument on behalf of the so-called will of the epoch, first expressed in the early 1920s ("The building art is always the spatially apprehended will of the epoch, nothing else"),[20] was characteristic of nineteenth- and twentieth-century German thought, in which will (*Wille*) was a central philosophical preoccupation. And the position he later granted to spirit (*Geist*) was just as common among his countrymen. Ritchie Robertson, reviewing Wolf Lepenies's *The Seduction of Culture in German History*, noted "the vast, vague territory called 'Geist' ('spirit') where boundaries between religion, thought and poetry become blurred."[21] Thus, we take note of Mies's almost insistent references to "the spirit" toward the end of the 1920s.

A final observation pertinent to the Weissenhofsiedlung: To the extent that functionality was one of the New Architecture's objectives at Stuttgart, it is hard to defend the rapid deterioration of most of the houses—stunningly, within as little as a year or two. In short, Weissenhof was never a triumph of *Sachlichkeit* and functionalism, but of the *image* of modernism.[22]

. . .

Of further consequence at Weissenhof was the deepening of Mies's relationship with Lilly Reich, a woman of talent and versatility who has lately emerged in the literature as a figure of independent stature, especially as a furniture designer.[23] Reich was born June 16, 1885, to a well-to-do Berlin family. She graduated at eighteen or nineteen from a girls' school—of presumably high quality—and became skilled in Kurbel embroidery, a Jugendstil machine sewing technique. The rest of her personal history in the first decade of the century, including possible study with Josef Hoffmann at the Wiener Werkstätte, is less clear. She worked as an exhibition designer for the Wertheim Department Store in Berlin before enrolling in 1910 at Die höhere Fachschule für Dekorationskunst (The Advanced Trade School of Decorative Art), also in the capital. Her teacher was Else Oppler-Legband, a student of van de Velde's. In 1911, while studying with Oppler-Legband, she was responsible for furnishing thirty-two rooms of a Berlin youth center, and a year later for a workers' apartment and two stores displayed in the exhibition Die Frau in Haus und Beruf (Woman at Home and at Work). This work led to her election to the Deutscher Werkbund in 1912.

Reich was one of the designers and organizers of the section "Haus der Frau" ("House of Woman") in the 1914 Werkbund exhibition in Cologne. During World War I, she opened a dressmaker's shop in Berlin, concentrating on her own designs, which also included furniture. Her devotion to the Werkbund and her professional accomplishments were sufficient to earn her a seat on the organization's board of directors in 1920. Indeed, she was the first woman to serve on the board. Thereafter, she helped assemble two significant exhibitions: the first, Kunsthandwerk in der Mode (Fashion Craft) for the Association of the German Fashion Industry at the Staatliches Kunstgewerbemuseum, Berlin, and the second, a collection of over 1,600 objects exported in 1922 to the Newark (New Jersey) Museum for the purpose of showing the best of German design in the United States. By 1923 she was living in Frankfurt am Main and active in the affairs of the Werkbund House, which had opened in 1921 on the grounds of the International Frankfurt Fair. It was there, in 1926, that she

played the central role in the design and assembly of the exhibition Von der
Faser zum Gewebe (From Fiber to Textile).

Reich, who met Mies no later than 1924 (the first year from which their correspondence survives), occupied a singular position in his career, and he in
hers[24] (fig. 4.5). She was the only woman with whom he developed a close,
even dependent, professional rapport. That they were lovers is presumed by
all who knew them. In the recollection of a woman who knew them both: "She
had an exceptional gift for organization and for accounting, which Mies possessed not at all—that was part of his charm—but without her he would have
been quite lost."[25] Reich was his close associate from 1925 until he immigrated
to the United States in 1938. Just before that she was responsible for the exhibition of textiles in the German section of the international pavilion of the Paris
World's Fair (Arts et Techniques) in 1937. Mies contributed designs to the same
building. And she spent several weeks collaborating with him professionally
during a single visit to Chicago, in 1939.

Reich continued thereafter to manage Mies's business in Berlin. She maintained his office and remaining personal and professional records through
the harrowing conditions of World War II and as late as 1947, the year of her
death. Mia Seeger remembered that Mies and Reich shared a small apartment
in Stuttgart during the preparation for Weissenhof. In all his life following the
breakup of his marriage, Reich was the only woman except his daughters with
whom Mies shared quarters. After Weissenhof, when he resumed full-time residence in Berlin, she took an apartment there, and they lived apart.

Reich was no beauty, but she was impeccably groomed, as one might expect of a professional *couturière*. When Mies's daughters traveled to Berlin to visit him, Reich was quick to express disapproval even of the understated manner in which Ada turned them out. They would be hauled off to Braun's and there costumed strictly and expensively, according to Reich's preferences, with Mies's approval. Not surprisingly, the girls failed to appreciate these pains. All three of them disliked Reich, finding her cold and hard even by the antiromantic standards of the time.[26]

It did not matter to Reich. She was professional, intelligent, disciplined, and endowed with a sensibility as refined as Mies's. She recognized his authority—in this respect she was a traditional European woman—and spent much time and energy attending to details and administration. Her professional thoroughness, turned by love for him into personal solicitude, eventually caused him to retreat. Mies, as already noted, cherished nothing in his life more than his independence, and when he immigrated to the United States he effectively closed her out of his life. She suffered for it, and in a significant sense he paid for his freedom; he never found a later collaborator whose artistry so complemented his own.

During the halcyon years of their relationship, Reich played a significant role in Mies's development of a new language for interior design, and in their joint exploration of the newest materials and technology, especially in exhibitions for industrial companies. Her chief assignment at Weissenhof was organizing and installing an exhibition of the latest furnishings and appliances, staged in Stuttgart at the Gewerbehalle Stadtgarten. In concert with her, Mies began to recognize and react to a condition that Weissenhof would demonstrate: modern architecture was well in advance of modern furniture. Pioneering efforts by Frank Lloyd Wright and Charles Rennie Mackintosh in the first decade of the century and by Gerrit Rietveld in the second had been significantly advanced only as late as 1925, by designers of the Bauhaus. In that year Marcel Breuer, inspired by the handlebars of his new bicycle, designed the first tubular steel chair, naming it the Wassily, after his Bauhaus colleague Kandinsky, who had admired it. The Wassily was a landmark, not just as an effective abstraction of the traditional four-legged lounge chair, but because it celebrated the cubic geometry that by mid-decade the Bauhaus practiced collectively. Most important, it used gleaming, chrome-plated tubular steel, expressive of machine technology and the aesthetic of standardization.

After the Wassily came the cantilever chair, in which the seat floats on the continuous loop of a tubular frame. In 1926 Mart Stam, the Dutch architect invited to Stuttgart, designed and fabricated the first modern cantilever chair, an assembly of gas pipes and fittings. He exhibited an improved version in his house for the Weissenhofsiedlung. Mies unveiled his own similar design at Stuttgart, and examples with and without arms were shown in several units of his apartment block. He acknowledged that his work postdated Stam's, which

he probably learned of when Stam discussed it at a meeting in Stuttgart in November 1926. Given Mies's doubtless limited prior experience with tubular steel, he must have developed his design quickly. It was distinctly superior to Stam's as a form. Mies was awarded a patent for his chair in August 1927.

Now known as the MR Chair (after its designer's initials), it is characteristic of Mies as his best (fig. 4.6). The metal frame and leather seat and back are enviably minimal, and the flow of curves into straights natural. The chair is remembered more for visual refinement than functionality; initially, it had the notorious tendency, later corrected, to involuntarily pitch the sitter forward during an attempt to rise. (Tripping sideways over the legs remains an occasional problem.) Mies and Reich designed other furniture for Weissenhof that had less to do with machine theory than with art, most notably several wood Parsons-type tables in luxurious veneers, as reductivist in form as his MR Chair, but inspired by materiality rather than technology.[27] Between 1927 and 1931, Mies and Reich spun out over a dozen variants of the MR concept, including additional tubular chairs, tables with tubular legs and glass tops, and other designs based on flat-bar steel. All this furniture was patented, but

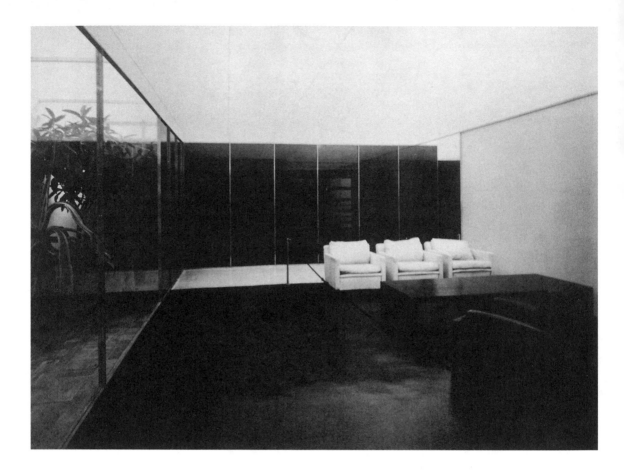

FIGURE 4.7.
Living Room of the
Plate-Glass Hall,
Stuttgart (1927).
Mies suggested the
idea for the hall to
the sponsors, the
Association of Ger-
man Plate-Glass
Manufacturers of
Cologne. The design
was by Mies and Lilly
Reich, who together
conceived three in-
terlocking "rooms"
walled entirely in
glass. Photo courtesy
of the Mies van der
Rohe Archive of the
Museum of Modern
Art, NY.

many items were "knocked off" almost immediately. Mies's authorized designs were manufactured by several German and non-German European companies under license, and a few, like the MR, were produced in the tens of thousands before World War II. Offsetting the income from royalties, Mies was much absorbed by patent litigation for the entire decade of the 1930s, and even after his immigration to the United States.[28]

For Stuttgart, Mies and Reich also designed the Plate-Glass Hall (also called the Glass Room or the Mirror Hall) (fig. 4.7). Even more than his Weissenhof apartment block, it ushered in the mature phase of Mies's European career that would follow at the end of the 1920s. The industry and craft exhibition at the Gewerbehalle, for which Reich organized her own show of furnishings and appliances, included two spaces that Mies designed with her: Hall 5 contained displays for the German Linoleum Works;[29] and Hall 4, termed the Plate-Glass Hall, featured three areas, each identified by sparse residential furnishings— living room, dining room, working room. These three subspaces flowed into a single large space bounded by freestanding walls of glass—Mies's most dramatic realization up to that time of the spatially dynamic plan that he first proposed for the Brick Country House. One of the glass panels was effectively an exterior wall, providing a view of what might have been the outdoors or a winter garden. The ceiling was a series of stretched fabric strips, permeable to the outdoor light and the sole source of illumination. The floors were covered with sheet linoleum of white, gray, and red that nearly corresponded with their respective "rooms." The glass likewise varied, in color and texture (gray, olive green, etched) as well as in degree of transparency, from clear to milky.

The viewer entered from Hall 5 into a vestibule, at a right angle to its long axis. There he or she could glance right and see, behind the glass of one of two sealed-in areas of the ensemble, a sculpture, *Female Torso, Turning* (1913–14), by Mies's late friend Wilhelm Lehmbruck. A turn to the left followed a curve at the end of the vestibule wall and into the living area, thence to the areas for working and dining. Exit was through another vestibule opposite the entry. The design was an avowed abstraction of a residential space, and a showpiece. It was practical in no respect save as prestige advertising for the Association of German Plate Glass Manufacturers of Cologne, the group that commissioned it at Mies's suggestion.

During the summer of 1927, Mies and Reich returned to Berlin, where in September in the Funkturmhalle they collaborated on the installation *Café Samt und Seide* (*Velvet and Silk Café*) that was part of the exhibition Die Mode der Dame. It consisted of a group of spaces defined by curved and rectilinear tubular steel framing, from which were hung ample lengths of fabrics. The rich chroma of the material—black, red, and orange velvet and gold, silver, black, and lemon-yellow silk—were Reich's selections, far more opulent than the modernist standards of the time, which tended to favor white. A group of Mies's chairs and tables occupied the open spaces between the draperies, where visitors could relax over coffee. The plan prefigured those that Mies would soon employ in the Tugendhat House.

. . .

After Weissenhof, Mies's reputation continued to grow—as planner, organizer, theoretician, and above all as one of the most prominent architectural talents of his generation. He had also proved to be an effective politician. In view of his modest beginnings and his uncompromising nature, it is remarkable that at Weissenhof he succeeded in imposing his artistic and administrative will on a company of powerful peers.

Yet even as the vanguard spirit thrived in these headiest of the Weimar years, resistance threatened. We have already encountered some of it in the attacks of Bonatz on the "suburb of Jerusalem." The forces of German right-wing nationalism, stymied by the success of Gustav Stresemann's pragmatic postinflation policies, never made their peace with the chancellor. The yearning to avenge Versailles was the virus of the German soul, waiting to be activated by some national adversity. In 1925 Adolf Hitler published the first volume of *Mein Kampf* and reorganized the Nazi Party that had been discredited two years earlier by the failure of his Munich putsch. This rebirth, at the very outset of Weimar prosperity, was accompanied by reaction within the architectural profession. Paul Schultze-Naumburg, an architect who before World War I had been a progressive, led a crusade in the later 1920s against the New Architecture, at first arguing that it was an impractical way of building but later, with increasing vehemence, associating it with "un-German culture," and linking it to the poisoned soil of bolshevism. Schultze-Naumburg had allies, including Konrad Nonn, who attacked the Bauhaus in the pages of his journal *Zentralblatt der Bauverwaltung*, and Emil Högg of the Dresden *Hochschule*, who published equally shrill denunciations of the Ring.

Responding to Weissenhof's positive press, opponents were galvanized. The colony, they claimed, was a publicity stunt with little or no aesthetic merit. It was denounced as *ungemütlich*, and its organizers identified as elitists indifferent to German tradition. Indeed, once in power, the Nazis, acting on their opposition to modernism in the arts, commissioned plans in 1938 that would have razed the entire Weissenhofsiedlung in favor of an immense complex for the German Army High Command. Only the decision to move the command's headquarters to Strassburg in 1941 averted demolition. One of the wonders of the modernist movement of the 1920s is that it went on, however transformed, to lead the architecture of the Western world following World War II, a generation after it had been brought low by the Nazis and artistic conservatives in Germany and thrown into doubt throughout the rest of the world.

. . .

Mies was never a utopian, and his devotion to the aesthetic dimension of his work led him to elevate the value of material effects. Reich's influence was again significant. Recalling the fabrics she contributed to the exhibition Die Mode der Dame, one could allow metaphorically that it was a silken trail that led him to his next important commission.

The assignment was unusual, for it consisted of *two* major houses designed as an ensemble. Josef Esters and Hermann Lange, managing directors of the Verseidag, the large silk-weaving mills in the Rhineland city of Krefeld, probably came to Mies through Lilly Reich, though there may have been earlier contacts, perhaps between the Langes, who were collectors of modern art, and avant-garde elements in Berlin, or through the Krefeld Museum, or through museum officials in nearby Duisburg, where Mies had exhibited in 1925.[30] In any event, late in 1927 Lange took the lead in selecting Mies to design houses for himself and his business partner for adjacent lots (numbers 91 and 97) on the south side of Wilhelmshofallee in an exclusive new development outside the old city. The houses were designed in about a year, and were constructed simultaneously, with groundbreaking late in 1928 and completion early in 1930.

The Esters and Lange Houses are direct developments of the experimental, open-plan Brick Country House of 1924 and of Mies's lately realized Wolf House (figs. 4.8 and 4.9). Like the Wolf House, they present unornamented, cubical, brick-clad massing to the street, where an inconspicuous entry, vertical circulation, and services cluster. Both houses open up on the opposite elevation, where a series of interlocking first-floor dining, living, and study spaces offer views of gardens and landscape. The garden elevations on both levels feature large windows set into flat brick walls. Balconies and terraces are oriented toward the south and the sun. Following the example of Wolf, the extensive gardens are treated as semihardscape architecture, with basketweaved pavers and brick retaining walls and stairs terracing into the grounds. The second floors of both houses are organized around single-loaded corridors with bedrooms facing south, but are otherwise conventional. Both houses feature large, unadorned rooms and the outsized spaces appropriate to a noble dwelling. Mies paid special attention to the display of the owners' collections of painting and sculpture.

In recollections late in life, Mies stated: "I wanted to make [these houses] much more in glass, but the client[s] did not like that. I had great trouble"[31] (fig. 4.10). It is clear from the ample record of drawings and documents—and notably from earlier concepts, in Mies's pastel renderings—that his ambitions were frustrated. Relative to what was built, the initial schemes for both houses offer greater variety in massing, with bracketing single-floor wings and third floors (a third floor was provided for structurally, but not built, for Esters) and, as Mies remembered, almost continuous floor-to-ceiling glazing of the garden elevations. These early perspectives are for buildings not even obviously of brick; instead, we read primarily an assembly of interlocking glazed cubes. The garden-side windows as built are still enormous, and both houses feature the novel and technically daring *Senkfenster* (a large window that can be lowered electrically into a trough), made famous less here than later, at the Tugendhat House. Unlike the load-bearing brick of the Wolf House, at Esters and Lange the decision to employ an exterior brick expression combined with the large windows required the introduction of complex, concealed structural

FIGURE 4.8
(*facing, top*).
Josef Esters
House, Krefeld
(1930). Street el-
evation. The Lange
and Esters Houses
were designed to-
gether, and stand
next to each other
on the south side
of Wilhelmshofal-
lee. Photo courtesy
of the Mies van der
Rohe Archive of the
Museum of Modern
Art, NY.

FIGURE 4.9
(*facing, bottom*).
Josef Esters House,
Krefeld (1930). View
from the garden.
Note the extension
of the brick paving
and partial-height
walls—the "archi-
tecture"—into the
landscape. Photo
courtesy of the
Mies van der Rohe
Archive of the Mu-
seum of Modern
Art, NY.

FIGURE 4.10
(*above*).
Mies touching up a
charcoal drawing
of the Josef Esters
House, 1928. Private
collection.

steel, notably as lintels but also for lateral bracing. Thus, the brick walls are enclosure but not the only structure, with the advantage that door and window openings could be placed almost at will.

In his later career, Mies mostly edited these two houses out of his oeuvre. We can speculate about why. The reductivist brick-clad massing is severe. Though the English bond walls are exquisitely realized and rich in texture, they are also relentless. The windows, designed by Mies and beautifully detailed and proportioned, are nonetheless too numerous, too much alike, and, especially on the street elevations, too freely disposed.

In spite of Mies's "great trouble" with clients Esters and Lange, he went on to design a factory for them, built 1931–35, and was associated with the Verseidag organization as late as 1937, when he designed a major office complex that was never built. In the mid-1930s he also designed a house for Hermann Lange's son, Ulrich, leading us to conclude that his "great trouble" must have been much qualified. And even if these houses are not masterworks, we have plenty of evidence that Mies made a large investment in their realization. The interior detailing of both houses is but one example, as dozens of beautiful working drawings attest. Everything is designed as if conceived for the first time—exterior, interior, and closet doors, window frames and mechanisms, bookcases, radiator covers, interior stone sills, freestanding and built-in furniture, even the steel driveway gates and their diamond-lattice infill. Indeed, the interiors of these houses for the first time employ Mies's—and Lilly Reich's—mature vocabulary of interior detailing. Millwork shows the typical "Miesian" reveals, with clear profiles and shadow lines and careful proportioning of the often rich materials. Doors and windows and their frames are detailed as carefully as the furniture. In the end, neither house was comprehensively furnished by Mies—as would soon be the case at Tugendhat—and the furniture Mies did design for Esters and Lange was not reproduced, or even much admired, until in 2003 the Knoll Corporation introduced its line of "Krefeld Furniture," based on a chair, ottoman, and side table Mies and Reich designed but, except for the table, never again employed.

. . .

In 1928 Mies received a new commission from Eduard Fuchs, the man responsible for the Liebknecht-Luxemburg monument completed two years earlier. Fuchs now wanted an addition to the house he had purchased from Hugo Perls. Mies was obliged to unite a neoclassical building with a new element reflecting his work of the later 1920s. He provided an asymmetrically planned gallery wing that features a terrace reached by a stair at the rear of the gallery. Five French doors offer a view of the garden, inviting a walk to the left to take in the Schinkelesque loggia of 1911. Mies matched the exterior color of his addition with the yellow-tan of the original.[32]

Four other Mies designs from the years 1928 and 1929 were prepared for competitions: in Berlin, for the S. Adam Department Store; in Stuttgart, a project for a Bank and Office Building; and again in Berlin a Second Friedrichstrasse Office Building and the reconstitution of the Alexanderplatz. None of his work was selected, nor were any of the projects built. They have attracted relatively little attention, partly because of the surpassing excellence of the German Pavilion at Barcelona and the Tugendhat House, designed at about the same time, and because none of the four is compelling by itself. Nonetheless, each warrants comment, especially in view of their implications for his American period.

Since 1923, Mies had worked on small-scale projects in which he attempted to render interior space dynamic and to break down traditional barriers between interior and exterior. Glass and the freestanding wall were the primary means of achieving these ends, which in one- and two-story houses encouraged a reaching out into space. In large, multistory buildings, this type of planning was not applicable. As early as the Friedrichstrasse Office Building project of 1921, Mies had proposed a continuous glass exterior that qualifiedly erased the distinction between inside and out, but the multistory program demanded a regular plan based on a structural frame. In the Glass Skyscraper project, the frame lacked clarity and rationality because of an informal plan, and Mies thereafter imposed a more "objective" order on his proposals for tall buildings.

Seeking to update its image, the Adam Department Store, in business in Berlin since 1863, invited several prominent architects to offer designs for a mid- or high-rise building to replace its existing facility at Leipzigerstrasse and Friedrichstrasse. Mies's competitors included Hans Poelzig, Heinrich Straumer, and Peter Behrens, each of whom honored the client's request that the new building emphasize verticality. Mies had a different idea. "You have indicated in your requirements that in general a building with vertical articulation would conform to your tastes. May I say in all frankness that in my opinion a building has nothing to do with taste but must be the logical result of all requirements that result from its purpose. Only if these are established can one speak of the intrinsic forming of a building." Then, in one of his earliest adumbrations of functionally flexible, so-called universal space (a term used by his followers but not by him), he added: "You need layered floor levels with clear, uncluttered spaces. Furthermore, you need much light. You need publicity and more publicity."[33]

Mies proposed a rectangular block of eight floors with a rounded corner and a setback at the top floor for a terrace. With a steel structure the interior could be open, with the outer walls entirely of glass. The walls on the ground floor, pulled back to provide covered walkways, were to be of clear glass, while opaque glass, suitable for signage, would cover the remainder of the façade. Georg Adam, co-owner of the firm, favored Mies's proposal. "Wide window panes with little support in between, light, and air, that's what businessmen demand from architects," said Adam. Nonetheless, the competition was suspended and no selection was made. The old building remained in place, and was eventually demolished.[34] This was Mies's first realistic proposal for a glazed exterior wall. "Neither wall nor window but something else again, quite new," said the critic Curt Gravenkamp of the Adam project. "It achieves the ultimate possibilities of a material [glass] already millennia old. . . . Modern architecture weds a building to the landscape, binds the interior with the space of the street."[35]

The "Bank and Office Building" competition, sponsored by the Württembergische Landesbank, called for a multiuse building with a banking hall, stores, and offices. The site in central Stuttgart was near the now iconic railroad station completed in 1927 from the plans of Paul Bonatz, Mies's nemesis at Weissenhof. Together with Friedrich Eugen Scholer, Bonatz won the bank commission. Mies's entry, which received honorable mention, used the same concept as the Adam design. Based on an open plan, with uninterrupted floors once again offering "universal" space, it proposed a glass-and-steel wall. Transparent glass would have been used on display windows at ground level, while upper stories were to be clad in opaque glass, again for advertising.

Choosing to separate the bank from the general office building, Mies proposed an eight-story volume facing Lautenschlagerstrasse, with retail at street level and offices above, and at the rear, a three-story building for the bank. Between the two would be a court and four towers with stairways and toilet rooms.

The remaining two unbuilt competition projects of the late 1920s returned Mies's attention to the Alexanderplatz, and specifically to the site meant for his high-rise design of 1921. On this occasion he responded to a 1929 competition sponsored by the Berlin Traffic Authority. The official objective, nearly a duplicate of the 1921 program, was for a tall building of manifold function that would add a variety of commercial and recreational services to downtown Berlin. Mies's project was easily distinguishable from the other entries, especially in its generalized regularity. The architects who shared the top prize, Erich Mendelsohn and the team of Paul Mebes and Paul Emmerich, proposed a tall four-sided tower rising from a ground-hugging, three-sided base. Mies proposed three curved slabs with convex faces to the street, in effect a trihedral mass about a central core, ascending without setbacks to a flat roof and a rooftop garden. The façade was to be organized in alternating transparent and opaque (brick) bands. The nine-story tower would include offices, stores, and a hotel, with underground access to the subway. None of the submissions were built.

A competition for the redevelopment of the Alexanderplatz was approved by the Berlin City Council in 1928. It grew out of a proposal by Martin Wagner, the head of Berlin's planning department, and was intended to improve automobile circulation. Six firms, with some of the architects teamed, were invited to make proposals: Peter Behrens, Hans and Wassily Luckhardt with Alfons Anker, Paul Mebes and Paul Emmerich, Mies, Heinrich Müller-Erkelenz, and Johann Emil Schaudt.

First prize went to the Luckhardts and Anker, who, like all the competitors except Mies, submitted plans based on Wagner's model, a symmetrical grouping of buildings conforming to the existing roadways. Mies, who finished last, paid no attention to the competition rules. He proposed a grouping of seven slablike buildings arranged asymmetrically, dominated by one seventeen-story tower (fig. 4.11). The ensemble addressed the circular core of Alexanderplatz, but almost as if the streets were incidental. The individual buildings were austerely stereometrical, similar in elevation to the Stuttgart bank building.

Mies was influenced in this period by the city planning concepts of Ludwig Hilberseimer, one of his closest friends. The two had met at Hans Richter's in the early 1920s, and had worked together on G, though Hilberseimer remained truer longer to a tough functionalist line. When Walter Gropius resigned the directorship of the Bauhaus in 1928, to be replaced by Hannes Meyer, a left-wing architect with previous connections to Swiss functionalist group ABC, Hilber-

FIGURE 4.11.
Urban redevelop-
ment proposal for
Alexanderplatz,
Berlin-Mitte (1929).
Despite the affirma-
tions of Ludwig Hil-
berseimer, an early
and faithful cham-
pion of Mies's, later
critics have found
little to praise in
this scheme.

seimer joined the Dessau faculty. His 1927 book on city planning, *Großstadt-architektur* (Architecture of the Metropolis), presented an uncompromising *Sachlichkeit*. Le Corbusier's ideal of a city consisting of widely spaced towers surrounded by greenswards and elevated traffic—thus cleansed of the ancient "mess" of streets, lanes, alleys, and tenements—was translated by Hilberseimer into perspectives of forbidding length and chilling emptiness.

There is more than a little of that overpowering antisepsis in Mies's Alexanderplatz project. Hilberseimer was Mies's staunchest defender in the press. Accusing the managers of the Alexanderplatz competition of seeking a design that closed the plaza and created "an effect reminiscent of classicism," he maintained that "Mies van der Rohe's project is the only one of the designs submitted that breaks through this rigid system and attempts to organize the square as an independent shape. The traffic lanes retain the circular form, yet Mies has designed the square by grouping freestanding buildings according to architectural principles alone. By opening the streets wide, he achieves a new spaciousness which all the others lack."[36]

· · ·

The zenith of Mies's European career can be fixed at May 26, 1929, when King Alfonso XIII and Queen Victoria Eugenia of Spain inaugurated the newly com-

FIGURE 4.12.
German Pavilion,
International Expo-
sition, Barcelona
(1929). Mies (*in top
hat at middle right*)
accompanies King
Alfonso XIII of Spain
following the inaugu-
ration ceremony,
May 26, 1929.

pleted German Pavilion at the Barcelona International Exposition[37] (fig. 4.12). As architect of the pavilion and chief of all German exhibits at the exposition, Mies was prominent in top hat, tails, and spats as the king and queen offered a ceremonial champagne toast. The moment may have been brief, but for the forty-three-year-old Mies it was unalloyed triumph. The world has forgotten this one among so many international commercial expositions, but the pavilion Mies conceived as representative of Weimar Germany remains vivid in memory, among the handful of iconic architectural masterworks of the twentieth century. Demolished at the end of the fair but reconstructed between 1981 and 1986, it is—we can now use the present tense—Mies's greatest single work. He achieved in one creative act a building altogether novel and hauntingly timeless, an inimitable statement of pure architectural abstraction. Its significance was instantly apparent, and remains so; that it belongs among the few modern buildings to stand comparison with the greatest architecture of the past is a judgment of comparable historical record.

Mies had a thin record of realized modern work well into the 1920s. But he was sufficiently well known and highly regarded that the Weimar government selected him to supervise the design and installation of all German exhibits at the Barcelona fair, a national pavilion building only one among them. Mies's uncompromising commitment to architecture as high art—and to forms free of ornament and historicism—also made him a natural choice. In the ten years since the war, Germany had become peaceful and prosperous, culturally accomplished and internationally oriented. German design at Barcelona was to reflect these new conditions. In a speech marking the opening of the German exhibitions in Barcelona, Commissar General Georg von Schnitzler, who selected Mies for the commission, stated: "We wished here to show what we can do, what we are, how we feel today and see. We do not want anything but clarity, simplicity, honesty."[38] Mies gave the commissar clarity and honesty, but the route of his endeavor was anything but simple.

Mies was awarded the Barcelona commission at the beginning of July 1928, less than a year before the opening of the fair. At the outset a national pavilion was not even part of the brief. In a 1959 interview, Mies described how it came about:

> It is very curious how buildings come to pass. Germany had the task of putting on an exhibition at Barcelona. One day I received a call from the German government. I was told that the French and British would have a pavilion and Germany should have a pavilion, too. I said, "What is a pavilion? I have not the slightest idea." I was told: "We need a pavilion. Design it, and not too much glass." I must say that it was the most difficult work which ever confronted me, because I was my own client; I could do what I liked. But I did not know what a pavilion should be.[39]

These lines have been much quoted, often with an amusing misprint: "Design it, and not too much *class*."[40]

Mies responded with atypical speed and decisiveness. In spite of the usual financial problems and tangled lines of authority typical of a government commission, he was able to develop solutions quickly and get them approved. By October he had a half-dozen assistants working in an annex to his Berlin atelier, some of whom moved to Barcelona as construction commenced. Endemic to the government assignment was not only a near-impossible schedule but funding so shaky that the already rushed construction was shut down for sixteen critical days early in 1929. Here von Schnitzler was the project's hero, for he not only ran interference for Mies but for long stretches all but funded the project out of his personal resources. And like most design work for exhibitions, many details were unfinished at the opening. Sections of the exterior were painted to resemble stone, for example, because not enough had been ordered, and the pavilion's office space and miscellaneous furnishings were incomplete well into the fall of 1929.

Mies's concept materials are lost, but it is likely that he worked alone and intensively before asking assistant Sergius Ruegenberg to prepare the base for a plasticine model on which various walls and roofs might be tested. Early on Mies decided on a rich palette of materials, and special papers and textures were prepared for evaluation in the model. Based on these experiments, the developing schemes were captured in interim plans and perspectives, by both Mies and Ruegenberg, and then revised and refined. Several planning grids were tested, but the building was never organized on a single grid. Rather, it was planned around multiple reference systems for walls, columns, benches, the reflecting pools, and the site overall. The solution was generically related to themes first explored in the Brick Country House project. But now it was in three and not two dimensions, for a building sure to be realized. Indeed, the July 1928 minutes of the Werkbund refer to the government's official request for nothing more (or less) than a *Repräsentationsraum*, best described in English as a prototypical space of formal or ceremonial purpose, in this case celebrating Germany.

For the pavilion, Mies was free of many of the typical demands of constructability too, because an exhibition building was likely to be temporary. Some of the explanation of Mies's alacrity with the design no doubt also rested with Lilly Reich, whose responsibility for the exhibition halls relieved him of the burden of detailed design, organization, and outfitting.

Mies was always keenly interested in the siting and context of his buildings, and the German Pavilion was no exception. Stretched across the north-facing hill known as Montjuich, the Barcelona fairgrounds had been laid out in a classic Beaux-Arts plan by Catalonian architect Josep Puig y Cadafalch. Site work began in 1915. Many buildings were constructed there during the next fifteen years, but due to economic and political complications a Barcelona international exposition was delayed until 1929. The main axis of the fairgrounds, culminating in the domed National Palace, was flanked by vast exhibition buildings and crossed at about the midpoint by a wide, grand plaza. Mies selected the western end of this secondary concourse for his pavilion. In plan a rough rectangle longer on its front, the pavilion was sited at a right angle to the plaza, fronting a formal grouping of trees and fountains and parallel to a row of freestanding classical columns, looking through to another pavilion, representing the city of Barcelona, at the far end. Behind the German Pavilion a slope of embracing shrubbery rose to the Spanish Village. Immediately to the south stood the massive walls of the palace of Alfonso XIII, with its counterpart, named for Victoria Eugenia, across the main axis. The German Pavilion

FIGURE 4.13 (*following, top*). German Pavilion, International Exposition, Barcelona (1929). View of the exterior looking southwest. Because the pavilion was demolished shortly after the end of the fair, the photographs commissioned by Mies, of which this is one, effectively constituted the visual history of the building. Mies had the pavilion photographed before the word *Alemania* was affixed to the dark marble wall *at right*.

FIGURE 4.14 (*following, bottom*). German Pavilion, International Exposition, Barcelona (1929). View looking north from the office to the pavilion "interior," with the larger reflecting pool *at right*.

was initially planned for the space between these two huge buildings, across the axis from the French Pavilion; but Mies persuaded the Spanish authorities to change to the eventual site, which was advantageous in several respects. "[It appears] virtually obvious," wrote the critic Walther Genzmer, "that the main orientation of the pavilion should be perpendicular to the palace wall, that in contrast to the considerable height of that wall the pavilion be quite low, and that in contrast to the calm unbroken surface of the wall it be kept open and airy."[41] Mies had chosen an exclusive site, commanding in its long approach.

The pavilion is a single-story, asymmetrical assembly of freestanding and partially engaged walls of dressed stone panels over steel framing (fig. 4.13). The rest of the enclosure is steel-framed plate glass. The superstructure is set atop a paved podium, and is partially covered by a planar, all-white roof (also internally of steel) with broad eaves. The spaces captured or defined or sometimes only suggested by these elements are chaste, dynamic, and inviting of movement (figs. 4.14–16). Mies designed and installed glass doors for the pavilion, but each day during the fair they were laboriously removed and stored for reinstallation at night, further evidence that "inside" and "outside" were conflated. The base of the pavilion recalls the podium of a classical temple, but the smooth stone-and-glass planes that emerge from this base glide past each other, floating below and slipping out from under the line of the roof, altogether unclassically. A stair penetrating the podium offers entry parallel to the long "front" of the building, which is especially beckoning at this distance. At the top of the stair, a travertine terrace and a large reflecting pool come into view.

Entry to the quasi interior requires a U-turn. Amid the prevailing asymmetry is a set of eight regularly spaced columns, each of cruciform section and electroplated in chromium, standing free of the several stone walls, like guards attending. The structural solution is ambiguous, and possibly deliberately so, with contributions from both the columns and the many walls. Deeper into the interior, we discover a spectacular stone wall ten feet high and eighteen wide, built of eight bookmatched slabs of a ravishing marble called onyx doré, glowing golden, with spectacular veins from dark gold to purest white. This is unmistakably the main event. To the left of the onyx wall, a milk-glass light is lit from within. Parallel to the milk-glass wall is a long glass-topped table, with a second, smaller version in front of the onyx, and to the right a pair of steel lounge chairs placed side by side, each with cushions of white kid leather. We know that Mies designed the pavilion "around" this onyx grouping, because he purchased the raw slab himself, at enormous cost, in the fall of 1929. Acquired at a Hamburg stoneyard, the massive block had been reserved for the ballroom of a new transatlantic liner, but Mies succeeded in snatching it away.

As part of the government's program, Mies was asked to reference the

FIGURE 4.15.
German Pavilion,
International Expo-
sition, Barcelona
(1929). View looking
north toward Georg
Kolbe's sculpture,
Dawn. Compare this
photograph with a
sketch by Mies of
a 1935 project that
remained unbuilt
(fig. 5.13).

black, red, and gold of the German national flag. He chose to do so abstractly, as we would expect, with a rich black carpet, brilliant scarlet drapery, and the gold of the onyx. He sidestepped the request to include images of eagles (the national symbol), but assented to the name Alemania on a front-facing exterior wall, lettered in black to a design by his friend Gerhard Severain. Mies stage-managed a long delay in the installation of the lettering, so that almost all published images of the building are free of signage. Indeed, Mies's own letterless photographs so fully defined the pavilion that when it was recon-structed, *Alemania* is once again nowhere to be seen.

Materials are uniformly sumptuous.[42] To the impression of free-flowing space are added polychromy and opulent surface, plus another category of experience: the play of reflections from the five varieties of marble, the vari-ous types of glass set in chromed frames, and most of all the two reflecting pools, the larger lined with polished black river rock. Through the bottle-green

FIGURE 4.16.
German Pavilion,
International Expo-
sition, Barcelona
(1929). View of the
double-sided onyx
wall, two "Barcelona"
chairs, and several
ottomans.

glass is a standing bronze figure, accessible via a left turn to a platform at the edge of the second pool, which is lined with black glass. The figure, *Dawn*, by Mies's contemporary Georg Kolbe, appears to rise from the water at the far end, drawing one across the pavilion. The Tinian marble wall enclosing the pool emerges from under the roof to define the northern end of the building, balancing the enclosing travertine wall at the south. The Tinian leads back again along the west side of the pavilion to the central space or, alternately, between a gray glass plane and a small garden immediately to the west of the podium and into the terraced area. Another exit leads to the garden path and a stair to the Spanish Village.

All that Mies had first postulated in the Brick Country House about the potential interaction of inside and outside space was realized at Barcelona. His debts to both Wright and van Doesburg are manifest. But a rich materiality, detailed with patrician reserve, is Mies's alone. Other influences are evident:

from Lilly Reich, the bold colors and rich drapery, and from Le Corbusier—specifically from the entry to the first floor of his single-family house at Weissenhof—the revelatory 180-degree turn at the top of the stair.

The exhibition halls, which Mies supervised but Reich designed,[43] were another demonstration of high artistry. Mies's mastery at Barcelona was demonstrated across the full range of his "building art" (*Baukunst*): for the German Pavilion he was architect, interior designer, landscape and hardscape designer, and furniture designer par excellence. He designed two glass-topped, steel-legged tables that, as it happened, barely stood up, but he also created a chair (and ottoman) that turned out to be *the* chair of the century—the Barcelona chair[44] (fig. 4.17). Though the building was demolished when the fair came down, the chairs most surely survived. At least six were fabricated for the fair, along with eight or more ottomans, and these were retained by Mies and Reich and either used by them or transferred to other projects. As documented by Tegethoff,[45] the chair and ottoman were used by Mies and Reich in several mostly modest projects in the early 1930s—but famously in the Tugendhat House—and even made an early appearance in the United States through the patronage of (and duplication by) Philip Johnson. Large-scale production would wait until the designs were resurrected and adapted for American fabrication in stainless steel beginning in the 1940s. To this day they are produced in quantity by their authorized manufacturer, the Knoll Corporation, and by countless others as knockoffs. Mies described his design intent in a 1964 letter:

> It was in the Pavilion that the king and queen of Spain took part in the Exposition's opening ceremony. In this context the Barcelona Chair could not be just a chair—it had to be a monumental object as well, but a monumental object which would not block the special flow of the building.[46]

For each side, the chair's frame consists of two rolled (curved) steel bars, originally chrome-plated but later mirror-polished stainless steel, one the long arc of a circle, the other a shorter, flowing *S*. The two cross in a welded joint, forming a seat, back, and legs. The two "leg" elements are connected by three transverse bars. Two diagonally welted leather cushions, one for the seat, supported by wide straps of belting leather screwed to the frame, the other for the back (also with straps, similarly attached), complete the chair.[47] The form, though utterly transformed by Mies, resembles Roman curule chairs as revived by early nineteenth-century neoclassicists, including Schinkel, and is related to premodern "folding chairs" probably unknown to Mies. Mies made a large number of test prototypes for the Barcelona chair—so many, in fact, that he invited his staff to help themselves to the rejects.

Structurally (and practically), the Barcelona chair is possible only in steel. The frame, of bar stock about three-eighths of an inch thick, is improbably slender when viewed from the sides, and the weld where the bars cross seems entirely natural, though the elegantly sculpted fillets are the product of very high craft. The chair appears to be light—the cantilevered seat floats as if unsupported—but as anyone who has attempted to move one will attest, it is stubbornly heavy. Over time the costly straps that carry the upholstered seat and back are sure to stretch and eventually break. The width of the chair is lavish—three-quarters of a meter, suitable even for Mies's substantial girth. But it is too low for many users, and for some, difficult to climb out of. Tegethoff overstates when he asserts that the chair is "primarily distinguished by the fact that it is almost never used for sitting."[48] In spite of these qualifications, the Barcelona chair has become an undisputed marker of elegance, grace, and luxury, with a price to match. No other "designer" chair comes close to its ubiquity in institutional and high-end private interiors.

Mies continued his experiment with chromed flat-bar framing in his less famous Tugendhat chair, the flat-bar Brno chair, and the Dessau or Tugendhat "X-table." As in the case of the Barcelona chair, manufacturing en masse would wait until the late 1940s, when Mies was lobbied to revisit these pieces by his American staff. At that time the chairs and table were redetailed for fabrication in polished stainless steel. Before that, a few stainless pieces were authorized to be custom-made by Chicago metal artisan Gerald Griffith.[49]

The last days of the Barcelona fair were less felicitous than the first; the world financial crisis of October 1929 abruptly intervened. The German Pavilion had weathered several smaller economic storms by the time the fair opened, and spirits had soared when international critical response proved almost unanimously enthusiastic. But by the time the exposition closed in January 1930, the atmosphere had soured enough that the German government, tone-deaf to the accolades, sought to recoup through a sale what some officials considered the pavilion's exorbitant costs. Just six months into its life, it was disassembled. The steel was sold for scrap, and the onyx and other marbles, as well as the chromed columns and other components, were returned to Germany for recycling.

Thereafter, and for a half century, the pavilion was represented through photographs, the most well known of which were commissioned by Mies. He closely controlled their reproduction, and many were retouched. Some views were forever lost. The building was never comprehensively documented, no doubt because as an exhibition pavilion it was changed and refined up to and even after the last minute. After many false starts, beginning as early as just after World War II, the Spanish government finally succeeded in shepherding to completion a superb reconstruction timed to coincide with the 1986 centennial of Mies's birth. The work was led by the architects Ignasi de Solà-Morales, Cristian Cirici, and Fernando Ramos. The reconstructors had to face the requirement that a new building be permanent. Careful and successful consideration was given to correcting original flaws, including a sagging roof widely commented on in 1929–30, as well as securing and fabricating the appropriate marbles and especially the onyx. The work is impressively documented in a well-illustrated book by the supervising architects.[50]

· · ·

The days of the Weimar Republic were numbered, as were those at the pinnacle of Mies's European career. At the close of the Barcelona fair his office was still busy, chiefly with work on a large house that had come to him indirectly through the agency of Eduard Fuchs. In 1928, when Mies's addition to the Fuchs House was just completed, Fuchs was in social contact with a well-to-do, just-married Czech couple, Fritz and Grete Tugendhat. Grete (née Löw-Beer) had been born and raised in Brno, Czechoslovakia (in German, Brünn—today in the Czech Republic). Her family were upper-class Jews and members of the prominent ethnic-German minority in Czechoslovakia, where they founded and owned a major textile manufactory. Grete had spent most of the 1920s in Berlin while married to her first husband, Hans Weiss. During this period she had circulated in the art world and gotten to know Fuchs, who was, it will be remembered, a collector, art historian, and art-world impresario. After Grete's divorce, she returned to Czechoslovakia and met and married Fritz Tugendhat, also Jewish and also a textile manufacturer. Her father had promised her the wedding gift of a new house in Brno, for which he also provided a prime piece of land carved from his large in-town estate. The choice of an architect was left to the newlyweds. The Fuchs house, though traditional, had impressed Grete. She learned that it had been designed by Mies van der Rohe. "I had always wanted a spacious modern house with clear and simple forms," she recalled, "and my husband had been almost horrified by the interiors of his youth, stuffed with trinkets and lace."[51]

Thus, Mies was called on to meet with the Tugendhats, who reacted as others before: "From the first moment we met him," Grete reported, "it was clear to us that he should be the one to build our house, so impressed were we by his personality. . . . The way he talked about his architecture gave us the feeling that we were dealing with a true artist."[52] At Mies's suggestion, the Tugendhats traveled to Guben to inspect the Wolf House, which stood atop a slope similar to theirs. They were vastly impressed. From Grete's recollections, we know that they also inspected some of Mies's premodern houses, and that they were familiar with the Weissenhofsiedlung from publications. But the couple had no knowledge of the Barcelona Pavilion—as yet unbuilt—when they selected Mies.

In September 1928, Mies traveled to Brno to inspect the Tugendhats' site, a broad, sloping parcel with a commanding view of the city and its hallowed Spielberg castle. He returned to Berlin and fell to work, even as he continued with the several Barcelona commissions. Thus, the pavilion and the Tugendhat House, sharing so much in spirit and detail, were designed almost at the same time, though the pavilion had progressed into working drawings by the time Mies returned from Brno.

"Towards the end of the year," Mrs. Tugendhat reported,

Mies let us know that the design was ready. Early afternoon on New Year's Eve we expectantly entered his studio. We were due for a New Year's Eve celebration with friends, but instead the meeting with Mies went on until one o'clock in the morning. First we saw the plan of an enormous room with a curved and a rectangular free-standing wall. Then we noticed little crosses at a distance of about five meters from each other, and asked what they were. As if it were the most natural thing in the world, Mies replied, "Those are the iron supports, which will carry the whole building."[53]

The steel structural frame of Barcelona was to be repeated at Brno, and to the same end: elegant walls of rich materials would delimit a new kind of flowing interior space, made possible by the order of an independent structural-steel grid.

Grete Tugendhat claimed that the couple "had in mind a much smaller and much more modest house"[54] than what they ended up with, which was a large house indeed. In addition to their personal needs, their requirements included an apartment for the family chauffeur and his wife and suites for a governess, a cook, and two other servants—elements implying more than a "modest house." Out of this program came a three-level house with a *footprint* of 8,000 square feet, with over 10,000 square feet of finished interiors and another 3,000 of paved terrace (fig. 4.18). The basement and main level are tucked into the slope. The upper level, of 3,500 square feet and primarily for bedrooms, engages the street to the rear and shelters the entry. The street façade is divided into a residential volume and a smaller service wing and garage (fig. 4.19). The services include the chauffeur's apartment on the upper level and a kitchen and servants' quarters immediately below. The space between the two wings is roofed by a thin slab that unites the composition and frames a view to the Spielberg castle. The bedroom compound is itself divided into two blocks oriented long side to the street, one containing a pair of children's rooms and the governess's room (which could double as a guest room), the other the separate bedrooms of the parents, with a direct connection to the children's area. The bedroom blocks slide not quite past each other, so that the vestibule between them is connected to an open terrace (on the roof of the main floor) by a short corridor. All bedrooms except that of the governess open onto the terrace with its sweeping southwest view. The terrace doubled as an easily monitored play area for the children. The planning even in these private areas is informal, and obviously indebted to Barcelona. Mies originally wanted to "express" the structure in freestanding columns on this level too— they are a main feature of the living spaces, as we shall see—but the Tugendhats thought they would "bump into them" in the domestic spaces, and Mies agreed to place them inside walls. This was one of very few compromises he agreed to make. (When Fritz Tugendhat suggested that Mies's floor-to-ceiling doors would likely warp—as it turned out, they never did—Mies refused to yield: "Then I won't build.")[55]

A curved, frosted-glass wall at the upper-level entry frames a spiral stair that descends to the main living area, a single room of almost 3,000 square feet, bounded on the south and west by walls of glass and containing, as Grete Tugendhat accurately described, "a curved wall and a rectangular freestanding wall."[56] Normally accessed from the stair, the space also opens to the outdoors via a terrace at the west-facing corner. Entry from the garden below is gained via a stair running parallel to the south elevation of the main level,

FIGURE 4.18.
Tugendhat House,
Brno, Czechoslova-
kia (1930). View of
the main living space
one level below the
street, which in this
view is behind and
above. The house
had a sumptuous
budget, to which
Mies responded with
a creative outpouring
unmatched in his Eu-
ropean work.

FIGURE 4.19.
Tugendhat House,
Brno, Czechoslovakia
(1930). View from the
street looking west,
with the entry *at cen-
ter*. Like the sites of
many of Mies's Euro-
pean houses, the Tu-
gendhat property is
steeply sloped (away
in this view), and
entry to the house is
gained from what is
nominally the "rear."

FIGURE 4.20
(*facing*). Tugendhat
House, Brno, Czecho-
slovakia (1930), in-
terior. View of the
main-level living
space looking south-
east, with the onyx
wall and adjacent
cruciform columns *at
center*. At right, fac-
ing away, are three
Tugendhat chairs.
Left of the onyx wall
is Fritz Tugendhat's
"study," an area de-
fined mostly by its
furniture and use.
The floors are white
linoleum, intended
to complement the
white plaster ceilings.

penetrating a podium in the exact manner of Barcelona. Here one enters the house after a U-turn on the terrace at the top of the stairs.

The main living space is punctuated by a grid of structural-steel columns, each cruciform in plan section and not identical, in either section or cladding, with the cruciform columns of the Barcelona Pavilion (fig. 4.20). These columns grow out of the basement-level structural-steel framing and pass through the living space to support the upper-level steel structure and its terrace. The exact dimensions of the structural grid, 4.9 by 5.5 meters, have no obvious rationale.

Standing free of the columns at the center of the room is a wall of onyx doré, described by Mies as "the color of a young girl's hair, honey yellow with white

strands."[57] Closer to the garden is a full-height wall of millwork, slightly more than a half circle in plan, veneered in vertical-grained, bookmatched panels of black and light-brown Makassar ebony. The veneers are said to have been hand-picked by Mies during a trip for this purpose to Paris. These two "walls" define various functions within the main space. The onyx wall, also book-matched and detailed like the one at Barcelona, though not as thick, acts as a virtual hearth. It also separates the living room from Fritz Tugendhat's "study" just behind, a gracious open-plan area anchored by a Mies-Reich–designed desk and bounded near the entry by a low, glass-doored sideboard. The ebony wall more directly defines a traditional domestic space, in this case what the drawings term a dining niche (*Essnische*), centered on a round table and partially shielded from view from the main space but open to the garden vista (fig. 4.21). At the western end of the space, an interior glass wall set back from the façade extends nearly the width of the building, forming an airy winter garden. As at Barcelona, a single piece of sculpture stood in the Tugendhat

FIGURE 4.21.
Tugendhat House,
Brno, Czechoslo-
vakia (1930). View,
looking north, of the
radiused Makassar
ebony wall that di-
vides the dining area
from the rest of the
main floor. The din-
ing table (*middle
left*) is in its smallest
configuration, here
with five Brno chairs,
which were designed
for the house in both
tubular and flat-bar
versions. Contrast
with figure 4.23,
which shows the plan
of the same table in
its expanded form.

House: a female torso by Wilhelm Lehmbruck. This elegant piece was installed at one end of the onyx wall.

Two other major passages in the great space can be identified by function, though they are distinguished from each other primarily by the placement of furniture. Opposite the onyx wall and to the north of the study, a library oc-cupies a large niche framed by two stub walls; and just around a corner, sep-arated by a long cabinet, stood a grand piano, placed against a wall but im-plicitly defining a "music room." These elements did nothing more than qualify the fundamental perception of a grand, unitary interior. The onyx and Makas-sar walls and the carefully placed furniture suggest an identifiable domestic program, but the space is not quite so dynamically flowing as that under—and out from under—the roof at Barcelona. The experience is contained and not centrifugal, though the connection to the outside is a far stronger theme. And since this is a real house and not a "representative space," it had to be enclosed.

The glazing on the west and south functions as enclosure, though in places not quite. The glass wall on the south, 55 feet long, gives onto the winter gar-den. The west wall, over 80 feet long, literally opens on the garden (fig. 4.22). The individual floor-to-ceiling lights of these walls are enormous—15 unbro-ken feet horizontally inside their bronze frames[58]—and every other one on the west side can be lowered electrically into the basement by means of the fa-

FIGURE 4.22. Tugendhat House, Brno, Czechoslovakia (1930). Southeast view from the garden-side exterior stair looking into the main living space. Two of the enormous windows along this elevation are the famous *Senkfenster*, which can be lowered mechanically into the basement. Photo courtesy of the Mies van der Rohe Archive of the Museum of Modern Art, NY.

FIGURE 4.23
(*facing*).
Tugendhat House, Brno, Czechoslovakia (1930), reflected plan of dining table, showing the twice-expandable tabletop. The largest configuration accommodates eighteen. The curved "wings" and their supports and the extra chairs were kept in storage when not in use. The central support is a chromed cruciform patterned after the house's columns. Note the curved, cantilevered serving shelf beginning at nine o'clock on the curved wall.

mous *Senkfenster* mechanism, first installed in the Krefeld houses two years before.[59] The large living space is functionally almost a terrace, and the dining area as well can open directly to, and only a few feet from, the outside. The Tugendhats reported that the house performed perfectly; the heating and an air-conditioning system provided year-round comfort, and even in winter the great windows were often lowered to embrace the afternoon sun.

It is the rhapsodic flow of space that makes the first floor of the Tugendhat House so immediately arresting. But the effect depends just as surely on an array of perfectly coordinated architectural elements, including Mies's disciplined proportions, the quiet order of the chromed columns, the sumptuous and minimalistic use of materials, an array of custom furniture, and an environment of obsessive design detail. The onyx wall, at 60,000 Reichmarks, cost as much as a handsome middle-class home of the time. Mies chose seamless white linoleum—then a luxury material—for the floor of the main space, mirroring the white plaster ceiling. Travertine is used for flooring at Tugendhat only in the entry hall of the upper level, the winter garden, and selectively for the south terrace and stairs. In front of the onyx wall lay a hand-woven natural wool carpet, and behind it, in the study, one of brown wool. Draperies—black raw silk and black velvet on the winter garden wall and beige raw silk on the west wall—can be drawn so as to close off the entire space from the outdoors. Drapes on tracks can also divide subspaces from the whole.

Central to the house was the design of new furniture and fixtures, accomplished, to be sure, with the cooperation and generosity of the Tugendhats.[60] Mies and Reich produced more new furniture and custom millwork for the Tugendhat House than for any other project of Mies's career, and except for the servants' quarters the appointments in all rooms were custom, down to the doorknobs[61] and light fixtures. Mies and Reich even designed a custom metal ladder for the library.[62] Some of the millwork is exceedingly complex, most notably the dining table. It is fixed in the floor atop its own chrome-plated, cruciform pedestal set at the center of the curved ebony wall, which is built to a radius of 7 meters. In its normal configuration the dining table, 1.4 meters in diameter, seats eight, but it can be expanded in two stages to diameters of 2.2 or 3.3 meters—accommodating up to eighteen—using curved leaves and an under-table telescoping mechanism that incorporates additional legs (fig. 4.23). The dining niche also includes a 20-inch-wide *vert antique* serving shelf, curved in plan and cantilevered from steel brackets buried in the ebony wall.[63]

Two chairs were reemployed for Brno: the MR with and without armrests and the new Barcelona chair and ottoman. In order to provide a modern, domestic lounge chair as comfortable as traditional overstuffed examples—as well as one with arms—Mies designed the Tugendhat chair, which uses flat steel bar as a sprung cantilever leg that yields a satisfyingly resilient bounce (fig. 4.24). The cushions are much like those of the Barcelona chair, supported

CHAPTER FOUR

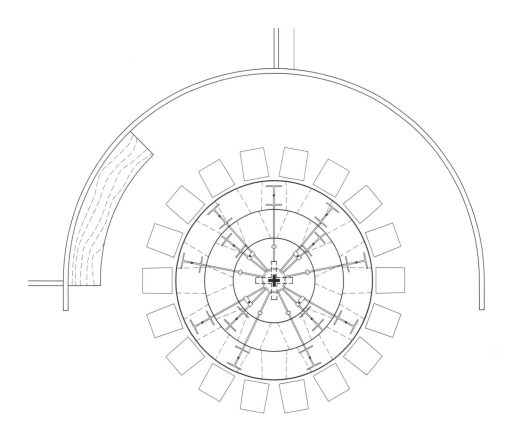

between the steel framing by leather straps. To adapt the MR side chair with arms for use as a dining chair, Mies designed the Brno chair, which features a flatter bow from arm to floor, allowing the chair to be located closer to a table (fig. 4.25); both tubular and flat-bar versions of the chair were developed. Another piece newly designed for the Tugendhats, and later ubiquitous, was the X coffee table, a cross of four L-shaped chromed bars that carry a square top of twenty-millimeter–thick, bevel-edged glass[64] (fig. 4.26). The tabletop is of Platonic perfection: in plan, one meter to a side.

Furniture design for the Tugendhat House was not limited to the interiors. The terrace off the children's rooms was furnished with a custom bench and integral trellis, a half circle in plan like the ebony wall of the dining niche. A similar linear bench, another larger trellis, and custom-designed planters were also provided. Two concrete dining tables were designed but not executed. To make them appear only to touch the terrace, the supports were to have been concealed below the level of the rooftop pavers. Railings, fencing, gates, and light fixtures were designed and detailed by Mies and his staff.

Though the interiors and furniture are justly famous, and for the modern period the house is the architectural equivalent of a *Gesamtkunstwerk* (total artwork), Fritz Tugendhat, for one, had to be brought along. Mies, in

a 1959 interview, recalled: "Later [Herr Tugendhat] said to me: 'Now I give in on everything, but not about the furniture.' I said 'This is too bad.' I de-cided to send furniture to Brno from Berlin. I said to my superintendent: 'You keep the furniture and shortly before lunch call him out and say that you are at his house with furniture. He will be furious, but you must expect that.' He [Tugendhat] said, 'Take it out,' before he saw it. However, after lunch he liked it. I think we should treat our clients as children, not as archi-tects."[65]

Mies would labor on in Germany for eight more years, but the Tugendhat House proved to be his last major European house. The Tugendhats, cos-mopolitan and politically liberal, were able to flee Brno for Switzerland in 1938, a year before the Nazi takeover of Czechoslovakia. But the parents of both Fritz and Grete, and many others of their families, perished in the Holo-caust. Fritz stayed behind in Brno for a few months, and amid the trying times was able to save some of the furniture. With the onset of the war, the house suffered one depredation after another. As the property of Jews, it was seized by the Nazis in 1942 and nearly razed. The remaining furniture was comman-deered and placed at auction, as was Jewish property in Czechoslovakia uni-versally. In 1944, during the collapse of the Wehrmacht on the eastern front,

Red Army troops took over the house. The Russians are said to have ridden horses up and down the garden stair and roasted oxen on a spit set up in front of the onyx wall. The Makassar wall disappeared, as had the Lehmbruck torso at a date unknown. The house still stands, for a time one of the most grievous casualties suffered by the modern movement during its post-1933 extremity. Another in a series of restorations—at last, one of high quality—was completed in 2012.

Unlike the Barcelona Pavilion, the Tugendhat House was not widely covered in the German press, and it gained international exposure only with the Museum of Modern Art show of 1932, where it was featured by Philip Johnson, who had toured it with Mies. But from the start, the house was the subject of at least minor controversy. Justus Bier, in an article in *Die Form* titled "Can

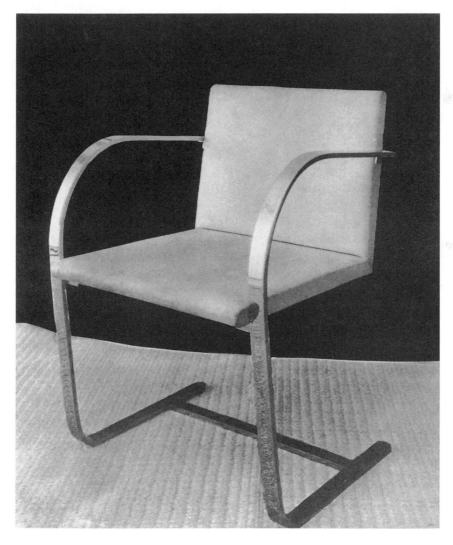

FIGURE 4.25.
Brno chair, flat-bar version (1930). The Brno was a "flat-fronted" modification of the MR design intended to serve as a dining or desk chair. The flat-bar version is almost too heavy to move. Photo courtesy of the Mies van der Rohe Archive of the Museum of Modern Art, NY.

FIGURE 4.26.
X-table, Tugendhat
House, Brno, Czecho-
slovakia (1930). The
glass top is one me-
ter on a side. The
horizontal leg ele-
ments meet at a
welded joint similar
to that connecting
the crossing com-
ponents of the legs
of the Barcelona
chair (designed ear-
lier). Photo courtesy
of the Mies van der
Rohe Archive of the
Museum of Modern
Art, NY.

One Live in the Tugendhat House?," offered a negative assessment.[66] It was, he maintained, a showpiece, not a home, its "precious" spaces and ostentatious furnishings suppressing both intimacy and individuality.

Die Form published rebuttals by the Tugendhats themselves, Grete writing in a letter to the editor that "[she had] … never felt the spaces as being precious, but rather as being austere and grand, not in a way that oppresses, but rather liberates."[67] To this Fritz Tugendhat added:

> It is true that one cannot hang any pictures in the main space, in the same way that one cannot introduce a piece of furniture that would destroy the stylish uniformity of the original furnishings—but is our "personal life repressed" for that reason? The incomparable patterning of the marble and the natural graining of the wood do not take the place of art, but rather they participate in the art, in the space, which is here art.[68]

Clients and critic were at one with Mies himself in granting highest priority to the spiritual component of architecture, a principle Mies had been emphasizing since before the Weissenhofsiedlung. Bier regretted that Mies was not working on projects "that engage his ability, which is equal to the highest tasks of architecture, in the proper place, namely, where it is intended to build a home for the spirit, and not where the necessity of living, sleeping, and eating requires a quieter, more muted idiom."[69] Grete Tugendhat, perhaps the judge with the best credentials, nonetheless claimed that Mies was "doing justice to the primarily spiritual sense of life of each and every one of us as opposed to mere necessity."[70]

.   .   .

In January 1929, while Mies was at work on the Tugendhat House, the renowned painter Emil Nolde, whom Mies had met in Hellerau while courting Ada, commissioned a house for himself and his wife, in Berlin-Zehlendorf. Nolde set down a tight schedule, and soon he was badgering:

> If ... you do not give me a guarantee by [April 13] that we will be able to move into the house by September 15, 1929—whereby I am allowing for two weeks beyond the deadline you promised, namely the end of August—I must conclude that you are not in a position to keep to the promise, as indicated above, that you have repeatedly made me. I would then be forced, unfortunately, to do without your services. This would disappoint me most especially, for I value you highly as an artist.[71]

Mies completed his design on time—by April 13—but for reasons unknown the house was never built. The drawings show a one-story steel construction with walls of masonry infill and a partial basement. There are walls of glass and a grid of cruciform columns, and several versions of a plan divided into living, working, and support areas. The living room looks out through a winter garden akin to that of the Tugendhat House. The entry leads through a vestibule to the servants' quarters, the living room, and a gallery of one hundred square meters that in turn gives onto the artist's atelier. The atelier is windowless, but may have had a skylight.

.   .   .

The year 1930 separated Mies's most important and celebrated works to date—the Barcelona Pavilion and the Tugendhat House—from a period of professional frustration and financial reversal. The collapse of the Nolde project was the first in a series of setbacks, and even projects he was able to win came to unprofitable ends. Among significant disappointments was a 1930 competition entry for the remodeling of Karl Friedrich Schinkel's Neue Wache

FIGURE 4.27. Neue Wache War Memorial project, Berlin-Mitte (1930). Like the Monument to the November Revolution (fig. 3.13), Mies's competition entry was intended to evoke emotion, though not through conventional devices like wreaths or garlands or sculpture. A single black quadrilateral stone slightly depressed in the floor was to carry the laconic inscription DEN TOTEN (To the Dead). The monolith was to be at the center of a below-grade, stone-walled room in Schinkel's New Guard House in Berlin (see fig. 2.7). Through a rear exit, a group of trees would have been visible. Mies's entry was not selected.

(New Guard House) in Berlin (fig. 4.27). The government had decided to transform the building into a memorial to the German dead of World War I. The lower level was to be used for a commemorative installation. Mies proposed a grandly scaled, cubical space walled in Tinian marble, with a slight depression near the center of a travertine floor. There a low black slab would be inscribed on its edges with the German eagle and the legend DEN TOTEN (To the Dead). The power of the concept lies entirely in monumental understatement. But the jury awarded the top prize to Heinrich Tessenow.[72]

Next came the failure of Mies's entry in a limited competition for a golf club in Krefeld. Invitation to participate was tendered in August 1930. Mies offered two proposals. The first shows the clubhouse, including changing rooms and instructor and caretaker apartments, built into a knoll that was probably to be artificially created. At the top of that rise is a circular, open pavilion ringed by slender columns — like nothing else in Mies's catalog. An angled, freestanding glass wall mounted nearby was intended to protect the pavilion from the wind and to fulfill the conditions of the competition, which called for a veranda both covered and uncovered. A wide stair leads to a terrace at the foot of the knoll.

Mies's decision to replace this proposal may have been inspired by its striking (and unexplained) distance from his normal manner. Whatever the reasons, his second offering is characteristic. A single building built on a flat ground plane is made up of three wings, sheltered and centrifugally organized around a terrace. One wing contains social rooms and a large reception hall; a second, changing rooms, administrative offices, and apartments; and a third, a linear outdoor space accommodating parking.

The unfolding international financial crisis prompted the club's directors to reduce their program, and Mies agreed to participate in a second competition. Due to what he claimed was a tight schedule, he was granted a postponement of the submission deadline. Since the records have been lost, it is not known whether he produced a revised design. It may be that the crisis caused a premature end to the competition.

Political Crises and the End of the Bauhaus: 1930–36

5

I am not a world improver; never was, never wanted to be. I am an architect, interested in building. **MIES,** describing his politics

The Bauhaus is supported by forces that are fighting our forces. It is one army against another, only in the spiritual field. Nazi official **ALFRED ROSENBERG**

The totalitarian states depend upon the favor of the masses. We are obliged to dance painstakingly on a wave, and if the wave should not support us, we would disappear overnight. I can do nothing for Mies, since the masses that stand behind us are driven by very different ideas, and if I were to recommend Mies, well, that wouldn't be viewed favorably at all.
JOSEPH GOEBBELS, Nazi Propaganda Minister, speaking to Lilly von Schnitzler, 1933

Mies's 1931 design for an apartment in New York City was by itself a modest success. The client was a twenty-four-year-old American, Philip Cortelyou Johnson, Cleveland born, Harvard educated, competent in German, precocious, opinionated, and lately associated with Alfred H. Barr Jr., the erudite young director of New York's Museum of Modern Art. Johnson was touring Europe in the summer of 1930, devoting most of his time to a study of the New Architecture, a subject then little known in the United States. His guidebook was Gustav Platz's 1927 *Baukunst der neuesten Zeit*.[1] There for the first time he encountered the work of Mies, who he decided was a better architect than Le Corbusier or J. J. P. Oud, the two modernists favored by Johnson's friend Henry-Russell Hitchcock. A year earlier, in 1929, Hitchcock had published *Modern Architecture*,[2] and two years later, in 1932, Johnson, Hitchcock, and Barr would mount MoMA's now legendary exhibition of international modern architecture. While the Johnson apartment was Mies's first completed work in the United States, the MoMA exhibition constituted his initial public appearance.

The 550-square-foot apartment, at 424 East Fifty-Second Street, consisted of a foyer, a living room with a fireplace, a bedroom, and a kitchen with dining nook. Judging from photographs and drawings, the professional assignment was ordinary interior design, but with custom-made pieces of Mies's and Reich's furniture and custom-designed millwork (the hand of Lilly Reich is in evidence on most of the surviving drawings).[3] In the living room, the fireplace was addressed in an asymmetrically formal arrangement of two Barcelona chairs, one Tugendhat chair, a Barcelona ottoman, and a low couch (also sometimes called a daybed) around a Parsons table. A grand piano stood against the wall opposite the fireplace, with an MR-style piano bench by Mies. The couch, which is still manufactured by Knoll International,[4] was designed for the Johnson apartment.[5] Though undeniably beautiful, it is a curious structural hybrid, with a sculpted wood frame supported on chromed (later stainless) tubular-steel legs. Recent scholarship has attributed the design of the daybed to Lilly Reich, who in her independent furniture designs often worked with the tube-to-wood combination.[6] In the living room the double-hung windows (and the radiators) were screened wall to wall by full-length draperies. The custom millwork included two sets of bookshelves, a leather-topped desk and a dresser for the bedroom, and a long, narrow wooden cabinet for flat art storage in the living room. Tubular steel was employed for the vertical supports of bookcases installed in the bedroom, as well as for the legs of Johnson's desk (the same motif was used for the Tugendhat House). All the furniture and millwork was manufactured in Germany. As Johnson no doubt desired, the apartment was among the most advanced private interiors in the country. Characteristically, he did not hesitate to display a photograph of his own living room in the 1932 MoMA exhibition.

It was Johnson, then, who effectively introduced Mies to the New World. For the next four decades, the two men would carry on a relationship marked by warmth and polar chill, intellectual accord and personal animosity. The germ of it was the genuine admiration felt by a bright, rising young man of privilege for an illustrious older one seemingly in danger of eclipse. Johnson represented wealth and institutional authority in America, a land of boundless material resources; Mies had risen from humble origins to high professional rank by virtue of talent, in a country that had witnessed little social mobility. Johnson engaged Mies's attention largely because Mies always gravitated toward cultural power, especially if it gravitated toward him. At the same time, Mies's pride must have counseled him to keep his distance. There was plenty of cause for both attraction and conflict in a relationship that grew turbulent within a year.

"We used to go to Schlichter's all the time," Johnson recalled, "and I'd pay for him. It was frightfully expensive and he had no means of support that I could see. In 1930 he had only my apartment to do. He did it as if it were six skyscrapers—the amount of work he put into that apartment was incredible."[7] Johnson's reference to "no means of support" may account for his later contention that Mies was in financial distress, although in view of Mies's customarily deliberate behavior—and his pride—he probably did nothing to correct Johnson's assumption. Indeed, Mies had been hired by the Bauhaus at an annual salary of 11,200 Reichmarks, a substantial sum at the time.[8] Johnson again:

[Mies] loved to drive in the country. That was one way I knew I could get to see him.... His favorite buildings were the *Hallenkirchen* (hall churches), up north toward Stettin, toward Lübeck.... [The *Backsteingotik* (Gothic in brick)] was where he felt most at home, in the *Hallen*, the tall churches.

I used to try to get him to talk about Schinkel. But he would just say yes, if I got enthusiastic, and would never really discuss it, even though he did that early thing [the Perls-Fuchs House] that looks like the Persius house. When I first found that [building] I jumped for joy and said, "Oh, you know Persius." He didn't. At least not by name.[9]

Regardless of Johnson's frustrations, his admiration for the architect only grew. Together they visited the almost completed Tugendhat House, which, Johnson claimed, Mies had never seen.[10] Deeply impressed, Johnson later made certain that Mies was given a major place in MoMA's exhibition, and even invited him to install the show. Mies was held in equally high esteem by Barr, who, having visited Berlin in 1930, must have done a lot to solicit the assistance of one of the museum's most important benefactors, Mrs. John D. Rockefeller Jr. Early in 1931 Johnson wrote her from Berlin: "It is extremely encouraging to know that when the time arrives, probably in September, for the show to be designed, that we have the greatest architect to do it. Your cooperation and interest mean a great deal to us, especially in this preliminary period."[11]

Mies's attitude toward Johnson's attention and the exhibition itself seems to have vacillated between cordiality and indifference. In July, complaining about Mies's all-too-frequent inaccessibility, Johnson wrote: "Mies is having a fit of being very hard to get hold of, and there is just nothing to be done. Repeated calls only make him mad."[12] But only days later Johnson found him "very eager to design a new house especially for us."[13]

Did Mies really behave with such caprice? What we know of him suggests it. He was fully capable of hauteur, especially toward a young man who may have pressed too hard. We have little evidence beyond Johnson's irrepressibly gossipy letters of what may have been going on in Mies's mind during the darkening days of 1931. In what respects was the Bauhaus "falling apart rather badly," as Johnson said?[14] Why did Mies never go ahead with his design of a house for the MoMA show after "absolutely promising to send a model from Berlin by October 15?"[15]

"More modest show," Johnson scribbled on the margin of a memo late in 1931. "Mies not coming, no installation."[16] Reduced ambitions point to reduced financial means all around. Johnson nevertheless had reason to presume that Mies would be more available toward the end of 1931 than toward the beginning. His expectation that Mies would come to the United States to install the MoMA exhibition is consonant with the August closing of the one event of the year on which he, Mies, had labored earnestly.

It may be overdramatic to assert that the Berlin Building Exposition was Mies's swan song in Germany. But the full-scale exhibit of a house for a childless couple that he introduced at the Berlin Fair Grounds at the Reichskanzlerplatz in 1931 was his last built work—or, more accurately, built *model*—in the manner of his late 1920s "style": small scale, lovingly detailed buildings characterized by an open plan and the interlocking flow of indoor and outdoor space. Not even in his vigorously active second life in the United States did he do anything so apparently uncompromising. Further, while it was not without intimation of the future, prefiguring some of his residential projects of the later 1930s, none of these works, save the modest Lemke House, were realized.

The exposition was his last major organizational assignment as a spokesman for the New Architecture. Conceived in 1926 as a vehicle for the display of the latest advances in city planning, architecture, and construction, it was to have been a permanent feature of Berlin life, and would have included an entire model community. By the beginning of 1930, the international economic crisis had forced a major rethinking, so that by May 9, 1931, when it opened, the show had been reduced to model structures and trade-fair exhibits housed indoors in a single hall. Exactly a year before the opening, Mies had been selected to be "artistic director" for the fair's most important architectural component, an exhibit called *The Dwelling in Our Time*. As he had done at Weissenhof, he selected the architects and coordinated their contributions. Houses by the Luckhardt brothers, Hugo Häring, Marcel Breuer, and Lilly Reich were featured along with apartments by, among others, Walter Gropius, Ludwig Hilberseimer, and Otto Haesler. Individual rooms were outfitted by Josef Albers and Wassily Kandinsky. A gallery that circled the hall housed a materials exhibition organized by Reich.

Mies's one-story house for a childless couple was the Barcelona Pavilion recast as a residence, with less expensive materials and without dressed stone (fig. 5.1). The freestanding columns, for example, were round steel pipe. Though nominally a dwelling for two, the house was enormous, with 3,400 enclosed square feet under a 5,000-square-foot roof and with a total hardscaped footprint of almost 8,000 square feet. The structure consisted of a three-by-five set of freestanding columns disposed over a 5-by-6-meter grid and bracketed by unengaged, full-height walls, some of which extended into the surroundings. Interior functions were suggested by stub walls or millwork elements, and hanging fabric dividers replaced conventional doors. Only the baths and services were enclosed, the latter with conventional windows as opposed to the otherwise ubiquitous frameless glazing. The living-dining area was surrounded on three sides by expanses of glass, one unit of which could be lowered electrically into the ground, merging inside and out in one of Mies's

FIGURE 5.1.
Full-scale model
house for the Berlin
Building Exposition
(1931). Mies's long-
standing interest in
conflating indoors
and out can be in-
ferred from the mod-
el's garden "rooms"
and adjacent court-
yards. Mies's house
was connected by a
long, freestand-
ing wall to a smaller
house (not seen in
this view) credited
solely to Lilly Reich.

now familiar gestures. The bedroom, with separate beds in a palatial layout, opened to expansive exterior courts and a reflecting pool with another sculpture of a standing female figure, again by Georg Kolbe. One white plaster wall escaped to connect with a smaller house by Lilly Reich and to create a garden area between, evoking the walls darting off to infinity in Mies's project for a Brick Country House.

Hitchcock visited the exposition late in 1931, Johnson early in 1932. Both wrote reviews, and both agreed that Mies's house together with his furnishing of a bachelor's flat in one of the apartment houses were the most successful entries in the show. The Americans then returned for the February opening of MoMA's *Modern Architecture—International Exhibition*. Johnson was responsible for the installation. More than fifty architects were included. The catalog, published under the supervision of Johnson, Hitchcock, and Barr, featured essays on the major Europeans, Gropius, Le Corbusier, Mies, and Oud, as well as such Americans as Raymond Hood, Howe and Lescaze, the Austrian-born Richard Neutra, and Frank Lloyd Wright. Mies was represented by the Barcelona Pavilion, the Tugendhat House, the Hermann Lange House, and Johnson's apartment.[17]

The exhibition received mixed reviews from the critics in New York, where

144 / 145

the New Architecture as a movement was now seen for the first time. None-theless, controversy meant attention. Edward Durell Stone, who in 1939 de-signed the first new building to house the Museum of Modern Art, later said that the Johnson-Hitchcock-Barr exhibition "did for architecture what the fa-mous Armory Show had done for painting.... I know of no single event which so profoundly influenced the architecture of the twentieth century."[18] John-son and Hitchcock followed their success with a book, *The International Style*, in which they identified three hallmarks of the "style": "There is, first, a new conception of architecture as volume rather than as mass. Secondly, regular-ity rather than axial symmetry serves as the chief means of ordering design. These two principles, with a third proscribing arbitrary applied decoration, mark the productions of the international style."[19] In a second edition of 1966, Hitchcock reflected on the term and the definition and recognized that neither fit quite so neatly all the work included in the show, or all the able designers they downplayed or omitted.

. . .

Mies assumed the directorship of the Bauhaus in September 1930. Agreement has never been reached as to how many times he was offered the position, or why he accepted it. Scholars at the Bauhaus Archive in Berlin believe that Gropius asked him to take the job in 1928, prior to the appointment of Hannes Meyer, and that Mies turned him down.[20] Elaine Hochman, who has studied the period closely, believes this is simply a rumor. She cites a letter she re-ceived from Gropius's wife, Ise, according to whom Gropius brought Meyer to the Bauhaus with the intention of turning over the directorship to him when-ever Gropius wanted to leave: "When it turned out that Hannes Meyer was so left-oriented ... the mayor [Fritz Hesse of Dessau, where the Bauhaus was located] dismissed Meyer and asked Gropius to return and direct the school again. Gropius declined.... It was then and not earlier that he proposed to Mayor Hesse to ask whether Mies might want to take over."[21]

Mies's reasons for "taking over" are murkier still. The claim that he was in dire financial straits is attributed, by Hochman, to Philip Johnson.[22] In steady contact with Mies after meeting him in the summer of 1930, Johnson would seem a respectable witness. Yet he evidently did not take into consideration the substantial sums Mies had received for his work on the Barcelona Pavil-ion and Tugendhat House; for Barcelona, for example, Mies received an hon-orarium of 125,000 Reichmarks, and though he had work there in addition to the pavilion design, his fee was nevertheless more than *one-third* the cost of the lavishly appointed building. Georgia van der Rohe offers her memory of the effect of those two commissions on her father's reputation—"in one stroke, world renowned"[23]—and his lifestyle: "Mies lived luxuriously. The spacious

Berlin apartment, where he dwelt alone, was equipped with furniture he had designed for Barcelona.... [T]he floor was entirely laid with elegant white linoleum. Huge dark blue drapes of Shantung silk could be moved in front of the windows from wall to wall, like a theater curtain."[24]

Recalling that "for such a lordly existence a butler was an obvious necessity,"[25] Georgia adds to the evidence that Mies was not in need of a salary from the Bauhaus at the time of his appointment. She is less informative about what followed at the professional level, and while that subject takes nothing away from her recollections of Mies's circumstances, it is a fact that after the completion of the Tugendhat House his career suffered a sudden reversal. That development may account for Johnson's recollection.

The prehistory of Das staatliche Bauhaus, as it was formally known, is traceable to the English Arts and Crafts movement and the Deutscher Werkbund. Central to the concerns of these movements was the development of industrialism in western Europe and the appropriate cultural responses to it. The nineteenth century German architect Gottfried Semper had argued that technological change could not be reversed and, as an alternative to keeping the traditional crafts alive, advocated the schooling of a new type of craftsman capable of exploiting the machine in artistically viable ways. Even older institutions joined the ranks of the champions of reform in art education. As early as 1915, with World War I in progress, authorities in the provincial city of Weimar cultivated hopes of reopening the local Kunstgewerbeschule (the Grand-Ducal Saxon School of Arts and Crafts) as soon as possible following the cessation of hostilities. In turn the Grand-Ducal Saxon Academy of Fine Art, dating from 1860, also embraced educational reform, and a merger with a reopened Kunstgewerbeschule was proposed. The academy's officials believed that the new institution should be headed by an architect. In 1919 a contract was concluded with Walter Gropius, who had earlier played a significant role in the affairs of the Werkbund and was party to the plans for the new Weimar school.

Gropius's call for the educational unification of what had theretofore been separated became a core principle of the Bauhaus. Incoming students were obliged to complete a basic course, the *Vorkurs*, in which the objective was to turn away from traditional art and instead experiment with natural materials, color, and abstract form. Pictorial works of art were subjected to analytical study. Students then enrolled in a workshop of their choice in such crafts as weaving, printing, metalworking, and cabinetmaking. They were first "apprentices" and later "journeymen," terms recalling the guild system. Gropius replaced the academic title of professor with the craft-historical term *master*, a rank granted students upon completion of their course of study. Apprentices were taught by masters of the crafts—the so-called workshop masters—and also by fine artists, the "masters of form," who would guide students toward individual modes of expression.

Architecture was not part of the curriculum until 1927. While Gropius at the outset had made "the complete building" his ultimate educational goal, he believed that students should take up problems in architecture only after they had mastered theory and gained skill in craft and design. By 1926, when the Bauhaus moved into a building of his design in Dessau, Gropius considered that goal attained, and a year later a department of architecture was established, equal in rank with the workshops. He hoped to appoint Mart Stam as head, but the Dutch architect preferred practice to teaching and turned him down. An offer was then made to Basel architect Hannes Meyer, who accepted. Gropius had earlier demanded that political sentiment play no role in departmental governance. Yet once on the faculty, Meyer turned out to be an activist Marxist. As Gropius later told it, Meyer "was scheming to keep his intentions to himself until he was in the saddle."[26]

Meyer concentrated his energies almost exclusively on the architecture department. True to Marxist principles, he emphasized practical over speculative endeavor and encouraged collective solutions rather than personal experiment. He helped in the formation of a trade union school in Bernau, near Berlin. Practical, inexpensive "people's furniture" was produced, and Bauhaus wallpaper designs were developed. Among his major faculty appointments were Ludwig Hilberseimer, who supervised projects in mass housing and city planning; and Walter Peterhans, who taught photography. These two men would later find their way to Chicago and major roles in Mies's life.

While these developments may be counted among Meyer's achievements, his tenure is remembered for divisiveness and dissent. Many of the faculty were alienated not only by his politics but by his radical functionalist aesthetic and his determination to insinuate sociology into all Bauhaus activities. Oskar Schlemmer quit in 1929, while Josef Albers, Wassily Kandinsky, and Paul Klee suffered the progressive isolation of the fine arts from the curriculum. In 1930 matters came to a head. Following charges that Meyer had given money to striking miners in the name of the Bauhaus, on July 29, 1930, Mayor Hesse formally requested his resignation. Hostilities erupted again, this time with attacks coming from the Left, supportive of Meyer, as well as from the Right. Midway through the year, Mayor Hesse, acting on the recommendation of Gropius — who from without was trying to salvage the school's reputation — approached Mies and offered him the directorship. Mies accepted.

Mies was a man of neither the Right nor the Left, nor even of the center — he was an artist. Thus, it was assumed he might keep the political dogs at bay without compromising the progressive standards of the school. Though he was identified with the design of houses for the rich, there was no question about his talent or integrity.

In Berlin in this period, Mies continued to cultivate the image of the Grand Seigneur, one to which he had aspired ever since he saw Peter Behrens convincingly act the part. He dressed impeccably, with a preference for dark suits set off by bowlers and homburgs. For a brief spell he wore a monocle. His natural reserve deepened into magisterial aloofness and the impression of a monumental personality. In his midforties he became heavyset.[27] He had also become an inveterate cigar smoker, a habit directly related to his death, in 1969, from esophageal cancer.

Mies ran the school as his own man. Given the reflexive quarrelsomeness of the Bauhaus, his arrival produced an angry response from many students: the putatively democratic atmosphere of the school had been invaded by an elitist taskmaster. In noisy meetings in the school cafeteria, the students voiced their indignation at the dismissal of Meyer, demanding that Mies appear and defend himself. They had challenged the wrong man; Mies called in the Dessau police and directed them to remove the students from the building. Mayor Hesse then closed the school for several weeks. Mies officially expelled all the students, with the offer to reinstall only those who, in one-on-one interviews with the new director, expressed a desire to rematriculate. Five of the expelled students were banished from Dessau altogether.

Mies, in his 1968 interview with Dirk Lohan, recalled the situation:

> We had had a meeting with the various Bauhaus masters. After we threw the students out, they were just hanging around the corridors talking, in a standup convention. I called the faculty together because I wanted to ask them, "Do you find this a normal state of affairs for a school? Are you content with your people? I want to hear yes or no." They weren't sure they should express themselves. So I said, "Yes or no. Other answers don't interest me." Then I went from one to another in a circle and put the question to each of them. In the end it was obvious. "Of course it's no school; nothing but disorder. We are unable to teach." ... So I said, since it has come to this, that no one knows what the rights and the duties of the students and the teachers are, we'll have to clear things up. I don't remember if I asked whether they agreed with me, but in any case I called the mayor [Hesse] and said, "We are closing the Bauhaus for a couple of weeks in order to produce a clear constitution."
>
> I had been asked by Gropius and the mayor to take over the school, with the agreement of the administration in Dessau. ... I came here to return order to the school, to clean it up. ... Hannes Meyer ... wanted to make the school politically Communist. I was in no way in favor of that. I am not a world improver; never was, never wanted to be. I am an architect, interested in building and in problems of form.[28]

The Bauhaus charter conceived by Gropius was annulled, and another adopted. The 170 students were invited to reenroll when the school reopened. Work resumed the following semester.

Under Mies's stolid direction, the Bauhaus was turned into something ap-

FIGURE 5.2.
Mies, cigar in hand,
with students at the
Dessau Bauhaus,
about 1930. Private
collection.

proaching a school of architecture, operating with little of its former rambunc-tiousness and much midnight oil (fig. 5.2). The crafts workshops lost their erstwhile autonomy as Mies redirected activities toward the discipline of in-terior design. Klee resigned to take a professorship in Düsseldorf. Kandinsky stayed on, having argued about the curriculum with Mies, who agreed to retain color theory—at the same time reducing Kandinsky's teaching load.

The agreement Mies struck with the City of Dessau enabled him to consult on municipal planning and awarded him all patents and licenses developed by the school. Hilberseimer's influence increased. Lilly Reich was appointed to head the weaving workshop. She and Mies shared an apartment at the Bau-haus, spending three days a week there, the rest in Berlin. Hilberseimer was in charge when Mies was absent.

Mies left most of the administrative tasks to Reich or Hilberseimer, and made no effort to mediate internal institutional disagreements.[29] He restricted his teaching to advanced students, whom he assigned ostensibly simple prob-lems like a one-story, single-bedroom house or a house facing a walled garden. "The very simplicity of these houses," wrote his student Howard Dearstyne, in justification of Mies's teaching approach, "is their chief difficulty. It is much easier to do a complicated affair than something clear and simple."[30] Mies was more likely to tell a student "Versuchen Sie es wieder" (try it again) than to criticize—or encourage—in detail. If Hannes Meyer might have regarded such practice as so much formalistic fussiness, Mies had his own opinion of his predecessor. As Gropius remembered, his reaction to Meyer's materialistic worldview—that "all life is a striving after oxygen plus carbon plus sugar plus starch plus protein"—was direct: "Try stirring all that together: it stinks!"[31]

Mies's contractual responsibilities at the Bauhaus included unspecified ar-chitectural consulting as requested by the City of Dessau. In 1932 in this con-nection, a little-known but certainly Miesian work, the *Trinkhalle* ("refresh-

FIGURE 5.3.
Trinkhalle, Dessau
(1932). Mies inserted
this "refreshment
stand" into a wall
surrounding four
houses designed by
Gropius for his Bau-
haus faculty. It sur-
vived in GDR Dessau
until 1969.

ment stand" or "kiosk"), was completed. Properly, it was neither stand nor kiosk; in today's parlance it might be termed an "intervention." Behind an existing, curving, white stucco wall two meters high, Mies inserted a small enclosure with a single rectangular opening capped by a cantilevered canopy (fig. 5.3). Service was through a pair of sliding glass lights, behind which the work space was accessed by a new opening around the corner. The wall was the work of Walter Gropius; it surrounded four houses the former Bauhaus director had designed for the Dessau faculty a few years before.

We know about the *Trinkhalle* in detail chiefly through the testimony and photographs of Eduard Ludwig, a student at the Bauhaus and Mies's assistant for the project. (Ludwig would play a crucial role in the preservation of Mies's papers and drawings during and after World War II.) Mies appears never to have spoken publicly about the *Trinkhalle*, at least in his American period, though Dessau-era documents under his signature confirm his authorship.[32] The *Trinkhalle* and parts of its enveloping wall survived in East German Dessau until 1969. Today the location is memorialized by a humble plan outlined in brick (fig. 5.4).

Refreshment stands of all varieties—often ornate trifles—had been common in German cities for decades. Mies's was characteristically distilled. Dismissing commercial architectural appliqué, he inserted into existing fabric a solution of minimal means and maximum visual impact. The service opening, slightly set back in the otherwise undifferentiated white wall, was marked by an overgenerous all-white canopy. This new element floated atop the wall and provided shelter both at and beside the window. At the bottom of the opening

was the suggestion of a serving shelf or counter, hardly thicker than the window frame itself. By concealing the door around the corner, Mies both isolated and highlighted the locus of service.[33]

In the tiny *Trinkhalle* we see Mies practicing as a minimalist, something he rarely did in Germany or the United States. In Germany he was primarily a master of open-plan design and the rich, reductivist surface. In America he embraced a new architecture, one flowing "out of construction" and with "a clear structure." Neither of these positions is minimalist, except in the trivial sense that they both reject historicist ornament. Mies almost never designed for minimal member sizes, minimal numbers or types of components, or minimal means or inputs. On the contrary, most of his work is spatially lavish and, where he could afford it, materially rich. It is the *expression* of simplicity at which he aims. In its extreme reduction of materials, means, and message, the *Trinkhalle* is therefore exceptional.

. . .

Mies did not see the MoMA exhibition, occupied as he was with his responsibilities at the Bauhaus. From the beginning of his tenure he had been confronted with political conflicts he wanted to sidestep. In addition to the strife generated by the Meyer affair, the condition of the German economy had grown grave enough by 1932 to awaken memories of the worst days of 1919. Street fighting—the clearest sign of the increasing polarization of politics—was again common. In the national elections of July 31, 1931, to which an unprece-

Political Crises and the End of the Bauhaus

dented number of citizens responded, more than half the electorate endorsed parties expressly committed to the overthrow of the republic.

The Bauhaus spun toward its doom. Blows rained on it from architects promoting a traditional national style, led by Paul Schultze-Naumburg, and from the local Nazis, who demanded not only the closing of the school but the demolition of the Gropius buildings that housed it. Under pressure from the national government, Dessau Social Democrats abstained from a crucial city council vote in the summer of 1932. The Nazis won the day.

Seeking to cultivate the appearance of fairness, the victors announced that a committee of experts, headed by Schultze-Naumburg, would visit the school's regular end-of-term exhibition and formally decide whether the Bauhaus warranted further municipal funding. The progressive faculty and students rejected the idea. Mies, whose behavior seems to have been naive or headstrong or both, insisted on proceeding with the show, even though he persuaded only a few of his own students to participate. Matters were not helped by Kandinsky's determination to display a few of his geometric abstractions, paintings certain to displease the committee, which needed only a few minutes to view the undersized display before rendering a final, fatal judgment.

The Bauhaus was shut down on the first of October. In negotiations with Mayor Hesse, Mies—this time acting not at all naively—concluded a legal agreement that effectively transformed the school into a private institution. His salary was guaranteed until March 31, 1933, and half of it thereafter for two more years. Since it was Mies's intention to move the school to Berlin, the City of Dessau gave up its rights to the name Bauhaus, securing it to Mies as director. Patents and equipment were likewise remanded to him.

In late October 1932, the Bauhaus reopened in Berlin-Steglitz, with a faculty of Albers, Hilberseimer, Kandinsky, Peterhans, Reich, Friedrich Engemann, Hinnerk Scheper, and Alcar Rudelt. Its quarters were an abandoned telephone factory in an unprepossessing neighborhood at the southern limits of the city. Mies came up with 27,000 Reichmarks of his own money to make the rent. Renovation was confined to painting the interior white. Mies claimed, even late in life, that he and his colleagues had warmed to the place, which they considered "not so pretentious" as Dessau.[34] Though he succeeded in reopening the school, enrollment fell short of the hundred students he had planned for. He reinstated the Dessau curriculum, and a measure of calm descended. For virtually the first time in its history, the Bauhaus seemed united in spirit. The most festive events in the short history of the Berlin Bauhaus were the Fasching (Carnival) Balls of February 18 and 25, for which students and faculty made a great show of redecorating the building with gaudy colors and lights.

In retrospect these balls may have been equivalent to a jazz funeral. Political quarrels reemerged. Leftist students protested the move to Berlin, calling the privatization a "flight into the desert" and asserting that Mies had assumed the directorship for "egotistical reasons." On the morning of April 11, Mies arrived at the Bauhaus to find the portal locked and the building cordoned off by police. The Nazis, who had taken over the government in Berlin two months before, initiated a search for documents that might link the school with the Communist Party.

In 1952 Mies recounted the incident in an interview with six design students from North Carolina State College:

> Our wonderful building was surrounded by Gestapo—black uniforms, with bayonets. It was really surrounded. I ran to be there. And a sentry said, "Stop here." I said, "What? This is my factory. I rented it. I have a right to see it."
>
> "You are the owner? Come in." He knew I would never come out if they didn't want me to. Then I went and talked to the officer. I said, "I am the director of this school," and he said, "Oh, come in," and we talked some more and he said, "You know there was an affair against the mayor of Dessau and we are just investigating the documents of the founding of the Bauhaus." I said, "Come in." I called all the people and said, "Open everything for inspection, open everything." I was certain there was nothing there that could be misinterpreted.
>
> The investigation took hours. In the end the Gestapo became so tired and hungry that they called their headquarters and said, "What should we do? Should we work here forever? We are hungry and so on." And they were told, "Lock it and forget it."
>
> Then I called up Alfred Rosenberg. He was the party philosopher of the Nazi culture, and he was the head of the movement. It was called the Bund deutscher Kultur. I called him up and said, "I want to talk with you." He said, "I am very busy."
>
> I understand that, but even so, at any time you tell me I will be there.
>
> "Could you be here at eleven o'clock tonight?"
>
> Certainly.
>
> My friends Hilberseimer and Lilly Reich and some other people said, "You will not be so stupid as to go there at eleven o'clock?" They were afraid, you know, that they would just kill me or do something. I am not afraid. I have nothing. I'd like to talk with this man.
>
> So I went that night and we really talked, you know, for an hour. And my friends Hilberseimer and Lilly Reich were sitting across the street in a café window so they could see when I came out, if alone, or under guards, or what.
>
> I told Rosenberg the Gestapo had closed the Bauhaus and I wanted to have it open again. I said, "You know, the Bauhaus has a certain idea and I think that it is important. It has nothing to do with politics or anything. It has something to do with technology." And then for the first time he told me about him-

self. He said, "I am a trained architect from the Baltic states, from Riga." He had a diploma as an architect from Riga. I said, "Then we certainly will understand each other." And he said, "Never! What do you expect me to do? You know the Bauhaus is supported by forces that are fighting our forces. It is one army against another, only in the spiritual field." And I said, "No, I really don't think it is like that." And he said, "Why didn't you change the name, for heaven's sake, when you moved the Bauhaus from Dessau to Berlin?" I said, "Don't you think the Bauhaus is a wonderful name? You cannot find a better one." He said, "I don't like what the Bauhaus is doing. I know you can suspend, you can cantilever something, but my feeling demands a support." I said, "Even if it is cantilevered?" And he said, "Yes."

He wanted to know, "What is it you want to do at the Bauhaus?" I said, "Listen, you are sitting here in an important position. And look at your writing table, this shabby writing table. Do you like it? I would throw it out of the window. That is what we want to do. We want to have good objects that we do not have to throw out of the window." And he said, "I will see what I can do for you." I said, "Don't wait too long."

Then from there on I went every second day for three months to the headquarters of the Gestapo. I had the feeling I had the right. That was my school. It was a private school. . . . And it took me three months, exactly three months, to get to the head of the Gestapo. He must have had a back door somewhere, you know. And he had a bench in the waiting room not wider than four inches, to make you tired so that you would go home again. But one day I got him. [Mies did not identify him by name.] He was young, very young, about your age, and he said, "Come in. What do you want?" I said, "I would like to talk to you about the Bauhaus. What is going on? You have closed the Bauhaus. It is my private property, and I want to know for what reason. We didn't steal anything. We didn't make a revolution. I'd like to know how that can be."

"Oh," he said. "I know you perfectly, and I am very interested in the movement, the Bauhaus movement, and so on, but we don't know what is with Kandinsky." I said, "I make all the guarantee about Kandinsky." He said, "You have to, but be careful. We don't know anything about him, but if you want to have him, it is O.K. with us. But if something happens, we pick you up." He was very clear about that. I said, "That is all right. Do that." And then he said, "I will talk with Göring, because I am really interested in this school." And I really believe he was. . . .

That was before Hitler made a clear statement. Hitler made this statement in 1935 at the opening of the Haus der deutschen Kunst, the House of German Art, in his speech about the cultural policy of the Nazi movement. Before, everybody had an idea. Goebbels had an idea; Göring had an idea. You know, nothing was clear. After Hitler's speech the Bauhaus was out. But the head of the Gestapo told me he would talk with Göring about it and I told him, "Do it soon." We were just living from the money we still got from Dessau. Nothing else came to us.[35]

Finally I got a letter saying we could open the Bauhaus again. When I got this letter I called Lilly Reich. I said, "I got a letter. We can open the school again. Order champagne." She said, "What for? We don't have the money." I said, "Order champagne." I called the faculty together: Albers, Kandinsky ... they were still around us, you know, and some other people: Hilberseimer, Peterhans, and I said, "Here is the letter from the Gestapo that we can open the Bauhaus again." They said, "That is wonderful." I said, "Now I went there for three months every second day just to get this letter. I was anxious to get this letter. I wanted to have the permission to go ahead. And now I make a proposition, and I hope you will agree with me. I will write them a letter back: 'Thank you for the permission [to] open the school again, but the faculty has decided to close it!'"

I had worked on it for this moment. It was the reason I ordered the champagne. Everybody accepted it, and was delighted. Then we stopped.

That is the real end of the Bauhaus. Nobody else knows it, you know. We know it. Albers knows it. He was there. But the talk about it is absolute nonsense. They don't know. I know.[36]

The North Carolina interview, while valuable as Mies's recollection, failed to mention this letter from the Gestapo:

Strictly confidential:
State Secret Police
Berlin S. W. 11, July 21, 1933

Prinz-Albrecht-Strasse 8

Professor Mies van der Rohe
Berlin, Am Karlsbad 24

Regarding: Bauhaus Berlin-Steglitz
In agreement with the Prussian Minister for Science, Art, and Education, the reopening of the Bauhaus Berlin-Steglitz is made dependent upon the removal of some objections.

1) Ludwig Hilberseimer and Vassily Kandinsky are no longer permitted to teach. Their places have to be taken by individuals who guarantee to support the principles of the National Socialist ideology.

2) The curriculum which has been in force up to now is not sufficient to satisfy the demands of the new State for the purposes of building its infrastruc-

ture. Therefore, a curriculum accordingly modified is to be submitted to the Prussian Minister of Culture.

The members of the faculty have to complete and submit a questionnaire, satisfying the requirements of the civil service law.

The decision on the continuing existence and the reopening of the Bauhaus will be made dependent on the immediate removal of the objections and the fulfillment of the stated conditions.

By order: [signed] Dr. Peche
Chancery staff[37]

Over the years, historians have paid a good deal of attention to a 1934 proclamation that appeared in the *Völkischer Beobachter*, the Nazi Party newspaper. An excerpt:

We believe in this leader ["Führer"], who has fulfilled our fervent wish for unity.

We trust his work, which calls for sacrifice beyond all carping sophistry; we place our hope in the man who, beyond man and things, believes in God's providence.

Because the writer and artist create for the people with equal devotion, and because he brings the same conviction ... we belong to the leader's followers.... The leader has called upon us to stand by him in trust and faith. None of us will be missing when an affirmation of trust is needed. The nation will never dissolve when it remains united and true.[38]

Mies was one of the signers, together with artists Ernst Barlach, Emil Nolde, and Erich Heckel, conductor Wilhelm Furtwängler, composers Richard Strauss and Hans Pfitzner, and a host of other notables of both the Right and the Left. Mies's willingness to profess faith in Hitler has given reasonable cause for the unforgiving response of later generations. Still, a qualifying note should be added. During 1934, the year of the proclamation, Nazi attitudes toward the arts ranged from Rosenberg's hostility toward modernism to Goebbels's promotion of it, and Hitler's alternating embrace of consensus and a tendency toward vacillation. While it is not certain, it is also not hard to imagine that Mies, whose practice was languishing at the time, simply accepted the dominance of National Socialism as a fact in hopes that it would swing toward the modernist position and allow him to pursue his career.

. . .

Nazi cultural policy was seldom simple or clear-cut. Right-wing *völkisch* sentiment saw the modern arts as pernicious and pathological, expressions of a rootless, *undeutsch* urbanism for which the International Jew was the symbol. Yet Nazism could just as easily identify itself with modernity, science, and advanced technology. Among all the arts, architecture was gripped most tightly in a vise of contradiction. The Nazis fumed over Walter Gropius's Bauhaus building in Dessau, threatening to tear it down, and going so far as to add a sloping roof to the studio wing. Yet they also built the superbly efficient, visually *sachlich* Autobahn. Hitler's personal preferences ran to a pre–World War I neoclassicism. But Hermann Göring commissioned buildings for the air force that were indistinguishable from the most matter-of-fact 1920s modernism.

The professional and financial comfort that Mies enjoyed in 1930 had come to a grievous end by the time the Bauhaus closed in 1933. His investment in the building in Berlin left his finances exhausted. He could no longer afford a butler and maid, and was obliged to maintain his apartment himself. His failure to secure professional work continued. Between 1931, when he finished the house for the Berlin Building Exhibition, and 1938, his last year in Germany, he worked on a number of houses, of which only one was built, the 1932–33 Lemke House in Berlin.

What might have been a major work, and the most compelling of his European residential designs after the Tugendhat House, is the Gericke House project, a competition entry put together in just three weeks during the summer of 1932. Herbert Gericke, wealthy director of the German Academy in Rome, had taken the unusual step, for a private citizen, of initiating an invited, unpaid competition for the design of a house intended for a superb site overlooking Berlin's Wannsee. The brief, as if tailored for Mies, called for a house "in the simplest form of our period and pleasantly connected with the landscape and with the garden."[39] The competition, administered by Werner March (who would design the 1936 Olympic Stadium in Berlin), included Mies, Bruno Paul, and two others no longer known.[40] The site had been occupied by a nineteenth-century villa, now demolished. Three terraces and some foundation walls remained, framed by stands of old trees. A few weeks after submitting his proposal, Mies learned that Gericke had rejected it (and the others) in favor of his own design. Keenly interested in the commission, Mies offered, in writing, to rework his proposal without fee. Gericke rejected this offer too, and in a letter to March explained why:

> I had to refrain from commissioning an architect of genuinely artistic abilities because I did not wish to get into intellectual boxing matches over the shape of each piece of molding and each doorknob.... My respect for independent artistic work prevented me from expecting a man like Mies van der Rohe to concede to my very detailed suggestions that probably run counter to his own artistic ideas.[41]

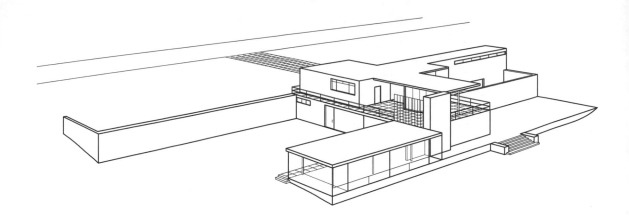

FIGURE 5.5.
Gericke House
project (1932). Con-
jectural perspective
drawing. The single-
level rectangular vol-
ume (*at front center*)
is almost entirely
glazed and prefig-
ures Mies's Farns-
worth House then
seventeen years in
the future. Though
the Gericke proposal
incorporates many
elements from the
Tugendhat House,
including entry from
the upper level via a
glassed-in circular
stair, the interplay of
exterior and interior
"rooms" and vistas is
unprecedented.

In a letter of the same date to Mies, he was astonishingly frank:

The unpretentious house that I am now building, derived purely out of my personal experiences and intended for my personal use, is so different from the [competition proposals] that I saw no way to bridge the gaps between my own ideas and those of others.... It seems to me that the great number of unfortunate dwellings constructed recently are a result of compromise between clients and architects. In this case it would have been all the more disastrous inasmuch as the so-called client had a very specific (probably bad) image of the completed house in mind.

Mies knew nothing of Gericke's ambivalence when he set to work on a design. A large number of Mies's sketches survive, as do plans and elevations worked out by his assistants, so that the building, though a concept, is well represented (fig. 5.5). The program was on the scale of the Tugendhat House. Mies disposed it over two floors plus a basement, with entry, servants' quarters, and children's rooms on the upper level, and a lavish master suite as well as living and dining areas on a lower, main level. Circulation between levels is by a winding stair like that at Tugendhat. Both floors open generously and variously on hardscaped outdoor terraces, some of them walled, presumably atop existing foundations. The major plan components are disposed in quasi-independent volumes integrated with the landscape. The plan evokes the exactly contemporaneous Krefeld Golf Club, with programmatic volumes overlapping or touching at a corner in a dynamic pinwheel. Of special note is the living room volume, on the lower level but set apart as a single-story appendage, organized on the now-familiar Barcelona/Tugendhat columnar grid but bounded on three sides by enormous glass lights, some of the *Senkfenster* type, prefiguring the all-glazed prism of the 1951 Farnsworth House.

Original in the Gericke project was a free plan interlocked on multiple levels, more naturally integrated into its sloping terrain than either the Tugendhat or Wolf Houses. The semidiscrete volumes broke new ground in defining outdoor rooms and in offering framed vistas to the exterior, across outdoor terraces and back into other interiors. We have no detail about materials and finishes, and no idea whether Mies would have been able to control the furniture and furnishings. What remains is a singular example of Mies's mastery at this point in his European maturity.

· · ·

The desperate state of Mies's fortunes in the early thirties is evident in a recording made in 1974 by Ludwig Glaeser, then curator of the Mies van der Rohe Archive of the Museum of Modern Art. The voice is that of Lilly von Schnitzler, wife of Georg von Schnitzler, the government official who commissioned Mies's designs for the Barcelona fair. Frau von Schnitzler:

> Long spans of time passed for Mies in which he had nothing to do. He kept himself busy, but only by reading and sketching a lot. And on one occasion, when he came by, it was obvious that he was in dire straits. He said, "Frau von Schnitzler, my back is to the wall. I'm no longer getting any commissions, I'm forced to change things around and reposition myself somehow, because I'm simply at the end of the line, materially. But since you have so many connections, can't you help me somehow?" And unfortunately I had to tell him that my husband and I didn't have any connections to the Nazi Party, and besides, he wouldn't be welcome there anyway.[42]

Contrary to her representation to Mies, the Schnitzlers did have access to Nazi officials, and in 1933 Lilly made one significant effort on Mies's behalf— though, as she predicted, it proved futile. Seated at a dinner party next to Joseph Goebbels, the Reich propaganda minister, she struck up a conversation, requesting that he provide some assistance to Mies, whose exceptional gifts she cited. "Yes," Goebbels replied,

> Mies is the most significant German architect, after Troost. [Paul Troost, a neoclassicist, was at this time Hitler's favorite architect.] But Frau von Schnitzler, you seem not to know that the totalitarian states depend upon the favor of the masses. We are obliged to dance painstakingly on a wave, and if the wave should not support us, we would disappear overnight. I can do nothing for Mies, since the masses that stand behind us are driven by very different ideas, and if I were to recommend Mies, well, that wouldn't be viewed favorably at all.[43]

(Goebbels's professed fealty to the masses stands in sharp contrast with the power that had accrued to him, for at the time he was in complete charge of Germany's radio, press, cinema, and theater.)

By comparison with the major commissions of the late 1920s, Mies's house for Karl and Martha Lemke at Oberseestrasse 60 in Berlin-Hohenschönhausen is a footnote. His personal finances had deteriorated so rapidly that when the Lemkes approached him in February 1932, asking for a small house on a tiny budget and an almost impossible schedule—substantial completion was demanded within the calendar year—Mies accepted. The result, which survives in a magnificent restoration completed in 2002, is a modest masterwork, all the more poignant because it was Mies's last realized residential commission before his immigration to the United States in 1938.

Karl Lemke was the director of a large commercial printing company that specialized in quality art books. Eduard Fuchs was among Lemke's customers, and it was Fuchs who had suggested Mies. The Mies literature often identifies Lemke as a Communist, but there is no evidence for the claim. He was a successful printer, and as such he produced materials of all political stripes, including, later, publications for both the National Socialists and, after World War II, the Soviet military administration.[44] The Lemkes, who had no children, had purchased two small lots bordering an artificial lake created in the nineteenth century when the Hohenschönhausen district in far eastern Berlin was first developed. Their program was modest: a living room, bedroom, guest room, a study or workroom for each, and the typical services. For landscape and garden design, the Lemkes engaged the eminent Karl Foerster.

An initial two-story solution was rejected. Mies then produced a one-story, flat-roofed building, which he pushed to a corner of the site close to the street to make the most of the rear yard and lake view (figs. 5.6 and 5.7). The roughly L-shaped plan encloses about 1,725 square feet—still a substantial single-family house by the standards of the day. Each leg is organized around an L of its own. Living and service spaces occupy the leg parallel to the street, and the bedroom and study, connected to the living room by a wide hall, are rotated to the privacy of the rear. The plan is efficient, befitting the budget, but the design is still recognizably Miesian in its interlocking volumes, pinwheel organization, and especially in the carefully considered sightlines inside and out. The load-bearing brick walls are mostly opaque to the street and sideyards, save for punched windows with sills at waist height. On the garden elevations, they open with wide expanses of steel-framed glazing to a paved terrace. The house wraps the terrace on two sides and a partial third, establishing an outdoor room and a strong visual center for house and landscape.

Like all of Mies's work, the Lemke House is beautifully detailed. It was furnished with Mies's tubular chairs and tables and with custom furniture and millwork by Mies and Lilly Reich. Some of the Lemkes' rugs and furniture were incorporated into the Mies-Reich interior. The custom interiors are all the

FIGURE 5.6. Lemke House, Berlin-Hohenschönhausen (1933). View looking southwest. *At right*, the street elevation; *at left*, the main but side entry and garage. The street elevations are mostly opaque, but the rear opens to an expansive yard and views to a lake. The house, which was Mies's last in Europe, was magnificently restored by the German government in 2002.

FIGURE 5.7. Lemke House, Berlin-Hohenschönhausen (1933). Rear elevation, view looking northeast. The house is an *L* in plan. From within, each leg offers a view into the other and onto an outdoor paved courtyard.

more remarkable because Lemke's budget was only 16,000 Reichmarks (the Tugendhat House, as we have noted, cost over 1 million Reichmarks just two years earlier). By today's standards, the quality of materials and workmanship is astounding. The exterior walls are salmon-orange clinker brick, laid up in English bond capped at the roof by a brick-thin line of stone; the floors are oak herringbone parquet; the door to the terrace is custom steel and bronze (similar to doors designed for Esters and Lange) and integral with the full-height glazing. It is no surprise that the almost total renovation and reconstruction of the house sponsored by the German government in 2000–2002 cost over 2 million DM.

The Lemkes occupied the house until almost the end of World War II, when it was commandeered by the invading Red Army. After the war they were never able to regain possession of their property, and they eventually moved to West Berlin. In the GDR period, up to 1989, the house was used by the State Security Service (the Stasi), and even casual exterior photography was prohibited.[45] In spite of many depredations the solid construction survived, and in 1990 the house and grounds, derelict and barren, passed to the reunified Germany. In the same year, Frau Lemke died, and the surviving Mies-Reich furniture, some of which she and her husband had been able to save, was willed to Berlin's Kunstgewerbemuseum. Today the house is a state museum and gallery, and once again, as at first, a remarkable work of art, rendered even more so by the constraints of its design and budget and the calamities of its history.

.   .   .

Beginning around 2003, a considerable amount of journalistic literature has been published concerning the Heusgen house, an early-1930s residence in Krefeld, Germany, claimed by several respected authorities to have been designed by Mies. Other observers, ourselves among them, doubt that authorship.

The house was owned by Karl and Milly Heusgen, who had a son, Manfred. Like Hermann Lange and Josef Esters, Karl Heusgen was an executive in Krefeld's Verseidag velvet and silk industry. In 1930, before the Heusgens' marriage, Milly Geissen purchased a wooded, almost two-acre parcel on Hülser Talring, north of the center of Krefeld. In February 1932 she obtained a building permit for a private residence. Construction began shortly thereafter, and she and Karl Heusgen, now married, took occupancy in January 1933. The extant building records were signed by Rudolf Wettstein, who may or may not have designed the house. The destruction of Krefeld's archives during World War II has frustrated further investigation into the origins of the design.

The two-story house is sited on a gentle rise well removed from the street. Its construction is white painted stucco over structural steel. At the south end of the long front, or east-facing, elevation, the living room opens through floor-to-ceiling windows to a sloping lawn. To the right is the entry, gained by a right turn beyond a stub end of the front facade. It provides access to the living room as well as to a circular stair leading to second-floor bedrooms, served by a single-loaded corridor illuminated by twenty east-facing strip windows. A first-floor extension to the west is occupied by a dining room with its own floor-to-ceiling windows. The short south side of the house has yet another set of the same windows. A lower-level garage abuts the blank north side.

Karl Heusgen died in 1968. In 1972 Milly Heusgen hired Krefeld architect Karl Amendt to undertake an exterior restoration. According to Amendt, Frau Heusgen told him that Mies was the designer, but claimed that she had not wanted it known for fear of an influx of pilgrims.[46] Amendt honored her wish. Following her death in 1981 and that of Manfred Heusgen in 1999, Amendt purchased the house and undertook an investigation of its history, as well as further restoration.[47] His conviction that Mies was the designer has been bolstered by the testimony of two recognized scholars: Christian Wolsdorff of the Bauhaus Archive, and the architectural historian Jan Maruhn. Because there are no documents connecting Mies to the house, the arguments of Wolsdorff and Maruhn depend on factors that both men regard as characteristic of Mies's work. Maruhn and his coauthor Werner Mellen argue for Mies as designer in their pamphlet *Haus Heusgen: Ein Wohnhaus Ludwig Mies van der Rohes in Krefeld* (The Heusgen House: A Residence by Ludwig Mies van der Rohe in Krefeld), published in 2006 in various periodicals and widely on websites.[48]

Maruhn observes that the plan of the Heusgen house is close to that of Mies's Berlin Building Exposition house of 1931, and the massing is "similar to various [Mies] sketches of these years."[49] The organization of open-plan living, service, and bedroom spaces, especially the single-loaded corridor on the second floor, typify Mies, he says. The entry is hidden, like that of the Tugendhat House, and the entry door is Makassar, a favorite Mies material. Interior doors are room high, a device Mies favored. The steel structure is generically the same as that of the Esters and Lange Houses, and of the Tugendhat House. Maruhn even argues that the Heusgen house is connected to nature via the extensive glazing, and is, in this respect, "masterfully" Miesian.

Maruhn believes that these design strategies were known in detail only to Mies and his staff. He also cites what others have acknowledged: that the house resembles student work from Mies's Bauhaus. It is plausible that the Heusgen house was designed by a Mies student or a member of his staff. A case against Mies as the architect rests on something as simple as the look of the house, both by itself and when compared with his other works of the period. The front elevation is confused, with three different fenestration strategies, in combination neither open nor closed to the street. The row of windows on the second floor produces a monotonous rhythm. In the rear, the second story is visually too heavy for the columns supporting it, and on the south these same columns support nothing but a slender roof where no support is needed. The columns are round steel pipe, a type used in Mies's model house at the Berlin Building Exposition, but in all of his other modern European residential projects Mies used custom-made cruciform columns. (Mies continued proposing the cruciform column for projects he worked on during his early American career.) Finally, Mies's well-known sensitivity to the proportion of parts to whole is unfailingly evident in the contemporaneous Gericke and Lemke Houses and the other house projects of the early to mid-1930s—yet strikingly absent from the Heusgen house.

Maruhn seeks to account for the absence of any published record of the house by suggesting that Mies may have regarded it as unworthy of publication. But that hardly reinforces the claim that it was the work of a master. In any event, the issue may soon be resolved. Christiane Lange, Hermann Lange's granddaughter and a respected architectural historian, has recently completed extensive research on Mies's several Krefeld projects, and published a monograph in 2011.[50] She believes that Mies's employee Willi Kaiser, who worked on-site at the Esters and Lange Houses and also on the Barcelona Pavilion, was significantly involved with the Heusgen project. He is said to have left for Switzerland in 1932, which would explain the timing of Wettstein's signing of the documents. In her 2011 monograph, Lange hedges on attributing the Heusgen house to Mies, but in November 2011 she announced that she had "proof" that "the Villa Heusgen is not by Mies."[51] She did not elaborate, except to say that she will publish her latest findings in 2012.

. . .

As 1933 wore on, Mies decided to accept private students in his Berlin studio; and in September, with the same motive, he and Lilly Reich rented a cottage on the terrace of a hillside vineyard near Lugano, in the Ticino canton of Switzerland (fig. 5.8). They were joined there by five students and two of the students' wives. Mies's assignment: choose a site in the immediate area and design a house for it.

During a stay of six weeks, the group visited the Triennale exposition in Milan. One of the students, Howard Dearstyne, reported:

> We were not much impressed by it. Following this, we gravitated to the huge square before the Milan Cathedral.... I suggested to Mies that we cross the plaza and see the inside of the fantastic structure (with which I was well acquainted). He refused to budge. Though he was a profound admirer of the Gothic, he would have no truck with this mongrel example of it.[52]

Upon his return to Berlin following the stay in Lugano, Mies produced several schemes for mountain houses probably inspired by his Alpine experiences. Scholars identify candidate sites for these projects not in Switzerland
but in Merano in the South Tyrol. The most legible, depicted in a dozen perspective sketches, is in its several versions an L-shaped, one-story volume embracing an ample courtyard, the whole atop a bluff. The exterior wall is glazed
toward the courtyard with, in some sketches, a battered, rough-hewn stone
exterior facing the downhill sides. There are no plans or scaled drawings in the
surviving material, and in the end the scheme or schemes barely command attention. But another, possibly related project, the "Glass House on a Hillside,"
though represented by only a single, originally tiny (4½-by-8-inch) sketch, is,
thanks to a wall-sized blow-up featured in Mies's 1947 show at the Museum of
Modern Art, among Mies's most celebrated graphical musings. Probably executed in 1934, the scheme depicts, in elevation and with extreme economy
of line, a trussed glass box of indeterminate structural material supported at
one end on a sloping grade and at the opposite end by one or perhaps a pair of
freestanding columns. The design is avowedly visionary, and might have been,
originally and literally, a "napkin sketch." But by 1947, Mies had turned it into

the "Mountain House, Tyrol, Austria," in which form it would greatly influence, by their own admission, Philip Johnson, Charles Eames, and a host of lesser lights. Though the Mountain House has elements in common with the 1937–39 Resor House — as noted by critics in 1947 — in its uncompromising abstraction it is far more powerful than the unbuilt Resor.

. . .

In addition to Dearstyne, whose book *Inside the Bauhaus* is the fullest eyewitness account of the school by an American, another American student from the Berlin Bauhaus who studied privately with Mies, John Barney Rodgers, would go on to teach with him at Armour Institute of Technology in Chicago.[53] As draftsman, architect, and translator, Rodgers assisted Mies in his transition to the United States, and even before Mies's immigration became something of a spokesman. Describing a series of lectures on modernism he gave at Princeton University in 1935, Rodgers told Ludwig Glaeser that "[they were as close] as I can come to the notes I took on Mies's talks when I studied with him in 1934 and 1935."[54] Never published, Rodgers's lectures offer an understudy's snapshot of Mies in his fiftieth year:

> Mies van der Röhe [*sic*] reached his present position through the power of his own thinking. . . . He speaks and acts with conviction and force because the thoughts which actuate him are his own and have been developed by long years of sincere and thoughtful work. . . . [T]he dominant impression he gives is one of tremendous physical and mental force and leadership. He has always had to fight for his convictions, but never more than in the present period of government inspired reaction.[55]

In a lecture titled "Dynamic Design," Rodgers explained Mies's design philosophy:

> In architecture, as in literature, an idea to be effective must be simply expressed. It is therefore desirable to keep all elements as simple as possible. Let a wall count as a wall, and be clear and unbroken and not chopped up into small pieces, none of which count, by doors and windows. If it be free standing let it be free standing, completely surrounded by space. All forms, whether voids or solids, should be kept simple and distinct. They should not be obscured by furniture or architectural incrustations. The lines and proportions of furniture count most when they are free standing, liberated in space. This same reasoning applies to the house as a whole.
>
> There is nothing as unimportant to the architect as ornament. In the past successful ornament always came when a style was mature, to embellish and emphasize design. Modern architecture is far from that stage at present,

and since our decorators have not developed an appropriate ornament which can ... be said to embellish or enhance anything, most modern architects prefer to omit it entirely.... They prefer to rely on the color and texture of natural materials rather than spoil their surfaces with modernistic ornament.[56]

And finally, Rodgers described Mies's teaching about "order":

The human mind craves order. It seeks to coordinate and arrange the chaotic facts of nature into a logical system in order to comprehend them.... This habit of mind is so ingrained that any design which is completely disorganized and unrelated is not only unpleasant but positively disturbing.... Therefore, an architectural design must be ordered. There must be a reason, practical or aesthetic, behind every decision resolved during its creation. The finest architecture will have this integration carried out in the finest details.[57]

. . .

On February 9, 1933, less than two weeks after Hitler's accession, Mies was one of thirty architects invited by the Reichsbank to participate in a competition for a major expansion of the bank's central Berlin facility. The enterprise was intended to memorialize the Reich's then grandiloquent economic optimism. The competitors represented the full range of architectural practice in Germany: Gropius and Mies at one end of the spectrum and the very conservative Wilhelm Kreis at the other. In May 1933, a jury including Peter Behrens and Paul Bonatz awarded prizes to six projects, Mies's among them, and though the entries were displayed and published, nothing ensued.

The winners tended toward a cautious modernism, with Mies's the most advanced. He made a serious effort to accommodate the bank's detailed program, and to provide the offices and vast banking halls with ample natural light. He proposed a ten-story block, probably but not certainly of structural steel, totaling an astonishing 1 million square feet. In a single sweeping curve, Mies's "addition" would front the existing bank buildings across a narrow street, and in the opposite direction offer three open-plan office wings that converge toward the River Spree. On most floors the three wings, each only about 40 feet wide, flank light wells open to the sky (fig. 5.9). The curved front was to be dominated by a 350-foot-long swath of double-story glazing enclosing an immense entry hall at the second and third levels. Above would be tripartite strip windows. Alternating with wide brick spandrels, the strip system was to wrap the other elevations in an undifferentiated pattern that evoked the Concrete Office Building of a decade before (fig. 5.10). No fewer than three rooftop gardens were specified, the largest of which was labeled "for the officials [*Beamte*]." These gardens would have offered close-up views of the dense core of old Berlin.

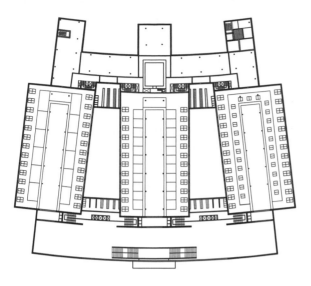 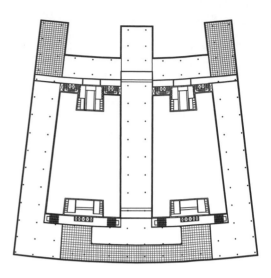

FIGURE 5.9.
Reichsbank project,
Berlin-Mitte (1933).
At left, a lower-level
plan, showing three
large banking halls
accessed by a grand
circulation con-
course. *At right*, an
upper floor, all of-
fices, with generous
internal courts.

In an article titled "Architecture in the Third Reich," published in the fall
of 1933, Philip Johnson took up the question of the political implications of
the Reichsbank. "What [Germany's] new buildings will look like," he said, "is
yet completely unknown." Then, reviewing the factions vying for the attentions of the party—the conservatives (Schultze-Naumburg, Troost), the "half-
moderns" (Schmitthenner), and "the young men in the party, the students and
revolutionaries who are ready to fight for modern art," Johnson continued:

> There is only one man whom even the young men can defend and that is Mies
> van der Rohe. Two factors especially make Mies's acceptance as the new ar-
> chitect possible. First Mies is respected by the conservatives.... Secondly
> Mies has just won (with four [*sic*] others) a competition for the new buildings
> of the Reichsbank. If (and it may be a long if) Mies should build this building
> it would clinch his position.
>
> A good modern Reichsbank would satisfy the new craving for monumen-
> tality, but above all it would prove to the German intellectuals and foreign
> countries that the new Germany is not bent on destroying all the splendid
> modern arts which have been built up in recent years.[58]

Johnson lived to regret his overly optimistic view of the Nazis. And Mies,
too, must have been chagrined by his tardiness in learning from the new government's purge of the progressive building administrations in Berlin and
Frankfurt, which took place even as the Bauhaus was being shut down. Late in
1933, a body called the Reichskulturkammer was established at the behest of
Goebbels. Mies became a member.[59] During the previous year, Goebbels had
made a point of publicly opposing the militantly intolerant attitude toward
the modern arts represented by Alfred Rosenberg's Kampfbund für deutsche
Kultur. The Reichskulturkammer was assembled to advance Goebbels's posi-

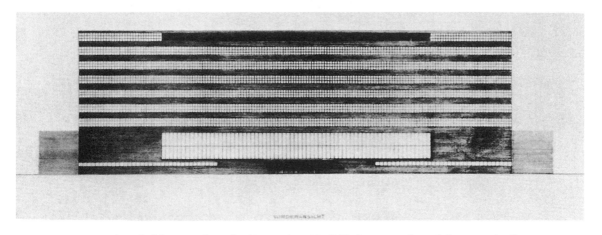

FIGURE 5.10.
Reichsbank project,
Berlin-Mitte (1933).
West elevation, op-
posite the River
Spree. The nine-
story building is 360
feet wide.

tion. In his speech at the November 16, 1933, inauguration of the organization, he attacked conservatism, declaring: "German art needs fresh blood. We live in a young era. Its supporters are young, and their ideas are young. They have nothing more in common with the past, which we have left behind us. The artist who seeks to give expression to this age must also be young. He must create new forms."[60] There was just enough encouragement of the modern arts in that statement to hearten their champions, although it is worth recalling Goebbels's disingenuous remarks to Lilly von Schnitzler, made during the same year, 1933, already cited here.

As matters developed, Goebbels never fought for any of the ideals expressed in his November 16 speech. Nevertheless, for a time, mostly in 1934, Mies could have rationalized his membership in the Reichskulturkammer, which imposed on its members no stylistic restrictions—though it required proof of "racial purity"—and even provided him with an invitation to participate in another competition, for yet another exposition pavilion.

· · ·

On June 8, 1934, Mies and five other architects were invited to "contribute a trial solution for the [German] exposition buildings for the 1935 Brussels World's Fair." Like the Barcelona Pavilion, the Brussels building was intended to represent Germany, this time with a structured brief. The many requirements included the use of Nazi symbols and a long list of industrial and cultural exhibits intended for display in a single large building. Hitler personally reviewed and then rejected all the submittals.[61] Mies's employee Sergius Ruegenberg claimed that during the review, Mies's drawings, summarily rejected, ended up on the floor.[62] Though Ruegenberg's information was secondhand, Dirk Lohan reported that "Mies told me several times that Hitler, probably with Albert Speer, reviewed the designs for the competition and was so displeased with Mies's modern design that he angrily pushed the drawings aside

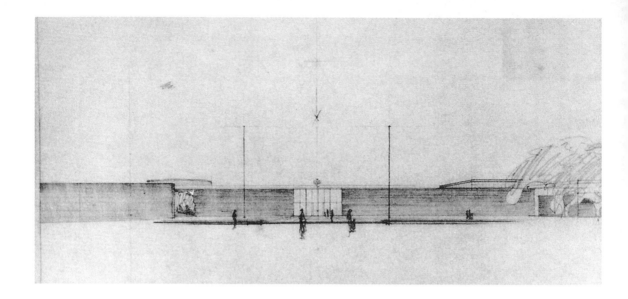

FIGURE 5.11.

German Pavilion project, International Exposition, Brussels (1934). Main elevation. This project has stirred more political heat than any other of Mies's European efforts—at the expense of more serious architectural investigation. The stimulus is the inclusion of a swastika in several of his drawings and the consequent contention that Mies was sympathetic to the Nazis. Lost in the noise is the fact that the brief required that symbol. Photo courtesy of the Mies van der Rohe Archive of the Museum of Modern Art, NY.

and when they fell to the floor Hitler walked on them. Mies said that from then on he knew he would never be allowed to do any work under the Nazi regime."[63] In a remarkably short time, a building by Hitler favorite Ludwig Ruff and his architect son Franz Ruff was in fact begun, only to be abandoned when Germany pulled out of the exhibition in late 1934.

Mies put together his entry in less than a week, and his submittal, which included presentation drawings and model photography, remained with the government and is lost. Nothing about the competition was published, and the work is known only through sketches and in-progress plans and elevations. Though the brief called for "an exhibition building [expressing] the will of National-Socialist Germany through an imposing form [symbolic of] National Socialist fighting strength and heroic will,"[64] in the written part of his submittal Mies argued, even more abstractly than usual, for an "essential" building, appropriate to "what an exposition should be, to a factual [sachlich] but effective visual display of things, to a real picture of German achievements."[65] What he offered was effectively the Barcelona Pavilion made giant, housing myriad exhibits in an otherwise austere building discreetly adorned with a few underscaled Nazi symbols—among them, here and there, a swastika (fig. 5.11). Mies resolved the overelaborate program by proposing a mostly walled main hall of open plan, eight bays to a side (fig. 5.12). To this volume were appended various forecourts and semiattached and independent outbuildings, some also quite large. The total area under roof was to be 15,500 square meters (166,840 square feet), and associated public space and gardens were to cover another 11,700 square meters (125,900 square feet)—about thirty-two times the area of the Barcelona Pavilion.[66]

Within the main hall, Mies organized the plan around his signature cruci-

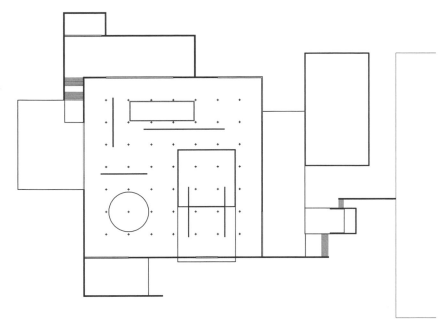

FIGURE 5.12.
German Pavilion
project, Interna-
tional Exposition,
Brussels (1934). Re-
constructed conjec-
tural plan. The area
of the square en-
closing the colum-
nar grid is approxi-
mately 100,000
square feet.

form columns, pin-connected at the smooth ceiling, under which were sheltered the typical grouping of freestanding walls, reflecting pools, and suggested interior volumes. A special exhibition space, which the program termed
the Court of Honor, was reached axially from the entry through a pair of tall,
bracketing stone walls. The focus, certainly heroic, was an atrium open to the
sky, framed on three sides by dark glass and partial-height walls, evocative
of Mies's 1930 competition scheme for Berlin's Neue Wache. The rest of the
interior, reached from the quasi-central atrium, was generic Miesian space,
accommodating whatever the program might require. In the surviving drawings the exterior of the building is only suggested. Evident were enormous expanses of windowless brick walls, most rising sheer to the roof. The roof structure, obviously a critical element in a building of this scale, was only hinted at
in one or two sketches.

. . .

Among efforts of the 1930s that did materialize was a contribution to the National Socialists' first major exhibition, Deutsches Volk—Deutsche Arbeit,
which opened in Berlin April 21, 1934. The event was intended to celebrate
both the history of the German people and contemporary German technology. Hans Weidemann, a party member well disposed to modernism, was appointed by Goebbels to direct the show. Weidemann admired Mies's work, and
invited him to assume responsibility for the exhibition's architectural displays.
According to Elaine Hochman, Weidemann sought approval of his plan from

FIGURE 5.13.
Hubbe House
project, Magdeburg
(1935). Mies arrived
at the final design
for the Hubbe House
after an enormous
number of prelimi-
nary studies and
several changes in
direction. The result
mediates between
enclosure and open-
ness by the use of in-
terrupted courtyard
walls.

Hitler himself, who reacted to photographs of the Barcelona Pavilion with un-
qualified animosity. In the end, Mies retained only the section of the exhibition devoted to mining.[67] The Nazis allowed his involvement, but omitted his
name from the catalog.

Mies produced an exhibit that consisted mainly of three large walls—in fact
they were displays of material—one of rock salt, one of anthracite coal, and
one of bituminous coal. The pale pink and beige of the rusticated rock salt
contrasted with the intense black of the anthracite and the more nearly matte
brown of the bituminous. Especially notable were the flawless "bonding" of
the anthracite and the horizontal coursework of the rock salt. To common sub-
stances like salt and coal, Mies brought the same refinement that marked his
use of luxurious stone and glass in the Barcelona Pavilion and Tugendhat House.

. . .

Mies may have made the acquaintance of Margarete Hubbe as early as 1926,
when she applied for membership in the Werkbund during the period when
Mies was vice chairman. But it was not until early 1934, probably through her
friend Emil Nolde, that she approached Mies to design a large house for an island in the Elbe River in Magdeburg. The roughly square, two-acre property
was adjacent to buildings on the side away from the river. There was dense development to the immediate south; the island was in fact an urban district. For

reasons unknown, Hubbe sold the property and abandoned the project in mid-1935, but not before Mies had generated, even by his standards, an enormous number of alternate schemes and, finally, a fully resolved design depicted in models and presentation plans (fig. 5.13). Elevation studies were probably not as advanced, and may be lost. The only written document related to the project is a brief published notice signed by Mies:

> The house was supposed to be built on the Elb-Insel in Magdeburg, under lovely old trees [and] with a broad panorama of the Elbe.
>
> It was an uncommonly beautiful building site. Only the position of the sun presented difficulties. The lovely view lay to the east [toward the Elbe], whereas to the south the view was utterly without charm, almost a disturbance. It was necessary to balance out this flaw by the layout of the structure.
>
> Therefore I extended the living area of the house toward the south by means of a garden courtyard surrounded by walls, thus obstructing the view while at the same time preserving all of the sunlight. Downstream, on the other hand, the house is completely open, flowing freely over into the garden.
>
> In so doing I not only followed the site conditions, but achieved a nice contrast of quiet seclusion and open expanse as well.
>
> This layout also suited the residential needs of the client. For though she was going to be living in the house alone, she wanted to be able to maintain a casual social life and hospitality. The inner arrangement of the house is designed for this purpose as well, once again offering the necessary privacy in conjunction with fullest freedom of open spaces.[68]

Margarete Hubbe, like almost all of Mies's European residential clients, was wealthy, and able to afford an enormous open-plan residence lavishly embraced by walled courtyards and ample gardens. From the evidence of almost five hundred surviving sketches, the house would have been a major statement. The program included just two bedrooms, one for Frau Hubbe and one for guests, a service wing including two modest bedrooms for servants, and a living and dining area, glazed on three sides, featuring a massive floating fireplace of ashlar blocks. Services and bedrooms had load-bearing walls, but the living and entry spaces were carried on cruciform columns disposed in a grid not quite square (7 by 6.5 meters), encompassed by Mies's typical detached walls. The enclosed area was a roomy 5,000 square feet, sheltered by another 2,000 square feet of cantilevered eaves. The essentially T-shaped plan was then wrapped by an orderly rectangle of full-height walls, the whole covering almost 11,000 square feet of dwelling, garden, and paved courtyard. Little wonder that Mies was able to achieve both "privacy" and the "fullest freedom of open spaces."

The Hubbe House is fully equal to Mies's best work. The sprawling entry faces the river and the view, and access to the all-glazed living space is gained via the usual carefully planned though circuitous route. Views from the rambling main space are controlled by the courtyard walls and the floating fireplace but, just as Mies claimed, the southern and eastern exposures fully invite the sun. To the north, Frau Hubbe's bedroom and study are glazed to a garden court but closed off by walls from the distant, "disturbed" view. South of the living/dining space, the service wing elevation is almost fully opaque to the east. The dining area opens to a very large courtyard framed on three sides by walls and on the fourth by the Elbe. Several sketches propose figural sculpture for the courtyard. The nonriver elevations appear to be closed except for a few large, rectangular lights for bedrooms and services on the west, in the manner of the Krefeld houses. Materials and colors are not discernible from the surviving documents, and we are not even sure if the courtyard walls were to be brick. Indeed, there are other tantalizing mysteries, including the furniture, which in one limpidly beautiful sketch includes club-type chairs and a vaguely Biedermeier chest. There is almost no information about the demise of the Hubbe project, save for a letter by Reich to J. J. P. Oud stating that the house was not built because Frau Hubbe sold the property.

Contemporaneous with the Hubbe project is a related design produced during 1935 for the newly married Ulrich Lange, son of Hermann. The site is in Krefeld-Traar. In a personal letter from early 1936, Lilly Reich referred to the project as "small" when mentioning its abandonment, though like the Hubbe project it is anything but, at least in the last of its several revisions. It is a courtyard scheme as large as Hubbe, with tall, embracing brick walls in a plan rectangle of almost 12,000 square feet. Within these walls, Mies disposed a flowing, L-shaped interior, somewhat smaller than at Hubbe but with the typical elements: a large master suite at the distal end of one plan leg, separated by servants' bedrooms, services, and a long corridor from living and dining space in the other leg of the plan. Living and dining are again a square box, this time glazed on two sides. The living area is organized around the same grid used for Hubbe, but Mies replaced several of the expected cruciform columns with the stub ends of brick bearing walls. Within the living space, the kitchen is screened by a wall, probably of millwork, thrust into the main volume, in this instance uncharacteristically serpentine in plan. Views beyond the courtyard are tightly controlled, with only one wall of the living space open to a distant vista. Mies provided a one-car garage tucked in the far corner of one of the courts. The vehicular path is through the courtyard via a hairpin turn, effectively concealing the garage from the street. The street elevation is a quiet—some might say dull—brick band punched by a series of plain, square lights. The roof is flat, with modest cantilevers.

The final and possibly an earlier version of the project were refused a building permit by the local authorities. By this time under Nazi control, the Krefeld building department rejected the project under an "unsightliness law" used to block modernist work. The Lange family was able to use its influence to gain approval, though on condition that the house be screened from the street by an earthen berm. Various reports confirm that Mies, resentful of these manipulations, withdrew.[69] There is no record of Ulrich Lange's immediate reaction, although remarkably, he tried to restart the project as late as 1949, only to be turned down in his appeal to the American Mies "because of too much work."[70]

The Hubbe and Ulrich Lange Houses, had they materialized, would arguably have established a new European housing type, the modernist courtyard villa. Both projects were standard Miesian open-plan dwellings — large residential versions of the Barcelona Pavilion — inserted into walled surrounds with large paved and landscaped courts.

. . .

On May 24, 1937, the International Exposition of Arts and Techniques Applied to Modern Life opened in Le Palais International in Paris, remaining there through November 26. Works of both Mies and Lilly Reich were on view. Under the byline of Jean Badovici, an architect and editor of *L'Architecture Vivante*, the exhibition catalog, *Architecture de Fêtes* (Editions Albert Morance, Paris, probably 1938), featured illustrations of the German section of the exposition's international pavilion, all of which was credited to Mies. They show two structures, one with a curved glass wall framed by slender strips of metal, designed to display synthetic materials and precision equipment, the other a flat wall of glass partitioned in a grid, showing metallurgical tooling and machines. Mies may have been in Paris on the occasion of the exposition.[71] Lilly Reich's contribution consisted of the design of the German textile industry exhibit, also located in the international pavilion.[72]

Mies's last design in Germany prior to his immigration to the United States involved another commission from Krefeld. The Esters and Lange Houses of the late 1920s were followed in 1930–31 by an unremarkable, strictly functionalist design for a Verseidag factory building, realized in two campaigns between 1931 and 1935. In 1937 Mies designed a much larger, four-story administration building, like the factory of white stucco over a steel superstructure. Similar in plan to the Reichsbank project of 1933, the scheme is undistinguished. According to John Barney Rodgers, the design was incomplete as late as the summer of 1938, and the project was soon abandoned due to concrete shortages caused by the construction of fortifications along the Reich's western border.

America Beckons: 1936–38 [6]

I am willing to accept an appointment, but not to make myself a candidate for a chair. **MIES**, to Harvard's Joseph Hudnut

Order as the definition of the meaning and measure of being is missing today; it must be worked toward, anew. **MIES**, 1938

The path that led Mies from Berlin to Chicago was strewn with detours and dead ends. We have remarked on his lowly state in 1935, with the latest failure of the Hubbe and Ulrich Lange Houses. He was not alone among his colleagues in suffering professionally from the accession of the Nazis. As early as March 1933, two months after Hitler assumed power, Erich Mendelsohn responded to government-sponsored anti-Semitism by leaving Berlin and moving to London. A year later, Walter Gropius also found his way to the British capital, as did Marcel Breuer in 1935. Neither returned to live in Germany. Mendelsohn, Gropius, and Breuer had jobs awaiting them in London. By the beginning of 1936, the pattern was clear, but Mies remained in Berlin, professionally stymied.

In December 1935, he received a telegram from Alfred Neumeyer of Mills College in Oakland, California, inviting him to teach there the following summer.[1] The salary and travel expenses were generous. Prior to his own immigration in 1934, Neumeyer had been an art historian and university lecturer in Berlin and had met Mies on several occasions. But the position required English, and Mies had no knowledge of the language.

Shortly thereafter, fate made a move of its own. One day early in 1936, two Chicago architects, John Holabird and Jerrold Loebl, were walking along Michigan Avenue when they encountered David Adler, a professional colleague. In the course of their conversation, Holabird and Loebl mentioned that they were members of a committee at Armour Institute of Technology seeking a new director for its architecture program. They were looking for someone with a modern educational outlook to replace director Earl Reed, a Beaux-Arts-oriented educator who intended to retire at the close of the 1935–36 academic year. Adler, whose work was of the traditional, eclectic society type, remarked that he personally found Mies van der Rohe "the finest of the modernists and a brilliant designer." Neither Holabird nor Loebl knew of Mies, so Adler invited them to step into the Burnham Library of the Art Institute of Chicago, just a few yards away, where he showed them photographs of the Barcelona Pavilion.

A courtship was set in motion. On March 20, 1936, Holabird wrote to Mies:

We have in Chicago an Architectural School forming a part of the Armour Institute of Technology. The School is housed by itself in the Art Institute of Chicago, has 100 to 120 students and is, by reason of its location, more or less independent of Armour Institute.

The Trustees and President of Armour Institute are very anxious to secure the very best available head of the Architectural School with the idea of making it the finest school in this country. . . .

Amongst others I wrote to Richard Neutra in Los Angeles. He suggested the possibility of interesting Walter Gropius or Josef Emanuel Margold as he felt that the best was none too good for Chicago. . . .

In talking the matter over with the Advisory Committee, I thought that as we were considering the possibility of a European heading this school that I would like to ask if you would, under any conditions, consider such an appointment. . . . If we are to consider the best I would naturally turn to you first.

The School itself can be made anything that the proper man might wish; he would have a free hand with the authorities of the Institution. He could organize the School in such a manner that he could [also] establish his private practice.[2]

Mies waited a month before responding. He knew nothing about Armour beyond what Holabird had written, and perhaps only a little more about Chicago. On April 20 he wired Holabird: "Thanks for the letter. Am interested. Letter follows."[3]

The letter, sent May 4, 1936, expressed his interest in the Armour position but appended conditions that he be free to give the school a "basically new form" as well as continue his private practice of architecture in Chicago.[4] A week later, probably without having received Mies's message, Holabird wrote again: "I sincerely hope that you can arrange to take this position. . . . With you as head, this should be the finest school in America."[5]

Mies responded May 20, 1936:

On 20 April I sent you a cable to let you at least know of my interest in your proposal. Today I wish to thank you sincerely for the confidence you have shown in me.

I was interested to learn of your plans for reorganization of your Institute's architectural school and of its promise. I welcome your intentions, as I am certain of their justness and worth. They have led me to follow up your suggestions and earnestly to deliberate the thought of guiding such a school.

Since by reasons of my experience, I have certain definite conceptions about the organization of a school of architecture, I would like to know more particulars about the present structure of the school.... I would also like to know whether additions and reorganization of the teaching staff may be possible, the extent of the present budget of the school, whether practical workshops for training purposes can be found and finally, the relation, if any, of the architectural school to the Art Institute....

I should like to take over the work, however, only if the possibility is there to find a basically new form for such a school, in keeping with the spirit of the times.[6]

On May 12, President Willard Hotchkiss added his own letter, declaring that he "was very glad to note your interest," adding that a definite offer could not be made "without the authority of the Board of Trustees."[7] Mies probably did not understand that trustee ratification was a matter of form. His response to Hotchkiss was abruptly negative. He declined the Armour proposal, stating: "A change of curriculum would have to be so fundamental as to extend beyond the present framework of [your] architecture department."[8]

On July 2, Hotchkiss answered with patience and courtesy, offering assurances of good intentions but allowing that only Mies's personal acquaintance with the Chicago situation would be properly instructive. Would Mies consent to give a course of lectures at Armour in the fall or winter? "You would then be in a better position to decide whether we have here the kind of opportunity for creative work that would attract you."[9]

Mies took three months to reply. Meanwhile there had been encounters with other solicitous Americans. At about the same time, Hermann Lange invited him to design a major textile exhibition scheduled for Berlin in 1937. Mies took the bird in hand. On June 20, before his receipt of Hotchkiss's July 2 letter, Mies had received Alfred Barr, who had traveled to Europe with two objectives: to discuss the role Mies might play in the design of a proposed new building for the Museum of Modern Art, and to apprise him of the possible offer of a chair at Harvard University. In the latter capacity, Barr was the emissary of Joseph Hudnut, dean of the architecture faculty, who, having set himself the goal of introducing modernism into American architectural education, nursed hopes of securing the services of a gifted European. Hudnut's candidates were Mies, Gropius, and Oud.

Mies had now been approached by two of the most significant cultural institutions in the United States, and Armour's proposal faded. "Your museum plans interest me," he wrote Barr; "it could be a rare and wonderful assignment."[10] But it proved a will-o'-the-wisp. Barr was forced to withdraw his offer as early as July 19, when he wrote Mies from Paris: "I have tried very hard to have our museum bring you to America as collaborating architect on our new building but I am afraid I shall not succeed. Believe me, I am very disappointed in my defeat. It has been a hard battle.

"In any case, I hope most sincerely for a favorable outcome of your conversation with Dean Hudnut."[11]

On July 21, Hudnut wrote Mies: "I am greatly pleased to learn [from Barr] that you are interested in the possibility of accepting a chair at Harvard University.... I look forward ... to seeing you in Berlin on about the sixteenth of August."[12] Mies did not know that on the same trip Hudnut planned to meet with Oud, who turned him down, and Gropius, who did not. As to his true feelings about Mies prior to their meeting, Hudnut was ambivalent. Mies was a superb architect, better than Gropius. But Gropius was more cultured and polished, more flexible, and probably a better teacher, with the added advantage that he spoke English. Hudnut may have also been aware of an article by George Nelson, who profiled Mies in the September 1935 issue of the architectural journal *Pencil Points*: "Mies, the academician, the former professor of the Bauhaus, has no use whatever for schools, and delights in listing the outstanding men in architecture who never saw the inside of one."[13]

But the meeting with Hudnut went well, judging from the letter he sent Mies on September 3, from London:

> I should like as soon as I reach Cambridge to make a final request to the President of the University in respect to the appointment of a Professor of Design. I hope that I may receive from you a letter telling me that you are able to consider favorably the acceptance of a chair should this be offered you by the President....
>
> It would be foolish to pretend that there will not be opposition to the appointment of a modern architect as Professor of Design. In Berlin I tried to make clear to you the cause of this opposition — which is based in part on ignorance and in part on a difference in principles — and since my visit to Berlin, I have received letters which promise an opposition even more serious than I expected.
>
> The President, however, has assured me of his sympathy with my plans and I have every reason to suppose that I can successfully carry them out.
>
> The President suggests that my chance of success may be improved if he is able to present to the Senate at least two names, each of which is acceptable to me. This is a customary procedure at Harvard, where the Board of Overseers expects always the privilege of considering an alternate.[14]

Most of this was on page one. The first paragraph of page two read: "I should like, therefore, to propose not only your name but also that of Mr. Gropius. If for any reason this does not meet with your approval, I hope that you will tell me so frankly." Mies told him so, frankly enough: "Your letter has taken me aback. It forces me to the unpleasant decision to curtail the agreements I made to you in my letter of September 2. I am willing to accept an appointment, but not to make myself a candidate for a chair. If you stand by your intention to submit several names to the President of the University, kindly omit mine."[15]

Once again, as in the years with Behrens, Gropius stood in the way, though in this instance Mies positioned him there. He could have reasoned that Harvard would decide in his favor because he was—was he not?—artistically superior to Gropius, but his own precipitate action bore out another of Hudnut's worries, that Mies was hardheaded.

Gropius received the appointment on February 1, 1937.

. . .

Later the same year, Mies learned that his role in the Berlin textile exhibition had been canceled. Hermann Göring had taken over patronage of the show, and assigned the project to the architect Ernst Sagebiel, designer of the Tempelhof Airport and much in favor with the Nazis. In the meantime, Earl Reed had retired from Armour. Following his departure, the acting chairs of the Department of Architecture were, successively, Loebl and Louis Skidmore, who had just started a practice in Chicago with Nathaniel Owings.[16]

In New York, Mies's fortunes were once again affected by the director of MoMA. Barr was close to Helen Lansdowne Resor, a MoMA trustee and vice president and director of the J. Walter Thompson Company of New York, then the world's largest advertising agency. Like her husband, Stanley Resor, head of the Thompson Company, Mrs. Resor cultivated an interest in modern art and architecture. In the early 1930s, the couple had commissioned American architect Philip Goodwin to design first a guest cabin and then what was intended to be a large summer house for their Snake River Ranch in Wilson, Wyoming, near Jackson Hole. A service wing for the proposed house was under construction in 1936 when the Resors fell out with Goodwin and released him. Early in 1937, Mrs. Resor approached Barr with the idea of hiring Mies to complete the unfinished Goodwin commission. Barr was predictably enthusiastic for Mies, and wrote to him on the Resors' behalf. Mies may or may not have answered—the record is unclear—but in July 1937 he did respond to the Resors' telegram from Paris inviting him to meet at the Hôtel Meurice to discuss the project. The encounter was congenial, with Helen Resor reporting in a letter to Barr the next day: "I like him immensely [and] have great respect for him."[17] The two-day meeting concluded with an invitation to Mies to come to the United States as the Resors' guest. He was to inspect their site and consider the commission. Mies returned to Berlin and in a matter of days was aboard the SS *Berengaria*, traveling in the company of Mrs. Resor and her two children, arriving in New York August 20.

Mies made no attempt to communicate with Armour Institute while he was in the United States, and even after Harvard hired Gropius there were evidently no second thoughts about Chicago. Sometime in 1937, Mies was also approached by the Vienna Academy with the likelihood of an offer of a post lately vacated by Peter Behrens. While reports from Vienna suggest that he liked the idea, it evaporated with the Nazis' annexation of Austria in 1938.[18]

Mies was greeted in New York by John Barney Rodgers, the young German-speaking American architect who with his partner William Priestley had studied at the Berlin Bauhaus. Rodgers acted as interpreter. Priestley also made himself useful; he was working on a project in Chicago at the time, and through him Armour learned of Mies's whereabouts.

Mies tarried only briefly in New York before heading west with Mrs. Resor. During a daylong layover in Chicago, he was met by Priestley and two young architect friends, Gilmer Black and yet another ex-*Bauhäusler*, Bertrand Goldberg. The three "showed [Mies] all the Richardson, Sullivan, and Wright we could find," Priestley remembered, adding, "I talked to John Holabird, who was most anxious to see him when he returned [from Wyoming]."[19]

On the return leg, Mies made the required change of trains in Chicago, where he was met again by Priestley and Goldberg. They took him on an auto tour of Frank Lloyd Wright houses in suburban Oak Park, after which Priestley invited him to a meeting the next day with representatives of Armour Institute. Mies agreed to attend. It is possible that his willingness was affected by a pair of letters he had received from Michael van Beuren, a former Bauhaus student, who sent them before he learned of the Harvard decision. (Mies had shown van Beuren some of the correspondence from Armour.) Van Beuren had taken it on himself to report on the situation at Harvard and Armour:

> I saw Rodgers and Priestley in New York. They both believe it is better for you in Chicago than in Boston. The people [in Chicago] have more initiative; they get more naturally and directly to the point of things. Here [in New York] as well as in Boston issues are far more theorized and more influenced, through personalities and tradition, by *unsachlicher* politics.[20]
>
> At Armour you could do what you want ... the people [there] repeated their promise of absolute freedom to the department head, plus assistants to take over administrative work if he wants more time for himself....
>
> But the school is small, as yet insignificant, no stature. And the location is miserable. You should see what an example it is of America's fantastic inconsistencies. Chicago's "grandest" building, its great temple of art, the Art Institute ... is an ostentatious relic of the cultural ambition of the last cen-

tury.... But in the School of the Art Institute everyone works in tunnels beneath the temple ... while the Armour school of architecture sits on the roof of the temple.... The studios snake along under the skylights of the attic.... In the summer, you roast. On the other hand, Boston:

Boston, self-anointed "hub of the universe," has allowed New York to fracture some of its spokes in the last fifty years. Lately it is a proud "foin" city, which all in all does not love our century.

[About Harvard]: the location, the spaces, the whole school, all are elegant; the entire layout looks well-to-do. You can work comfortably there.

[But] the difficulties ... ridiculous ... and serious. All the big shots, among them worthy gray heads who haven't had a chance to design a palace since the Depression, have their own recommendations for the professor's chair. Hudnut is young and new at his post ... arrayed against him are all the cranks who smell something—they want "no more foreigners." ... About Gropius Hudnut tells me honestly that he likes him, that Gropius has so many "ideas" ... but above all he [Hudnut] wants you ... he has limited his list to your name and intends to stick with that.... He admits that the fame of Gropius's Bauhaus is great and that it counts with the opposition.[21]

Armour had lost none of its ardor. On three consecutive days, Mies lunched at the Tavern Club, first with John Holabird, then with Dean Henry T. Heald, and finally with James D. Cunningham, chairman of the Board of Trustees. On the last day, a formal offer as director of the architecture program was submitted, and Mies accepted, subject to an agreement to be ratified after he completed his proposal for departmental and curricular changes.

Mies next expressed the desire to meet Frank Lloyd Wright, whereupon Holabird instructed Priestley: "*You* phone Wright. I don't want to give the old bastard a chance to badmouth my architecture." Priestley's call to Spring Green, Wisconsin, found Wright at home. "Mr. Wright," said Priestley, "Mr. Mies van der Rohe is in Chicago. He would like to meet you."

"I should think he would," snapped Wright. "He's welcome."[22]

This account, recalled by Priestley in 1982, differs from another record of Mies's efforts to meet Wright. The Frank Lloyd Wright Foundation owns a telegram from Mies to Wright, dated September 8, 1937: "Am in Chicago for tomorrow only would like very much to drive to Taliesin and pay my respects if convenient to you STOP your telephone reported out of order please wire reply Blackstone Hotel Chicago."[23]

The accounts differ in detail, but all agree that Wright's welcome was cordial. Wright made a point of detesting European architects, and the bigger they were, the more he detested them; they were always taking credit for ideas they had filched from him. He had already been approached earlier in the 1930s by two of the very biggest of them—Gropius and Le Corbusier—and

had rejected both in their efforts to visit him. Each time, he was unconsciona-bly rude.[24] With Mies on this occasion, and on all later ones until relations be-tween the two men cooled, he never misbehaved. Now he was positively ex-pansive, not just because Mies came as a pilgrim paying his respects—Gropius and Le Corbusier had done so too, and been insulted for their pains—but be-cause Wright genuinely admired Mies's work. He was especially impressed by the Barcelona Pavilion and the Tugendhat House, products of an individual sensibility distinguished from the horde of Bauhaus functionalists. And it did not hurt that Miesian space was indebted to Wright, who saw Mies as the only European with the good sense to follow his lead and the independence to cre-ate something original in the process.[25]

Mies was awed by what he saw at Taliesin, Wright's vast compound, de-signed and built between 1902 and 1925. He walked out on the terrace that commanded a sweeping view of the rolling Wisconsin landscape and ex-claimed, "Freedom! This is a kingdom!"[26] He applauded the siting of the buildings, and motioned with his hands to acknowledge the interpenetrat-ing masses he had known from books and now experienced firsthand. Wright was genuinely drawn to Mies, whose natural reserve now and then gave way to a warmth all the more attractive for being rare and spontaneous (fig. 6.1). An afternoon's visit lasted four days. "Poor Mr. Mies," Wright commiserated. "His white shirt is [quite] gray!"[27] After Priestley, Goldberg, and Black returned to Chicago, Wright summoned a chauffeur and personally conducted Mies through the Johnson Wax Building in Racine, Wisconsin, under construction at the time, and then back to Chicago via his Unity Temple in Oak Park, Coonley House in Riverside, and Robie House on the city's South Side.

. . .

The Resor ranch consisted of a group of rustic cabins near the Snake River, in brushy flatland with classic views of the Grand Tetons—an untraveled European's very picture of the big-sky American West. When Mies reached the property, he found the partial two-story service wing of a large house, constructed as the first phase of a grand summer residence meant to span an artificial tributary of the Snake River. Four concrete piers were already in place across the creek, the center pair awash and the set temporarily decked as a bridge in anticipation of a structure to come. The completed service wing occupied the east bank of the waterway. The architect, as mentioned, was Philip Goodwin, who as a MoMA trustee was among those who had worked to deny Mies the commission for the museum's new building. The Resors may have dismissed Goodwin, but enough of his building was up that Mr. Resor insisted on Mies's accommodating his design to it. Mies may or may not have known about these circumstances before his visit. Nevertheless, and in spite of the language barrier—Mies spoke not a word of English, the Resors were entirely without German, and now there were no translators present—he was able to signal his reservations about both the site and the preexisting conditions. He spent most of his few days' stay contemplating the site and the light, often perching himself atop the temporary plank bridge. He then returned via train to New York, again by way of Chicago. By coincidence, during some of his stay with the Resors he was boarded in the same modest cabin with the painter Grant Wood.[28]

Mies's debt to Rodgers and Priestley mounted after he returned to New York. It was in their office that he worked on the Resor House through the fall and winter of 1937–38, at the same time composing an educational rationale and putting together a curriculum for Armour. (Rodgers and Priestley were translators for both efforts.) During this time he was obliged to be careful in offering any public communication about the reasons for his visit to the United States, since he was "in the country on a tourist visa and his continued stay would be jeopardized if it was discovered that he was working as an architect."[29]

The Resor House turned out to be another unbuilt project of the 1930s, but it was Mies's introduction to America—his reason, at first, for coming at all—and it had a real chance of being realized. Over six months, with Rodgers and Priestley as staff and with American engineers, Mies worked through a number of schemes to produce, in March 1938, a set of construction documents for a two-story, steel-framed house set above the waterway. The design incorporated and subordinated the original Goodwin wing. Under Rodgers's supervision, the drawings were let for bid, but on April 5, while aboard the SS *Queen Mary* en route to Germany, Mies received a wire from Stanley Resor:

FIGURE 6.2. Model of the second scheme for the Resor House project, Jackson Hole, Wyoming (1938). This scheme is effectively an abstraction and idealization of Mies's initial two-story design that was required to incorporate an unfinished structure by the Resors' previous architect, Philip Goodwin. Photo courtesy of the Mies van der Rohe Archive of the Museum of Modern Art, NY.

"I am sorry on account of business conditions I shall not build on my property at Wilson, Wyoming."[30]

The reasons for Resor's decision are unclear.[31] When bids were received a few weeks later, the project came in at twice the Resors' budget, and contractors and suppliers had already raised technical issues about the enormous glass lights and even their shipping. Later still, Resor had another change of mind, offering Mies the possibility of a renewal of work for a smaller building.

The house Mies designed in 1938 is the first of two distinct versions of the Resor project. After Mies took up his duties at Armour, revisions continued intermittently as late as 1943, when a spring flood washed away the piers and, in combination with World War II, finished off the project for good. These post-1938 revisions generated models and drawings of a single-story house no longer incorporating the Goodwin wing—a house that became more a promotional exercise for Mies than anything real (fig. 6.2). This second house became the well-known Resor House, however, because it was widely published and ended up prominently featured in Mies's 1947 MoMA show. But what about the first—and real—Resor House?

Mies's solution for the first Resor House is mostly a recycling of the Tugendhat plan, with more modest finishes and materials and a dollop of what Mies must have considered American rusticity. On the upper level, crossing the stream and supported by the existing piers, the house is a steel-framed rectangular box. Atop the bank at one end is Goodwin's two-story service wing, with the kitchen on the upper level. Opposite, on the west bank, Mies developed a complementary but strictly rectilinear two-story volume housing an entry, utilities, a garage, and offices on the lower level; above, three clustered bedrooms adjacent to circulation and an open porch. Between the two-story bookends is a grand living-dining-study on the second level, fully glazed to vistas on the long elevations. The interior is a Tugendhat-type open volume, right down to the cruciform columns, freestanding walls, and the disposition of appropriately traditional furniture. A massive double-sided fireplace stands in for the onyx walls of Europe. Of rusticated local stone, it was envisioned by Mies as a backdrop for freestanding sculpture, exactly as at Barcelona or Tugendhat. The exterior of the house was to be clad with cypress planks over steel framing and thick insulation. Windows and floor-to-ceiling lights were to be framed with custom bronze extrusions. The views would have been extraordinary, as Mies's famous collages attest. Full-sized detail drawings for the glazing and exterior wall and roof sections are technically dazzling, as is the entire set of construction documents executed by Priestley and Rodgers. A single sheet detailing the spiral stair is said to have been drawn by Mies himself.

In spite of the lavish care in working out over eight hundred preserved sketches and drawings, this first version of the house is unconvincing. The living space, though organized in a standard Miesian dynamic, is sandwiched between two architecturally static service elements at each end. Mies was unable to make anything volumetrically compelling out of the two-story stack, primarily because the lower-level volumes are fixed by the pier locations and the Goodwin footprint. The roofed second-level balcony reads not as an independent space but a cavity. The composition is further compromised by an ambiguous structural solution, with four of the columns exposed as freestanding cruciforms in the living space and the other four buried in walls. The massive fireplace may or may not have been part of the structure, for it runs floor to ceiling, adding to the ambiguity.

It is worth reflecting on the record of the *second* Resor House project. Free of the program, Mies reconceived the house as a one-story box, glazed mid-elevation on the long sides and clad by wood-plank walls on the short. The main interior space, floating above the water, is a museum-like grouping of vertical planes and artwork. The house had become an abstraction, yet it is the Resor we remember, reflecting and celebrating Mies's continuing search for unitary architectural space.

. . .

In late 1937 while in New York, Mies had a chance encounter with Walter Peterhans, the gifted photographer who had been on the faculty of the Bauhaus during Mies's tenure. Now living in Brooklyn, Peterhans was down on his luck, a circumstance that prompted Mies to offer him, then and there, a position on the Armour faculty. In February 1938, before returning to Germany to conclude his affairs, Mies made one last trip to Chicago, where he met with Heald and others at Armour to discuss his new program. On March 31, directly before his departure on the *Queen Mary*, Mies recommended the addition of three new faculty: Ludwig Hilberseimer, still in Berlin and lacking a connection that might have provided him earlier passage to the United States; Walter Peterhans in New York; and John Barney Rodgers. Each was accepted. Of the "old" faculty, Mies proposed to retain three—Charles Dornbusch (architectural design), Sterling Harper (history of architecture), and Albert Krehbiel (drawing and watercolor)—provided they were "prepared to work with us on carrying out the new educational program."[32] Salary negotiations had already been concluded: Mies asked for $10,000 per annum but ended up with $8,000—by the standards of Depression-era America, still a handsome sum.[33]

Back in Germany, Mies attended to business and made his farewells. His apartment and studio were undisturbed. His sole remaining employee, Herbert Hirche, was working mostly for Lilly Reich. Mies's daughters were no longer living with their mother, who had returned earlier from the South Tyrol to Bavaria, where she paid typically close attention to the girls' schooling, sending them first to an academy in Garmisch-Partenkirchen and later providing them with house education in Icking, under the guidance of a tutor from Munich, Wolfgang Lohan.

In 1935, the trough of Germany's Depression, Ada moved to Berlin, and lived for a while in one room before she found an apartment. Mies is said to have supported her from his own resources. Georgia began a career as an actress. Marianne was courted by Wolfgang Lohan, whom she married in 1937. In 1938 they became the parents of Dirk, Mies's first grandchild. Karin and Ulrike followed, in 1939 and 1940, respectively. Waltraut had taken her *Abitur* at Birklehof, a branch of the Salem Gymnasium, Georgia's alma mater. Thereafter, she began study in the history of art at the Ludwig-Maximilian University in Munich.

Reich labored on. She had continued to watch over Mies's affairs in his absence. Now he would be gone even longer, and maybe for good. Would he, could he, did he even want to take her to America? Might he return to Berlin? And what, if anything, did he think he owed her? If doubts about his own future lingered, the Nazis made decisions for him. By 1938 intraparty arguments over tolerance for modern art had been resolved in favor of the ultra Right. Ratification at the public level had already taken the form of the Nazi-sponsored Entartete Kunst (Degenerate Art) exhibition, which leveled official condemnation at 650 pieces of modernist painting and sculpture by the likes of Max Beckmann, Ernst Ludwig Kirchner, Paul Klee, Emil Nolde, Gerhard Marcks, and Ernst Barlach, all of which had been produced in Germany from 1918 to 1933. Between its July 1937 opening in Munich and its dissemination as late as 1941 to a dozen large German and Austrian cities, the exhibition was seen by over two million.

Sibyl Moholy-Nagy, an art historian who lived in Germany at the time, recalled events of the period:

On 15 May the president of the Prussian Academy of Fine Arts, Max von Schillings, requested in a letter to each progressive member their resignation in May 1937 as a "dignified solution" to irreconcilable differences. On May 18 Mies wrote a letter to von Schillings refusing to resign, since "such a step in times like these might cause misinterpretations." He remained a member of the fanatically "gleichgeschaltete" [accommodating] Academy until July 1937, although it was responsible for the infamous traveling exhibition "Entartete Kunst."[34]

Given his own artistic reputation and his association with Jews and leftists, Mies was in more danger in 1938 than he had been before he left for the United States. In August 1938, shortly before his planned departure from Berlin, he was summoned to the local police station to pick up his emigration visa, preparation of which had required the temporary surrender of his passport. He was afraid to go lest he be detained and his travel plans upset or voided. His former assistant Karl Otto went in his stead to retrieve the passport and visa.[35] When Otto returned, he found Mies under rough interrogation by two Gestapo officers who had made an unannounced call and were aggrieved to discover that Mies did not have his passport.

Papers in hand, Mies managed to placate the officers, but as soon as they left he decided to change his schedule, pack a single suitcase, and leave immediately. Hirche saw him off at the train station, one soul more than was present when he arrived in the capital thirty-three years before. "Hirche," said Mies, "come soon yourself."[36] A figurative full circle was completed when Mies's train arrived in Aachen. After a brief meeting with his brother Ewald, he used the latter's passport (his own had been taken from him by the two Gestapo officers), crossed into Holland, and made his way to The Hague. There, after the sympathetic German consul issued him another passport, he succeeded in booking passage to New York. Via the SS *Europa*, he again set foot in America on August 29, 1938.[37]

Architect and Educator: 1938–49

Ladies and gentlemen, I give you Mies van der Rohe. But for me there would have been no Mies. **FRANK LLOYD WRIGHT**, 1938

The long road from material through function to creative work has but one goal: to create order from the desperate confusion of the present time.
From **MIES'S** inaugural address, 1938

I don't belong to the people who cannot live alone. **MIES**, to Lora Marx

How helpless we are all delivered up!
LILLY REICH, in a letter to Mies from wartime Germany

When he arrived at Armour Institute of Technology for the beginning of the 1938–39 academic year, Mies's direct experience of Chicago had been limited to his brief stops in the two years previous. In his mind and in fact, Chicago and Berlin were a matter more of contrast than comparison. Berlin was the capital of a country, Chicago not even of an American state. With a population of three million, Chicago was a metropolis, though less than half as populous as New York City. At over four million, Berlin was the largest city in Continental Europe, and culturally a world city. Yet Berlin and Chicago developed in remarkably similar ways. Both were late arrivals in the chronology of their respective nations, attaining major metropolitan status in the late nineteenth century. Chicago's population was 299,000 in 1870 and 503,000 a decade later, despite the Great Fire of 1871. Berlin in the same period grew by one-third, to 1,122,000. By 1910 the population of each was two million. In 1868 the medieval walls of Berlin came down and several once-independent communities, including Wedding, Moabit, and Gesundbrunnen, were absorbed. Chicago was never walled — excepting its earliest days as Fort Dearborn — but a similar major annexation took place in 1889, when the area of the city was expanded by a factor of five.

Chicago's kinship with Berlin was noted by the statesman and industrialist Walther Rathenau, already quoted here as an admirer of the American skyscraper. Rathenau's identification of Berlin as "Chicago on the Spree" is recorded by the historian Gerhard Masur, who adds that "many considered [Berlin] the most American of all the European cities . . . well on its way to becoming one of the greatest manufacturing centers in Europe."[1] The same can be said of Chicago in the American context.

When Mies arrived, much of the work of the "first Chicago school of architecture" was still to be seen,[2] but early twentieth-century commercial architecture had embraced historicism akin to counterparts in Berlin and Europe. Art Deco architecture appeared briefly in Chicago at the turn of the 1930s before the Depression stifled commercial construction. A form of modernism had made its appearance at the 1933–34 Century of Progress Exposition, but virtually all of it was taken down, with little lasting influence.

Mies's first Chicago address was the Stevens Hotel. Completed in 1927 to a design by the venerable Chicago firm Holabird & Roche, the Stevens (now the Chicago Hilton and Towers) is loosely classical, typical of the traditionalism of the period. It fronts Grant Park across the city's great boulevard, Michigan Avenue, a half-mile south of the Art Institute of Chicago, where Armour's architecture school held classes. As Mies made his way along the avenue, he passed Adler & Sullivan's world-famous Auditorium Building of 1889 and two major works by Daniel Burnham, the Railway Exchange Building (1904) and Orchestra Hall (1905). It was in the Railway Exchange that Mies first took space for his practice.

He lodged at the Stevens for a month, and then moved across Balbo Drive to the older Blackstone Hotel (1908), one of the city's most storied hostelries. For the next three years he lived in a single room, befitting a man of privacy and self-containment, though worlds away from the easy cosmopolitanism of his rambling Berlin apartment. He socialized, to be sure, but just as in Germany he resisted intrusions. His requirements were martinis, Havana cigars, and a few fine suits. In 1941 he moved to 200 East Pearson Street, a stately, ten-unit, neo-Renaissance building. There he purchased a two-bedroom, third-floor apartment, where he lived the rest of his life.

Reich was able to send one large collection of belongings and professional papers prior to the outbreak of World War II, but the greater portion of Mies's possessions and records remained in Germany. From Reich's shipment Mies assembled a small exhibition of his work for the Art Institute of Chicago in 1938. It consisted of enlargements of photographs and drawings and newly constructed models of two clusters of "court houses" and the Hubbe House.

On November 20, 1938, Armour hosted a gala dinner to celebrate Mies's appointment. The venue was the Red Lacquer Room at the Palmer House. Four hundred filled the Beaux-Arts ballroom, among them officials of the country's leading architecture schools, ranking architects, and a swath of Chicago society. (Armour charged the assembled three dollars per head.) Mies is said to have requested that Frank Lloyd Wright introduce him. Wright agreed to appear, though he knew that many of the attending professional brotherhood cared no more for him than he for them. His remarks were preceded by statements from Armour board chairman James Cunningham, Henry Heald (since May 1938 Armour's president), and several academic notables. Wright rose at last, irritable and bored, and began with uncourtly allusions to the state of the profession as manifested by those attending. Next he took credit for Mies: "Ladies and gentlemen, *I* give you Mies van der Rohe. But for me there would have been no Mies—certainly none here tonight. I admire him as an architect, respect and love him as a man. Armour Institute, *I* give you my Mies van der Rohe. You treat him well and love him as I do. He will reward you."[3] (Heald's version of Wright's parting sentence was "God knows you need him!")[4]

Wright promptly exited, followed by a train of his acolytes, even as Mies was moving to the dais. The conflicting testimony of witnesses leaves us uncertain as to whether Wright's was a deliberate act of upstaging or, as his colleagues later insisted, an exit for a pressing out-of-town engagement. Heald had the last word: "After the dinner was over, I found him at the bar, where he'd been waiting out the rest of the program."[5]

Mies delivered his 1,150-word address in German—he was altogether without English—and with some contretemps, since his interpreter, who had not examined the text beforehand, so botched the translation that John Barney Rodgers was obliged to replace him midstream. The ending gives some flavor of the whole:

> We want an order that grants each thing its proper place according to its nature.
>
> This we wish to do in so consummate a way that the world of our creations will blossom from within.
>
> More we do not want; more we cannot do.
>
> Nothing will express the aim and meaning of our work better than the profound words of St. Augustine:
>
> "Beauty is the radiance of truth."[6]

In a detailed analysis of the address, Fritz Neumeyer attempted to trace Mies's ideas to the writings of, among others, Romano Guardini, Georg Simmel, Max Scheler, and Henri Bergson, all of whom Mies had read in the 1920s and 1930s. Neumeyer argued that the address is a *summum* of Mies's intellectual position as expressed in notebooks, speeches, and writings from as far back as the mid-1920s: "Nowhere else [than in this address] is the logic of the Miesian building art expressed more clearly and more emphatically."[7]

Emphatic it may be, but the inaugural address is hardly clear. Like almost all of Mies's published professional expression, it is aphoristic, proclamatory, and devoid of sustained argument. In his analysis, even Neumeyer was reduced simply to quoting long sections of the speech; with its compressed language it is, sentence by sentence, almost beyond explication.

Mies's message is nevertheless discernible. It reaches its climax in his declaration of "but one goal"—educational, though applicable to society at large—"to create order from the desperate confusion of the present time." Mies expanded on the same theme in a January 31, 1938, letter to museum curator Carl O. Schniewind:

> In contrast to the extraordinary certainty apparent in [today's] technical and economic realms, the cultural sphere, moved to no necessity and possessed of no tradition, is a chaos of directions, opinions. . . .
>
> It should be the natural responsibility of the university to bring clarity to this situation. . . . The countless "masters" of our profession, [all forced to be] significant personalities, can hardly find the time to deepen their own philosophical understandings.
>
> Things by themselves create no order. Order as the definition of the meaning and measure of being is missing today; it must be worked toward, anew.[8]

Here Mies stated, privately but as directly as he ever would, the fundamental principle of his mature worldview: "Order [is] . . . the meaning and measure of being." This principle can be traced through centuries of Western philosophical and religious thought, and it may have been the independent product of Mies's own philosophical probing. But it could equally well have had its proximate source in his private artistic struggles, or in the "desperate confusion" of interwar German culture, politics, and economics, or in the concatenation of any number of challenges personal or professional.

Mies's commanding embrace of "order" accounts for most of the corollary material of the address: the student "personality" must be "molded," for the unformed student is assumed to possess only "irresponsible opinion"; education must "lead us from chance and arbitrariness to the clear lawfulness of a spiritual order"; we gain "clear understanding of . . . material[s]" in the world of "primitive building"; we must "learn about our goals . . . to analyze them clearly"; we "want to illuminate the possible orders and lay bare their principles."[9]

Themes of the inaugural address were reflected in key elements of Mies's curriculum for the Illinois Institute of Technology (IIT was founded in 1940 with the merger of Armour and Chicago's Lewis Institute). In addition to the study of and praise for "primitive building," Mies's teaching would focus on the fundamentals of the "handy" brick and the "right use" of elemental building materials like wood, concrete, and steel—to "give each thing what is suitable to its nature." (Here he sounded like Wright.) The first years of undergraduate education under Mies would be likened by some critics to nothing more than "trade school" training, but Mies, speaking in 1960, made it sound perfectly reasonable:

> When I came here to the school and I had to change the curriculum, I was just thinking to find a method which teaches the student how to make a good

building. Nothing else. First, we taught them how to draw. The first year is spent on that.... Then we taught them construction in stone, in brick, in wood, and made them learn something about engineering. We talked about concrete and steel. Then we taught them something about functions of buildings, and in the junior year we tried to teach them a sense of proportion and a sense of space. And only in the last year we came to a group of buildings. And there I see no rigidness in the curriculum at all. Because we try to make them aware about the problems involved. We don't teach them solutions, we teach them a way to solve problems.[10]

For the student of architecture and for Mies's teaching, as he stated in the address, mastery of materials and "functionalist factors" are never enough; "means must be subsidiary to ends and our desire for dignity and value." Ultimately, Mies seems to say, "order," "clarity," and even a deep engagement with the "the spirit of our time" are not sufficient to yield "creative work."[11] That is for the artist, who must act: "What I have said is the ground on which I stand; that which I believe and the justification of my deeds. Convictions are necessary, but in the realm of one's work they have only limited significance. In the final analysis it is the performance that matters.... That is what Goethe meant when he said: Create, artist, do not talk."[12]

A key fact about Mies's professional development as of 1938 is revealed by what is *not* in the inaugural address. To be sure, he uses the word *structure* four times, referencing the structure of "the epoch," structural "connections" in old wooden buildings, the "wealth of structure" observed in stone buildings, and the structure of the "carrying and driving forces of our time." But nowhere does he mention that a building should have a "clear structure," which would become *the* defining architectural principle of his American career. At the beginning of that career in 1938, Mies had thus far failed to articulate it, as the address confirms. It would emerge in his 1942 IIT Metals and Minerals Building, and then fully with his 1944 project for the institute's Library and Administration Building.

As discussed earlier, in the 1960s Mies acknowledged that he "went modern" under the influence of Dutch architect Hendrik Berlage: "I saw and studied carefully Berlage. I read his books and his theme that architecture should be construction, clear construction."[13] In 1961, in an interview with staff architect Peter Carter, Mies gave a fuller explanation—with the benefit of much hindsight—and provided an important clarification about the differing meanings of the word *structure* in English and German:

Berlage was a man of great seriousness who would not accept anything that was fake and it was he who had said that nothing should be built that is not clearly constructed. And Berlage did exactly that. And he did it to such an extent that his famous building in Amsterdam, The Beurs, has a medieval character without being medieval. He used brick in the way the medieval people did. *The idea of a clear construction came to me there, as one of the fundamentals we should accept.* We can talk about that easily but to do it is not easy. It is very difficult to stick to this fundamental construction, and then to elevate it to a structure.... I must make it clear that in the English language you call everything structure. In Europe we don't. We call a shack a shack and not a structure. *By structure we have a philosophical idea. The structure is the whole from top to bottom to the last detail—with the same ideas.* That is what we call structure.[14]

Mies's most important student, Myron Goldsmith, who tracked Mies in his own distinguished career, stated it even more clearly: "[A] building should be a coherent work of structural art in which the detail suggests the whole and the whole suggests the detail."[15] For Gene Summers, a key member of Mies's American staff, structure ultimately meant this:

> If you look at everything that he has said and you try to come down to what he's all about, it really is structure. His most important contribution was that one should express the essence of architecture.... He clearly felt ... that the essence of our society at that time, of our civilization ... was a combination of science and economics.... That's what technology is.... Mies ... put all of his goals in any building he designed towards that.... He reasoned that structure is the one thing you have to have. You can do a lot of buildings with walls, without walls—most of them, of course, with, because you have [an] environment to make.... The one thing you do have to have is structure. Therefore, the refinement, the development and the expression of ... structure is ... the most important aspect of all of his work and his ideas.... That's what the school was all about and that's what his work later was all about. *He really didn't clearly develop that until he got to the United States. It was starting in Europe. You could see the beginning of it, but it was really in the United States that he got that clear direction.*[16]

We have another indicator of when Mies began to articulate the structural cause. In a 1944 book by Hilberseimer, *The New City: Principles of Planning,*[17] the publisher announced a book by Mies van der Rohe, "in preparation 1944," to be titled *Architecture: Structure and Expression.* As with Mies's other flirtations with book-length writing, this title never appeared. Though the concepts of "order" and "spirit" would remain central to Mies's written and spoken vocabulary until the end, "a clear structure" became his core professional value. It is *the* principle, in its German sense—along with its built examples—for which he is and will be best remembered.

Having arrived a foreigner in Chicago at the moment that separated the enervation of the Great Depression from the dislocations of World War II, Mies could hardly expect to find private work waiting for him. For most of the first decade of his American career, he depended for sustenance on his academic salary.[18] Though it is sometimes represented that he took the Armour directorship with the understanding that he would design a new campus, there was in fact no such agreement. In 1938, unbeknownst to Mies, the very survival of Armour was in question. Nonetheless, it was the university, in the person of then thirty-five-year-old Henry Heald, that provided Mies with his first Chicago commission: a master plan for the redevelopment of Armour's South Side campus. Mies proudly recalled the arrangements in a 1959 interview: "[Heald] said to me one day, 'Mies, you had better think about a campus.' That was all the commission I had. We never made a contract as long as he was there."[19]

Heald believed that Armour's survival as a technological university required a modern curriculum, serious research programs, and a new physical plant. His task was complicated by Armour's location in one of Chicago's most distressed neighborhoods. In the decades bracketing World War I, African Americans in great numbers moved to Chicago from the South, many seeking employment in and around the Union Stock Yards a short distance from Armour. Since the late nineteenth century, the city's racial partitioning had effectively confined African Americans to two ever more crowded "black belts"—one of which engulfed the Armour campus. In the summer of 1919, a full-fledged race riot in Armour's immediate area resulted in the deaths of fifteen whites and twenty-three blacks, and injury to over five hundred people. In the aftermath, many Armour faculty who had lived close to or on campus decided to move, and the school sought several times to relocate.

When Mies arrived, the Armour campus occupied nine acres around the intersection of South Federal and Thirty-Third Streets, bounded by Thirty-First Street on the north, Thirty-Fourth Street on the south, State Street on the east, and the tracks of the Rock Island Railroad on the west. All its buildings dated from the late nineteenth or early twentieth century. The surrounding district, once a dense mix of commercial and residential buildings, was in a state of long-standing dilapidation, a condition Mies must have been aware of from the time of his first visit to Chicago in 1937. Myron Goldsmith, who was a third-year undergraduate at Armour when Mies arrived, said that "[Mies] was aware in the early years how frighteningly depressing Chicago was, especially the area around IIT. It was one vast slum that was gradually cleaned out, [with] people living in the utmost depravity."[20] These facts prompted the latest proposal, of 1930, to relocate the school. That also proved futile, and after a 1935 decision to remain, the campus was enlarged by the purchase of thirty additional acres. For a generation thereafter, nineteenth-century brick walkups and wood-framed cottages—most on twenty-five-foot-wide lots—still stood on the "newly" acquired parcels, though eventually all were razed. The expanded campus included the frontage along both sides of State Street between Thirty-First and Thirty-Fifth Streets, an area known as the Stroll, once the very center of Chicago's jazz scene. During the 1920s, King Oliver, Louis Armstrong, Duke Ellington, Bessie Smith, and Jimmie Yancey, among many others, made the Stroll one of the liveliest entertainment precincts in the United States.

The 1930s—the Depression years—were unkind to the Stroll and to the university it bordered. The jazzmen moved to larger theaters and dance halls farther south, and the decline of the neighborhood along State Street continued. Armour's decision to expand the campus gradually displaced many who had lived in the area for decades. At the time, this strategy was seen as a proactive way of simultaneously eradicating slums and making the school's own physical plant and surroundings more attractive and safe. With the support of the City of Chicago, Armour was anticipating government programs of the post–World War II period, which gave high national priority to the publicly financed upgrading—or complete rebuilding—of urban neighborhoods officially designated as slums.

Mies's plan for the Armour campus was preceded by another and followed by yet another. In 1937, prior to Heald's appointment as Armour's president, the school hired the Chicago firm of Holabird & Root to prepare a plan for expanding the campus. Despite John Holabird's enthusiasm in pursuit of Mies, his firm's plan was traditional. Buildings were to be grouped around courtyards on either side of an axial thoroughfare, with the main entrance from the west through the columns of a proposed classical propylaeum that crossed Thirty-Third Street opposite an elevated train platform four blocks east. A second plan, by Alfred Alschuler, a Chicago architect and Armour trustee, dates from late 1940—later, that is, than Mies's first plan. Although Heald held Mies in high regard, his letter of January 9, 1941, had the effect of marginalizing Mies's plan. With the public presentation of the campus plan expected in a few days, Heald quietly wrote Mies that

> the Board of Trustees has decided out of respect for Mr. Alschuler to use a sketch he prepared before his death....[21] I do not want you to feel that, because the board is using Mr. Alschuler's sketch, it represents any reflection on your work in connection with the program. It happens that [Alschuler] had prepared a sketch which shows a partial development with certain old buildings in use and which is not as comprehensive as the general program on which you have been working, and the Board felt that at this time it would be best to show the picture in that way.[22]

Very likely a product of institutional political infighting, Alschuler's plan was published in the *Chicago Daily News* of January 13, 1941. Mies persisted with his own planning, which finally received official backing from Heald. The Alschuler plan, showing the most important buildings in neoclassical style, was shelved. Heald announced to the trustees on October 13, 1941, that Mies had produced "an outstanding plan for a modern campus, and working drawings are now being developed by the firm of Holabird & Root."[23]

Mies began work on what we will term his initial campus plan in late 1938 or early 1939. He was assisted by Rodgers and Priestley. "We had to build school buildings, and often we didn't know [how] they would be used," said Mies. "So we had to find a system that made it possible to use these buildings as classrooms, as workshops, or as laboratories."[24] Rodgers undertook a study of classroom and laboratory requirements that led to Mies's decision to adopt a planning module of twenty-four feet. This module was deemed suitable for offices (one-half module square), classrooms (one module square, or fractional and whole-number multiples thereof), laboratories (one by two modules), and overall building dimensions. Mies also adopted a half multiple of the module—twelve feet—for the typical building floor-to-floor height, which was reasonable for constructability but probably only coincidentally related to the planning module.

Mies embraced the 24-foot module not just for the planning of individual buildings, but also as an *ordering principle* for the campus. "We came to a system of 24 feet," he said, "so I drew a network of 24 feet by 24 feet all over the campus. The crossing points were the points where we put columns. Nobody could change that. I had some fight about it, but I stuck to it. So you could connect the buildings at any place and you still had a clear system."[25] As it turned out, almost without exception the campus buildings were and remained freestanding, and "connections" were few.[26] Yet Mies's rationale is questionable. Even for a new campus planned as a unity, there is no necessary link between the plan dimensions of individual buildings and their siting relative to one another. Mies may have been influenced by the existing street grid in and around the campus, as well as by the large-scale order imposed by Chicago's eight-blocks-to-a-mile orthogonal grid. From the remarks quoted above, we know that he was aware that his "system" might be foiled, and that he hoped to prevent it. But large-scale gridded planning was foreign to the old Europe from which he came. He had never proposed it for the siting of his European buildings.

For the initial plan, Mies proposed consolidation of the six city blocks of the existing campus into two nearly square "superblocks" on either side of a new east–west main axis along Thirty-Third Street (fig. 7.1). The superblock scheme assumed the closing of Dearborn and Federal Streets, major thoroughfares that ran for miles north and south of the campus. Two key elements of the

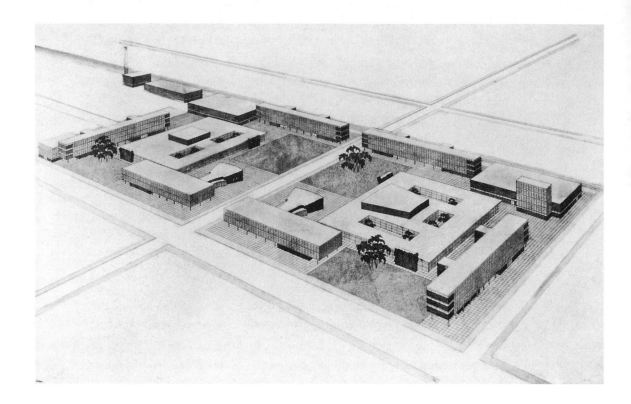

FIGURE 7.1.
Mies's initial cam-
pus plan (1939–40)
for Armour Institute
of Technology, Chi-
cago (later Illinois
Institute of Technol-
ogy); George E. Dan-
forth, delineator.
Aerial perspective
looking southwest.
Thirty-Third Street
runs from lower left
to upper right. Photo
courtesy of the Mies
van der Rohe Archive
of the Museum of
Modern Art, NY.

program—a library building to the south and a student union with auditorium to the north—occupy the approximate center of each superblock, with classroom and laboratory buildings disposed at the edges. Mies either assumed demolition of several Armour buildings (including the storied "Main Building" [1891–93], which survives), or elected to ignore them in his presentation.

Mies poured enormous effort into developing building solutions appropriate to a technological university. He borrowed from the last decade of his European experience—especially for building elevations—though the examples he could draw from, chiefly the unbuilt Reichsbank and the Verseidag factory, were not especially relevant. A wide range of exterior systems was proposed, including those with strip windows; gridded, glazed curtain walls; brick skirts and spandrels; and the taller end-bay spandrels, also in brick, that Mies continued to favor in design but would never implement. Most of the secondary buildings were raised on *pilotis* of cruciform section (dear to Mies since Barcelona). For these buildings only a lobby and exposed stair towers extended to grade. Most notably, back-to-back auditoria associated with the laboratories were shown as semidetached volumes, fan-shaped in plan and with raking roofs.

In a comprehensively illustrated essay in her 2001 exhibition catalog *Mies in America*, Phyllis Lambert offers the fullest examination in print of the development of Mies's campus plans.[27] Although her assessment is respectful and detailed, she argues that the first plan—that just described—is "extraordinarily agitated and complicated,"[28] and asserts that "in order to arrive at the final IIT campus scheme of 1941," Mies "[sought] simplification, to eliminate the frippery and excessive [number of] building types."[29] The second scheme, described below, is certainly a simplification of the first. Nonetheless, Lambert fails to acknowledge that for the first plan Mies was *inventing* a campus, without a detailed program or budget, for a university just then formed from the consolidation of two long-standing institutions. At this point he had had no experience with American construction. Mies also surely understood that a technologically progressive *image* was the chief aim of the exercise he had been assigned. Heald sought to reinvent the school, and he turned to Mies both for ideas and for their convincing expression. Real building—and reality—would come later.

In this light, the first plan is among the most advanced expressions of architectural modernism in the United States up to that time. In the context of Chicago's dense South Side, the superblock offered a realistic framework for creating—necessarily over time—a visually integrated academy still connected to the city around it. The several proposed building types were a response to programmatic variables—a work in progress. And the buildings envisioned are unprecedented. They are free of historicism and, as Mies may not yet have understood, in advance of the technology required to build them. The auditoria, though later viewed as "too expressionistic" by Mies,[30] are nonetheless, again for the United States at this time, radically modern. Mies proposed to concentrate resources in the symbolically important library and student union buildings, for which he imagined soaring, single-story, all-glazed prisms, each with multiple interior courts. It is ironic that though these signature buildings survived into the second, revised campus plan and remained central to IIT's ambitions for the next twenty years, neither was built to a Mies design, nor were they realized, in less successful forms, until after Mies's 1958 dismissal as architect of the campus.

One of the key elements of the initial campus plan is the proposed elevation of almost all classroom and laboratory buildings on *pilotis*. The concept of elevating whole buildings was new for Mies.[31] For Armour it appears to be without narrow programmatic justification; but in 1938, as symbol, such ground-plane transparency, especially at the scale of a superblock and for a coordinated set of buildings, was unprecedented.

Mies fundamentally revised the initial plan during 1940–41 (fig. 7.2). The changes were driven by two major developments: consummation of the merger between Armour and Lewis Institutes[32] to form IIT, and a decision by the City of Chicago to disallow the closing of Dearborn and Federal Streets, effectively barring a superblock scheme. With typical clarity and brevity, Mies recalled his process in a 1960 interview: "I made one design for the campus—

FIGURE 7.2.
Second (revised) campus plan for Illinois Institute of Technology, montage (1941). Aerial view looking northeast. This part of the dense South Side of Chicago would soon be all but destroyed by a combination of urban renewal and continued physical deterioration. Photo courtesy of the Mies van der Rohe Archive of the Museum of Modern Art, NY.

it was not built — where I removed most of the streets, so that I could place the buildings freely there. I was told by Henry Heald, the president, that it could not be done at that moment. They would not permit me until much later to remove the streets. So I was confronted with the past. I had to develop a plan in that normal block pattern, and I did that."[33] In the revised plan, Mies simplified the building volumes and eliminated the appended auditoria. As in the first plan, about half the buildings would be elevated, though in the end none were built that way. Plan symmetry is relaxed, except for the buildings on the blocks fronting Thirty-Third Street, where it is strictly maintained. Because the "reintroduction" of streets resulted in smaller blocks (versus the superblock), the library and student union buildings are reduced in size, and each now has a single interior court.

For the revised scheme, the most significant planning change was the proposed siting of several buildings parallel to and ajog each other. On either side of Thirty-Third Street, this created a number of smaller greenswards bounded by buildings on three or four sides. Critics have interpreted this as an example of — or even a quote from — the compositional style of Dutch artist Piet Mondrian.[34] And since the concept is clearly reflected in what was eventually built — notably in the siting of Alumni, Perlstein, and Wishnick Halls — it is frequently cited as one of Mies's major innovations in campus planning. But because the first plan's superblocks are almost square, Mies was able to dispose buildings at right angles to each other, which we assume was his preferred solution. Parallel siting and the "sliding" of one building past the next (always with the long dimension of the building north to south) are arguably functions of the smaller *rectangular* blocks to which Mies now had to adapt.

CHAPTER SEVEN

The second campus plan also reflects Mies's understanding of the severe financial constraints under which the new IIT operated. Only two significant buildings were built during World War II, after which campus improvements invariably depended on successful fund-raising for a specific project. Indeed, during Mies's tenure IIT never came close to raising enough money at one time to fund a coordinated building campaign. Had it done so, Mies's campus would surely have benefited from the informed prioritizing typical of more financially secure institutions, and he might well have realized his library and student union buildings. Much later, Mies would characterize the campus plan as the "biggest decision I ever had to make."[35] Though for Mies the "big decisions" were architectural, politics and money turned out to be variables of equal importance. Heald summed it up in his own reminiscence of Mies: "There were many times ... when I felt that he deserved a better client, or at least he deserved a wealthier one!"[36]

. . .

We return to the summer of 1939, when initial planning for the campus was under way. At the invitation of a friend of William Priestley's, Chicago lawyer E. M. Ashcraft, Mies was to vacation at a north-central-Wisconsin hideaway called Pike Lake Lodge. He asked John Barney Rodgers and Armour undergraduate George Danforth to come along, where work on the plan continued. Priestley and Walter Peterhans also appeared, though intermittently. There was a woman in the party too—none other than Lilly Reich. In July she had arrived in New York, where Mies met her; they traveled together by train to Chicago.[37]

For a few weeks in the north woods, the little community was elysian. Work progressed, professional camaraderie was close, and leisure hours were cheerfully free of bourgeois constraints: liquor was readily available, and swimming was comfortably in the nude. Evenings passed pleasantly as Ashcraft and Priestley, both musicians, offered impromptu jazz. Now and then they were joined by the renowned trumpeter Jimmy McPartland, encamped nearby. McPartland fascinated and mystified Mies, who was usually indifferent to music.

"Why is it," he once asked Danforth, an accomplished pianist, "that you like chazz?"

"Because it is so improvisational," came the reply.

"*Tja*," returned Mies, "but you must be careful with improvisation, no?"[38]

During the late summer or early fall of 1939, the following letter was received at the Chicago office of the Federal Bureau of Investigation. It was written by an unidentified businesswoman from the Chicago suburb of Glencoe.

I have just returned from Pike Lake Lodge, Wisconsin and while there [I] was very suspicious of four Germans who were staying there. The leader was supposed to be a marvelous architect from New York. He had two younger men there and a woman secretary who had just come over from Germany. They spoke nothing but German and spent their time over drawings. I may be wrong but they impressed me as spies, perhaps drawing plans of our country for the woman to take back to Germany. If you are interested I can tell you more about it.[39]

The letter precipitated an eight-month investigation. As reported by the FBI, the woman stated that she had grown alert to the possibility of undercover activity "due to the fact that she had just seen the movie 'Confessions of a Nazi Spy,'" a 1939 film starring Edward G. Robinson as, of all things, an FBI agent. The Milwaukee office of the FBI sent agents to Pike Lake to obtain registration information on Mies and his colleagues. At no time then or later did the bureau speak with Mies. It turned up cables from Pike Lake Lodge arranging ocean-liner reservations for the woman's return to Germany—Reich's name was not yet known—but they were inaccurate.[40] Inquiry into Chicago police records revealed nothing. On November 10, 1939, the agents determined from the records of the Blackstone Hotel that Mies was resident there, at six dollars a day, and two days later they confirmed that he was head of the department of architecture at Armour Institute. It was also determined that he and his associates regularly sent air-mail letters to Germany. The probe continued until the following spring.

Two passages from the FBI reports illuminate Mies's personal and political sentiments at this early point in his American career. (The FBI did not yet know that "van der Rohe" was not Mies's full last name.) One: "[Blank] stated that VAN DER ROHE did not make a practice of expressing his viewpoint to everyone whom he met, but among his close friends he did not hesitate to express his dislike for the Hitler regime, and stated that it had practically ruined him financially in Germany, and he further stated that he was quite content, now that he is living in the United States, and has no desire or plans of ever returning to Germany." Another: "[Blank] advised that he had talked on many occasions with VAN DER ROHE on various subjects and on politics he could say that VAN DER ROHE had stated to him that he was opposed to the present dominant political party in Germany. However, [Blank] advised that VAN DER ROHE had not been sufficiently interested in his opposition to actively fight it."[41]

The FBI concluded that Mies was not a spy, stating: "Inasmuch as it was not deemed advisable to personally contact any of the subjects, and as no violation of the Espionage Statute seems to be apparent, this case is being closed." The date was November 24, 1939.[42] But reporting continued until at least 1964. In 1946 Mies's name had turned up in a pamphlet titled *We Need You*, distributed by the Chicago branch of the Independent Citizens Committee of the

Arts, Sciences and Professions, an organization claimed to be a Communist front by the House Committee on Un-American Activities. The FBI file does not disclose what action followed (large sections of the report are blacked out), but Mies was evidently free of further governmental suspicion during the McCarthy scare of the early 1950s. The file concludes with records of a White House request, signed by Kenneth O'Donnell, a figure of consequence in the Kennedy administration, for a background check on Mies in connection with a potential appointment to the Advisory Committee for the [1964] New York World's Fair.[43] In response, the FBI provided a summary of all the investigations going back to 1939.[44]

Late in August 1939, Mies and his colleagues prepared to take their leave of Pike Lake Lodge. The mood grew dark as the radio reported news of the imminence of war in Europe. We presume that Reich wanted to stay with Mies, far from the bleak haunts she had left. It is believed by most of his friends that he did little to persuade her to remain, chiefly because, as we have further presumed, he felt the need to be free of her and her commanding personality. Besides, it could be rationalized that she had responsibilities back in Germany that required her return. Whatever passed between the two in the waning days of August at Pike Lake, she was gone before Nazi Germany invaded Poland on September 1. She took the train to New York, only to discover that the liner *Bremen* had slipped away under cover of darkness to avoid pursuit by the British. She managed to get back to Berlin by September 22, when, faithful as ever, she resumed her correspondence with Mies. She never saw him again.

Letters were exchanged until June 1940, when the mails were permanently interrupted by the war. They mostly concern business, chiefly Mies's European furniture patents, from which he still received remuneration, and over which litigation continued.[45] His letters to her are lost; we know of their frequency and scope only from hers to him. Reich wrote Mies as she did everything else with and for him—thoroughly and solicitously. Her affection is obvious from the way she cares for his business affairs and reports on the lives of Ada, Georgia, Marianne, Waltraut, Ewald, and various old colleagues. Her tone is level, yet now and then she gives way to the pain of the war and her hopeless distance from Mies.

Mies's side of the correspondence is surprising for its volume. He sent at least twenty-two letters in less than a year, a remarkably faithful correspondence in view of the fact that Marianne reported that "I got no more than three or four letters from him in my entire life." He was no less dutiful in sending food packages to Reich and the family as well as friends. (He resumed shipments for members of his family after the war.) Reich complains gently when he does not write, and in a letter of June 12, 1940, which she supposes will be her last to him, she addresses the fact that she has lost him:

I am powerfully reminded of the last days and hours in Chicago. I fear my instincts did not deceive me, despite the fact that I wished nothing more, both
then and now, than to be proven wrong. I am sad that I have received only
the slightest word from you in the last weeks, and that pertaining solely to
business affairs. Perhaps you have no time, perhaps you have sent more letters than I know. That the mail connections stop now makes it all the harder
to bear.

I suspect we have more to worry about with you. I will hear nothing from
you, know nothing about you. Will you try to find a way to be in touch? I am
happy that you have friends now, and it comforts me somewhat that I was
once with you over there. How helpless we are all delivered up![46]

Her instincts were right. Mies had evidently made his decision before she
left the United States; it was too much to ask of him that he compromise himself for her or anyone else. Loneliness was the price of the quest. He later told
Lora Marx: "I don't belong to the people who cannot live alone."[47]

. . .

In spite of the fact that Mies had completed one building for IIT by 1942, his
campus plan came close to being abandoned outright. In 1943 the trustees
learned of the availability, at a bargain price, of the Stevens Hotel. The War
Department had owned it since the beginning of World War II, using it as a bar-
racks and for training. Discussions ensued, based on the fact that the building could accommodate the entire university as well as house its students.
Though a "considerable sum of money" had already been expended to improve the South Side campus, "it is believed," the Board of Trustees minutes
of July 9, 1943, stated, "that all the money invested can be realized if the property were sold." One can only speculate on what this might have meant for
Mies's career. But the Stevens was sold to another entity, to become the latest
chapter in the history of IIT's many attempts to relocate.[48]

Much has been written about Mies's curriculum for Armour and IIT. Most of
it is descriptive, noncritical, and often hagiographic. And though Mies wrote
a few pieces describing his American program and educational philosophy—
most notably the aforementioned 1938 inaugural address and one or two
statements for university publications—his most comprehensive description
is a Bauhaus-inspired chart developed for Armour at the beginning of his tenure in 1938, later revised and widely reprinted.[49] Like most graphical representations of ideas, it is subject to multiple readings, and it necessarily contains
nothing in the manner of rationale.

As we have noted, Mies's professional rhetoric tended toward aphorism,
often of the fewest words. Thus, in connection with Mies—even on T-shirts

sporting his cigar-smoking silhouette—we witness the retailing of "Less is more," "God is in the details," and "almost nothing [*beinahe nichts*]."[50] But out of context, these statements are meaningless. Indeed, the most well known is not even his. In a recorded exchange with architecture students in 1960, Mies was asked about the "origin of your phrase ['Less is more']." He replied: "I said it ... I think I said it first to Philip [Johnson]. Oh, I think where I heard it first was from Peter Behrens. Yes. You know it is not original, but I like it very much."[51] About Thomas Aquinas, one of his favorite philosophers, he was equally matter-of-fact: "Aquinas ... says 'reason is the first principle of all human work.' Na, when you have grasped that once, you know, you can act accordingly. So I would throw everything out what [meaning 'that'] is not reasonable."[52] In common with most of Mies's "principles," however, these pronouncements are consistent with a very wide range of outcomes.

An irony of Mies's involvement in architectural education is that he was by nature and experience dismissive of formal education. His undergraduate program for IIT reflects not only this bias but another. For Mies, architecture at the highest level—perhaps the only level of interest to him—cannot be taught, at least widely, and certainly not to the young, even eager, undergraduate. His curriculum was therefore both rigorously basic and arduously additive. In practice, the talented undergraduate ended his or her four (later five) IIT undergraduate years with superb but basic professional skills and a portfolio that looked very much like the work of his or her fellow students, and of Mies van der Rohe. According to Gene Summers, Mies privately expressed limited hopes for his program: "If he could get ten architects a year out of his college ... then he would have enough good architecture sprouting up around the country.... That was early, and then later he said, 'God, if I can get ten architects all together.'"[53]

But A. James Speyer, Mies's first graduate student and a longtime member of his faculty, stoutly defended IIT's undergraduate curriculum:

> The curriculum was orderly, working from simple to complicated, from easy to difficult. It was planned to train a student to become an architect in the most direct fashion where the student might come in without any knowledge of architecture and emerge, if not as a great artist, at least as a thoroughly trained architect.... He knew how to draw, how to build, how to plan, and he was assured of a basic professional status. If he was an artist, he could elevate any one of these professional assets to the level of fine art. I think that it was without question ... the best and most basic curriculum that I could imagine.... I think that it is exactly the opposite of most architectural school curricula in that it is so, I repeat, simple and direct in evolution, whereas the temptation in so many schools is the reverse.

Mies always felt that it was very damaging for a student to be put into a situation where he could not find a solution.... This really retarded him rather than advancing him. Mies's belief was that everything proceeded in the architectural school as step after step. You would start to draw black lines on white paper. You might do nothing but draw a fine line, a medium line, and a heavy line. But, by the time you had mastered the art or craft of drawing those lines so that you could make a line any weight you wish, and make a rough line or a smooth line, you had made great progress. Then you could maybe think about how to put the lines together and draw a square, or get a compass and draw a circle, or make a complicated composition of crosshatched lines. Then you might go into color.... And then you go into construction. It's an evolution.[54]

Thomas Beeby was educated at Cornell and Yale, and taught at IIT in the early 1970s. During this period he also worked under Gene Summers and was thoroughly immersed in the Miesian idiom. He later moved away from modernism, and offered this view of Mies's curriculum:

> Jacques Brownson ... came to the attention of Mies when he was in his first year. Jacques, who had trained as a carpenter, was [helping to put together a show in S. R. Crown Hall], working in his methodical, precise and workmanlike way.... Mies became interested in having Brownson work for him because Mies thought he had the right attitude about architecture—that it's workmanship and workman-like attitudes versus [artistry], which Mies didn't have a lot of patience with, except with himself. I don't think that he wanted the people around him to be particularly artistic. The curriculum of the school remains terribly vocational and purposely unintellectual ... I think Mies actually was training people to work in his office. I have a sense that in the cultural displacement of leaving Europe he didn't feel [American] society had a cultural milieu where artists could build things. I think he felt that this was sort of a roaring wilderness where he had to start over again and train people on the most basic level to be tradesmen. Some of them might become artists, but in the meantime he had to raise the lowest level to where people became useful as architects. I think it's [an incorrect] assessment of our society, but it makes sense if you think of where he was coming from.[55]

One of Mies's beliefs—equally applicable to architectural education—was beyond dispute. Architecture was plain hard work. Reginald Malcolmson, a student of Mies's, reported this memorable exchange between Mies and his faculty colleague Alfred Caldwell:

> Caldwell ... would [often] act as a kind of straight man to Mies.... He would ask him leading questions.... He asked him one day in Crown Hall when we first moved in, "How important do you think it is for students to have talent?" And Mies sat and thought for a while, and said, "I will tell you. I have seen many talented, gifted people in my lifetime, hundreds of them, maybe even a

thousand, but talent is only cream in your coffee." He said, "So many people I've known that were very gifted, they were too lazy and they just didn't work it all out. There's no reason to rest on your talent. If you don't present it, then it gets nowhere."[56]

Mies's IIT graduate program, beginning with two or three students a year in the late 1930s and early 1940s, did produce advanced work. Its standards and format were mostly developed by Ludwig Hilberseimer. Graduate students of that era had already completed a professional degree in architecture, and though many came up from the IIT undergraduate program, by the late 1940s Mies was attracting graduate students from around the world. The product of an IIT master's degree was a "thesis," usually a fully worked-out building design briefly described in text and represented by presentation drawings and photographs of a professional-quality model (built by the student). The student was encouraged to place his or her work within the context of architectural, cultural, and economic history. Thesis topics were most often "representational" buildings, such as theaters, museums, or arenas. Graduate students worked with an advisor and one or two other faculty or outside professionals, functioning like project architects working under a principal in a real design office, and with considerable independence. After Mies's retirement, Myron Goldsmith and his student—and later faculty colleague— David C. Sharpe were advisors for a series of graduate theses examining the confluence of engineering and aesthetics in tall and long-span structures— work for which the school became renowned in the 1960s and beyond.

With IIT as his base, Mies had multiple professional advantages; in the early years the best students, trained in his methods, moved into his office or through it on their way to larger firms and bigger (and livable) paychecks.[57] It was easy for Mies to explore new ideas in the low-cost, low-pressure environment of academia. And as talented graduates moved into the workforce, Mies's methods and persona took on storied status. Except in the war years, when he personally taught classes, Mies's classroom contact with students— particularly undergraduates—was limited. And though he was nominally an advisor for master's thesis projects in the 1940s and early 1950s, the work of thesis supervision was mostly done by Hilberseimer, who was beloved of students in their oft-repeated testimonies. There are dozens of reports from students of this period describing Mies's actual "teaching" as, typically, long periods in silent contemplation of a drawing or model, sometimes in front of an eager group, punctuated, after harrowingly extended but wordless scrutiny, by a quiet, "*Ja*, try it again," or "*Ja*, you could do that," or, more positively, "Keep working on it."

There is evidence somewhat to the contrary. Paul Pippin, a graduate student in 1946–47, described Mies's classroom performance this way:

[We were assigned] the design of a house, entirely on our own, over six weeks. Mies kept our drawings for a week. We were advised that he would meet with us on a certain day to begin a discussion of our designs. He had an assistant put the drawings of one student in front of him and the crit[ique] began. He would make a comment—then there would be a long pause—then another comment, until the entire design had been reviewed and evaluated. Each individual crit went on for two continuous hours or more, and the total critique took a number of days. [Mies made no attempt] to play the great master—quite the contrary, he was very "low key," even shy, but powerful in his convictions. . . . He said "I want to say there is no such thing as genius. It is just hard work. If you will work for me, I will work just as hard for you." He gave his time freely and the sessions [might] cover several hours. It was more of a warm, friendly encounter than a critique from the professor.[58]

Nonetheless, it was not in Mies's nature to correct or attempt to refine a student's work in anything like what goes on in today's academic studio environment.[59] Instead, he *led* by the force of his own intellectual and artistic gravity, and by the example of the IIT campus as it rose around him.

. . .

During World War II, Mies and his two principal professional associates at IIT, Hilberseimer and Peterhans, had fewer students but more time of their own. Mies remained busy with the first new campus buildings. Hilberseimer concentrated on educational administration and on his writing about architecture and city planning.[60] And the polymath Peterhans became a teacher of consequence, chiefly through a course of instruction of his own devising that became legendary. Early on, Mies had expressed concern about the lack of visual sensitivity of Armour's architecture students. He later wrote:

Sometime [after 1938] I made the startling discovery that although the students appeared to understand what I said about the importance of proportion, they did not demonstrate the slightest sense of it in their exercises. I realized that their eyes simply could not see proportion. This problem was discussed with Peterhans and we decided to introduce a new course especially designed for training the eyes and forming and maturing a sensitivity for proportion. . . . To achieve this end, Peterhans developed the course called Visual Training. The effect . . . was a radical change in the whole mental attitude of the students. All fussiness and sloppiness disappeared from their work; they learned to discard any line that did not fulfill a purpose, and a real understanding of proportion emerged. Although specially gifted students sometimes produced plates that would have enriched the collection

FIGURE 7.3.
From left to right,
architect Erich
Mendelsohn, with
IIT faculty Walter
Peterhans, Ludwig
Hilberseimer, and
Mies, across from
Orchestra Hall and
the Pullman Build-
ing (the latter de-
molished), about
1940.

of a museum, the purpose of the course was never to produce works of art, but to train the eyes.[61]

Peterhans was the most broadly educated of Mies's American colleagues (fig. 7.3). Born in Frankfurt in 1897, he grew up in Dresden, where he studied machine design before following a similar program at the *Technische Hochschule* in Munich. In 1920 he enrolled in philosophy at the Ludwig-Maximilian University in Munich, moving a year later to the Georg-August University in Göttingen, where until 1924 he studied philosophy, mathematics, and art history. He then moved to the State Academy for Graphic Arts and Book Production in Leipzig. His versatility in the visual arts prepared him for a faculty position at the Bauhaus, from 1929 to 1933, when the school closed. During his tenure at Armour/IIT as professor of visual training, he was also a member of the Committee on Social Thought at the University of Chicago. He was a lecturer at the Hochschule für Gestaltung in Ulm in 1953 and at the Hochschule für bildenden Künste in Hamburg in 1959.

Peterhans's dual commitment to science and art derived from his father, a Zeiss optical engineer who gave him a quality camera and taught him optics. His creative work, mostly in photography, was characterized by obsessive precision of technique. He often labored for weeks on the production of a

FIGURE 7.4.
Ludwig Hilberseimer
teaching, ca. 1960.
Photo: IIT Archives
(Chicago). Used by
permission.

single, still-life photo. Given this background, as well as his experience at the Bauhaus, he was perfectly suited to developing the ends and means of the IIT Visual Training course.

Peterhans conceived a program of ten exercises to be completed over four semesters. The student was instructed to manipulate a variety of abstract designs presented in the basic visual elements—line, form, value, color, and texture. As an example, a 20-by-30-inch white board with one thin, black vertical line crossed by one similar horizontal line yielded four rectangles, which the student manipulated in an effort to produce the most convincing layout of lines and rectangles. Each effort was critiqued in group discussion. This elementary exercise led to more complicated arrangements involving curving and diagonal lines and color and texture.

Peterhans believed that training in the Beaux-Arts had placed an over-emphasis on the student's *painted* presentation of a design. He thought this worked against any understanding of the properties of the underlying individual elements. Thus he chose to isolate those elements in exercises. He acknowledged that his course was indebted to his Bauhaus association with Paul Klee, and specifically to Klee's "Pedagogical Sketchbook" of 1925. Peterhans conducted the Visual Training course from 1939 until his death in 1960. A similar course has been maintained to the present.

. . .

As noted, Mies's association with Hilberseimer dated to the 1920s and the *G* circle, and in 1938 Mies brought him to Armour as professor of city and regional planning (fig. 7.4). Born in Karlsruhe in 1885, Hilberseimer studied at that city's *Technische Hochschule* and in 1910 moved to Berlin, where he practiced architecture. He was associated with avant-garde causes in Germany, notably the Arbeitsrat für Kunst, the Novembergruppe, and the expressionist-oriented gallery Der Sturm. In 1931 he became a director of the Deutscher Werkbund. He also devoted himself to criticism, all of it sympathetic to progressive movements.

Despite the variety of his interests, Hilberseimer's career in Germany is remembered mostly for his work in city planning. By 1924 he had produced a Project for a High-Rise City (*Hochhausstadt*). The plan has stirred not a little controversy. Though influenced by Le Corbusier's "Ville contemporaine" of 1922, Hilberseimer's High-Rise City consisted of two parts: at a lower level, a nest of business activity and automobile traffic, and at a level above, a residential city where vehicular traffic was prohibited. The objective was an environment protective of pedestrians and especially children. As delineated, the buildings were endlessly similar slabs, rising in a cityscape devoid of anything natural. Critical response has ranged from acutely negative, with Richard Pommer claiming in 1988 that "the drawings ... still have the power to bring on a shudder,"[62] to that of Vittorio Magnago Lampugnani, who in 2001 responded defensively: "Hilberseimer was not attempting to provide views of some fictional ideal city, but simply schemata."[63] Howard Dearstyne, who studied with Hilberseimer at the Bauhaus and was a longtime faculty colleague at IIT, said this about his teacher's drawings:

> They looked bald and poverty-stricken, almost amateurish. Hilbs was altogether lacking in facility as a draftsman, unlike his colleague Mies van der Rohe, who was a supremely talented architectural delineator. Hilbs was apparently aware of this deficiency.... He once told me that architect friends in Germany used to accuse him of putting in the windows of his architectural drawings with a rubber stamp.[64]

Hilberseimer offered his own acid judgment: "The repetition of the blocks resulted in too much uniformity. Every natural thing was excluded: no tree or grassy area broke the monotony. Taken as a whole, the design for this high-rise city was wrong from the start. The result was more a necropolis than a metropolis, a sterile landscape of asphalt and cement, inhuman in every aspect."[65] Hilberseimer wrote those words in 1963, nearly forty years after the High-Rise City project. In his late work in the United States, he specialized in large-scale *regional* planning. He also became an early and ardent environmentalist. Yet his critics remained unimpressed, charging him with an unremitting preference for abstract principles over human considerations.

Little came of Hilberseimer's American exertions beyond a singular collaboration with Mies on Lafayette Park in Detroit, discussed in detail below. As a figure of distinction in the history of Armour and IIT, Hilbs (as he was always called) is remembered most affirmatively for his writing, his inquisitiveness, and his gifts as a teacher.[66] As a writer, he enjoyed the distinction of receiving lavish professional praise from Mies himself. In a foreword to Hilberseimer's 1944 book *The New City: Principles of Planning*, Mies praised his colleague in terms he would use over and over in the United States. The rhetoric is unmistakable, and if we substitute *architecture* for *city planning*, Mies might equally well have been speaking of himself:

> Reason is the first principle of all human work. Consciously or unconsciously L. Hilberseimer follows this principle and makes it the basis of his work in the complicated field of city planning. He examines the city with unwavering objectivity, investigates each part of it and determines for each part its rightful place in the whole. Thus he brings all the elements of the city into clear, logical order. He avoids imposing upon them arbitrary ideas of any character whatsoever.
>
> He knows that cities must serve life, that their validity is to be measured in terms of life, and that they must be planned for living. He understands that the forms of cities are the expression of existing modes of living, that they are inextricably bound up with these, and that they, with these, are subject to change. He realizes that the material and spiritual conditions of the problem are given, that he can exercise no influence on these factors in themselves, that they are rooted in the past and will be determined by objective tendencies for the future.
>
> He also knows that the existence of many and diverse factors presupposes the existence of some order which gives meaning to these and which acts as a medium in which they can grow and unfold. City planning means for the author, therefore, the ordering of things in themselves and in their relationship with each other. One should not confuse the principles with their application. City planning is, in essence, a work of order; and order means—according to St. Augustine—"the disposition of equal and unequal things, attributing to each its place."[67]

Aside from Hilberseimer's writings on city and regional planning, his most important book is his 1956 monograph *Mies van der Rohe*, the first monograph on Mies after Philip Johnson's 1947 MoMA catalog.[68] Author and subject had worked together for more than thirty years, and the authority of the book is supported by friendship, collegiality, and shared professionalism. On every page, Hilberseimer all but spoke for Mies: "[Mies] has arrived at structural clarity, the requisite of steel architecture, and found a harmony between the material means and his spiritual aims."[69]

... Structure, while not in itself architecture, can be a means to architecture, if the builder understands the organic principle of order which relates every part of the building to the whole, according to its importance and value.

[Mies's] architecture, though dependent on structure, is infinitely more than structure. It grows out of and elaborates structure, but attains a transcendence of the material into the realm of the spiritual ... Mies van der Rohe has achieved this ... with a material as prosaic as steel, steel as it comes from the mill, the same steel that had always before been hidden behind the "architecture."[70]

Hilberseimer also celebrated what he called Mies's "new architectural language," which he asserted is "understandable to everyone."[71] It was Mies's "greatest achievement ... developed out of the very nature of steel."[72] He even anticipated criticism: "A [Mies] building looks simple only because the problems involved have been solved with clarity."[73] Appearing at the peak of Mies's American renown, Hilberseimer's book reflected the confidence and exuberance of the school of Mies at high tide.

Mies's relationship with Hilberseimer was not symmetrical. Mies would listen when Hilberseimer expressed his opinion, but when he disagreed, he was certain to go his own way. The best-known instance involved site planning for Mies's apartment towers at 860–880 North Lake Shore Drive in Chicago. One of Hilberseimer's cherished principles was that a building should be sited to optimize the natural illumination of its interior. To that effect, he offered counsel that Mies simply chose to ignore; the buildings were sited based on factors geometric, programmatic, and urbanistic—but not solar.

Hilberseimer was modestly eccentric. He was known to walk about the city on a schedule and at great distances, including regularly walking the six miles to and from his apartment to IIT. He was not cowed by officialdom, or as Lora Marx expressed it, he was "hopelessly tactless." She remembered Mies's embarrassment when Hilberseimer "spoke disrespectfully to some high labor leader in Detroit" during work on their joint project at Lafayette Park.[74] Hilberseimer was outraged when Mies was dismissed as IIT's campus architect, but he soldiered on, teaching for almost another decade under the directorship of his former student George Danforth. Danforth, who loved Hilberseimer (and was executor of his estate), said it between the lines: "When he thought a course wasn't right, he felt perfectly free to say something about it, no matter who was annoyed."[75]

In one respect, Hilberseimer eclipsed Mies: as a studio and classroom teacher. From all accounts, he was a unique combination of rigor and warmth. Mies recognized his talent: "I ... have often wondered what qualities make him such an excellent teacher. The absence of any formula or personal whim certainly contributes to the value of his work. He uses the Socratic method of asking questions and leading students, through an analysis of their answers, to an understanding they appear to reach themselves."[76] In the words of one of his students of the 1950s, "He wasn't a teacher who, in a discussion or a critique, would get you in a corner, so to speak, and let you out of it easily. He would force you to your knees, as it were. And yet at the same time it was done very gently. What he wanted you to do was to think about issues; to know what you were talking about, to be careful what you were saying and how you were saying it."[77] It is impossible to imagine any student speaking that way of Mies. Reginald Malcolmson—a student and intimate of both—summed it up: "Mies was the head of the school; Hilbs was its heart."[78]

Proof of that may be found in an IIT tradition honoring Hilberseimer: the annual faculty-student dinner meeting of the "Allies of the Republic of Hilberseimer," on or near the winter solstice, a date reflecting Hilberseimer's conviction that on the shortest day of the year at least four hours of sunlight should reach the major rooms of any building. Started in 1940, "Hilbs' Day" continued with the guest of honor for twenty-six years and, remarkably, in his memory, into the twenty-first century.

. . .

Among Mies's faculty, the American Alfred Caldwell occupied a unique position. He is best known as a landscape architect, responsible for, among other works, the landscape design for Mies's campus. But he was an architect too, with an independent practice during most of his career and long tours of duty as a professor in the IIT College of Architecture and at other universities. As documented by his biographer, Dennis Domer, Caldwell was also a poet, essayist, environmentalist, and sage[79] (fig. 7.5). He produced exquisitely detailed architectural and landscape drawings that are today as coveted by collectors as those by Mies. He was the most colorful character among Mies's colleagues, a galvanizing lecturer with a booming voice and a legendary temper that was leveled regularly at the world around him.

Born in St. Louis in 1903, Caldwell moved with his family to Chicago in 1909. He enrolled at the University of Illinois in 1921 to study landscape architecture, but dropped out. Shortly thereafter, he began to practice landscape architecture in Chicago with a partner, George Donoghue, who financed the business. Caldwell then made a fateful and, as matters developed, eminently fortunate decision when he applied for work with Jens Jensen, the fabled landscapist famous for employing native midwestern species and creating naturalistic rock formations. Jensen became teacher and model as well as employer, and in the 1920s the two men were responsible for a number of ambitious landscapes for prominent private clients. Jensen's friendship

with Frank Lloyd Wright led to visits by Caldwell to Taliesin, and Wright's in-fluence was soon entwined with Jensen's, evident in Caldwell's celebrated WPA-era landscape and building designs for Eagle Point Park in Dubuque, Iowa.

Working for the Chicago Park District in the second half of the 1930s, Caldwell designed major parks, including Promontory Point in Hyde Park and the landfill extension of Lincoln Park north to Hollywood Avenue. One day in the fall of 1938, three men — Mies, Hilberseimer, and Peterhans — were walk-ing through Lincoln Park when they came across a lily pond and surrounding garden and structures that greatly impressed them. Mies presumed it was by Wright, but Caldwell, who happened to be there working, proudly corrected him. Thus began Caldwell's connection with Mies, and a brief matriculation as an IIT architecture student. He sat for his architect's license in 1940.

One afternoon in 1944, Caldwell received a telephone call:

> Somebody with a guttural voice said, "This is me." . . . I said, "This is Ardwell 4982. You have the wrong number" and I hung up. . . . The phone rang again pretty soon and the man said, "This is me." Then I recognized he wasn't saying

"This is me," he was saying "This is Mies. . . . Vould you be villing to teach our young architects?" He said "Come to my office tomorrow afternoon." I came and he talked to me and he said it would only take part of the time. Mies was so smooth, making it very agreeable. He said, "I don't know how much time it will take, you have to find out. It's nothing much." He exhausted my life in actuality, but that was the way he put it.[80]

Caldwell was hired, the first new full-time, Chicago-based faculty member to teach under Mies. His teaching specialty was construction.

Later in his career, Caldwell served on the faculty of the School of Architecture at the University of Southern California. There he taught philosophy, literature, and history as well as architecture and landscape design. In 1981 he rejoined IIT as the Ludwig Mies van der Rohe Professor of Architecture, a post he retained until his death in 1998 in Bristol, Wisconsin.

A New Architectural Language: 1946–53

Then when everything was finished, the people from the Metals Building, the engineers, they came and said "We need here a door." And the result was Mondrian!
MIES in 1960, denying that he was influenced by the painter Piet Mondrian

Architecture is not a cocktail. **MIES**

At IIT Mies tested his ideas in work he assigned to students. He had done this at the Bauhaus as well, but in Chicago the process intensified now that campus buildings were to be realized. The method had little in common with Beaux-Arts education, though in its way it was fully traditional, for it was based on Mies's beloved image of medieval masters and apprentices working together, impersonally, toward a common goal.

In 1942 student Paul Campagna brought to Mies's attention a photograph of the interior of the Martin Bomber Plant near Baltimore, designed for war production by the Detroit firm Albert Kahn Associates. The Kahn office specialized in no-nonsense factories, in this case an immense, column-free space spanned by great steel trusses. Mies elected to design a project based on the photograph. He conceived the installation of a concert hall inside the great factory (fig. 8.1). Using collage-montage technique, he proposed a number of arrangements of walls and ceilings, horizontal and vertical, flat and curved, standing and hanging, together intended to define a venue for musical performances within the far larger building. He was unconcerned about the obvious acoustical problems. This was a postulation—materially unfeasible, but rich in implications. The Concert Hall stood squarely between his German and American oeuvres, incorporating elements of each equally and separately. The planes, slipping into and around space that in turn flowed and curled around them, were vestiges of the spatial dynamism of the 1920s, while the great factory hall in which this was to take place represented structure at large scale, the focus of his later work.

In 1943 the American journal *Architectural Forum*, preparing a special issue on postwar architecture, approached several prominent architects for hypothetical designs of buildings of the future.[1] Mies was asked to design a church. He agreed to participate, but assigned himself a museum. The result was a project now known as the Museum for a Small City, which in the words of his

FIGURE 8.1.
Collage of Concert
Hall (1942), Mies's
pictorial response
to the interior of Al-
bert Kahn's Martin
Bomber Plant in Bal-
timore. Impressed
by the plant's enor-
mous clear-spanning
trusses, Mies pro-
posed an arrange-
ment of vertical and
horizontal planes
that defined a focal
space within a larger
open plan. This is an
early example of his
fascination with "uni-
versal space." Photo
courtesy IIT Archives
(Chicago).

prospectus "should not emulate its metropolitan counterparts. The value of such a museum depends upon the quality of its works of art and the manner in which they are exhibited."

The first problem is to establish the museum as a center for the enjoyment, not the internment, of art. In this project the barrier between the art work and the living community is erased by a garden approach for the display of sculpture. Interior sculptures enjoy an equal spatial freedom, because the open plan permits them to be seen against the surrounding hills. The architectural space, thus achieved, becomes a defining rather than a confining space. A work such as Picasso's *Guernica* has been difficult to place in the usual museum gallery. Here it can be shown to greatest advantage and become an element in space against a changing background.[2]

Mies went on to highlight his celebration of space and simplicity of form: "The building, conceived as one large area, allows every flexibility in use. The structural type permitting this is the steel frame. This construction permits the erection of a building with only three basic elements—a floor slab, columns and a roof plate."[3]

The well-known collage, executed by George Danforth, shows an open plan with Aristide Maillol's *Night* in front of and to the right of the *Guernica*, which acts as a freestanding wall. To the left, Maillol's *Young Girl Reclining* rests before the glass wall, behind which are a wooded area and a pool. The plan incorporates a free arrangement of the gallery walls evocative of Mies's German work, and several interior courts, which became standard in his designs for IIT. He also included a mezzanine, a sunken seating area, and an auditorium. It was the last of these elements that appears to have followed the lead of the trusswork of the Martin Bomber Plant. To provide column-free space, Mies proposed a pair of exposed trusses from which part of the roof is suspended, a step toward the clear-span structures that were to occupy so much of his energy in the United States.

· · ·

In 1941 Mies's campus plan began to generate actual building. To some observers, these works looked like mere factories. Others admired the fine proportions and sophisticated detailing. Mies himself recalled the exceptional quality of some of the German factories of the late 1920s and early 1930s. Theodor Merrill's Königsgrube works in Bochum (1930), for example, had appeared in Johnson and Hitchcock's *International Style*. Also published by 1933 were Fritz Schupp's Zollverein Colliery near Essen (1932) and the boiler plant designed in 1927 by Erich Mendelsohn for the Mosler Publishing Company in Berlin. These three works exemplified a characteristically German industrialization of the vernacular half-timbered house. In February 1933, *Architectural Forum* reported on the huge Zollverein Colliery: "Every structure in the extensive establishment is built upon an iron framework and covered with glazed brick, in Germany, called clinker.... [This system] promised even with buildings which vary in form and size and purpose throughout the whole complex a general impression of uniformity."[4] Mies believed that an impersonal—and *economical*—architecture of industrial connotation could satisfy both the practical and symbolic requirements of a technological institution of varied purpose and the potential to grow.

Mies's master plan for IIT gave only modest hints of his imminent self-reinvention as a champion of structural expression. The buildings that the plan depicts are placeholders, of undoubted modernity, though they are not primarily structurally expressive. Nonetheless, early on in his other efforts we begin to see steel detailing of remarkable aesthetic power. It is first suggested with the aforementioned Museum for a Small City, and then fully formed with the heroically scaled steel skeleton and steel-to-brick detailing of the Library and Administration Building, a design completed by 1944. In these two unbuilt projects, trusses and long-span girders, respectively, made possible the column-free and nearly column-free interiors that are lodestones of Mies's American oeuvre.

It is easy to forget that Mies's IIT campus plan depicts an imagined, *completed* institution. In 1940, and for years to come, much of the campus was a patchwork of dilapidated commercial and residential buildings. Old Armour buildings were also present, but Mies consistently omitted them from models and aerial perspectives. The order and location in which new buildings were

FIGURE 8.2.
Minerals and Metals
Research Building,
Illinois Institute of
Technology, Chicago
(1942). View looking
southwest. *At right*,
the infamous "Mon-
drian wall," which
critics claimed was
based on de Stijl
compositions of the
Dutch artist. Mies vig-
orously debunked this
theory. The north wall
was later subsumed
in a building addi-
tion by Mies. Photo:
Joseph J. Lucas.

actually built turned out to be a function of available funding, IIT bureaucratic infighting, a world war, and after the war the complex dynamics of a rapidly growing technical university.

Mies's first building for IIT was a three-story construction of the most practical sort—a foundry hall with offices and laboratories and a five-ton moving crane. It is at the western edge of the campus, on a narrow lot abutting the tracks of the Rock Island Railroad. Called the Minerals and Metals Research Building, it was commissioned in March 1941 and constructed between November of that year and February 1943 (fig. 8.2). Mies, assisted by Danforth as draftsman, constituted the design team.

Although there has been considerable speculation as to why and how Mies first adopted an architectural language of exposed structural steel, it is easy to see why he began with steel for Minerals and Metals. For all the campus buildings into the early 1950s, Mies associated with the Chicago firm Holabird & Root, which prepared construction documents and provided mechanical and structural engineering. For Minerals and Metals, a structural-steel frame of heavy rolled sections was the obvious solution for function, cost, and constructability—especially to accommodate the crane—and Holabird was surely the source of the technical advice Mies required. With the structural system a given, Mies had only to refine the program, organize the plan, and compose and detail the building exterior. The City of Chicago Building Code allowed nonfireproofed steel for foundry-type buildings, which Mies exploited for simplicity of construction and—for the first time in his career—a self-consciously clear structural expression. It so happened that clear, rational construction also suited IIT's bare-bones budgets.

The Minerals and Metals plan is unremarkable, except that it departs from the 24-foot module posited for the new campus. Given the narrow site, Mies chose to dispose the three-story building in 24-foot bays north to south, but in off-module bays, roughly 22 and 42 feet wide, east to west. Offices and labs face east, and the foundry hall occupies the full north–south dimension on the west, shielding the offices from the noisy tracks. Mies chose to set the brick-and-glass east and west walls just *outside* the structural-steel frame, but to *infill* the structural steel wide-flange columns and beams on the north and south with two interlocking wythes (a wall two bricks thick) of buff brick. On the north and south elevations, the off-module plan generates an asymmetrical composition of steel and brick, which includes two additional exposed steel stiffeners needed to brace the brick. For some, these elevations again evoked the paintings of Mondrian. It was a notion that stuck. Mies was irritated by the claim—he didn't depend on "artists" for his ideas—and he made a point of rejecting it:

> People claim that I was influenced by Mondrian in the first building for the IIT campus, the Metals Building. But I remember very well how it came about. Everything was donated for this whole building. The site—we had 64 feet from the railroad to the sidewalk. Somebody gave them a traveling crane—it was 40 feet wide, so we needed 42 feet from center of column to center of column. The rest was laboratories…. Everything was there—we needed steel bracing in the wall, the brick wall. It was a question of the building code. You can only make an eight-inch wall so big, otherwise you have to reinforce it. So we did that. Then when everything was finished, the people from the Metals Building, the engineers, they came and said "We need here a door!" So I put in a door. And the result was Mondrian![5]

The "problem" of locating an enclosing wall relative to a building's structure—sometimes solved in Mies's European work by separating the two—would become, for the American Mies, a source of inspiration and the subject of intense investigation. For the long elevations of Minerals and Metals, Mies adopted a seven-foot-high skirt of continuous double-wythe brick. Above are translucent strip windows, five per bay. Behind the glass are Mies's first wide-flange mullions, all but hidden from the outside. Stair exits and a central pair of floor-height doors complete the east elevation. The strip-windows are similar to those depicted on buildings of both the first and the final campus plans, but Mies would never use them again; the long brick skirt of Minerals and Metals cracked at the column lines because of differential movement of the brick, which was locked to the steel behind. Mies would later adopt a campus standard for brick infill of no more than a twelve-foot width (with notable exceptions).[6] Other key ideas from the campus plans were dropped before Minerals and Metals and never employed—chief among them the open ground floor supported on *pilotis* and the special glass banding and distinctive brick wrapping the narrow ends of long, curtain-walled buildings.

The elevations of Minerals and Metals are an expression of the plan. Because the Flemish bond of the brick skirt and end-wall infill is used to interlock the two brick wythes, in Mies's understanding it too is "objective." (Later campus buildings employ the visually richer—and slightly more expensive—English bond, for the same objective reason.) And in a design decision that would carry through all of Mies's IIT steel buildings, he elected to paint the exposed steel "Detroit Graphite black," a product developed by the Detroit Graphite Company as far back as the late nineteenth century for painting railroad cars, bridges, and ships. The primary pigment was pure graphite, and shortly after application the paint took on a slightly chalky, highly stable nonreflective surface. Although Mies did consider colors other than black for campus buildings and his later commercial buildings in steel, it is likely that in addition to selecting black as representative of steel, he also favored it because almost all buildings in central Chicago in the 1940s were already stained black by the polluted air of the coal-fired metropolis.[7]

Minerals and Metals at its birth was arguably in the vanguard of modernist architecture in the United States. Due to the advent of World War II and the virtual suspension of private construction, it may have had little competition, but it was still an extraordinary debut for the American Mies, not least because it signaled his own professional growth.

.   .   .

Mies began work on a classroom building, at the time called the Metallurgy Building, early in 1942. It was studied in both steel and concrete, where the design remained when suspended in mid-1942. During 1943 he designed two of the eventual three units of the concrete-framed, two-story Engineering Research Building, completed in late 1944. This building is notable for the use of wood-framed windows detailed to look like steel, a material not normally available in wartime. Then in early 1944, the administration asked Mies to begin work on a major building—a key element in his campus plan—with the dual purpose of housing the university library and its administrative and executive offices. It was to be called the Library and Administration Building. Almost at the same time, IIT reauthorized Mies's work on the Metallurgy Building, adding to its program classrooms and labs for chemical engineering. It was renamed the Metallurgy and Chemical Engineering Building, but later became Perlstein Hall.

Both the Library and Administration Building and Perlstein were conceived as steel structures, and as Phyllis Lambert has demonstrated,[8] the two designs were developed "interdependent[ly]." The Library and Administration

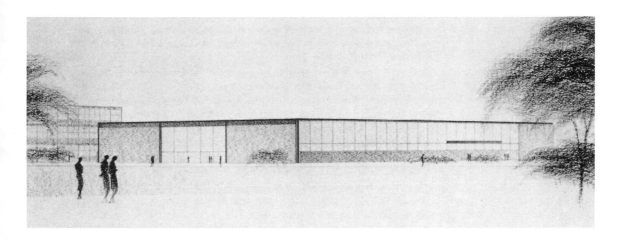

Building was not built, but Perlstein was, completed late in 1947, some eigh-teen months *after* the Navy Building (see below), a classroom building de-signed and built on a "fast track" for the United States military and completed in May 1946. In almost all details, Perlstein was the model for the "earlier" Navy Building.

The Library and Administration Building was an almost fully worked-out design[9] (fig. 8.3). In contrast to the workmanlike Minerals and Metals, Library and Administration was to be, in Mies's terms, a high-status "cultural build-ing." Working with the assistance of staff architect Edward Olencki and a few students,[10] Mies initially gave the project most of a year of his time. He stud-ied proposed steel connections with full-sized, painted-wood models or with full-scale drawings, and he imagined the exterior and interior in innumerable perspective sketches and in presentation drawings (typically prepared by the students). With the experience of Minerals and Metals, and his "discovery" that standard hot-rolled steel could be transmuted into architectural art, Mies now tested and expanded this vocabulary, and for the first time placed it in the service of the symbolic and experiential power of gigantic, undifferentiated space—space appropriate to and representative of the cultural challenge as he conceived it.[11]

The building is nominally of one floor, 24 feet floor to ceiling. A broad, mostly open mezzanine was to house the university's executive offices. Thus, the building was legally permitted to be of single-story, nonfireproof construc-tion, and its steel structure could be exposed inside and out. In plan the build-ing is a single "room" 312 feet long and 192 feet wide, of thirteen 24-foot bays north to south and three 64-foot bays east to west (the latter again in viola-tion of the 24-foot campus module). Counting the mezzanine, the floor area is 73,000 square feet (with additional, low-height floors for book stacks, one of which was below grade), for the time an enormous unitary interior. Mies had already used a 42-foot clear span for the foundry hall of Minerals and Met-

A New Architectural Language

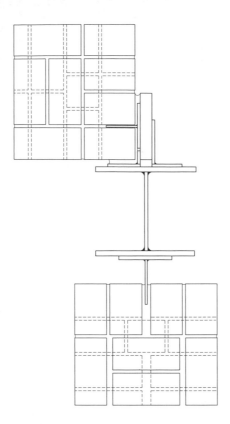

als—forced by the requirements of the moving crane—but for the Library
and Administration Building he proposed a longer, lighter but deeper steel
section, a standard wide flange (often incorrectly called an I-beam) of then-
maximum 36-inch depth. Sections of this size were normally used for bridges
or special conditions in factory buildings, but here, for the first time, Mies employed a major wide flange chiefly for its architectural character. Following his
own model at Minerals and Metals, as well as quoting Perlstein Hall (then in
design), Mies proposed skirt and end infill walls of multi-wythe buff brick. The
exterior was to be more than 50-percent glazed, using the largest plate glass
units then available, roughly 12 by 14 feet. The high, nominally unbraced end
walls called for brick bond of four wythes, a system Mies also proposed for
the 6-foot-high skirt but in five-wythe construction, probably to allow a wide
sill for the glazing above. Building corners, column-to-beam connections, and
inside-the-wall mullions were to be fashioned in novel concatenations of steel
beams, angles, and plate, continuously welded to create plastic forms of evident beauty (fig. 8.4).

The Library and Administration Building was also distinguished by the clear
resolution of its complex program. The reading room and multitiered library
stacks were to occupy roughly the north half of the building. Near the center
was to be a large interior courtyard, glazed on three sides and open to the sky

(Perlstein has a similar, smaller interior court). The university's administrative offices were to occupy most of the south half of the main floor, wrapping the courtyard south, east, and west. Prefiguring the modern, open-plan corporate office, main-floor spaces are partitioned with freestanding, eight-foot-high walls, open to above. At the center of these offices floats the partly cantilevered mezzanine, housing the presidential and vice-presidential offices, a large conference room, and space for administrative staff. Private mezzanine offices were to look down onto the interior court and to the library and reading room beyond. At the main entry, Mies provided a "waiting hall" of over six thousand square feet. The mezzanine, intended as a symbol of administrative authority, was to be accessed by a single floating stair, elegantly beckoning.

Mies studied the interior in fastidious detail. He understood the acoustic challenges of such an enormous, multiuse space, and proposed an expansive acoustical ceiling in spite of the fact that it concealed much of the great steel superstructure. Millwork is suggested for the high-status mezzanine offices. Toilet rooms and other services were to be neatly concealed under a pair of inconspicuous mezzanines flanking the stacks. Below these mezzanines are the reserve book room on one side and study rooms and library offices on the other. (These floors are "expressed" in a floating spandrel on the exterior.) The reading room was to occupy only the two northernmost bays of the building, an area of just over nine thousand square feet. Mies eschewed the traditional focal grandeur of a library reading room; the *entire* program, and not just the reading room, is subsumed in an effectively single grand space.

On matters technical, the Library and Administration Building may have been less successful. Air-conditioning was unavailable, and would be, generally, for more than a decade (IIT would not adopt it until the 1960s). Heat gain from the tremendous expanse of clear glass would have been uncontrollable. The building envelope is uninsulated, though this was standard for the time. Lighting at ceiling elevation would surely have been inadequate. The list can go on. In any event, following its presentation in late 1944, the scheme was roundly criticized by the university librarian, Nell Steel, and by acoustical and mechanical consultants unsympathetic with the design. Mies patiently defended his scheme as functionally and technically complete, but by mid-1945 he had lost momentum and the project was officially "postponed."[12] Over the next two decades, it suffered a slow death.

. . .

With the war still on, IIT was approached in early 1945 to construct a Naval Science Building (later renamed Alumni Memorial Hall). Mies was given a detailed program and a preliminary layout prepared by others, with the charge of producing construction documents by early summer. The design drew heavily

on the plans and details already in hand for Perlstein Hall, and the new building was rushed to completion by May 1946. Under wartime controls, it was allowed to be constructed in steel, which was all but required for an internal clear-span equipment arena specified by the U.S. Navy. Mies again employed brick skirt infill (now with plaster on the interior),[13] this time in twelve-foot runs, with custom steel sash above, identically for the two floors. The two-story classroom construction required fireproofing, and Mies elected to locate the steel wide-flange columns inside the line of the exterior wall, and to encase this "real structure" in concrete. It was then "expressed" on the exterior by mullions fabricated from a combination of smaller wide flanges and steel plate and angles. Panels were infilled in English bond, with shallow, half-brick reveals where brick meets steel. The corner is "turned" by the now iconic assembly of two wide flanges at the column centerlines and an eight-inch angle welded between (figs. 8.5 and 8.6). The exposed steel, both at the corners and along the typical bay, stops short of the ground, where brick is continued to grade. While it has often been observed that the above-grade termination of the exterior steel was a way of "representing" its nonstructural character, it also has a practical explanation: when separated from grade, the steel is less likely to rust.

Photographs of the Navy Building at its completion show it amid mounds of construction rubble and flanked by remaining nineteenth-century urban fabric. In new condition, it was sleek and stunning. The elevations were ordered by the module, the component parts elegantly proportioned. The buff brick

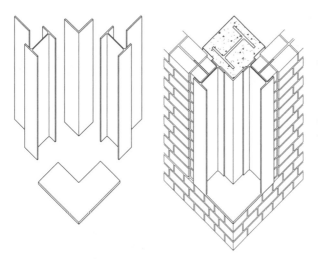

FIGURE 8.6.

Details of the corner of the Navy Building, Illinois Institute of Technology, Chicago (1946). *Left*, exploded view of the standard rolled-steel shapes brought together, by welding, *at right*. The wide-flange section encased in concrete "behind" the corner (*right*) is one of the building's "real" columns.

and black steel framing became canonical, but were then novel. The steel-framed windows were crisply integral with the façade. Building-standard Venetian blinds further organized the exterior.

Perlstein Hall came later, employing the new technology of aluminum-rather than steel-framed windows for the first time on campus. It is programmatically more complex than the Navy Building, with an expressed, clear-span laboratory at one end and conventional offices, classrooms, and an internal auditorium at the other. With the completion of Perlstein, Mies's campus vocabulary was essentially complete (fig. 8.7). Later classroom buildings would add a story, and a few of special type, like the Chapel, the Commons, and Crown Hall, would deviate from the norm. But characteristically for Mies, a problem "solved"—always with great labor and abiding patience—became a solution appropriate to continued reuse, and with these three earliest campus buildings, Mies and IIT had a new tectonic vocabulary and a representational architecture, as Mies would have expressed it, "appropriate to the epoch."

. . .

An early project for a private client was the first of many clear-span solutions that Mies would test on and beyond the IIT campus. In 1945 he received an inquiry from Joseph Cantor, a real estate developer and the prosperous owner of movie houses in Indianapolis, who desired an "amusement building" of "open plan."[14] By early 1946, the project had become a "drive-in" restaurant. In complying with Cantor's request that the building "stand out" along a major commercial strip, Mies proposed a fully glazed, single story plan rectangle with a clear-span roof cantilevered along each long side. The roof was suspended from two powerful trusses set 48 feet apart and spanning 120 feet in the plan's long dimension (fig. 8.8).

FIGURE 8.7.
Wishnick Hall (1946),
originally the Chemistry Building, Illinois
Institute of Technology, Chicago. View
looking northeast,
showing the typical
exterior treatment of
Mies's campus architecture. The twelve-
and twenty-four-foot
module is easily distinguished. Wishnick
received a comprehensive refurbishment and rehabilitation ending in 2010.
Photo taken in 2011.

The project was canceled late in 1950, and is known today mainly in photographs of a model constructed by Edward Duckett, Mies's gifted model maker, which was produced chiefly for display in the 1947 MoMA show. Some two hundred drawings and sketches also survive. All the drawings are by Myron Goldsmith, who was both the project architect and its structural engineer. Several plan variants exist, but the probable "final" scheme is organized on a 12-by-8-foot structural grid, with a 4-foot square for interior planning. The enclosed space is apportioned about two-thirds to restaurant seating and one-third to kitchen and services. The two Pratt trusses leap across ten 12-foot modules, with one truss panel fully outside the envelope for 12 feet at the kitchen end, which was to face the highway. The conventionally steel-framed roof is cantilevered 16 feet on the long sides, no doubt with the benefit of sheltering a single row of cars, though the site plan shows parking for a total of 175 cars, all but thirty in conventional aisles removed from the building. Dining room capacity was a surprisingly large three hundred. It is unclear whether Cantor or Mies ever contemplated genuine drive-in curb service, though the large seating capacity in the dining room argues for a traditional walk-in restaurant (fig. 8.9). The various seating layouts show arrays of freestanding partitions symmetrical about the long axis but freely disposed, with

some schemes prefiguring the layout of Crown Hall's interior, still a decade in the future.

Goldsmith carefully studied and sized the ten-foot-tall trusses, their steel columns, and the purlined steel roof, as if the building were headed for construction. Design of the exterior glazing was less advanced, and mechanical systems and details were apparently barely considered, though air-conditioning was noted on the plans. Goldsmith acknowledged that Mies wanted "a big statement" with the trusses, but it is curious that they span the "wrong," long dimension of the building, just as it is unclear why the restaurant needed to be column free (as opposed, for example, to an open plan with widely spaced columns).[15]

. . .

Internationally, the mid- to late 1940s witnessed a sea change in the arts of the West: a revitalization of modernism that would lead to its hegemony. Eclipsed for well over a decade, modernism shone forth again when conditions hostile to it—the Depression and the rise of totalitarianism—were overcome. Two points of view fundamental to modernist thinking were revived: abstraction

A New Architectural Language

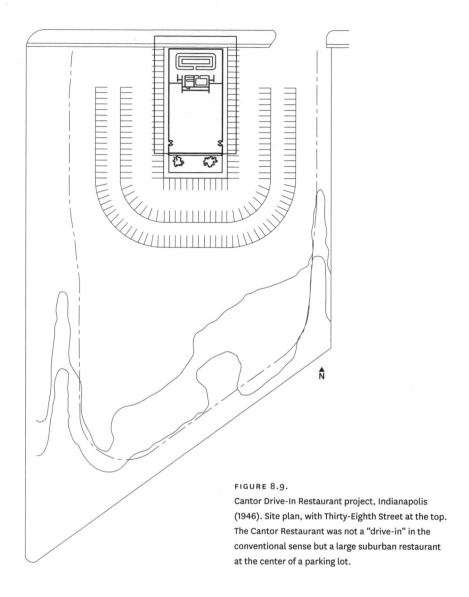

FIGURE 8.9.

Cantor Drive-In Restaurant project, Indianapolis
(1946). Site plan, with Thirty-Eighth Street at the top.
The Cantor Restaurant was not a "drive-in" in the
conventional sense but a large suburban restaurant
at the center of a parking lot.

became the favored expressive language, and internationalist sympathies replaced the nationalisms of the 1930s and 1940s.

There were differences, to be sure. For one thing, the new modernism neither sought nor proclaimed a utopian union of art and politics. The economic
and political cataclysms of the century had convinced all but the most inflexible ideologues that utopia was not possible in the contemporary world. The
United States, the country where the modernist revival most firmly took hold,
was mostly indifferent to political ideologizing. Both tradition and military triumph saw to that. The Americans in their now-dominant world position were
not interested in political lessons from the Europeans, but they were eager
to learn about art from the many first-generation European modernists who

fled to the United States to escape the war. These refugees—Mies and Gropius, Piet Mondrian, Thomas Mann, and Arnold Schönberg, to name but a few in the arts—were received by their American hosts with hospitality bordering on reverence.

This set of circumstances was ideally suited to Mies, and he to it. He was an abstractionist, with no national sympathies and no political ideology, a perfect Prometheus of the new modernism. Just as naturalism in painting was increasingly perceived as a superficial, leftover cosmetic of history that concealed the body and bone of art, its equivalent in architecture—ornament or composition identified with any historical period—was regarded as a disguise. Mies was now in a position to put that conviction to work. For if the *Zeitgeist* was technology, then steel-and-glass construction was the appropriate form of modern building for the modern city, especially the modern American city. Since this conclusion was arrived at "rationally," there was no room for caprice or for "self-expression" in an architecture properly practiced. "Architecture," Mies would declare over and over, "is not a cocktail." And even if one sensed arbitrariness in his characterization of what is "rational," it was difficult to argue the point in the sight of those walls at IIT, which *looked* so incontrovertible in their tectonic logic. Paradoxically, though, they looked that way because they were given form by an unimpeachable *artistic* sensibility.

The 1940s

9

But this note is to say that I wouldn't want to hurt your feelings—even with the truth. You are the best of them all as an artist and a man.
FRANK LLOYD WRIGHT, in a 1947 letter to Mies

He was invariably courteous, in his own monosyllabic way, yet he trod roughshod over any involvements—emotional or otherwise—that might interfere with his priorities.
KATHARINE KUH, on Mies's way with people, especially women

Mies met Lora Marx on New Year's Eve 1940 at a party in Chicago hosted by Charles and Margrette Dornbusch[1] (fig. 9.1). A willowy beauty recently divorced from Chicago society architect and art collector Samuel Marx, Lora showed up in the company of one of Mies's German-speaking friends, the architect Helmut Bartsch, who had asked her if she minded a third in their party. The third was Mies. As to what followed, we have the testimony of Lora and her friend, the gallerist Katharine Kuh, both of whom agreed that Lora and Mies were drawn to each other suddenly and electrically. "Love at first sight," Lora's view, was corroborated by Kuh's recollection of an "absolutely beautiful" Lora and an unmistakably smitten Mies.[2]

Mies waited a week and then phoned Lora.[3] Thus began a relationship that lasted, with one significant interruption, from then until Mies's death. Lora was the antithesis of Lilly Reich, comely, serene, and yielding, a sculptress but hardly an artist as accomplished as Reich. Fourteen years younger than Mies,[4] Lora also proved to be a woman he could tolerate having around for a long time. Like Reich, she maintained a separate residence for all the years she was close to him, and she put up with his occasional peccadilloes. She played no role in his professional life, either as inspiration or irritant, and cared for him selflessly into his pain-filled old age.

Mies and Lora seized the day. It was the 1940s, the most boisterous period of their romance, and by consensus of all associated with Mies, a decade awash in booze. For a while it was because of the war, and later because of the victory. Mies and Lora drank; his students drank; the architects and artists, Americans and Europeans, residents and visitors and friends. Once Mies and Lora, partying with the architect Alfred Shaw and his wife, Rue, all of them besotted, pooled the ladies' lipsticks and reworked the face and form of a marble nymph in the lobby of the Blackstone Hotel. Hans Richter and the gal-

232 / 233232 / 233

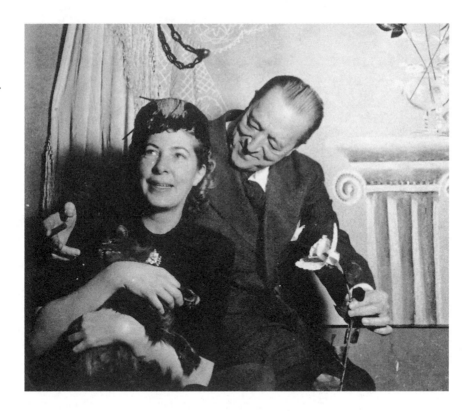

lerist Curt Valentin showed up in Chicago one night and stayed long enough at Lora's for Valentin to tumble down a flight of stairs dead drunk.[5] Faculty and students mixed at parties, often far into the night. The most famous such occasion came later, in the mid-fifties, when Mies and students and members of his staff descended on a splendid old Highland Park mansion where one of their number, Peter Roesch, was living and looking after the place. The group staged a twelve-hour candlelight party that lasted until dawn.[6]

Lora helped Mies find his apartment at 200 East Pearson Street (fig. 9.2). It was big enough for a guest, though except for his daughters, who first arrived in the late 1940s, Mies usually had the place to himself. His universe was mostly within a few miles, and he traveled by cab; later, when he became less mobile, a student or someone from his office would take him around. He acquired his first automobile—a yellow Oldsmobile—as late as the 1950s. Lora drove it; Mies neither learned nor tried. He had no interest in making his apartment an architectural showcase, though he did go to the trouble to have all the walls painted white (fig. 9.3). In 1941 he installed shelves supported on concealed steel brackets cantilevered from either side of the wall that separated his bedroom from the living room. They were fourteen feet long and nineteen inches deep, with a *verde issorie* top for the living room and travertine for the bedroom.[7] He also had a modest custom table and some MR Chairs, but nothing as glamorous as a Barcelona chair.[8]

N

FIGURE 9.2.
Plan of Mies's apart-
ment (*shaded area*)
at 200 East Pearson
Street, Chicago. The
ten-unit building was
designed by Robert S.
de Golyer, 1916–17.

One day in 1947, Lora realized that she was an alcoholic. She decided to quit, cold turkey. "Mies was fascinated by the fact that I stopped as suddenly as I did, but it didn't affect the quantity of his intake."[9] She sought out Alcoholics Anonymous and attended meetings for years, long enough for Dirk Lohan, who arrived in the early 1960s, to remember her schedule—weekly, on Thursdays. Fearing that she could not stay sober as long as she was with Mies, Lora broke off the relationship. The separation lasted a year. Whatever their troubles, after Mies's death Lora warmly recalled that Mies considered the years from their meeting until 1947 "the best of his life." In those same years, she confessed, "I was hung over most of the time."[10]

Alcohol and cigars were Mies's more constant companions.[11] It is an open question whether he was clinically alcoholic, but evidence against is considerable. At IIT and in his office, he was always the center of attention, but he was never reported by anyone to be impaired. He rose late out of habit, and not, so far as we know, because of drinking. His consumption was always social, though Lora reported that before 1947 "Mies and I rarely quarreled, and only when we both got drunk." Donald Sickler, who worked in his office from 1953 to 1963 and frequently acted as Mies's driver, never saw him drunk, even after what he knew had been a liquid lunch.[12]

It is fair here to mention Mies's lively sociability, especially with students and his professional staff. Though in discussion everything revolved around architecture—and to a lesser extent art or philosophy—Mies was easily ap-

CHAPTER NINE

234 / 235

proachable, and seems to have excluded no one when a group formed for lunch or in some other casual setting. Gene Summers remembers that Mies was a loyal presence when deadlines pushed office hours late into the night. On more than one occasion, he stayed almost until dawn. Naturally, he became a father figure to many of the young men, and the occasional young woman, who worked for him. From his earliest days as Mies's first employee, George Danforth remembered Mies's advice to "skip lunch and buy art," and he followed through.[13]

Something of a cult did grow up around Mies. Danforth reported the typical homage of impressionable student to Olympian master: in imitation of Mies, students sketched with soft leads.[14] They also paid keen attention to the timing of his appearances, so as to be in place and ready at the oddest hour.[15] And there was the inevitable cigar smoking and martini drinking. Students wore jackets and ties, and so did the office staff.[16] It was all serious business, modeled after Mies's own on-the-job demeanor.

. . .

In 1947, the Renaissance Society of the University of Chicago mounted a retrospective of the work of Theo van Doesburg, Mies's associate from the art wars of the 1920s. Recounting the event in *My Love Affair with Modern Art*,[17] Katharine Kuh remembers Mies's approach to design and his attitude toward women:

> Mies asked me to pick him up at his office on South Wabash Avenue late one October afternoon in 1947. We were due at a dinner sponsored by the Renaissance Society . . . to celebrate the opening of a Theo van Doesburg exhibition. Because of his affection for both van Doesburg and his widow, Nelli, who had come from Europe for the occasion, Mies had agreed to design the installation, which reaffirmed his credo of "Less is more." Relying solely on a harmonious spatial balance to set off and integrate van Doesburg's clean, Constructivist compositions, he confessed that the most time-consuming part of the job had been adjusting the labels. . . .
>
> After a rather prolonged cocktail hour, the president of the Renaissance Society asked Mies if he knew what was delaying Nelli van Doesburg, since the dinner in her honor couldn't start without her. Mies was thunderstruck. "*Mein Gott*," he said. "I forgot her!" The poor lady was waiting in his apartment on the North Side, where she was staying and where he had neglected to tell me to pick her up. He was almost sadistically amused by the episode. Nelli, in a fetching black dress cut low in front, eventually arrived via taxi and found herself at the head of a long table with Mies beside her. She addressed no word, not even a nod, to him.

Later, en route to Mies's apartment, their silence was palpable, quivering on her part with unsaid accusations. Mies, who regardless of any situation, never seemed worried by guilt or personal incidents, finally suggested, tongue in cheek, that I "chaperone" their reconciliation over a nightcap and thus help restore Nelli's equanimity. He always mellowed over his own excellent whiskey, and she, when not upset, was an entertaining, exuberant companion and a woman of considerable determination, but no match for him. Indeed, few women were, perhaps because of the unattainable attraction he was for them. He was invariably courteous, in his own monosyllabic way, yet he trod roughshod over any involvements—emotional or otherwise—that might interfere with his priorities.[18]

Kuh's recollection of "excellent whiskey" is one more confirmation of Mies's hospitality, notably to European émigrés like himself. During a Max Beckmann exhibition at the Art Institute of Chicago in the winter of 1948, the artist was Mies's guest of honor at a party attended by a number of the city's cultural leaders. A day later, Beckmann dined at Pearson Street, closing the evening with Mies, Walter Peterhans, and several others in the warmth of a striptease bar on North Clark Street. Richard Neutra appeared in town, and the brothers Naum Gabo and Antoine Pevsner. And always the bottle tilted.

But these shows of friendship were matched by the disaffection Mies bore toward László Moholy-Nagy, who had also immigrated, indeed to Chicago, where in 1937 he opened a school that he called the New Bauhaus. As the last director of the German Bauhaus, Mies knew that the name legally belonged to him, and he resented what he regarded as Moholy's usurpation.

Mies may have been better off without the name. The Bauhaus, even in the United States, seemed cursed to a short life because of the endless animosities among its protagonists. Excepting friendships with Hugo Weber, the designer Konrad Wachsmann, and the photographers Aaron Siskind and Harry Callahan, as well as occasional attendance at the lecture-appearances of Buckminster Fuller, Mies turned a cold shoulder to Moholy and his school, even when it was reorganized under the name Institute of Design (called ID). Mies did not change his mind after Moholy's death in 1946, when Serge Chermayeff became director. In the words of George Danforth: "Chermayeff wanted to establish another architecture department. It made Mies really hit the top in a way that I never saw him blow up before when he found out that Chermayeff was doing projects under some title ["shelter design"] which was really architecture."[19] In 1952 ID was officially incorporated into IIT, but there was still no peace among the bumptious ID staff, which broke into open rebellion following policy and personnel changes rung in by a new director, Jay Doblin, in the mid-1950s. The school found itself, literally and figuratively, in the basement of the new architecture school, Crown Hall, in 1956.

In 1947 the Museum of Modern Art staged a full-scale retrospective of Mies's work that brought him to the attention of the wider public for the first time.[20] Again he had Philip Johnson to thank; the exhibition was Johnson's idea. Following World War II and service in the army, Johnson returned to the museum. There, in alliance with Alfred Barr—and energized by ambition and the application of his own considerable charm—he managed to assume uncontested leadership of the Department of Architecture. Early in 1946, he decided to mount a major exhibition on Mies. The decision was audacious: Mies had been in the United States less than a decade, much of it clouded by war, and only a couple of his American buildings had been completed. The show covered his whole career, and Johnson wrote the accompanying monograph, the first on Mies.[21] Research was made more difficult, because most of Mies's personal and professional papers were still in Germany, and worse still, in the Soviet sector. During the war, the drawings and records Mies had left in Berlin had been packed by Lilly Reich and Mies's Bauhaus student Eduard Ludwig and shipped for safekeeping to Ludwig's parents in Mühlhausen, Thuringia, which later became part of the GDR. For practical purposes, then, they were irretrievable (but see below for the 1963 repatriation of this material).

Undeterred, Johnson consulted everything in print, debriefed Mies's professional staff in Chicago, and queried Mies himself, whose cooperation was not always assured. By December 20, 1946, Johnson was confident enough to promise Mies "the most important exhibition the department has ever held."[22] He secured a generous budget and more space—some five thousand square feet—than the museum had allocated to any previous architecture show. Johnson was even successful in persuading Mies to design the exhibition—as he was unable to do for the international modern architecture exhibition of 1932—though at the predictable price of wheedling and cajoling Mies into observing deadlines he sometimes ignored. Some of what went on between the two can be gleaned from a 1985 Johnson interview:

> I remember [Mies] called me once from Chicago—a very unlikely event in those days. He said, "Will you tell me if those columns in the Museum have chamfers at the corners?" I said, "No." Mies said, "Well, that's fine because we won't have to have anything but the columns. Leave them." Then he came here and, of course, he held it against me all the rest of his life.... We had to sheetrock all the corners. Or plaster in those days.[23]

The installation was worth the effort. Mies created an effectively column-free space by screening the four gallery columns behind monumental floor-to-ceiling photomurals. The murals acted as walls, organized in a pinwheel composition that recalled his European open plans (fig. 9.4). The show consisted

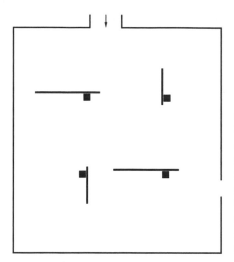

FIGURE 9.4.

Schematic plan of the exhibition *Mies van der Rohe* at the Museum of Modern Art, New York (1947). Exhibition design by Mies. The allotted area, about five thousand square feet, was the largest MoMA had given to an architectural topic up to that time. Characteristically, and with minimal means, Mies was able to create a dynamic plan in an otherwise undistinguished, windowless space.

of drawings, photographs, and presentation models purpose-made by Mies's staff. They ranged from the Kröller-Müller House project of 1912 through the best-known built and unbuilt designs of the 1920s, to projects and buildings in progress from the mid-1940s, including the Farnsworth House, the Cantor Drive-In Restaurant, and buildings from IIT. A full-sized model of a wall section of the Library and Administration project stood in one of the corners. Furniture was also displayed, together with drawings of a so-called conchoidal chair from the early 1940s, a body-fitting, curvilinear form intended to be made from plastic. The exhibition's graphics were designed by none other than Gerhard Severain, Mies's childhood friend, who had remained in Germany.

Johnson's wide-ranging text cited the influence of Karl Friedrich Schinkel and Peter Behrens on Mies, whose career he systematically traced to the years before World War I. "Mies considers the Riehl house too uncharacteristic to publish," wrote Johnson, who added, insistently: "Designed in the then popular traditional eighteenth-century style with steep roofs, gables and dormer windows, it was distinguished from its contemporaries only by fine proportions and careful execution."[24]

If this last remark conveyed Johnson's opinion of a single work, another passage, offered as fact applicable to more than a few of Mies's designs, was inaccurate. Because the catalog was the first full treatment of the architect's career in any language, and published by the highly respected Museum of Modern Art, Johnson's text was for decades widely regarded as authoritative in filling significant lacunae in Mies's oeuvre of the 1930s. "From 1931 to 1938," Johnson wrote, "Mies developed a series of projects for 'court-houses' ... in which the flow of space is confined within a single rectangle formed by the outside walls of court and house conjoined. The houses themselves are shaped variously as L's, T's or I's and their exterior walls, except those forming part of the outside rectangle, are all of glass."[25]

In a 2001 essay titled "From Bauhaus to Court-House," Terence Riley examines Johnson's claim in detail and concludes that ten drawings of "courthouses" were misinterpreted: "Three are misidentified sketches for other projects; three are drawings made by IIT students, and related, most likely, to the work of Mies's students at the Bauhaus; three are drawings made by IIT students and based on earlier projects, unidentified or of unclear origin, by Mies; and one is a project developed by a number of Mies's students at IIT."[26] Though not disputing Mies's central role in developing the court-house idea, which is evident especially in his sketches for the Hubbe House project of 1935, Riley shows that the idea had served principally as an exercise Mies gave his students. Johnson's mistake may be partly attributable to the aforementioned limits of his research and Mies's occasional lack of cooperation in conversation.

Yet there is a postscript, illuminating Johnson's ever-mercurial disposition. At about the time he conceived the show, early in 1946, a new fascination with symbolic and monumental architecture, especially that of French neoclassicist Claude-Nicolas Ledoux, had begun to intrude on his commitment to Mies and modernism. In April Johnson wrote to J. J. P. Oud: "Most architects and critics think that Mies's slogan of '*beinahe nichts*' [almost nothing] has gone so far that there is really *nichts*. I don't know.... History will tell us and tell us no doubt very soon."[27]

History did just that, in a way that justified Johnson's effort if not his doubts. Reaction to the exhibition was decisively affirmative. *New York Times* critic Edwin Alden Jewell was full of praise, especially for the installation's "breathtaking largeness of effect."[28] Writing in *Arts and Architecture*, a rising star of American design, Charles Eames, acknowledged Mies's achievement but, like Jewell, focused on the uncommon merits of the installation design: "Certainly it is the experience of walking through that space and seeing others move in it that is the high point of the exhibition."[29]

Even Wright materialized at the opening. The act signified homage, though he did what he could to make himself cynosure and chief critic. He strode into the gallery late, cape flowing, and quickly and publicly delivered himself of a criticism of Mies that is best related, together with Mies's response to it, in the exchange of letters that later passed between them:

My dear Mies:

    Somebody has told me you were hurt by remarks of mine when I came to see your New York show.... But did I tell you how fine I thought your handling of your materials was?

    ... You know you have frequently said you believe in doing "next to nothing" [*beinahe nichts*] all down the line. Well, when I saw the enormous blow-ups the phrase [*sic*] "Much ado about 'next to nothing'" came spontaneously from me.

Then I said the Barcelona Pavilion was your best contribution to the original "Negation" and you seemed to be still back there where I was then.

This is probably what hurt (coming from me) and I wish I had taken you aside to say it to you privately because it does seem to me that the whole thing called "Modern Architecture" has bogged down with the architects right there on that line. I didn't want to classify you with them—but the show struck me sharply as reactionary in that sense. I am fighting hard against it myself.

But this note is to say that I wouldn't want to hurt your feelings—even with the truth. You are the best of them all as an artist and a man.

You came to see me but once (and that was before you spoke English) many years ago. You never came since, though often invited.

So I have no chance to see or say what I said then and say now.

Why don't you come up sometime—unless the break is irreparable—and let's argue.

Sincerely, Frank[30]

Mies replied:

My dear Frank:

Thank you so much for your letter.

It was an exaggeration if you heard that my feelings were hurt by your remarks at my New York show. If I had heard the crack "Much ado about next-to-nothing" I would have laughed with you. About "Negation"—I feel that you use the word for qualities that I find positive and essential.

It would be a pleasure to see you again sometime in Wisconsin and discuss this subject further.

As ever, Mies[31]

The two personalities are captured in their brief lines: Wright alternately warm and aggressive in criticism, fellowship, and above all vanity; Mies inclined to modesty, distance, and privacy. Mies counterpunched only once ("qualities that I find positive and essential"), though that was enough to stake a position. The mutual esteem was genuine; Wright would never have invited anyone else to Taliesin more than twice who failed to show up more than once, and Mies would scarcely have bothered to answer and make light of anyone else's reproach. Yet the signals of eventual separation are evident. Wright recognized Mies as the best practitioner of modern architecture, but wanted no part of the movement, admitting his own struggle "hard against it." Within a few years, the two men passed the point where either heard the other.

During the run-up to the 1947 MoMA exhibition, Mies was in New York often enough to renew ties with the museum crowd. He socialized with the curator and critic James Johnson Sweeney, whom he had met in Berlin in 1933.

FIGURE 9.5.

Georgia van der Rohe (born Dorothea Mies), circa 1945. Photo: Hildegard Steinmetz.

A decade later, Sweeney would tender Mies the commission for an expansion to the Houston Museum of Art (which Sweeney would head). And Johnson introduced him to the sculptress Mary Callery, an alluring woman who was on Mies's arm at the exhibition opening. A mostly long-distance dalliance followed that lasted more than a decade, but required nothing serious from either party.[32]

· · ·

Postwar life in Germany underscored Mies's good fortune in having made Chicago his home. Ada had suffered through most of World War II in Berlin. There, in the worst of times, the best of her spirit emerged. She concealed several Jews in her small apartment in the Bayerischestrasse, most notably a Dr. Levy and his wife. In an effort to find their way to what they hoped would be security in Switzerland, they were met in Munich by Waltraut, who escorted them to the border. After two attempts at crossing failed, they were apprehended by the Nazis and are believed to have perished.[33]

In 1942 the Allied air forces stepped up their raids on Berlin, and Ada managed to remove her possessions from her apartment only days before it was destroyed. That same year Georgia (fig. 9.5), already a rising young actress in the local Regensburg troupe, married the director of the *Stadttheater* there, Fritz Herterich. They had a child, Frank, born November 1943. By then Ada, having lived for a time with friends in Berlin, had joined them in Regensburg.

Marianne, together with her seven-year-old son, Dirk, and daughters, Ulrike and Karin, was forced to flee Rathenow early in 1945, when bombing

FIGURE 9.6.
Mies's middle daughter, Marianne, in 1935 at age twenty. Photo by Greta Bruhn, the sister of Marianne's mother, Ada. Photo courtesy of Dirk Lohan. Used by permission.

leveled the town. Dirk was able to save only his teddy bear. Several months later, with the war ended, they were in Halle in the Soviet zone. A series of anxious moves followed, in the course of which Wolfgang Lohan, freed from prisoner-of-war camp, succeeded in bringing his family west to Salem, where he secured a teaching position at the *Gymnasium*. By 1951 they were settled in nearby Freiburg. Waltraut meanwhile matriculated at the Ludwig-Maximilian University in Munich, and amid the grim circumstances of the time completed a doctorate in art history in 1946.

In Germany the later 1940s were a desperate time. The country was a physical and spiritual wasteland at the mercy of its conquerors, who contended against one another more, and more portentously, than in 1919. The arts failed to revive as they had after World War I. For a time, Marianne (fig. 9.6) helped support her family by making dolls and exchanging them for American cigarettes. Georgia worked for Amerika Haus and the public relations office of the US military government, shuttling between Munich and Regensburg. Following the destruction of her studio in 1943, Lilly Reich moved to Saxony but returned to Berlin once the war was over. Resuming her letters to Mies, she asked him to send anything that might help her equip her atelier—paper, ink, the simplest tools.[34]

Toward the end of 1948, Georgia and Waltraut, with Mies's financial assistance but without an invitation, sailed for the United States and made their way to Chicago. There they encamped in his apartment—in Waltraut's case for the next two years. After eight months of study at the Goodman School of Drama, Georgia returned to Munich, where Ada joined her yet again. Ada's condition had deteriorated, and in 1951 she died of cancer in a Regensburg

hospital. Waltraut stayed in Chicago for good, living with Mies and later alone, working in the library of the Art Institute of Chicago until her death, also of cancer, in 1959 (fig. 9.7). Marianne made a trip to the United States in 1950, spending four months with Mies and Waltraut. She returned to Chicago on several occasions, ministering to Waltraut in 1959 and living by herself from 1963 to 1975 following her divorce from Lohan.

Mies (and Lora) put up with these filial intrusions, but never gladly. Lora reported that friction was frequent between father and daughters, especially when more than one of the women shared his apartment with him. (They slept on couches in Mies's living room.) Mies was a nautilus; he would emerge to survey the world and enjoy his companions, then withdraw from it and them as and when he chose. Yet the metaphor must be qualified: he was not so much lacking in long-standing affection as he was in the ability, even the will, to express it. Waltraut worshipped him and devoted herself endlessly to him. He made little display of affection in return. Yet he was deeply proud of her gifts, evident as early as her graduation summa cum laude from the university in Munich. At her death, he clothed her body in his own academic robes and, following her cremation, drove to Wisconsin with Lora and Georgia. There they dropped her ashes into the Mississippi River. Said Lora: "Mies took Waltraut's death as he took all adversity—stoically, as if it were a fact from which there was, after all, no escape, no consolation."[35]

The 1940s

When Mies returned to Europe for the first time after the war, in 1953, he visited the Lohans in Freiburg. Dirk, then aged fifteen, was already a keen student of his grandfather's work. He was allowed to attend a luncheon with Mies and five or six local architects, and remembers how impressed he was when his grandfather, illustrating a point, casually drew on the tablecloth. For Dirk, a second highlight of the visit was a long ride with his grandfather through the Black Forest, just the two of them and the chauffeur of the elegant Horch automobile.[36]

. . .

During the period when his family and friends were struggling to survive in Germany, Mies was adjusting to changing conditions of a benignly different sort in the United States. The number of architecture students at IIT had dropped to about fifty by war's end, but the return of the armed forces promised a jump in enrollment. In 1945 classes were shifted from the Art Institute to a pair of spaces, one at Thirty-Seven South Wabash Street, where Mies had his own offices, and another at Eighteen South Michigan Avenue. Two years later, the department moved again, taking over most of Alumni Memorial Hall (the former Navy Building) on the IIT campus.

George Danforth rejoined the war-depleted faculty upon his return from service in 1946. By the early 1950s, Daniel Brenner, Jacques Brownson, Alfred Caldwell, William Dunlap, Earl Bluestone, Thomas Burleigh, and Reginald Malcolmson were among Mies's junior faculty. His professional staff also grew: Edward Olencki and Edward Duckett were joined in 1945 by Joseph Fujikawa and John Weese. In 1946 Myron Goldsmith hired on. Mies's business manager was German-born Felix Bonnet, who complained constantly, if justifiably, about the noise and dust of model-making that went on in the passage between Bonnet's desk and the drafting room. A two-year spell in 1946 and 1947 during which the office had little work ended when Herbert Greenwald brought in Promontory Apartments.[37] Thereafter, work was steady, though in the early 1950s, when Mies entered the most creative phase of his American career, his staff never exceeded ten.

Mies had more on his mind than building, though there was now enough of that. In 1951 he had had a grave falling-out with a client. By spring of 1952, the lawsuit he lodged against Edith Farnsworth and her subsequent countersuit precipitated an enervating and costly courtroom battle. Legally at issue was the question of who owed what to whom for the cost of a house Mies designed and built for Farnsworth. The real struggle was over bigger stakes—a clash of personalities of authority and will. The subject of their dispute, the house itself, is Mies's first American masterpiece.

I was famous before. She is now famous throughout the world.
MIES, of Edith Farnsworth, under oath

Mies reminded me of a mediaeval peasant.   **EDITH FARNSWORTH**, of Mies

I think the house is perfectly constructed, it is perfectly executed.
MIES, about the Farnsworth House, under oath

In 1945 Edith Farnsworth, a Chicago physician, purchased nine acres of an old farmstead bordering the Fox River near Plano, Illinois, sixty miles southwest of Chicago.[1] The seller was Colonel Robert R. McCormick, publisher of the *Chicago Tribune*. The sale price was $500 per acre.[2] A farmhouse and several outbuildings stood on the property, but Farnsworth wanted something new. In an unpublished memoir from the 1970s, she recalled her project's beginnings:

> One evening I went to have dinner with Georgia [Lingafelt] and Ruth [Lee][3] in their pleasant old-fashioned apartment in the Irving. Also invited that evening was the massive stranger whom Georgia, with her peculiarly sweet smile, introduced, as I slipped off my coat: "This is Mies, darling."
>
> I suppose he must have formed a few syllables as we had dinner, but if so, I do not remember them. My impression is that the three of us chatted among ourselves around the granite form of Mies. I related in detail, probably too much, the story of finding the property, the dickerings with Col. McCormick and the final acquisition of the nine-acre plot....
>
> All of this came to naught, conversationally speaking, and I concluded that Mies spoke almost no English; how much he understood remained problematical. We moved back to the sitting room after dinner and both Ruth and Georgia disappeared to wash the dishes.

Farnsworth continued, addressing Mies:

> "I am wondering whether there might be some young man in your office who would be willing and disposed to design a small studio weekend-house worthy of that lovely shore."

The response was the more dramatic for having been preceded by two hours of unbroken silence. "I would love to build any kind of house for you." The effect was tremendous, like a storm, a flood or other act of God. We planned a trip to Plano together, so that I could show him the property.... We set out for a day in the country, to inspect the property with a view to the ideal weekend house. It was either late autumn or late winter [of 1944–45] when I stopped at 200 East Pearson to call for Mies, and he came out wearing an enormous black overcoat of some kind of soft, fine wool which reached well down toward his ankles. Installed beside me in the little Chevrolet he put up only feeble resistance to the advances of my white cocker who sprawled across his knees for the duration of the trip.

Finally we reached the dooryard of the farmhouse and I could open the car doors. The emergence of Mies and the cocker was spectacular, as it turned out that the latter had yielded most of his white coat in a soft frosting over the black wool of that splendid overcoat, and we had nothing on board with which to remove it.

We walked down the slope, through the frozen meadow grass and dormant brush, and I worried for fear a European might be unable to see the beauty of the mid-west countryside at so unfavorable a season; but midway down, Mies stopped and looked all around him. "It is beautiful!" he said, and I didn't doubt the spontaneity of his exclamation.[4]

This is the beginning of the tale as remembered by Farnsworth, then in her seventies. Remarkably, we have Mies's quite different version of the same events, offered in 1952 as testimony in the action *Van der Rohe v. Farnsworth*:

Question, to Mies: Will you state what your conversation was with Dr. Farnsworth that evening?

Answer, by Mies: After dinner Dr. Farnsworth said that she had a site in Plano, and she would like to talk with me about a house she had planned there and then we were left alone and we talked about the site. She told me she wanted to build a small house and asked me if I would be interested in doing that. I said normally I don't build small house but I would do it if we could do something interesting.

Q: Did you explain what you meant by "interesting"?

A: No.[5]

Mies added that he learned that before she met him, Farnsworth had asked Chicago architect George Fred Keck to design the house. Keck, said Mies, would undertake the project only on condition that he "can do what he wants, and she didn't seem to like that."[6]

．　．　．

Edith Brooks Farnsworth was born to Chicago wealth in 1903. Her father, George J. Farnsworth, was an executive in lumber companies in Wisconsin and Michigan. As a young adult she studied English literature and composition at the University of Chicago and violin and music theory at Chicago's American Conservatory of Music. Electing to pursue music, she traveled to Italy to study with the violin virtuoso Mario Corti.[7] In time she decided she lacked the talent the instrument demanded, but she learned Italian, an interest she cultivated late in life as a translator of modern Italian poetry.[8]

In the early 1930s, back in Chicago, she turned to medicine. She entered Northwestern University Medical School in 1934, and received her MD degree in 1939. She opened a practice and served on the staff of Passavant Memorial Hospital. With the outbreak of World War II, she took on patients of male physicians who had entered the armed forces, thereby accelerating, by her own acknowledgment, her professional success. She became an accomplished clinician and researcher. Her concentration was nephrology, where she made contributions to the development of the natural hormone ACTH and its synthetic counterpart, cortisone, both effective in the treatment of nephritis. She also wrote papers on hypertension, anemia, and cirrhosis. Despite these accomplishments, Farnsworth is now remembered for the house that bears her name, since what Mies created and she facilitated turned out to be far more "interesting"—to use Mies's term—than either of them could have imagined.

Farnsworth's memoir offers a sometimes intimate account of the early phases of the house and her relationship with its architect:

> We began to see each other from time to time and to make frequent Sunday excursions out to Plano.... As the warm weather came on we had to cut pathways through the weeds and meadow grass down to the shore.... From the bank we studied various sites for the house and drove a few tentative stakes.
>
> "Mies, what building materials were you thinking of for the house?"
>
> "I wouldn't think of the problem quite like that. I wouldn't think, We'll build a brick house or a reinforced concrete house. I would think that here where everything is beautiful, and privacy is no issue, it would be a pity to erect an opaque wall between the outside and the inside. So I think we should build the house of steel and glass; in that way we'll let the outside in. If we were building in the city or in the suburbs, on the other hand, I would make it opaque from outside and bring in the light through a garden-courtyard in the middle."[9]

Farnsworth also explored Mies's personality: "Mies reminded me of a mediaeval peasant, and aspects of his nature which later proved themselves as cruel, during those years seemed simply clumsy. He never showed the trivial courtesies—or the greater ones, for that matter—and it never occurred to him to call a taxi or otherwise facilitate the safe return of any unescorted female visitor."[10] Farnsworth's assessment of Mies is interwoven with an account of her own intellectual cravings:

> There was a certain metaphysical vein which enhanced the standard topic of Mies himself.... I read Guardini, as he urged, and tried to lend myself to the concept of *liturgy* as an element in the "hierarchy of values," or a mystic dimension of religion, or a sitting-up exercise in the hygiene of the soul—as almost anything which might enrich my own awareness, presumably by showing me how Mies had been enriched....
>
> At this stage in our relationship I took it for granted that our views on all such matters were the same. The impression was heightened by the discussions we had after Mies had read [Erwin] Schrödinger's book, *What is Life?* I lent him that disciplined, lucid treatise by an eminent physicist, thinking that whatever might be his metaphysical views, he could only admire a kind of heroic abstemiousness in Schrödinger's reduction of life to observable crystals, organic or inorganic....
>
> "Don't you approve of the Schrödinger book, Mies?"
>
> "It is unspiritual. What about man and his hopes for immortality? Does Schrödinger think that I can sit staring at the snowflakes on the window or the salt crystals on the dinner table and be satisfied? I want to know what I have to expect after death."
>
> "Probably Schrödinger does too, but writing as a physicist and deleting the questions of the natural longings of human beings for a hereafter, he still offers to man the very considerable dignity of the observer of life. We don't have to sit and get rained on—"
>
> "That's not enough!"
>
> I was struck with the force of Mies's preoccupation with death and it lent a mystic context even to the project of the house by the river, and an indefinable dimension to the personality of Mies.[11]

In his testimony, Mies reported conversations about the possibilities of a house of brick or stone, and recalled a site visit during which he proposed an all-glass solution:

> I remember on one trip we were discussing the house, how it should be, and she asked me if I had ideas about it and after looking around in the different directions for the views possible I said "if I would be to build here for myself I think I would build in glass because all the views are so beautiful that it is hard to decide which view should be preferred."[12]

Mies decided to locate the new house squarely *in* the floodplain of the river, just a few feet from its banks, even though there was higher ground elsewhere on the property. He testified:

> We discussed the advantages and disadvantages of both places and I proposed to Dr. Farnsworth to build close to the river where there were beautiful old trees. She was afraid that the river would go over the bank, but I still stuck to this place because I thought that [the problems could] be overcome in one way or the other.[13]

He produced, by his own hand (as he testified), [14] not a series of exploratory pencil sketches—his usual manner—but a watercolor, an elevation view of a one-room building of steel and glass elevated on widely spaced piers. The interior included an asymmetrically placed service core, one element of which was a floor-to-ceiling drum, a comfortable chair, and a single, low table. Except for the drum, the house would be built essentially as depicted, down to the size of the columns and the thickness of the floor and roof—though at this stage the screened porch was a vague stub with a single stair at its far end. Mies described this earliest design:[15]

> It was in principle a similar construction as we have now, only we did not think of it in the high classification as it is now.... Then we were talking about a steel construction, not welded, but bolted and on a more simple house—we were thinking even if we could do a lot of the work with the students on it.... [And] at this time we were thinking about a concrete floor, [and plywood for the core].[16]

Mies requested information from the Illinois State Water Survey concerning the highest flood stages of the Fox River. Informed that such records were not kept, he was advised to "interview old settlers in that vicinity."[17] He decided to set the top of finished floor five feet above grade, two feet higher than the highest stage reported by old-timers.[18]

Design and construction of the Farnsworth House is dated in the literature 1946–51, a long time even for a special house. But according to Myron Goldsmith, project architect and structural engineer for the house, between 1946, when the design was conceived, and early 1949, when work on the construction documents commenced, nothing much was accomplished. Unbeknownst to Goldsmith, Mies was the major factor in this delay. It was he, and not so much Farnsworth, who was concerned about costs. He testified:

> *Question, to Mies*: In 1946 did you draw any plans for this house, you or your office?

> *Answer*: No, I don't think we did.... I was against building then because of the uncertainty in the construction market.... It was difficult to get real cal-

FIGURE 10.1 (*facing*).

Edith Farnsworth consulting with My- ron Goldsmith in the Mies office in 1950. Goldsmith and Farns- worth are examining a hardware catalog. This photograph, taken with a Brownie camera by Edward Duckett, was placed into evidence at the *Van der Rohe* [sic] *v. Farnsworth* hear- ing. It contradicted Farnsworth's con- tention that she had not been informed of many features of the house. Note Gold- smith's white coat, typical of those worn in the Mies office to protect street clothes from graphite dust.

culated prices from any contractors.... They guessed more than they really figured out, or put too high a safety factor in it.[19]

Goldsmith, in a narrative prepared at the request of Mies's attorneys, contin- ued the chronology:

> I came to work for Mies the first part of May 1946.... I saw a sketch Mies had made [the watercolor described above].
>
> At about the end of May 1946, I worked on the house for about three weeks. I made some calculations for the structure and worked on various methods of constructing the house. At this time we had in mind a relatively primitive construction.... I made a rough estimate [for the cost of construction] which amounted to about $40,000–45,000....
>
> I dropped the house and did not do any more on it until 1949. During the interim the only work done on it was in connection with the 1947 exhibition at the Museum of Modern Art. [Alfred] Caldwell worked several weeks on it [as a freelancer] in the summer of 1947. When we took up the work in 1949, we pretty much started from scratch.... I devoted almost my full time to it until April 1951.[20]

It was during 1949–51, then, that Mies's concept evolved into an all-welded structure with high-quality interior features. Much of his office (then num- bering four or five) worked on design development, building full-sized mod- els of structural elements and five different models of the entire house. Gold- smith: "It was a thing in which he was interested because he had full control over it.... It was understood that it would be built as beautifully as it could be done." Goldsmith assembled a time sheet summarizing the project, for which the office charged an astonishing 5,884 hours—three man-years—not counting weekends at the site, some of which were recreation, but many of them work.[21] Not included in Goldsmith's tabulation was Mies's labor, which was never tracked. Goldsmith made about one hundred trips to the site in the course of the work,[22] usually by train to and from Plano, then hitchhiking or walking the two miles back and forth from town[23] (fig. 10.1).

In the spring of 1949, Farnsworth received an inheritance of $18,000, which moved Mies to acquiesce in proceeding with the detailed design. Of conse- quence in the decision was another house, designed by Philip Johnson for himself and finished in New Canaan, Connecticut, in 1949. Johnson had been inspired by the Farnsworth concept, which he knew from the 1947 MoMA exhi- bition and from visits to Mies's office in Chicago, where a model of the house sat on Mies's desk.

Mies's notes record this decision:

> Dr. Farnsworth was eager to proceed with construction and in the winter of 1948 and spring of 1949 pushed me very hard.

In the spring of 1949 Philip Johnson told me that his house, which was of similar type and size, would cost him about $60,000.

I told this fact to Dr. Farnsworth and made it clear that I thought we could not build the house for less than $50,000.

She informed me that her assets were $65,000 but that she did not want to spend it all for [security] reasons. Later she told me that she had inherited $18,000 and now we could build the house as we would want to build it.

Early in June 1949 Mr. Goldsmith made estimates of houses of various sizes in order to set a size for the working drawings.[24]

Goldsmith made cost estimates for houses of three sizes: 84 by 30 by 10 feet, at $69,250; 77 by 28 by 9 feet, at $59,980; and 77 by 28 by 10 feet, at

$60,980. Agreement was reached for a scheme measuring 77 by 28 by 9½ feet, by which Mies hoped to limit the cost to around $60,000—roughly equal to Johnson's outlay.

Not surprisingly for so unconventional a house, Mies failed to interest local contractors in the project, and decided to assume the role of general contractor himself. His office sourced and paid for materials and labor and prepared detailed monthly statements of the outlays. The decision to replace a bolted with a welded steel frame had already been made, but in Goldsmith's words, "the floor had been the basis of much discussion and I got samples of many alternate materials. We had limestone, bluestone, marble, tile, precast concrete slabs, etc.... Mies liked travertine, not only for its appearance but because it was a good material for the purpose.... Dr. Farnsworth finally decided to use travertine and later I remember how pleased she was that she made that decision."[25]

These observations reflect the still cordial relationship of architect and client in the summer of 1949. The cost estimate had risen to $65,000, but the added expense, reflected in the selection of the most desirable materials for the core walls and the floor, seemed justified and understood.

Farnsworth had reached her own high tide: "For me the summer was marvelous because it fulfilled my ideal that persons trained in different fields of the arts and sciences should seek to understand the ideals and principles common to all fields of advancement and to lend their loyalty and support."[26] Mies's feelings about moving forward—characteristically muted—are captured in his testimony about the decision:

> Question, to Mies: All right ... you said that she said "is it not wonderful I have inherited some money, now we can go on and we can build the house as good as we want"?—and did you make any response to that, or did she say anything further on that subject, or about the house?
>
> Answer: No, I was as pleased as she was.
>
> Q. Did you say so?
>
> A. She could see that, yes.[27]

. . .

We have drawn on the trial transcript in advance of discussing the litigation in detail because the testimony is so richly illuminating. But we are still speculating as to how matters deteriorated. Goldsmith, next to Mies closest to Farnsworth, never completely understood what went wrong; nor, because witnesses were barred from sitting in court, did he ever hear the testimony that might have enlightened him.

Some of Farnsworth's distress was surely due to the rising cost of the house, which would climb to $74,000, well above the $60,000 Mies had set for himself at the start of detailed design. Then there was the matter of a fee for Mies's services, and a possible separate charge for his work as general contractor. Here their relationship was anything but comfortable; there was no discussion at all. Mies sent monthly statements of outlays for materials and construction labor, but never invoiced for fees. Goldsmith, well aware of Farnsworth's concerns about the budget, carefully monitored costs. That Farnsworth expected that bad news as well as good would come directly from Mies was also pivotal; Goldsmith recounted that near the end of construction, price spikes caused by mobilization for the Korean War pushed up electrical costs by "several thousand dollars." "I went to Mies and said, 'Mies, this is what has happened, it's terrible news. How shall we tell Dr. Farnsworth?' I don't know why he said it but he said, 'Goldy [Goldsmith's nickname], you tell her.' I don't know if already their relationship was in trouble.... I called her and told her. I remember she said, 'Why didn't Mies tell me?' She thought he had deceived her ... she suspected the worst."[28]

Goldsmith singled out another contentious issue—the selection of draperies. Mies had proposed Shantung natural silk. Samples were ordered and mock-ups prepared, along with other fabrics suggested by Farnsworth. She finally accepted Mies's recommendation, but not before offending him by seeking advice from another architect. Goldsmith: "She said something like 'I don't like the Shantung natural silk color. I discussed it with Harry Weese and he thought it should be brown.' I don't know if I reported this to Mies or how he knew. He said: 'If I would have known that she would be so difficult I would never have touched the house,' something like that. That was his background."[29]

If this much is known, a key detail is not—the nature of the personal relationship between Farnsworth and Mies. The spectacle was fascinating: two distinguished professionals, both single, socializing and working so closely together as to suggest—what? A dalliance? A romance? And what of Lora Marx, steering clear of Mies and alcohol in 1947, as reported, or of Mary Callery in New York, who that same year accompanied Mies at the opening of his MoMA retrospective, which Farnsworth also attended? It was fertile ground for rumors and fetching speculation. Lora Marx, speaking with one of us in 1980, claimed that "there was a short 'little thing' between them but no real affair—strictly professional."[30] But Marx was hardly disinterested. The hostility that developed between Farnsworth and Mies may have grown from the disappointments of mutual emotional involvement, or from intellectual and professional rivalry. We know that as the project neared completion, Farnsworth increasingly pressed her demands, especially about interior appointments that were still to be decided on.

A dramatic new element in this debate is information contained within the 3,500 pages of the trial transcript *Van der Rohe v. Farnsworth*, which we have recovered and analyzed for the first time.[31] The new material makes it clear that the Mies-Farnsworth relationship was in serious trouble long before the last stages of construction, when the breach was palpable to all. The following testimony covers what at first appear to be trivial topics from the period when construction was just beginning. Farnsworth's attorney, Randolph Bohrer, is questioning:

> *Question, to Mies*: Didn't Dr. Farnsworth tell you at your apartment at the time that they were preparing to get materials for the footings of the building, in which she told you she was out to Plano, and she heard a conversation between Mr. Freund and Mr. Goldsmith; and Mr. Freund[32] wanted to use local gravel [to build a temporary road into the site], and Mr. Goldsmith wanted to use crushed limestone; and that she was quite perturbed about it, because Mr. Freund said the limestone was far more expensive after it was hauled a long distance, and gravel was available at a nominal cost, and it could be obtained locally? Do you recall a conversation in which something like that was talked about?
>
> *A. by Mies*: Yes, but it was in Plano.
>
> *Q.* What was this conversation?
>
> *A.* As I recall, Mr. Goldsmith would have preferred a gravel—not gravel, crushed stone—he was discussing with Freund if he could get it, and Freund said it was far away, and he doesn't know if he can get it, and then they decided to use gravel.
>
> *Q.* And you had no discussion with Dr. Farnsworth about this?
>
> *A.* I think that Dr. Farnsworth said, "I don't know why they talk so much about that."
>
> *Q.* And you don't remember Dr. Farnsworth saying that she wished you wouldn't have him out on the job? That is, Goldsmith.
>
> *A.* No.
>
> *Q.* That she thought he might be incompetent?
>
> *A.* No, that was another discussion in my apartment one evening. . . . That was quite early. I think shortly after we ordered the steel [mid 1949].
>
> *Q.* But before you had erected the steel or put in the footings?
>
> *A.* Yes, I think so. We were discussing—she was talking about her people in the Passavant Hospital, and she was complaining about the work in my office,

and then she said: "Why don't you change that —" and so on, and I said "Listen, that is my affair, and it is not your affair, and if I would not have ordered the steel I would not build the house."

Q. Isn't it a fact that that conversation was one in which Dr. Farnsworth said she thought that Mr. Goldsmith was using poor judgment and had no idea of costs, and you told her that you . . .

A. I told her she should keep out of my office, it is my affair.

Q. That's right, and that medicine was her affair?

A. I don't know if I told her about medicine.

Q. But you told her not to butt in about what was used there?

A. No. [It] was a general discussion. She was not satisfied with the work in her laboratories. . . . And then she started to talk about I should change my office, and I said: "That is none of your business. . . ."

Q. Didn't she tell you in that same conversation, that . . . Goldsmith . . . didn't seem to know what he was doing and that he was irritating Mr. Freund? And consuming most of his time?

A. . . . I don't remember that but certainly Mr. Goldsmith is a very careful man. . . . I would say that Dr. Farnsworth certainly can't judge Mr. Goldsmith.[33]

We have clear evidence, then — at least from Mies's point of view — of a micro-managerial battle between client and architect. Remarkably, in the face of his own immense interest, Mies threatened to cancel the project for a principle. But there was a practical problem; he had already ordered the steel, and was financially obligated.

. . .

The Farnsworth House is unlike any before: a steel-and-glass pavilion enclosing a single space free of internal structural elements. It is also the work of Mies van der Rohe at the height of his powers (fig. 10.2). In a remarkable passage from the trial, in replies to friendly questioning, Mies labored to explain:

Question, to Mies: Now, what is so good about this house?

A. I think the house is perfectly constructed, it is perfectly executed. It would be a lot of trouble to find a similar house or house similar to such a careful workmanship, and I think it is excellent design, too.

Q. Is that all?

FIGURE 10.2.
Farnsworth House,
Plano, Illinois (1951);
partial elevation view
looking north from
the banks of the Fox
River.

A. I think it is carefully designed, it is carefully constructed and it is carefully executed. We took the greatest care in choosing materials and selecting the pieces for the travertine, for the wood. In itself I think the house speaks for itself. Somebody has only to see it. . . .

Q. Didn't it have features in the house that were completely novel in the architectural world?

A. Oh, yes. We discussed that in front of the model [in earlier testimony].

Q. And didn't it use completely novel ways of placing and constructing equipment in the core?

A. Certainly, yes.

Q. And didn't it have a novel way of being suspended, the house?

A. Certainly, yes.

Q. Didn't it have a novel way in its overall construction?

A. I don't know that it was—I think the first time maybe, the first time that the floor and roof—is not directly supported but is suspended but that is—I would say a normal way of doing it under the circumstances.

258 / 259

Q. Was this unusual design to enable Dr. Farnsworth or any other person to live in the house in greater comfort or to enjoy life more than if living in any other type of house?

A. I am sure she does.

Q. I am asking you if it was designed by you for that purpose?

A. Certainly, yes it is.

Q. And you think it does that, don't you?

A. Certainly I think it does, and she has as far as I know told a lot of people that she is very pleased with the house.

Q. Now, you received as you testified a little while ago, considerable publicity about this house?

A. She too. I was famous before. She is now famous throughout the world.

Q. And one of the demonstrations of your fame is the fact that so much publicity to this house and so much space and publicity in magazines and newspapers, isn't that right?

A. Oh, no. That is for her, yes. People expected work from me what [meaning *that*] would be about—what [that] would have about this quality.[34]

With the Farnsworth House, Mies brought his American structural vocabulary to ultimate refinement. The house is a glass-walled rectangular prism supported above grade so as to clear the level of occasional floods. The long side faces north to a grassy rise, the south to the wooded riverbank. The roof and floor are bounded by fifteen-inch-deep steel channels turned flat side out, supported on each long side by four steel columns welded to these channels. (The W8 × 48 columns, nearly square in section, are usually used for steel foundations.)[35] The exterior between floor and roof is, with the exception of a pair of glass doors and two hopper windows, quarter-inch-thick polished plate glass. The main floor area is 2,216 square feet, but only 1,540 are enclosed, with the remainder a porch.

Access is by a steel stair with travertine treads at the river side of the expansive terrace. (A second stair on the north was eliminated to save money.) The terrace lies parallel to the house but slides to the west, and is carried above grade at about half the height of the main floor. Another stair ascends from terrace to porch, where a right turn is required for entry through a pair of glass doors located close to the middle of the west wall.

The major element of the interior is a freestanding, asymmetrically placed core containing a galley kitchen, two bathrooms separated by a utility space, and a generous fireplace. A freestanding wardrobe suggests a sleeping area. The "living room," which spreads before the fireplace with a view to the river, is similarly suggested. Cross ventilation can be conjured by opening the doors and the two hopper windows, the latter located at the base of the east wall opposite the entry. Originally, there was no air-conditioning—the house was mechanically ventilated by four concealed fans, including a whole-house exhaust fan sandwiched into the floor below the sink.

The stone floor is laid out on a 24-by-33-inch rectangular grid. It acts as a radiator for under-floor heating tubes, and conceals plumbing and electrical service to the kitchen, bathrooms, and utility space. A shaft from the core extends to the ceiling, accommodating exhaust from the heaters, kitchen, and baths as well as the roof drain. This drain, together with plumbing and electrical service, descends into a stack, painted black, which except for the columns is the only connection between house and ground.

Structure and space reflect the evolving preoccupations of Mies's American years. What remained from the European career was the plan asymmetry, evident in the major elements of porch and terrace, and in the placement and programmatic uses of the core. Roman travertine, Mies's ideal material for an important space, is used for both interior floors and exterior decking—a powerful unification of interior and exterior. Mies personally selected the travertine slabs and the veneer flitches for the millwork. The steel structure, made unitary by welded and ground joints, was sandblasted and smoothed to planar perfection (and to prepare it for painting) and painted white (fig. 10.3).

While the major components of the house were of modern manufacture, they were assembled and finished by craft methods. The house is unmistakably "modern" in its abstracted geometry and lack of ornament, yet it is history that Mies abstracted as surely as he did structure. The building has reminded some of an eighteenth-century country pavilion, others of a Shinto shrine. The white coating and carefully concealed welds deny the steel its industrial origins, transforming the piers into something akin to classical columns. The utilitarian wide flange is transformed into a spiritual object, an expression of the potential of the industrial epoch (fig. 10.4).

The house is more temple than dwelling, and rewards aesthetic contemplation ahead of domesticity. Technology sometimes proved unequal to it in a strictly material sense. In cold weather, the noninsulating glass lights were clouded by condensation, for the simple reason that the glass was not washed by a moving column of warm air. In summer, notwithstanding the immense black maple just outside, the sun turned the interior into a cooker. Cross ventilation availed little, interrupted as it was by the core and other millwork. Against the heat, the silk draperies were largely ineffective. The house was designed from the beginning for a screened porch, and a screen door to the main space was considered unnecessary.

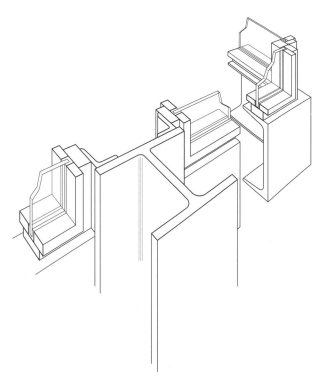

FIGURE 10.3.
Farnsworth House, Plano, Illinois (1951); cutaway perspective of the steel structure at the intersection of a column and the floor. To frame the glass, Mies used "stops" of rectangular steel bar stock in a manner akin to traditional wood window framing. Note the complex assembly of steel components necessary to "turn the corner" (*far right*).

Mies was content to condense and regularize the open plan. The interior is given life by the complex flow of spaces defined by the core and wardrobe. Exploration and observation are equally rewarded. Nature may change, but the frame is frozen in geometric perfection. In none of Mies's buildings did he come closer to the dematerialization of architecture leading to the expression of a fixed and supersensible order. The Farnsworth House is to his American career what the Barcelona Pavilion was to his European period: the apotheosis of a worldview. But here it is no longer characterized by the dramatic conditionality of his early years but by a newly urgent, "objective" maturity.

. . .

Farnsworth first stayed in the house overnight on New Year's Eve 1950. A few details remained unfinished, and work continued until the end of the following March. Lawyers got involved earlier. On August 8, 1950, Mies received a letter from Farnsworth stating that "no further financial commitments can be endorsed beyond the amount quoted in [your] statement of August 1."[36] In that regular monthly statement, Mies had reported that his expenses for materials and construction totaled $69,686.80. Consistent with his past practice, professional fees were not listed.

Farnsworth's letter was drafted by Chicago attorney Randolph Bohrer. Farnsworth had earlier treated the fifty-nine-year-old Bohrer for blood pres-

FIGURE 10.4.

Farnsworth House, Plano, Illinois (1951); wide-flange column supporting the terrace. View from above. The column is attached to the terrace fascia member by plug welds, which were ground smooth after completion. The column and fascia appear merely to touch. The effect is further enhanced by the termination of the column below the top of fascia steel.

sure and kidney problems, and it is likely that he credited her with saving his life.[37] We know from Farnsworth's memoir that one day in the course of his hospitalization she casually mentioned disappointment with her new house. Bohrer offered to do anything he could to "help [her] with this problem."[38]

In spite of the August 8 letter, Farnsworth continued to pay Mies, and even ordered additional items. She apparently believed that their social relationship could and would continue. But near the end of February 1951, according to Mies's testimony, Farnsworth, in a telephone call initiated by Mies, accused him of deceiving her about the cost of the house. After stating that "she could not talk to [me] that way," Mies hung up. It was their last contact until the trial.[39]

In a June 4, 1951, letter to Mies, Philip Johnson offered his own views of the client, the house, and the "situation":

> Edith was very charming to me [when I saw her recently] and was vociferous in her praise of the house. She did not mention your name, but said nothing about having any trouble during the building. I think she will calm down quickly now, and I only hope she does before too much furniture is installed.[40]
>
> There is no way I can tell you how much I admire the architecture. Your bril-

liant solutions of the problems that have been plaguing all of us for years are breathtaking. The steel connections are so inevitable, so clean, so beautifully executed, that I believe no one will ever improve on them. Their problems are solved once and for all. Their execution also is a wonder to me. I am amazed that you found workmen to execute them so well. I cannot be specific, because each one is as good as the next. It exhausts me to even imagine what work you have been through.[41]

Here matters stood until the appearance of Robert Wiley, a business consultant, friend, and real estate development partner of Johnson's. In casual conversation, Mies had complained to Johnson that his office was struggling financially. Johnson recommended Wiley, who soon enough arrived to review Mies's books. Among other problems, Wiley spotted the $4,500 balance due on construction costs for the Farnsworth House. Setting out to collect it, he approached Bohrer, now Farnsworth's representative, but made no headway. Eventually, he convinced Mies to meet with Bohrer. As Mies testified, he told Bohrer that if Farnsworth would pay the $4,500, he would waive any professional fee and "consider the matter closed." Bohrer replied that Farnsworth was "willing to settle" for $1,500. We do not know if Wiley himself then suggested a lawsuit—Goldsmith thought it likely—but through Wiley Mies was put in touch with the Chicago law firm Sonnenschein Berkson Lautmann Levinson & Morse. Senior partner David Levinson interviewed Mies, and recommended that he sue. Goldsmith later said, "I think this was one of the most unfortunate things that could have happened."[42]

Levinson surely knew that Farnsworth and Bohrer would fight back. He probably did not know at this time about Bohrer's health or Farnsworth's role in his treatment. As it turned out, Bohrer pursued the case with extraordinary zeal, and probably without charge to Farnsworth. In the early 1950s, Bohrer practiced with his son Mason, who had recently graduated from Harvard Law School, but Sonnenschein was (and still is) a major Chicago law firm, with substantial legal firepower. After depositions of Mies, Goldsmith, and Farnsworth, taken in Chicago, the trial was set for Yorkville, Illinois, the seat of Kendall County, where the house had been built. Both sides associated with local attorneys. For Mies, local counsel included young William C. Murphy, who had also just graduated from Harvard, where he and Mason Bohrer had been classmates.

Both sides agreed on what was even then an unusual format: instead of a hearing before a judge or judge and jury, the court appointed a Special Master in Chancery, usually an attorney with trial experience, who alone heard the case. Each side paid half the Master's fee and expenses. The Master was charged to deliver recommendations to a judge about how the case should be decided, and a formal Master's Report was prepared for this purpose. Each

side could object to the Master about his conclusions, and could raise these
objections and other points of appeal to the reviewing judge. Typically, the
judge would hold a hearing to consider the parties' arguments and to review
the Master's Report. Next, a decision would come down, usually adopting the
Master's recommendations. This decision, too, was subject to appeal. These
many steps conspired to make mischief later in our story.

The Special Master for *Van der Rohe v. Farnsworth* was Jerome Nelson, a
Kendall County attorney who had grown up in nearby Aurora (fig. 10.5). He
graduated from the University of Illinois College of Law in 1936, served in the
FBI through most of World War II, and in 1944 joined the Marine Corps. For two
years he participated in postwar military tribunals in Okinawa. In the 1970s, he
was twice elected Kendall County State's Attorney. Nelson's son Robert characterized his father as "a country lawyer" who "considered a hearing with ste-
nographers a big deal."[43] *Van der Rohe v. Farnsworth* was Nelson's only experience as a Master in Chancery.[44] It is clear in the record, and corroborated by
Murphy, that Nelson was impressed by Mies's persona and achievements—
a reflection of the personal magnetism Mies enjoyed throughout his life. According to Robert Nelson, also an attorney, his father remembered the case
as "one of the highlights of his life."[45]

For the hearing, Levinson turned the case over to Sonnenschein litigator
John Faissler. Memoranda between Levinson and Faissler reveal how they felt
about Bohrer's tactics and personality and even their client.[46] Faissler was
suave and seasoned, and his interaction with Nelson was consistently positive. (Faissler remained Mies's personal attorney for the rest of his client's

life.) Bohrer, by contrast, comported himself in "high dudgeon," as Murphy reported and the transcript confirms. Murphy added that Mies's legal team nonetheless considered Bohrer a "worthy adversary," though he was "often more angry than informed."[47]

The hearing commenced May 23, 1952, and ran until July 3. The testimony consumed twenty-five days, every one of which Mies attended. Farnsworth appeared only for her own testimony and cross-examination—three days in all. This is significant, since Farnsworth got most of her information about the proceedings from Bohrer, who was hardly a disinterested reporter. We know from Farnsworth's memoir that Bohrer boasted to her about his performance in court—and we now know that the facts were mostly otherwise.

Though the pleadings are dense, the case can be summarized as follows:[48] Faissler (representing Mies, the plaintiff) argued that Mies was owed approximately $3,500 for unpaid out-of-pocket construction costs. (Farnsworth had already paid Mies about $70,000.) In addition, he argued that Mies was owed $16,600 for the value of his architectural and general contracting services, based on a reasonable and customary fee for such work. In spite of the fact that Mies had never invoiced Farnsworth for his fees, Faissler argued that the parties had had a contract "partly express and partly implied," of which Farnsworth was fully aware, including her "understanding" that a fee would be charged. Bohrer (representing Farnsworth, the defendant and counterplaintiff) reacted in a legally proper and standard way—he developed counterclaims. He argued that Mies represented that the house could be built for $40,000, and that in the course of design and construction he had fraudulently concealed its rising cost. Related to the claim of fraud, but not technically alleged by Bohrer, was his contention (probably his genuine belief) that Mies had produced a "botched" piece of work. Bohrer claimed the house was unsuitable for habitation, evidence of Mies's obsession with "building art" at the expense of everyday professional competence. Bohrer asked that his client be paid approximately $35,000, roughly the difference between what he alleged she was "promised"—a $40,000 house—and what she had already paid.

In his testimony, Mies comes across as confident, professional, and in possession of the facts. He sometimes patiently acts the educator as he describes details that Bohrer misunderstands or misrepresents. In testifying about his professional dealings with his client, Mies argues explicitly that he had been careful to address her needs and concerns. He recounts his attempts to delay construction until Farnsworth could afford it. He describes office meetings and design presentations in which she was given numerous options for materials, finishes, and features. The decision to use travertine, which consumed about 20 percent of the budget, was carefully considered. To get the best price for the stone, Mies even wrote to his brother Ewald, who was still in the marble business in Germany. Ewald's price, at cost, was higher than in the United States.[49]

Farnsworth's testimony is hesitant. In support of Bohrer's theory of the case, he questioned her at length about budget discussions and her knowledge of the design and construction process. To support the counterclaim, she was forced to assert that she had been promised a $40,000 house; that she continued almost to the end to believe that promise, because she was ignorant of the work of the office; that she was manipulated and deceived by Mies; and that she had failed to read the monthly statements Mies had issued. In a few cases, she claimed not to recall important incidents. Photographs of her in the office, including one in which she is examining plans and documents with Goldsmith, were introduced by Mies's attorneys, and damaged her case.[50] Goldsmith, who had admired Farnsworth, lamented many years later: "Disappointingly, Farnsworth lied about everything."[51]

Bohrer questioned Mies about the budget, the various states of the plans and specifications, and the means by which cost estimates were made. He claimed that Mies never produced a complete set of contract documents, and that the budget was a "moving target."[52] In reply, Mies explained that he and Farnsworth had agreed that the plans and specifications would be developed "step-by-step." A house as special as this one could not be designed, documented, and bid as a single "package" like a school or office building. Mies cited the $60,000 cost of Philip Johnson's Glass House as evidence that Farnsworth's house could not have been built for less. He had shared Johnson's figures with Farnsworth. Mies reduced the size of the house by 10 percent during 1949 solely to reduce the cost. (Farnsworth not only knew of this change, but asked Mies to assure her that it would not compromise the design.)[53] And most spectacularly, Mies and Faissler produced a project budget in Farnsworth's hand that totaled $65,000. The $40,000 story collapsed.

That left Bohrer with the claim of fraud, which carries with it a high standard of proof,[54] which he did not come close to demonstrating. Testimony clearly showed the care that Mies, Goldsmith, and the rest of the office showered on the project. Bohrer alleged various design and construction defects. He concentrated on the mechanical systems, where Mies might have appeared vulnerable; but the testimony of William Goodman, a mechanical engineering professor at IIT and Mies's regular consultant for mechanical design, demonstrated, as Nelson later put it, the "skill and due care required of him by law." Bohrer's strategy included a campaign to ridicule and humiliate Mies and Goldsmith, but he himself often appeared uninformed about routine details of design and construction. It may have given Bohrer satisfaction to grill the architect, but Nelson bought none of it, as one of the "Conclusions of Law" in his Master's Report forcefully states:

14. It was proved by preponderance of the evidence that plaintiff [Mies] exercised the skill and due care required of him by law in the performance of his services; that there were no substantial defects in the designing, planning, supervision or construction of the house.[55]

Mies was on shakier ground when it came to his "contract" with Farnsworth. As we have noted, in over five years of professional association and close friendship, neither of them had ever discussed a fee. Farnsworth once sent money to the office with a note attached, commenting that this $1,000 was "toward a fee," but that was the extent of it. Late in the project, she asked Goldsmith what she should do about a fee, admitting that "[Mies] has never said anything about it. . . . What do you think I should do about it?" Goldsmith replied: "Why don't you ask him?"[56] She never did. From the start, Farnsworth suggested that the house be made available to Mies from time to time. Perhaps in her mind that constituted compensation. But Mies's actual manpower investment in the house turned out to be enormous, and even a "usual and customary" fee would not nearly have covered his costs. In the end, though, the "informal" contract was probably damaging to Mies's case (see below).

At the conclusion of a Master in Chancery proceeding, both sides typically produce their own "suggestions for findings of fact and conclusions of law." Each side uses this document to reargue their case, and to marshal evidence from the trial supporting their side that the Master might draw on for his report. Final oral arguments[57] were not made until January 30, 1953, six months after the conclusion of testimony, and the Master's Report followed on May 7, nearly a year after the hearing.

Nelson came down for Mies on every point, borrowing large chunks of Faissler's suggestions.[58] Of his forty-five "findings of fact," the following is typical of his dismissal of Bohrer's position:

[In finding 35, Nelson reported] that plaintiff [Mies] did not represent to defendant the cost of the house would not exceed $40,000 or any other specific amount, nor did plaintiff represent to defendant that a house substantially in the likeness of the model delivered to defendant could be constructed for a sum not to exceed $40,000. . . . Plaintiff made no representation whatever that the cost of the house would not exceed any specific amount.

[In finding 38, Nelson stated] "that plaintiff made no false representation whatever to the defendant," and (from point 39) ". . . plaintiff at all times acted in good faith."

Nelson concluded that Mies was entitled to $12,934.30 plus "the costs of this proceeding."[59] The exact sum was the result of a complex calculation that effectively awarded Mies his unpaid out-of-pocket costs and a reasonable, though hardly handsome, professional fee.

Bohrer offered objections to the Master's Report, and produced a point-by-point refutation of Nelson's conclusions. Faissler's much briefer document corrected some points of fact. After weighing both, Nelson convened a hearing in which he dismissed all of Bohrer's objections.

In the next and usually final step, a judge reviewed the report, the testimony, and the evidence and rendered a legal conclusion. This task fell to Circuit Judge Harry C. Daniels, who held a one-day hearing at which both sides, with Nelson present, reargued the case. In a memo to Levinson, Faissler reported that Bohrer "trotted out all his old arguments." Faissler thought Judge Daniels was in "pretty full sympathy" with Nelson (and Mies).[60]

At this point, the trail is partially lost. Daniels never rendered his opinion, despite arguably improper attempts by both camps to influence him. Two inexcusable years passed. In 1955 the case was reassigned to a Judge Abrahamson. He held a hearing in which he discussed weaknesses on both sides of the case and expressed interest in having the parties settle. He noted the lack of a written contract between Mies and Farnsworth, an observation that may have been intended to offer Farnsworth some relief. He also made it clear, according to Faissler's notes, that he was not interested in reading a 3,500-page record. After two weeks of negotiation, both sides reported that a settlement was impossible—neither would pay the other anything—and Bohrer signaled that he was prepared to appeal.

In considering settlement, Mies struggled with himself about an external annoyance. Farnsworth, stung by the glowing reception of the house in the professional and popular press, had started her own campaign.[61] She gave interviews in which she disparaged both architect and house, and she succeeded, secondhand and probably unintentionally, in touching the nerve of postwar anticommunism. In the April 1953 issue of the popular and influential Hearst magazine *House Beautiful*, in an article titled "The Threats to the Next America," editor Elizabeth Gordon extended Farnsworth's argument against the house into an attack on the International Style and the Bauhaus. Gordon associated Le Corbusier with the former, Walter Gropius with the latter, and Mies with both. She called Mies's architecture "cold" and "barren," his furniture "sterile," "thin," and "uncomfortable." Gordon had "talked to a highly intelligent, now disillusioned woman [she did not quote Farnsworth by name] who spent more than $70,000 building a 1-room house that is nothing but a glass cage on stilts."[62]

The title of her piece suggested, too, that European-inspired modernism had already succeeded well enough in the United States to elicit the sort of nationalistic harangue that Paul Schultze-Naumburg had lodged against the New Architecture in Germany during the 1920s and 1930s. But the consequences were clearly different: the United States never suffered the kind of total right-wing ascendancy that Germany experienced. Nevertheless, Gordon's sentiments were echoed in the quoted words of Frank Lloyd Wright: "These Bauhaus architects [with whom Wright now identified Mies] ran from political totalitarianism in Germany to what is now made by specious promotion to seem their own totalitarianism in art here in America. . . . Why do I distrust and defy such 'internationalism' as I do communism? Because both must by their nature do this very leveling in the name of civilization."[63]

Against this background, Mies suggested to his attorneys that he was willing to settle for nothing "if she would just stop slandering us." Levinson told Mies they were powerless to stop Farnsworth's campaign, but urged that given the Master's favorable report, "she has got to pay you something."[64] With Randolph Bohrer on vacation,[65] Faissler's team was able to deal with his son Mason, who convinced Farnsworth to pay "a small amount." Faissler suggested $2,500, about the difference between the Master's original award and the cost of an appeal. Mason Bohrer agreed. After five years of struggle, the frontline battle was over. We do not know Mies's legal costs, though something over $20,000 is a reasonable guess. Remarkably, the settlement nearly split the difference between Mies's original request for $4,500 and Farnsworth's counter to "settle" for $1,500. And by one critical measure, Randolph Bohrer succeeded spectacularly in defending his client. He shielded her from a significant financial penalty and a painful repudiation in a court of law.

· · ·

In spite of her statement that the house was "uninhabitable," Farnsworth made it her country retreat for twenty years. In 1968, interconnected events led to her decision to sell the property. The first was an action by Kendall County to replace the 1884 Fox River bridge downstream from her property. To accommodate a new bridge and to improve its alignment, the north approach was to be razed and shifted to the east about 175 feet, taking two acres from Farnsworth's property. The bridge and road would be visible from the house, especially in winter. Farnsworth expressed herself to the *Chicago Tribune*: "[The bridge] will pass within 180 feet of the house. Just think, any of these Hell's Angels who seem to be riding around could shoot right into the house—it's all glass."[66]

In an attempt to stymie the county's plans, Farnsworth retained William C. Murphy, the junior member of *Mies's* legal team fifteen years earlier. She remembered and liked him.[67] After the location of the new bridge had been established, a county conservation official mentioned to Farnsworth that Native American artifacts had been discovered on her property. Farnsworth engaged archeologists to confirm the find, which they did, stating that the "site [was] definitely prehistoric, probably at least 2,000 years old, and 'very significant.'"[68] Armed with this information, Farnsworth and Murphy tried to offer the two condemned acres to the Illinois Department of Conservation. Farnsworth never heard from the state, and the gambit failed.

As a follow-up, Murphy developed a more generous proposal in a May 25, 1968, letter to Kendall County's elders:

> If the Board of Supervisors will rescind its ordinance of the 5 Mile Bridge through the Farnsworth property, Dr. Farnsworth will deliver a deed to the County of Kendall dedicating all of her property for park purposes, but reserving a life interest therein to herself, on condition that during her lifetime no roads, bridges or approaches thereto be built on her property by any governmental body or other person without her express written consent first had and obtained....
>
> The bridge can be built elsewhere, but once this offer is rejected, the people of this County will lose a park forever.[69]

If Murphy's offer had been accepted, the house would have become part of the park, and the record would be very unlike what ensued.[70] But the board declined. Farnsworth then made a last effort—in perhaps the ultimate irony—arguing through Murphy that the house and land together constituted an important work of art that the new bridge would destroy. She demanded $250,000 in damages, but a jury of local citizens was unmoved. Her sole consolation was an award of $17,000 for the two acres she was forced to cede.

In the next act, though some details remain uncertain, it is hard to avoid speculating about connections direct and indirect. A great admirer of the Farnsworth House was a wealthy British real estate developer, Peter Palumbo, who had learned of it as a schoolboy. In the early 1960s, grown to manhood, he decided to develop an office building on a parcel he controlled in London. In 1967 he offered the project to Mies, who accepted (see our discussion of the Mansion House project in chapter 13). While visiting Mies in Chicago in 1968, he sounded out Dirk Lohan on whether Mies might design a house for him on land he owned in Scotland. Lohan suggested that Palumbo simply purchase the Farnsworth House, which was at the time listed for sale in the real estate section of the *Chicago Tribune*. Lohan drove him to see the house that very day.[71] Palumbo made contact with Farnsworth, and after some back and forth they agreed on a price of $120,000.[72]

In 1971 Farnsworth left Chicago for Italy. She purchased a villa in Bagno a Ripoli, near Florence, and set about writing a memoir, translating modern Italian poetry, and composing poems of her own. She published three books featuring the work, respectively, of Albino Pierro, Salvatore Quasimodo, and Eugenio Montale, the last of these winner of the 1975 Nobel Prize in Literature, to whom she became close. Palumbo remembers visiting her in Florence, where with eloquence and vigor she recited verse for him. She died in Italy in 1977, aged seventy-four.

Palumbo purchased the property in 1968, but by agreement Farnsworth occupied it for three more years. Until he sold the house in 2003, he was an ideal owner: London remained his principal residence, his visits were occasional, and he retained a full-time caretaker for the Fox River property. Farnsworth had insisted on screening the deck. When Palumbo took over, the screening was loose and full of debris, and he removed it. Since Mies's intention to design furniture for the house had been thwarted,[73] Palumbo purchased modern Mies furniture and an important original, a black glass table that had been in the Barcelona Pavilion. He also commissioned Dirk Lohan to design a desk for the living area, a table for the dining area, and additions to the fireplace that prevented ash from falling and flying as it had in Farnsworth's time. He installed air-conditioning too, which Lohan achieved by concealing the equipment on the roof and in the core.

Palumbo retained the services of English landscape architect Lanning Roper to redesign the grounds that Farnsworth had left mostly unattended. Roper placed new trees east and west of the house, leaving a meadow to the north, where he planted thousands of daffodils. He cared for the majestic black maple to which Mies's design so carefully responded. Palumbo complied with Mies's wish to keep the core walls of the house free of artwork, but sculpture, he presumed, was acceptable, both indoors and out. Along a looping path across the property, he eventually displayed monumental sculpture by Henry Moore, Richard Serra, Anthony Caro, Claes Oldenburg, and Andy Goldsworthy, as well as a piece of the Berlin Wall and several London telephone booths.

Even with his resources, Palumbo could not control the weather. As early as 1954, the river had risen to flood the house. The core, furniture, and draperies were damaged, but the structure was unaffected. Though there were more floods during the Farnsworth years, the worst occurred in July 1996, when the area received 18 inches of rainfall in 24 hours. No one could reach the house to rescue the interior appointments, which were at the mercy of the river once two of the great glass lights yielded to the turbulent water. The core was damaged beyond repair. Furnishings were destroyed, and some of the art was swept downstream. The water crested 4 feet 10 inches above the floor. Palumbo was away at the time. He called on Lohan to prepare a full-scale restoration, which cost half a million dollars.

In 2000, now sixty-five years old, Palumbo decided to sell. Recent cancer surgery and a serious heart condition drove him to his decision. With news of the sale came rumors that the house could be sold to someone who might move it. Reacting to this threat, Chicago architects Helmut Jahn, Ronald Krueck, and George Larson sought the support of John Bryan, a Chicago businessman and arts patron. Reasoning that the ideal purchaser would be the State of Illinois, Bryan initiated a campaign to win the support of then governor George Ryan. He met with the editorial boards of major Illinois newspapers to apprise them of the exceptional qualities of the house. Ten affirmative editorials followed. The governor was then approached, and he agreed to make $7.5 million available from a discretionary fund. But in 2002 Ryan decided not to seek reelection. The sale was formally rejected when the next attorney general, Lisa Madigan, disallowed it on account of the state's poor financial condition.

Palumbo had waited two years for a decision. Now the money would have to be raised privately. Bryan and his group set up a connection with the National Trust for Historic Preservation and the Landmarks Preservation Council of Illinois. The parties approached Palumbo and offered to make the purchase. He now wanted $10 million, and though Bryan presumed he would accept less, Palumbo turned him down and selected Sotheby's to auction the property.

The auction was scheduled for December 12, 2003. By the morning of the day before, $3.6 million had been committed to Bryan's group, less than Sotheby's low estimate of between $4.5 and $6 million. Most of the funds from Bryan's group consisted of pledges of $500,000 from Bryan and $1 million each from LPCI and NTHP. Early that afternoon, LPCI president David Bahlman received a phone call from Jack Reed, a wealthy architecture buff who lived in Mies's Promontory Apartments. Reed pledged $500,000. Bahlman also met with Fred Eychaner, a Chicago television executive who owned a house designed by Japanese architect Tadao Ando. Eychaner had come to New York undecided: he might contribute, or he might make a bid on his own. After meeting with Bryan, he pledged $750,000.

On the following morning, Bryan's team strategized with gallerist Richard Gray, an acknowledged master at bidding. Jack Reed added $250,000 to his pledge of the day before. Bryan then offered to double his $500,000 if LPCI would double its own $1 million. It was agreed that the second million would be borrowed against proceeds of the future sale of adjacent lands to be owned by NTHP. The auction had attracted a national audience, its attention seized by an architectural masterpiece whose fate hung in the balance, the cause of preservation, and the rarefied realm of high-level bidding. At the auction, Bahlman recorded the action:

> At about 5:30 bidding starts on lot 800 [the Farnsworth House]—starts at 3.5 million, slows at 4.5, reaches 5 and two bidders drop out. At 6 million tension rises. Bryan negotiates with Eychaner for a resolute 500 and ability for another 250. Bryan instructs Gray to go to 6.5 and no higher. Gray goes to 6.7 [Bryan to Gray: "Dick, I hope you know you're on your own."] Last two bids on his [Gray's] own. Gavel comes down at 6.7 million. All in booth cheer and hug.[74]

We are not decorating. This is structure. We put up what has to be built, and then we accept it. **MIES,** about 860–880 North Lake Shore Drive

Mies had no interest in or even the slightest remote thought of efficiency of an office as far as getting a job done. That just didn't enter his mind.
GENE SUMMERS, Mies's chief lieutenant in the 1950s and 1960s

So I said, incredulously, one day to Mies, "Do you mean you can raise this family with children, parents in this open plan . . . ?"
MYRON GOLDSMITH, project architect of the Fifty by Fifty House, questioning Mies

By 1958 and for the last decade of his life, arthritis confined Mies to a wheel-chair. Only with extreme effort could he hoist himself on crutches and move about. His pain was partially relieved by tedious medical interventions, as well as by his drinking. But these years of physical decline were also those in which his fame and professional influence peaked. This and the following chapter catalog and critique the most important built work from Mies's mature American career. Residential projects are discussed first, with the major commercial and institutional work treated in chapter 12.

.   .   .

Mies's student Y. C. Wong worked for him in three stints between 1950 and 1957 and for Skidmore, Owings & Merrill for one year during the same period. "It was complicated at SOM. Much larger, and you were not supposed to get your hands on everything. In Mies's office you'd just do whatever you can do."[1] Mies never had a large office, but as the 1950s progressed, his practice did enjoy steady growth. In 1952 it relocated from 37 South Wabash, in Chicago's Loop, to a loft outside the central business district at 230 East Ohio Street (fig. 11.1). In 1959 Mies doubled his Ohio Street space to about ten thousand square feet when his staff reached thirty-five—then as now only a medium-sized firm. Joseph Fujikawa directed the firm's "developer work," and Edward Duckett, who had established the model shop, remained its master. Among other key staff, William Dunlap left Mies for SOM in 1951, and helped turn it into the most powerful Miesian practice in the United States. Two of Mies's most

FIGURE 11.1.
The Mies office, in a
loft building at 230
East Ohio Street,
Chicago, in 1956.
Mies is in the dark
jacket. He employed
graduates of IIT ex-
clusively, and almost
all were forty years
his junior. Frank
Scherschel/Time &
Life Pictures/Getty
Images.

gifted students, Jacques Brownson and Myron Goldsmith, became central figures in the ascendancy of a collective Miesian architecture known as the Second Chicago School.[2] Like Dunlap, Goldsmith became an SOM partner, and
Brownson a designer for C. F. Murphy Associates, the favorite firm of Mayor
Richard J. Daley. In the mid-1950s, Gene Summers emerged as Mies's chief
office lieutenant, though Fujikawa remained powerful (fig. 11.2). Summers's
elevation — staff roles and professional rank were never formalized in Mies's
office — was the product of an exceptional design talent, a strong, business-
like will, and a tireless work ethic.[3] Like Brownson, but later, he moved to C. F.
Murphy Associates, where as head of design in the late 1960s and early 1970s
he was responsible for several major buildings.

During the 1950s, Mies's regular professional consultants included structural engineer Frank Kornacker, landscape architect (and IIT professor) Alfred
Caldwell, mechanical engineer (and IIT engineering professor) William Goodman, and New York lighting designer Richard Kelly. Ludwig Hilberseimer re-

FIGURE 11.2. Gene R. Summers, then twenty-eight years old, with Mies in his Chicago office in October 1956. Mies is examining a marble sample proposed for the long benches on the Seagram Building plaza. A model of the plaza and the lower floors of the tower is in the background. Frank Scherschel/Time & Life Pictures/Getty Images.

mained ally, confidant, and publicist, continuing to teach and write until his death in 1967. As Mies yielded to advancing age and physical disability—he was absent from the office for extended periods—he (usually with Summers) concentrated on a few projects, among them pavilions for the Bacardi Company in Cuba and the New National Gallery in Berlin. Summers, who also assumed the key role of contract negotiator, exercised authority that brought a new level of professionalism and productivity to the office.

. . .

A single professional relationship formed in Chicago during the 1940s proved to be the most important of Mies's career. It began when he was approached by a twenty-nine-year-old rabbinical scholar turned real estate entrepreneur, Herbert Greenwald. If the 1947 MoMA exhibition established Mies's wider reputation as a designer, it was Greenwald who enabled him at last to realize major buildings.[4] In turn, the work Mies went on to produce—both innovative and economical—was a no less significant stroke of luck for Greenwald (fig. 11.3).

While a student of philosophy at the University of Chicago in the late 1930s, Greenwald worked for a summer for Chicago architect John Holsman. The experience led him to form his own real estate firm, the Herbert Construction Company. By 1946 he had completed three nondescript mid-rise apartment buildings in suburban Evanston. He had also gained the financial support of Samuel Katzen, a lawyer and investor and one of a group that controlled a parcel on Chicago's South Lake Shore Drive suitable for an apartment building. Katzen put Greenwald in charge of its development, and Greenwald in turn assigned himself no less a task than to secure "the best architect in the world."[5] He approached Wright, who demanded a $250,000 retainer. The prospect was too rich for Greenwald, so he approached Eliel Saarinen, who was too busy with Cranbrook Academy in Bloomfield Hills, Michigan. Greenwald's next candidate, Harvard's Walter Gropius, also declined, but suggested that Greenwald hire "the father of us all," Mies van der Rohe, who was already in Chicago.[6] After three "greater" architects failed him, Greenwald at last approached Mies. Like Mies, he was a devoted student of philosophy, and an intellectual kinship was quickly established.

Born in St. Louis in 1915, Greenwald left home at the age of fourteen because, according to his son Bennet,[7]

his father's brutality was unbearable.... He went east because he could get into Yeshiva University [in New York] to study for the rabbinate. He always said he was waiting for the bush to burn and the stick to turn into a snake, but it never happened. He became disillusioned by the greed and irrespon-

FIGURE 11.3. Mies and client Herbert Greenwald in 1956, studying models of buildings for Lafayette Park in Detroit. Greenwald brought to completion Mies's first large-scale commercial works. Greenwald died in a plane crash three years after this photograph was taken. Frank Scherschel/Time & Life Pictures/Getty Images.

FIGURE 11.4
(*facing*).
Promontory Apart-
ments, Chicago
(1949), Mies's first
realized high-rise
building. East eleva-
tion, view from the
sidewalk. Note the
column setbacks as
the tower rises. Un-
coordinated pen-
etrations of the brick
spandrels for air-
conditioning units
were introduced
in the 1950s and
1960s—to the un-
happiness of Mies
and his staff. For fire
protection, proxim-
ity to the building *at
right* required that
Promontory's side
walls be windowless.

sibility of his fellow students. But [he] loved the ethics of the religion. He was well-trained and a good scholar. . . . So he looked around for a university and he found [the University of] Chicago, which at that time was a hotbed of ideas—the whole Great Books approach. He ran out of money, so he didn't finish.

According to Greenwald's son, "he went into business to make an impact on the landscape."[8]

With what became Promontory Apartments, the course was set for a historic partnership. Much of the work of Mies's office during the 1950s was Greenwald's, including projects in Chicago and Detroit. Later, studies and proposals were made for developments in New York, San Francisco, and around the country. Not surprisingly, early in their relationship Greenwald was in awe of Mies. Joseph Fujikawa characterized Greenwald "in the early days" as "completely beholden to Mies on architectural issues." Bruno Conterato agreed: "Sometimes I felt that Herb would almost go overboard in complimenting Mies for a decision. I remember Herb saying, 'Mies, you've done it again!'"[9] Nonetheless, Greenwald soon emerged as his own man—and the key figure in Mies's professional fortunes.

. . .

Completed in 1949 on a lakefront site in Chicago's Hyde Park neighborhood, the twenty-two-story Promontory Apartments was Mies's first realized tall building (fig. 11.4). He began working on it in the fall of 1946, when he was sixty years of age, and when his staff numbered four or five. Technically, Mies was design consultant to architect-of-record Pace Associates, a new firm headed by Mies's student Charles Genther. With its exposed concrete structure, Promontory is atypical of Mies's better-known later towers—those with metal-and-glass exterior walls that became his signature American work. And even before it was completed, Promontory was overshadowed by Mies's steel-skinned Lake Shore Drive Apartments, under construction by 1949 on a more prominent site at 860 and 880 North Lake Shore Drive.

For fifty years after its completion, books and articles repeated the claim that Promontory was intended to be built in steel, that it was to have had a steel or aluminum exterior wall, and that it was built in concrete because of budget limitations or the postwar steel shortage. The argument seemed amply supported by three drawings in which the front elevation is rendered in floor-to-ceiling, mullioned glazing. The drawings, made in 1947 at Mies's direction by Myron Goldsmith, were widely published, thanks to Mies himself.[10] The concept was indeed Mies's, but the "Promontory steel versions" were studies after the fact, as Goldsmith reported. They were done before the 860 project

materialized, and incorrectly came to represent a potential somehow unrealized at Promontory.

Promontory was nonetheless a pathbreaking building. It was Chicago's first modern high-rise apartment building, structurally typical of concrete-framed towers of the 1920s and 1930s, but modern because the exterior was without ornament. Promontory was Greenwald's first use of the "cooperative" method of financing, standard in New York but rare in Chicago; he would use it again at 860. In a "co-op," apartments are offered as shares in a corporation that owns and operates the building. Technically, the shareholder leases a unit from the building corporation. Because the corporation has collateral—the building itself—it can readily borrow. A developer typically financed half of a co-op's value, and charged the buyers the other half as the purchase price of their shares. The owners took on the burden of servicing the development debt in return for a below-market price going in. Banks at the time would not write mortgages for co-ops, so purchasers had to pay cash. Consequently, only the relatively well-off could participate.

Though the construction budget was severely squeezed, Promontory's unit mix was luxurious—two- and three-bedroom apartments only, an artifact of the co-op format. Mies adopted a conservative 16-foot, 6-inch structural module along the eight-bay front, with two 17-foot bays front to back. Four apartments faced both east toward the lake and west toward the city. To increase the unit count, two apartments were added to each floor, one each in a short plan leg, resulting in a double-T plan overall. From the lake, the building appears to be a prismatic slab, but from the west it looks like the rear of a standard 1920s apartment block. Key elements of Mies's "clear structure" are the slight column setbacks at floors 7, 12, and 17, reflective of the reduced loads at higher elevations. These setbacks are "expressed" on the exterior rather than buried inside a masonry wall, which had been standard practice. The edges of the floor slabs are also exposed, so that the full concrete cage is legible.

In spite of the double-T plan, Mies provided a mostly transparent ground floor. Here Promontory is recognizably "Miesian," and of real distinction. In the late 1940s, there was no demand for enclosed residential parking. Thus, the large rear yard was used for on-grade parking, accessed by drive lanes under the north and south bays of the tower. This scheme followed the example of Chicago's prewar lakefront apartment buildings, as did the inclusion of ground-floor apartments (where the legs of the Ts housed three-bedroom units). Between the Ts, Mies created a surprisingly open lobby, glazed floor to ceiling east and west and opening on the west to a small court that screened the parking area. The glazing on the east is set in from the exterior, which creates an inviting arcade. The spatial flow is open, and the tower appears to float overhead (fig. 11.5). The effect is further enhanced by the open drive aisles and by clearstory glazing of two service areas that face the street.

The ostensibly modest lobby is beautifully detailed. The interior walls are beige brick, just as at IIT. At each of the elevator lobbies, Mies provided a cantilevered birch shelf, floating just free of the wall and supported by concealed steel bars. For the mail room he designed a freestanding steel-and-glass mailbox structure hovering above floating translucent-glass shelves. He also designed a pair of austere wood-framed benches with honed travertine seats, custom-designed sconces for the hallways, and custom lettering for the house numbers.

Mies was characteristically thorough in testing alternate unit layouts. As built, the apartments were conventional, and the aluminum-framed glazing was limited to the area above the rather high spandrel. Yet in the design studies, there are open-plan layouts and even freestanding millwork dividers between "rooms." Because the sides of the tower were to be adjacent to buildings or buildable lots, the Chicago Building Code required fire-rated and therefore solid sidewalls, which effectively prohibited glazed living spaces wrapping the building's corners. Living rooms were therefore located adjacent to the two cores, with bedrooms pushed to the extremities of the plan. This meant shorter common corridors and slightly larger units. Each apartment has a small dining alcove, but internal circulation is meandering.

FIGURE 11.5.
Promontory Apart-
ments, Chicago
(1949); view of the
colonnade, looking
north. Mies would
go on to make the
colonnade a sig-
nature of his glass-
walled towers. This
is its first appear-
ance in built form.

Quite the contrary is evident in one surviving set of alternate plan studies, where Mies tested an all-duplex scheme in a plan layout of a single, slender T^{11} (fig. 11.6). There are ten nearly identical apartments, each nineteen feet
wide, with what we would today describe as a "loftlike" living room, an open
kitchen on the first level, and a private stair leading to an upper floor. There
the master bedroom faces east, and one or two smaller bedrooms face west.
The seven units facing the lake are accessed by a single-loaded corridor along
the west wall. On the "upstairs" floors a common corridor is not required, and
this space is captured for bedrooms and their western exposure. The core
houses the two elevators, a connecting corridor between the main plan ele-

Residential Work

Duplex - Upper Level

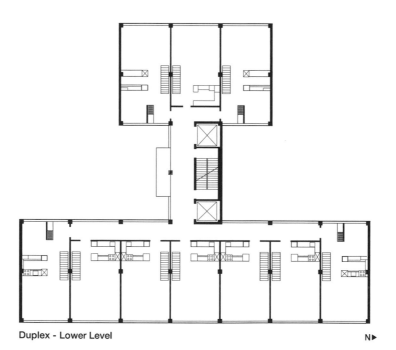

Duplex - Lower Level

N▶

ments, and a scissors stair. The scheme is both a brilliant site solution and an exciting statement about the possibilities of high-rise living.[12]

Mies did not invent the combination of brick spandrel and exposed concrete frame, but Promontory was nevertheless a much-publicized and highly influential application of that system. It was also irresistibly economical: the

FIGURE 11.6
(*facing*).
Promontory Apart-
ments, Chicago
(1949), alternate
scheme with a
T-shaped plan
and duplex units.
Above, the upper
duplex level, with
the bedrooms and
a bath, but with-
out a common cor-
ridor. *Below*, the
living rooms, kitch-
ens, internal stairs,
and corridor. The
scheme is remark-
ably contempo-
rary, and was no
doubt far ahead
of the market in
post–World War II
Chicago.

exposed structure could serve as part of the exterior envelope, along with easily constructed spandrels below inexpensive infill windows. In the 1950s, this
system became the chief rival of technically more advanced (and more expensive) curtain walls, of which Mies himself was a pioneer. When it came time for
high-rise public housing, then, a concrete frame with brick spandrels was the
obvious choice. Promontory-like elevations of no aesthetic merit appeared all
across Chicago and much of the rest of urban America. Except for its location
and its middle-class occupancy, Promontory came to have much in common
with some of the twentieth century's most controversial urban architecture.

.   .   .

With Promontory under way, Greenwald set his sights on other locations along
the Chicago lakefront. In mid-1948 he asked Mies to study options for adjacent
parcels about a half mile north of Promontory, among a group of prewar residential towers known as Indian Village. The south parcel, north of Hyde Park
Boulevard between Cornell and East End Avenue, was vacant. The other, north
across East Fiftieth Place, was occupied at a corner by a twenty-seven-story,
stone-clad, 1920s apartment building.

Three months later, the land for what would become the Lake Shore Drive
Apartments (860–880 North Lake Shore Drive) became available, and Greenwald abandoned the Indian Village project, called the Algonquin Apartments,
in favor of the better site on Chicago's North Side. Greenwald's inability to secure financing for Algonquin contributed to his decision.[13] Mies designed a
twin-tower scheme for the north Algonquin parcel, prepared a presentation
model, and completed alternate plans for apartments and lobbies for what is
now identified in the literature as Algonquin Apartment Buildings Scheme No. 1.
With Mies's peripheral involvement, a *second* Algonquin project, designed by
Pace Associates, was realized. Now referred to as Scheme No. 2, these six
fourteen-story buildings are also called the Algonquin Apartments. They are
almost universally and incorrectly said to have been "designed by Mies van
der Rohe."[14]

The Algonquin No. 1 designs were the first freestanding towers Mies had a
chance to realize[15] (fig. 11.7). The model photographs show no context, and
the buildings appear to be isolated and bilaterally symmetrical. The proposed
interiors clustered kitchens and adjacent living rooms in the middle three
bays of opposite sides, where for the first time Mies specified limited floor-to-
ceiling glass for a residential high-rise.[16] The other pair of opposite sides had
bedrooms at the perimeter, and the exterior was similar to Promontory, with
all-brick spandrels below aluminum-framed glazing.

In this period, lenders were wary of all-glass exteriors, and even the 860–
880 "glass houses" turned out to be difficult to finance. Developers were also

FIGURE 11.7. Algonquin Apartment Building project, Chicago, (1948), model. The elevations are based on those of the Promontory Apartments, though a few bays (*middle left side*) are glazed floor-to-ceiling. The modest height, square plan, and large, expressed columns combine to produce an uninspired composition. Photo: Hedrich-Blessing; Chicago History Museum, HB-11601-B. Used by permission of the Chicago History Museum.

uncertain that the market would accept modern apartments, and the Algonquin exteriors in part reflect this. In other respects, the buildings closely followed Promontory; the concrete frame with brick infill was almost identical, column sections were progressively reduced on the exterior, and the ground floors were set back (on three sides only) to squeeze in a pair of one-bedroom apartments opposite the lobby.

It was fortunate for Mies's reputation that Algonquin No. 1 was canceled. Joseph Fujikawa, who developed the apartment plans for Algonquin, 860–880, and many later towers, thought the buildings were "clunky."[17] They were to be 200 feet tall but 85 feet wide—squat even by nineteenth-century standards. The combination of 16-foot, 6-inch column spacing and its exterior expression wrapped the buildings in a veritable concrete harness. Four of the twenty intercolumn elevations were entirely bricked in. The structural system was already an anachronism, the column-and-slab high-rise cage having evolved only modestly in fifty years. Not ten years later, Mies pioneered modern flat-slab construction at the Esplanade Apartments, using concrete spans of 21 feet and columns interior to the building envelope. The "structural expression" of Algonquin appeared even to contradict Mies's own principles. Copying the "logic" of progressively setting back the columns as practiced at Promontory led at Algonquin to massive right-angled buttressing at the corners—as Mies well knew, these are the very columns that carry the *least* load.

These problems were swept away at 860–880 North Lake Shore Drive, soon on the boards and from the beginning intended to be steel. But by 1951, when that project was almost complete, Algonquin No. 2 was also finally out of the ground. As related in an oral history, Charles Genther, head of Pace Associates, resurrected the Algonquin project in the form of six fourteen-story buildings spread over both the parcels Greenwald had studied in 1948. Genther knew that Algonquin No. 1 had been too large to finance. One lender later suggested a phased construction of several buildings, each of which was small enough to qualify for its own mortgage. Genther and Greenwald then restructured the deal as a six-tower scheme. Genther claimed to have retained Mies as the design architect for Algonquin No. 2, and a few drawings from the Mies Archive include conceptual elevations and common-area details for the buildings that were built. But in the same interview, Genther boasted that he himself had "design[ed] the building[s] [with mechanical engineer John Holsman] at lunch on a paper napkin."[18] The studies that Mies's office did provide were probably untouched by Mies himself. He never claimed authorship for Algonquin No. 2.

. . .

The structural-steel and steel-and-glass-walled towers at 860 and 880 North Lake Shore Drive are among the most celebrated and influential buildings of all time (figs. 11.8 and 11.9). At first they were called the Lake Shore Drive Apartments, and colloquially the "Glass Houses." Now usually referred to together as "860," the two were so much copied and are so well known that it is now difficult to conjure their originality.

The architectural vocabulary of steel and glass as realized at 860 had been under development by Mies since the early 1940s, beginning with the IIT Metals and Minerals Building and the unbuilt Library and Administration Building, where Mies brought it to a first maturity, and in prototypical built form with the Navy Building. He had also worked with students on these same problems. In these buildings and studies and in the Farnsworth House, conceived in 1946 but not then constructed, Mies had tested the use and expression of "architecturally exposed" or "architecturally welded" steel, where hot-rolled plate and standard rolled shapes, in combination, yielded new architectural forms and possibilities. As we have noted, Mies had conceived a steel exterior wall with wide-flange mullions even before the completion of Promontory. That concept was an extension to multiple stories of the column-to-fascia connections of the Farnsworth House. When the opportunity came to construct and clad a tall building in steel, and to push for an all-glazed solution, Mies was ready.[19]

In a trade press interview just after the buildings were completed, Mies described his method: "We are not decorating," he asserted. "This is structure. We put up what has to be built, and then we accept it."[20] This is the heady language of Mies the objectivist—and a caricature of the real work of design. But of all his works, 860 may make the strongest case for what Mies believed was an objective architecture—a building art (Mies always preferred *Baukunst* to *Architektur*) that leads by reason and reiterative labor to a set of correct solutions to the problems of building. These "problems" encompass programming, siting, the economics of construction, structural and environmental performance, and the representational and spiritual imperative to make art.[21]

The 860 site is a trapezoid, with the diagonal to the east, fronting Lake Shore Drive. The land had been reclaimed from the lake early in the twentieth century. Due to the Depression and World War II it had never been built on, though prewar towers were close by. In mid-1948 Greenwald was approached by Chicago's McCormick family, in the persons of Robert H. McCormick senior and junior, who at the time controlled the north half of the eventual site and contiguous land to the west. The McCormicks offered to partner fifty-fifty with Greenwald on a development, contributing the land and the McCormick family's prestige. Greenwald provided youthful energy and a design team already proven at Promontory.[22]

Through bequests that went back decades, Northwestern University controlled the other half of the Lake Shore Drive frontage between Chestnut and Delaware Streets. The powerful McCormicks were able to trade their plot to the west for Northwestern's, with an important condition: they agreed to con-

FIGURE 11.8. Lake Shore Drive Apartments, 860–880 North Lake Shore Drive, Chicago (1951). View looking northeast. Note the 1950s automobiles in the foreground. (The south elevation of 860 [*at right*] is being painted.) Photo: Hube Henry, Hedrich-Blessing.

struct *two* residential towers with an opening between so that Northwestern could profit from the lake views of a future building on the parcel to the west. Such a building was realized at 260 East Chestnut Street in 1964, a forty-two-story tower with lake views between and over 860–880.

After study with massing models — simple wooden blocks, to scale — Mies elected to dispose identical towers at right angles to each other. The three-by-five-bay 880 tower, with its long axis north to south, was pushed toward the north and west property lines, and 860 (five bays east to west) toward the south and east. The 860 building was also shifted one structural bay to the east relative to 880. This simple adjustment opened the southwest corner of 880 to city views and the northwest corner of 860 to the lake, and provided space for an inconspicuous ramp from Chestnut Street to two levels of parking below grade.

Column-to-column dimensions were analyzed for both structural and planning efficiency. (Frank J. Kornacker and Associates was the structural engineer.) Schemes with 21- and 22-foot square bays were the most studied, and the 21-foot version was selected for the combination of structural efficiency, accommodation of the residential layouts, and precise fitting of buildings to site. (Two bedrooms just squeeze into a 21-foot bay.) North to south, the site was filled exactly with the eight total bays of the two towers and a 48-foot space between. Critics have noted the Mondrianesque planning at 860, but the studies demonstrate that given a self-imposed requirement for two identical towers, the solution was highly constrained.

Each tower is just 7,000 square feet per floor, and only 40 percent of the site is occupied by the buildings. With parking below and the towers' first floors set back on all sides, only 15 percent of the site is built at grade. The glass of the first-floor walls, clear and frosted, further dematerializes the buildings at grade, especially when softly illuminated from inside at night.[23] Adjacency to the limitless vista of Lake Michigan further heightens the effect, and the meeting of the orthogonal city grid and the "natural" diagonal of the lakefront is brilliantly mediated by the floating, paired prisms.

By the late 1940s, Mies had fully articulated his belief that architecture is "clear structure." This principle, chiefly realized in architecturally exposed steel and almost wholly a product of his American career, constitutes a remarkable example of artistic growth in maturity. The IIT campus buildings completed before 860 progressively approached this goal, but it was at 860 that he achieved for the first time a clear structure that was, *by itself*, powerful enough to carry all the representational aspirations of Mies's "building art." All of this came in his sixty-fifth year.

At twenty-six floors, the 860–880 towers are not really tall, and steel moment frames suffice.[24] The riveted steel structure is technically indistinguishable from those used in countless skyscrapers of the 1920s. But through various subtle maneuvers, Mies was able to produce a technologically progressive *expression*. It was not simply that he omitted the masonry cladding and the ornamental regime that had reigned since the very beginning of the high-rise in the United States—though he did that. Rather, he created a novel exterior wall, exploiting the new technology of shop- and site-welded architectural steel to reduce the building envelope to ordered essentials. The result, for the first time, is a high-rise, structural-steel frame legible (and therefore *expressed*) through an exterior wall.

The effect was achieved by complex means, elegantly and economically realized.[25] The typical 10-foot floor-to-floor dimension provides for an 8-foot, 4½-inch-high ceiling. The ceiling is vermiculite plaster fireproofing, with the space above for structural-steel floor beams carrying corrugated sheet-steel decking topped with concrete. The ceiling-to-floor sandwich is closed to the exterior with a 20-inch-high spandrel of steel plate. The columns, all W14 sections but of various weights,[26] are held just inside the edge of the floor slab so that one face meets the plane of the exterior. The column face, like the spandrel, is clad in steel plate, with the "real" column behind and fireproofed by an interior plaster surround. The exterior wall is thus a grid of intersecting spandrels and columns all in the same plane, each "line" of which is a band of steel roughly 2 feet wide. The grid gives almost equal legibility to horizontals and verticals, except that the verticals, "representing" the real columns behind, are visually favored when extended to grade. At the first-floor colonnade, the columns are free of the exterior wall on all sides. Mies boxed them crisply with steel cladding. Absent the glass and mullions, which we discuss below, the exterior is entirely painted steel plate three-sixteenths of an inch thick, welded edge to edge where column covers and spandrels meet. For the first time, a tall building was covered in apparently seamless steel. Technically, the fact that the *structure* is steel is incidental; the columns and floors may just as well have been reinforced concrete.

The 860–880 towers are often called the first steel-and-glass skyscrapers, but this is inaccurate. They are the first tall buildings with an architectural-steel exterior wall. The windows, floor to ceiling and four per bay, are polished plate glass carried in off-the-shelf, extruded aluminum frames that infill the steel wall. Mies chose to further "clad" the exterior in a series of W8 wide-flange "mullions." The inside-facing flange of the mullion is welded to the crossing spandrel. The aluminum window frames, also restrained top and bottom, are affixed to the back of the mullions. The windows were tilted into place from the inside after the steel exterior was in place.

A memorable controversy surrounded another "mullion," also a W8, welded continuously to the steel cladding of each column. "All of us were asking," said Bruno Conterato, "why do we have mullions on the columns? Structurally you don't need them. And it kept gnawing at Myron [Goldsmith] particularly. One day we said 'Myron, why don't you ask Mies?' So Myron went into his office and asked. Mies answered: 'Because it looks better that way.'"[27] Joseph Fujikawa was equally troubled: "One thing that Mies had always striven for [was] to be objective, to have a reason for everything you do. But what was the reason for putting a mullion on the column? You didn't need it except for the aesthetics, for the emotional."[28] In an admiring review of his recent work in the November 1952 *Architectural Forum*, Mies explained his decision:

> Now first I am going to tell you the real reason, and then I am going to tell you a good reason by itself. It was very important to preserve and extend the rhythm which the mullion set up in the rest of the building. We looked at it on the model without the steel section ["mullion"] attached to the corner column and it did not look right. Now the other reason is that this steel section was needed to stiffen the plate which covers the corner column so this

plate would not ripple, and also we needed it for strength when the sections were hoisted into place. Now of course, that's a very good reason, but the other reason is the real reason.[29]

The architectural wide-flange mullions and the rhythm they establish are, in addition to the steel cladding itself, the signature Miesian element invented at 860. They cast deep, crisp, constantly changing shadows, and serve to open and close the wall as the viewer changes position. Because the column covers and corner enclosures are in the plane of the exterior wall and the mullion spacing is constant, windows adjacent to columns must be narrower than the two at the center of each bay.[30] This sets up another layer of textural richness. There is also an apparent paradox: these may be the first "glass houses," but the actual area of glazing as a percentage of the exterior is slightly less than half. The buildings are an exercise in planar and layered steel detailing, and not maximal glazing, demonstrating once again that Mies was not a minimalist but a structural artist seeking the appropriate *expression* of contemporary technology.

Much has been made of the beautiful proportions of the exterior wall of 860, though some observers, including those who worked on the design, argued that they are a consequence of the plan, the floor-to-floor height, and the structural solution.[31] Mies studied the wall in the greatest detail, and called on both Ludwig Hilberseimer and Walter Peterhans to advise him. Peterhans made color studies to test alternates to the chalky-black "Detroit graphite" paint Mies had come to love; even a yellow scheme was discussed and then dismissed. Mies had a full-scale wooden model of a corner of one floor of the exterior installed in his crowded office, where it straddled a drafting table. The tight-fitting steel jacket wrapping the colonnaded columns (where the wide-flange steel is heaviest and thickest) was adopted to make them appear as slender as possible, as well as to minimize their intrusion into the apartments. Indeed, the sober steel cladding serves yet another symbolic purpose, for we readily imagine that the columns standing before us are solid steel. Nevertheless, Mies chose not to reduce the width of the column covers at higher floors, where the steel section is smaller, nor did he signal that the corner and other perimeter columns are lighter than those in the interior. His interest was in the expression of a structural frame of idealized simplicity.[32]

Apartment layouts were also of deep interest to Mies. He had not been able to achieve much with Promontory's plans, and he recognized that 860's nominally all-glazed exterior and three-by-five-bay building plan offered significant opportunities for the interiors. Lenders and real estate professionals, not to mention the buying public, were by various indications not quite ready for floor-to-ceiling glass, and Robert McCormick Sr. was especially wary. Indeed, the presentation model and sales brochure show operable lower lights of *translucent* glass wrapping the short sides of the buildings. Concerns about bedroom privacy were especially contentious. Remarkably, all-clear glazing was not finalized until construction was under way.[33]

The developers decided that with two buildings they could segment their market. The 880 building was designed for "singles," with eight one-bedroom units per floor, and the 860 building for families, with four three-bedroom units per floor. Mies pushed for open plans, and Fujikawa was able to complete a design for the 880 building's units. There were no interior doors except for baths, and, predictably, the open plan made the one-bedroom units appear larger. A much-reproduced presentation drawing of the full-floor 880 building unit plan is often mistakenly represented to be the condition as built. In fact Robert McCormick Sr., hardheaded and personally noncommittal toward Mies, quashed the 880 open plan even before Mies could complete similar studies for 860.[34] That act precipitated a crisis in which Mies nearly resigned. He decided to persevere because the massing and exterior had come together well, and, he reasoned, the interiors could always change. In any event, there had been great difficulty in resolving an open plan with three bedrooms. Dozens of layouts were tried. The surviving sketches show the confusion,[35] with bedrooms pinwheeling at the corners and indirect circulation similar to that at Promontory. The unit plans that were eventually accepted were conventional, with living rooms on the corners wherever possible (all of 860's units, and all except the noncorner units at 880). Visual order on the exterior was achieved by the provision of a double curtain track; the outside track was to carry building-standard light-gray draperies, and the inside, if used at all, left to the unit owner's wishes. Air-conditioning had been considered and recommended by Mies, but was rejected for cost reasons.

Mies focused considerable attention on the lobbies and entry canopies, and on the plaza and canopy connecting the two buildings. The lobby walls and floors are clad and paved, respectively, in honed Roman travertine, and the plaza, continuous with the lobby floor under the storefront, is also paved in travertine, a lavish gesture for the time. Gerald Griffith produced custom Barcelona chairs, ottomans, and X-tables for both lobbies. A landscape plan by Alfred Caldwell was only partially implemented—Caldwell facetiously claimed that the budget allowed for a single tree—though he refreshed the plantings on a real budget some forty years later.[36] The steel canopies at both entries and the longer version connecting the towers are internally braced steel boxes, canted slightly up and away from the buildings in the case of the entries, and carried by handsome exposed-steel brackets more associated with bridges than buildings.

That Mies was able to place the parking below grade is another piece of good fortune. Parking in an above-grade "bustle" (the typical solution for large apartment buildings in Chicago) would have destroyed the composition. Just five years later, across the street at 900–910, Greenwald was unable to resist a single-level parking structure in its "front yard," which he could equally well have forced at 860. The 860–880 lawn remains to this day the only abstract planar landscape on Chicago's Lake Shore Drive.

Greenwald lived for a time at 860, and so did Charles Genther, Mies's architect-of-record. The Mies office customized units for both men, and for dozens of other buyers. Mies himself considered taking an apartment—and sketched a plan for unit 21AB, a northeast-corner lakeside combination of two one-bedroom units in the 880 building.[37] Yet with the host of difficulties the buildings and their owners were to endure in the near term, it was best that he stayed away. The glass was at the heart of the problems, whether it was the blistering heat or the bucket brigades conducted by unhappy owners during rainstorms. It may have been understood to be the price paid by pioneers, but within a couple of years lawsuits had been filed, and the owners dismissed Robert McCormick Jr., who had stayed on as managing agent. Unit air conditioners started to appear—many through the exterior wall—and the heat was somewhat tamed; but the windows were beyond improvement until modern sealants and the permanent freezing of the once-operable upper lights made reasonable peace with the water.[38] Indeed, widespread systematic leaks in the exterior wall—the product of what Fujikawa would much later describe as "an infantile stage of curtain wall design"[39]—must be judged an embarrassment.

In spite of the flaws, which were addressed or deflected as much as possible, 860 was an enormous success—first for Mies, who had created it out of his own intellectual resources, and for Greenwald, who would go on with Mies to spin out profitable adaptations, improvements, and imitations for the next decade. Critics and other informed observers recognized it as an original, masterly work of architecture. Asked whether Mies knew at the time that he had created something uniquely important, Goldsmith, who was on the scene but did not work on 860–880, replied:

> I think so. I think Mies, though he didn't go around saying so, had a great quiet idea of himself, and he did everything because of this idea. He did everything [professional] as if his life depended on it, as if everything was a matter of life and death. He knew the importance of his reputation. I'm sure he knew. In the way he looked at [the buildings] in models he was very pleased with it. He invited people to see it.[40]

The buildings were also a milestone in postwar Chicago real estate. Greenwald proved that modernist residential architecture could attract buyers and be put up at a profit. The project carried no premium for its architectural excellence (indeed, Robert McCormick Jr. thought it had been significantly undersold),[41] and Greenwald was quick to realize that a good site, the Mies imprimatur, and an efficient, not-too-modern plan constituted a formula worth repeating.

. . .

The Mies-Greenwald team continued to study sites up and down the lakefront. After a few false starts, Greenwald and his partner Samuel Katzin[42] were able to acquire the block just north of the 860–880 apartments for what was then the highest price ever paid for residential land in Chicago. Greenwald had advanced his education both with and since 860, and what became the Esplanade Apartments (later known as 900–910 Lake Shore Drive) would be rather more Greenwald and marginally less Mies (fig. 11.10).

Completed in 1957, Esplanade was the first large project for which Mies's office completed both the design and the construction documents. Heretofore, Mies had always associated with other architects, dividing the standard 6-percent-of-construction-cost fee so that one-third went to him and two-thirds to an associated "architect-of-record" (and the consulting engineers). The design architect controlled the project, but the architect-of-record, usually larger and better staffed, did the labor-intensive work of preparing the construction drawings and specifications. Mies never cared about managing his own or his staff's time; he worked until he was satisfied,[43] and his fees were all but squandered. The growth afforded by Greenwald's work coincided with an agreement Mies made with Joseph Fujikawa after the completion of 860. Fujikawa had worked for Mies for almost ten years, and felt he was ready to have his own firm. Mies persuaded him to stay, promising him independence and control of the Greenwald work. When Esplanade came along, Mies was already deeply involved in Seagram. Fujikawa took on the Chicago project, leading the office team and managing day-to-day contact with the client.

In planning, massing, and a host of details, Esplanade is a reprise of 860. But it was designed five years later, and in the interval building technology had advanced and market demands shifted. Mies and Greenwald were eager to exploit the newest technologies. Thus, Esplanade was the tallest concrete building yet constructed in Chicago, and the first with a flat-slab concrete frame. It boasted the city's first central air-conditioning for a residential tower; one of the first unitized, anodized aluminum curtain walls; and Chicago's first large-scale use of tinted, heat-absorbing glass.

The high cost of the land, coupled with Greenwald's greater experience, led to a search for new efficiencies vis-à-vis 860. The floor-to-floor height was reduced by using the concrete frame, so that three additional floors were achieved in a little less total height. Studio apartments were inserted on the plan ends of the 900 building, adding two "bonus" units per floor but compro-

FIGURE 11.10.
Esplanade Apart-
ments, 900–910
North Lake Shore
Drive, Chicago
(1957). View look-
ing southwest. The
single-level garage
structure is just
visible *at bottom*.
There are also two
levels of parking
below grade. The
longer 900 slab is
at left.

mising the corner two-bedroom units.[44] It was decided to run the mechanical risers up the outside face of the columns, where they do not interrupt the
concrete slab or take space from units, forcing the exterior wall well outboard
of the columns. With the dark glass, the exterior reads as an uninterrupted
plane, an effect quite different from 860, where the clear-glass envelope and
column-spandrel grid highlight the structural cage. The exterior detailing
tends away from simplicity, especially in the layered aluminum cladding of
the colonnade columns. The exterior wall uses an extruded aluminum mullion conceptually similar to an off-the-shelf, steel wide flange. When Mies first
saw the partially erected curtain wall during a return trip from working on the
Seagram Building in New York, he objected to the gaps in the mullions at each
floor. They were there for good reason, since aluminum moves with tempera-
ture three times as much as steel, and Fujikawa was concerned that if connected continuously, like those at 860, the mullions might buckle. But they
were not visually continuous, and to Mies they "didn't look good."[45]

Like the 860 site, Esplanade's is a trapezoid, but it covers a full block east
to west and is therefore deeper. Three three-by-five-bay towers were initially
studied, but the sightlines were crowded, and Mies proposed linking two of

Residential Work

the towers on their short ends. This left one three-by-five-bay tower (the 910 building), and at a right angle to it the long slab of 900, now three by ten structural bays. The massing is less satisfying than the right-angle mirroring of 860 and 880. As mentioned above, the addition of enclosed parking in Esplanade's front yard closes the groundplane vista that is so impressive at 860. Compensation is afforded by a private sundeck atop the parking.

Esplanade, like 860, is constructed on a 21-foot column grid. Not by coincidence, the 900–910 towers are sited 21 feet west of the west column centerline of 880. Esplanade has a first-level colonnade like 860, but given the state of concrete technology at the time, the required sectional area for concrete colonnade columns was too great, and so it was decided to construct them in steel. Once they rise above the first two floors, these columns switch to concrete. Compared with 860, other details at Esplanade disappoint: there are no canopies marking the entrances; the plaza space between the towers, so openly ceremonial at 860, is reduced to a service drive; the 900 lobby is narrow, and with terrazzo floors but marble walls, both lobbies lack 860's serene integration of travertine inside to out. Most seriously, the long 900 slab and its eight bays of enclosed space at the ground floor negate much of what makes the soaring 860–880 pair so exceptional.

These shortcomings are mostly unnoticed by buyers. Real estate values at 900–910 are significantly higher than at 860–880. The market rewards the improved technology of the newer buildings, including especially the central air-conditioning, but also the more visually consistent exterior wall, better elevators, and even the garbage chutes so famously omitted at 860 (intentionally so, according to Mies, who is said to have believed at the time that garbage chutes were "unsanitary"). The market is equally untroubled by the arcane comparisons of steel versus concrete frame, or any of the other myriad but subtle visual differences between 860–880 and 900–910. Indeed, the two developments are often confused in books about architecture, even in those entirely devoted to Mies.

.   .   .

Esplanade was sibling to an even larger Greenwald project planned as four towers, the Commonwealth Promenade Apartments farther north on Lake Shore Drive. Only the southern pair was completed (now known as 330 and 340 West Diversey Parkway). Except for a clear anodized aluminum exterior and overall dimensions, the buildings are almost identical to Esplanade. The original roughly three-acre site was a rectangle, and the four buildings were to be sited parallel to one another and, in their long dimensions, perpendicular to the lake. The north and south buildings were to be shifted four bays to the east to open views from the central pair. A rectangle in the middle of the complex was to be occupied by a single-level, at-grade garage, and the towers were to be linked by a baywide covered promenade running from the south to the north property lines. There were even studies for an identical complex to be mirrored to the east, which would have created a large courtyard interior to an ensemble of eight buildings, but the site to the east was never acquired. The parallel siting is inferior to the planning at 860 and Esplanade—though Mies always liked parallel tower blocks—but it made sense as a real estate decision. The whole might have been convincing if realized, but the two-building torso is an unsatisfying remnant.

As a businessman, Greenwald might force his architect's hand, but when it came to aesthetics he could also act on principle. Mies proudly noted that Greenwald had "turned down twelve million dollars in mortgage money for Commonwealth Promenade and Esplanade because the lender wanted a masonry spandrel and other modifications.... This," he said, "takes courage."[46] Still, an alternate presentation model reflected the continuing unease about glazing.[47] It shows marble spandrels on the long elevations and full-height marble panels in the north and south bays of the end elevations. Only the central end bay is floor-to-ceiling glass. The result is a jumble, and the solution, which was rejected, reflected Mies's long-standing uncertainty about special treatment for the short elevations of a rectangular prism.

· · ·

By the end of the 1950s, Greenwald had begun to use other architects. Mies's practice, too, by then included large assignments for other clients and other countries. Among the firms Greenwald worked with was the Chicago office of Skidmore, Owings & Merrill. In 1958 he commissioned SOM to design a hotel for a site on South Michigan Avenue in Chicago. In pursuit of financing, he flew to New York on February 3, 1959.

Though the L-188A Lockheed Electra was new and the instrument approach into LaGuardia apparently routine, the American Airlines turboprop plummeted into the East River almost a mile short of the runway. Pilot error was blamed. The forty-three-year-old Greenwald, his secretary, and 63 others of the 73 aboard perished.[48] Mies spoke at his funeral. Greenwald's death stopped work on projects of his sponsorship—the northern two towers of the Commonwealth Apartments were the immediate victims—and Mies was forced to lay off half his staff.[49]

· · ·

At Greenwald's death, his single major urban-renewal project, Lafayette Park in Detroit, was substantially incomplete. The seventy-eight-acre redevelop-

ment was never realized in its original 1955–56 form, and his designers—Mies, planner Ludwig Hilberseimer, and landscape architect Alfred Caldwell— would never again work together at this scale. In one sense this was a great misfortune, since the project came closer than anything Mies ever did to putting his version of modern architecture in service to the American city. But he finished enough of it to prove his purpose, the partial realization of which continues to be judged a success.[50]

In concept Lafayette Park exemplifies the hopeful but mostly futile programs of urban renewal subsidized by the federal government—but typically planned and constructed by private developers—in the 1950s and '60s (figs. 11.11 and 11.12). These programs rested on the assumption that the overcrowded, dangerous, and dilapidated neighborhoods in so many inner cities could be remade by replacing large sections of "obsolete," usually nineteenth-century urban fabric with lower-density residential parks. On airy, sunlit meadows, apartment buildings, town houses, schools, and community centers would rise, free of vehicular traffic that was consigned to thoroughfares encircling the parklands or to routes at lower levels.

This was Ludwig Hilberseimer's plan for the new city as it materialized in Lafayette Park, the single instance in which he and Mies collaborated professionally on a major built work. Hilberseimer in turn owed much to Le Corbusier, whose city planning ideas of the 1920s developed in part out of the same post–World War I revolutionary mood that had produced European modernist architecture.

Despite the vision of a new metropolis as the setting for a new architec-

FIGURE 11.12.
Town houses and a
high-rise apartment
building at Lafay-
ette Park, Detroit
(1956). Caldwell's
landscape, then
just planted, to-
day dominates this
view. Photo: Baltha-
zar Korab, Ltd.

ture, urban renewal failed in the United States, largely because the financial interests of private developers conflicted with the aspirations and prescriptions of social planners, who possessed insufficient political power to control them. Corbusian residential parks destroyed neighborhoods along with neighborhood slums. The sense of community that was a natural consequence of well-trafficked streets was lost in the windy greenswards, which put people at unmanageable distances from services and one another. The problem became critical in low-income housing, generally racially segregated projects that turned into nocturnal no-man's-lands. Urban renewal became identified with housing for the poor, since people of means could and did select environments offering freedom of movement and a choice of services and amenities.

Located half a mile from downtown Detroit, Lafayette Park was intended to appeal to middle-class people, most of them professionals who wanted to stay in the city. The complex consists of three building types disposed at the edges of the site, enveloping a nineteen-acre clearing intended by Caldwell to

Residential Work

evoke a prairie landscape. Other housing types were considered but rejected, including six-unit clusters of courtyard houses and two-story walk-up apartments. As built, single-story row houses look onto individual rear yards enclosed by brick walls. Two-story houses, their exposed fronts and backs steel framed and fully glazed, are also set in rows, with end walls of brick. Parking for the low-rise units is outdoors, but Hilberseimer lowered the parking grade by three feet, so that cars almost disappear from view. Dominating the development are three twenty-one-story apartment towers, the last two finished as late as 1963. (The plan had called for either six or eight towers, depending on which version is considered final. Many other buildings, tall and low, were completed later to mostly unsympathetic designs by others.) Characteristically for Mies, the three types were sited loosely ajog of one another. A system of closed-end streets prevents through traffic while providing vehicular access to each building.

Lafayette Park incorporates elements of the "settlement unit" Hilberseimer advocated in Germany and the United States. It was conceived as a pedestrian-scaled collection of mixed building types—each oriented for optimal solar exposure—that would include home and work in proximity, as well as educational, recreational, and cultural amenities appropriate to the unit's population. (The target population varied depending on environmental, geographical, and other factors.) The settlement was organized to separate vehicles and pedestrians. Hilberseimer studied and illustrated his settlement unit both as a decentralizing replacement for large cities and for use in existing urban fabric. Since 1940 Caldwell had assisted Hilberseimer in the publication and dissemination of these ideas, chiefly in the role of master draftsman.[51]

Though Hilberseimer's planning concepts were generally respected, one of his most cherished principles—"proper" solar orientation—was simply ignored, even for the low-rise units, because Mies rejected it (as he had for 860–880). Given the tight budgets imposed by Greenwald, even Caldwell's landscaping, now considered one of the glories of Lafayette Park, was nearly sacrificed for a few thousand dollars. Although a small number of specimen trees were saved when the site was cleared, in the end Caldwell made do with saplings and plant detritus from a nearby bankrupt nursery. Greenwald and his staff were similarly strict with the construction budget: on the towers, for example, the ground-floor columns and the exposed corners all the way up are unclad concrete.

Though stopped short of completion, the Mies-Hilberseimer plan remains a model of successful urban redevelopment. The mixed building types, good construction quality, and fee-simple ownership of the low-rise units each contributed to this success. Lafayette Park was eventually taken over and filled out, if not completed, by other developers with other architects. Mies's later exercises in urban planning were confined to commercial or governmental superblocks, where Hilberseimer's settlement unit was not relevant.

. . .

In 1951–52 Mies's office designed a 2,100-square-foot house in Elmhurst, Illinois, for Robert McCormick Jr., Greenwald's partner in the development of 860. Joseph Fujikawa was the project architect. In plan the house consists of two rectangles, each 26 feet deep: one is seven 5-foot, 6-inch modules wide and the other eight. The two units overlap by one module. The south contains the living room and master suite, and the north the kitchen, dining room, and three more bedrooms. Wide-flange beams supporting precast-concrete roof panels span the 26-foot plan dimension. A carport is tucked against the middle end wall.

The end walls of each plan unit are buff brick, and the long elevations on both sides are floor-to-ceiling steel and glass, with mullions similar to those at 860. (They were *not* actual units of the 860 wall, as is often claimed; the McCormick mullions are slightly beefier than those at 860, and the module is three inches larger.)[52] The structure is ambiguous in its relationship of load bearing to frame action. Only the living room and a study next to the master suite participate in an open plan. The rest of the interior has conventional rooms. McCormick by this time was a Miesian modernist — he was immensely proud of 860 — but he was not ready for the master suite without a door that Fujikawa proposed. He claimed he had to go to Mies for the door, which was freely granted.[53]

Although the McCormick House was intensely custom, it looked prefabricated, and Greenwald and McCormick imagined that it might be a model for manufactured housing. Greenwald asked Mies to investigate. A design was generated and working drawings prepared.[54] A 1,200-square-foot plan rectangle of ten modules of the McCormick scheme was proposed: 55 feet wide and the same 26 feet deep. Land was selected and a site design completed for four buildings, each on conventional lots. A marketing flyer was prepared, but nothing came of it, and the site was later acquired for the development of O'Hare International Airport. It is hard to imagine a more unlikely real estate venture than a subdivision of custom steel houses — by Mies — made to look, but not cost, off the shelf.

. . .

The Fifty by Fifty House was a further exploration of steel single-family housing nominally suitable for the general market. Mies worked on the single-story, all-glazed structure with Myron Goldsmith, who recalled that similar houses had already been studied at IIT.[55] The Fifty by Fifty House, so named because of its plan dimensions in feet (40- and 60-foot square versions were also studied), is documented in concept sketches by Mies, no less than twenty surviving presentation plans by Goldsmith, and photographs of a model constructed by Edward Duckett. The interior — of which there were many variants — was organized around an off-center core, with a kitchen, two bathrooms, a utility room, and a fireplace. A double bed was perpendicularly adjacent to the right-hand core wall. Two single beds shared a space to the left. One quadrant provided sitting and dining areas and another a closet. (Curiously, the planning grid is 3 feet, which does not divide exactly into 50.) The model showed a white fascia at the roof, the same fifteen-inch channel used for the Farnsworth and Mc-Cormick Houses. The roof structure is of exposed-to-below crossing beams.

Sketches by Mies illustrate the two support schemes considered, one with a single column at the midpoint of each of the four sides, the other with paired columns on opposing walls. Goldsmith explored options with and without walled rooms, some with moveable walls and some engaging the exterior. He considered possibilities for the number of occupants, suggesting up to four children, with consideration for the problem of "one person sick," accommodation of a guest, and even "the possibility parents [might] remain in bed while children are up."[56]

The house would never have served as a workable residential prototype. The two-way, all-welded roof structure alone would have been prohibitively expensive, and the interior was immoderately spacious. (But in order for the open plan to work, the house had to be large.) American families with children would never have accepted the lack of privacy that Mies's generalized interior implied. Goldsmith "thought it was a huge step to suggest [it for a family], so I said, incredulously, one day to Mies, 'Do you mean you can raise this family with children, parents in this open plan and adjust some walls?' '*Ja*,' said Mies, 'There's distance, and it reminds me of some ski lodges or on a yacht or sailboat.' He thought it could be done if you had a venturesome client."

"The Fifty by Fifty House was an abstract[ion]," Goldsmith stated in a 1986 interview.

> At that time Mies was very interested in architecture just as background for people, to try to reduce the architecture as much as possible to nothing.... He said he had visited the United States Plywood Company to pick some plywood for something and loved this big empty warehouse. What a wonderful house it would make, this space where you could just live. How all the problems are solved, one sees the glimmer of this in some of the lofts that are being done now, unified, very high spaces, solving the elements like sleeping and everything at an absolute minimum. Mies had the same idea. This was the

idea of the Fifty by Fifty House, of how far you could go in one unified space and how you could live within it.[57]

It warrants mention that the exterior of the house, of immense butt-glazed units (and therefore without mullions), was by Goldsmith. He thought that Mies would not have liked it.

American Apogee: Commercial and Institutional Work 1950–59

The clearest structure we have done, the best to express our philosophy.
MIES'S opinion about Crown Hall

You made them, you made their firm, and they pay you back by stealing your work.
LUDWIG HILBERSEIMER to Mies in 1959, upbraiding the staff of Skidmore, Owings & Merrill

He was a groan-and-grunt man. **PHILIP JOHNSON**, of Mies

By the time it turned fifty in 2006, Mies's Crown Hall, designed for and still housing IIT's College of Architecture, had become an official landmark three times over. It received the significant legal protections of City of Chicago landmark status in 1996, ten years before it was officially eligible, and in 2001 was placed on the National Register of Historic Places and made a National Historic Landmark. These designations will ensure that one of the twentieth century's most important buildings is preserved, effectively unaltered, for posterity.

The site, at the northwest corner of State and the former Thirty-Fourth Streets, had been reserved for an "architecture department" in Mies's campus plan, but it was 1950 before IIT finally began to raise money for a building with this purpose. The long gestation is tied to the history of the site, which involves key issues of social and urban history and the presence of another building legendary in its own right. Occupying the site was the Mecca, a large apartment building completed in 1892 to a design of Willoughby J. Edbrooke and Franklin Pierce Burnham of Chicago. At the time of its construction, luxury apartment buildings were beginning to challenge the supremacy of the substantial single-family house, especially on the city's still fashionable Near South Side. Built for $800,000—an enormous sum, given that sixty years later Crown Hall cost about the same[1]—the Mecca originally had ninety-eight apartments and twelve retail stores. Its U-shaped plan was centered on a landscaped courtyard facing Thirty-Fourth Street. The two four-story wings featured skylit galleried atria, the first of their kind in a Chicago apartment building.

Demographic developments following the turn of the twentieth century

FIGURE 12.1 (*facing*). The new 3410 South State Building (originally Institute of Gas Technology—North Building), Illinois Institute of Technology, Chicago, 1951. View looking north, with the city's Loop in the far distance. To the north across Thirty-Fourth Street is the storied Mecca apartment building, soon to be demolished to make way for S. R. Crown Hall. The dilapidated surroundings are evident. Wallace Kirkland/Time & Life Pictures/Getty Images.

worked to the ill fortune of the Mecca. As discussed above, migration from the South that led to the rapid growth of Chicago's African American population contributed to racial tensions and neighborhood deterioration. By the mid-1940s, no fewer than fifteen hundred people were crowded into the Mecca, which was routinely described as "the most notorious slum in America."[2] On account of its location, Armour Institute got involved, and in 1938 trustee Alfred L. Eustice, acting on his own, purchased the building. Three years later he deeded it to IIT, which initiated plans for demolition.[3]

The university soon encountered determined opposition from tenants and their sympathizers. The battle lasted more than a decade, but in 1952 IIT succeeded in razing the building. By that time, many of Mies's designs had been built, including the 3410 South State Building, just across Thirty-Fourth Street

Commercial and Institutional Work

(fig. 12.1). In December 1954, ground was broken for the new architecture building.

The Mecca was legendary long before it was pulled down. Reginald Malcolmson, a Mies student and later a key faculty administrator, remembered:

> On the site of Crown Hall was this enormous apartment house … a big slum building, actually. Very dramatic. If you walked into the court inside it, it was like a setting from a Tennessee Williams play.... It was built in a style almost like Elmslie in the flat Roman brick that was used in Sullivan's day so much, and by Sullivan himself.... It had been a great building at one time, and it had simply gone into decay and decline.... It had a kind of macabre grandeur.[4]

In his long career, Mies had never designed a school of architecture. He had run the Bauhaus in the Gropius building in Dessau, and in Berlin, as we have noted, in a converted warehouse. His first venue at Armour was the attic of the Art Institute of Chicago. Later, he moved the IIT architecture department to Alumni Memorial Hall, a building he had designed, though not for the study of architecture. Thus, the prospect of a new building that would reflect his principles—architectural, educational, and spiritual—made Crown Hall a dream project.

Effort toward an "architecture design and planning building" began in 1950. Early that year, at Mies's direction, Joseph Fujikawa first prepared studies and drawings "for fundraising." Elevations and perspectives of the several preliminary schemes show a building consistent with campus architecture already in place: brick infill panels below steel-framed, large-scale glazing, derivative of precedents set as early as the Library and Administration Building. The interior is columnated, albeit with spans on the order of 60 feet. A mezzanine and basement are also indicated, again evoking the Library project. This concept was maintained into the summer of 1952, at which time the university elected to postpone construction of another project, a student union, and instead "secure funds for ID-architecture" first.[5] "ID," IIT's Institute of Design, was also in need of facilities, and it was decided that the building that would become Crown Hall would house both departments.

Mies worked rapidly during the summer and fall of 1952 to confirm the program and work out a solution. His chief assistants were Fujikawa, Goldsmith, and David Haid. Haid and Donald Sickler would shepherd the project through construction. A superb model was ready for presentation to university officials in November. It is best known from a much-reproduced photograph in which a dour but elegantly attired Mies stands behind and above the model, as if offering it on a platter. Malcolmson accompanied Mies to the IIT trustee presentation: "Mies was called in. He explained the model, he explained the drawings and so forth, and then they asked him to leave the room and they would discuss it. And then they asked him to come back again, and do a little

more explaining. And he said to me, 'As if there was something wrong with it!'"[6] Mies's self-confidence, so dryly—if not to say contemptuously—delivered, was one thing; the university's fiduciary responsibilities were another. Though the trustees' minutes acknowledge the "advanced design," they also indicate that the proposal was "of such [an] extreme nature and the cost so far in excess of amounts planned that the matter should be held in abeyance for the time being."[7] As it turned out, almost two more years would pass before the building was finally approved, with the last third of the $750,000 construction budget coming from the Arie and Ida Crown Foundation, along with the naming rights for family scion Sol R. Crown. Another key contribution came from Charles Genther, Mies's one-time student and the managing principal of Pace Associates; Pace produced the construction documents pro bono.

Completed in 1956, S. R. Crown Hall is officially a one-story building, though with a programmatically rich, partially above-grade lower level (fig. 12.2). The two levels total 52,800 square feet. The main floor is a glass-walled rectangular room 120 feet north to south and 220 feet east to west. The ceiling height is 18 feet. Four wide-flange columns spaced 60 feet apart rise along the two long elevations to carry each end of the six-foot-deep steel plate girders that span the roof north to south. The roof diaphragm is hung from the underside of these girders. The building is organized on a 10-foot module, with the glazing unit, of paired translucent glass lights below and a single clear light above, carried by wide-flange steel mullions with steel bar-stock stops (fig. 12.3). Because the columns and mullions are, visually, roughly the same size—the columns are W14 sections, the mullions W8s—and because the columns and

Commercial and Institutional Work

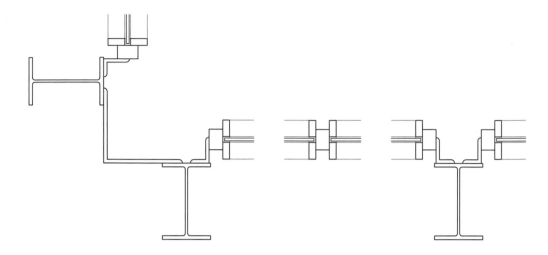

mullions are outside the line of the glass, the building, especially from inside, appears to be supported by nothing other than its diaphanous glazed wall. Inside, the edge of the acoustical tile ceiling is held back from the exterior by about a foot, so that the ceiling appears to float.

Crown Hall's clear-span structure is a spiritual ideal made real. It has no programmatic justification, but as a representation of the potential of Miesian steel-and-glass architecture it approaches an idealized perfection. By the mid-1950s, Mies had been trying to realize a major clear-span building for a decade. He had proposed one for the Cantor Drive-In Restaurant, the Fifty by Fifty House, and simultaneous with Crown Hall's development and on a grand scale for the Chicago Convention Hall and the Mannheim Theater competition, as we discuss below. With the requirement to house the Institute of Design, Mies was able to rationalize a large floor plate—26,400 square feet for the architecture department—while providing a second level of the same ample footprint for ID. The lower level was also used to house back-of-house functions for both departments, including toilet rooms, mechanical spaces, and service entrances.

The lower level is a conventional, concrete-walled box exposed 6 feet above grade. It supports a main-level concrete floor on a 20-by-30-foot grid of concrete piers. Services are grouped in the center, with circulation and exiting surrounding, and standard classrooms and workshops at the perimeter. Four-foot-high, translucent-glass clearstories run along the entire lower-level perimeter, by day flooding it with softly filtered natural light. Lower- to upper-level circulation is via a central "stair hall" bracketed by two of Mies's most exquisite stairs. The lower-level layout has been altered over the decades, especially after the Institute of Design's departure in 1989, when the College of Architecture took over the entire building. The history of these successful remodelings suggests that the advantages of a clear span for future planning flexibility—one of Mies's principal justifications for the open plan—are overstated.

Much has been made of the fact that the main floor is raised, podium-like, with observers citing precedents in Greek and Roman architecture. To be sure, Mies's other campus buildings rest mostly at grade, and entry is without ceremony. For Crown Hall, Mies took advantage of the elevated entry to install a lavish porch, 60 feet wide and 30 deep, framed in steel and paved with Roman travertine. Access from grade is by five 30-foot-wide, floating travertine treads, with a second set of six leading up from the porch to the main doors. The porch and stairs are pure aesthetic gesture—modeled on those of the Farnsworth House—and are unique in Mies's work for IIT. For the north stairs—at the historically most-used "back door"—Mies provided opposing stairs of concrete and steel that hug the exterior.

That the main entrance faces south seems a curiosity, since the area north of Crown Hall is an open greensward, and Thirty-Fourth Street was long ago vacated. But a "future Mechanical Engineering Building" had been planned to rise only sixty feet to the north, just across the existing service drive, and the frontage on Thirty-Fourth Street was natural for drop-offs. The anticipated close proximity of another classroom building may also have influenced Mies's selection of translucent glass for the lower eight feet of Crown Hall's main-floor glazing.

While the initial planning for Crown Hall employed the standard campus vocabulary and its twenty-four-foot module, as built it represents a major exception in Mies's campus plan. Gene Summers reflected on this issue in a 1987 interview:

> When Mies did the architecture building he broke with what he intended originally to do on the campus. He had a design for the arts and architecture building that was a steel structure with a brick infill that would have tied in with the first buildings on the campus. For him to have [gone] to this totally steel and glass building with the structural system he used ... I personally thought was the wrong thing to do.... [The campus] should have been more unified. The irony ... [is that] he built it, and certainly Crown Hall is one of his best buildings.... I think the whole concept of the campus with its modular system both in planning and ... within the structure of each individual unit was the very kernel of the whole idea, and then he changed it for that building. That's what great artists do sometimes.[8]

Summers's observations reflect his knowledge of later developments; campus buildings by other designers strayed even further from Mies's standards. The key point remains: for Crown Hall, Mies "the artist" allowed himself new freedoms in pursuit of what he believed were great goals. Some of those freedoms—like the adoption of a ten-foot module in favor of the standard twelve/twenty-four—may have been motivated by practical concerns, such as limiting the size of individual glass lights. Others, including the structural solution, represented opportunities too promising even for an objectivist to resist.

The main floor is ostensibly freely organized. Originally, three key functions were envisioned for its center: an exhibition space, flanked east and west by freestanding millwork partitions and the two stair openings; an administration area north of the exhibit space and closed by similar partitions on three sides; and, opposite the northern entry, a library, also demarked on three sides by freestanding millwork walls. Tucked between the library and administration areas were janitors' closets and a coatroom. Over time the school's administration has decamped to the lower level, and these once-differentiated functions have coalesced into generalized exhibit space. White-painted storage cabinets were an early addition on the main floor. The other principal vertical features inside the space are a pair of floor-to-ceiling shafts, three by thirteen feet in plan, which carry plumbing vents, roof drains, and other mechanical systems to and from the roof.

The rest of the main floor was originally occupied by steel and wood drafting tables designed by Mies's office. Early photographs show them neatly aligned but adrift in the ocean of space. The building was not originally air-conditioned, and climate control was problematic. White Venetian blinds were the primary solar control. The modest vents at the base of each lower light were the sole source—along with open doors—of fresh air. The acoustics turned out to be benign. "I like to work in this building," said Mies. "There is never any disturbance in the acoustics, [except] when the Professor becomes emotional. He should not do that. Otherwise we have no disturbances."[9]

For the exterior wall of Crown Hall, the paired lower lights were originally quarter-inch-thick, sandblasted plate glass, except for those to either side of the main doors, which were clear, polished plate, offering the only direct outside views to grade. Above in each module was a single light of polished plate glass, about 9 feet wide and 10 feet high. Mies was able to use quarter-inch glass even in the upper lights, but only by reducing the height of the building by 2 feet (20-foot-high ceilings, as initially intended, are shown in the model), avoiding the thicker glass that would have been needed for the original design.[10] Glass was held in place by steel stops, exactly as at Farnsworth, which allowed the slender frames and crisp shadows that Mies prized. But the system was thermally inefficient and onerous in maintenance, with breakage and reglazings a plague. Due to revisions in the Chicago Building Code, renovations have been required to increase glass thickness in the upper lights, first (in the 1970s) to three-eighths of an inch and then (in 2005) to half-inch plate. The lower lights were also replaced in the major renovation of 2005.

About Crown Hall Mies famously said, "[It is] the clearest structure we have done, the best to express our philosophy."[11] Jacques Brownson offered his understanding in 1994: "Every [structural] member is like a tree.... The tree is a structure that works in continuity. Crown Hall is [just like this,] a building in which all of the members, in effect, transmit the forces. If you start to take it [apart] piece by piece, they become individually relatively weak. But as soon as you put them all together, they become a strong ... unified structure."[12] Ludwig Hilberseimer, writing in 1956 not about Crown Hall but about the Library and Administration Building, offered a mostly aesthetic explanation: "[Because] the [American] architecture of Mies van der Rohe is based on structural elements and not on superimposed forms, each part, each detail, becomes important in itself, as well as in relation to the whole. Steel ... is used in the fixed shapes that come from the rolling mill. The different members are joined together ... without a single arbitrary addition of anything superfluous. A maximum of effect, rich in architectural refinements, results from a seeming minimum of effort, as the details illustrate."[13]

Brownson's technical analysis is neatly balanced by Hilberseimer's artistic apology, and both aid our understanding. Nevertheless, the *actual* structural behavior of Crown Hall is anything but clear. Mies conceived a visually powerful structure in his original model, and Frank Kornacker, an exceptional engineer, was able to turn that *image* into a safe building, albeit by many tricks of his trade. The building does partake of multiple structural redundancies, just as Brownson indicates, though he would have us believe that these systems must function jointly to yield a safe design, which is not the case. Contrary to appearances, Kornacker's structural solution is solidly conservative, as the following analysis demonstrates.

We begin with the main columns. Each is rigidly fixed to structural elements of the foundation at two key points: to the steel fascia where the foundation wall emerges, and then 6 feet higher, where the concrete floor slab of the main level meets the exterior. These two connections fix the column base, making it a pure cantilever. The columns appear to be 24 feet high (the height of the exterior), but the cantilevered portion is only 18 feet long. The longer the cantilever, the larger the required structural member. Analysis indicates that the columns can resist all the lateral (wind) loads on the building exterior without any stiffening from the frame action of the walls and without any contribution from the portal frame formed by the plate girder. This is even true for lateral loads that accumulate against the narrow elevations, where the columns are oriented on their weak axes.[14]

The wide-flange mullions, also 24 feet high but with only 18 feet standing free, are also cantilevers. They, too, are rigidly attached to the steel fascia panels below and above the basement lights, so that they act as rigid frame elements in the plane of the wall. The mullions alone can *also* resist all the lateral forces acting on the building.

The plate girders spanning the roof are Crown Hall's structural signature. They are welded to the top of their supporting columns, which creates true portal frame action. Portal frames are laterally rigid, and at Crown Hall they certainly resist lateral loads, though only in the north–south direction. (They provide no frame action east to west.) From the discussion above, we can see that the portal action is *not* critical to the building's lateral system. The plate girders could just as well have had pinned connections at their ends, in which case they would behave as simple spans. Here Mies evidently deemed the visual impression of a fixed portal even more important than "structural clarity."

As engineering, Crown Hall's structure is bold only in the use of the *upturned* plate girder; buckling of the girder's top flange controls the structural design, and Kornacker's rigid end connections and the welding of all main roof purlins to the bottom flange of the girder counter potential rotation. The plate girders' depth-to-span ratio, 1 to 20, is conservative. Mies also considered trusses for Crown Hall, but trusses of 120-foot span offer no advantage in cost or structural depth over plate girders.

Although the roof is usually described as cantilevered for 20 feet at each end (the plate girders are held back that distance from the east and west elevations), the action is that of beams resting on bearing walls, because though the purlins are welded continuously under each plate girder, the distal ends are fixed to the top of the end walls. The 20-foot span appears bold from the exterior, but it is in fact short for the steel employed.

Nonetheless, after more than half a century Crown Hall still *appears* magical. Vertical support seems effortless, especially from inside through the diaphanous glass. The ceiling appears to float, or even to disappear, especially in daylight. From inside, the snow-white glow of the lower lights dissociates the building from the ground, while the view through the clear upper lights is of treetops and sky, of indeterminate elevation and place. At night from outside, the shimmering building floats, separated from the ground by its internally illuminated lower level.

Crown Hall is the largest interior space Mies had realized up to that time, and while he rationalized it as he always had, namely, that it was by its very generality forever adaptable to changing purposes, he had another end in mind too. The building was a materialization in modern form of the *Bauhütte*, the shelter of centuries past where master builder, workmen, and apprentices met, planned, taught, and learned in concert. As a shared space, it implied goals and methods held in common by its users—in short, shared *values*. The "chaos of directions" of the modern world that Mies lamented in his 1938 letter to Carl O. Schniewind might here be put to order by the formative, clarifying mind, working communally, objectively, and impersonally.

In the United States, Mies did little to actively seek work. He and his key staff responded to inquiries and encouraged repeat business, and he was attentive to the press, if not encouraging. Even then there were exceptions: graduate student Paul Pippin recalled that "one day in the design studio Mies's secretary came in to say a newspaper reporter was outside and would like to interview him. Mies replied, 'You know what to tell him. Say I am not here.'"[15] Exhibitions of his work, under his control, were Mies's primary promotional vehicle. He was averse to even a whiff of professional competition, as Goldsmith recounted: "I don't know of any case where he was competing for a job, where somebody said 'I'm talking to you, Mies, and I'm talking to SOM [Skidmore, Owings & Merrill].' . . . I think he very well may have, during the years I [worked for him], withdrawn if they were considering anybody else."[16] On the subject of soliciting clients, Joseph Fujikawa confirmed that Mies was "a real [old European] professional . . . I remember we had one potential client who seemed to Mies kind of dubious, and I suggested to him that the simplest thing to do would be to ask for a retainer. . . . Mies chewed me out! 'We don't do that here!'"[17]

As for entering competitions, which his staff now and then suggested, Mies was equally adamant: "They know what we can do."[18] An exception to the rule was his decision in late 1952 to enter an invited competition for the design of a new German National Theater, sponsored by the City of Mannheim—a replacement for a nineteenth-century building destroyed in World War II. Mies was motivated by the participation of his prewar employee Herbert Hirche, now an advisor to Mannheim's mayor. Hirche suggested Mies, who was the only competitor from outside Germany. There were four local firms and five of national stature, including that of Mies's friend Rudolf Schwarz. Mies must have been pleased to have Hirche working on the inside.

Mies began the Mannheim project just as he was completing the schematic design for Crown Hall.[19] Goldsmith was project architect and structural engineer, with David Haid and Edward Duckett assisting. Daniel Brenner worked with Mies on the interiors. The site, Mannheim's Goetheplatz—not the location of the destroyed theater—measures roughly 90 by 200 meters, and is bounded on all sides by roads.[20]

The program called for theaters of 1,300 and 500 seats, each with its own entry, and ancillary facilities including administrative offices for the National Theater and a large restaurant. Mies proposed a building 80 by 160 meters in plan, nearly filling the site. Entry to back-to-back theaters was to be on opposite ends, with a huge back-of-theatrical-house between. Typical of the 1950s, there was no requirement for parking.

Mies elected to house the complex in a scaled-up, two-story adaptation of Crown Hall. "I came to the conclusion," he said, "that the best way to enclose

FIGURE 12.4.
National Theater
project, Mannheim,
West Germany,
model (1953). The
Mannheim Theater
competition entry
was Mies's first Eu-
ropean effort follow-
ing his immigration
to the United States
fifteen years before.
In the 1950s, he pro-
duced his most am-
bitious clear-span
works, only one of
which, S. R. Crown
Hall, was realized.
The Mannheim
Theater would have
had seven open-web
trusses supporting a
roof that covered two
large theaters. The
proposed building
would have enclosed
more than five times
the area of Crown
Hall. Photo: Bill
Engdahl, Hedrich-
Blessing.

this complicated spatial organism was to cover it with a huge column-free hall of steel and colored glass"[21] (fig. 12.4). The module was increased from Crown Hall's 10 feet to 4 meters; instead of plate girders, seven open-web trusses were to span the 80-meter narrow plan dimension—more than the *length* of Crown Hall. The ground floor was to be 4 meters high and the second an astounding 12. Seating for the theaters was to be nestled between the floors, with the upper tiers spilling into foyers open to below at each end. The second floor was to be bounded by a great promenade 10 meters wide and 12 high, interrupted on the north by the restaurant.

In architectural competitions the goal is to win, and it is common practice to overreach. The inevitable economic and technical challenges can and must be tackled later. And because Mies's proposal was not built, it can be forgiven for certain extravagances. Thus, at the ground floor on the long sides, and extending well beyond the building at both ends, Mies called for a 3- and 4-meter-tall base veneered with Tinian marble. The giant trusses were to be of all-welded stainless steel, on a scale never before used in a building. Perhaps the greatest extreme is the quantity of enclosed space, in which the theaters and back-of-house elements all but swim. The second-level promenade alone covered a quarter of the enormous floor. The rear of the main theater had no physical enclosure at all; it was to be boldly cantilevered into the 18-meter-high foyer beyond and below. Actual seating would have occupied less than 5 percent of the proposed floor area.[22]

Acoustics would surely have been a problem; the huge volumes, hard surfaces, and open-to-below upper tiers of the larger theater each posed special problems. The all-glazed exterior, though grand, does nothing to enclose the second floor specialty areas, none of which, for theatrical use, need or welcome natural light. Most problematic is the rationale for a clear span. Neither the program nor Mies's solution require it. The largest *required* clear span in Mies's scheme is for the upper tiers of the large theater, about 32 meters. The smaller theater spans 24. Mies nonetheless elected to span the entire 80-meter-wide volume—hardly an objective solution. A few columns hidden in walls could have carried the roof.

According to his staff, Mies was delighted with his solution. He even worked one night until dawn to help meet the competition deadline.[23] In June 1953 the City of Mannheim announced a shortlist of Rudolf Schwarz and Mies. But members of the jury also suggested a second round, in which they solicited a submittal from Frankfort architect Gerhard Weber, who had not been invited to the first round. No revisions were requested of Mies, however. The next month, upon Mies's trip to Europe, he made the extraordinary—for him—effort to personally lobby for the project, and met with Mannheim's mayor, who asked him to revise his design. After three months thinking about it, Mies quietly bowed out. Goldsmith said, "His thinking went something like this: 'I have made my design, they know what I can do, it was stupid of them to run another competition for minor changes.'"[24] The project was awarded to Gerhard Weber, whose building, designed with full knowledge of Mies's scheme and completed in 1957, stands on the Goetheplatz today. By contrast with Mies's vision, it is a middling effort.

. . .

In the fall of 1953, the South Side Planning Board of Chicago invited Mies to design a fifty-thousand-seat convention hall for a site west of Lake Shore Drive between the Loop and IIT. The invitation came through Raymond J. Spaeth, the board's chairman and an IIT vice president.[25] The SSPB, though not empowered to commission a building, sought a compelling proposal in the hope that the city and state might embrace it or something similar.

Chicago desperately needed a new facility for the hundreds of conventions, expositions, and other events it hosted across the city, and the Illinois legislature first voted to fund such a building in the summer of 1953.[26] In anticipation, the SSPB called for a large, flexible structure on a site close to downtown. A motley district of commercial and industrial buildings plus scattered and mostly tatterdemalion housing, the development area seemed perfectly appropriate by the planning standards of the day.

Mies undertook the design as a project within IIT, not as the work of his office. He selected three graduate students, Yujiro Miwa, Henry Kanazawa, and Pao-Chi Chang, who worked as a group and produced a joint master of architecture thesis.[27] Site design, parking, and links to public transportation were barely studied, though today they would be critical for such an enormous project. Some of the program was shunted to subsidiary buildings that remained ciphers. For the hall—there was always only one—Mies appears to

FIGURE 12.5.
Chicago Convention
Hall project (1953).
Version with exte-
rior wall of glass and
metal panels. For
scale, note the fig-
ures standing next to
the second column
from the left. Photo:
Hedrich-Blessing.

have focused exclusively on a clear-span solution, considering a dome and a system of three-hinged arches before settling on a square-plan roof of two-way trusses covering 520,000 square feet (fig. 12.5). The volume, too, was gargantuan, a box 720 feet on a side with a clear interior height of 85 feet. There appears to be no programmatic justification for this clearance.

The roof is an all-welded, two-way grid of 30-foot-deep steel trusses on 30-foot centers (fig. 12.6). Each truss is built up of W14 wide-flange chords and webs. Member sizes and truss depth increase toward the center, as expected, but visually the system is homogeneous. The scheme recalls the Martin Bomber Plant Mies admired and used in his 1942 Concert Hall collage, but the two-way truss is far more sophisticated than the half-as-long one-way system in Baltimore. The roof is a diaphragm, point-supported along its perimeter by massive trusses built in the plane of each wall. Five units to a side and 60 feet deep, they are expressed inside and out, spanning 120 feet between giant, cone-like supports.

At the corners, the trussed wall opens to grade under matching, 60-foot cantilevers. Infill panels are set between the exposed structural members, yielding identical wall elevations inside and out. Mies studied wall units of both marble and aluminum panels. True to the symmetrical ground plan, access is on all sides through a glazed wall set back at ground level. The main floor is depressed 10 feet from grade so that on entry the entire space would be visible. To accommodate objects or internal construction of any weight, there was no basement. At the perimeter of the vast interior are 17,000 tiered seats. Moveable main-floor seating increases capacity to 50,000.

The real work of design was in repeated study of specific problems — variations in the dimensions and components of the roof, in the expression of the in-wall diagonals, in the material of the skin, and so on. This was Mies's stan-

FIGURE 12.6.

Mies, studying a large student-made model of the Chicago Convention Hall's two-way roof in 1953. A full model of the building is visible in the distance, above Mies's head.

dard way of working, in his office and the school. His three students dutifully produced superb models and perspective drawings that captured the project's overwhelming scale. Mies surely believed that his concept was eminently practical; such a volume, precisely because it was undifferentiated, could accommodate any and all activities appropriate to it, from conventions to trade shows to sports events. Subdivision, he asserted, could be achieved by free-standing or hanging partitions.

Nothing Mies had ever done was as intellectually adventurous or as tectonically bold as the unbuilt Convention Hall. From within, the soaring roof alone would have inspired awe. From the exterior, the trussed wall structure would be grandly legible. Mies's ability to produce architectural art by what appeared to be the most uncompromisingly rational means was never so manifest. By comparison, a monumental project like the Reichsbank was sluggish and earthbound.

With the publication of the Convention Hall design, Mies's reputation as the great rationalist of modern architecture was powerfully advanced. Yet within the heroic scope of the work was a paradox: except for the odd indoor sporting event—which in any case the hall was not really intended for—there was no reason for the clear span he proposed. He could have placed a columnar grid within the hall, adopting large but reasonable spans to achieve the flexibility he prized.[28] He selected the clear span not out of force of reason and logic but out of passion and will. Certain that his architecture was rational, he carried it to an irrational extreme. Very likely in no other way could he have produced a space so daring.

Mies always characterized his task as problem solving, based in necessity. "There are certain rules," he said. "The great historical epochs restricted themselves to very clear principles, yet they were certainly able to do anything, and that is the only way you can make important architecture."[29] From a major figure of the modern architectural revolution, this sounds unmodern and un-revolutionary, and in 1951 he admitted as much: "I am not a reformer. I don't want to change the world. I want to express it. That's all I want."[30] Mies was a system builder in an age suspicious of systems, and part of his genius was his skill in reconciling opposing positions. His system was not a set of rules but a method for seeking and finding an architecture in harmony with modern times. It was his will, firm and final, that convinced the world of the 1950s that he was a man of reason. Yet without the simple excellence of his architecture, even his will and the charisma that radiated from it would not have been enough to win the acclaim he garnered. It became conventional wisdom to acknowledge that Mies's architecture, because it was reasonable and systematic, was therefore the most teachable. The stillborn design in the Miesian manner that transformed the American cityscape in the 1950s and 1960s suggests otherwise.

.   .   .

Mies's 1951 design for the Arts Club of Chicago is his only American work executed in a building he did not design,[31] and the sole instance in which he used—in this case *reused*—traditional furniture. It is, at this writing, also the only American work by Mies that has been demolished.[32] That act riveted the attention of the architectural world, and led to an exchange of views to be reported here in brief.

Founded in 1916, the Arts Club is a private institution devoted to exhibitions, concerts, lectures, and kindred programs in the arts. It has operated in several downtown Chicago locations. In 1947 the club was forced to vacate the Wrigley Building when it lost its lease. During the same year the club's president, Rue Shaw, invited Mies to design a new club space in a building at 109 East Ontario Street. He commenced work early in 1948, offering his services without charge. An agreement was reached that enabled Mies to modify the street entry and window openings for what would become the club's second-floor space. The project was in design over a two-year period, and the club took occupancy in the fall of 1951.

A small ground-floor lobby included an elevator and a new stair that led to the main rooms above, which consisted of an art gallery, a dining area, and a lounge that doubled as an auditorium. The materials were simple: walls painted white except in the gallery, where they were millwork; floors of black

wood parquet; and floor-to-ceiling draperies of raw silk in black, smoke gray, ivory, and saffron yellow. The signature element was the stair, an inspired abstraction of diagonals, verticals, and horizontals engaged with two floating landings (fig. 12.7). The steel stringers and bar-stock railings were similar to those in Mies's classroom buildings at IIT, but painted white. With lushly carpeted treads and the surrounding walls clad in travertine, the composition was immensely assured.

The leased space at 109 East Ontario was not the only Arts Club designed by Mies. In 1989 plans for a one-story Arts Club *building* were discovered in the MoMA collection.[33] They are dated August to November 1949—during the period when the Ontario space was in design—and they probably represent an

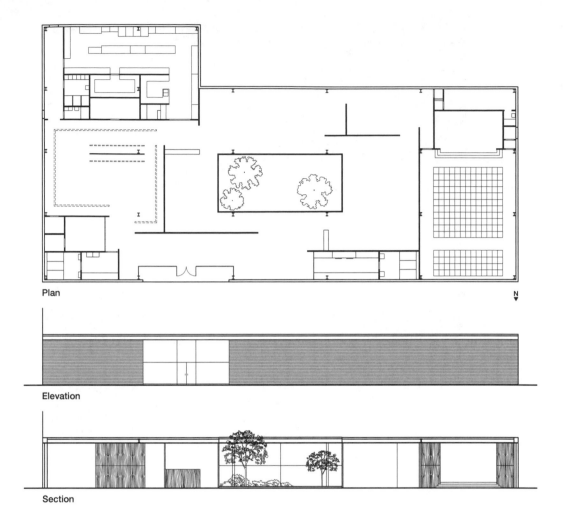

Plan

N

Elevation

Section

alternate scheme for a freestanding building then still a possibility (fig. 12.8). A site plan shows the proposed building on a corner, with existing buildings abutting either side, but there are no street names.

Except for a glazed entry, the two exposed elevations are uninterrupted brick. The 10,000-square-foot structure is of steel, in a three-by-five-bay rectangular grid, each bay 30 by 25 feet, with columns exposed in the interior and set in slightly from the exterior wall. The roof edge is a steel channel. The interior is open in the manner of the plan of the Barcelona Pavilion. Program areas flow into each other, loosely marked by freestanding walls of partial or full height. Each of the foyer, lounge, dining, and conference areas opens to a glazed interior court. A gallery and lecture hall fill out the narrow end of the plan. Materials are specified: floors of terrazzo, interior walls of plaster and millwork, and the inside of the exterior in continuous face brick.

In 1990 the Arts Club was forced to recognize its diminishing financial resources and the imminent loss of its Ontario Street lease. New owners had taken over the property with the intention of razing the club's building and three others on the same block—hence the club's need to find another home in a building of its own, which would be tax exempt. To finance the plan—at a time when the art market was strong—the officers decided to sell Constantin Brancusi's *Golden Bird*, a sculpture the club had purchased in 1927 for $1,200. A transaction consisting of a sale and partial gift in the amount of $12 million was struck with the Art Institute of Chicago.[34] The Arts Club was able to gain a new building, and the city's prime art collection took possession of an internationally acclaimed work of art.

Preservationists then made their own move. On May 9, 1994, Terence Riley, chief curator of the Department of Architecture and Design of the Museum of Modern Art, wrote the Arts Club, advising that it "look for ways in which [Mies's] space might be preserved as and where it is." He added that "the incorporation of the space into the [developer's] proposed new building should, in fact, pose no serious structural or design problems." Riley's letter prompted the club and its friends to address the international architectural community. Letters were solicited urging the preservation of the Mies space, and it was hoped that the Commission on Chicago Landmarks and the City Council might be persuaded to name it a landmark.

By the fall of 1994, the preservationists had focused their campaign on Chicago developer John Buck, who controlled the property. Armed with a demolition permit that had been granted months before, Buck had no intention of changing his mind. In a dramatic hearing in which he played the oppressed, the Landmarks Commission voted against landmark status for the Mies interior. The entire block was taken down in 1996. By this time the Arts Club had acquired a prized parcel nearby, at 201 East Ontario Street. Chosen by a club committee, Chicago architect John Vinci designed a new two-story building that partly follows Mies's plan, incorporates the celebrated stair, and again redeploys the furniture.[35]

· · ·

Mies's IIT buildings were built with modest budgets, and most suffered modifications and sometimes redesigns at the order of university administrators. The austerity of Mies's IIT work is bound up with its ungenerous funding.[36] The architect's achievement under these constraints is doubly remarkable, and no building on the campus better exemplifies these struggles than the Robert F. Carr Memorial Chapel of Saint Savior. Completed in 1952, it is Mies's only work in service to religion (fig. 12.9).

Planning commenced in 1949. Two buildings were proposed: a chapel and a parish house with quarters for a chaplain, a meeting room, and administrative space. The first studies were based on the 24-foot campus module, with

FIGURE 12.9.
Robert F. Carr Memorial Chapel of Saint Savior, Illinois Institute of Technology, Chicago (1952). The only building by Mies serving an ecclesiastical purpose. Early planning called for two buildings: a chapel and a connected parish house. Budget cuts reduced the built scheme to a single—some say severe—building. Photo: Hedrich-Blessing.

FIGURE 12.10
(*facing*).
Three alternate concepts for the Carr Memorial Chapel at IIT, Chicago, each showing a pair of buildings (1952). Two of the alternates are organized as a courtyard group. All the chapel buildings in these drawings are of structural steel, in contrast with the built scheme, which is of load-bearing brick construction. These are excellent examples of the way Mies explored the many possibilities of almost every commission.

a 3,000-square-foot chapel four bays long and one and one-half wide. The 2,300-square-foot parish house was to be two bays square. The pair share a partially walled compound (fig. 12.10). Mies's perspective sketch of the chapel interior[37] indicates a steel superstructure bracketed by opaque sidewalls, with roof beams expressed above the side aisles and columns up and down the walls, a low platform supporting a table-like altar, and behind that a flat wall displaying only a cross.

Budget and program reductions led to the elimination of the parish house. The chapel's nave was reduced from four bays to three. This revision preserves the structural-steel frame, now spanning two bays or 48 feet, for an *increase* of area to 3,400 square feet. The scheme also employs Mies's standard expressed steel with buff brick infill. It was carried well into the construction document phase before it, too, was judged too costly. Mies again reworked the design, this time almost from scratch, abandoning the 24-foot module to produce a 2,220-square-foot building 37 by 60 feet in plan, with load-bearing brick carrying steel beams that support a precast concrete roof.

Carr Memorial Chapel as built is a simple—some say excessively plain—rectangular brick prism, with sidewalls wrapping each end to meet full-height, steel-framed glazing. The walls are eighteen feet tall—a comfortable maximum for unbraced load-bearing brick—but the short nave, the lack of exterior illumination from the side or above, and the flat, rectilinear roof framing defeat any experience of verticality. Well-chosen materials produce the main effect. The altar is a solid block of unfilled Roman travertine, resting on a six-inch-thick platform of three large blocks of the same material. Behind the altar hangs a curtain of raw Shantung silk, foil to a mirror-polished crucifix of

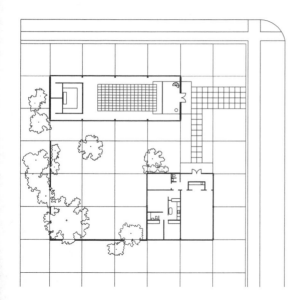

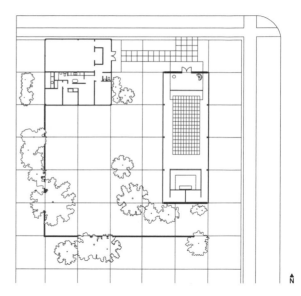

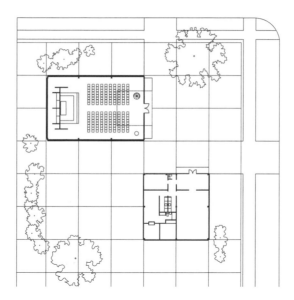

solid stainless steel. The sidewalls, inside and out, are perfectly laid up English bond, inadequately washed by the simple interior lighting.[38] The floor is dark terrazzo. Many surviving studies show a small cross centered atop the front parapet—the only exterior indicator of a religious purpose—but it was not included in the final design.

Mies and his staff paid typically close attention to details: a design exists, unexecuted, for a pair of three-fingered candelabras, companion pieces to the stainless steel cross; for square-backed pews in quartersawn white oak, also unbuilt; and for two wall seats, effortlessly cantilevered from the brick sidewalls, built and in place to this day (see fig. 14.6).

Commercial and Institutional Work

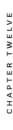

CHAPTER TWELVE

Mies's Chapel has suffered hard luck and not a little controversy. In the mid-1990s, significant sections at the top and corners of the brick sidewalls broke away, and remained unrepaired for years. The special materials and finishes, beautiful as they are, are not in harmony with traditional ecclesiastical art. The building is underscaled, underilluminated both day and night, and poorly furnished. Nevertheless, and in spite of a budget almost no other architect (or style) could have accommodated, Mies created a demonstration piece for what he believed was an objective architecture, as if to declare that special buildings—even religious buildings—need not depend on representative art or traditional decorative regimes.

. . .

Another small but important building of the same period is the IIT Commons Building, completed in 1953 as a campus center and dining hall (fig. 12.11). In Mies's era, IIT was never able to raise the money for his Student Union, which, with the Library and Administration Building, was to have been one of the two centerpieces of the campus. The Commons Building was intended to serve until the larger building could be built. In the early 1960s the student union program, including a major auditorium, was finally realized as Grover M. Hermann Hall, to a design by Skidmore, Owings & Merrill. Thereafter, the Commons housed various services, among them the IIT bookstore, a convenience store, and the campus post office.

The Commons Building is a single-story, structural-steel pavilion with basement, skirted with buff brick infill and glazed above. The structural grid is 24 by 32 feet, seven narrow bays wide and three wide bays deep. The same footprint could have been achieved with "standard," square 24-foot bays, seven wide and four deep, but Mies stretched the module on the narrow, side elevation to permit his favored odd number of bays per side and to provide wider "leasable" spaces.

The structure appears utterly simple: wide-flange columns rise to a grid of same-sized, wide-flange roof beams, where members intersect in beautiful site-welded joints. The roof is precast concrete plank. Because of the single-story construction type, the steel did not require fireproofing. Exterior columns are expressed on both sides of the infill brick enclosure. Unlike the multipart corners at Alumni and Perlstein Halls, for Commons a single wide flange was deemed sufficient to turn the corner.

The Commons stands in the shadow of the Chicago Transit Authority's Green Line elevated railway. Though less than 50-percent glazed, it is stunningly transparent, and the open plan has survived innumerable modifications and a half century of hard use. The controversial amalgamation of the Commons Building with Rem Koolhaas's 2004 McCormick Tribune Center has done little to compromise the integrity of this understated gem.

. . .

Mies formally and voluntarily retired from Illinois Institute of Technology in 1958, aged seventy-two, though it is arguable that he yielded most of his academic duties much earlier. The growth and increasing geographic range of his practice during the 1950s, his global renown, and his arthritis all contributed to his decision to step down. Regarding his role as IIT's architect, the school's administration, for its part, had chafed for some time under what it perceived as Mies's inattention to campus assignments. There is little doubt that Henry Heald's successor as president, John Rettaliata,[39] neither understood nor appreciated the eminent architect in his midst.[40] In 1958, shortly after Mies's retirement and without notice, Rettaliata relieved him of the campus work, turning it over to Skidmore, Owings & Merrill, the very firm that had most fashioned itself in the Miesian mold.

The record offers an extraordinary inside view of the administration's position as it separated itself from Mies. In a matter-of-fact memorandum filed among the Mies office papers at the Library of Congress, Joseph Fujikawa reported on a meeting with IIT vice president of facilities, the aforementioned Raymond J. Spaeth:

Memorandum re Luncheon Meeting with R. J. Spaeth on August 5, 1958

Writer met with above to discuss IIT administration's action in going to other architects for the design of new campus buildings; i.e. SOM doing the Union Building.

Spaeth gave as some of the reasons:

1. Our office did not produce work fast enough.
2. Felt we no longer had any strong interest in campus:
    a. Mies limited in attention to campus work.
    b. Felt they had to work with a "junior architect"[41] rather than a senior.
3. Did not like the idea of associate architects on campus buildings and consequent "divided responsibilities."
4. Experiencing a degree of mechanical problems, leakage, etc. in our buildings.
5. "Always a battle" to get something which they considered practical and functional in design.

Said "sooner or later" the administration felt that they would have to involve other architects in campus design; thought that "this was as good a time as any."

Asked Spaeth if Mies'[s] retirement from department head position influenced their thinking. He didn't think so.

Said he tried to point out implications of other firms doing work on campus to Building Committee but made little impression and no support. Board's attitude was that they were not "building a monument to Mies" on campus.

Spaeth thought idea of open space as in Architecture Building was not suited to needs of IIT. "Administration is quite conservative." Feared Mies['s] design for Student Union would be too radical (said that the Building Committee did discuss Mies's preliminary design for Student Union building). Feared concept was too radical. Administration wanted series of closed spaces to carry on a number of unrelated functions simultaneously.

Also made comment that libraries did not like large reading rooms but preferred smaller study rooms.

Liked to have more "color" in buildings.

Spaeth said he personally could and would have worked with us but felt certain that it would entail [a] great deal of effort, "constant battle," and the school would end up with something which they felt did not completely meet their requirements. "The Architecture Building exposed the administrative offices to direct view upon entering building."

Admitted that a mistake was made in not consulting Mies before making move. Has gotten [a] number of critical letters which have made administration rather uncomfortable.

Said Mies could still get Library Building if Mies and Rettaliata "worked things out together when they met."

Joseph Fujikawa[42]

Many of the themes expressed above are elements in the widespread negative reaction to architectural modernism that peaked in the United States at the end of the 1960s. In the case of IIT, Mies's single most important client, the problems were not theoretical. Rettaliata felt that he was getting neither attention nor service, that he had to wage "a constant battle" to get what he got, and, worst of all, that for IIT's purposes the products were *conceptually* flawed. It is something of a shock to learn that at least some in the IIT administration scorned the very idea of Crown Hall, a building, then as now, considered a masterpiece. It is less surprising that they growled about "building a monument to Mies," though the concept is anathema to everything Mies stood for as both architect and educator.

It is doubtful that Mies would have added much of significance to the campus had he kept control. The Library and Administration Building was still unbuilt, and it probably would not have emerged in anything like its original form, or in a new but equally original version, had Mies been able to "work things out" with Rettaliata. It is certain that Mies felt rejected and humiliated by the institution he had made famous. According to Lora Marx, he was "contemptuous" of the part played by SOM.[43] In his own mind the decision was his to make, especially since Rettaliata had not been party to the conception of the new campus.

The Skidmore people were uneasy in their inheritance. In his 1991 oral history, William Hartmann, partner in charge of SOM Chicago during this period—and a friend of and deeply respectful of Mies—told his firm's side of the story:

For whatever reason, and I don't know the reasons, [Rettaliata] told me that they were going to change architects for the campus. I deplored it and all that, and they asked that we become the architects. I deplored it and argued against it, and IIT said they were adamant about it, and if we weren't going to do it, somebody else was going to do it.... Frankly, it wasn't a job that [SOM] would want to have very much at all....

However ... I felt that we had more Miesian disciples than anyone in our office. A great number of them, and that if any group could undertake to carry out Mies's design philosophy that SOM could, and that it was in the best interest of the campus for us to do so. I discussed this with Mies, and I discussed it with all my partners.... In fact, as I recall, we offered to do something we've never done with anyone else. We offered to just do working drawings from Mies's designs. We offered that, and Mies said, no, he thought it would be best if he was not involved. There was absolutely no problem between us about this whole subject.... I think he was grateful that we took over — I really think we could do better Miesian buildings and follow his precepts and ideas and objectives better than anybody else.[44]

Speaking for SOM, Gordon Bunshaft wrote to Mies, presenting what was in essence Hartmann's position. Mies replied with characteristic concision: "Thinking over the whole problem of IIT, I feel it would be a mistake to accept your friendly proposal. The campus is an idea which should be finished as planned. If this will not be done, I have to accept its torso."[45]

Shortly thereafter, George Danforth organized a dinner at the Chicago Club in celebration of Mies's birthday. As Alfred Caldwell reported:

I sat next to Mies for a moment before I left because it was his party.... Then Hilberseimer picked a fight with three or four Skidmore people ... with Willy Dunlap [who had once worked for Mies] and this other fellow, this big wheel, Bruce Graham. "Why are you here, at Mies's birthday party, you, you, you — pointing to three Skidmore people — ? You are his enemy, you have taken his campus away" ... Hilbs repeated it, using his pipe like a pointer. Mies was embarrassed and said, "Oh, Hilbs, stop it." Hilbs said, "I won't stop it, Mies. They've stolen your work. You made them, you made their firm, and they pay you back by stealing your work." Willy Dunlap became very hostile to Hilberseimer and said, "The same old payola, get another record," and all this stuff. I joined in because I can't stand to see the old man insulted.... I said, You made it. You took the job that he really wanted more than anything in his whole life. They said, "We're very sorry about it." I said, If you're sorry, do something about it. Resign your jobs in protest. They said to me, "Would you do that?" I said, Certainly I would do it. Bruce Graham said, "Go ahead, do it." I said, All right, I'll do it. I'll do it tonight in protest. I went home, I wrote a letter to Rettaliata, a very nice letter. It said, "Much to my regret I am obliged to resign because you have discharged Mies van der Rohe as the architect of the campus."[46]

Thus ended Mies's IIT career, and, for the next twenty years, Caldwell's too. SOM assumed the campus work,[47] which it retained until new construction ended — for a generation — in the early 1970s. The first academic buildings to go up under SOM were loosely based on the example of Crown Hall. Each of the two large pavilions, Hermann Hall and the John Crerar Library (renamed the Paul V. Galvin Library in 1985), feature overhead plate girders supported by sculpted interior concrete columns. Exterior walls and miscellaneous detailing were loosely derived from Mies. But as Hartmann later said, "it was no prize, because we knew no matter what was done, it was going to be subject to severe criticism."[48]

. . .

As we have noted, in the United States Mies adopted a comfortable, old-school professionalism, patient in the belief that work would come. For what turned out to be his most famous American building—the New York headquarters for Joseph E. Seagram and Sons Corporation—his strategy was ideal. He did nothing to actively seek it, nor would he have won it without the advocacy of two headstrong individuals, one of whom he would meet, and first impress, over lunch.

The story begins in 1954. After a short marriage to Belgian banker Jean Lambert, Phyllis Bronfman Lambert had moved to Paris to start afresh. The daughter of Samuel Bronfman, chief executive officer of the Seagram Corporation, she happened upon a newspaper article about an office building planned for a site on Park Avenue in midtown Manhattan. Depicted was a model of the building, prepared by the Los Angeles firm of Pereira & Luckman, a large, experienced, and busy office. The client was her father. The new Seagram headquarters was to be completed by 1958, the company's hundredth anniversary.

Lambert was aghast; her father had publicly proclaimed his commitment to a building of the highest quality. She returned to New York to express her feelings. Meeting with his strong-willed daughter, Bronfman chose to argue neither for the design nor with her. Instead, he suggested that she conduct a search for the kind of architect she was insisting on—one capable of producing a work of historic significance. She accepted the assignment, promising that in six weeks she could conduct the necessary research and make a recommendation.

As a Bronfman, Lambert had access to important people, and she began by seeking out Alfred H. Barr at the Museum of Modern Art. He suggested that she discuss the problem with Philip Johnson, who at the time was about to leave the museum to resume his architectural practice. Johnson was captivated. The combination of Seagram money, the anniversary event, and the Park Avenue site was irresistible, especially against the background of a building boom that was producing a lot of shoddy work. As it happened, one new building of exceptional quality—SOM's Lever House, completed in 1952—stood at the corner of Fifty-Third Street and Park Avenue, diagonally across from the Seagram site. This only added to the challenge.

In short order Lambert and Johnson, now a team, set out to identify and evaluate the best architects. "We listed those," she remembered, "who should but couldn't—Paul Rudolph, Eero Saarinen, Marcel Breuer, Louis Kahn—all good but with insufficient experience—then those who could but shouldn't: the big firms, including Skidmore, all competent enough but indebted in every case to someone more original. Lastly, those who could and should. On that list were Wright, Le Corbusier, and Mies."[49]

According to Lambert, Johnson never so much as suggested himself for the job. He arranged interviews for Lambert with Saarinen, Breuer, I. M. Pei, Walter Gropius, and, finally, Mies. The choice quickly came down to Le Corbusier—whom she did not interview—or Mies. Johnson, who had long ranked Mies above Le Corbusier, may or may not have influenced Lambert, but the matter was finally settled after a trip the pair made to Chicago, where Lambert first went to see 860–880 North Lake Shore Drive, and then met Mies for lunch. In a 2005 interview she recalled:

> I came to Chicago and met Mies at the Pearson Hotel, and we had lunch there. First, though, I went to see 860. . . . The extraordinary presence of that building was just overwhelming. I just thought it was absolutely marvelous. . . . The question I asked everybody [about the Seagram project] when I met them was never "Would you like to do the building?"—that would have been a silly question—but "Who do you think *ought* to do the building?" and people would say, well, Le Corbusier, you know he's an important architect, but to do a building in the United States—of course he had already done one—he wouldn't be able to deal with all of the complications and things like that. Well, Mies just said, "Obviously, that's simply nonsense. Le Corbusier is a great architect, and that's not a problem at all." So [Mies] was the only person who was really generous. Mies was being Mies, that's all—I can say that now. He was very charming, as you can imagine, and very interesting. . . . So I was impressed by 860, and also interested because everybody who I talked to, Yamasaki, Pei, everyone, and Eero Saarinen, talked in terms of Mies. It was always "I do this differently from Mies, I do that differently from Mies . . ." I was very conscious that the mandate was to do a tall building on Park Avenue. So if somebody had not done [a high-rise], maybe if [Mies] had done just Promontory, I don't know what [my] reaction would have been, but I certainly wouldn't have been wowed the way I was by 860.[50]

Lambert announced *her choice*—a German expatriate Chicagoan unaccustomed to front-page coverage—and prepared to return to Paris. Informed of the recommendation, Lou Crandall, chairman of the senior Bronfman's favorite construction company, the Fuller Company, raised his concerns about Mies's arthritis.[51] Crandall felt Mies should have a continuous local presence to oversee the design operation and provide continuity in the event that he could not complete the work. Kahn & Jacobs had already been selected as architect-of-record—indeed, the construction and engineering team had worked to-

FIGURE 12.12.
Philip Johnson, Mies, and Phyllis Lambert in the mid-1950s. Behind them is a photograph of the Seagram Building presentation model. Photo courtesy of the Mies van der Rohe Archive of the Museum of Modern Art, NY.

gether on many New York projects—so Crandall was comfortable in suggesting a partner for Mies.

Mies deftly solved the problem by forming a joint venture with Philip Johnson. He thereby acquired the services of a well-known figure in the New York art world who was also a devoted follower. On October 18, 1954, the two men together signed a contract with Seagram. Mies did not foresee that Johnson would begin to reject his discipleship even before the Seagram assignment ended. For now, however, Johnson was more than prepared to play the understudy. Lambert concluded that she also needed to remain in play. Mies and Johnson were now *her* architects, and this was her project. She needed to protect them from the forces of compromise, as well as administer an occasional booster shot to her father. By the end of the year, with Lambert as director of planning, the threesome had taken over an office at 219 East Forty-Fourth Street and were ready to move ahead (fig. 12.12).

The mid-1950s building boom was the biggest in New York since the 1920s. Following the Great Depression and World War II, a massive, pent-up demand for new office space had developed, a pressure heightened by the return of economic prosperity. A tropical growth of skyscrapers was spreading over Manhattan, invading even the once exclusively residential precincts of Park Avenue. Most of the new buildings were in the traditional New York ziggurat form, shaped by zoning regulations dating from 1916, though variations of the tower slab became popular following the favorable response to Lever House. But none of the newest buildings approached Lever House for innovation or quality.

Commercial and Institutional Work

The Seagram commission had its lofty goals built in, not least by a budget primed for a lavish outcome. Mies was granted financial freedoms enjoyed by no other skyscraper designer of the era; the project had double the typical square-foot construction budget of a first-class commercial office building, and it would come in at four times the square-foot cost of the 860–880 buildings. Mies responded with the full creative force he almost always brought to bear when a client treated him well.

The siting and massing of the building deserve special acknowledgment, since Mies, like other and lesser modernists, has been routinely criticized for designing buildings as self-referential "objects," independent of and presumably superior to their contexts. For some of his later projects, this criticism may well be accurate. It is decidedly not true of the Seagram Building.

In 1951 Seagram purchased the land along the east side of Park Avenue between Fifty-Second and Fifty-Third Streets. The twelve-story Montana Apartments (1914), part of the Park Avenue residential street wall, were razed to make way for the new tower. New York zoning prohibited buildings from rising from the sidewalk without setbacks above prescribed heights—hence the ziggurat form—with the exception that on 25 percent of a zoning lot, a tower could rise to unlimited height. The Seagram site as initially assembled allowed a tower floor of only eight thousand square feet, too small for a modern office building. After study, the company decided to acquire and demolish an apartment building on East Fifty-Third Street contiguous with the eastern edge of the property, increasing the size of the zoning lot and, just sufficiently, the tower's allowable floor plate.

In December, Lambert wrote:

[Mies] has a cardboard model of Park Avenue between 46th and 57th Streets with all the buildings on the Avenue and some going in the blocks and then he has a number of towers for different solutions that he places in the empty place of the old 375 [the Park Avenue address], and this model is up on a high table so that when sitting in a chair his eye [*sic*] is just level with the table top which equals the street—and for hours on end he peers down his Park Avenue trying out the different towers.[52]

Mies rejected a ziggurat instinctively, as well as two other concepts: a point tower of square plan and a slab, like Lever House, perpendicular to Park Avenue. He settled on a shaft of rectangular plan, three structural bays east to west and five north to south, with the long dimension parallel to Park Avenue (fig. 12.13). The tower is set back from the frontage a remarkable ninety feet. The north and south elevations are also held back thirty feet from the side streets. This strategy allowed an apparently prismatic tower on the model of one of the 860–880 buildings, but of twice the height. But a three-by-five-bay

FIGURE 12.13. Seagram Building, New York (1958), view looking east. Though the tower is a *T* in plan, the building from this vantage point appears to be a soaring, prismatic shaft. Fifty years later the Seagram Building is all but lost amid neighboring towers. Photo by Ezra Stoller.

plan came at the expense of significant unused floor area relative to that permitted.

With the tower set back and of almost adequate area (see below), Mies had transformed the frontage by manipulating the ultimate New York luxury, space. At the time the Seagram plaza was conceived, there was no comparable privately owned, open urban space anywhere in midtown Manhattan with the exception of the Rockefeller Center mall and the special case of the United Nations. Mies recognized that the street wall along Park Avenue made it nearly impossible to actually see any individual building except from the opposite side of the street. A plaza offered visual and spatial relief.

Across Park Avenue stands the Racquet and Tennis Club, a neo-Florentine palazzo completed in 1918 to a design of McKim, Mead, and White. In creating the plaza, Mies relieved the general density all around while at the same time establishing a dialogue with the Racquet Club. It is solid masonry; the Seagram Building, glass. The former is four ample stories built to the edge of the sidewalk; the latter, at thirty-nine stories, majestically set back. Both buildings are symmetrical about a common axis. Thus, in similarities of planning and contrasts of mass, volume, height, and spatial displacement, the two buildings participate in one of the most arresting architectural dialogues anywhere.

There is further synergy of tower and site. With the grade of Fifty-Second and Fifty-Third Streets dropping to the east, Mies chose to set the plaza on a low podium accessible from Park Avenue by three steps.[53] The expanse of pink granite paving, 90 by 150 feet, is uninterrupted except for a flagpole—the sole expression of asymmetry—and, left and right, symmetrical, shallow pools. The plaza is closed at the side street by a long banquette of solid Tinian marble that, together with the podium, creates a subtle isolation from the surrounding traffic even as the vast opening unites the plaza with the building masses around it.

The Seagram Building rears up beyond. The planning module is 4 feet 7½ inches, of which six units make an efficient span in structural steel, 27 feet 9 inches. The glazed first floor terminates at elevation 28 feet, with the bronze-and-glass curtain wall above set in front of the steel skeleton. Sheet-bronze spandrels enclose the slab edges and ceiling-to-floor sandwich. The mullions are T-shaped extrusions, imitative of the steel wide-flange sections used for mullions at 860, but with the supreme refinement possible with extruded bronze. Columns set in from the exterior reinforce the vertical thrust of the wall, while the pink-gray tinted glass affects a unity among the competing forces on the surface. The whole volume shines with the tranquil, matte finish of precious statuary.[54]

Beyond a stand of ginkgo trees flanking the short sides, Mies extended the

FIGURE 12.14.
Seagram Building,
New York (1958),
ground-floor
plan. *At right*, the
"bustle"; *at center*,
the tower (*dashed
outline*) with eleva-
tors; and *at left*, the
plaza and its two
pools. Only 52 per-
cent of the valuable
site is built on.

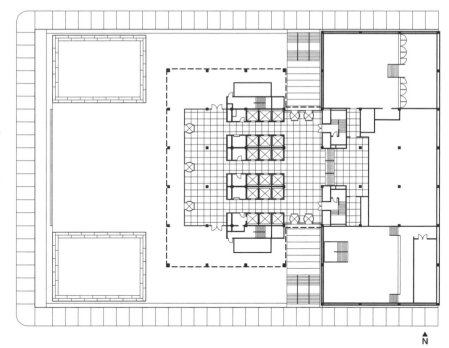

N

east face of the tower with a "spine," one bay deep and three wide, which rises the full thirty-nine stories. He also added a three-bay-deep, ten-story-high "bustle" flanked by a pair of three-bay-deep, four-story wings. On both sides, between the wings and the tower, a gap the width of the spine provides space for a side entrance. The spine, bustles, and wings increase floor area without compromising the tower's prismatic form, especially when viewed from the plaza. Thus, Seagram's "underbuilt" floor area, while not totally recovered, was mostly remedied. The appended volumes have a further advantage. The Seagram program called for a major public space on the ground floor. Mies provided a large room in each of the opposing wings: a bar to the south and a restaurant to the north. Hidden transfer girders allow the clear-span rooms (55 by 55 by 24 feet) that are not normally achievable within the columnar grid — and at the lowest level — of a skyscraper.[55]

The building's main entry is signaled by a cantilevered canopy centered on the Park Avenue elevation. The glass walls of the lobby bring the sweeping plaza inside, in a further refinement of the similar transition at 860. In contrast to the asymmetrical disposition of the 860–880 twins, at Seagram the powerfully axial building and plaza offer a single, psychically formal entry, as if the building were a classical edifice (fig. 12.14). This axis is reinforced by the four elevator cores, regularly spaced and perpendicular to the line of entry. Between the middle elevators, a passage leads to a stair at the rear, thence to a landing from which a pair of low passages empty with dramatic sudden-

FIGURE 12.15
(*facing*).
Seagram Building,
New York (1958), sec-
tion of the typical
tower corner column
(*lower left*), and a
section at the reen-
trant corner of the
plan *T* (*upper right*)
showing the bronze
curtain wall infilled
with thin serpen-
tine panels. Contrast
the Seagram corner
with that of the much
simpler, single-story
Crown Hall (fig. 12.3).

ness into the public spaces to the north and south. Lobby walls are dressed in bookmatched travertine, the ceilings finished in gray tesserae, a glass mosaic, and the floors in granite.

The Seagram tower together with its plaza is the most nearly classical building Mies designed in the United States; indeed, circulation is almost Beaux-Arts. Gene Summers reported that a need for elevator capacity sufficient to the thirty-nine-story occupancy persuaded Mies to break the grid and move the elevators forward half a bay.[56] Philip Johnson marveled—given Mies's oft-stated desire for clarity of structure—at both the use and the concealment of the transfer girders in the wings.[57] In order to achieve adequate lateral bracing, the engineers demanded concrete shear walls for the north and south elevations of the tower's spine. Mies elected to conceal them with a screen of serpentine stone panels set behind a network of mullions and spandrels that imitate the glazed elevations (fig. 12.15).[58]

In detailing the tower, Mies exercised the care and devotion for which he was famous; Johnson recalled the infinite pains Mies took in designing the termination of the front flange of the bronze mullion, specifying a small additional lip so that the flange would be suitably robust. Indeed, it is in the detailing and material richness that Seagram is far more than a refinement of 860. With Seagram's bronze wall, Mies in some ways reverted to his European self, adopting and manipulating precious materials as if by handicraft means. The Seagram mullions *look like* wide-flange shapes, but they could have been *any* extrudable section, limited only by fancy and the allowable sectional dimensions. Mies also chose to frame each spandrel with bronze extrusions mitered at the corners, adding depth, texture, and stiffness at the cost of considerable complexity compared with 860's plate steel spandrel. Mies was certainly entitled to improve on or even copy himself. Whether the example he set by doing so was ultimately positive—for Seagram, like 860, would be "knocked off" by the less talented, or greedier, or both—is subject to debate.

For the Seagram project, Mies established an office outside Chicago for the only time in his mature career. He engaged a nominal equal partner in Johnson (also a first and only event), and even established a New York residence, at the Barclay Hotel. His main assistant from Chicago for most of the time was Summers.[59] The rest of the professional team was supplied by Kahn & Jacobs and by Severud engineers, who, under Johnson and Summers, provided the necessary technical support. Mies remained stern and sovereign, capable of following his precepts with religious fidelity, but also of traversing territory foreign to our image of him. Even his pride conflicted—at least for a time—with his dedication to the very project in which he had invested so much. Construction had already begun on the Seagram Building when he received a letter from the New York Department of Education reminding him that he did not have a license to practice architecture in the state of New York, and that he would not

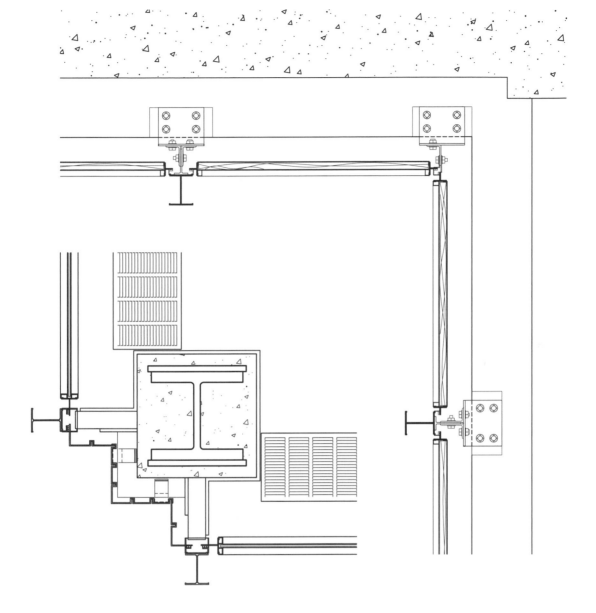

be granted one until he showed proof—of all things—of high school equivalency, after which an examination would follow.

On learning of this, Mies mounted a great, silent fury. According to Summers, he lost little time in clearing out his suite and returning to Chicago. Weeks passed, during which there was little communication between him and Johnson, whom he had instructed simply to stay on the job. He remained indifferent to efforts by people of influence to intercede. Meanwhile, Summers wrote to the cathedral school in Aachen, which furnished Mies's records. This simple step proved to be all that was needed to persuade the New York Board of Registration to waive the examination and issue Mies a license, though nothing else or less would have been sufficient in his eyes. In any event, Mies was not the architect-of-record, so he probably did not need New York registration—or any professional license.

If at the age of seventy he was rich enough in years and laurels to indulge his pride, he could do the same with his impulses, especially when it came to relationships. He was far more patient, for example, with his client Sam Bronfman than he was mindful of the feelings of his associate Johnson. (Lambert recalls, colorfully, that Mies and her father, on first meeting, "smelt each other like animals," the first ritualized step in establishing what became a deep mutual respect.)[60] When Bronfman, studying the model of the Seagram Building, inquired irritably why "the columns showed," Mies politely invited him to lean over so that he could see "how nice it is to look at the columns through the lighted lobby."[61] Mies even made a special trip to Bronfman's home in Tarrytown, where he argued, gently and successfully, against a last-minute proposal to enclose part of the plaza to make space for a bank.[62] Johnson was treated with less deference. During the Seagram period, he was already beginning in his own work to abandon the Miesian credo in favor of a sculpted, streamlined neoclassicism. Mies despised it, though he was more offended by what he believed was an act of defection and a lack of principles.

One evening in the winter of 1954–55, Johnson invited Lambert and Mies to dinner at his compound in Connecticut, where they spent several hours in the glass house. As the evening wore on and the liquor flowed, Mies's tongue loosened. He told his host in no uncertain terms that the house was badly detailed. Johnson apparently chose not to return the volley, but a later remark had precisely that effect: "Mies, I see what you see in Behrens. But I don't understand what it was in Berlage that interested you so much."[63]

Mies was astounded by the sacrilege. "He talked quietly when he was really angry," recalled Johnson. "At about 10:30, he got up and said, 'I'm not staying here tonight. Find me another place to stay.' And I laughed. And about ten minutes later he said, 'I don't think you understand, I'm not staying in this house another minute.'" One thing was clear enough: "I think he felt that my bad copy of his work was extremely unpleasant. He also deeply resented my inquisitive attitude, making him verbal when he wasn't. He was a groan-and-grunt man."[64] Mies was put up for the night at Robert Wiley's house down the road, and never returned to New Canaan.[65]

In the short run, Mies and Johnson continued to get along. "He went right back to New York, and we went right on as if nothing had happened," said Lambert. But Mies's displeasure with Johnson turned permanent. Dirk Lohan, in his 1968 interview, asked Mies about Johnson as he knew him during the early 1930s, when the two men first met.

Lohan: Was he an art historian or an architect?

Mies: Neither. Nothing at all. He had only studied at Harvard and later struck up a connection with the Museum of Modern Art. So now and then he would call himself a historian, if he wanted to emphasize a point.

Lohan: Why did he study with Gropius and not here in Chicago?

His voice heavy with sarcasm, as if he were remembering an assortment of past grievances, Mies responded:

Harvard is a very special school, isn't it, where only fine people go? (They just went on strike, didn't they, the fine people!) [Mies was referring to one of the student uprisings of the late 1960s.] Well, he [Johnson] was earlier at Harvard, as a poor student. Gropius, after all, was not *so* bad that Philip would want to give up his alma mater!

Lohan: I only meant that he had been with you so often in Berlin.

Mies: He did come around here [Chicago] from time to time. He would snoop through all the details and copy them. The mistakes he made in the details occurred because he hadn't worked them through, but just sniffed around them.[66]

In sum, Mies's later opinion of his former associate was harsh, and he was not the kind of man to modify it. Nonetheless, Johnson's contributions to the Seagram Building were real. He was responsible for some of the best interior appointments, most notably the Four Seasons bar and restaurant, both of which featured Mies's furniture. The décor of the Four Seasons, including Marie Nichols's elegant metallic draperies and Johnson's own installation of a central pool, constituted a masterly completion of a noble space. Johnson also designed the elevators and the glass-roofed canopies leading to the side entrances. He secured a Richard Lippold sculpture for the bar and the Picasso tapestry, *Parade*, for the landing that issued into the restaurant and bar. For Seagram, Mies was well served by a man of Johnson's talents. And for Johnson's budding career, it was no less fitting that he departed the shadow of the master when he did.

Worldwide Practice: The 1960s

Less is a bore.
ROBERT VENTURI, in *Complexity and Contradiction in Architecture* (1966)

You have to give this much to the Luftwaffe: When it knocked down our buildings it didn't replace them with anything more offensive than rubble.
PRINCE CHARLES, on modern architecture in Great Britain

Despite his disability, Mies traveled widely during the 1950s and 1960s. Professional assignments required his presence, and there were occasional vacations, in the United States and abroad. A 1957 swing through the upper Mississippi River country, taken with Lora, Waltraut, and his eighty-year-old brother Ewald, included their chance discovery of a Minnesota hamlet called Miesville (founded in 1874 by one John Mies, who was not related to their family). In the spring and summer of 1959, Lora joined him on a second postwar trip to Europe and his first visit to Greece. They were accompanied by A. James Speyer, Mies's first graduate student and a longtime member of his IIT faculty. In Athens Mies paid the Parthenon his highest compliment by rising early to give it, together with the Acropolis, all the time required. He studied the sacred shrines for what seemed to Lora an age, then returned to his hotel to ponder them from the balcony of their room. Delphi and Epidaurus followed (figs. 13.1 and 13.2). A half century earlier, on his trip to Italy with Joseph Popp, he had been disturbed by the unrelenting Mediterranean light; now the same atmosphere seemed benign. With the help of Karl Friedrich Schinkel and Peter Behrens, Greece had become one of the "great epochs" so crucial to Mies's worldview, and the golden light of the south essential to the splendor of Greek architecture. A Gothic cathedral, he told Lora—however much he loved it— would "look like an old spider web here."[1]

Mies's official purpose on the 1959 trip was to accept the Gold Medal of the Royal Institute of British Architects in London and membership in the Academie d'Architecture in Paris, two of the many awards he received during his final years.[2] Three years before, he had been elected a fellow of the American Academy of Arts and Sciences, and in 1957 the German Federal Republic had made him an honorary senator of its Academy of Arts.

A special occasion awaited him on the 1959 trip. Returning to Aachen for

FIGURE 13.1.
Mies with cane
at the fourth-
century-BC theater,
Epidaurus, Greece,
in 1959. Photo cour-
tesy of A. James
Speyer.

FIGURE 13.2.
Mies and Lora Marx
at Nafplion, Greece,
in 1959. Even while
on vacation, Mies
wears jacket and
tie. Photo courtesy
of A. James Speyer.

the first time since 1938, he was invited to sign the city's golden book, and a boulevard was named for him.[3] "Next to Charlemagne," exulted a German newspaper, Mies "is very likely Aachen's proudest son."[4] A reunion with Ewald and sisters Maria and Elise, described by Lora as warm and touching, rounded out the journey (fig. 13.3).

Nonetheless, in the thirty years of Mies's professional life in the United States, 1959 was also the most tumultuous. IIT had abruptly dismissed him as campus architect; the deaths of his daughter Waltraut and steadfast client Herbert Greenwald took from him two of the most important people in his life; and, as already mentioned, when work dried up after the suspension of Greenwald's projects, Mies's prospering office of carefully chosen IIT graduates had to be cut by half.[5]

·   ·   ·

During Mies's 1959 vacation, Gene Summers was informed that the US government had selected a consortium of Mies and three large Chicago firms to design a new federal courthouse complex for Chicago. Summers and Joseph Fujikawa had submitted a routine qualifications application some months before, and now, as if from nowhere, came an enormous commission that effectively saved the firm. Though Mies was not officially designated the lead designer, the other three joint-venture architects—Schmidt, Garden & Erikson, C. F. Murphy Associates, and A. Epstein and Sons, Inc.—quickly agreed among themselves that Mies should act as the design architect.

With his usual initiative, Summers set to work in Mies's absence, and planning and massing options were ready for review when Mies returned. As it

FIGURE 13.4
(*following*).
Federal Center,
Chicago (1964–
75). View looking
south–southwest.
The single-story
post office is at
lower right. Photo:
Hedrich-Blessing;
Chicago History Mu-
seum, HB-39277-T.
Used by permission
of the Chicago His-
tory Museum.

FIGURE 13.5
(*page 345*).
Architects Bruno
Conterato (*fore-
ground*) and Joseph
Fujikawa in the Ohio
Street, Chicago, of-
fice with Mies in
1956. Both Con-
terato and Fujikawa
became partners in
the Office of Mies
van der Rohe and
its successor firms.
Mies's loft offices
were carefully pre-
pared for this im-
portant *Life* maga-
zine photo shoot;
the desks, for ex-
ample, are unusu-
ally neat. Frank
Scherschel/Time &
Life Pictures/Getty
Images.

turned out, both the planning and the detailed design for the Federal Center would fall to Summers. Bruno Conterato, one of Mies's most trusted—and patient—senior staff, assumed the role of project director for what became a fifteen-year-long assignment (fig. 13.4). Two of the three Federal Center buildings were not completed until five years after Mies's death, and a decade after Summers left the office (fig. 13.5). Conterato was the project's unsung hero, providing managerial continuity and the political savvy to see it through.[6]

The government's property included the full block then occupied by Henry Ives Cobb's U.S. Post Office and Courthouse (1905), and the half block to the east across Dearborn Street. The program called for 3 million square feet of offices, enough to cover the 4.6-acre site lot line to lot line with a fifteen-story building. The Cobb courts had to remain in uninterrupted session, so it was clear that the first new building—for courtrooms—would be built on the east side of Dearborn Street. After completion of the new courthouse, the Cobb building was demolished in 1965, but funding problems and the Vietnam War postponed completion of the rest of the complex for almost a decade.

Summers identified three alternate site and massing strategies, in concert with Mies's by then standard procedure of offering three schemes to a client. Scheme A was the boldest—a single 56-story skyscraper of 44,000 square feet per floor, housing the complete courtroom and office program on the half block east of Dearborn. The huge tower was to face a full-block plaza to the west, open except for a single-story post office. Since it was unlikely that the government would select or be able to fund Scheme A, Scheme B offered an initial 30-story building east of Dearborn (containing the twenty-one required courtrooms) and a future, possibly taller tower for administrative offices sited to the west along the north side of Jackson Boulevard. A single-story post office filled out most of the rest of the block, leaving about half the ground area for two semiconnected plazas. Scheme C was similar to B except that the full block was to be occupied by two approximately 30-story towers set side by side and perpendicular to the courtroom building. This group of three similar buildings enclosed a plaza internal to the full block, with the post office subsumed in one of the towers.

Mies favored Scheme A, both for the full-block plaza and for the single tower's boldness and simplicity. Fujikawa thought that for political reasons alone, the federal government would never construct what would have been the tallest building in Chicago. It was also assumed that the government would never agree to the perceived extravagance of a full-block plaza. Summers argued for Scheme B as most likely to meet these objections, especially if the program were to change (which it did, as he predicted).[7] Scheme B was handsome, with superb views of the "wall" of older buildings that effectively created a grand, outdoor room. Mies "always liked" Scheme C's "equal-height buildings side by side,"[8] but it became the throwaway scheme, principally because it was deemed unlikely that three "equal" towers could satisfy a changing program.

Worldwide Practice

Scheme B was closest to the project as built—albeit with a forty-five-story second tower—but the single tower of Scheme A, fronting an immensely valuable open urban block, was conceptually and artistically more daring. It could have been conceived and seriously proposed by no other architect.[9]

For the Federal Center, interior planning was a principal challenge. A 4-foot, 8-inch planning module was selected, and it was decided that the exterior would be steel (and not aluminum, which Mies reportedly would not use to clad a steel structure).[10] As with the 860–880 North Lake Shore Drive buildings, the Federal Center mullions are standard wide-flange sections, and spandrels and column covers are steel plate (though unlike 860, the glass is tinted gray). The novel program components are the two-story courtrooms within the high-rise building, which Summers placed on the *upper* ten floors, where low-rise elevators drop away. He proposed a modest exterior articulation for the courtrooms—something like two-story-tall windows—but Mies elected to maintain the regularity of his then standard wall. In any event, the courtrooms were interior to the plan, and had no windows.

The first tower, now the Everett McKinley Dirksen United States Courthouse, has thirteen 28-foot bays north to south, and four east to west. In elevation the almost-square slab, 383 feet high and 368 feet wide, became the powerful east "wall" of the later plaza across Dearborn. The 1.3-million-square-foot tower meets the ground in the typical wraparound colonnade, and with the elevator cores pushed to the northern and southern ends of the plan, the ground plane around and through the lobby is strikingly open. Services are hidden midblock to the east, with two and one-half subgrade levels accessed by a ramp from Jackson Boulevard.

By the 1960s, steel curtain walls were both technically obsolete and more expensive than aluminum ones, which Mies had pioneered at Esplanade and Commonwealth. Indeed, his office would finally turn to bronze anodized aluminum for the exterior of Chicago's IBM Building, constructed with a steel frame and completed in 1974. But with the Dirksen Building, the entire Federal Center was committed to the steel skin, and the forty-five-story Kluczynski Building, opened in 1974, would be the last Mies high-rise with an all-steel exterior. On a square-foot basis it was also far more expensive than its IBM cousin. The "epoch of glass and steel," so heralded by Mies and his followers, was to last, for the paradigmatic high-rise, less than twenty years.

The 1973 United States Post Office, a single-story building framed with exposed steel, was originally proposed as a clear-span version of the Crown Hall type, and later as a clear-span pavilion similar to what became the Berlin New National Gallery. But soil conditions at the site were found to require costly footings for a structure with so few concentrated loads, and it was eventually decided to build with a conventional columnar grid, though of a still imposing 65-foot span. Summers reported that the switch from clear span to grid required almost no change to the interior layout, again demonstrating that Mies's clear-span concept was, for practical purposes, a conceit. The very tall mullions of the Post Office are spaced at 9-foot, 4-inch centers (double the towers' 4-foot, 8-inch module and that of the plaza's granite paving), matching the ground-floor storefronts of the two towers and further reinforcing the transparency of the ground plane. In Mies's work, the purity of this expression is realized so completely nowhere else. The interior clear height of 27 feet is one and one-half times that of Crown Hall, though the square-plan Post Office is slightly shorter (200 versus 220 feet) than Crown Hall's long dimension. The interior volume, though interrupted by a stone-clad core and flanking millwork, is even more powerful than Crown Hall's interior, because of the increased height, the larger area under roof (38,000 versus 22,000 square feet), and the looming proximity of tall buildings on all four sides.

The remarkably fitting steel stabile, *Flamingo* by Alexander Calder, was selected after Mies's death and installed in 1974. Architect Carter Manny, a C. F. Murphy Associates principal, was the prime mover in the Calder acquisition.

Gene Summers, by then also with Murphy, was in charge of the siting.[11] The plaza has become the downtown site of choice for all manner of public demonstrations (and especially for protests directed at the federal government), as well as for musical performances, a weekly farmers' market, and an array of celebrations. The center is an integral component of Chicago's downtown, especially because of its invitingly permeable edges and extensive colonnades. But it also maintains a grandeur and dignity appropriate to its special status, which is most clearly conveyed by the combined elegance of black steel and gray tinted glass mated to the organizing grid of massive granite pavers. It was Mies's mature architectural vocabulary and its supreme flexibility for program, building type, and urban context that made possible this powerfully representational complex.

. . .

By the late 1950s and throughout the 1960s, Mies's practice was worldwide. Beginning in 1964, for example, Mies was design consultant for two other superblock developments, both in Canada. The first was Toronto's Dominion Centre, a three-building commercial complex in the city's old financial district. The site area and program were remarkably similar to those of the Federal Center: a 5.5-acre site — in this case uninterrupted by streets — with 3.1 million square feet of offices and the requirement that the project be phased. By 1968 two towers had been completed: one of 56 stories, the Toronto Dominion Bank Tower, and another of 46 stories, the Royal Trust Tower. For the Dominion Bank, Mies, with Summers, chose to accommodate the retail banking functions in a freestanding one-story pavilion, square in plan and almost exactly the area of Crown Hall. The complex was connected by a concourse level for shopping and services, with two levels of parking below. (Chicago's Federal Center has below-grade parking but lacks a public concourse.)

The Toronto buildings are structural steel, with steel skins of wide-flange mullions and steel spandrels. A five-foot module was selected, along with a highly flexible (for interior planning) 30-by-40-foot bay. The taller tower is three wide bays by eight narrow, and the shorter three by seven — proportions superior to those of the Federal Center, where the narrow dimension of the towers is four short bays, an even number Mies usually avoided. The Toronto towers overlap by one bay, just as at Chicago's 860, and their outsize height — 731 and 600 feet — yielded a pair of rectangular prisms in exquisite repose. Three more towers by other architects, similar but shorter than the originals, have been added to the Dominion Centre, so that today Mies's original ensemble is difficult to read.

The banking hall is roofed by a steel waffle structure supported at the perimeter by cruciform columns on ten-foot centers. Several features first developed for Crown Hall are rendered here with finer materials: the service shafts are faced in green Tinos marble, the floor is St. John's granite, and the ceiling lighting is integrated into the structure, so that the underside of the roof diaphragm appears to flow into the supporting exterior wall.

Phyllis Lambert suggested Mies for the Toronto commission, but she was not involved in the best-known of Mies's several projects in her hometown of Montreal. Westmount Square was commissioned by the Montreal Development Company, a private enterprise, with Mies as design consultant to the Canadian architect-of-record. The 3.5-acre site is Mies's only superblock incorporating mixed residential and commercial use. The project consists of three 21-story towers—two with apartments and one for offices—as well as a 2-story office building, a shopping concourse, and below-grade parking. The towers are concrete with aluminum curtain walls. Tower core walls, lobby floors, and the entire plaza are clad in Roman travertine.

Completed in 1968, Westmount Square pioneered dense mixed-use development in its fashionable neighborhood two miles from central Montreal. But unlike the Dominion Centre, which is a superbly detailed, near-model commercial development, Westmount (admittedly, built with a much lower budget) reads today almost as a Mies knockoff. It is in deteriorating condition, and it seems unlikely that it will ever receive the kind of careful attention—or money—a competent exterior restoration now demands.

. . .

Opened September 15, 1968, Berlin's New National Gallery was the last project in which Mies had significant personal involvement. Though design work started in 1962, the concept had been developed five years earlier for an unbuilt project, the Bacardi Company Administration Building (Ron Bacardí y Compañía Administration Building) in Santiago, Cuba. Soon thereafter, Bacardi became the basis for another unbuilt project, the Georg Schaefer Museum in Schweinfurt, Germany. The New National Gallery was therefore a third iteration of the Bacardi scheme.

The commission for the Bacardi Office Building project in Cuba—sometimes called "Bacardi Santiago" to differentiate it from the realized 1961 Bacardi Administration Building in Mexico City—was awarded in 1957 by the president of Bacardi Rum, José M. Bosch. Bosch had learned about Mies from a profile in the March 18, 1957, issue of *Life* magazine. Titled "Emergence of a Master Architect," the nine page spread, timed with the near completion of the Seagram Building, was the most lavish national press Mies had ever received.[12] According to Summers, "[Bosch] came in the office and said he had seen the story in *Life*.... He said he saw a picture of Crown Hall, and he said 'I'd like to have a building just like that, big space, open space.'"[13] He had come to the right place.

By the time Mies and Summers arrived in Havana on their way to the building site in Santiago, Mies had already settled on a Bacardi building based on Crown Hall. According to Summers, preconceptions grew less secure on their first night in Cuba, when Mies observed the rusting balcony railing at his Havana hotel "in that wonderful salt-laden sea air." On the following day, confronted with the withering Caribbean sunlight, Mies "realized that this was definitely not Chicago, where the light and warmth of the sun is welcome within a building most of the year."[14] Crown Hall, its glazed walls flush with the edge of a roof hung from steel, was wrong as a point of departure.

Summers went on to report another observation Mies made during the return trip to Havana and the same hotel. Relaxing in the garden court surrounded on three sides by a veranda on wooden columns, Mies noted that the enclosing wall of the lobby was

> fifteen feet [in] from the columns.... It was a nice proportion, a nice space, and it shaded the building wall. Mies leaned forward in his chair, in a very characteristic way, and said, "What if we reverse it? Let's put a walk under the roof [of the Bacardi building] on the outside of the glass line." With that he asked me to make a sketch, which I promptly did on the back of the cocktail napkin—it was a large square roof supported by columns only on the exterior edge, with column centers at about ten feet and with the glass line back 30 feet from the roof line. I passed the sketch to Mies and he quietly looked, while puffing on his Monte Cristo cigar—he said, "No, it looks like a consulate—one that Gropius would do—there are too many columns—take some out." Back to the cocktail napkin. This time with only two columns on each side, Mies said, "That's it. Let me have that."[15]

In the completed design, Bacardi Santiago is a square pavilion with an enclosed area 138 feet per side—a single main-floor room of 19,000 square feet. Interior height to the bottom of the roof structure is 23 feet. The flat roof, 5 feet deep, extends 20 feet beyond the glazing (fig. 13.6). Eight concrete columns, two per side and cruciform in section, are pin-connected to the all-concrete roof at its edge (fig. 13.7). The concrete exterior was intended to be white or gray, with the window wall framed by steel bar stock clad with extruded bronze. The roof is a post-tensioned monolith of two-way, poured-in-place concrete beams, with increasing section toward the center. Antecedents can be found in the Convention Hall and the Fifty by Fifty House. The set-in ground floor, chosen here for shading, is also a feature of most Miesian towers. The single monumental room, the "universal space" symmetrical in plan and typical of Mies's American work, is subdivided for office use, in the manner of the European Mies, by two freestanding marble walls, several millwork dividers, an off-grid, millwork-clad mechanical stack, and one set of stairs to the basement (fig. 13.8). The building is partially screened by brick "garden walls" rem-

FIGURE 13.6. Ron Bacardi y Compañía project, Santiago, Cuba (begun 1958, halted early in construction 1960). Model. The project was canceled on account of Fidel Castro's Cuban Revolution. Note the wide stair at a right angle to the podium, in the manner of similar sequences at Barcelona and the Tugendhat House, among others.

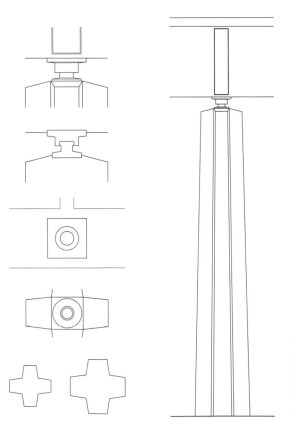

FIGURE 13.7.
Ron Bacardi y Compañía project, Santiago, Cuba. Elevation and section details of one of the concrete columns and its pin connection to the concrete roof (1958).

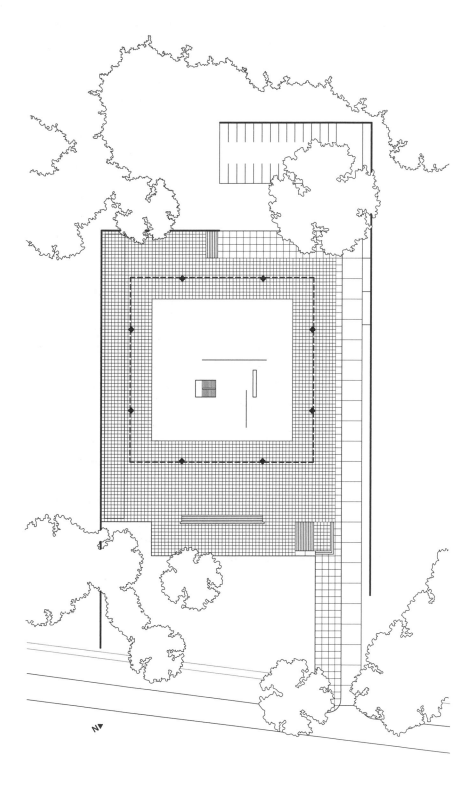

FIGURE 13.8. Ron Bacardi y Compañía project, Santiago, Cuba, site plan (1958). The interior shown here is truly "beinahe nichts," that is, almost nothing.

iniscent of the Barcelona Pavilion, and set on a podium that encloses a partial basement, where additional program elements and back-of-house functions are accommodated, exactly as at Crown Hall.

For the complex engineering, Mies's office worked with Bosch's engineers, Sáenz-Cancio-Martin, led by Luis Sáenz. The project had proceeded through working drawings and site preparation had begun when construction was abruptly halted in September 1960 after Fidel Castro assumed power in Cuba; Bosch, who at first supported Castro, changed his mind and fled the country, never to return. Summers, reflecting on the project thirty years later, considered it "one of the most important buildings ... in all of Mies's later years. It was probably the clearest structure, and that's what it was all about."[16] Indeed, "the Cuba building," as Mies called it, was too important to remain "in the drawer."

In 1959 Mies's grandson Dirk Lohan, then an architecture student at the *Technische Hochschule* in Munich, married Heidemarie Schaefer, daughter of Georg Schaefer, a wealthy Bavarian industrialist and owner of the world's most important private collection of nineteenth-century German art. Schaefer housed his collection in a castle near Schweinfurt, but he nursed ambitions to build a modern museum in that city for its permanent display. To be called the Georg Schaefer Museum, both building and collection would one day be donated to the City of Schweinfurt.

In the only project of Mies's American career in which family connections played a central role, Lohan persuaded his new father-in-law to offer the project to Mies. Surprisingly, Mies had never designed a freestanding art museum; the Cullinan wing for the Houston Museum of Art (see below) had been an addition only, and his European work for collectors was all residential. But during most of 1961 Mies was in poor health, and rarely came to the office. In February 1961, Summers therefore initiated the design work, beginning with a trip to Schweinfurt to meet with Schaefer and Lohan. In the course of the year, Summers developed a scheme similar to the IIT Commons Building (which he had worked on in his early days with Mies)—a single-story, columnated square three modules to a side, each about sixty-five feet column to column. The central square featured a lower level for sculpture. Referencing the predominant architectural material of Schweinfurt, on all sides Summers provided a tall, red-brick skirt with large lights above.[17] Only the entry was glazed to grade. After the usual thorough study, the office produced a model, and in December 1961, before leaving for Germany to present it to Schaefer, Summers showed it to Mies at his apartment. According to Summers, Mies said little other than "*Ja*, good luck." Schaefer liked the proposal, and sent Mies a telegram expressing his satisfaction.

The next act is best told by Summers: "Several weeks after I'd come back,

then Mies was feeling better, and he came in the office and he said, 'Gene, let's look at the model again of Schweinfurt.' We had a model of it; it was a nice model, and Mies said, 'Ya, why don't we do the Cuba building?' I gulped and stammered around a bit, but then if he wanted to do the Cuba building, we'll do the Cuba building."[18] Still in discomfort, Summers duly reported to Schaefer that Mies wanted to try another scheme. He also had to contact Bosch, since the Bacardi building, though halted, might someday restart. Bosch graciously released his scheme. Summers then produced a "Bacardi" in steel—appropriate for a country that had a highly developed steel industry—which was eventually presented to Schaefer. He preferred the original scheme (as he stated to Summers, but not to Mies), and the project stalled (fig. 13.9).

. . .

Notwithstanding his commitment to Schaefer, Mies was available to listen to the City of Berlin when in March 1961 it contacted him with the offer of another, much more ambitious museum. Initially, the Berlin building was to have housed art owned by the city, although soon enough plans changed: the museum would also accommodate the formidable Prussian collection of nineteenth- and twentieth-century art, one of the finest of its kind, much of it in storage since World War II. For Mies, the prospect of designing such an important building as part of an entire cultural center in the city of his first professional maturity was immensely appealing. As an examination of the program and space requirements made clear, conditions were nearly ideal for another Bacardian scheme (fig. 13.10). Recognizing the force of Mies's intentions and the place of Berlin in Mies's career, Schaefer gallantly released him from all obligations to Schweinfurt.[19]

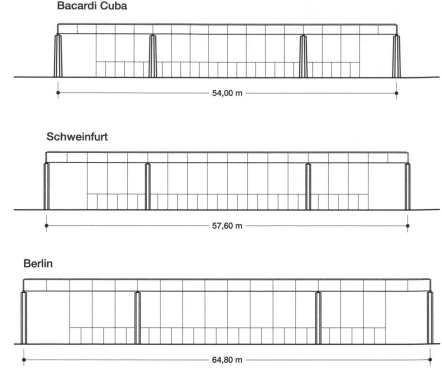

Bacardi Cuba

54,00 m

Schweinfurt

57,60 m

Berlin

64,80 m

• • •

In the summer of 1962, following deliberations in the Berlin Senate, Mies was formally designated architect of the New National Galley *and* of an exhibition hall intended for changing displays of contemporary art. The two spaces would be part of a single building. Mies's work was slowed in its early stages by a flare-up of his arthritis and weeks of hospitalization, after which he was again absent from his office for long periods. But he was determined to carry the project through. Even while in the hospital in 1963, he exercised close control as the design was developed in his office. Schematic studies in model and drawings were prepared as usual, and for ultimate control the working drawings—a typically beautiful set, this one in German—were prepared in Chicago. At the Berlin groundbreaking ceremony in 1965, which Mies attended, he insisted on lifting himself out of his wheelchair and onto crutches to strike a stone tablet with a hammer, in hopes that the building would serve as the "appropriate frame of a noble endeavor."[20]

The New National Gallery stands within several hundred yards of the site of Mies's old apartment at Am Karlsbad 24 (fig. 13.11). It occupies part of the city's Kulturforum, a development of cultural institutions intended at the outset to include a state library and Hans Scharoun's Philharmonic Hall. The museum's site, the Kemperplatz, slopes gently from west to east. On that account, and

FIGURE 13.11. New National Gallery, Berlin (1968). Partial elevation. Mies's last work, and his first in Berlin since well before immigrating to the United States in 1938, it is based on the Bacardi Cuba project—a black vitrine grown from a white one. The roof is an orthogonal grid of six-foot-deep steel girders twelve feet on center. It was assembled on site and raised as a single piece by eight hydraulic jacks at column centers. Photo: David L. Hirsch.

to accommodate the program, it was decided to construct on two levels. The lower level houses the permanent collection in a series of enclosed galleries, along with building utilities and services. A walled courtyard to the west provides extensive outdoor space for sculpture. The level above, intended for temporary exhibitions, is a 27,000-square–foot, column-free space, 166 feet 4 inches square and 27 feet 9 inches in height, glazed on all four sides, its flat roof projected 20 feet beyond the enclosing walls. The roof is supported on eight matte-black cruciform steel columns, two to a side, each of which taper gently upward to pin connections at the edge of the roof.

The all-welded roof is an orthogonal grid of unfireproofed, exposed plate girders 6 feet deep, spaced at 12-foot intervals (fig. 13.12). Upper flanges for the plate girders were omitted so that the webs could be welded directly to a top plate that is continuous across the roof. Since the bottoms of the girders were to be exposed—for Bacardi and Schaefer, a drop ceiling was intended to conceal the deeper midspan structural members—they needed to appear dead flat, and this was achieved by selective use of thicker bottom flanges, thicker webs where necessary, and higher-strength steels as required. In addition, the great roof was cambered at its center and also at the corners to achieve an

FIGURE 13.12.
New National Gal-
lery, Berlin (1968).
Main-hall entry. The
low millwork wall
and stairs to the
lower level flank the
open area beyond the
main doors. Photo:
David L. Hirsch.

absolute level appearance. The amount of camber was agreed on by combin-
ing the results of performance calculations by German engineer Hans Dienst
and further visual adjustments arrived at by examination of large-scale models made in Mies's office. Camber at the corners was used to counteract the
appearance that a flat roof sagged at cantilevered corners—a lesson learned
from one of the large Bacardi models. Mies himself made the decision to introduce 5 centimeters of additional camber at the corners, based on study of
a giant, 1:5 scale model of the roof edge (42 feet long) erected in the Chicago
office. Other key decisions were studied in multiple models; no fewer than
six were made to study the column, for example, and the entire building was
modeled at 1:50 to assist with interior appointments and details.[21] For the New
National Gallery, Mies took steel detailing—indeed, an all-steel architecture—to the point of ultimate visual refinement.

For site circulation, access to the granite-paved podium is mainly via a
broad stair centered on the east elevation, though there are secondary stairs
at the northwest and southeast corners. The square plan is echoed in the
square coffers of the roof grid and in the granite paving. The immense interior—broken only by a pair of marble-sheathed mechanical shafts, a few low,

millwork walls, and stairs leading to below—evokes an implicit infinitude of movement in all directions beyond the transparent walls. The cost of that effect, which Mies did nothing to mitigate, was the arrangement of the downstairs galleries in an unimaginative series of artificially illuminated spaces.

The great room is a mostly inflexible, inhospitable arena for the display of any but the largest objects. In the inaugural exhibition, Piet Mondrian's paintings were hung on large white panels suspended from the ceiling. In ensemble the panels themselves were an impressive study in weightlessness, but the paintings were drowned in the ocean of surrounding space. Mies barely bothered to rationalize his solution. "It is such a large hall," he declared, "that of course it means great difficulties for the exhibiting of art. I am fully aware of that. But it has such potential that I simply cannot take those difficulties into account."[22] These words are a measure of the intensity, not to say the willfulness, of Mies's belief that the structurally objective clear span was the ultimate expression of the epoch.

Witnesses remain enthralled by the memory of Mies's appearance at the building site in 1967, when the vast roof was raised by eight hydraulic jacks placed at the points along the perimeter that would ultimately be supported by columns. Mies gravely watched the entire nine-hour operation. The jacks were precisely synchronized, and during the lift the 1,250-ton roof was never more than two millimeters out of level. The great plate was raised just enough that the columns could be secured to their foundations, and was then lowered onto the pins.

Mies had spent his life resisting distractions—moral, political, romantic, even conversational—but he was never more concentrated than on that chilly April morning of his eighty-second year. Even the champagne reception in honor of the occasion—of himself, that is—left him in a state of bored irritability, to which he gave voice when called on to deliver a statement. It was pure Mies—compact, disdainful of ceremony but respectful of labor, and flavored with the accents of his youth:

> It was agreed that nobody would speak more than five minutes. What humbug that was! I want to thank the men who worked the steel, and those who did the concrete. And when the great roof raised itself up without a sound, I was amazed!![23]

Mies was too incapacitated to return to Berlin for the official dedication in September 1968. Yet his presence in the city was now reestablished, in the form he valued most. Even though his massive black vitrine had grown directly out of a white one meant for the Caribbean sunlight, its relationship with the legacy of Karl Friedrich Schinkel was no less apparent. The Altes Museum stood nearby, secure on its own podium, fronted by its own classical colonnade, even though its then location behind the wall in East Berlin left it separated from the New National Gallery by an ideological gulf far greater than a few city blocks. Mies's design had created an immaterial but unbreakable connection with a tradition and a master he first came to revere sixty years before.

· · ·

In 1962 Dirk Lohan, twenty-four years of age and newly graduated from the *Hochschule* in Munich, moved to Chicago, where he joined Mies's office and quickly rose to a central place in his grandfather's personal and professional life. However much sway Gene Summers had with the master, he could not match Lohan in two crucial respects: he was family, and he spoke German. He was not Mies's only grandson; Georgia had two boys, Frank and Mark. But Lohan's new profession was his grandfather's, and in the isolation of his later years Mies could not help appreciating the attentions of a cultivated young European who took on the identity of the *Stammhalter* Mies never had. Mies's singular abilities and introverted unworldliness had long made him attractive to those who wanted to care for him while nourishing themselves in his light. He was quite prepared to accept such care, but only up to the point that Ada and Lilly Reich, to name but two, had earlier exceeded. Lohan made no such error; thus, Mies found it easy to feel warmth for his young grandson while suffering not at all from the threat of strangulating love.

Unavoidably, a rivalry developed between Lohan and Summers, the latter secure in his experience and Mies's professional trust, but at a growing disadvantage on the personal level. Blood won out. As work on the New National Gallery progressed, Summers's role as Mies's closest associate was slowly taken over by Lohan. Summers accepted the situation with typical cool resolve. "We were at a good and firm point in office fortunes," he recalled. "Various projects were in hand and underway. So I said to Mies one day that I wanted to leave."

"I wish you'd stay a few more years," replied Mies.

"But then I might have to stay longer."

"Well," said Mies, his thoughts returning to his last hours with Peter Behrens in 1912, "I appreciate that. I had to make a similar decision once. When do you want to go?"

"In two weeks."[24]

· · ·

In May 1966, Summers set up his own office about a block from Mies's and made his first hire, a young German studying at IIT named Helmut Jahn. The two worked together for less than a year before Summers was recruited by C. F. Murphy Associates, which had been selected by Chicago mayor Richard J.

Daley to design a new convention hall to replace one destroyed by fire in January 1967. Opened in 1960, the first McCormick Place had been the object of heated civic controversy, not because of its palpable inferiority to Mies's own unbuilt Convention Hall, but because it took up a swath of Chicago's traditionally open lakefront. And the city was determined to erect the replacement building on the same spot.

Summers demanded that C. F. Murphy make him "partner in charge of design of all [their] projects and not just McCormick Place," and to his surprise the firm agreed. He also stipulated that Mies "become a joint venture partner in charge of design on McCormick Place," to which the firm also assented. He carried this offer to Mies. "I explained my situation and that one condition of my joining their firm was that he would design McCormick Place. He said 'Gene, you should join their firm. You will get big buildings to work on, you should do McCormick Place, thank you but I wouldn't do the building with all of the controversy; it could be the Parthenon and it would be criticized.'"[25] Mies well knew that he was in no position to undertake a project as complex as it was discordant.

Mies made no effort to see Summers after their professional parting. But as always, it was the work that mattered. "The structure was up," recalled Summers, "and he was sick. He had Lora Marx call . . . and she said, 'Mies had asked me to drive him by McCormick Place. We did, and he just wanted me to call you and say he thinks that's a good building.' For him to do that was a major concession. He didn't do those things and that just wasn't his character."[26]

. . .

In 1966 Philadelphia architect Robert Venturi published *Complexity and Contradiction in Architecture*, in which he proclaimed a theoretical position at odds with the modernist viewpoint most famously represented by Mies: "I like elements which are hybrid rather than 'pure,' compromising rather than 'clean,' distorted rather than 'straightforward,' ambiguous rather than 'articulated,' perverse as well as impersonal, boring as well as 'interesting,' conventional rather than 'designed,' accommodating rather than excluding, redundant rather than simple, vestigial as well as innovating, inconsistent and equivocal rather than direct and clear." Any doubt that Mies was a prime target of these sentiments was quickly erased: "More is not less." And later: "Less is a bore."[27]

Venturi's book was a product of the 1960s, characteristic of that period's shift in political, economic, social, and aesthetic priorities. The Vietnam War, racial tensions, urban instability, and the ascendancy of youth and popular culture are all background to Venturi's opposition to what he regarded as modernism's suffocating values of simplicity and clarity. The book had an immense impact on the profession, and in the 1970s and 1980s was a major source of the thinking that drove the postmodernist movement to freely embrace stylistic elements from all phases of architectural history. Names such as Ricardo Bofill, Michael Graves, Charles Moore, and Robert A. M. Stern, as well as Venturi and his partner, Denise Scott Brown, began appearing frequently in the critical press. Philip Johnson himself joined in; his most notable contribution was the AT&T Building in New York, a high-rise capped by a pediment based on Chippendale furniture. With his gift for the *mot juste*, Johnson offered his encapsulation of the PoMo stance: "You cannot *not* know history."[28]

. . .

In 1962 Peter Palumbo had not yet met Edith Farnsworth, but as we have reported, his admiration of Mies would lead to his purchase of the celebrated house. Long before, the Palumbo family had gained control of a plot in the city of London, suitable for an office building. Palumbo:

> I wrote to [Mies] and told him that I was something of an admirer of his work and would he consider a commission for London. I got a cable by return saying "delighted to consider London commission. Please meet me Chicago office next Monday morning 10 A.M., Mies van der Rohe."
>
> I went to Chicago and saw Mies, with some trepidation I may say, and found him to be immensely sympathetic, not at all frightening. He could see that I knew a good deal about his work and I think that this was part of the reason he responded to me.
>
> I told him that he must understand from the outset that anything he designed was unlikely to be built until 1986, because of the leasehold situation on the site. [A lengthy leasehold would not be retired until that date.] He understood by that at once that what I was offering him as a commission would be built posthumously. I think it rather intrigued him, because he had never been asked to do anything like that, and he said to me, "well, how far do you want me to go with it?" I said that "I want you to go all the way."[29]

With British-born Peter Carter as project architect, Mies began work on the assignment late in 1964. He flew to London, where he made a detailed examination of the site—a roughly rectangular parcel bordered by Poultry and Walbrook, divided diagonally by Queen Victoria Street, and addressed by several well-known buildings: George Dance the Elder's Mansion House (1739–52), residence of the London Lord Mayor; the Church of St. Stephen Walbrook (1672) by Christopher Wren and John Vanbrugh; and Edwin Lutyens's Midland Bank (1936). Also involved was one of London's most heavily trafficked intersections, as well as a network of underground concourses with access to five subway lines. These conditions influenced the siting of the intended building in a new city square to be created by rerouting Queen Victoria Street and razing several nondescript buildings fronting it. Palumbo:

> The crucial material, which [Mies] fastened onto right away, was the underground survey which showed a nightmare of complications: statutory undertakings, travelator, subway system, sewers, drains, post office cables, ducts, tunneling. Mies took one look and said, "I want to get as far away from this as I can. I don't want to have to thread the foundations this way and that, and cantilever, and so on. Let us make life simple." The conditions underground dictated the siting of the building at the extreme western end of the site, where there were no complications underground. By doing so Mies had opened up at the base of the building an area of land stretching from the building to the Mansion House, while revealing the other sides of the square, already there. I remember Holford [London architect William Holford, who played a secondary role in the decision] saying when he saw the plan: "That is a stroke of genius."[30]

The architectural critic of *The Spectator*, Stephen Gardiner, concurred: "Suddenly—amazingly—something has been put right, the jungle has been cut down: a piece of *real* town planning has been done and stands a pretty good chance of being carried out."[31]

For the Mansion House Square project, Mies worked with his most generous budget since the Seagram Building. He envisioned a twenty-story, 290-foot-tall prismatic tower (fig. 13.13). The building was to have a steel frame with a skin of bronze and bronze-gray tinted glass and cores clad with travertine, with lobby and plaza paved in Cornish granite.

The working drawings were ready by 1967, and were presented to the architect for the Greater London Council, to the City Architect and Planning Officer, and to Lloyds Bank, which expected to occupy the building with the headquarters of its overseas department. Following Palumbo's 1968 request for planning permission, the project was approved. An exhibition at the Royal Exchange was mounted later that year. Consisting of models, photomontages, and material samples of the office tower and new city square, the show attracted 30,000 people, of whom 3,325 accepted the invitation to offer an opinion about what they had viewed. A majority favored the project. Other commentators were divided. Was the building too close to St. Paul's Cathedral? Did the square replace a crowded neighborhood with a rewarding openness or was Lutyens's Midland Bank never intended to be viewed frontally, as the reconfigured square would allow?

The nearly twenty years between the presentation of Mies's design and the expected retirement of the leasehold worked against the project. The City of London and the Greater London Council, two groups that had supported Pa-

FIGURE 13.13.
Mansion House
Square project, Lon-
don (1967). Model.
Developer Peter Pa-
lumbo commissioned
the design and pro-
vided Mies with a
handsome budget.
Construction had to
await the retirement
of a leasehold twenty
years in the future.
During that time, the
postmodernist move-
ment developed its
criticism of Mies and
Miesian modernism.
London authorities
denied approval for
the project in 1986.
Photo: John Donat.

lumbo's application in 1968, opposed it in 1981. Traditionalists now added their antimodernist sentiments, among which the most publicized was a speech delivered by Prince Charles at Hampton Court Palace in 1984, on the 150th anniversary of the Royal Institute of British Architects.

The prince minced no words in attacking the modern architecture that had gone up in the United Kingdom, especially in London, since World War II. Mies's Mansion House Square was not mentioned, but little doubt was left that it belonged in this category. The following line was widely quoted: "You have to give this much to the Luftwaffe: when it knocked down our buildings it didn't replace them with anything more offensive than rubble." The prince's message was congruent with postmodernism, which grew internationally in the 1980s, inspired by a belief that modernism's indifference to historical ornament had robbed architecture of one of its most valuable legacies. There is no way of measuring how much the speech influenced the eventual ruling against the Mansion House Square project, handed down in May 1985 by Patrick Jenkins, Britain's environment minister. Jenkins acknowledged the boldness of the development, but argued that its anticipated domination of the surrounding neighborhood was unacceptable.

. . .

With his long and debilitating bouts of arthritic illness, Mies's mortality increasingly intruded on those close to him. Indeed, the future of his office had been a point of discussion between Mies and Summers as early as 1962, even before the arrival of Lohan. At that time Summers's own concerns about succession "had been brewing for a couple of years." He continued the story in his oral history:

> Mies had talked to me on two or three different occasions about having Joe Fujikawa, Bruno Conterato, and myself become partners with him. I was really aghast at the whole idea, and he didn't talk to them about it. . . . I said, "Mies, you can't do that ... it's ridiculous. I cannot see somebody being a partner with Frank Lloyd Wright, and I certainly can't see it with you. . . . I don't think it's good for you, and I don't particularly think it's good for us. . . . What sense does it make when something happens to you that Joe or Bruno or I have ourselves as partners? We're all in design. . . ." We got along fine, there weren't any conflicts, but on the other hand we didn't need each other. Six or eight months later he brought it up again, and I said the same thing. He brought it up again probably another six or eight months after that.[32]

Summers's account that Mies "didn't talk to [Fujikawa and Conterato]" about the firm's organizational future is corroborated by Fujikawa's own report of staff unrest:

> In the early sixties, we were asking for more pay. We said, "Gee, Mies, we can't live on what we're making." Mies, at that time, had a business manager, so I remember we all went up to Mies's apartment on Pearson Street, and somebody made the ill-advised statement of saying, "Well, if I were a partner ..." When Mies heard that, he really taught us all a lesson. He said, "If I want a partner, I'll go out and get my partner. I wouldn't have to rely on any of you for it."[33]

After Summers left the office, Lohan also questioned his grandfather about its fate. Persisting in the face of Mies's progressive infirmity, in 1969 Lohan finally worked out an agreement to form the Office of Mies van der Rohe, a partnership including Mies, Joseph Fujikawa, Bruno Conterato, and himself. After Mies's death that same year, the new firm continued until 1975, when its name was changed to FCL Associates. In 1982, with FCL flush with work and grown to one hundred staff, Fujikawa and senior architect Gerald Johnson, who both wanted a smaller organization, separated to form Fujikawa Johnson Associates, Inc. Dirk, with Conterato, founded Lohan Associates.[34]

Was Less Less? 1959–69　　14

People say how do you feel if somebody copies you.... I say that is not a problem to me. I think that is the reason we are working, that we find something everybody can use. We hope only that he uses it right.　**MIES**, recorded in 1960

I go a different way. I am trying to go an objective way.　**MIES**

Certainly it is [neither] necessary nor possible to invent a new kind of architecture every Monday morning.
MIES, in a 1960 speech to the American Institute of Architects, San Francisco

Mies stands for discipline, and this is becoming a lost architectural virtue.
ADA LOUISE HUXTABLE, *New York Times*, February 1966

A commonplace of Mies criticism is that most of the work of his last decade is formulaic and dull. Gordon Bunshaft, a friend and admirer, expressed it this way:

> I think Mies was a really great architect, and he built three or four magnificent buildings: the Tugendhat House, the Barcelona Pavilion, and the greatest office building built at any time, his Seagram Building ... [the result] of years of refinement of detail, without a client, without a building.... I think he got too many commissions afterwards and they got a little repetitious.[1]

Gene Summers and Joseph Fujikawa also spoke to the issue. In a 1996 interview, Fujikawa said: "I think after 860, [Mies] felt he'd solved the problems of the high-rise apartment house, because [with] all subsequent buildings, he really had just a casual passing interest in what went on."[2] Summers characterized Mies in his late years as follows:

> [At] this time [from the Federal Center onward, after the late 1950s] Mies didn't take part too much in all these buildings as far as the day-to-day detailing. I would go in and I would ask him about a specific detail that I thought was important, and I wanted to know whether he agreed with that or not. He just was old at this time, and it's a misconception to think that he was creating during that period.... Creation takes hard work, and he wasn't capable of doing that, but he was certainly capable of making a decision.[3]

Mies was fifty-two when he embarked on his American journey; and his reputation was not firmly established until the completion of 860–880 North Lake

Shore Drive in 1951, when he was sixty-five. After he returned from New York and his work on the Seagram Building (in 1956, two years before the building was completed), though he retained his immense authority, he was not an active participant on most projects. Thus, the tall buildings after Seagram and all institutional work from around the time of the Convention Hall—with exceptions, like the Berlin New National Gallery—are best considered the collective work of his architectural staff, rather than works of the master as implied in the firm's official name, Mies van der Rohe – Architect.[4]

In the United States, when Mies was deeply involved in a project—as he was for his smaller-scaled modernist work in Europe—the result was compelling. The IIT campus plan, the IIT prototype buildings, the unbuilt Library and Administration Building, the Farnsworth House, then 860–880 up to and including Crown Hall and the Seagram Building—each embodies significant development of his architectural language. Each also met the highest standards for architectural detailing, which we discuss in a short essay at the end of this chapter.

Mies was forthright about what he considered the "danger [of] doing with [something] what you like,"[5] what he considered the superficial "play with forms," and his disdain for innovation for its own sake. In a recorded 1960 interview, speaking extemporaneously, we hear his deep voice (and still less than perfect English):

> I will tell you something. You know you find often in books they have nothing to do with architecture, very important things. That is Schrödinger, you know, this physicist. He talks here about the general principles, and he said "The creative vigor of a general principle depends precisely on its generality." That is exactly what I think when I talk about the structure in architecture. It is the general idea. It is a single solution, but it is not meant as that. You know I don't want to be interesting, I want to be good ...
>
> Sometimes people say how do you feel if somebody copies you and so on. I say that is not a problem to me. I think that is the reason we are working, that we find something everybody can use. We hope only that he uses it right.
>
> [Speaking of great artists, like Michelangelo,] I am quite sure it is an individualistic approach and I don't go this way. I go a different way. I am trying to go an objective way.[6]

In these words lies a paradox, and it is at the heart of the question about the merits of Mies repeating himself. Despite his rhetoric, Mies was a supreme innovator, and though influenced by others, he developed his architectural language essentially by himself. This is one reason—in addition to the excellence of his art—that we admire his work and study his career. But once Mies created a prototype solution, he shifted his energy and talent to the next challenge; as new commissions arrived, his staff mostly *applied* successful prototypes to the next task. With little room for innovation within Mies's well-established language, staff architects were left to test their skills by adjusting prototype forms to meet specific programmatic and technical requirements. Mies neither expected nor demanded innovation from his staff, but he hoped for creative implementation of his principles. The magisterial self-discipline of his own creative process eventually stifled further creativity in his office. The result was repetition, which opened the field to other architects to critique and displace the Miesian language.

In this book we have covered Mies's major buildings and projects mostly chronologically. Consistent with that format, we next discuss some of the many less noteworthy built projects of Mies's final years—projects in which his staff took the lead.

. . .

Colonnade and Pavilion Apartment Buildings, Newark, New Jersey, 1960

An important urban-renewal project and another venture of Herbert Greenwald's, the Branch Brook Park Redevelopment Project ("Newark" in the literature) consists of three twenty-one-story apartment buildings. Colonnade is the largest, a rectilinear prism three structural bays wide and twenty-two long (over *twice* the long dimension of Mies's 900 North Lake Shore Drive building). It commands the top of a slope three blocks from the perpendicularly oriented Pavilions I and II, each three bays by ten. Greenwald had hoped to acquire the area between Colonnade and the two Pavilions for a park and a commercial building, but could not strike a deal. Apartment buildings by other architects were constructed there, all since replaced by low-rise housing.

The Newark buildings closely follow the Lafayette Park model. They use the same flat-slab concrete construction, aluminum curtain wall, and clear glazing, with integral air-conditioning at the spandrel.[7] According to Joseph Fujikawa, the Lafayette details "proved to be a practical and economical solution, and Mies saw no reason to change them."[8] Said another way, Lafayette Park was already so cheap that Newark could not be made cheaper. Even with these constraints and in the difficult environment of Newark, Colonnade and Pavilion were and remain safe, desirable housing more than fifty years after their completion. Colonnade is especially sought after for its views of the midtown Manhattan skyline twenty miles to the east.

The question remains whether this kind of repetition was good, bad, or something in between. For reasons political and economic, the Lafayette and Newark projects were difficult to achieve, but they were built. They provided modern housing in two inner cities where it was scarce or nonexistent. If neither is remarkable as architecture, both were financially and socially successful. Mies was right: "Certainly it is not necessary nor possible to invent a new kind of architecture every Monday morning."[9] For an objectivist, it would also be irrational.

Home Federal Savings and Loan Association, Des Moines, Iowa, 1963

The Home Federal building that was built is less interesting than a dramatic preliminary scheme partly modeled on the Cantor Drive-In Restaurant. It featured a rectangular two-story volume with an all-glazed, double-height upper floor cantilevered on four sides. The roof was to be hung from exoskeletal trusses spanning the long (like Cantor, the "wrong") direction. The banking hall had a vast, four-sided floating mezzanine. A subsequently much-published presentation model shows the steel exterior and the huge trusses in white, a first for Mies in a commercial building.

By the 1960s, the "Cantor scheme" had been "pulled out of the drawer" many times, although Gene Summers attested that Mies "loved nothing more than to reuse an old scheme."[10] But in this case, the Cantor solution was too much building for the Des Moines bankers. The spacious banking hall was rejected in favor of adding tenant space, and the plan was made square, three forty-foot bays to a side.[11] The building was built with three stories above grade, a standard first-floor colonnade, and an exterior wall similar to that used at 860–880.

Even after the scheme was reduced, bank executives were still wary of costs. This is reflected even in small matters. A waiting-room kiosk for the parking lot attendant — in plan twelve by sixteen feet — was designed and detailed in steel and bearing-wall brick, a lovely example of how Mies's vocabulary succeeds at the smallest scale (fig. 14.1). But the scheme was rejected, and the kiosk was constructed of wood.[12]

Mies's office produced superb details even for second-tier buildings, as the Des Moines project demonstrates. His staff designed not just the typical bank interiors like teller stations and transaction desks, but millwork cabinets, free-standing partitions, custom paneling, file cabinet surrounds, stone-topped conference and dining tables, granite benches, custom signage for inside and out, and even the main-floor wall clock. Mies had little involvement in the Home Federal project, which is credited chiefly to Gene Summers.

Bacardi Administration Building, Mexico City, 1961

Though the headquarters building intended for Santiago, Cuba, was canceled, a second project for the Bacardi Company was completed in 1961 in Mexico City. It is a two-story, steel-framed pavilion with a steel-and-glass exterior wall (again modeled on 860, with the very same mullions) in Mies's favorite three-

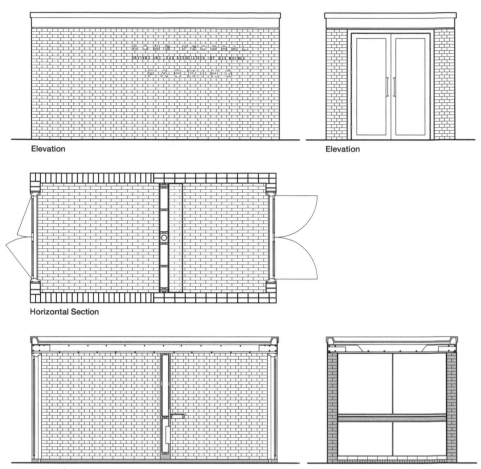

Elevation

Elevation

Horizontal Section

Vertical Section

Vertical Section

FIGURE 14.1.
Unbuilt version of
parking lot atten-
dant's facility, Home
Federal Savings and
Loan Association,
Des Moines, Iowa
(1963). Elevations,
plan, and longitu-
dinal and latitudi-
nal sections. Mies's
architectural vo-
cabulary could en-
noble even utilitarian
structures.

by-five-bay plan (fig. 14.2). In a 1964 interview, Mies explained the two-story solution: "The highway [close to and in front of the building] is higher than the site. So if we [had] built a one-story building there, you would see only the roof. That was the reason that we made a two-story building there."[13]

The interior features an expansive open well that leads via a pair of stairs to a tall second floor of open offices. The stairs and both levels are paved in travertine, the stair treads a lavish four inches thick. The entrance hall is set far in from the façade above, and is glazed on all sides. Two cores housing mechanical systems descend from the second floor outside the line of the first-floor glazing.[14]

In some respects, the result is compelling. The open well creates a grand, triple-height space, bounded on the upper level by a band of circulation that surrounds and effectively expands the well. Eight powerful, wide-flange columns penetrate this space, the central four supporting the upper level but just touching the opening as they ascend. The mostly open-plan offices were conventional Mies, but they must have fully satisfied José Bosch, who asked only

FIGURE 14.2.
Bacardi Office
Building, Mexico
City (1961). *Above,*
the second, open-
plan office level;
below, the ground
floor.

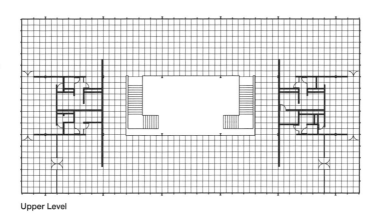

Upper Level

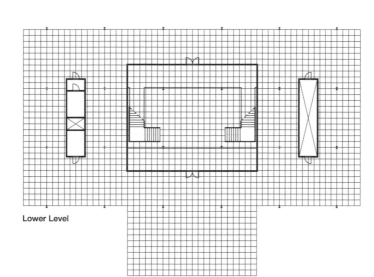

Lower Level

for "an ideal office . . . in which there are no partitions, where everybody, both officers and employees, see each other."[15]

There are shortcomings, mostly on the exterior, where the tall second floor seems not to float but glower. The module is six feet (180 centimeters), five to a bay. Two modules are cantilevered on each long end, but visually the cantilever is too short or simply unnecessary. The narrow elevations, without cantilevers, are satisfying. The main-floor glazing is expansive, but solar control requires that the draperies remain closed, which deprives the building of transparency. The elevation studies survive, and they reveal all these problems.

One Charles Center, Baltimore, 1962

In 1959 plans to revitalize the derelict Charles Center district in Baltimore led to the construction of a group of commercial buildings and apartment blocks in an urban-renewal development that included, ahead of its time, preservation of several historic buildings. Among the new buildings, the most distinguished is Mies's twenty-five-story One Charles Center, completed in 1962. The developer was Metropolitan Structures, successor to the Greenwald organization.[16] The building is a mostly typical example of the high-rise commercial architecture that emerged from Mies's office in the 1960s, echoing the Seagram Building but without bronze or a Park Avenue address. The concrete-framed tower is a stubby *T* in plan, also akin to Seagram, with which it shares curtain-wall details, executed in bronze anodized aluminum. The plan is curious, since the similar shape at Seagram was used to increase an otherwise small floor plate and to provide for the placement of shear walls, neither of which was an issue in Baltimore. The sloping site allowed for a beautiful two-story exterior stair, shamelessly demolished during a 1983 renovation. A 1990s renovation added site furniture and other plaza features unsympathetic to Miesian reserve.

The curtain wall at One Charles Center is exceptional for one exquisite detail, unique in Mies's oeuvre, but typical of his fanatical attention to detail. At the reentrant corner between the main slab and the projecting *T*, a "negative volume" of area equal to the typical column section is introduced (fig. 14.3). This deep cavity allows the panels and mullions to terminate in an inside (reentrant) corner where otherwise unique wall components would be required.[17] In common with many of Mies's best details, it is an example of necessity generating art. According to Donald Sickler, the project architect, Mies worked closely with him on this detail.

Highfield House, Baltimore, 1963

Highfield House is a fourteen-story apartment building and another Baltimore project of Metropolitan Structures. The structure is reinforced concrete, never Mies's favorite material when exposed. To save money,[18] a curtain wall was rejected. The structure employs upturned concrete beams at the perimeter, but otherwise the stepped columns and brick infill follow the example of Promontory. Concrete technology had steadily improved in the almost twenty years since Promontory, an advance reflected in the much longer bays at Highfield House (23 feet, 6 inches versus 16 feet, 6 inches). With the tall but wide glazing and the short brick spandrel (only 14 inches high), the elevations are strongly horizontal and well proportioned. The building was painted white, perhaps to contrast with Baltimore's ubiquitous red brick. Though Highfield House remains sought after as real estate, as architecture it is distinguished background.

2400 North Lakeview Avenue, Chicago, 1964

The twenty-eight-story apartment building known as 2400 Lakeview is a concrete flat-slab tower with a clear anodized aluminum curtain wall and gray

tinted glass. The design was led by Joseph Fujikawa. In order to accommodate parking under the tower, four 25-foot, 10-inch bays are disposed north to
south. This allows three vehicles to just fit between columns. In the east–west
direction the bays must be shorter, and at 15 feet, 6 inches, six are required.
This results in an almost square floor plate, 95 by 105 feet, a difficult configuration for optimal unit layouts. The narrow east–west column spacing generates awkward rooms. The deep floor plate favors living rooms at the middle
of the elevations, where they are generally only three 5-foot, 2-inch modules

Was Less Less?

wide. In many cases, apartment rooms are too narrow and deep, with kitchen and dining areas far from windows.

At 270 feet, the blocky tower seems chopped off. Visually, it should have been ten floors higher. Fujikawa recalled that Mies was especially unhappy about the elevator penthouse, which he considered "too squat." The site is crowded with surface parking and enclosed by high brick walls, interrupting the ground plane and spatial flow. Mies's tall buildings require space around them, and the best ones—860, Seagram, the Federal Center, Toronto—possess it. In this respect, 2400 tends toward Esplanade, where too much of the towers touch the ground.

Meredith Memorial Hall, Drake University, Des Moines, Iowa, 1965, and Richard King Mellon Hall of Science, Duquesne University, Pittsburgh, 1968

Designed between 1961 and 1965, these two buildings share plan concept, structural systems, and many details. While both have back-to-back auditoria internal to their ground floors—reminiscent of the albeit expressed auditoria of Mies's initial plan for IIT—the programs are different. Meredith is a classroom building, based on a 22-foot, structural-steel grid. Its two floors total only 44,000 square feet. There is no colonnade, and the building has an internal courtyard of 5,200 square feet. Mellon is a much larger laboratory building. The structural grid is 28 feet, typical of a commercial office building. It has twice the footprint and four times the total area of Meredith. Mellon has no internal courtyard, but like all of Mies's larger buildings, it has a colonnade. There is yet another difference of note: Meredith went up without incident, but Mellon's four-story steel frame, not yet securely bolted, was blown down in a weekend windstorm in May 1966.

For both buildings the exteriors, painted black, are of the 860 type, though neither has operable lights. The upper three floors of Mellon Hall are laboratories, which require few or, for those internal to the plan, no windows. To meet this requirement, areas that are glazed in the standard Mies wall are infilled with steel panels for the bottom two-thirds of what would normally be glass. The steel panels are not simply "glazed in" in lieu of glass, but are set outside the glass line with an insulated panel that is surrounded on four sides by a two-inch-wide, two-inch-deep reveal. This reveal visually separates the panel from the rest of the spandrels and column covers, preserving the rhythm and organization of the façade. All the long elevations are treated this way, but on the narrow ends the center three bays are fully glazed and the outer two infilled with steel. In the face of this special requirement, Mies's office apparently saw no reason to rethink the standard 860-type wall, but was able to adapt it in spite of the fact that for Mellon it needed to be 90-percent opaque.

To be sure, Meredith and Mellon are the products of a formula, but each is a successful application of that formula to a different and difficult problem—how to make, as Mies would say, a "good building." Ada Louise Huxtable, in a survey article on Mies in 1966—just as these buildings took form, and just as architectural "fashion" was about to change—addressed this issue: "Mies stands for discipline, and this is becoming a lost architectural virtue. He stands for logic, which is now a contortionist's trick. He stands for style, in its highest and most valid meaning of the expression of standards and techniques of a particular historical time."[19] A Meredith or a Mellon from Mies twenty-five years earlier would have been a sensation. They are often discounted as tired and repetitive, though in Huxtable's sense they still have "style."

School of Social Service Administration Building, University of Chicago, 1965

Uniquely among Mies's works, the SSA Building incorporates three interior levels within a single-story elevation. Paired entries lead without vestibules to a tall, expansive lounge space, from which elegant twin stairs lead down to an English basement with classrooms and offices, and up to a library and additional administrative space. The 120-by-200-foot plan is about the same area as Crown Hall. The module is the same too, but with three structural bays by five and columnar grid spacing at an airy 40 feet (and 20 feet for the concrete lower level). There are four nearly identical elevations. The building fronts Sixtieth Street, relatively far from the heart of the campus several blocks to the north. It is isolated both physically and stylistically on a campus famous for its neo-Gothic quadrangles, and is less well known than some of the university's other forays into midcentury and later modernism.

Of note at SSA is the use of steel columns built up to form cruciform sections, both for interior supports and as part of the exterior wall (fig. 14.4). Mies and Gene Summers—the latter chiefly responsible for the SSA design—had been studying cruciforms in both steel and concrete for the several clear-span projects they worked on together in the late 1950s and early 1960s. The form became treasured. For SSA, Summers designed a cruciform composed of four wide-flange sections welded to form a box. The cruciform's wide-flange components are of the same section as the wall's mullions. The webs make up the arms of the cruciform, and the outboard flanges complete a graceful, slender analog to a Gothic pier. At the exterior, one of the cruciform's four wide-flange arms is outside the line of the glass, aligned with the regular mullions. Thus, the exterior column and all the other mullions read in plane. The solution is not rational as structure, since a column in the plane of the wall is not subject to the same lateral forces from all directions (like, in principle, one on the interior). A slightly larger wide flange would have been more "objective" at these locations, which was Mies's usual practice. The interior design, especially of

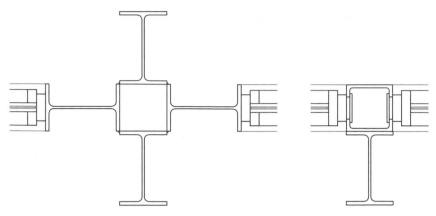

FIGURE 14.4. Social Services Administration Building, University of Chicago (1965). Detail section of the exterior wall. *At left,* a cruciform column made up of four wide-flange sections welded to form a box. The outboard wide flange of the cruciform matches the typical mullion, *at right.*

the main hall, employs the Miesian vocabulary of buff brick walls, extensive custom millwork, and exposed interior steel. The maturity and sophistication of Summers's solution is apparent in every detail.

Martin Luther King Jr. Memorial Library, Washington, D.C., 1968

The King Memorial Library came in the office at the end of 1964. Summers worked on the design with project architect John (Jack) Bowman. Mies had never completed an independent library building, and at this time his beloved, unbuilt IIT Library and Administration Building was twenty years in the past, and clearly inapplicable as a model. Instead, Summers adopted (and adapted) the 860-type exterior wall, which the office had used successfully for several low, large buildings.

Originally called Washington, D.C.'s New Downtown Central Library, the King Library is not a federal facility, and did not have the generous budget typical of federal projects in the nation's capitol. Even in his American work, Mies depended on rich materials for rich effects, or, where materiality could not be a factor, spatial or structural interest, or simply beautiful details. But in the King building, there are no special spaces or interior sequences, little connection of inside to out, and no sense of quality.

The building fills the 65,000-square-foot site. The structural bay is 30 feet square, with only three window divisions. With boxed-in columns at the ground-floor colonnade and the four-story height, the exterior wall is neither vertical nor horizontal, and the proportions fail to satisfy. The building cannot be seen from farther than across the street, which makes it appear boxier still. No doubt the provision of underground parking combined with the required library floor loading made the 30-foot span the largest practical, but a longer bay would have improved proportions and established a satisfying horizontality. An interior court might also have helped, for the floors are deep and the interior unrelenting.

The King Library has been little loved by patrons and critics, and is currently under threat of replacement. Even in a change of use the bones are eminently salvageable, and all involved could surely endorse a sensitive revitalization for a building that is structurally sound and readily adaptable.

Cullinan Hall, Museum of Fine Arts, Houston, Texas, 1958 and 1974

Mies's first project for the Museum of Fine Arts in Houston was Cullinan Hall, a gallery addition begun in 1954 and completed in 1958. David Haid, who had worked with Mies on Crown Hall, was project architect. The result was an amalgam of earlier ideas, with Crown Hall themes dominating. The existing museum consisted of a 1924 Beaux-Arts pavilion, rectangular in plan, and a pair of not-quite-matching wings, splayed to the wide (northern) end of a pie-shaped plot. Mies elected to fill in the area between the two wings with a tall volume, the north façade of which is gently curved in plan. The wall, glazed at the center, has buff brick on either side to conceal stairs that connect to the old building. The new space is mostly gallery, with the roof carried by four exoskeletal plate girders, also splayed in plan. The architectural steel was painted white as a concession to the neoclassical building.

Between 1965 and 1968, the office designed the still larger Brown Wing, completed in 1974, after Mies's death. It dissolved the Cullinan wall and extended the building still farther toward the wide end of the site. All steel was then painted the familiar black. The new roof was again carried by plate girders, although because the Brown Wing is supported on a columnar grid, the grandest space within the museum remains the remnant of Cullinan. In one of the exhibitions staged there by James Johnson Sweeney, the director of the museum, paintings were hung on panels suspended by wires from the ceiling. Mies envisioned a variation of Sweeney's technique for exhibitions in the New National Gallery in Berlin.

IBM Office Building, Chicago, 1974

Begun in 1966, the IBM Building is the largest of Mies's Chicago structures. Bruno Conterato led the project. It commands a spectacular site at a jog in the Chicago River one block west of Michigan Avenue, but its east elevation has been blocked by Skidmore, Owings & Merrill's ninety-two-story Trump International Hotel, completed in 2009. The IBM Building (now known as AMA Plaza) is the sole example of Mies's commercial work in which a structural-steel frame is enclosed in an anodized aluminum curtain wall, in this instance of dark bronze color, a system that Mies had been philosophically opposed to for a structural-steel tower.

The client's demands for improved environmental performance controlled the design of the curtain wall, the first by Mies with thermal breaks and insulated glass. With the first OPEC oil embargo of 1973 and the subsequent run-up in energy costs, IBM's investment in this advanced exterior was doubly wise. Before IBM, Mies's buildings were designed with little or no attention to thermal efficiency. Glazed steel walls carry cold into the interior, and though insulated glass had been available from the early 1950s, owners typically rejected it for its poor return on investment, and Mies did not employ it. The solid brick walls of IIT's campus architecture also connect the outside directly to the inside, and even these relatively thick brick enclosures provide only minor insulation value.

The decision to proceed with aluminum for IBM was wise for another reason. The exterior has required very little maintenance in forty years, while its fraternal twin (roughly the same size and almost as tall), the Kluczynski Building at the Federal Center, has already undergone a major and costly restoration of its all-steel exterior.[20] The handsome garage to the north of IBM, built shortly afterward to a design by Mies's one-time employee George Schipporeit, is clad in visually sympathetic Cor-Ten steel.

Nuns' Island Esso Service Station, Montreal, 1969

Metropolitan Structures undertook several projects in Montreal in the late 1960s and after, including apartment buildings on Nuns' Island in a new development it pioneered. Mies's office handled the Nuns' Island work. The service station designed as part of this assignment is unremarkable except for its tenuous association with Mies van der Rohe. Mies was seriously incapacitated during this period. He probably knew little or nothing about the service station. Nonetheless, it has gained attention as the quizzical main character in a film about Mies, *Regular or Super*,[21] that was distributed in the United States and Canada in the mid-2000s. From the talking heads that surround it in the film, it is hard to draw any conclusions about how Mies himself might have viewed the building.

Mies's Detailing

With the possible exception of the declaration "Less is more," the assertion that "God is in the details," though not securely attributable to Mies, is nonetheless a remark closely associated with him in the public mind. What are these details, and how might God "inhabit" them? Surprisingly, in print the subject has not been much discussed. In Peter Carter's 1974 book, *Mies van der Rohe at Work*, he briefly treated Mies's detailing, stating some rules and citing examples. There has been little other serious commentary.

As we have observed, Mies's lifelong devotion to craft originated in his family's trade, in his experience working construction, and in his formative professional encounters with the polymath Bruno Paul. For Mies's early, traditional houses — which appear to have had adequate budgets — detailing was a function of the style, which dictated exterior decorative flourishes, an interior design at least loosely coordinated with the exterior, and the incorporation of furniture and finishes true to both. In sophisticated form he first encountered this kind of architecture with Paul, as we have seen, and in the Riehl House he had all but mastered it by the age of twenty. As part of Mies's apprenticeship, he also developed a profound reverence for drawing, much of which, as ever, was the work of detail. His accomplishments were reinforced by the recognition of his talent, but also, surely, by his pleasure in doing. In spite of his later dependence on study models (always prepared by his staff), for Mies drawing and design were one.

In the 1920s, when he took up the self-imposed challenge to create an architecture "expressive of the age," Mies's effort was mostly conceptual, and his graphical representations schematic. The five projects of the early 1920s that opened up this new world were pointedly vague; Mies would have said that details were beside the point. With the Wolf House, the Weissenhofsiedlung, and the Esters and Lange Houses, he was forced — or forced himself — to create a new language of exterior detailing and interior design. Indeed, he aimed to conflate the two. In association with Lilly Reich, during the mid- to late 1920s, four key activities were intertwined: exhibition design, furniture design, millwork design, and a new type of detailing in natural stone.

Mies and Reich understood that exhibitions were among the shortest routes to putting their theorizing into practice. The Werkbund was a major sponsor. German industrial design first matured in the 1920s, and a host of new products, including an array of specialty glass, hardware, and consumer products, was just becoming available. Many of these items were their own best advertisement, and Mies and Reich recognized that they could display them effectively with little apparatus. Graphics were necessary, but with clarity and style graphic clutter could be much reduced. Mies and Reich did not invent the modern exhibition, but they were recognized as among its most significant pioneers.

As exhibition designers they had a singular advantage: they could outfit their work with modern furniture of their own design. As we have noted, Mies produced his first modern pieces for the Weissenhofsiedlung, for both his own building and the exhibits, after having been inspired by — or co-opting — an idea of Mart Stam's. Mies's first chair, the MR, was only nominally a copy of Stam's, for unlike Stam's it was suave and sculptural. The means were astonishingly appropriate to the idea of the chair, for they appeared to be of the simplest sort: a tanned-leather hide wrapped around a continuous loop of steel pipe, the whole a cantilever. Nothing could have been simpler, but nobody had given it elegant form until Mies. With the MR accomplished, it was a short step to a family of tubular pieces, including an armchair, side tables, beds and benches, and the somewhat later chaise longue. For furniture at the Barcelona Pavilion, the goals were more rarified. Using flat steel bar and leathers both traditional (for the upholstery) and beyond (for the straps, in belting leather), Mies made the leap to a welded frame, albeit with mechanical fasteners for lapped corners. Soon enough there were variations, like the Tugendhat chair and the flat-bar and tubular Brno, as well as the X-table, another essay in crossing, welded flat-bar steel. The table has been impossible to improve on.

The design of furniture almost always involves experiment. We do not know if Mies did much of his own research and development beyond what he could accomplish in his studio. But there were plenty of craftsmen available to do that work, heirs of a long tradition Mies understood and respected. Characteristically, having "solved" his furniture problem, Mies seems to have put the effort of only a couple of years behind him—after age forty-five, he never produced anything like his European pieces again. But he employed them almost continuously thereafter as an integral component of interiors varied in other details, like the consummate millwork he and Reich produced beginning with the Esters and Lange Houses, and for the Wolf House too, though we know less about it because the house was destroyed. Mies's millwork included custom built-ins, desks and tables, freestanding walls and wall panels, doors and framing, window casing, bookcases and storage units, shelves and benches, and even wood flooring. Hardware was also invariably custom, from doorknobs to clocks. Esters, Lange, and Tugendhat exemplify the entire range.

Mies's millwork building blocks are the rectangular wooden section and the veneered panel, from which walls and built-ins and miscellaneous framing were assembled. Milled sections are typically joined together by blocking or with rabbets or miters—all traditional methods—and they are the key to understanding Mies's well-known reveals. At important joints or where dissimilar materials meet—in walls or built-ins, typically, but also around doors and windows—he left a gap, the so-called *reveal*, for the practical reason that it facilitated fitting, and the aesthetic reason that it highlighted the joint, which was slightly widened and placed in shadow. Reveals establish rhythm and scale, and above all they articulate the components that are arranged to create Mies's all-important order (fig. 14.5). The wood reveal became a signature, and Mies employed it promiscuously. Just as a fine brick wall by its nature generates texture of human scale (for it is necessarily built *by hand*, with the

FIGURE 14.5.
Engineering
Research Build-
ing, Illinois Insti-
tute of Technology,
Chicago (1944).
Elevation view of
the intersection of
a poured-in-place
concrete column
with the English
bond brick exte-
rior wall. Note the
reveal, which high-
lights the line where
dissimilar materials
meet. Interruption
of the brick pat-
tern requires three-
quarter-length
stretchers at the
column.

"hand-sized" brick), so the reveal modulates and humanizes the many materials that Mies employed, not just as an effect, but as the very means for building. For Mies and his followers, the reveal replaced the traditional solution to
the handling of joints, which was to conceal them with molding or a "cover"
strip. Mies's reductivist reveal was not always easy to build, but its conceptual
simplicity was compelling.

The rectangular wooden section — never beveled or rounded over or in any
way specially shaped — remained fundamental. Its surface was elementary,
its edges and shadows crisp, and its applicability universal. For Mies it was the
same with stone. All of his stone, however rich, is laid up not as true masonry,
in bearing walls with pointed joints, but in panels or sometimes as blocks
(for benches, typically), as if it were wood. (It is honed or polished rather like
wood too.) This is only partially because it was expensive, and had to be used
as veneer.[22] In the modern world, stone structures were anachronisms. For
Mies stone was surface, rich and ravishing or quietly patrician, as need and
desire dictated. Freed from tradition, it could be organized in *modern* ways,
as bookmatched panels, with plain joints or with reveals, in slender freestanding walls and as seamless, endless, lavish paving. As surface, different stones
could even be rationalized for the same installation. There are, as we know,
five types at Barcelona. Panelized stone, often of large dimension, became the
unit of modular design.

None of Mies's large-scale European projects were built,[23] and his exterior
vocabulary remained tied to the brick or stucco-over-block walls he used for

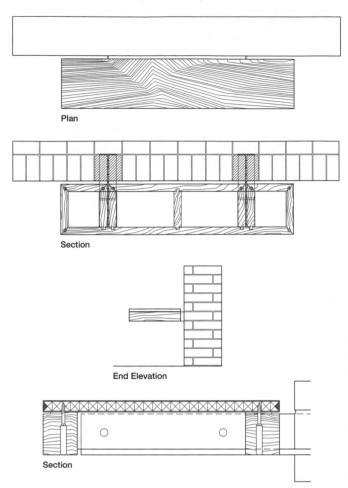

Plan

Section

End Elevation

Section

FIGURE 14.6.
Plans and sections
of wall-mounted,
cantilevered seat at
the Robert F. Carr
Memorial Chapel,
Illinois Institute of
Technology, Chicago
(1952). For Mies, even
"minor" details are
lovingly resolved.

residential work. Though he proposed a number of glassy exteriors in competition entries of the 1930s, he never had to make any of them real. He had seen the work of those who had, most notably the big glass walls of the Bauhaus Building in Dessau, and he must have known that technology was not yet up to the task. When he arrived in the United States and had to put up buildings for IIT, he faced the problem of designing and detailing an economical, modern exterior. He fell back, in a way, on what he knew, which was the vocabulary of brick and of the millwork detail, for the latter of which he now substituted hot-rolled steel — bars, angles, channels, and the soon-to-be-iconic wide flange, all abundantly available in his new country. The struggle played out in the 1944 Library and Administration Building, where he first experimented with enormous glass lights wedded to skirts and full-height walls of brick. He discovered that steel need not be confined to structure. It could be incorporated into the very fabric of a wall, in the expression of columns and beams, in framing for windows and the stops for glass, for the erstwhile cornice, for corners, and most reductively as simple cladding with steel plate, each plate welded edge to edge, seamlessly, to the next. All this vocabulary was derived from the modularized components of his European *interiors*.

Mies was devoted to the idea that there is a set of elementary materials appropriate for modern buildings—in the United States, as he said repeatedly, "architecture comes out of construction." He identified these materials—wood, concrete, and steel—and embraced them for his curriculum. But there were other important yet not so elementary materials, like brick, glass, and the versatile new postwar material, aluminum. In the end, categorization was arbitrary. For the Farnsworth House and Library and Administration Building—his genuine breakthroughs—steel is substituted for wood. The Farnsworth structure is a collection of off-the-shelf steel, assembled with the transformative technology of welding. It is nonetheless analogous to work in wood, assembled both in the shop and on-site. The real work was handwork, just as with wood. It was Mies who manipulated steel and made great architecture of it, and not something inherent in it as an "elementary" component of construction.

After the completion of the Farnsworth House and its scaling up for 860, Mies was essentially finished creating. He had successfully adapted his European vocabulary to the new materials and methods of fabrication available to him in the United States. For larger buildings, in any event, the choices of materials and methods were made mostly by the marketplace. His American interiors, corporate and institutional, still used the interior design template and the furniture he and Reich had developed a generation before. Both were updated, especially with the assistance of Edward Duckett, who was as fanatical about detailing (and about drawings and furniture) as Mies, and of Gene Summers and other dedicated staff. Every American building, no matter how humble, partook of the master's vocabulary, in things large and small (fig. 14.6). Each is an amalgam of beautiful, hard-won solutions to the "problems" of detail.

Recessional: 1962–69

What would bother me would be Johnson claiming that I was chiefly responsible for one of his buildings.
MIES, on hearing that Philip Johnson was taking credit for the Seagram Building

I have very little time to be for something. I have absolutely no time to be against anything. **MIES**

I have to wait that [until] the music dies out. **MIES**, on staying up late alone

Mies's home life in the 1960s was simple, quiet, even monastic (fig. 15.1). Financially comfortable, he continued to have little use for any but a few material pleasures. He always had companions, as the visits of intimates and Lora Marx's faithfulness guaranteed. Before his eyesight failed,[1] he and Lora occasionally took in a movie, far less often a concert or recital—the singer he most admired was Marian Anderson—and never the theater. Mies and Lora had their own circle of friends apart from IIT. Together they saw a good deal of Alfred and Rue Shaw, the former an architect whose companionship—though not his work—Mies enjoyed, the latter, as already mentioned, president of the Arts Club of Chicago.

They also took vacations, staying in Tucson several times, preferring the Pueblo-style Arizona Inn.[2] Except for necessary business trips, Mies remained confined to his apartment by his arthritis. He could sit for hours, not only by himself but in the company of others, rapt in immobilized silence and thought. In the late 1950s and early 1960s, Gene Summers was a regular dinner guest, reporting on office activity and acting as Mies's conduit for design approvals and the occasional administrative decision. Mies also saw a good deal of Phyllis Lambert, who, having matriculated as a graduate student in architecture at IIT in the early 1960s, had her own apartment at 860 North Lake Shore Drive, two blocks from Mies's. In the latter half of the 1960s, Dirk Lohan (fig. 15.2) was in constant attendance, and only a little less so his mother, Marianne.

But always these visitors departed at the end of an evening, leaving Mies to himself and his reflections. He studied as he always had—much the same philosophical fare—but with an increasing interest in physics and cosmology.[3] As ever, he sought his own way. Lora described him to one of us as "an avowed atheist,"[4] and while he was no friend of psychoanalysis, the one book

FIGURE 15.1
(*facing*).
Mies in his apartment in 1956 with painting by Paul Klee and sculpture by Pablo Picasso. The cove at the ceiling is one of Mies's "unnecessary literalisms," but one he was not moved to change.

FIGURE 15.2.

Architect Dirk Lohan, son of Marianne, Mies's daughter, in 2005. Lohan has had a significant career, first as a young architect in Mies's office, and then as a principal in successor firms to his grandfather's. Photographer unknown. Used by permission of Dirk Lohan.

he read by Sigmund Freud, at Lora's suggestion, was an attack on religion itself, *The Future of an Illusion*. He may have been looking for the confirmation of a higher system in the theoretical postulates of science—thus his further reading in Julian Huxley, Karl von Weizsäcker, and Sir Arthur Eddington. Yet he maintained his engagement with theology, adding to his library texts by his Roman Catholic friend Romano Guardini.

· · ·

Mies acquired a substantial personal library during his American years, now mostly preserved at the rare book room of the library of the University of Illinois at Chicago.[5] As told by Gene Summers in a talk to architecture students in New York during the Seagram period, "Mies made the remark that he learned a lot by reading. . . . He said, 'You know, I used to have three thousand books in Berlin. When I came to the United States I couldn't bring them all. I whittled it down to three hundred books. Of the three hundred there are probably thirty that are really worth keeping.' Then somebody said, 'Well, what are the thirty?' [Mies] said, 'You know, you're lazy. You have to read the three thousand before you know what the thirty are.'"[6]

Reginald Malcolmson, Mies's chief administrative assistant at IIT for many years and himself a bibliophile, said this about Mies's reading:

> When young, [Mies] read Nietzsche and Schopenhauer. Latterly, he read Schrödinger, Whitehead and Guardini. . . .
>
> Much has been made of Mies's references to Augustine and Aquinas in de-

scribing the aims of his work, but no attention has been paid to two philosophers and creative thinkers who, in my opinion, had a more profound and formative influence on his work—Plato and Goethe. . . . In Plato he found confirmation and clarification of viewpoints he had already arrived at in his own work. It is often so with creative artists, but in Goethe he recognized an attitude to life that he not only admired, but also loved to quote. If in Plato's dialogues he saw the operation of reason as an analytical tool and the goal as harmony, in Goethe he saw the emphasis on becoming—the creative process and the sense of organic unity.[7]

Historians and critics alike sometimes make broad claims about the genesis of works of art. In the case of Mies, scholars with excellent credentials have contended that he designed some of his buildings with the intention of expressing, in built form, a philosophical position, and that his buildings are architectural translations, from word into form, of his thinking, as derived, for example, from that of Romano Guardini.

It is tempting, especially in the case of Mies, who read and quoted philosophy his entire life, to evoke a causal connection between what he read and what he designed. But there is no *evidence* that the philosophy of Guardini or Rudolf Schwarz or anyone else was the source or the starting point of the design of any of Mies's works; nor is there reason to believe that Mies designed by anything other than his own formal intentions "to solve architectural problems," as he always described his work, unless they were derived to some degree from the acknowledged influences of other architects, like Schinkel or Paul or Behrens or Wright. This applies also to Saint Thomas Aquinas and Saint Augustine, two other philosophers frequently cited in discussions of presumed influence on Mies's architecture.

Joseph Fujikawa, who knew him professionally as well as anyone, offered this view of Mies's interest in philosophy: "He did quote . . . philosophers and I'm sure, even though he didn't personally say so, he made a real effort to read as much as he could of their works. My general impression is that he was trying to confirm ideas which he himself had. I think the things he believed in, he found these historical figures who said the same thing. I think it reinforced his own convictions. . . . He read philosophy primarily for that reason."[8]

. . .

During World War II, as reported above, important professional material from Mies's Berlin atelier was packed by Lilly Reich and Eduard Ludwig, Mies's Bauhaus student and assistant, and shipped to the Mühlhausen home of Ludwig's parents in Thuringia, a province later incorporated into the German Democratic Republic. Reich's solicitude in this regard was completely in character, and Ludwig was no less devoted and energetic. After the war he began an extensive, mostly one-way correspondence with Mies. His letters include graphic reports of the destruction visited on the German capital; recollection of days at the Bauhaus; detailed reports on Mies's family and former colleagues; and his efforts in the 1950s to persuade an unpersuadable Mies to return to Germany for good. During those years, Ludwig maintained his own practice in Berlin. He produced five elegant "Atrium Houses" for the 1957 Interbau Exposition there and, famously, his 1951 design for the Berlin Airlift Monument at Tempelhof Airport, a sixty-five-foot tall concrete sculpture known to Berliners as the "hunger claw."

As early as 1951 and in many letters thereafter, Ludwig mentioned the possibility of the return of the Mühlhausen materials. Nothing was accomplished until 1959, when Hans Maria Wingler, an art historian, Bauhaus researcher, and in 1960 the founding director of the Bauhaus Archive (then in Darmstadt, today in Berlin), obtained East German permission to visit Mühlhausen, under the pretext of carrying on research in medieval sculpture. Wingler made his way to the Ludwig home, where he opened and examined the five boxes. He reported their contents to Mies: drawings, photographs, correspondence, project files, competition papers, periodicals, and Bauhaus documents. The value of the material was obvious. Negotiations between the West and East German states dragged on for four years. During this period, in December 1960, the fifty-four-year-old Ludwig was killed in an auto accident on the Berlin Autobahn. From Chicago, Dirk Lohan continued to press for the return of Mies's property. Late in 1963, the general secretary of the Academy of Arts in West Berlin, Freiherr von Buttlar, and his directorial counterpart at the German Academy of Arts in East Berlin, Otto Nagel, effected a transfer of the crates to West Berlin — though not before the East Germans had removed all material pertinent to the Dessau Bauhaus, claiming it to be "state property." Finally, in December, the treasure arrived in Chicago, where Mies, to the exasperation of his staff, let it sit unopened for weeks. And according to staff testimony, the single box labeled "Lilly Reich" was never opened by Mies.[9]

The contents were at last duly and formally examined, shortly after Mies and the Museum of Modern Art had begun discussing the possible donation of drawings he had lent for the 1947 New York exhibition. In the course of these and subsequent talks, Mies, who did not care to see his work edited, let it be known that he would give the museum more, not fewer, of his professional materials, including the Mühlhausen papers and his American professional files. The result was the official establishment of the Mies van der Rohe Archive, a division of the museum's Department of Architecture and Design. This cache contains over 20,000 items, most notably drawings and project correspondence. In his will, Mies bequeathed 22,000 other documents, chiefly personal and professional letters unrelated to specific buildings, to the Library of Congress.

. . .

Mies owned a modest collection of art assembled over a period of fifty years, beginning shortly after World War I. Earlier, we contrasted his indifference to painting during his 1908 trip to Italy with his decision in 1919 to purchase a Kandinsky. We suggested that the Kandinsky may have been among the first evidence of Mies's shift toward the avant-garde at the turn of the 1920s.

In his European years, however, he was hardly a serious collector. When he moved from Berlin to Chicago, the only paintings of consequence in his possession were the Kandinsky and a 1934 nude by Max Beckmann, *Alfi mit Maske* (*Alfi with Mask*). The Beckmann was a fiftieth birthday gift (March 27, 1936) from friends and colleagues. The choice of Beckmann was made by Lilly Reich, who sent her assistant, Herbert Hirche, to call on the painter and select something from his studio. It was Beckmann himself who, in a show of friendship, not only made the final choice but lowered the price and joined the celebration.

Thus, an architect who had designed houses for the well-known collectors Helene Kröller-Müller, Erich Wolf, Eduard Fuchs, and Hermann Lange was himself unmoved (and unable) to follow their example—until he emigrated. Once in the United States, he began to make occasional purchases, aided by advice from a number of former Berlin gallerists, notably Karl Nierendorf and Curt Valentin, both reestablished in business in New York. (Mies had known them in Germany.) During his 1937–38 stay in New York working on the Resor House project, he socialized with Nierendorf, Valentin, and J. B. Neumann, another former Berlin dealer who had been in the United States since 1923. Mies visited Nierendorf's exhibition, *Three Masters of the Bauhaus*, which featured work by Kandinsky, Lyonel Feininger, and, in greater quantity, Klee. From that show he purchased five Klee paintings,[10] and by late 1940 his Klee holdings included five oils and ten watercolors. More were added later, for a total of at least twenty paintings, the most by any artist in his collection. Klee was Mies's favorite painter, though with at least one exception, not just because he valued his work as high art. IIT graduate student Paul Pippin recalled a class visit to Mies's apartment: "We came to one room with a Klee painting and Mies said 'I bought that because anyone brave enough to call it a painting deserves to have it bought.'"[11]

By the middle of the 1950s, the collages of Kurt Schwitters began to appear in his collection (fig. 15.3). Klee and Schwitters had in common a taste for freewheeling fantasy very unlike Mies's own dedication to order and reason.

But Mies's motives in favoring both men surely went beyond any such consideration. In comments made to George Danforth in the late 1930s, he recalled Klee with special admiration, calling him "a visionary painter" who, together with Braque and Picasso, was "possibly [one of the] three greatest painters at the moment." Friendship was another factor in Mies's collecting. Klee was on the faculty of the Bauhaus when Mies was the school's director. Then at the height of his powers, Klee was producing a steady flow of inventive work. He moved to Berne in 1933, but even then Mies maintained contact:

> [He] went to visit Klee after they had closed the Bauhaus, and Klee was not well. He was in Switzerland. He came into the house. Klee always loved cats, and Mies sat down and this big cat came over and jumped in his lap. Klee was startled and Mies said he said, "My God, this cat never goes near anybody." . . . Klee thought this was some omen that here was a special friend. [Mies] loved that [story].[12]

Mies owned fourteen collages by Schwitters, each composed mostly of snippets of paper—fragments of tickets, receipts, envelopes, calendars, and kindred detritus—that the artist found around the house or on the street. They are organized with a constructivist sensitivity to geometric form. Mies acquired them well after he had purchased the last of his Klees, which may be why, in conversation with the architect Paul Schweikher at about this time, he addressed the informal question, "Mies ... what do you like the best?" with the informal answer, "Oh, that is easy: My Schwitters, my martinis, and my cigars."[13] Nonetheless, all remaining evidence points to Klee as the artist Mies most highly esteemed—first and last.[14]

In Chicago Mies made studied contact with the city's art world. As we have noted, in the 1938–39 season the Art Institute of Chicago staged an exhibition of his work, organized by the museum's director, Daniel Catton Rich. Mies was a frequent visitor to the Michigan Avenue gallery of Katharine Kuh, one of the few places in the city that showed modern art. There he purchased Klee's *Rückfall einer Bekehrten* (*Relapse of a Converted Woman*), which, together with Kandinsky's *Herbstlandschaft* (*Autumn Landscape*), he later gave to Lora Marx. In 1952 he assisted with the installation of a show of Schwitters organized for the Arts Club of Chicago by the New York dealer Sidney Janis. This encounter led to his first purchases of Schwitters's work.

During the Seagram period, Mies renewed contact with the New York art world. Gene Summers recalled a tour of the Manhattan galleries. Mies had asked him to look for art on behalf of a Chicago investment counselor, and while at the Saidenberg Gallery Summers found a number of pieces by Picasso, Fernand Leger, and Juan Gris. At Summers's suggestion, Mies visited the gallery, where he purchased Picasso's *Buste de Femme* (*Bust of a Woman*) for himself. Once the work was in his possession, he noticed, with delight, that Picasso had scrawled on the back of the canvas the date of the painting's completion—"27 III 1956," Mies's seventieth birthday.[15]

Disinclined to buy art solely as an investment, Mies made a substantial exception in 1956 when he bought from J. B. Neumann a folio of ninety prints by Edvard Munch that he never hung in his Chicago apartment. In 1963 Chicago dealer Allan Frumkin negotiated the sale of the prints to the Art Institute of Chicago, where they were incorporated in the Clarence Buckingham Collection.

Mies was held in high regard by the younger generation of Chicago painters, sculptors, and graphic designers. In 1950, together with Clement Greenberg, Lester Longman, and Ernst Mundt, he was invited to serve on the jury of Exhibition Momentum, a group show organized by the city's art students to protest a decision by the Art Institute to exclude students from the museum's annual Chicago and Vicinity show. The experience brought him in touch with a group of postwar Chicago artists, one of whom, H. C. Westermann, was an especially gifted sculptor and the carver of *Butterfly*, an exquisitely crafted wood relief that Mies bought in 1957. Dirk Lohan, who now owns the work, remembers that Mies was attracted to it because it reminded him of Klee's technique. Westermann was the only American, indeed the only sculptor, in Mies's collection. Several years later, the purchase of a painted portrait of Mies by the Swissborn Hugo Weber concluded his collecting. Following his death, Mies's collection was divided and endowed to his two surviving daughters.[16] Marianne willed her portion to her son, Dirk Lohan, and daughter, Ulrike Schreiber, and Georgia lent hers, over time, to several museums.[17]

· · ·

Ludwig Mies van der Rohe died four decades prior to the publication of this book, and the ranks of those who remember him from personal observation have diminished accordingly. Yet there are enough firsthand recollections to provide a personal portrait of the man, many from a treasured source we have drawn on throughout this book: the oral history program of the Department of Architecture at the Art Institute of Chicago. Begun in 1983, it is a collection of professionally edited interviews with architects of significance to Chicago and its region. Many had ties to Mies or were influenced by him, while some reacted against him.[18] The narrative that follows draws from this material, from other private and published memories, and from our own interviews and personal and professional interaction with Mies's Chicago circle.

Almost universally cited by those who knew him was Mies's even temperament. Office colleagues Joseph Fujikawa, Edward Duckett, and Donald Sickler testified that over their combined decades of interaction with Mies, they seldom saw him upset, raise his voice, or engage in rude or overbearing behavior.[19] A precocious twelve-year-old formed the same impression. Tim Samuelson, today the official historian of the Chicago Cultural Center, made a call on Mies at his Ohio Street office in 1962. Having developed a youthful passion for architecture, Samuelson hoped to meet with Mies and persuade him to prevent the impending demolition of Henry Ives Cobb's 1905 Federal Building, which occupied part of the site of Mies's Federal Center project. The boy encountered the expected roadblocks, but was finally ushered into Mies's office. There, as he recalls, he addressed Mies: "The old building is so wonderful.... Can't you move your own building to another spot, so that no damage is done to such a beautiful piece of work?"[20]

Mies listened thoughtfully. "I hope that some day you will look at the new building and admire it as much as the old one." Realizing he had done what he could, Samuelson next fixed his attention on a nearby model of a tall building that was attended by toy cars and little strips of paper fashioned to look like figures. "How do you do that?" he asked. Mies took a piece of paper and patiently demonstrated the technique. With that the visit ended. Samuelson acknowledges that today he does indeed "look at the new building and admire it as much as the old one."[21]

Mies was still in good health when this description appeared, without byline, in the November 1952 issue of *Architectural Forum*:

> He is ... robust, not precious. He is a formidably shy man of 66 with massive shoulders, a daring chin now well upholstered in flesh and an expression of gravity which differs greatly from the urgent mobility of Le Corbusier's face, or the wise nobility of Wright's. His eyes, set in areas of intricately pleated and plumped skin, seem distant. In a meeting with Mies there are numerous, faintly hopeless stillnesses, when he withdraws behind a cloud of cigar smoke, while ideas and images simplify themselves in his mind.[22]

Though Mies expressed himself adequately in English, a language he used for thirty years, he remained more comfortable in German. Several colleagues made the same observation. Bruce Graham found him slow in English, though in German anything but.[23] Lohan, fluent in both languages, believes that Mies's reputation for taciturnity was the product of sustained unease in his adopted language. In German, Lohan recalled, he was "lively and more articulate," and never at a loss for words.[24] Fujikawa remembered Mies's difficulties with names: "He would introduce me to someone and say, 'This is Mr. Fuji-cago!' Mixed up with Chicago.... For years he called me Mr. Fujicago."[25]

Reginald Malcolmson had a different theory about the master's famous reticence:

> [Mies] had a habit of letting people talk their heads off.... [Y]ou ... would hear sense and nonsense vying with one another over some considerable period ... and he had the ability to sit through that.... He seemed to be impervious to it. And then you had the feeling that when he started to talk he'd already gauged that people had about talked themselves out. So now he could make some kind of impact by saying things that would either sum up what had to be said about it or would inject into it something that nobody had mentioned before.... And he did that very many times, so I am inclined to think that it was deliberate.... It was a studied way with which he could make an impact on people by holding his fire until the right moment.[26]

Werner Buch, a German who studied with Mies at Armour Institute at the end of the 1930s, remembered that "he spoke a very nice German, very calm, almost colloquial, but when he spoke English his Aachen background came through so clearly that it seemed he spoke English with a Low German accent." Buch also noted that Mies employed his adopted tongue in a most persuasive way, due less to linguistic finesse than force of personality:

FIGURE 15.4.
Mies revisiting Crown
Hall in the mid-
1960s, surrounded
by students and col-
leagues and armed
with his constant
companion, a cigar.
Behind Mies, framed
by the millwork wall,
is Hugo Weber's 1961
bust of the architect.
Photo courtesy of
Dirk Lohan.

He stood there quietly, and then he said one sentence, which of course was a platitude. But when he said it, the wheels began to turn and these plain words, in themselves totally insignificant, quickly connected with our recollection of Mies's work. He may have said something like "You will have to learn dat a church different ist from an industrial building." ... Everyone nodded with understanding. The amazing thing was that when Mies said something like that, and in the form and the way he said it, and with all that backed it up, we were all spellbound.[27]

Peter Roesch, a longtime IIT professor, has a contrasting recollection. As a student recently emigrated from Germany and still struggling in English, he attended a Mies lecture but missed nearly all of what was said. At the end, he asked for assistance from a nearby American student, who replied: "I couldn't understand his English any better than you could."[28]

Yet Mies had another way of communicating: the projection of authority, partly physical, partly verbal. James Hammond, a Mies student and later a noted Chicago architect, said it this way: "[Mies] was monumental and approachable, and people hung on his words and remembered them and almost inscribed them"[29] (fig. 15.4). For Gene Summers, it was more than charisma:

It was more as if God were over there on the other side of the table. It sounds a little silly ... but there was that feeling. He had this presence about him.... He didn't impress you with his talk. He wouldn't talk unless a question was really asked.... He always had a beautiful blue or brown suit on, mainly blue, with his gold watch fob coming out and his cigar.... You knew there was someone there and there was just no nonsense.[30]

Earlier, Summers experienced a different side of the monumental Mies: "Even with [only] six people in the office, I worked for a couple of years and he didn't even know my name."[31] Mies could also be less than grand: Edward Duckett and Joseph Fujikawa agreed that in all the years they worked for him, "there was one thing [we] never really forgave him for. If someone messed up, was undependable or something of that nature, no matter what that person did for the rest of their life, Mies never really trusted them.... [He] never forgave them, [and] never forgot it. It was just not in his psyche. He just couldn't live with it. That doesn't mean he mistreated anyone, but in a way it ended your opportunity or future with him."[32]

Malcolmson called Mies "an enigmatic personality, the exemplification of a witticism of Oscar Wilde: 'Simplicity is the last refuge of a complex mind.' And he had a complex mind, as well as an overpowering sense of intuition."[33] Malcolmson, equally fascinated by Ludwig Hilberseimer, said this about Mies and Hilbs as teachers:

> There is no question Mies and Hilbs, to some extent, were in their own persons exemplars.... Mies had a great deal of what I call the old German virtues. He was always punctual. Hilbs too, even more so. You never saw Hilbs or Mies sloppily dressed. Never. They were always on stage and very conscious of it.... They set a kind of example to people of devotion to serious interests. They had a way of discussing things with young people that conveyed the seriousness of the discussion, very simply and very effectively.[34]

Nonetheless, there is ample evidence, as noted earlier, that Mies was neither an eager administrator nor a gifted teacher. In Europe and the United States, he left the day-to-day operation of his schools to subordinates, preferring to concentrate on projects of interest to him and on his own professional work. Fujikawa:

> I don't think Mies was a leader.... He set an example by just doing things which made you respect him, in a sense you felt in awe because of his creative talent.... I don't think he would have made a good army general.... [Hilberseimer] was more of a born teacher than Mies. Mies had a lot to offer, but [he] was first and foremost an architect. And I guess since he had thought so much about architecture, he was a good teacher. But Hilbs had a gift for teaching, just as someone might have a gift for music or language.[35]

Mies did have a sense of humor, and it could occasionally bite, though it tended to be overshadowed by his customary neutrality of mood. Robert McCormick, Herbert Greenwald's partner in the development of 860–880 North

Lake Shore Drive, invited Mies and Walter Gropius to his home in Elmhurst, Illinois, which Mies had designed. In the course of a long evening, Gropius applauded an emerging trend in professional practice: one could now design projects for many different places, and have a local, associate architect handle the details. "But Gropius," McCormick recalled Mies's rejoinder, "if you vant to make a baby, do you call in the neighbors?"[36] And William Murphy, assistant counsel during the Farnsworth trial, remembered a lunch at the Aurora Country Club with Mies and several club members. A discussion of the cost of the recently completed clubhouse building produced a consensus: "around a million." Mies eyed his companions and with a sly smile said: "I could do it for two."[37] Roesch recalls the report of one of Mies's colleagues that Philip Johnson had been heard taking credit for the design of the Seagram Building: "Does that bother you, Mies?" "Not especially. What would bother me would be Johnson claiming that I was chiefly responsible for one of *his* buildings."[38]

We have claimed for Mies a normally unflappable manner. But normal is not constant. On occasion he was capable of choleric behavior. Lora Marx recalled occasions when Mies was "brooding about something. Suddenly he would explode. Whoever was in the way took the brunt. He would shout and wave his hands. And he wouldn't be frank about the source. I'd have to find out later."[39] As already reported, the best-known target of his professional antipathy was László Moholy-Nagy, dating back to Bauhaus days and escalating later when Moholy opened the "New Bauhaus" in Chicago in 1937. And Mies was no less displeased with Serge Chermayeff, the director of a later Chicago school directed by Moholy, the Institute of Design.

Mies's awareness of the ultimate uselessness of such enmity is suggested by a memory of Ambrose Richardson, an Armour graduate. Richardson recalled: "As Mies once said, 'I have very little time to be for something. I have absolutely no time to be *against* anything.'"[40] This principle applied equally to his professional practice and to his lifelong aversion to politics, in Germany and Chicago. It also informed his "horror of any kind of controversial situation," according to Malcolmson. "He was a very difficult man to position into a confrontation."[41]

As described several times in this text, Mies loved well-irrigated gatherings with colleagues and students. His prowess as a drinker was massive, as famously remembered as the identity of his favorite drink, the martini, a passion he cultivated in the United States.[42] Lora Marx recalled: "At dinner four martinis were standard. Then he would stop. 'Remember,' he would say, 'After you have had five martinis you never eat dinner' (which meant he wouldn't either)."[43] Yet he remained secondarily faithful to Steinhäger, a German gin he first drank during his apprenticeship in Aachen.[44] When surrounded by company, Mies eagerly stayed up until the wee hours, resisting the attempts of his guests to go home. The more he drank, the more volubly, and easily, he spoke English. Evidence of that—and more than that—marked Mies's conduct at Peter Roesch's all-night Highland Park party. He remained in his chair next to the fireplace for most of the affair, talkative to the point of loquacity—in English—while dandling Roesch's two children on his knees. And as dawn broke, Mies decided to make his way, arthritis and all, down the slope of a steep ravine to the shore of Lake Michigan to watch the sunrise.

Mies was seldom at the office before the close of the lunch period. He studied current work with unhurried concentration, discussing it in like manner with his staff, after which he returned to his apartment at the end of the afternoon. "Mies loved to draw," quoting Malcolmson again, "and admired excellence in drawing. Such skills were to him essential, and once, after an exasperating discussion with some of his office staff . . . he exclaimed, 'For heaven's sake, make a drawing; we are architects, not lawyers!'"[45]

. . .

Lora loved him unqualifiedly. She asked little of him, which was the best way to keep him as close as he was likely to be with anyone. Understanding his need for independence and solitude, she never lived with him, and always maintained her own household as well as a place in the country. He could be tender in his regard for her and, significantly, capable of small talk. She in turn treasured his attentions, and kept a record of his casual remarks.[46] She especially savored his eloquence in English:

Lora: "Is it raining?" Mies: "No, it's just mizzling."

Anticipating a trip: "Tomorrow night at this time I will be in Mexico, drinking Kweela."

Of a typical July weekend in Chicago: "It's such sticky, muffy weather."

After a new battery was installed in the car: "Did it spring on fast?"

Of a bright red sports car: "There is an alarm car."

Lora also documented his affections. Once, when she was bending over to fasten her boots, he said, as perhaps only an architect would: "You look nice even from the top. God must have pleasure to look at you." Snippets of table talk were likewise preserved:

On the subject of South American cuisine: "Twice my stomach pinched me."

Watching a "wild storm" over Lake Michigan: "Windcaps! How sharp they go ahead!"

On being used: "If I had known that, I would never have been the carrot in their vegetable soup."

Mies overhearing a phone conversation: "He was very excited. You could hear his brain clobbering. So metallic—like a typewriter."

Having just seen Edith Farnsworth on the street: "She looked like a stick in a field—against the birds (flapping hands)."

The morning after the 1964 presidential election: "He [Goldwater] looked like a wet cat."

Reacting to "terrible music on radio: 'When I hear music like that my shoes fall off.'"

At a friend's for lunch. "Small Japanese plum tree with small round flower bed at base of trunk. Mies: 'Everything here is on doilies.'"

And finally, she recorded the reflective Mies:

"Describing a girl ([aged] 30 during Nazi time) who owned and lent Mies a house ... in Tyrol in Sopra Bolzano: 'She was fanatically connected with the mountains. The whole of creation would have been nothing to her without the mountains.'"

"Regarding fame: 'It's like my relation to society. I don't want it, although I have nothing against the people. I like [want] the recognition, but I don't like the consequences. I *hate* the consequences ...'"

On Hilberseimer's terminal illness: "It is a pity we cannot just turn off our life-light."

On "staying up late, alone: 'I have to wait that [until] the music dies out.'"

. . .

Mies's recovery from his acute attack of arthritis in 1963 was short-lived. Mobility never returned but the pain did, so much so that in 1965 he confided to Lora his inability to concentrate. "The worst thing about pain," he told her, "is that it is boring."[47] Since his discomfort was made worse by the tautness of the musculature around his waist, his doctors decided on a surgical procedure in which they notched some of his muscles laterally, lengthening and thus relaxing them, bringing him the first pronounced relief from pain in years. While he never walked unassisted again, he was able to resume a moderate schedule of work.

Le Corbusier died in 1965, suffering a heart attack while swimming in the Mediterranean. Wright had died in 1959. Only Gropius and Mies remained from the great generation of European modernists born in the 1880s. The debt of the years was mounting, demanding more urgently to be paid. In the 1960s, Mies developed divergent strabismus, a condition known as wall-eye. It left him incapable of focusing for long on the printed page. He relied on Lora to read to him, which she did as diligently "as he would otherwise have done for himself. His intimacy with her and hers with him deepened, and one evening she laid her book aside and gently asked: "Tell me why you never married me?"

Mies heaved a great sigh. "I think I was a fool. I was afraid I would lose my freedom. I wouldn't have. It was a senseless worry." He paused. Then he asked: "Shall we do it now?"

"No," she replied, knowing him better than he knew himself. "It is rather too late for that; it would only spoil things. I guess I just wanted to know."[48] Lora was content with the responsibility to help him approach death in as much ease as possible.

The first symptoms of cancer of the esophagus appeared in 1966, shortly after a shower of congratulatory messages descended on him on the occasion of his eightieth birthday. Surgery was out of the question; his condition and age precluded it. Radiation reduced the size of the obstruction and gave him a measure of comfort. In 1968, Lora and Mies took "one last lovely trip" of several weeks to Santa Barbara, from which Mies returned looking tan and fit.[49] For about a year in 1968 and 1969, his physician, Dr. George Allen, kept him functioning by regularly dilating his esophagus, an unpleasant business that Mies endured with his usual stoicism.[50]

He died August 17, 1969, six weeks after Gropius. About two weeks before, one evening at dinner, Lora noted that Mies, who had a slight cold, was looking pale. She decided to spend the night, close to him, at his apartment. The next morning she found him in bed, trembling, gasping for breath, his fists clenched tightly under his chin. He was taken by ambulance to Wesley Memorial Hospital. What was thought to be a heart attack proved to be pneumonia. For two weeks, he drifted in and out of consciousness. Georgia flew in from New York. Marianne was already in Chicago. With both daughters at his side, Mies was ashen and inert when his breathing stopped. Lora and Dirk arrived shortly thereafter. The family entrusted Lora with the funeral arrangements, which she limited to a short service in the chapel at Graceland Cemetery. Dirk spoke briefly and the organist offered "O Haupt voll Blut und Wunden" from Bach's *St. Matthew Passion*. Mies's body was cremated, his ashes buried in a plot within sight of the graves of Daniel Burnham and Louis Sullivan.[51]

. . .

Two months later, the rest of the world offered its gesture of remembrance. On October 25, 1969, friends, colleagues, students, and admirers assembled in

Crown Hall at IIT to hear more Bach, this time from the cello of Janos Starker, and an encomium delivered by James Johnson Sweeney, former director of the Houston Museum of Fine Arts and a friend dating to 1930s Berlin. With striking appropriateness, he eulogized a philosophy as much as the man who lived it:

> Space, amplitude and a comfortable relationship among the parts—unity, order, form—were his basic requirements. A lack of order in any part hurt him....
>
> ... This is the bequest which Mies has left to all of us and particularly to Chicago: his vital, personal and inspiring patterns of order in a world which has suffered too long in recent years from the disregard of such a spiritual discipline.
>
> Today there is no need to stress the value of Mies's contribution, nor his stature as an artist. As the latter, he had the good fortune to live to realize the universal recognition ... being paid him. To the world he was a great architect and a modest, self-effacing man. To his intimates he will always remain what he always was to them, a benign monolith: a warm friend and a full human being.[52]

· · ·

Even as Sweeney spoke, a storm was breaking. Architectural modernism was in professional and critical retreat. According to its critics, during the 1950s and 1960s the modern movement had made common cause with corporate enterprise, its mission little more than abetting commercial power. The failure of urban renewal, the flight of the middle class from American cities, and the crowding of downtowns and suburban developments with banal boxes: all proved that bureaucrats and real estate interests had co-opted modernist planning and design. At the level of theory, disenchantment reared up. Many architects and critics had concluded that an "objective architecture"—to the extent it was pursued by the profession in attempted imitation of Mies—had produced not purity of expression but mostly sterility.

Not all—possibly none—of these grievances could be nailed directly on Mies's door. He did not think so: "There is obviously visible now a reaction to my approach in architecture. There is no question, but I think it is just a reaction. I don't believe it is a new approach.... The reaction is a kind of fashion."[53] Yet his influence made him a prime target of what became architectural postmodernism. He was his period's most impersonal rationalist, an authoritarian objectivist who had abjured even his own occasional impulses "to do something just because I like to." In an increasingly complex world where time was compressed by precipitous change and space could mean the sprawl of Dallas or the grid of Chicago, Mies's "objective" methods seemed impossibly passé.

. . .

With the oil shock of the early 1970s, architecture faced new challenges. The deep American recession of the mid-1970s, for example, all but stopped major commercial construction in Chicago from 1974, when Sears Tower and the Standard Oil Building were completed, well into the 1980s. With the revival of construction, there were again new buildings in a Miesian mode; indeed, modernism was never in full retreat. But the intellectual ground had shifted. Mies — his students spread to the wind — was now, it seemed, a figure of history. But the postmodern movement would in turn yield to new fashions in the 1990s, again after a downturn in construction in the late 1980s.

Yet before the turn of the twenty-first century, a new kind of modernism — again free of historicism, driven by new talent and ever-advancing technology — was again ascendant. By this time, Mies scholarship had reached a first maturity, and Mies, though no longer copied, was again revered. His major works have or will soon become protected landmarks, and several have already undergone meticulous restorations and even recreation. Thus he has passed to the status of icon.

Mies's place in architectural history is assured not by the infallibility of his thinking but by the subtlety and refinement of his art — what we now understand, paradoxically, as a highly *personal* art dependent on one man's objectivity. If he did not divine the epoch, he left his personal stamp on it, this most impersonal of artists.

Mies approached architecture as supplicant and master, with the humility of a novitiate and the certainty of one whose faith was confirmed by success. "The building art," he said, "is in reality always the spatial execution of spiritual decisions."[54] "Architecture is the real battleground of the spirit," he wrote in 1950. "Architecture wrote the history of the epochs and gave them their names."[55]

Acknowledgments

During the past half century, three American cultural institutions have collectively played the key role in documenting the life and career of Ludwig Mies van der Rohe. By donating his professional files to the Museum of Modern Art, New York, as well as drawings numbering in the thousands, Mies himself acted as the prime mover in the establishment of the museum's Mies van der Rohe Archive. Three years earlier, in 1965, he gave the Library of Congress a cache of material, more personal than professional, of comparable importance. And beginning in 1983, the Chicago Architects Oral History Project, under the auspices of the Art Institute's Department of Architecture, has documented the careers and opinions of nearly one hundred architects, most with ties to Mies.

We are grateful for discussions with architect Dirk Lohan, Mies's grandson, who was especially close to the architect. Among the interviewers who have given spirit to the Art Institute's oral history program, Betty Blum is preeminent. Mies's students and longtime colleagues who made themselves available to us for interviews include the late Jacques Brownson, the late Bruno Conterato, the late Edward Duckett, the late Joseph Fujikawa, the late Myron Goldsmith, the late Philip Johnson, the late Edward Olencki, Peter Roesch, George Schipporeit, David Sharpe, Donald Lee Sickler, and the late Gene Summers. We also learned much from the late George Danforth, whose knowledge of Mies was comprehensive. Phyllis Lambert granted us a long interview; we thank her, too, for providing access to the incomparable files of the Canadian Centre for Architecture in Montreal.

In America and Europe, we have relied on the testimony of those who knew Mies well or knew others who knew him well: curators John Zukowsky and the late Katharine Kuh; developer Peter Palumbo; foundation director and architect Carter H. Manny; historians Tilman Buddensieg, Dietrich von Beulwitz, Wolf Tegethoff, and David van Zanten; theater director Margit Kleber; and Robin Goldsmith.

At the Illinois Institute of Technology, thanks to university archivist Catherine Bruck. At Lake Forest College, thanks to Nancy Bohm, Susan Cloud, Richard Fisher, and Arthur H. Miller, and at the Farnsworth House to Executive Director Whitney French. For editorial counsel, we salute the late H. David Matson.

A unique place in our acknowledgments belongs to the late Lora Marx, Mies's companion from their meeting in 1940 until his death in 1969. In a series of conversations with Schulze in the early 1980s, she recalled aspects of Mies's personality and her relationship with him that are centrally important to the record.

We thank Marc Boxerman and architects Gene Summers (again), Dirk Lohan (again), Donald Lee Sickler (again), and especially Algis Novickas for their scrupulous reading of the manuscript. Finally, we thank June Sawyers, who prepared the index, and our editors at the University of Chicago Press: Executive Editor Susan Bielstein, Anthony Burton, and Sandra Hazel.

(Drawings in this book, unless otherwise indicated, are by one of us [Windhorst], and are based on graphic material preserved in the Mies van der Rohe Archive.)

Appendix A: Protégés

What else is possible? Regardless of how bad you think it might be, put it on paper.
MIES, on problem solving

I wish I had done it. **MIES'S** opinion about Jacques Brownson's Civic Center

By the 1950s—and especially after the completion of the Seagram Building—Mies was widely regarded as the most influential architect in the United States. As we have noted, a broad movement of Miesian architects and architecture was quickly labeled the Second Chicago School. Since 1938 Mies and his IIT faculty had trained a generation of architects, and some of the best had now begun to occupy positions of authority in major Chicago firms. And from the mid-1950s, distinguished buildings in the Miesian idiom were reaching completion, mostly in Chicago, but also in New York and other American cities.

Mies's ultimate influence was far wider than these earliest individual buildings, though that story—beyond our scope—is still being written. In this appendix we select five outstanding works of Mies's Chicago protégés, and discuss their history as it directly connects to Mies.

. . .

As we have noted, Myron Goldsmith was Mies's most important student. His masterwork, completed in 1962, is the McMath-Pierce Solar Telescope at Kitt Peak National Observatory near Tucson, Arizona (fig. A.1). Goldsmith—"Goldy" to Mies and his staff—has figured prominently in this book, thus far chiefly for his work in Mies's office between 1946 and 1953. He was in his late twenties when he began working for Mies, but he enjoyed a senior status as an architect, engineer, and intellectual. He left Mies to study with Italian architect-engineer Pier Luigi Nervi. Goldsmith asserted that during the time he worked for Mies, they were not really close—"we certainly weren't friends at this time"—but there is no question that Goldsmith's departure was a professional setback to Mies.[1]

In 1955 Goldsmith moved to Skidmore, Owings & Merrill's San Francisco office, where he was chief structural engineer, and in 1957 to SOM's Chicago office as a designer. He worked under Bruce Graham for the next decade, and

FIGURE A.1.
McMath-Pierce
Solar Telescope,
Kitt Peak, Arizona
(1962). Designed by
Myron Goldsmith of
Skidmore, Owings
& Merrill. *At right*,
the shorter box with
three associated
masts is a later in-
strument (by others).

was made a partner in 1967. From 1961 until his death in 1996, he was professor in the IIT College of Architecture, where he established himself, with the possible exception of Alfred Caldwell (and Mies and Hilberseimer), as the school's most eminent figure.

Goldsmith recalled Mies's influence as it related to the Kitt Peak project:

> If you look at [Mies's] work, it seems to me that he explored for a long time.... The idea of exploring many solutions to a problem is Miesian. He would not hesitate to make a dozen models or a thousand sketches of something ... to explore it.... On the telescope there were ... ten or fifteen models of different solutions made and some of them were visually nicer than the others.... They led to others and finally there was just one that was preferred. Happily it was, of all that we explored, the most reasonable in cost. It all came together. It was very Miesian, trying to make architecture out of the facts, the plan, the planning limitations, the limitations of normal structures, not fantastic structures.[2]

The telescope is sited atop a seven-thousand-foot peak in south-central Arizona. In a 1994 interview, Goldsmith described the project:

> It came out of the blue, with a phone call from the University of Michigan. "Come and see us about a telescope." They called because of [SOM's] reputation technically. A lot of these scientific projects had run into terrible difficulties. They were often just sort of cobbled together by the astronomers. And this was complex. The skin had to be uniformly cooled to eliminate atmospheric distortion. And it was a rush job.

APPENDIX A

The instrument was designed to study the surface of the sun. To cut atmospheric distortion we had to minimize the amount of telescope exposed to the elements. But the mirror had to sit 100 feet above grade, and it couldn't move more than a few thousands of an inch. We had to have something like a 300 foot focal length. You can get this by folding the light path, but every time you reflect it you cut quality. With the huge straight shaft continuing in a long underground tunnel we eliminated a couple of reflections. To simplify guidance the shaft is parallel to the solar axis. It's a precise angle for that latitude. And we had the idea that if the tube were turned at a 45 degree angle it would present a streamlined shape to the wind. We made a model and tested it with an electric fan and some smoke, and sure enough the smoke went around, and that's how we got that shape. It was partially dumb luck that this beautiful sculptural form emerged. But we had a lot going for us, that wonderful isolated site on the mountain, and the big dimensions.[3]

Goldsmith's "beautiful sculptural form" is a five-hundred-foot-long trussed structural-steel tube of square section, tilted up and two-thirds buried in the mountain. The exposed end is supported by a similar square-sectioned post. A heliostat and sixty-inch-diameter mirror are carried high above grade on a concrete tower isolated from the external structure. These instruments transmit an image of the sun to an observation chamber below. The exterior is a windscreen covered by a double copper skin, with chilled water circulating between inner and outer walls. The entire enclosure is painted white to reduce solar gain. Of breathtaking scale and mightily solitary astride the mountain, the McMath-Pierce Solar Telescope was widely acclaimed a triumph of architectural minimalism, just at the time that minimalism as an art movement was entering the American mainstream.[4] But as the architecture critic Allan Temko noted: "[Goldsmith's work] is far more than the minimalist sculpture it has widely influenced ... At the summit of an Arizona mountain, which to the Indians was sacred to the sun, the Kitt Peak Solar Observatory unlocks secrets of the cosmos, and yet reveals further mysteries beyond. The spare logical structure, which physically could not be more different from the chapel at the hilltop of Ronchamp, belongs by paradox to the same high realm of philosophic inquiry."[5]

· · ·

Chicago's one-hundred-story John Hancock Center (1968) is *not* the work of Goldsmith—or even, technically, that of a Mies student—though Mies and Goldsmith by influence and Goldsmith in person were entwined in its origins (fig. A.2). Hancock was designed by SOM's Bruce Graham and a colleague,

structural engineer Fazlur Khan. Of dozens of major buildings Graham designed over a forty-year career, Hancock is his most important. It was Khan's
breakthrough to world renown.

Graham received his professional education at the University of Pennsylva-
nia, but his work grew out of studying Mies, whose influence in Chicago and
at SOM was at its peak in the late 1950s and early 1960s. Witness the reaction of Natalie De Blois, a seasoned designer who transferred from New York
to Chicago in 1961 and worked under Graham: "I was flabbergasted when I got
to Chicago. I found out that everybody talked about nothing but Mies van der
Rohe. Everything was Mies. There were people [in the SOM office] who had
done detailing in Mies's office; there were people who studied with Mies at
I.I.T. I was not familiar with Mies ... I didn't understand Mies. I just sat down
and went to work."[6]

Fazlur Khan, a native of Bangladesh, was educated at the University of
Dhaka and the University of Illinois. Goldsmith was close to both Graham and
Khan, and in 1961 he recruited Khan to teach with him in the graduate program

at IIT. The two went on to produce historically significant research throughout the 1960s and 1970s.

In 1953, under Mies, Goldsmith completed a master of architecture thesis titled "The Tall Building: The Effects of Scale." He postulated that for buildings, a given structural system is appropriate for a range of physical scales, and that when the scale of a construction moves beyond a given range the structural system must change. He applied this principle to his own concepts for very tall buildings—he proposed a concrete superframe skyscraper of eighty stories—and asserted that new structural systems would be necessary as buildings exceeded then typical heights. He also described and illustrated several tubular systems for the lateral bracing of very tall buildings, including an all-steel, X-braced tube.

Goldsmith and Khan, working in 1962 with IIT graduate student Mikio Sasaki, tested the X-braced tube in a thesis project for a skyscraper for Tokyo, an area of high seismic activity. As both well knew, for tall buildings earthquake forces act primarily laterally, and are similar to those generated by wind. Using theoretical and physical models, Khan confirmed what Goldsmith had theorized: an exoskeletal trussed tube is exceptionally efficient at resisting lateral loads. Up to that time, very tall buildings like New York's Empire State had been constructed of ever more massive rigid steel frames. While the structure of a thirty-story, pre–World War II steel building might weigh twenty-five pounds per square foot of building area, for the Empire State Building the figure jumped to over sixty. Such a system could not be scaled up indefinitely. Goldsmith called this "the scale problem."[7]

SOM was awarded the Hancock commission in 1962. Graham asked Goldsmith to work with him on the project, but Goldsmith declined, citing other work. He said it was "the worst mistake I ever made."[8] Hancock was to occupy most of a full block facing Chicago's North Michigan Avenue, two blocks south of the Drake Hotel. The program anticipated *two* large towers, one for offices and one for apartments. The office tower was to be about forty stories and the apartment building sixty, but they would be roughly the same height, because offices must be taller floor-to-floor. Massing models were prepared—just as in Mies's office—and the permutations of siting, shape, and height were tested. Two large buildings did not fit comfortably on the site, and it also became evident that maintaining views between and around closely spaced towers was problematic.

According to Graham, the client suggested stacking the models, and asked if a single tower of one hundred stories might work.[9] Khan responded with the X-braced tube he had already studied at IIT. To marry the large lease spans required for offices with the smaller floor plates appropriate to apartments, Graham fashioned a giant tapered tube.[10] He clad and expressed its steel structure with black anodized aluminum panels infilled with bronze tinted glass.

Inland Steel Build-
ing, Chicago, by
Skidmore, Owings &
Merrill (1957). The
first tall building con-
structed in central
Chicago after the De-
pression and World
War II, Inland was a
demonstration piece
for the steel technol-
ogies then being ad-
vanced by its owner.

Mullion spacing followed the 860–880 North Lake Shore Drive model, with the plan module maintained across column and corner enclosures that were sometimes five feet wide. The structure weighs twenty-nine pounds per square foot, so that the tower's great height was purchased mostly by brain power.

· · ·

Graham's earliest work also followed Miesian models, notably at the Gunner's Mate School at Great Lakes Naval Training Center, Great Lakes, Illinois (1954), and shortly thereafter for the headquarters of Kimberly-Clark in Needham, Wisconsin (1956). His other great Miesian building after Hancock—though chronologically earlier—is Inland Steel (1957), the first commercial tower built in Chicago's Loop after the Great Depression and World War II (fig. A.3).

It was codesigned by Walter Netsch, who was at the time also lead designer for the United States Air Force Academy in Colorado Springs, SOM's marquee project of the 1950s.

Inland Steel was a test bed for innovative planning and new steel technology. For a modern office building, the service core is typically midplan, as the term implies; but for Inland it is removed to a quasi-freestanding tower that is connected by corridors to the main building. With columns mostly outboard of the exterior wall and three-foot-deep floor beams, Inland offered unprecedented sixty-foot-wide, column-free floors. In a dramatic departure from Mies's painted steel, and in an obvious nod to the owners, the architects clad the building in stainless steel sheets,[11] with slender, box-sectioned stainless steel mullions carrying insulating bottle-green glass. The windowless twenty-five-story service tower is also wrapped in panels of stainless steel, each band the height of a typical spandrel. The great spans, cantilevered end bays, and shimmering exterior wall combine to produce an airy building evocative of the optimism of architectural modernism and the wider culture of postwar America.

. . .

Graham also figures in the creation of the Chicago Civic Center (now the Richard J. Daley Center), completed in 1966 to a design by supervising architects C. F. Murphy Associates and associate architects SOM and Loebl, Schlossman, Bennett & Dart (fig. A.4). Murphy's lead designer was Jacques Brownson. For the Civic Center, Brownson headed the special office set up by the three firms to produce the project, and there is little doubt that he was responsible for almost every detail, large and small. But early on Graham and other SOM architects, including Arthur Takeuchi, another Mies student, were significantly involved in programming and conceptual design, and especially with the decision to create one and not two buildings (as suggested by government officials) to house the complex program.[12]

Brownson earned his professional degrees at IIT. His own house in Geneva, Illinois, was the subject of his 1954 master's thesis under Mies and structural engineer Frank Kornacker. Brownson built the steel, glass, and brick-infill house himself, starting without any experience in the welding or erection of structural steel. Though contemporaneous with the Farnsworth House, Brownson's is anything but a copy.[13] With its four steel portal frames, it has more in common with Crown Hall than with the Farnsworth House, and though little celebrated today, it is the most distinguished of the many houses by Mies's students.[14]

Brownson taught at IIT from 1948 until 1959. He then joined C. F. Murphy and stayed for six years. He designed Continental Center (1962), an elegant,

FIGURE A.4
(*facing*).
Chicago Civic Center (now the Richard J. Daley Center) (1966), designed by Jacques Brownson, a Mies student and faculty colleague. Mies told Brownson, "I wish I had done it." The much-admired building was made a Chicago landmark in 2002, fourteen years *before* it was officially eligible. Joseph Fujikawa, a longtime Mies lieutenant, thought the Civic Center was the finest building in Chicago.

twenty-three-story long-span tower at 55 East Jackson Boulevard in Chicago's Loop, and then the Daley Center. (Both buildings are now official Chicago Landmarks.) In 1966 Brownson became department chair at the University of Michigan School of Architecture, but returned to Chicago in 1968 as managing architect for the city's Public Building Commission. During the 1970s, he was a planning official for the State of Colorado.

The Daley Center is a courthouse serving the second most populous county (after Los Angeles County) in the United States. The program called for seven different types of courtrooms as well as judges' chambers and jury and conference facilities.[15] The windowless courtrooms are internal to the plan, with public circulation at the northern and southern perimeter. Judges' chambers open to the exterior on the east and west elevations, and connect to the courtrooms across private corridors. Given the complex spatial requirements and the perceived need for future flexibility, it was decided to introduce very long spans to create column-free interiors. Graham, Goldsmith, and Brownson, too, argued for the long spans, which when coupled with the reduced number of required caissons represented a reasonable premium over traditional column spacing. At 87 feet, the east-to-west bays required 5-foot, 4-inch-deep Warren trusses for floor beams, and even the north-to-south bays, at 45 feet, could not be spanned with simple beams. The deep floor system and tall interiors resulted in a 650-foot building with only thirty-three floors—briefly the tallest in Chicago. The structure and its cladding are entirely welded, and the exterior appears to be a seamless, poured-on sheath.

So-called weathering steel, under the trade name Cor-Ten, was used to clad columns and walls.[16] The floor structure is expressed on the exterior in what appear to be gigantic plate girders, which are in fact an exterior covering built up of Cor-Ten plate and stiffeners aligned on the module. The twelve perimeter columns (there are four more internal to the plan) are giant cruciform sections also built up from heavy steel plate and filled behind the Cor-Ten skin with concrete. The columns step back three times on the way to the top, reflecting the reduced dead loads, after Mies's manner at Promontory. The windows are bronze-tinted plate glass.

The building is avowedly gigantic, and the strongly horizontal exterior rich in texture, both at large scale and in detail. In these respects, it is unlike anything by Mies. Mies's walls, especially in his larger, post-860 buildings, tend toward flatness and always read vertically. The vast spans of the Daley Center, by contrast, call for depth in the wall precisely because, on this scale, we expect massive members. The expression is rational, though strictly it may be unnecessary, and Brownson got the proportions and shadowing just right. The cruciform columns are no more efficient than standard square-sectioned built-up steel, and were certainly more costly. They are especially impressive at the ground-level colonnade, where they lift the giant building effortlessly,

FIGURE A.5
(*facing*).
McCormick Place,
Chicago (1971), de-
signed by Gene Sum-
mers of C. F. Murphy
Associates. Summers
worked for Mies for
sixteen years—and
briefly had his own
firm—before he was
recruited to design
McCormick Place by
the Murphy office.
View mostly of the
underside of the can-
tilevered roof.

and where the ruddy Cor-Ten can be seen up close and touched. The elegant drains surrounding the base of each column—necessary to keep the stream- ing Cor-Ten from staining the granite plaza—are typical of Brownson's excep- tional detailing. The Cor-Ten louvers at the mechanical floors provide addi- tional texture and interest.

The Daley Center's patrician scale and half-block plaza were and remain unprecedented. They represent Chicago design, construction, and civic pa- tronage at one of its most energetic and—for world architecture—influential moments.[17] Mies lived long enough to see the completed building, and ac- cording to Brownson told him "I wish I had done it."[18] Brownson elaborated:

> He called me one day and asked me if I would take him to see the Civic Cen- ter.... I think he really respected the scale ... and [our] approach to [the] building problem. He could sense that ... there were people who were in- volved with that building at one time or another [who] had been his students, almost all of them [in the important roles].... When he saw the building com- ing up out of the ground and he saw those very long spans and the detailing of the ... spandrel beams, he said that here was architecture. He said you could sense it immediately.

Asked how he felt when Mies said these things, Brownson replied: "I was taken aback and couldn't say very much. He never said very much about any build- ings, except the ones that were being worked on."[19]

· · ·

The Daley Center was soon joined by the major Chicago work of Gene Sum- mers—his 1971 McCormick Place, an 800,000-square-foot convention cen- ter erected on the foundations of the "first" McCormick Place, destroyed by fire in 1967 (fig. A.5). Since Summers's building, McCormick Place has been expanded three times and by approximately 2.5 million square feet, but his is still the only architecturally distinguished component of the complex. This is credit to Summers's design talent, but also to the rich and highly adapt- able vocabulary—that of Mies van der Rohe—in which Summers so effec- tively worked.

Summers took his first professional degree from Texas A&M University in 1949. He decided to pursue graduate studies at IIT after a class trip to Chicago and a tour of the IIT campus. A group introduction to Mies was decisive: "There was a seriousness and a presence about him that I had never encountered," Summers recalled, echoing many others' impressions of their first meeting with Mies.[20] At IIT Summers attracted the attention of Edward Duckett, who worked in Mies's office and taught at the school. A recommendation followed, but Mies urged Summers to complete his graduate degree before starting full

time. His master's thesis was complete by 1951, and once in the office he captured key assignments: first as construction administrator for the Robert F. Carr Memorial Chapel at IIT, and then, at age twenty-five, as de-facto project architect for the Commons (both 1953). After military service in Korea, he returned to Chicago in 1956. Mies asked him to work on the Seagram Building, which took them to New York and put them in intimate contact. Among Summers's later work for Mies, as described elsewhere in this book, were Bacardi Santiago (1960), the Georg Schaefer Museum project (1962), the Chicago Federal Center (1964–75), Toronto Dominion Centre (1968), and the New National Gallery in Berlin (1968).

In 1966 Summers left to start his own practice, but he was soon hired by C. F. Murphy Associates (then Chicago's most prolific office after SOM).[21] In 1974 he formed a California-based development company with business partner Phyllis Lambert, through which the two pioneered development in Silicon Valley and restored and expanded the historic Biltmore Hotel in Los Angeles (1978). In 1984 Summers moved to France to concentrate on sculpture and furniture design, but returned to Chicago in 1989 to become dean of IIT's College of Architecture. Three years later, he resumed private practice in California.

Among Mies's American inner circle, Summers was most clearly his own man; he was consistently energetic and creative over a long, influential, and memorable career. That career is the subject of *Gene Summers Art/Architecture*, edited by Werner Blaser, testament to Summers's devotion to the profession and to Mies. In his large projects, most of which date from the decade prior to 1975, Summers's personal quest for innovation, especially in detailing, is evident in his use of the wide-flange mullion rotated into the plane of an exterior. There it generated a texture quite distinct from Mies's by-then-clichéd wide-flanged walls. An excellent example is Summers's Rehabilitation Institute of Chicago (1973).

For the new McCormick Place, Summers produced two complete schemes before a third was accepted. The better of the two rejected proposals combined the several program elements (chiefly the hall proper and the 4,350-seat Arie Crown Theater) under a single, 1,200-foot-long roof carried by suspension cables between bridge-like towers.

Completed in 1971 mostly atop the earlier foundations, the built scheme is superior to anything preliminary. It houses the major program components in two glazed volumes under a single roof. The roof is carried on a grid of thirty-six cruciform columns spaced 150 feet apart. The main hall is a single 300,000-square-foot room with only eight interior columns. In its simplicity, real (not merely "expressed") structural clarity, and proven programmatic flexibility, it is perhaps *the* ultimate Miesian universal space. The 1,350-by-750-foot space-frame roof is cantilevered 75 feet on all sides. The exterior columns are not in the plane of the glazing, but 25 feet outboard—a Miesian motif from as far back as Barcelona. The gray-tinted glass and matte-black steel of the main volume are complemented by a podium clad in subdued metallic gray brick.

Miesian precedents are everywhere in the structural details, but best studied at the roof nodes, where column and space frame meet. Here the roof framing—two-way Warren trusses—gives way to a "tree" of tapering T-sections and intersecting wide-flange diagonals. This tree is pin-connected to the top of an elegantly tapered cruciform column. This scheme is closely related to the columns and roof connections Summers designed for the concrete Bacardi Cuba project (see fig. 13.7). Throughout the three years of McCormick Place development, Summers was assisted by the young Helmut Jahn.

McCormick Place has its critics. Most have focused on the site, which is unnecessarily and inconveniently on the shore of Lake Michigan. When the first building burned, the city had a chance to reconsider the location, but for economic reasons it chose to retain the foundations and rebuild in place.[22] Even with the original 180-foot-wide opening between the main hall and the Arie Crown Theater, the Summers building has always been a barrier to lakefront sightlines. Now that that opening has been filled in by an enclosed pedestrian link to new parts of the complex west of Lake Shore Drive—to the considerable detriment of Summers's vision—sightlines to the lake are even worse. But the building retains its integrity and majesty, on a scale almost without equal.

. . .

The last of the important buildings of Mies's immediate followers to be examined here—Chicago's Lake Point Tower (1969)—is in some ways the most extraordinary (fig. A.6). The superlatives are many: it was the tallest concrete building in the world, and would remain the tallest all-residential building for thirty years; it had the first undulating curtain wall, and one of the city's first green roofs; and it was designed by two one-time Mies students, George Schipporeit and John Heinrich, then each in their thirties, neither of whom had ever designed a building on their own.

Schipporeit enrolled as a sophomore at IIT in 1955. He studied there for a year and a half, and fell under the spell of Alfred Caldwell. But he ran out of money and was forced to drop out. Caldwell nevertheless recommended him to Mies—chiefly because he was an outstanding draftsman—where among other projects he concentrated on the curtain walls for Lafayette Park in Detroit and the Pavilion and Colonnade Apartments in Newark. Schipporeit left in 1960 to work for the fabricator of the Newark curtain wall. Two years later, he was recruited by the developer William F. Hartnett Jr., an attorney who had represented Herbert Greenwald in the New York market. Hartnett had met Schipporeit through Mies's Newark projects.

In 1962 Hartnett was contacted by the Chicago Dock and Canal Trust, a century-old company that controlled lakefront property on the north bank of the main stem of the Chicago River. The once industrial area was becoming part of the commercial downtown, and Chicago Dock wanted to lease what became the Lake Point Tower site. To market the property, Chicago architects Perkins & Will prepared concepts for a phased development of 15- to 20-story towers. Hartnett thought the spectacular site demanded an equivalent solution, and himself proposed a single, 1,200-unit tower of cruciform plan. Schipporeit soon took over the design, and for assistance recruited John Heinrich, an IIT graduate then working as a construction manager at Lafayette Park. It took almost all of 1964 to produce a worked-out scheme for a 70-story con-

FIGURE A.6
(*facing*).
Lake Point Tower,
Chicago (1969),
by Schipporeit-
Heinrich, Inc. The
designers of Lake
Point Tower, both
then in their early
thirties, were en-
gaged in their
first independent
project. In the fore-
ground are locust
trees planted to a
design by Alfred
Caldwell.

crete tower enclosed by a Miesian-type, bronze anodized aluminum curtain wall. The proposed tower came to earth atop a block-long, brick-clad podium that was to contain parking for seven hundred cars.

Hartnett and his partner Charles Shaw were unable to secure financing for what would have been the largest single apartment building ever constructed. The project nearly fizzled before one of the team suggested cutting the unit count by "lopping off" one of the cruciform's wings. Thus was born today's tri-wing tower, originally with 880 units.

Based on his experience with Mies, Schipporeit developed a sophisticated variant on the Lafayette Park and Newark curtain walls. He expressed the required operable vent as a full-height, louvered spandrel that *concealed* the edge of the floor slab. Inside the wall was a continuous cabinet accommodating either an electric heating and cooling unit or a top-opening fresh-air vent. An independent operable window was therefore unnecessary. The exterior wall has the patrician elegance of Seagram, which is also uncluttered by operable vents—a configuration not normally possible where residential building codes require fresh air.

The literature has consistently cited Mies's Friedrichstrasse and Glass Skyscraper projects as the inspiration for Lake Point Tower.[23] Schipporeit and Heinrich certainly knew of them. But Lake Point Tower was originally conceived as a curtain-walled *cruciform*—and a rather dull one at that. It only morphed into a dynamic tri-wing form through a process of programmatic adjustment.[24] The family resemblance to Mies's projects is real but incidental. Nonetheless, Schipporeit and Heinrich, both then novice designers, could never have produced anything as accomplished as Lake Point Tower without Mies's architectural language. The standard mullioned wall was readily adapted to the undulating plan—indeed, it became even simpler, since the tri-wing plan lacked corners. But three wings did create problems. Schipporeit one day realized that the columns—square and rectangular in the original scheme—could and should be *round*—like nothing in Mies's work. In other respects, Mies was freely quoted: the core walls are clad in travertine; the tower is colonnaded even though atop a plinth; the palette is Seagram's, with the minor addition of green-glazed jumbo brick; and the green roof, a poetic expression of nature as a prairie park, is the work of Alfred Caldwell, Schipporeit's mentor.

Lake Point Tower is unlike any Mies project in one critical way: it is a "point tower," a tall building symmetrical in plan about a point. Mies's skyscrapers, all rectilinear prisms, are inserted into street grids and urban fabric, often brilliantly. But with Lake Point Tower, Schipporeit and Heinrich had the opportunity to place a megatower not just in a park, which had been a cliché of urban design since Le Corbusier, but on an urban "lake point" visible for miles. That it is novel, distinctive, and fully resolved was a great good fortune. Anything less would have been a missed opportunity of first order.

Appendix B: Mies's Career, in Publications and Exhibitions

Mies's buildings, projects, and career have generated a large volume of commentary and criticism. In this appendix, we review and assess the most important scholarship about our subject not already discussed above.

In addition to the buildings themselves, the best primary source about the architect is the Mies van der Rohe Archive at the Museum of Modern Art, established in 1968 pursuant to conversations between Mies and Arthur Drexler, then the director of the museum's Department of Architecture and Design. Following is a close paraphrase of Drexler's recollection of one of those conversations:

> After Philip Johnson's 1947 Mies show, I found a cache of Mies's drawings in dead storage, unaccessioned. I asked [Alfred] Barr to write Mies, requesting that he give MoMA the drawings. (I couldn't ask Johnson, because he had strayed from the fold, and Mies was edgy with him.) This was 1963. Mies agreed, and even suggested that MoMA could have more.
>
> I went out to Chicago to go through the pile of drawings he was offering me. I was looking for key drawings of projects, not any variations. Mies didn't like what I was doing. I must have gone through fifty drawings of mullions for Promontory.[1] He was displeased that I picked so few. "You know," he said, "they don't know we invented the mullion." I said, "Mies, the *world* knows you invented the mullion."
>
> In no way did I want all those drawings, though he never suggested we take them all. Thus choosing was difficult, because he didn't like my editing his work. Everything seemed important to him. At one point Glaeser [Ludwig Glaeser, appointed curator of architecture late in 1963] suggested we establish a Mies archive.... Mies added language in his will giving it all to MoMA, except personal correspondence and effects, which went to the Library of Congress.[2]

A catalogue raisonné of drawings by Mies and his office, now in the MoMA collection, was published by Garland under the title *The Mies van der Rohe Archive*. The initial portion, consisting of 7,000 European drawings, appeared in 1986, in four volumes edited by Drexler, with commentary by him and one of us (Schulze), while two more, edited by Schulze alone, came out in 1990. In 1992 thirteen volumes followed, reproducing 13,000 American drawings, edited by Schulze with commentary by him and George E. Danforth. The set was priced at $5,000 and targeted libraries. It is out of print.

We have already commented on the earliest known published references to Mies's work, a critique of the Riehl House: "Vom künstlerischen Nachwuchs" by Anton Jaumann in the July 1910 issue of *Innen-Dekoration*, Darmstadt. In the same year another article, "Architekt Ludwig Mies: Villa des Herrn Geheime Regierungsrat Prof. Dr. Riehl in Neu-Babelsberg," with no byline, featured a full set of photographs. It appeared in the first volume of the ninth year of *Moderne Bauformen*, Stuttgart.

When these articles appeared, Mies was twenty-four and unknown. Thus, it is remarkable that one year later, in 1911, he was mentioned in an American professional journal. The April issue of *Arts and Decoration* contained an illustrated commentary (no byline), "A Prototype of the New German Architecture." The subject was the Riehl House. The author based his comments on Jaumann's article, translated almost word for word from the German, with a personal conclusion: "To make a paradox one might almost say that its only fault lies in its faultlessness. It is so correct, architecturally speaking, that it almost seems a little cold, a little distant."[3] The architect's name—misspelled—is given as Ludwig Meis.

The next mention of Mies in the United States did not occur until he had joined the architectural avant-garde. The two skyscraper projects of the early 1920s elicited critical comment in the September 1923 *Journal of the American Institute of Architects*. Under the title "Skyscrapers in Germany," German critic Walter Curt Behrendt hailed both works, but two Americans disagreed: George C. Nimmons called the Glass Skyscraper "fantastic and impractical," and William Stanley Parker proposed the caption "A Nude Building Falling Downstairs."

The first European article exclusively about Mies appeared as late as 1927, when in *Das Kunstblatt*, Paul Westheim commented on the relation between Mies's work and Karl Friedrich Schinkel's in "Mies van der Rohe: Entwicklung eines Architekten":

Mies initially understood Schinkel as speaking a specific formal language as was generally held, but he soon discovered behind the classicist Schinkel that other Schinkel who had been, as to meaning, technology, and craftsmanship, the most eminent practical building master of his time, one who was never prevented by the ideals of the antique from planning his buildings as clearly and simply arising out of their proper frame of purpose.[4]

Mies first received institutional attention in the United States in the *Modern Architecture: International Exhibition* of 1932 at the Museum of Modern Art, curated by Barr, Henry-Russell Hitchcock, and Philip Johnson. During the same year, Johnson and Hitchcock published the companion book, *The International Style*. Several photographs of Johnson's New York apartment, designed by Mies and Reich, appeared in the October issue of *Vogue* (vol. 78, no. 7). The Barcelona Pavilion was discussed by Helen Appleton Read in "Germany at the Barcelona World's Fair," in the October 1929 issue of *The Arts*; by William Francklyn Paris in "The Barcelona Exposition: a Splendid but Costly Effort of the Catalan People," in the November 1929 *Architectural Forum*; and by Sheldon Cheney in his 1930 book *The New World Architecture*. European critics also covered the pavilion: Justus Bier in *Die Form* of August 15, 1929; Walther Genzmer in *Die Baugilde*, October 25, 1929; Guido Harbers in *Der Baumeister*, December 1929; and Nicolas Rubio Tuduri in *Cahiers d'Art*, December 1929. Johnson's article, "Architecture in the Third Reich," published in *Hound and Horn* (October–December 1933), argued that Mies was the German architect most capable of fusing modernism with an expression of the power of unity sought by the Nazis.

Mies's first solo American exhibition was at the Art Institute of Chicago in December 1938. The Mies-designed installation included photographs, drawings, and models. An essay by John Barney Rodgers accompanied the show, which traveled to the Albright Art Gallery in Buffalo, New York, in 1939. The dinner of October 18, 1938, in the Red Lacquer Room of the Palmer House in Chicago, at which Frank Lloyd Wright introduced Mies, was reported by Dorothy G. Wendt in the December 1938–January 1939 issue (nos. 6–7) of the *Monthly Bulletin of the Illinois Society of Architects*.

The first monograph on Mies, written by Philip Johnson and titled *Mies van der Rohe*, accompanied the retrospective curated by Johnson at the Museum of Modern Art in 1947. Expanded editions of Johnson's book, with coverage of Mies's most important American work, appeared in 1957 and 1978. Also in 1947, the Renaissance Society at the University of Chicago staged a small exhibition of Mies's work. The catalog included a statement by Ulrich Middeldorf, chairman of the university's Department of Art History.

Several important monographs were published during Mies's late career and shortly after his death. Among the most significant: *Mies van der Rohe* (1956), a scholarly panegyric by Ludwig Hilberseimer, and *Ludwig Mies van der Rohe: Furniture and Furniture Drawings* (1977), by Ludwig Glaeser. Peter Carter's *Mies van der Rohe at Work* (1974), which describes Mies's design methodology and teaching, also contains useful data on Mies's buildings, including their costs. Other early studies of the architect were written by Peter Blake (*Mies van der Rohe: Architecture and Structure*) in 1960, Arthur Drexler (*Ludwig Mies van der Rohe*) in 1960, Werner Blaser (*Mies van der Rohe: The Art of Structure*) in 1965,[5] and Martin Pawley (*Mies van der Rohe*) in 1970. In 1976 Wolfgang Frieg completed a doctoral dissertation, "Ludwig Mies van der Rohe: Das europäische Werk (1907–1937)," at the Rheinischen Friedrich-

Wilhelms-Universität in Bonn. It was the first full-scale treatment of Mies's European career.

A second museum-scale retrospective of Mies's work, including models, drawings, photographs, and furniture, was organized by the Art Institute of Chicago, where, in collaboration with the Graham Foundation for Advanced Studies in the Fine Arts, it was shown in 1968. The curator was A. James Speyer. Catalog entries were written by Frederick Koeper. The exhibition traveled to the Akademie der Künste, Berlin; the Walker Art Center, Minneapolis; the National Gallery of Canada, Ottawa; and the Amon Carter Museum of Western Art, Fort Worth, Texas.

By the time Mies died in 1969, he was routinely described as the most influential architect in the world, a reputation borne out by the publication that year of a boxed folio of thirty-one of his drawings in the collection of the Museum of Modern Art, with text and notes by Ludwig Glaeser.

In 1979 *Ludwig Mies van der Rohe: An Annotated Bibliography and Chronology*, covering the years through 1977, appeared under the byline of David Spaeth, a Mies student then a professor of architecture at the University of Kentucky.

A uniquely important study based on the collections of the Mies van der Rohe Archive was completed in 1981. Relying on the copious and unmatched material in the archive, German architect-historian Wolf Tegethoff wrote *Mies van der Rohe: Die Villen und Landhausprojekte*, with the English translation, *Mies van der Rohe: The Villas and Country Houses*, published in 1985. It is a monumental effort, unsurpassed in scholarship and vital to virtually all Mies research carried out since.

The archive was also a major source for *Mies van der Rohe: A Critical Biography* by Franz Schulze, the first complete account of the architect's life, published in 1985. Considerable new material has been unearthed meanwhile, necessitating the current volume, published as a revised and greatly expanded edition and coauthored with Chicago architect Edward Windhorst. Also appearing in 1985 was another monograph, more graphically focused, by David Spaeth.

Mies's centenary in 1986 was celebrated in several exhibitions, the most important, once again, by the Museum of Modern Art—another major retrospective, in this instance curated by Arthur Drexler. The catalog was never completed, because Drexler took ill while organizing the show. Before he died in 1987, he supervised the publication of *The Mies van der Rohe Archive*. Following Drexler's death, the museum decided to publish all of Mies's drawings in its collection, American as well as European, creating the aforementioned catalogue raisonné.

Two other centennial shows were mounted at the Art Institute of Chicago and Illinois Institute of Technology, respectively. The former, *Mies Reconsid-*

ered: *His Career, Legacy, and Disciples*, which traveled to Madrid, was accompanied by a catalog, later translated into Spanish, with "A Note on the Exhibition" by the editor, John Zukowsky. The catalog of the IIT exhibition, *Mies van der Rohe: Architect as Educator*, was edited by Rolf Achilles, Kevin Harrington, and Charlotte Myhrum.

The centenary was also observed in Europe. A major monograph unlike any other, *Mies van der Rohe: Das kunstlose Wort* by Fritz Neumeyer examines Mies's writings against the backdrop of architects like Peter Behrens and Hendrik Berlage and philosophers like Hegel and Nietzsche, who, Neumeyer argues, greatly influenced Mies. The English translation (*The Artless Word*), by Mark Jarzombek, appeared in 1991. Mies's centenary year also witnessed the reconstruction of the Barcelona Pavilion, recorded in *Mies van der Rohe: El Pabellon de Barcelona*, by Ignasi de Solà-Morales, Ignasi de Solà-Morales Rubio, Fernando Ramos, and Cristian Cirici. Their efforts are also chronicled in a seventeen-minute film, *Mies van der Rohe's Barcelona Pavilion*, produced in 1990.

In the wake of its 1986 retrospective, the Museum of Modern Art sponsored the 1989 publication of *Mies van der Rohe: Critical Essays*, edited by Schulze and written by several leading Mies scholars. Essays by Tegethoff, Richard Pommer, and Neumeyer are supplemented by an interview with James Ingo Freed, a Mies student who headed the architectural program at IIT in the mid-1970s.

Another important publication of 1989, *Architects of Fortune: Mies van der Rohe and the Third Reich* by Elaine S. Hochman, is even more politically oriented—and biased—than Pommer's scrupulously researched essay, which also treats of Mies's political sentiments. Hochman traces Mies's career during the four years he spent in Germany under the Nazi regime. She leaves no doubt about her admiration for Mies the architect, but she is equally unambiguous, and not altogether fair-minded, in her claim that he failed to free himself of the Nazi presence when he had the ability and occasion.

Of recent vintage are several monographs, each titled *Mies van der Rohe*, that cover the architect's entire career. The earliest (1990), untranslated, by the German Arnold Schink and subtitled *Beiträge zur ästhetischen Entwicklung der Wohnarchitektur*, is devoted chiefly to Mies's houses. Jean-Louis Cohen's compact study of 1994 (English translation 1996) was expanded in 2007. Claire Zimmerman's well-illustrated volume of 2006, subtitled *The Structure of Space*, establishes her as a creditable authority on Mies. Luiz Trigueiros and Paulo Martins Barata are editors of another book on Mies, published in Lisbon in 2000 and bearing the same title as Zimmerman's, with text (in Portuguese and English) by Yehuda E. Safran. Safran (2001) and Aurora Cuito (2002) are, respectively, authors of two other studies bearing the title *Mies van der Rohe*.

Two recent publications warrant mention even though Mies is not their chief subject. *The Weissenhofsiedlung*, by German scholar Karin Kirsch, appeared in 1989, and *Weissenhof 1927 and the Modern Movement in Architecture*, by American historians Richard Pommer and Christian F. Otto, was published in 1991. Both books give detailed attention to the roles played by Mies, his allies, and his opponents.

Other studies include *The Presence of Mies*, a 1994 publication edited by Detlef Mertins, with essays by Mertins, Phyllis Lambert, Neumeyer, K. Michael Hays, and others. Untranslated from the German are the thorough, well-illustrated *Mies van der Rohe: Möbel und Bauten in Stuttgart, Barcelona, Brno* (the 1990s, but no exact publication year); Rolf D. Weisse, *Mies van der Rohe: Vision und Realität* (2001); Adolph Stiller, editor, with Bruno Reichlin, Arthur Rüegg, and Jan Sapák, *Das Haus Tugendhat: Ludwig Mies van der Rohe* (Brünn, 1930; Salzburg, 1999); Christian Wolsdorff, *Mehr als der blosse Zweck: Mies van der Rohe am Bauhaus 1930–33* (2001); Max Stemshorn, *Mies und Schinkel: Das Vorbild Schinkel im Werk Mies van der Rohes* (2002); Johannes Cramer and Dorothee Sack, *Mies van der Rohe: Frühe Bauten* (2004); Ulrich Müller, *Raum, Bewegung und Zeit im Werk von Walter Gropius und Ludwig Mies van der Rohe* (2004); and Christiane Lange, *Mies van der Rohe: Architektur für die Seidenindustrie* (2011). Recent specialized work in English includes Mechthild Heuser, *Steel and Stone: Constructive Concepts by Peter Behrens and Mies van der Rohe* (2002); Christiane Lange, *Ludwig Mies van der Rohe and Lilly Reich: Furniture and Interiors* (2007); and Helmut Reuter and Birgit Schulte, editors, *Mies and Modern Living: Interiors, Furniture, Photography* (2008).

Publications on individual works include Franz Schulze's *Farnsworth House* (1997). Later discoveries, cited in chapter 10 of this book, render some of Schulze's study out of date. Equally at the mercy of those discoveries, but nonetheless written with elegance and insight, is Maritz Vandenberg's *Farnsworth House* (2003); Daniela Hammer-Tugendhat and Wolf Tegethoff, editor, *Ludwig Mies van der Rohe: The Tugendhat House* (2000); and Josep Quetglas's *Fear of Glass* (2001), which discusses the Barcelona Pavilion from novel viewpoints. Also noteworthy is Kent Kleinman and Leslie van Duzer, *Mies van der Rohe: The Krefeld Villas* (2005), and another book about the later career of the same two houses, Julian Heynan's *Ein Ort für Kunst* (1995).

Credit goes to Markus Jager for his essay "Das Haus Warnholtz von Ludwig Mies van der Rohe (1914/15)," which appeared in the *Zeitschrift für Kunstgeschichte* 65, no. 2 (2002), pp. 123–36. In 2006 the Mies van der Rohe Haus, devoted to exhibitions of Mies's work, was established at Mies van der Rohe Strasse 1 in Aachen.

Films about Mies have been produced by Georgia van der Rohe (1980, 1979) and by Michael Blackwood (1986), both titled *Mies van der Rohe*; by Joseph Hillel and Patrick Demers (2004), titled *Regular or Super*; by the art critic Robert Hughes, titled *Mies van der Rohe: Less Is More*, shown on BBC4 beginning in

2008; and by others as surveyed in Dietrich Neumann's "Mies Media," *Journal of the Society of Architectural Historians* 66, no. 1 (March 2007): 131–35. *Mies in Berlin* is a phonograph record of an interview of Mies by Horst Eifler and Ulrich Conrads, made by the American radio station RIAS Berlin in 1966.

An asteroid discovered in 1988 is named 24666 Miesvanrohe (1988 RZ3).

Regarding Mies's achievement and reputation, there are respected contrarians. One is Lewis Mumford, longtime architecture critic of the *New Yorker* and an early champion of modern architecture. In his review of the Museum of Modern Art's 1932 exhibition, he described the Tugendhat House as among "the most handsome objects in the show." Later, souring on what he called the aesthetic of the machine, he reversed himself, and attacked Johnson and Hitchcock for promoting the International Style. "From this," Mumford wrote,

> only a short step took the architect, with Mies van der Rohe to guide him, from the Machine to the Package. Mies van der Rohe used the facilities offered by steel and glass to create elegant monuments of nothingness. They had the dry style of machine forms without the contents. His own chaste taste gave these hollow glass shells a crystalline purity of form; but they existed alone in the Platonic world of his imagination and had no relation to site, climate, insulation, function, or internal activity; indeed they completely turned their backs upon these realities just as the rigidly arranged chairs of his living rooms openly disregarded the necessary intimacies and informalities of conversation. This was the apotheosis of the compulsive, bureaucratic spirit. Its emptiness and hollowness were more expressive than van der Rohe's [*sic*] admirers realized.[6]

British architectural historian David Watkin was equally negative, though he focused on the Mies of the early 1920s. In passages quoted from Mies's article in *G*, Watkin found "a menacing vision of the depersonalized, secular, mechanistic future."[7] (Mies's shift of direction in the late 1920s toward the spiritual, already noted here, was not considered by Watkin.)

In Charles Jencks's *Modern Movements in Architecture*, one of the first salvos of postmodernism, the author's fire was aimed at such early twentieth-century figures as Le Corbusier, Gropius, and Frank Lloyd Wright (Jencks praised Alvar Aalto). His view of Mies is announced in the title of chapter 2, "The Problem of Mies," which begins:

> The problem of Mies van der Rohe for critics and inhabitants of his architecture alike is that he demands an absolute commitment to the Platonic world view in order to appreciate his buildings. Without this commitment, the technical and functional mistakes which he creates are so damaging that one can no longer accept the Platonic form as being "perfect" or "ideal" or even "plausible."[8]

The two most ambitious Mies exhibitions of the twenty-first century, a pair of full-scale retrospectives, were accompanied by massive, fundamentally hagiographic catalogs.

Mies in Berlin, organized by Terence Riley of the Museum of Modern Art and Barry Bergdoll of Columbia University, opened at the Museum of Modern Art in New York in 2001, and traveled to the Staatliche Museen zu Berlin and the Fundacion La Caixa, Barcelona. Its companion volume by the same name is a major addition to the literature. The editing by David Frankel as well as the book design by Antony Drobinski of Emsworth Design, Inc. with Gina Rossi deserves high praise, and all the writers of the essays and illustrated statements live up to their professional reputations. The offerings of Barry Bergdoll and Rosemarie Haag Bletter are especially rewarding.

The second exhibition, *Mies in America*, curated by Phyllis Lambert, opened at the Whitney Museum of American Art, New York, in 2001, and traveled to the Canadian Centre for Architecture, Montreal, and the Museum of Contemporary Art, Chicago. The catalog was edited by Lambert, who also offers the fullest entry, a stellar addition to Mies scholarship.

Among the accolades, another voice was raised regarding the *Mies in Berlin* and *Mies in America* retrospectives, that of Martin Filler, best known for his writing on art and architecture for the *New York Review of Books*:

> As admirable as these two shows and their publications are, there remains an omission so major and so obvious that it is not merely the unacknowledged elephant in the room of this Mies revival, it is the veritable mastodon. In a two-part project [namely, the two shows] that is predicated around the turning point of Mies's career—his departure from Berlin to America in 1938—the architect's reasons for deciding to leave Germany, and indeed for choosing to linger there so long into the Hitler regime, are not mentioned at all.[9]

Filler concludes his review:

> Try as he might to rise above his own troubled epoch and to turn his back on the immediate in his pursuit of the eternal, Mies remained very much a product of his time and his place, of each time and every place in which he found himself. From the vibrant Weimar Berlin that stimulated his freest work, to the cautious modernism that he fine-tuned to ingratiate himself with the Nazis, to the boring and repetitive work that he churned out for corporate America at its conformist apogee, he was indeed the true architect of the century.[10]

But in a later book, Filler changed his position: "As a whole Mies's career must be seen as a heroic, and largely successful, undertaking—not least because his imprint has been so strong that it is unlikely ever to be fully effaced, dimmed though it had become after decades of debased adaptation of its most easily mimicked features."[11]

Notes

CHAPTER ONE

Translations from German are our own, unless otherwise indicated.

1. Mies van der Rohe, interview with Dirk Lohan (German-language typescript, Chicago, summer 1968); Mies van der Rohe Archive, Museum of Modern Art, New York.

2. Ibid.

3. Ibid.

4. Ibid.

5. In 1961, Mies stated: "As a young boy I went to the cathedral school in my hometown. It was a Latin school, but I was not very good and my father decided I should do some practical work and for this reason sent me to a kind of vocational school." This passage was edited out of the published interview, "Peter Blake: A Conversation with Mies van der Rohe," in *Four Great Makers of Modern Architecture: Gropius, Le Corbusier, Mies van der Rohe, Wright; The Verbatim Record of a Symposium Held at the School of Architecture, Columbia University, March–May, 1961* (New York: Columbia University, 1963; reprint, New York: Da Capo Press, 1970), pp. 93–104.

6. Mies, interview with Dirk Lohan, 1968, this and subsequent paragraphs.

7. The marker is at Lane 23, Number 213–215, West Cemetery, Aachen.

8. From the documentary film *Mies van der Rohe*, directed by Georgia van der Rohe, sponsored by Knoll International and Zweites Deutsches Fernsehen, Mainz, produced by IFAGE Filmproduktion, Wiesbaden; English version, 1979, German version, 1980.

9. In the brochure *Ludwig Mies van der Rohe und Ewald Mies in Aachen* (Aachen: Museum Burg Frankenberg, 1986), the design of "Haus Homburg," built in Raeren, Belgium, in 1936, is credited to Ewald Mies. Raeren is five miles south of the center of Aachen.

10. John Peter, *The Oral History of Modern Architecture: Interviews with the Greatest Architects of the Twentieth Century* (New York: H. H. Abrams, 1994), p. 158.

CHAPTER TWO

1. Kiehl's building was distinctive enough to be depicted in *American Architect* 96, no. 1753 (July 28, 1909): 34.

2. Mies, interview with Dirk Lohan (German-language typescript, Chicago, summer 1968); Mies van der Rohe Archive, Museum of Modern Art, New York.

3. Ibid.

4. Popp published the monograph *Bruno Paul* (Munich: F. Bruckmann, 1916).

5. Neubabelsberg, a mostly residential district, was joined with the village of Nowawes in 1938 to form the town of Babelsberg, which in turn was annexed a year later to Potsdam.

6. Mies, interview with Dirk Lohan, this and subsequent paragraphs.

7. Paul Mebes, *Um 1800: Architektur und Handwerk in letzten Jahrhundert ihrer traditionellen Entwicklung* (Munich: F. Bruckmann, 1908).

8. Most likely Haus Springer, the only Messel house in that community that stood before Mies made his trip to Italy.

9. Mies, interview with Dirk Lohan.

10. Mies, quoted in Peter Carter, *Mies van der Rohe at Work* (New York: Praeger, 1974), p. 174.

11. For the Riehl guest book, see "Weltoffenes Klösterli," *Frankfurter Allgemeine Zeitung*, March 11, 2002.

12. Barry Bergdoll, "The Nature of Mies's Space," in *Mies in Berlin*, ed. Terence Riley and Barry Bergdoll, an exhibition catalog (New York: Museum of Modern Art, 2001), p. 67.

13. Ibid., pp. 67–68. In the Klösterli guest book, the aesthetician Max Dessoir signed his name "in admiration of house *and* garden" (italics ours).

14. After World War II, the house was taken over by the German Democratic Republic, which used it as the administrative headquarters of the Film and Television Institute of Potsdam. The *Halle* was subdivided and the veranda enclosed.

15. Fritz Neumeyer, "Space for Reflection," in *Mies van der Rohe: Critical Essays*, ed. Franz Schulze (Cambridge, MA: MIT Press, 1989), p. 156.

16. On Behrens, see Stanford Anderson, *Peter Behrens and a New Architecture for the Twentieth Century* (Cambridge, MA: MIT Press, 2000); Fritz Hoeber, *Peter Behrens* (Munich: Müller & Rentsch, 1913); and Alan Windsor, *Peter Behrens, Architect and Designer* (New York: Whitney Library of Design, 1981).

17. On the AEG, see Anderson, *Peter Behrens and a New Architecture*; Tilmann Buddensieg with Henning Rogge, *Industriekultur: Peter Behrens and the AEG, 1907–1914* (Cambridge, MA: MIT Press, 1984); Hoeber, *Peter Behrens*; and Windsor, *Peter Behrens, Architect and Designer*.

18. Alois Riegl, *Spätrömische Kunstindustrie nach den Funden in Osterreich* (Vienna: Verlag Osterreichischen Staatsdruckerei, 1901).

19. Mies, much later in life, was also aware of this paradox: "You know, we architects are in this peculiar position. We should express the time yet build in it." "Peter Blake: A Conversation with Mies van der Rohe," in *Four Great Makers of Modern Architecture: Gropius, Le Corbusier, Mies van der Rohe, Wright; The Verbatim Record of a Symposium Held at the School of Architecture, Columbia University, March–May, 1961* (New York: Columbia University, 1963; reprint, New York: Da Capo Press, 1970), p. 97.

20. Mies, letter to Adalbert Colsmann, Langenberg, West Germany; Papers of Ludwig Mies van der Rohe, Manuscript Division, Library of Congress. Mies: "I don't know whether I wrote you that I was with Karl Ernst Osthaus and Heinrich Vogeler on a 1910 visit to the Deutsche Gartenstadt exhibition in London."

21. Ludwig Glaeser, interview with Schulze, 1980.

22. Anton Jaumann, "Vom künstlerischen Nachwuchs," *Innendekoration* 21 (July 1910): 266.

23. Discussed in detail in Anderson's *Peter Behrens and a New Architecture*, chap. 7, p. 300, n. 25. Tilmann Buddensieg, another Behrens scholar, believed that Mies "did the south wall" of the Turbinenhalle. Buddensieg, personal communication with Schulze, Berlin, 2003.

24. Dirk Lohan, interview with the authors, May 3, 2011.

25. Anderson, *Peter Behrens and a New Architecture*.

26. Dirk Lohan, interview with the authors.

27. Salomon van Deventer, letter to Helene Kröller-Müller, August 29, 1911; quoted in a letter of August 10, 1975, from van Deventer's widow, Mary, to Ludwig Glaeser. Mies van der Rohe Archive, Museum of Modern Art, New York.

28. Quoted in Winfried Nerdinger, *Richard Riemerschmid: Vom Jugendstil zum Werkbund, Werke und Dokumente* (Munich: Prestel, 1982), p. 413.

29. Mies in conversation with Horst Eifler and Ulrich Conrads, recorded by the American radio station RIAS (Radio in the American Sector), Berlin, October 1964 and produced on a phonograph record, *Mies in Berlin*, Bauwelt Archiv I (Berlin, 1966).

30. Kai Krauskopf, *Bismarckdenkmäler: Ein bizarrer Aufbruch in die Moderne* (Hamburg: Dölling und Galitz, 2002), pp. 165–68.

31. Riley and Bergdoll, *Mies in Berlin*, p. 158.

32. Quoted in Dietrich von Beulwitz, "The Perls House by Ludwig Mies van der Rohe," *Architectural Design* 53, nos. 11–12 (1983): 67. At this date Mies was not yet "Mies van der Rohe."

33. Ibid. According to von Beulwitz, who supervised the renovation of the Perls House in 1977, it was substantially altered: "The property and site had once been used by a commercial enterprise which produced medical and technical apparatus and, it was known, had done something similar during the war, designing measuring instruments for jet aircraft and V-weapons" (p. 63). Von Beulwitz added, in a personal communication with Schulze in June 1982, that following World War II interior changes were made in the house, including some commissioned by a society of anthroposophists, whose philosophy disdains the use of the ninety-degree angle. Diagonal "bridges" were placed in several of the corners of the rooms on the ground floor and upstairs.

34. Ibid., p. 67.

35. On the Imperial Embassy, see Tilmann Buddensieg, "Die kaiserliche deutsche Botschaft in Petersburg von Peter Behrens," in *Politische Architektur in Europa vom Mittelalter bis heute: Repräsentation und Gemeinschaft*, ed. Martin Warnke (Cologne: DuMont, 1984), pp. 374–97. Mies's sketch of the foyer is reproduced on p. 393.

36. Helene Kröller-Müller, letter to H. P. Bremmer, June 28, 1910; quoted in Salomon van Deventer, *Aus Liebe zur Kunst* (Cologne: Verlag M. Dumont Schauberg, 1958), p. 51.

37. On Behrens's project for the Kröllers, see Hoeber, *Peter Behrens*.

38. Helene Kröller-Müller, letter to Salomon van Deventer, March 18, 1911; quoted in van Deventer, *Aus Liebe zur Kunst*, p. 55.

39. Salomon van Deventer, letter to Helene Kröller-Müller, August 29, 1911; quoted in ibid., p. 1.

40. Tilmann Buddensieg, personal communication with Schulze, 1983.

41. Mies, in conversation with Horst Eifler and Ulrich Conrads, recorded by RIAS, Berlin, October 1964, and produced on a phonograph record, *Mies in Berlin*, Bauwelt Archiv I (Berlin, 1966).

42. Ibid. Mies was not exaggerating. The Kröllers' art collection eventually numbered 11,500 objects, most of them acquired on the advice of Bremmer. It included 93 paintings and 183 drawings by van Gogh.

43. The drawing is now in the collection of the Museum of Modern Art, New York.

44. The Meier-Graefe letter is in the Mies van der Rohe Archive at the Museum of Modern Art.

45. In a footnote to an article by Hugo Weber, "Mies van der Rohe in Chicago," *Bauen und Wohnen* (December 1950): 1, Mies is said to have visited the home of the critic Wilhelm von Uhde in Paris, and there to have seen cubist paintings for the first time.

46. Van Deventer, *Aus Liebe zur Kunst*, p. 70.

47. Helene Kröller-Müller, letter to A. G. Kröller, January 1913; quoted in ibid., p. 71.

48. Mies, letter to Helene Kröller-Müller, April 2, 1913; Archives of the Kröller-Müller Museum, Otterlo. Was there a romantic attachment between Mrs. Kröller-Müller and Mies? The suspicion is aroused, though hardly settled, by another passage in van Deventer's letter to Mrs. Kröller-Müller of August 29, 1911. Greatly impressed by Mies in his first meeting with him, van Deventer tried to persuade Mrs. Kröller-Müller to trust Mies in the latter's ongoing conflict with Behrens's assistant, Jean Krämer. Before he made the case for Mies, however, he wrote: "I sense from his words his great devotion to you and his wide-ranging perceptiveness; yet although the two of us in a few short hours developed a closeness that seems like an old friendship, and while everything he said reminded me of you, I somehow felt compelled to keep him at a distance from you. This was small of me, and just because it was small, I called to the heavens for help [presumably to be objective in his judgment of Mies as an architect] and I now want to write the following." What followed was van Deventer's argument in Mies's professional behalf. This passage is quoted in Mary van Deventer's letter of August 19, 1975, to Ludwig Glaeser, curator of the Mies van der Rohe Archive of the Museum of Modern Art.

49. Mies, "Frank Lloyd Wright," an appreciation written in 1940 for the unpublished catalog of the Frank Lloyd Wright exhibition held at the Museum of Modern Art (cf. Philip Johnson, *Mies van der Rohe* [New York: Museum of Modern Art, 1947], p. 105).

50. Georgia van der Rohe, *La donna è mobile: Mein bedingungsloses Leben* (Berlin: Aufbau-Verlag, 2001), p. 11.

51. Mary Wigman, interview with Ludwig Glaeser (Wigman changed her name from Wiegmann when she moved to Berlin after World War I), Berlin, September 13, 1972; Mies van der Rohe Archive, Museum of Modern Art, New York. She remained close to Mies after he separated from Ada. According to Wolf Tegethoff (*Mies van der Rohe: The Villas and Country Houses* [New York: Museum of Modern Art, 1985], p. 99), in the 1920s and 1930s she "often lived in [Mies's] studio when she was in Berlin."

52. Ludwig Mies, letter to Ada Bruhn, September 1911; quoted in Tegethoff, *Mies van der Rohe: The Villas and Country Houses*, p. 12.

53. Renate Werner, letter to Ille Sipman of the Building Centre Trust, London, Spring 1979. Copy in the collection of Franz Schulze.

54. Mies's daughter Marianne Lohan, in conversation with Schulze November 10, 1981, stated that her parents "sold the Werder property in 1916–17." But there is conflicting testimony that Mies was staying in Werder after the end of World War I.

55. Mary Wigman, interview with Ludwig Glaeser, Berlin, September 15, 1972; Mies van der Rohe Archive, Museum of Modern Art, New York.

56. Ibid.

57. It is thought by the family that the name was taken from Goethe's *Hermann und Dorothea*, a curious source, since it is a highly sentimental epic poem, the kind of literature young moderns of Germany might disdain.

58. Ada's daybooks were composed between 1914 and 1919. They are in the possession of Ulrike Schreiber, Mies's granddaughter.

59. Markus Jager, "Das Haus Warnholtz von Ludwig Mies van der Rohe (1914–15)," *Zeitschrift für Kunstgeschichte* 65, no. 1 (2002), pp. 123–36; special issue.

60. Renate Petras, "Drei Arbeiten von Mies van der Rohe in Potsdam-Babelsberg," *Deutsche Architektur* (Berlin, February 1974): 68.

61. For details of the Am Karlsbad building and Mies's apartment, see Andreas Marx and Paul Weber, "From Ludwig Mies to Mies van der Rohe: The Apartment and Studio Am Karlsbad 24 (1915–39)," in *Mies and Modern Living*, ed. Helmut Reuter and Birgit Schulte (Ostfildern, Germany: Hatje Cantz, 2008), pp. 25–39.

62. Georgia van der Rohe, *La donna è mobile*, p. 15.

63. Ada Mies daybooks, October 25, 1915, entry. The notebooks, cited here and in subseqent paragraphs, have never been published.

64. Ibid., December 1915 entry.

65. Manfred Lehmbruck, personal communication with Schulze, January 12, 1983.

66. Wilhelm Lehmbruck, "Who Is Still Here?"; quoted in Reinhold Heller, *The Art of Wilhelm Lehmbruck* (Washington, DC: National Gallery of Art, 1972), p. 198.

67. Entry from Ada Mies daybooks.

68. Julius Posener, letter to Schulze, December 1, 1982, in which he attributed this account to the Stuttgart architect Bodo Rasch, who knew Mies in the 1920s and had a minor role at the Weissenhofsiedlung. In her 2001 autobiography, Mies's daughter Dorothea, who became an actress and took the stage name Georgia van der Rohe, reported her own version of Mies's stay in Romania: "Only after my father's death did I learn from his trusted Knüpferlein [Elsa Knupfer] that during this time … he had a relationship with a German-speaking Transylvanian. He had a son by her, at about the time his third daughter was born. Never did he later recognize this son" (*La donna è mobile*, p. 15). Mies's grandson Dirk Lohan insists that there is no truth to Georgia's account. He states that his mother, Marianne, who knew Elsa Knupfer well, never heard any such report. He also states that Frank Herterich, one of Georgia's two sons, has told him that "[Georgia's] book is full of inventions and much of it cannot be taken as factual" (Dirk Lohan, interview with the authors, May 3, 2011). Since the only "evidence" that Mies fathered a son in Romania is the single secondhand report of Georgia, her claim cannot be supported.

69. Quoted from Ada's daybooks, July 1917 entry.

70. Ibid., spring 1919 entry.

71. Lora Marx, interview with Schulze, September 16, 1980.

CHAPTER THREE

1. Mies, letter to Ada Mies, February 25, 1920; quoted in Georgia van der Rohe, *La donna è mobile: Mein bedingungsloses Leben* (Berlin: Aufbau-Verlag, 2001), p. 18.

2. Ada Mies, letter to Mies; quoted in ibid., p. 19.

3. Lora Marx stated that "Mies never spoke much of Ada, either well or ill. He hadn't wanted children. He never divorced her, though she would have granted him one." Lora Marx, interview with Schulze, September 16, 1980. It is also possible that Mies may have rejected divorce because of its unacceptability in the Roman Catholic Church.

4. Paul Scheerbart, *Glass Architecture*, ed. Dennis Sharpe and trans. James Palmes (London: November Books, 1972), p. 41.

5. Walter Gropius, *Program of the Staatliche Bauhaus in Weimar*, published by the Staatliche Bauhaus, Weimar, April 1919; four-page leaflet with a title-page woodcut, *Cathedral*, by Lyonel Feininger.

6. George Grosz, quoted in Werner Haftmann, *Painting in the Twentieth Century* (New York: Praeger, 1965), p. 222.

7. Howard Dearstyne, in *Inside the Bauhaus*, ed. David Spaeth (New York: Rizzoli, 1986), claims that Richter introduced van Doesburg to Mies (p. 64).

8. For more on the Novembergruppe, see Helga Kliemann, *Die Novembergruppe* (Berlin: Gebrüder Mann Verlag, 1969), and Detlef Mertins, "Architectures of Becoming: Mies van der Rohe and the Avant-Garde," in *Mies in Berlin*, ed. Terence Riley and Barry Bergdoll, an exhibition catalog (New York: Museum of Modern Art, 2001), p. 110ff.

9. Hans Richter, letter to Raoul Hausmann, February 16, 1964; quoted in Hausmann's letter to the editor, "More on Group G," *Art Journal* 24 (Summer 1965): 350–52.

10. Theo van Doesburg, "Der Wille zum Stil, Neugestaltung von Leben, Kunst und Technik," *De Stijl* 5 (February 1922): 23–32 and (March 1922): 33–41.

11. Alexander Rodchenko, "Slogans," composed in 1921; quoted in German in Karginov, *Rodchenko* (London: Thames and Hudson, 1979), pp. 90–91.

12. Mies, interview with Peter Blake (typescript), Columbia University Oral History Project, 1960, pp. 94–95.

13. Gene Summers, quoted in Mertins, "Architectures of Becoming," p. 376, n. 14.

14. Walter Gropius, quoted in ibid., p. 107.

15. Cited in Bruno Möhring, "Über die Vorzüge der Turmhäuser und die Voraussetzung, unter denen sie in Berlin gebaut werden können," lecture to the Preussische Akademie des Bauwesens, December 22, 1920 (Berlin: Ernst Wasmuth, 1921), p. 6.

16. Adolf Behne, "Der Wettbewerb der Turmhaus-Gesellschaft," *Wasmuths Monatshefte für Baukunst* 7 (1922–23): 58–67. Behne's praise for "not conjuring any particular emotion" indicates just how extreme positions could be.

17. Max Berg, "Hochhäuser im Stadtbild," *Wasmuths Monatshefte für Baukunst* 6 (1921–22): 101–20.

18. Vittorio Magnago Lampugnani, "Berlin Modernism and the Architecture of the Metropolis," in *Mies in Berlin*, ed. Terence Riley and Barry Bergdoll, an exhibition catalog (New York: Museum of Modern Art, 2001), p. 42.

19. Berg, "Hochhäuser im Stadtbild," pp. 101–20.

20. Ibid.

21. Mies, "Hochhaus Projekt für Bahnhof Friedrichstrasse in Berlin," *Frühlicht* 1 (Summer 1922): 122–24. Mies's one-page text is on p. 124.

22. Mies, office correspondence to Don J. Burg, of Houston, Texas, February 21, 1951; box 21, Papers of Ludwig Mies van der Rohe, Manuscript Division, Library of Congress.

23. Wolf Tegethoff, *Mies van der Rohe: The Villas and Country Houses* (New York: Museum of Modern Art, 1985), pp. 32–33, 39–41.

24. Mies, "Building," *G*, no. 2 (September 1923): 1.

25. For a fuller, somewhat speculative discussion of Mies's name change, see Andreas Marx and Paul Weber, "From Ludwig Mies to Mies van der Rohe: The Apartment and Studio Am Karlsbad 24 (1915–39)," in *Mies and Modern Living*, ed. Helmut Reuter and Birgit Schulte (Ostfildern, Germany: Hatje Cantz, 2008), pp. 36–37.

26. Mies offered an account of the name change, under oath, June 2, 1952, during the Farnsworth trial (see chapter 10):

> Q: When did you change your name to Van der Rohe?
> A (by Mies): That must have been in the '20s, the early '20s . . .
> Q: Why did you add the name "Van der Rohe"?
> A: For no particular reason.
> Q: Wasn't it for the purpose of indicating some relationship to royalty? Prussianism?
> A: No. "Van der Rohe" is used in the Netherlands, and that is absolutely common there. You can see it that a butcher has that . . .
> Q: For what reason did you take that name?
> A: Because I liked it. . . . We came from this part of the country, and I added it to my name.

Van der Rohe v. Farnsworth, No. 9352 (Ill. Cir. Ct., Kendall County), trial transcript at pp. 713–15.

27. Georgia van der Rohe, *La donna è mobile*, p. 16.

28. Ilya Ehrenburg and El Lissitzky, April 1922; quoted in John Willett, *Art and Politics in the Weimar Period: The New Sobriety, 1917–1933* (New York: Pantheon, 1978), p. 76.

29. On *G*, see Werner Graeff, "Concerning the So-Called G Group," *Art Journal* 23 (Summer 1964):

28–82, and Raoul Hausmann, letter to the editor, "More on Group *G*," *Art Journal* 24 (Summer 1965): 350–52.

30. Hans Richter, letter to Raoul Hausmann, February 16, 1964; quoted by Hausmann in "More on Group G," p. 102.

31. For the full text of each of the six issues of *G*, in English, see *G: An Avant-Garde Journal*, ed. Detlef Mertius and Michael W. Jennings (Los Angeles: Getty Research Institute, 2010).

32. Ibid., p. 101.

33. Ibid., p. 103.

34. Ibid., p. 105.

35. Apparently first so designated by Philip Johnson, who, in his monograph *Mies van der Rohe* (New York: Museum of Modern Art, 1947), speaks of Mies's "five most daring projects" (p. 22).

36. A model also existed, known because Mies offered it for a show curated by van Doesburg.

37. Mertius and Jennings, *G*, p. 103.

38. Werner Graeff, "Concerning the So-Called G Group," 280–82.

39. Mies, letter to Theo van Doesburg, August 27, 1923; Papers of Ludwig Mies van der Rohe, Manuscript Division, Library of Congress.

40. "Von der neuen Aesthetik zur materiellen Verwirklichung," *de Stijl* 6 (March 1923).

41. Mies, letter to Friedrich Kiesler, March 22, 1924; Mies van der Rohe Archive, Museum of Modern Art, New York.

42. Paul Henning, public lecture sponsored by the Deutscher Werkbund, June 19, 1924; Mies van der Rohe Archive.

43. Mies, "Baukunst und Zeitwille," *Der Querschnitt* 4, no. 1 (1924): 31–32.

44. See Dietrich Neumann, "Haus Ryder in Wiesbaden und die Zusammenarbeit von Gerhard Severain und Ludwig Mies van der Rohe," *Architectura* 2 (2006): 199–219, and Gottfried Knapp in the *Süddeutsche Zeitung*, March 31, 2006. The address of the house is Zur schönen Aussicht 20.

45. On Walter Dexel see Tegethoff, *Mies van der Rohe: The Villas and Country Houses*, pp. 52–54.

46. Ibid., p. 52.

47. Ibid., p. 59.

48. Gesellschaft der Freunde des neuen Russlands, letter to Mies, January 12, 1926; Papers of Ludwig Mies van der Rohe, Manuscript Division, Library of Congress.

49. Mies, letter to Donald D. Egbert, February 5, 1951; copy provided by George Danforth. This and subsequent quotations by Mies also reprinted in Dietrich von Beulwitz, "The Perls House by Ludwig Mies van der Rohe," *Architectural Design* 53, nos. 11–12 (1983): 68.

50. Ibid. Liebknecht and Luxemburg were not "shot in front of a wall." Following their arrest in the Spartacist revolt, they were murdered en route to prison.

51. Hugo Perls, memoir; quoted by von Beulwitz, "The Perls House by Ludwig Mies van der Rohe," p. 68.

52. In 2002, proposals for the reconstruction of the Liebknecht-Luxemburg monument were made and resisted. The critic Anders Lepik of Berlin wrote in the *Frankfurter Allgemeine Zeitung* (March 12, 2002) that "nothing about the technical construction of the monument is known, nothing about its rear face, too little about its exact mass and details to produce a believable rebuilding.... In 1968, in connection with the opening of the New National Gallery in Berlin, the idea of reconstruction of the monument was presented to Mies, who decisively vetoed it." According to Arthur Drexler, Mies "declared [in 1968] that it would not be meaningful if erected on a different site." *The Mies van der Rohe Archive*, vol. 1 (New York: Garland, 1986), 342.

53. Hans Prinzhorn, letter to Mies, June 15, 1925; Papers of Ludwig Mies van der Rohe, Manuscript Division, Library of Congress.

54. Mathilde Meng, interview with Schulze, Heidelberg, 1982.

55. Mies wrote less and less as he aged. Donald Sickler, who worked in Mies's office from 1953 to 1963, recalled Mies's repeated editing of even routine letters (personal communication with Windhorst, 2007). They "became shorter and shorter, and often had to be rescued before they disappeared." Joseph Fujikawa had a similar view: "He'd search and think.... He was very careful about what he said and he wanted to be as precise as possible.... His speaking was like his buildings, he got down to the very essence of it" (Edward A. Duckett and Joseph Y. Fujikawa, *Impressions of Mies: An Interview on Mies van der Rohe; His Early Chicago Years 1938-1958* [n.p., 1988], p. 8).

56. Walter Gropius, letter to Mies, December 11, 1925; Papers of Ludwig Mies van der Rohe, Manuscript Division, Library of Congress.

57. Mies, letter to Walter Gropius, December 14, 1925; Papers of Ludwig Mies van der Rohe, Manuscript Division, Library of Congress.

58. Mies, letter to G. W. Farenholtz, December 7, 1925; Papers of Ludwig Mies van der Rohe, Manuscript Division, Library of Congress.

CHAPTER FOUR

1. Peter Bruckmann, statement to directors of the Deutscher Werkbund, March 30, 1925; Redslob Archive, German Federal Archive, Koblenz.

2. Mies, "Industrielles Bauen," *G* 3 (June 10, 1924).

3. Gustav Stotz, letter to Mies, September 24, 1925; Mies van der Rohe Archive, Museum of Modern Art, New York.

4. Mies, letter to Stotz, September 26, 1925; Mies van der Rohe Archive.

5. Mies, letter to Stotz, September 11, 1925, our italics; Mies van der Rohe Archive.

6. Both articles were published May 5, 1926: Bonatz's in the *Schwäbische Chronik*, Stuttgart, Schmitthenner's in the *Süddeutsche Zeitung*, Munich.

7. In May 1928, a group was formed with the name Der Block, in opposition to Der Ring. The traditionalist membership included Paul Bonatz, Paul Schmitthenner, Paul Schultze-Naumburg, German Bestelmeyer, Erich Blunck, Heinz Stoffregen, Franz Seeck, and Albert Gessner. Some years later, in 1932–33, Bonatz and Schmitthenner led in the organization and design of a housing colony built on principles opposed to those that animated the Weissenhofsiedlung. They called this project Am Kochenhof. Constructed a few blocks away from the Weissenhof, Am Kochenhof featured devices traditional to the German house, most notably the pitched roof.

8. Richard Döcker, letter to Mies, May 18, 1926; Mies van der Rohe Archive.

9. Mies, letter to Döcker, May 27, 1926; Mies van der Rohe Archive.

10. Mia Seeger, personal communication with Schulze, July 5, 1982, Stuttgart.

11. Max Taut, letter to Richard Döcker, February 9, 1927; Mies van der Rohe Archive.

12. Georgia van der Rohe, *La donna è mobile: Mein bedingungsloses Leben* (Berlin: Aufbau-Verlag, 2001), p. 33.

13. Cited in Richard Pommer and Christian F. Otto, *Weissenhof 1927 and the Modern Movement in Architecture* (Chicago: University of Chicago Press, 1991), p. 61.

14. Mies in *Die Form* 2, no. 2 (1927): 59.

15. Their program is thoroughly covered in Fritz Neumeyer's *The Artless Word: Mies van der Rohe on the Building Art*, trans. Mark Jarzombek (German edition, 1986; Cambridge, MA: MIT Press, 1991).

16. Romano Guardini, "Steps," in *Sacred Signs*, trans. Grace Branham (St. Louis: Pio Decimo Press, 1956), pp. 34–35.

17. Romano Guardini, *Letters from Lake Como: Explorations in Technology and the Human Race*, trans. Geoffrey W. Bromley (Grand Rapids, MI: W. B. Eerdmans, 1994), p. 95ff. Mies often marked passages in his books, but care must be taken in their interpretation. Sometimes no special meaning may be inferred, and selective citation can support a wide range of hypotheses.

18. Rudolf Schwarz, *Wegweisung der Technik und andere Schriften zum Neuen Bauen, 1926–1961*, ed. Maria Schwarz and Ulrich Conrads (Braunschweig and Wiesbaden: Friedrich Vieweg & Sohn, 1979), p. 24.

19. Rudolf Schwarz, *The Church Incarnate: The Sacred Function of Church Architecture* (in German, *Vom Bau der Kirche*), trans. Cynthia Harris, with a foreword by Mies van der Rohe (Chicago: Henry Regnery, 1958). Mies wrote only one other book foreword, to Ludwig Hilberseimer's *The New City: Principles of Planning* (Chicago: Paul Theobald, 1944). Mies occasionally passed on religious titles to staff architect Donald Sickler, a fellow Catholic. About *The Church Incarnate*, Sickler reports: "Mies gave me the book manuscript to read before he wrote the foreword. I told Mies that I did not understand the book. He laughed and said he did not either." Personal communication with Windhorst, June 1, 2011.

20. Mies, "Baukunst und Zeitwille," *Der Querschnitt* 4, no. 1 (1924): 1–32.

21. Ritchie Robertson, review of *The Seduction of Culture in German History* by Wolf Lepenies, *Times Literary Supplement*, April 7, 2006.

22. Damage to the Weissenhofsiedlung during World War II and its restoration are covered in Pommer and Otto, *Weissenhof 1927 and the Modern Movement in Architecture*, pp. 156–57.

23. On Reich, see Matilda McQuaid, ed., *Lilly Reich, Designer and Architect*, with an essay by Magdalena Droste (New York: Museum of Modern Art, 1996). Our summary of Reich's career chiefly follows this source.

24. The details of Mies's meeting Reich are not known. Pierre Adler, curator at the Mies van der Rohe Archive at MoMA, dates their meeting to 1924 (his "Chronology" of Reich is in McQuaid, *Lilly Reich*, pp. 60–61). The Werkbund Archiv states that she met Mies while working for the Frankfurt Messeamt (Trade Fair Office) as an exhibition designer, also in 1924 (Werkbund Archiv website, in German).

25. Lilly von Schnitzler, interview with Ludwig Glaeser, September 6, 1974; Canadian Centre for Architecture, Montreal.

26. Marianne Lohan, in conversation with Schulze November 10, 1981, stated: "I actively disliked her. I made no effort to like her. She was not a woman to us. I guess she was very intelligent and artistic, but we just resented that she tried to educate. She was not feminine. I think she and Mies were lovers, but Ada was beautiful."

27. The best study of Mies's furniture is Ludwig Glaeser's *Ludwig Mies van der Rohe: Furniture and Furniture Drawings from the Design Collection and the Mies van der Rohe Archive, the Museum of Modern Art* (New York: Museum of Modern Art, 1977).

28. For a 1931 catalog and price list of furniture by Mies and Reich, see Helmut Reuter and Birgit Schulte, eds., *Mies and Modern Living* (Ostfildern, Germany: Hatje Cantz, 2008), p. 160.

29. Wolf Tegethoff, *Mies van der Rohe: The Villas and Country Houses* (New York: Museum of Modern Art, 1985), p. 68.

30. Ibid., p. 61.

31. Mies, quoted in *The Mies van der Rohe Archive*, vol. 2 (New York: Garland, 1989), 2.

32. According to Dietrich von Beulwitz ("The Perls House of Ludwig Mies van der Rohe," p. 70), quoting Perls's memoir, he sold his house to Fuchs as follows: Fuchs, an avid collector of the works of Honoré Daumier, had offered the painter Max Liebermann a dozen Daumier prints in exchange for one of Liebermann's oils. Liebermann agreed, not once but many times over, until Fuchs had traded hundreds of Daumiers for fifteen Liebermann paintings. Fuchs then offered five of the Liebermanns to Perls in exchange for the 1912 Mies house. Perls accepted.

Dirk Lohan added a recollection of Mies himself. When Fuchs commissioned the Mies addition to his house, completed in 1928, he directed that a room in the basement be equipped with a secret exit. There Fuchs kept a packed suitcase in the event he might come under siege by right-wing elements. He in fact fled Germany quickly in 1936, when the Nazis sought him out. "The Nazis," wrote Perls, as quoted by von Beulwitz, "emptied his house. They needed several trucks to take away the 20,000 copper engravings, 10,000 books and hundreds of paintings and sculptures and store them for the Reich of the Grand Illusion."

33. Mies, quoted by Adrian Sudhalter, "S. Adam Department Store Project, Berlin-Mitte, 1928–29," in Terence Riley and Barry Bergdoll, eds., *Mies in Berlin*, an exhibition catalog (New York: Museum of Modern Art, 2001), p. 230.

34. Georg Adam, quoted by ibid.

35. Curt Gravenkamp, "Mies van der Rohe: Glashaus in Berlin (Projekt Adam, 1928)," *Das Kunstblatt* (April 1930), pp. 111–12.

36. Ludwig Hilberseimer, reply to Martin Wagner, "Das Formproblem eines Weltstadtplatzes," *Das neue Berlin* (February 1929): 39–40.

37. Wolf Tegethoff argues that the participation of Queen Victoria Eugenia is "unresolved," since she does not appear in photographs of the ceremony. He also debunks other "myths" associated with the ceremony; for example, that atop one of Mies's tables was a "golden book" that the king and queen were to sign, and the contention—supported, however, by Mies's own later statements—that the Barcelona chairs were intended to be "thrones." See Tegethoff, "The Pavilion Chair," in Reuter and Schulte, *Mies and Modern Living*, pp. 147–48.

38. Commissar General Georg von Schnitzler, quoted by Lilly von Schnitzler, "Die Weltausstellung Barcelona 1929," *Der Querschnitt* 9 (August 1929): 583.

39. Mies, interview with Cadbury-Brown (BBC), May 27, 1959. Later, Mies said that the IIT campus plan was the most difficult challenge he ever faced.

40. Mies, interview with Katharine Kuh, "Modern Classicist," *Saturday Review* 48, no. 4 (January 1965), pp. 22–23 and 61.

41. Walther Genzmer, "Der deutsche Reichspavillon an der internationalen Ausstellung Barcelona," *Die Baugilde* 11 (October 25, 1929): 1654–57.

42. For Mies's efforts to keep the pavilion free of signage, see Dietrich Neumann, "Haus Ryder in Wiesbaden und die Zusammenarbeit von Gerhard Severain und Ludwig Mies van der Rohe," *Architectura* 2/2006, pp. 215ff. Late in life Mies addressed the issue of rich materials: "Why shouldn't something be as good as possible, you know? I cannot follow the train of thought where people say, that is too aristocratic, that is not democratic enough. As I've said, for me it is a question of value, and I make things as good as I can." From the RIAS Berlin interview published on the phonograph record *Mies in Berlin*, Bauwelt Archiv, 1966.

43. The graphics were again by Severain.

44. In Germany, Mies used the term "pavilion chair" (*Pavillon Sessel*). In postwar production by the Knoll Corporation in the United States and elsewhere, it is called the Barcelona chair.

45. On the Barcelona chair, see Tegethoff, "The Pavilion Chair," pp. 145–73.

46. Mies, letter to I. D. Higgins, January 2, 1964; box 28, Papers of Ludwig Mies van der Rohe,

Manuscript Division, Library of Congress. Tegethoff, "The Pavilion Chair," p. 172, n. 3, suggests that the word *special* is a typographical error (made by Mies's secretary), and should read "spatial."

47. As manufactured by Knoll, the chair features welts in orthogonal rather than diagonal rows. The straps used for the back of the chairs at the pavilion may have been rubber and not leather, and they were arranged horizontally and not vertically, as became standard early on. See Tegethoff, "The Pavilion Chair."

48. Ibid., p. 171.

49. Edward Duckett, Mies's model maker, reworked the chair for fabrication in stainless steel. The originals were chrome plated. Duckett and Griffith worked hand in hand. They took advantage of the weldability of the new material to eliminate the original lap joint and fasteners in the frame at the front corners of the seat and at the top of the back. But they had great difficulty identifying an alloy with the appropriate "springiness." Duckett reported (personal communication with Windhorst, 1993) that his colleague Bruno Conterato, who was about the same size and weight as Mies, was recruited to test mock-ups. One sample lazily collapsed under Conterato, with Mies observing. Duckett said that Mies found it "tremendously funny." For more on Gerald Griffith, see *Interiors* 124 (November 1964): 74–75, 144, 146.

50. Ignasi de Solà-Morales, Ignasi de Solà-Morales Rubio, Cristian Cirici, and Fernando Ramos, *Mies van der Rohe: El Pabellon de Barcelona; The Barcelona Pavilion* (Barcelona: Gustavo Gili, 1993).

51. Grete Tugendhat, "On the Construction of the Tugendhat House," in *Ludwig Mies van der Rohe: The Tugendhat House*, ed. Daniela Hammer-Tugendhat and Wolf Tegethoff (Vienna: Springer Verlag, 2000), p. 5.

52. Ibid., p. 6.

53. Ibid.

54. Ibid.

55. Wolf Tegethoff, "The Tugendhat Villa: a Modern Residence in Turbulent Times," in Hammer-Tugendhat and Tegethoff, *Ludwig Mies van der Rohe: The Tugendhat House*, p. 61.

56. Grete Tugendhat, "On the Construction of the Tugendhat House," p. 6.

57. Mies, quoted by Tegethoff in Hammer-Tugendhat and Tegethoff, *Ludwig Mies van der Rohe: The Tugendhat House*, p. 68.

58. The main-level windows of the Tugendhat House were among the largest Mies designed. Even larger was a single light in a small rear addition to a house in Essen owned by the art collector Ernst Henke (constructed 1930; destroyed during World War II). That window was 9 feet high and 22 feet long. It was adjacent to a pair of glass doors, each 1 meter wide, completing a single wall of glass 9 meters long.

59. These lights were controlled by a single, custom-designed panel. Each window had its own three buttons, marked AUF (up), HALT (stop), and AB (down). Presumably, both windows could be operated simultaneously with the press of a pair of buttons, the same pair at the same time. For a drawing, see *The Mies van der Rohe Archive*, 2:487.

60. The best account of the furniture, including excellent photographs and details of its wartime dispersal and ultimate fate, is in Hammer-Tugendhat and Tegethoff, *Ludwig Mies van der Rohe: The Tugendhat House*.

61. *The Mies van der Rohe Archive*, 2:473–75.

62. Ibid., p. 422.

63. For the shelf in plan, see *The Mies van der Rohe Archive*, vol. 2 (New York: Garland, 1986),

p. 382. For a detail section, see p. 384. The specification "vert antique" is shown on the detail section. Other sources describe the stone as *verd Tinos*. See Jan Sapák, "Atmosphäre durch wertvolle Materialien: Eine Beschreibung," in *Das Haus Tugendhat*, ed. Adolph Stiller (Salzburg: Verlag Anton Pustet, 1999).

64. This table, often erroneously called the Barcelona table, is sometimes called the Dessau table because it appears in a 1930 photograph of Mies's apartment in Dessau, where he stayed during his directorship of the Dessau Bauhaus. The photograph is slightly earlier than the occupation date of the Tugendhat House. The X table is now often and correctly referred to as the Tugendhat Table. See Tegethoff, "The Pavilion Chair," p. 164.

65. Mies, interview with Cadbury-Brown.

66. [Justus Bier], "Kann man im Haus Tugendhat wohnen?," *Die Form: Zeitschrift für gestaltende Arbeit* 10 (October 15, 1931): 392–93.

67. Grete Tugendhat, "Die Bewohner des Hauses Tugendhat äussern sich," *Die Form* 11 (November 15, 1931): 437–38. English translation in Hammer-Tugendhat and Tegethoff, *Ludwig Mies van der Rohe*, pp. 35–36.

68. Fritz Tugendhat, ibid., pp. 36–37. Mies's early relationship with the Tugendhats was not so harmonious as his clients recollected. Mies acknowledged that Herr Tugendhat had liked the Perls House: "He expected something similar. He came to me and talked with me. I went there and saw the situation. I designed the house. I remember it was on Christmas Eve when he saw the design of the house. He nearly died! But his wife was interested in art; she had some of van Gogh's pictures. She said, 'Let us think it over.' Tugendhat could have thrown her out.

"However, on New Year's Eve he came to me and told me that he had thought it over and I should go ahead with the house. We had some trouble with it at the time, but we can take that for granted. He said that he did not like this open space; it would be too disturbing; people would be there when he was in the library with his great thoughts. He was a real businessman, I think. I said, 'Oh, all right. We will try it out and, if you do not want it, we can close the rooms in. We can put wooden scaffold pieces up.' He was listening in the library and we were talking just normally. He did not hear anything." *Architectural Association Journal* 75 (July 1959): 26–46.

69. [Justus Bier], "Kann man im Haus Tugendhat wohnen?"

70. Grete Tugendhat, "Die Bewohner des Hauses Tugendhat äussern sich."

71. Emil Nolde, quoted in Wolf Tegethoff, *Mies van der Rohe: The Villas and Country Houses* (New York: Museum of Modern Art, 1985), p. 99.

72. Tessenow's design, with a sculpted Pietà by Käthe Kollwitz, was constructed.

CHAPTER FIVE

1. Gustav Platz, *Die Baukunst der neuesten Zeit* (Berlin: Propyläen Verlag, 1927). A second, expanded edition was published in 1930.

2. Henry-Russell Hitchcock, *Modern Architecture: Romanticism and Reintegration* (New York: Payson and Clarke, 1929).

3. The drawings are reproduced in *The Mies van der Rohe Archive*, 3:121–37. Mies probably never saw the apartment. Two sketches with notes and dimensions in German documented the existing conditions.

4. Knoll has manufactured what it calls the Barcelona couch since 1953. Though the couch's cushion is similar to that used for the Barcelona chair, the couch had nothing to do with the Barcelona fair.

5. The daybed was also used for the Crous apartment in Berlin, which was exactly contemporaneous with the Johnson project. See Helmut Reuter and Birgit Schulte, eds., *Mies and Modern Living* (Ostfildern, Germany: Hatje Cantz, 2008), p. 198.

6. See Christiane Lange, "The Collaboration between Lilly Reich and Ludwig Mies van der Rohe," in *Ludwig Mies van der Rohe and Lilly Reich: Furniture and Interiors* (Ostfildern, Germany: Hatje Cantz, 2006), pp. 194–207, where Lange makes a convincing case for the primacy of Reich's contribution.

7. Philip Johnson, from conversation among Johnson, Arthur Drexler, and Ludwig Glaeser, December 1977; unedited transcript, published in Johnson's *Mies van der Rohe*, 3rd ed. (New York: Museum of Modern Art, 1978), p. 206. The talk about "six skyscrapers" was typical Johnson hyperbole; the surviving working drawings, for example, are a few sheets of unelaborated details.

8. Hans Wingler, *The Bauhaus: Weimar, Dessau, Berlin, Chicago*, trans. Wolfgang Jabs and Basil Gilbert (Cambridge, MA: MIT Press, 1969), p. 168.

9. Johnson conversation, in Johnson, *Mies van der Rohe*, p. 206.

10. Franz Schulze, *Philip Johnson: Life and Work* (New York: Alfred A. Knopf, 1994), p. 68.

11. Philip Johnson, letter to Mrs. John D. Rockefeller Jr., March 27, 1931; Mies van der Rohe Archive, Museum of Modern Art, New York.

12. Johnson, letter to Alfred Barr, July 11, 1931; Mies van der Rohe Archive.

13. Johnson, letter to Barr, July 1931; Mies van der Rohe Archive.

14. Ibid.

15. Johnson, letter to Barr, August 7, 1931; Mies van der Rohe Archive.

16. Johnson, memorandum to Barr, late 1931; Mies van der Rohe Archive.

17. The best secondary source on the show is Terence Riley, *The International Style: Exhibition 15 and The Museum of Modern Art* (New York: Rizzoli, 1992). Riley points out (p. 9) that "the catalog complemented rather than documented the exhibition."

18. Edward Durell Stone, quoted in Russell Lynes, *Good Old Modern: An Intimate Portrait of the Museum of Modern Art* (New York: Atheneum, 1973), p. 189.

19. Henry-Russell Hitchcock and Philip C. Johnson, *The International Style: Architecture since 1922* (New York: W. W. Norton, 1932).

20. Christian Wolsdorff of the Berlin Bauhaus Archive, personal communication with Schulze, 2000.

21. Elaine Hochman, *Architects of Fortune: Mies van der Rohe and the Third Reich* (New York: Weidenfeld and Nicolson, 1989), p. 328, n. 64.

22. Ibid., p. 83.

23. Georgia van der Rohe, *La donna è mobile: Mein bedingungsloses Leben* (Berlin: Aufbau-Verlag, 2001), p. 53.

24. Ibid., p. 54.

25. Ibid.

26. Gropius, quoted in Reginald Isaacs, *Walter Gropius: An Illustrated Biography of the Creator of the Bauhaus* (Boston: Bulfinch Press, Little, Brown, 1984), p. 165.

27. In a private letter to one of us (Schulze) dated June 17, 1985, Georgia van der Rohe said of her father, "Mies was never fat or obese. With very broad shoulders he seemed to have a wide frame. In German one would call his appearance 'gut durchwachsen'"—in literal English something like "well grown through."

28. Mies, interview with Dirk Lohan (German-language typescript, Chicago, summer 1968); Mies van der Rohe Archive, Museum of Modern Art, New York.

29. In addition to her other skills, Reich also "spoke very good English," and was therefore a key resource for the few American students then at the Bauhaus. Oral History of William Priestley, p. 8; Architecture Department, Art Institute of Chicago.

30. Howard Dearstyne, "Mies at the Bauhaus in Dessau: Student Revolt and Nazi Coercion," *Inland Architect* (August–September 1969): 16.

31. Hochman, *Architects of Fortune*, p. 93, quoting from Claude Schnaidt, *Hannes Meyer: Buildings, Projects and Writings* (Stuttgart: Verlag Gerd Hatje, 1965), p. 105.

32. See Helmut Erfurth and Elisabeth Tharandt, *Mies van der Rohe, Die Trinkhalle, sein einziger Bau in Dessau die Zusammenarbeit mit dem Bauhausstudenten Eduard Ludwig* (Dessau: Anhaltische Verlagsgesellschaft, 1995).

33. Howard Dearstyne commented on the *Trinkhalle* in *Inside the Bauhaus*, ed. David Spaeth (New York: Rizzoli, 1986), p. 236: "We students hailed it as another architectural triumph of the master. It turned out to be a financial flop because [too few] thirsty people passed by it."

34. Mies in conversation with Horst Eifler and Ulrich Conrads, recorded by the American radio station RIAS (Radio in the American Sector), Berlin, October 1964 and produced on a phonograph record, *Mies in Berlin*, Bauwelt Archiv I (Berlin, 1966).

35. The Haus der deutschen Kunst opened in 1937, not 1935.

36. Mies van der Rohe, "The End of the Bauhaus," in the student magazine *North Carolina State University School of Design* 3, no. 3 (Spring 1953): 16–18. Mies was invited to North Carolina State by Dean Henry Kamphoefner, who instituted a distinguished visitors' program that brought important modern architects to the American South.

37. Gestapo letter, July 23, 1933, to Mies from Dr. Peche; quoted in Wingler, *The Bauhaus*, p. 189.

38. "A Call by Cultural Leaders / Countrymen, Friends!," *Völkischer Beobachter*, August 18, 1934.

39. Cited in Terence Riley and Barry Bergdoll, eds., *Mies in Berlin*, an exhibition catalog (New York: Museum of Modern Art, 2001), p. 101.

40. The competition is covered in detail in Wolf Tegethoff, *Mies van der Rohe: The Villas and Country Houses* (New York: Museum of Modern Art, 1985), pp. 114–19. Tegethoff believes that March was the prime mover in initiating the competition, and that Gericke was "from the start . . . obviously only half-heartedly involved in the whole affair" (p. 114).

41. Ibid., p. 119, for this letter from Gericke and that which follows.

42. Lilly von Schnitzler, interview in German with Ludwig Glaeser, Canadian Centre for Architecture files "Glaeser Papers," p. 9; CCA, Montreal.

43. Ibid. p. 11.

44. For the lives of Karl and Martha Lemke, see Wita Noack, *Konzentrat der Moderne: Das Landhaus Lemke von Ludwig Mies van der Rohe* (Munich: Deutscher Kunstverlag, 2008), pp. 50–70. Noack's comprehensively illustrated monograph is definitive on the house and its history.

45. Oswald Grube, personal communication with Schulze, January 23, 2009. Grube was told of the restrictions against photography by the house's former GDR supervisor.

46. The rumor is by definition hearsay, and Amendt's later purchase of the house may in itself have led him to want to believe Frau Heusgen's attribution.

47. Amendt's restoration was awarded a prize from the City of Krefeld in 2002.

48. Jan Maruhn and Werner Mellen, *Haus Heusgen: Ein Wohnhaus Ludwig Mies van der Rohes in Krefeld* (Haldensleben: Mies van der Rohe-Haus Aachen e. V., 2006). The fifteen-page German-language pamphlet includes original plan drawings as well as a photo of a wood model.

49. Ibid., p. 8, this and the quotation at the end of the paragraph.

50. See Christiane Lange, *Mies van der Rohe: Architektur für die Seidenindustrie* (Berlin: Nicolai Verlag, 2011).

51. She is quoted in Hans Dieter Peschken, "Villa Heusgen ist nicht von Mies," RP Online (rp-online.de), November 10, 2011.

52. Dearstyne, *Inside the Bauhaus*, p. 250.

53. Dearstyne taught at IIT from 1957 until his death in 1970.

54. John Barney Rodgers, letter to Ludwig Glaeser, March 16, 1978; Glaeser files, Canadian Centre for Architecture, Montreal.

55. John Barney Rodgers, Princeton Lectures, Spring 1935; Glaeser files, "Lecture 1," p. 3, Canadian Centre for Architecture.

56. Ibid., p. 9.

57. Ibid., pp. 9–10.

58. Philip Johnson, "Architecture in the Third Reich," *Hound and Horn* 7, October–December 1933, p. 138.

59. It is not known when Mies joined the Reichskulturkammer, but an invitation to a Berlin Philharmonic concert of November 15, 1933, marking the ceremonial opening of the organization, as well as a program for that concert, are in the Papers of Ludwig Mies van der Rohe at the Library of Congress. As late as November 8, 1938, by which time Mies had already immigrated to the United States, a letter (signed Eckermann) was sent to his office in Berlin by the president of the Reichskammer der bildenden Künste, a division of the Reichskulturkammer, advising him that he was expected to add to his own proof of racial purity—previously provided—similar proof for his wife. The typescript of a public notice, dated January 20, 1939, and signed by Hauswald states: "On January 19, 1939 I visited the Reichskammer Blumeshof and confirmed that Herr Mies has been absent from Germany for a year and a half, for which period he was not required to pay his dues."

60. Joseph Goebbels, quoted in Barbara Miller Lane, *Architecture and Politics in Germany, 1918–1945* (Cambridge, MA: Harvard University Press, 1968), p. 176.

61. Hochman, *Architects of Fortune*, p. 223, quoting Albert Speer, at this time the Nazi's chief architect and a member of Hitler's inner circle.

62. Riley and Bergdoll, *Mies in Berlin*, p. 284. Claire Zimmerman, in her discussion of Mies's entry, states that Ruegenberg's claim "cannot be confirmed."

63. Dirk Lohan, interview with the authors, May 3, 2011.

64. Mathies, German General Commissioner of the 1935 Brussels World's Fair, in a draft of the commission, accompanying a letter to Mies June 11, 1934; Mies van der Rohe Archive, Museum of Modern Art, New York.

65. Mies, "Concerning the Preliminary Draft of an Exposition Building for the 1935 Brussels World's Fair" July 3, 1934; Mies van der Rohe Archive.

66. Ibid.

67. Hochman, *Architects of Fortune*, p. 203.

68. Mies, quoted in Tegethoff, *Mies van der Rohe: The Villas and Country Houses*, p. 121.

69. Ibid., p. 123.

70. Ibid., p. 121.

71. Karen Fiss, personal communication with Schulze, 2009. See her *Grand Illusion: The Third Reich, the Paris Exposition, and the Cultural Seduction of France* (Chicago: University of Chicago Press, 2009).

72. See Matilda McQuaid, ed., *Lilly Reich, Designer and Architect*, with an essay by Magdalena Droste (New York: Museum of Modern Art, 1996), p. 35.

1. Neumeyer made a similar offer to Walter Gropius for the summer of 1937. Gropius — by then already at Harvard — declined.

2. John Holabird, letter to Mies, March 20, 1936; Mies van der Rohe Archive, Museum of Modern Art, New York.

3. Mies, cable to Holabird, April 20, 1936; Mies van der Rohe Archive.

4. Mies, letter to Holabird, May 4, 1936; Mies van der Rohe Archive.

5. Holabird, letter to Mies, May 11, 1936; Mies van der Rohe Archive.

6. Mies, letter to Holabird, May 20, 1936; Mies van der Rohe Archive.

7. Willard Hotchkiss, letter to Mies, May 12, 1936; Mies van der Rohe Archive.

8. Mies, letter to Hotchkiss, undated; Mies van der Rohe Archive.

9. Hotchkiss, letter to Mies, July 2, 1936; Mies van der Rohe Archive.

10. Mies, letter to Alfred Barr, July 14, 1936; Mies van der Rohe Archive.

11. Barr, letter to Mies, July 19, 1936; Mies van der Rohe Archive.

12. Joseph Hudnut, letter to Mies, July 21, 1936; Mies van der Rohe Archive.

13. George Nelson, quoted by Cammie McAtee, "Alien #5044325: Mies's First Trip to America," in *Mies in America*, ed. Phyllis Lambert, Werner Oechslin, et al., an exhibition catalog (New York: H. N. Abrams, 2001), p. 148.

14. Hudnut, letter to Mies, September 3, 1936; Mies van der Rohe Archive, Museum of Modern Art, New York.

15. Mies, letter to Hudnut, September 15, 1936; Mies van der Rohe Archive.

16. Alfred Swenson and Pao-Chi Chang, *Architectural Education at I.I.T.: 1938–1978* (Chicago: IIT, 1980), p. 10.

17. Helen Resor, letter to Alfred Barr, July 1937; Resor Papers, MoMA Archive. Quoted by McAtee, "Alien #5044325," p. 157.

18. In his autobiography, *Architekt in der Zeitenwende: Clemens Holzmeister; Selbstbiographie, Werkverzeichnis* (Salzburg: Bergland-Buch, 1976), p. 101, Holzmeister writes: "As one of my last assignments at the Academy prior to the Anschluss, I had to find a successor to Peter Behrens. I decided on Mies van der Rohe, then in Berlin and already internationally renowned. Mies answered in a long letter, consenting in tone, on March 10, 1937.... But there followed the blow from the Third Reich, which reduced all our capabilities at the masters' schools." Dirk Lohan suspects that Mies wrote cordially to Vienna in order to let the record show that he was prepared to remain in a pan-German environment and was not interested in immigrating to the United States. Prof. Johannes Spalt, personal communication with Schulze, Vienna, November 25, 1982.

19. William Priestley, letter to John Barney Rodgers, September 1, 1937, quoted in Rodgers's letter to Nina Bremer, February 11, 1976; Mies van der Rohe Archive.

20. In later years, Mies concurred with van Beuren's characterization of Chicago: "Mies mentioned many times to us that in Chicago you felt they 'gave you a chance.'" Oral History of Reginald Malcolmson, p. 107; Architecture Department, Art Institute of Chicago.

21. Michael van Beuren, excerpted from two letters to Mies, October 21 and November 6, 1936; Mies van der Rohe Archive, Museum of Modern Art, New York.

22. William Priestley, interview with Schulze, January 25, 1982.

23. Mies, telegram to Frank Lloyd Wright, September 8, 1937; quoted in McAtee, "Alien #5044325," p. 190, n. 96.

24. Edgar Tafel, *Apprentice to Genius: Years with Frank Lloyd Wright* (New York: McGraw-Hill, 1979), p. 66.

25. Ibid.

26. William Wesley Peters, interview with Schulze, October 12, 1982.

27. Frank Lloyd Wright, quoted in Tafel, *Apprentice to Genius*, p. 69.

28. McAtee, "Alien #5044325," p. 160.

29. Ibid., p. 162.

30. Quoted in Wolf Tegethoff, *Mies van der Rohe: The Villas and Country Houses* (New York: Museum of Modern Art, 1985), p. 127.

31. Rodgers suggested that the commission may have been withdrawn because "Mr. Resor worried about the war and J. Walter Thompson's European clients." John Barney Rodgers, letter to Nina Bremer, February 11, 1976; Mies van der Rohe Archive, Museum of Modern Art, New York.

32. Mies, quoted by McAtee, "Alien #5044325," p. 183.

33. Lora Marx reported (interview with Schulze, in 1980) that Mies told her he had hoped to receive a $10,000 salary as director of the Department of Architecture at Armour. She stated that he reached that salary only just before retirement.

34. Sybil Moholy-Nagy, reply to Howard Dearstyne's letter; quoted in *Journal of the Society of Architectural Historians* 24, no. 3 (1965): 255.

35. Karl Otto, interview with Hans Schwippert, March 3, 1973, Berlin; Mies van der Rohe Archive.

36. Herbert Hirche, personal communication with Schulze, July 3, 1982.

37. Mies listed details of his passage in an "Application for Certificate of Arrival . . ."; box 62, Papers of Ludwig Mies van der Rohe, Manuscript Division, Library of Congress.

CHAPTER SEVEN

1. Gerhard Masur, *Imperial Berlin* (New York: Basic Books. 1970), p. 74.

2. In 1938 it was simply "the Chicago school." The "second" school would refer to Mies and his followers.

3. Frank Lloyd Wright, *An Autobiography* (New York: Duell, Sloan and Pearce, 1943), p. 460.

4. Henry T. Heald, "Mies van der Rohe at I.I.T.," in *Four Great Makers of Modern Architecture: Gropius, Le Corbusier, Mies van der Rohe, Wright; The Verbatim Record of a Symposium Held at the School of Architecture, Columbia University, March–May, 1961* (New York: Columbia University, 1963; reprint, New York: Da Capo Press, 1970), p. 106.

5. Ibid.

6. Mies, Armour Institute inaugural address, November 20, 1938; German-language typescript in box 61, Papers of Ludwig Mies van der Rohe, Manuscript Division, Library of Congress. Philip Johnson first published the address, in an incomplete translation, in his 1947 monograph *Mies van der Rohe* (New York: Museum of Modern Art).

7. Fritz Neumeyer, *The Artless Word: Mies van der Rohe on the Building Art*, trans. Mark Jarzombek (German edition, 1986; Cambridge, MA: MIT Press, 1991), p. 220 and passim, pp. 220–28.

8. Mies, letter to Carl O. Schniewind, January 31, 1938; Mies van der Rohe Archive. Schniewind was then librarian and curator of the Department of Prints and Drawings at the Brooklyn Museum.

9. Mies, Armour Institute inaugural address, November 20, 1938.

10. Mies, quoted in "Peter Blake: A Conversation with Mies van der Rohe," in *Four Great Makers of Modern Architecture: Gropius, Le Corbusier, Mies van der Rohe, Wright; The Verbatim Record of a Symposium Held at the School of Architecture, Columbia University, March–May, 1961* (New York: Columbia University, 1963; reprint, New York: Da Capo Press, 1970), p. 103. A contrasting firsthand view of Mies as educator was offered by the architect Ralph Rapson, who in the early

1950s served on an accreditation team reviewing Illinois Institute of Technology's architecture program: "Mies van der Rohe viewed the team's visit as something of an affront. When asked why he did not bring in outside lecturers, he replied simply: 'We know what we want to teach. We don't need other people to come in to tell us that.' He similarly explained the absence of an architectural library by stating that his faculty would decide what the students needed to see. He dismissed the need for courses in mechanical, electrical, and structural subjects by drawing a sketch consisting of a few vertical lines connected by a horizontal one, putting down his cigar, and jabbing at the drawings with his forefinger: 'This is the wall. This is the ceiling. That is your structure. Mechanical goes here. Electrical goes there.'" Rapson gave this interview in 1997; it is recounted in Jane King Hession, *Ralph Rapson: Sixty Years of Modern Design* (Afton, MN: Afton Historical Society Press, 1999), pp. 51–52. Rapson and his team voted *in favor* of accreditation.

11. Mies, Armour Institute inaugural address, November 20, 1938.

12. From an "address Mies gave [in the United States] in German, date and occasion unknown"; reprinted in Neumeyer, *The Artless Word*, pp. 325–26. If the address was given in German, the date is probably not long after 1938.

13. Mies, interview with Peter Blake (typescript), Columbia University Oral History Project, 1960, pp. 94–95.

14. Mies, quoted by Peter Carter in "Mies van Der Rohe: An Appreciation, This Month, of His 75th Birthday," *Architectural Design* 31 (March 1961): 97, our italics. The authors thank Dirk Lohan for discussions about the German meanings of *Struktur*.

15. Myron Goldsmith, in *Myron Goldsmith: Buildings and Concepts*, ed. Werner Blaser (Basel: Birkhäuser Verlag, 1986), p. 24.

16. Oral History of Gene Summers, pp. 15–16, our italics; Architecture Department, Art Institute of Chicago.

17. Published by Paul Theobald and Co., Chicago.

18. In an affidavit filed with his "naturalization papers," Mies listed, in addition to his IIT salary, his income from professional practice in 1945: $4,986. Box 62, Papers of Ludwig Mies van der Rohe, Manuscript Division, Library of Congress.

19. Mies, interview with Cadbury-Brown (BBC), May 27, 1959.

20. Oral History of Myron Goldsmith, p. 49; Architecture Department, Art Institute of Chicago.

21. Alschuler died November 9, 1940.

22. Henry Heald, letter to Mies, January 9, 1941; box 5 ("I.I.T."), Papers of Ludwig Mies van der Rohe, Manuscript Division, Library of Congress (cited by Phyllis Lambert in *Mies in America*, ed. Phyllis Lambert, Werner Oechslin, et al., an exhibition catalog [New York: H. N. Abrams, 2001], p. 267, n. 66).

23. "First Annual Report of the President to the [IIT] Board of Trustees," 1940, Henry T. Heald, October 13, 1941, p. 18; University Archives, Paul V. Galvin Library, Illinois Institute of Technology, Chicago. Holabird & Root served as Mies's associate architect for campus buildings from 1942 into the 1950s.

24. "Peter Blake: A Conversation with Mies," p. 96.

25. Mies, interview with Cadbury-Brown.

26. Only the Institute of Gas Technology—North Building (3410 S. State) and the 3424 S. State building were connected after the fact, *after* Mies was terminated as campus architect. An addition to the north elevation of the Metals and Minerals Building was constructed in 1958.

27. Phyllis Lambert, "Learning a Language," in Lambert, Oechslin, et al., *Mies in America*, pp. 223–330. The campus plans are discussed on pp. 223–275.

28. Ibid., p. 243.

29. Ibid., p. 235.

30. According to George Danforth, cited in Lambert, Oechslin, et al., *Mies in America*, p. 254.

31. It was done by Le Corbusier in the 1920s. Mies was well aware of it. He explored the idea in unbuilt projects like the Krefeld Golf Club.

32. In an article illustrating the new campus plan in *Architectural Forum* 76, no. 2 (February 1942): 14, the revision is described as "merging Mies with a merger." Illustration cited in Lambert, Oechslin, et al., *Mies in America*, p. 268.

33. "Peter Blake: A Conversation with Mies van der Rohe," p. 96.

34. The plan of the Brick Country House was also called "Mondrianesque" by many of Mies's Weimar contemporaries. The flowing interiors of the Barcelona Pavilion are generically similar to some of Mondrian's paintings. Mies always denied the influence, for his work in both Europe and the United States.

35. Mies, "Mies van der Rohe's New Buildings," *Architectural Forum* 97, no. 5 (November 1951): 104.

36. Henry Heald, "Mies van der Rohe at IIT," in *Four Great Makers of Modern Architecture: Gropius, Le Corbusier, Mies van der Rohe, Wright; The Verbatim Record of a Symposium Held at the School of Architecture, Columbia University, March–May, 1961* (New York: Columbia University, 1963; reprint, New York: Da Capo Press, 1970), p. 108.

37. Howard Dearstyne, *Inside the Bauhaus*, ed. David Spaeth (New York: Rizzoli, 1986), p. 251. Dearstyne met the couple in New York, where he led them on a tour of the World's Fair.

38. George Danforth, personal communication with Schulze, October 6, 1981.

39. Federal Bureau of Investigation, Chicago Report, September 15, 1939; FBI file no. 65-4656. The material was obtained through the Freedom of Information Act. Details are in Franz Schulze, ed., *Mies van der Rohe: Critical Essays* (Cambridge, MA: MIT Press, 1989), in an addendum to an essay by Richard Pommer, p. 146. Note the stereotyping of Reich as a "secretary" by the "unidentified *business*woman."

40. The ocean liner on which she intended to leave was the *Bremen*, not the *New Amsterdam*, as the agents reported.

41. Federal Bureau of Investigation, Chicago Report, October 26, 1939.

42. Ibid., November 24, 1939.

43. The Deputy to the Secretary of Commerce, Washington, DC, reports of December 28, 1961, January 4, 1962, and May 23, 1966. From FBI file no. 65-4656.

44. Mies's name, the many misspellings of which comprise a history of their own, appears in the FBI reports as "Nies van der Rohe," "Mies varber Hohe," and "Mies varder Rohe." In other contexts, misspellings have included "Miss van der Rohe," "Miles van der Rohe," and "Mr. Vanderroh." In the American press and even in scholarly publications (cf. the many books of Carl Condit), Mies was widely referred to as "Mr. Van der Rohe." During the Farnsworth trial (in the early 1950s—see chapter 10), the Special Master, the attorneys, and even his own staff called him Mr. Van der Rohe.

45. Ludwig Glaeser, *Ludwig Mies van der Rohe: Furniture and Furniture Drawings from the Design Collection and the Mies van der Rohe Archive* (New York: Museum of Modern Art, 1977), pp. 14–15, gives an overview of the litigation.

46. Lilly Reich, letter to Mies, June 12, 1940; Papers of Ludwig Mies van der Rohe, Manuscript Division, Library of Congress.

47. Lora Marx, interview with Schulze, 1980.

48. IIT's quest to relocate did not stop with the substantial completion of the main campus in the late 1960s. Active consideration was given to abandoning the campus as late as 1995.

49. See Leah Dickerman, "Bauhaus Fundamentals," in *Bauhaus 1919–1933: Workshops for Modernity* (New York: The Museum of Modern Art, 2009), for "the characteristic Bauhaus belief that there was no principle that could not be rendered diagrammatically" (p. 25).

50. The authors have found no evidence that Mies ever said "God is in the details." In *Meaning in the Visual Arts: Papers in and on Art History* (Garden City, NY: Doubleday, 1955), Erwin Panofsky quotes Flaubert: "Le bon Dieu est dans le détail" (p. 5). Mies may have read Panofsky—or even Flaubert (though not in French)—but there is no proof of that either.

51. Typescript, question-and-answer period following a speech to the Architectural League of New York, 1960; box 62, "Speeches," Papers of Ludwig Mies van der Rohe, Manuscript Division, Library of Congress.

52. From page 20 of an interview of Mies for the aluminum industry, New York City, 1960, recorded by Peter Associates; box 62, Papers of Ludwig Mies van der Rohe, Manuscript Division, Library of Congress.

53. Oral History of Gene Summers, p. 19.

54. Oral History of A. James Speyer, pp. 61–62; Architecture Department, Art Institute of Chicago.

55. Oral History of Thomas Beeby, pp. 40–41; Architecture Department, Art Institute of Chicago.

56. Oral History of Reginald Malcolmson, p. 135; Architecture Department, Art Institute of Chicago.

57. Bruno Conterato, who worked for Mies for fifteen years and became a partner in the follow-on firm, remembered signing on: "I asked him rather brashly, 'How much do you pay, Mies?' Mies knew I had just been at Skidmore [Owings & Merrill]'s office, and he said, 'What is Skidmore offering you?' I said, 'They want me to start at four dollars an hour.' Mies replied, 'We pay a dollar an hour to everybody in the office.' Then he thought a minute, and said, 'But if you need more money, why don't you work more hours?'" Recorded interview with Windhorst, 1993. The dollar-an-hour rule was not sacred; George Schipporeit started in 1956 for ninety cents an hour.

58. "Notes from a manuscript by Paul Pippin describing his graduate studies at I.I.T. under Mies," 1946–47, unpaginated typescript and longhand; Mies van der Rohe Archive. About Mies's "delivery," Pippin added: "[It] was very individual. He spoke at intervals after long puffs on his cigar, and then made a short, simple, direct comment, preceded by a slight smile. He always spoke that way during a crit and it was very effective though certainly not contrived for effect."

59. This is not to say that Mies did not explore for himself. Bruno Conterato recalled the early days of the office: "I was surprised by how he would try things, and ask us to draw something which we felt, why would he want to do this? This is crazy, this doesn't look good at all. But he would say, 'If we're going to make mistakes, let's do it on the drawing board, not on the building.' His method was to eliminate possibilities that were not good, and zero in on only the best." Recorded interview with Windhorst, 1993.

60. Hilberseimer's American publisher was Paul Theobald & Co., Chicago. His American books are *The New City: Principles of Planning* (1944); *The New Regional Pattern: Industries and Gardens; Workshops and Farms* (1949); *The Nature of Cities* (1955); *Mies van der Rohe* (1956); and *Contemporary Architecture, Its Roots and Trends* (1964). See also D. Spaeth and R. A. Fosse, *Ludwig Karl Hilberseimer: An Annotated Bibliography and Chronology* (New York: Garland, 1981).

61. Mies, quoted in Neumeyer, *The Artless Word*, p. 335.

62. Richard Pommer, "More a Necropolis than a Metropolis," in *Ludwig Hilberseimer: Architect, Educator and Urban Planner* (Chicago: Art Institute of Chicago, 1988), p. 17.

63. Vittorio Magnago Lampugnani, "Berlin Modernism and the Architecture of the Metropolis," in *Mies in Berlin*, ed. Terence Riley and Barry Bergdoll, an exhibition catalog (New York: Museum of Modern Art, 2001), p. 50.

64. Dearstyne, *Inside the Bauhaus*, p. 212.

65. Pommer, "More a Necropolis than a Metropolis," p. 17.

66. "I remember Mies saying, 'The thing about Hilbs, he thinks all the time.' And he did." Oral History of Ambrose Richardson, p. 43; Architecture Department, Art Institute of Chicago.

67. Mies, foreword to Ludwig Hilberseimer, *The New City: Principles of Planning* (Chicago: Paul Theobald, 1944), p. xv. Mies's text is also reprinted in Richard Pommer, David Spaeth, and Kevin Harrington, *In the Shadow of Mies: Ludwig Hilberseimer, Architect, Educator, and Urban Planner* (Chicago: The Art Institute of Chicago, in association with Rizzoli International Publications, Inc., 1988), p. 67.

68. Ludwig Hilberseimer, *Mies van der Rohe* (Chicago: Paul Theobald, 1956). One year before, Swiss artist Max Bill published a small book titled *Miës van der Rohe*, in Italian, number 12 in the series *Architetti del movimento moderno*, Milan.

69. Ibid., p. 49.

70. Ibid., p. 12.

71. Ibid., p. 60.

72. Ibid., p. 49. Gordon Bunshaft, Mies's friend and for decades Skidmore, Owings & Merrill's chief designer in New York, had a profoundly different view of Mies's triumph: "His life if he hadn't come to the States would have ended up with not much. He belonged to the United States because the United States at that time especially was essentially a steel construction country. That was what he was really geared for. Germany is not a steel construction country. You think of the Krupp works, but we did buildings there. They don't know anything about big steel." Oral History of Gordon Bunshaft, pp. 136–37; Architecture Department, Art Institute of Chicago.

73. Ibid., p. 49.

74. Lora Marx, interview with Schulze, September 23, 1980.

75. George Danforth, "Hilberseimer Remembered," in Pommer, Spaeth, and Harrington, *In the Shadow of Mies*, p. 15.

76. George Danforth, quoting Mies in ibid., p. 10.

77. Ibid., p. 11. Danforth does not reveal the identity of the student.

78. Ibid.

79. Dennis Domer, ed., *Alfred Caldwell: The Life and Work of a Prairie School Landscape Architect* (Baltimore: Johns Hopkins University Press, 1997). Caldwell's drawings are sampled in Werner Blaser, *Architecture and Nature: The Work of Alfred Caldwell* (Basel: Birkhäuser Verlag, 1984).

80. Oral History of Alfred Caldwell, p. 78; Architecture Department, Art Institute of Chicago.

CHAPTER EIGHT

1. "New Buildings for 194X," *Architectural Forum* 78, no. 5 (May 1943): 69–152, 189. Twenty-three architects participated, among the well-known Louis Kahn, Charles Eames, Pietro Belluschi, William Lescaze, Serge Chermayeff, and Hugh Stubbins.

2. Ibid., p. 84.

3. Ibid.

4. "The Zollverein Colliery in Essen: Schupp and Kremmer, Architects," *Architectural Forum* 53, no. 2 (February 1933): 148.

5. Mies, quoted in "Peter Blake: A Conversation with Mies," in *Four Great Makers of Modern Architecture: Gropius, Le Corbusier, Mies van der Rohe, Wright; The Verbatim Record of a Symposium Held at the School of Architecture, Columbia University, March–May, 1961* (New York: Columbia University, 1963; reprint, New York: Da Capo Press, 1970), pp. 100–101. The northern end wall was engaged (and permanently hidden) by a 1957–58 addition to Minerals and Metals known as the Metals Research Building. The "Mondrian wall" can still be seen on the south elevation of the 1942 building.

6. See the Chapel and Alumni Memorial Hall, where some brick panels exceed twenty-four feet.

7. Dirk Lohan, interview with the authors, May 3, 2011. The Detroit Graphite Company was purchased by the Velspar Corporation in 1930, but the Mies literature maintains the product name that references the original vendor.

8. See *Mies in America*, ed. Phyllis Lambert, Werner Oechslin, et al., an exhibition catalog (New York: H. N. Abrams, 2001), p. 291ff., and p. 329, n. 109.

9. See the 870 drawings in *The Mies van der Rohe Archive*, vol. 9 (New York: Garland, 1992), which is entirely given over to the Library and Administration project.

10. Olencki was Mies's second employee, after George Danforth, and like Danforth he became an educator. Olencki left Mies's office in 1948 to teach at the University of Michigan. He remained a committed Miesian.

11. Mies took the problem of "representation" very seriously. In a 1945 letter to the IIT administration, he answered various technical objections to his design for the Library and Administration Building. But in a final paragraph he addressed "what I think of importance: The Illinois Institute of Technology is going to build a new campus. That is a rare occasion—it happens seldom. The campus could be merely a conglomeration of buildings or it could be a unit, expressing the ideals of I.I.T. That is how I planned it. The school buildings should express in their objectivity the sincerity of the Institute, while the Administration and the Student-Union Buildings should be a symbol of its dignity." Mies, letter to Dr. Linton E. Grinter, June 12, 1945; Mies van der Rohe Archive, Museum of Modern Art, New York.

12. Cited in Lambert, Oechslin, et al., *Mies in America*, p. 329, n. 111. In his June 12, 1945, letter to the IIT administration, Mies asserted, "I thought I found a good solution for this difficult problem." He then cited the approbation of his professional peers: "My belief was backed by the best architects of the country ... who have expressed their admiration for the work we have done." Letter to L. E. Grinter; Mies van der Rohe Archive, Museum of Modern Art, New York.

13. In a discussion with Mies in the Navy Building, Reginald Malcolmson, then a new graduate student, said, "I'm impressed that you make the English bond with such exactitude. Would you make the same if it was a plastered wall [meaning plastered on the interior]?" Mies answered, "Let me tell you, if I had to build a wall I would make it an English bond even if it was plastered on all sides." Malcolmson said to himself, "I know I'm in the right place now." Oral History of Reginald Malcolmson, pp. 40, 41; Architecture Department, Art Institute of Chicago.

14. Cantor became a prominent collector of modern European art. Mies also designed a Cantor house and office building, both unbuilt. The Cantor house shares elements of the Resor House project—though for a rolling and waterless site—and the plans suggest an important result. In spite of the brief flurry of work—in the two years after World War II, Cantor was Mies's most significant private client—he and Mies seem not to have been close. Joseph Fujikawa recalled that Cantor sought out Mies because "the best architect in the world doesn't charge me any more in fees than any other architect." Joseph Fujikawa, "Mies's Office: 1945–1970," *A+U* [Architecture and Urbanism] (January 1981): 175.

15. Goldsmith, undated interview with Kevin Harrington, in Lambert, Oechslin, et al., *Mies in America*, p. 430, n. 170.

CHAPTER NINE

1. Dornbusch was on Armour's architecture faculty when Mies was made director. He was one of the three "old faculty" whom Mies retained.

2. Katharine Kuh, personal communication with Schulze, July 1979. Kuh opened Chicago's first commercial gallery for avant-garde art in 1936. She was later a distinguished curator at the Art Institute of Chicago.

3. Lora Marx, interview with Schulze, 1980.

4. Lora Marx was born in 1900 and died in 1989.

5. Lora Marx, interview with Schulze, 1980.

6. See below for additional details of this event.

7. The single sketch for this work—in Mies's hand—is in *The Mies van der Rohe Archive*, vol. 13 (New York: Garland, 1992), p. 67.

8. Jacques Brownson, in his early days as an IIT student, had this first reaction to Mies's apartment: "They gave me something to take up to Mies's apartment.... I didn't know who Mies was.... I rang the bell and I went up—oh, God, this is terrible—and Mies answered the door.... He was very gracious. He said, 'Come in,' and I gave him the package. He didn't say anything. I looked around, and I said, 'When are you going to move in?' It was so Spartan.... He just looked at me." Oral History of Jacques Brownson, pp. 65–66; Architecture Department, Art Institute of Chicago.

9. Lora Marx, interview with Schulze, September 23, 1980.

10. Ibid.

11. There are very few photographs of Mies *without* a cigar. When he taught, he would always show up with several.

12. Donald Sickler, personal communication with Windhorst, 1992.

13. The Arts Club of Chicago now owns the small Picasso etching that was Danforth's first "lunch money" purchase—for $50.

14. In the United States, Mies was attached to sketching on the 6-by-8½-inch Apex Figure Pad no. 68, "Perforated and Permanently Bound."

15. Mies's office secretary, Helen McConoughey, took it on herself to "call down to IIT" as Mies was heading out. Such intelligence was much coveted. George Schipporeit, personal communication with Windhorst, 2008.

16. Mies's American staff also took to wearing white coats, to protect their clothes from pencil dust.

17. Katharine Kuh, *My Love Affair with Modern Art: Behind the Scenes with a Legendary Curator*, ed. Avis Berman (New York: Arcade, 2006).

18. Ibid., pp. 69–70.

19. Oral History of George Danforth, p. 114; Architecture Department, Art Institute of Chicago.

20. Museum of Modern Art Exhibition no. 356. It ran from September 16, 1947, to January 25, 1948. During the show's run, Lilly Reich died in Berlin on December 11.

21. Philip Johnson, *Mies van der Rohe* (New York: Museum of Modern Art, 1947).

22. Philip Johnson, letter to Mies, December 20, 1946; Mies van der Rohe Archive, Museum of Modern Art, New York.

23. Robert A. M. Stern, ed., *The Philip Johnson Tapes: Interviews by Robert A. M. Stern* (New York: Monacelli Press, in association with the Temple Hoyne Buell Center for the Study of American Architecture, 2008), p. 112.

24. Johnson, *Mies van der Rohe*, p. 10.

25. Ibid., p. 96.

26. Terence Riley, "From Bauhaus to Court-House," in *Mies in Berlin*, ed. Terence Riley and Barry Bergdoll, an exhibition catalog (New York: Museum of Modern Art, 2001), p. 335.

27. Philip Johnson, letter to J. J. P. Oud, April 1946; quoted in Franz Schulze, *Philip Johnson: Life and Work* (New York: Alfred A. Knopf, 1994), p. 177.

28. Edwin Alden Jewell, "A Van Der Rohe Survey," *New York Times*, September 28, 1947.

29. Charles Eames in *Arts and Architecture* 64, no. 27 (December 1947): 27.

30. Frank Lloyd Wright, letter to Mies, October 27, 1947; Mies van der Rohe Archive, Museum of Modern Art, New York.

31. Mies, letter to Wright, November 25, 1947; Mies van der Rohe Archive.

32. Nonetheless, it was serious enough to elicit an exchange of artwork. Sometime in the 1940s, according to Arthur Drexler, Mies gave Callery the collage for his Concert Hall project (personal communication with Schulze, March 18, 1985). At an unknown date, she lent him a Picasso, a 1930 bronze sculpture of a seated woman, which he displayed in his apartment. The Picasso loan is cited in *Mies in America*, ed. Phyllis Lambert, Werner Oechslin, et al., an exhibition catalog (New York: H. N. Abrams, 2001), p. 124. For more on Callery (1903–1977) and her close relationship with Johnson, see Frank D. Welch, *Philip Johnson and Texas* (Austin: University of Texas Press, 2000).

33. Georgia van der Rohe, *La donna è mobile: Mein bedingungsloses Leben* (Berlin: Aufbau-Verlag, 2001), pp. 106–7. Marianne Lohan, in conversation with Schulze November 10, 1981, stated that "in the Nazi time [her mother] was courageous—she tried to hide Jews."

34. Marianne Lohan, personal communication with Schulze, November 10, 1981. Reich's post-World War II letters to Mies have not been located. See also the Oral History of Myron Goldsmith, p. 35: "After the war . . . Lilly Reich was trying to set herself up in business. They didn't even have needles and thread. Mies . . . spent a lot of time trying to get these things to her." Architecture Department, Art Institute of Chicago.

35. Lora Marx, interview with Schulze, September 23, 1980.

36. Dirk Lohan, interview with the authors, May 3, 2011.

37. Joseph Fujikawa was "sent over" to Skidmore, Owings & Merrill Chicago in 1947, but returned when Mies's work revived. Fujikawa stated that Mies was "too embarrassed to terminate our employment," and he and fellow staffer John Weese volunteered to leave. "Mies's Office: 1945–1970," *A+U* [Architecture and Urbanism] (January 1981): 175.

CHAPTER TEN

1. Van der Rohe v. Farnsworth, No. 9352 (Ill. Cir. Ct., Kendall County), trial transcript at p. 62 for the cost of the land; for the date of purchase, p. 35.

2. Plano was a McCormick factory town. Farnsworth's nine acres had been part of a *Chicago Tribune* experimental farm.

3. *Van der Rohe*, trial transcript at p. 81, for both last names. Ruth was Mrs. Edward Lee.

4. Edith Farnsworth Papers, Department of Special Collections, Newberry Library. Farnsworth's unpublished, unpaginated, handwritten memoir is in boxes 1 and 2. Subsequent references to her memoir draw on this source.

5. *Van der Rohe v. Farnsworth*, trial transcript at pp. 312–13.

6. Ibid., p. 313.

7. Corti (1882–1957) was a performer, teacher, and editor of violin music.

8. Edith Farnsworth, unpublished memoir; Edith Farnsworth Papers, Department of Special Collections, Newberry Library, Chicago.

9. Ibid.

10. Ibid.

11. Ibid.

12. *Van der Rohe*, trial transcript at p. 320.

13. Ibid., p. 316.

14. Ibid., p. 320. Edward Duckett corroborated Mies's testimony: "He did those ink washes of the Farnsworth House.... I fixed the paper and got it ready for him. He put a wash on two different sketches of the house with Edith Farnsworth standing right there watching. One scheme was on the ground and the other was with it raised up, the way it was eventually built." Edward A. Duckett and Joseph Y. Fujikawa, *Impressions of Mies: An Interview on Mies van der Rohe; His Early Chicago Years 1938–1958* (n.p., 1988), p. 18.

15. *Van der Rohe*, trial transcript at p. 322.

16. Ibid., p. 323.

17. Division of Waterways, State of Illinois, letter to Mies van der Rohe, June 8, 1945; Mies van der Rohe Archive, Museum of Modern Art, New York.

18. The finished floor of the house is 5 feet 10 inches above grade.

19. *Van der Rohe*, trial transcript at p. 327.

20. Variously cited in *Mies in America*, ed. Phyllis Lambert, Werner Oechslin, et al., an exhibition catalog (New York: H. N. Abrams, 2001), and on p. 508, n. 16.

21. Oral History of Myron Goldsmith, p. 66; Architecture Department, Art Institute of Chicago. By comparison, for a much larger project of the same period, the 860–880 North Lake Shore Drive apartment buildings, Mies's staff charged only 2,500 hours (with working drawings by an associate architect).

22. *Van der Rohe*, trial transcript at p. 1487.

23. Gene Summers, who was a junior assistant to Goldsmith on the Farnsworth project, recalled his own travel adventure to Plano. He was assigned the task of making full-scale models of the mullions for the Farnsworth House. "I built those mullions on a wood saw in the office. They were nine feet four inches high. There were two of them. I put them on my shoulders, took them to the railroad station and took them to Plano and walked from the train station to the house and installed them so that Mies could see them the following weekend." Oral History of Gene Summers, p. 22; Architecture Department, Art Institute of Chicago.

24. Memo by Mies: "The Important Facts of the Farnsworth House." Farnsworth trial papers of Sonnenschein Berkson Lautmann Levinson & Morse; Sonnenschein Nath & Rosenthal LLP, Chicago. On these topics there is almost identical, but longer, trial testimony: see transcript pp. 330–50, passim.

25. Myron Goldsmith, memorandum; Farnsworth file, Mies van der Rohe Archive, Museum of Modern Art, New York.

26. Edith Farnsworth, unpublished memoir; Edith Farnsworth Papers, Department of Special Collections, Newberry Library, Chicago.

27. *Van der Rohe*, trial transcript at p. 348.

28. Oral History of Myron Goldsmith, p. 67.

29. Ibid., p. 68.

30. Lora Marx, interview with Schulze, February 14, 1980.

31. A copy of the transcript was provided to the authors by Sonnenschein Nath & Rosenthal LLP of Chicago, the successor firm to Sonnenschein Berkson Lautmann Levinson & Morse, which represented Mies in the lawsuit. It was released to us with the permission of Dirk Lohan. Only a few dozen pages of the trial record are located at the Kendall County Courthouse. Over the years, researchers have sought the full transcript there, or have drawn on the limited material in the Mies van der Rohe Archive at the Museum of Modern Art, New York, which does not include the transcript. William C. Murphy, the last surviving attorney who participated in the case, suggested to us that the Sonnenschein firm might still have the transcript. He told us on October 13, 2005, that he had never personally seen it. As to its whereabouts, Murphy was right, though his memory was imperfect. He told us, for example, that one reason he believed Farnsworth's case "fell apart so quickly" (see below) was that "there had been no discovery," and Farnsworth's attorney, Randolph Bohrer, had been "taken by surprise" by facts he had not known. But the Sonnenschein firm's records include lengthy depositions of Mies, Farnsworth, and Goldsmith. Sonnenschein's records include all the many pleadings in the case; internal memoranda between Levinson (the partner in charge) and John Faissler (the trial attorney); correspondence between Sonnenschein and Murphy's firm, which was local counsel; and documents prepared by Mies and Goldsmith at the request of Sonnenschein. During the six-week trial nineteen witnesses were heard, and some five hundred exhibits were placed in evidence.

32. Karl Freund was the contractor for the foundations, and later built the millwork.

33. *Van der Rohe*, trial transcript at p. 1237ff.

34. Ibid., pp. 1178–81.

35. The nomenclature "W8 × 48" means a wide-flange section nominally 8 inches deep weighing 48 pounds per foot.

36. Copy in Farnsworth trial papers of Sonnenschein Berkson Lautmann Levinson & Morse; Sonnenschein Nath & Rosenthal LLP, Chicago.

37. William C. Murphy, interview with the authors, October 13, 2005, in his Aurora, Illinois, offices. Myron Goldsmith also believed this.

38. Edith Farnsworth, unpublished memoir; Edith Farnsworth Papers, Department of Special Collections, Newberry Library, Chicago.

39. *Van der Rohe*, trial transcript at pp. 829–30.

40. Johnson is referring to Farnsworth's (not Mies's) choice of furniture, as so far installed.

41. Philip Johnson, letter to Mies, June 4, 1951. Mies van der Rohe Archive, Museum of Modern Art, New York.

42. Oral History of Myron Goldsmith, p. 67.

43. Robert Nelson, interview with the authors, November 11, 2005, Aurora, Illinois.

44. According to his son, and also William Murphy.

45. Robert Nelson interview.

46. In internal correspondence about collecting the firm's fees, Levinson referred to Mies as a "difficult person." Faissler, who developed great affection for Mies, did not share Levinson's view.

47. William Murphy, interview with the authors.

48. The authors are grateful to James L. Cooper, partner in the Washington, DC, law firm Arnold & Porter LLP, for his review and interpretation of parts of the transcript.

49. Mies considered his brother an expert on stone. He turned to Ewald as late as the 1960s for advice in selecting stone for the New National Gallery in Berlin. Gene Summers recalled that Mies asked Ewald to advise him (Summers) about granites appropriate to the Berlin location. "Ewald took me to the cemetery. He said not only can you see [many] types but you can also see how they age" (Summers, personal communication with Windhorst, October 2009). Later, Dirk Lohan had similar experiences with Ewald on the same project. Silesian granite—quarried from what was then postwar Poland—was eventually chosen.

50. The photographs were taken by Edward Duckett, who had received a Brownie camera the previous Christmas.

51. Oral History of Myron Goldsmith, p. 70.

52. Mies's office made drawings for the individual trades, which were very detailed and produced as needed. A full set of construction documents was also prepared, but it was subject to continuous revision as the project progressed.

53. Goldsmith believed that it did, reducing the width of the galley kitchen and making the core relatively larger than desired. The model shown at the 1947 MOMA show was of the larger, original design, which was spacious enough to show a second bedroom area, presumably a guest bedroom, not included in the final design.

54. See *Van der Rohe*, Master's Report, p. 25, secs. 10 and 11.

55. Ibid., p. 26.

56. *Van der Rohe*, trial transcript at p. 1611.

57. The oral arguments, unlike the testimony, were apparently not transcribed.

58. Murphy said that Mies's lawyers were "surprised by the unanimity of Nelson's findings," and thrilled by the unusual "complete victory." Murphy, interview with the authors.

59. *Van der Rohe*, Master's Report, p. 26.

60. John Faissler, memo to David Levinson; Farnsworth trial papers of Sonnenschein Berkson Lautmann Levinson & Morse; Sonnenschein Nath & Rosenthal LLP, Chicago.

61. It is not known how she reacted to newspaper accounts of the Master's Report, which were explicit in recording Nelson's "judgment" and Mies's "victory." Though Nelson's findings were preliminary, the press treated them as final.

62. Elizabeth Gordon, "The Threats to the Next America," *House Beautiful* 95, no. 4, April 1953, p. 129.

63. Frank Lloyd Wright, quoted in Peter Blake, *The Master Builders* (New York: W. W. Norton, 1976), pp. 248–49.

64. David Levinson, note to the file, Farnsworth trial papers. In both Germany and the United States, Mies almost never spoke about his professional activity in the first person. Here, consistently, he refers to Farnsworth "slandering *us*."

65. Bohrer was on a three-month vacation to the Southwest "for his health," according to a "note to the file" by attorney John Faissler.

66. "Fox River Bridge Issue to Be Settled by Court," *Chicago Tribune*, May 2, 1968, sec. 3A, p. 2.

67. Murphy warmly recalled Farnsworth's playing the violin for him when he visited her at the house in connection with the bridge matter. Interview with the authors, October 13, 2005.

68. "Fox River Bridge Issue to Be Settled by Court."

69. Copy of letter provided by William C. Murphy, 2005.

70. On the south side of the Fox River opposite the Farnsworth House is Silver Springs State Fish and Wildlife Area. The Silver Springs purchase, originally of 1,250 acres, was completed in 1969. With the addition of Farnsworth's land, a combined park would have embraced both sides of the river.

71. Dirk Lohan, interview with the authors, May 3, 2011.

72. The asking price for the house and land was $250,000. Palumbo may have made other payments to Farnsworth beyond the amount listed in public records.

73. Mies's initial watercolor suggested traditional pieces. Goldsmith reported: "When things were going well . . . [Mies] even spoke about maybe designing some furniture for [the house], furniture that wasn't as elegant as the furniture that is now used [in the house by Peter Palumbo], like Barcelona chairs. He said, 'Maybe even using untanned leather, with the hair on it, and tanned skin.' I [got] the impression maybe more pillows on the floor, in [an] informal way." Oral History of Myron Goldsmith, p. 67.

74. Photocopy of handwritten notes titled "Farnsworth House Chronicle" by David Bahlman, prepared during the auction and dated December 14, 2003. Copy in possession of Schulze.

CHAPTER ELEVEN

1. Oral History of Y. C. Wong, p. 20; Architecture Department, Art Institute of Chicago.

2. The term is principally the coinage of the historian of technology Carl Condit, although according to Robert Bruegmann the term also arose in the architectural press in the early 1960s. See Bruegmann's "Myth of the Chicago School," in *Chicago Architecture, Histories, Revisions, Alternatives*, ed. Charles Waldheim and Katerina Ruedi Ray (Chicago: University of Chicago Press, 2005). Mies saw himself as part of the lineage of the "first" Chicago school, albeit with emphasis on the "structural clarity" of that earlier work; see, for example, Ludwig Hilberseimer's 1956 monograph: "It is surprising to see how faithfully [Mies's] work carries onward the Chicago school of architecture, originated by architects who aimed as he does, at a structural architecture. The two grew from the same roots." *Mies van der Rohe* (Chicago: Paul Theobald, 1956), p. 21.

3. Summers offered his own theory—probably in jest—about why he emerged as an office leader: "I had a closer relationship than anybody in the office with Mies, probably because I was from Texas, spoke slower, and he could understand me." Oral History of Gene Summers, p. 66; Architecture Department, Art Institute of Chicago.

4. With his early IIT buildings, Mies enjoyed a modest renown, chiefly among the architectural profession, before Greenwald came on the scene. But Greenwald's work offered Mies what he never had at IIT: the opportunity to realize high-rise buildings on prominent sites.

5. Lillian Greenwald, personal communication with Schulze, 2000.

6. But Joseph Fujikawa's memory differed: "[Greenwald] had, through reading publications, decided that the three greatest architects in the world were Frank Lloyd Wright, Le Corbusier and Mies van der Rohe. He rejected [Wright] after hearing from friends that he was very difficult to work with, and Le Corbusier seemed to eliminate himself because of distance." Joseph Fujikawa, "Mies's Office: 1945–1970," *A+U* [Architecture and Urbanism] (January 1981): 176.

7. Bennet Greenwald, personal communication with Schulze, 2007.

8. Bennet Greenwald, interview with Kevin Harrington, intended, according to Greenwald, for an archive prepared for IIT that was never realized.

9. Joseph Fujikawa, recorded interview with Windhorst, June 30, 1993. Bruno Conterato, recorded interview with Windhorst, July 26, 1993.

10. An article in the September 1947 issue of *Architectural Record* prints Goldsmith's drawing of Promontory with steel mullions. Mies's signature is appended to every page. The first edition of this book prints the Goldsmith drawing on p. 241, with the caption "Perspective of Promontory Apartments as planned with steel façade."

11. Reproduced in *The Mies van der Rohe Archive*, vol. 13 (New York: Garland, 1992), pp. 439–41.

12. Problems with the Chicago Building Code would have been inescapable. The lack of a corridor on alternate floors would probably have been disallowed, as was later the case when other architects tried it.

13. The project was not eligible for FHA funding, and was to be privately financed.

14. *The Mies van der Rohe Archive*, vol. 14 (New York: Garland, 1992), pp. 8–124, fails to clarify this difference, and drawings from both projects are mixed together, sometimes on the same page. A seventh, similar building at the southeast corner of the site was not part of Algonquin as built.

15. Mies's speculative towers of the early 1920s were also "exposed" on all sides. Promontory was an "infill" building.

16. In projects and models, he had been studying this problem for three decades.

17. Joseph Fujikawa, interview with Windhorst, June 30, 1993.

18. Oral History of Charles Genther, p. 26; Architecture Department, Art Institute of Chicago.

19. In a 1964 interview, Mies discussed the advantages of steel: "It is very strong. It is very elegant. You can do a lot with it. The whole character of the building is very light. That is why I like it when I have to build a building in steel construction.... If you build in steel it gives you a lot of freedom inside.... Inside you can really do what you like.... But you are not free outside." Interview with Mies in John Peter's *The Oral History of Modern Architecture: Interviews with the Greatest Architects of the Twentieth Century* (New York: H. N. Abrams, 1994), pp. 167–68.

20. Mies, quoted in *Architectural Forum* 97, no. 5 (November 1952): 94.

21. Responding to the question of whether he had been influenced by Japanese architecture, Mies stated: "I have never seen any Japanese architecture. I was never in Japan. We do it by reason. Maybe the Japanese do it that way, too." Mies, interview with Cadbury-Brown (BBC), May 27, 1959.

22. Other architects were apparently considered. Greenwald was also charged with arranging financing for the entire development. The design team was drawn entirely from Promontory, with Mies again officially "design consultant."

23. The lighting was by New York designer Richard Kelly, whom Mies met through Philip Johnson. Kelly would also work with both men on the more famous lighting scheme for the Seagram Building.

24. A high-rise "moment frame" provides the necessary lateral bracing using rigid connections between columns and beams. In the case of 860, these connections are L-shaped steel brackets. Buildings taller than 860 usually require lateral systems of shear walls, diagonal braces, or an all-concrete core.

25. The buildings are said to have cost 10 percent less than comparable traditional structures, but this figure has been picked up from Greenwald's marketing materials. It would be impossible to support the claim, since comparable, equivalent "traditional" buildings of the same era do not exist.

26. A "W14" section is nominally fourteen inches from outside of flange to outside of flange. There are many different sections (of lesser or greater strength) available for the same nominal size, depending on the thickness of the flanges and web. For example, the mullions at 860 are W8 sections, and weigh 21 pounds per foot, hence "W8 × 21."

27. Bruno Conterato, interview with Windhorst, 1993.

28. Joseph Fujikawa, quoted in *Mies in America*, ed. Phyllis Lambert, Werner Oechslin, et al., an exhibition catalog (New York: H. N. Abrams, 2001), p. 362.

29. Mies, quoted in *Architectural Forum* 97, no. 5 (November 1952): 99. In the Mies literature, this quotation has been recirculated endlessly.

30. Windows next to columns are nine inches narrower than the middle two.

31. Fujikawa was a strong proponent of this view.

32. He also concealed the large wind-bracing brackets within the ceiling-to-floor sandwich.

33. In wrapping the short ends of the towers, Mies carried the frosted glass into the long elevations for one bay on each side. This left three bays of floor-to-ceiling clear glass centered on the long elevation, precisely the width of the short. Mies's interest in "bracketing" the ends of buildings in special fenestration goes back at least to the first IIT campus plan of 1939.

34. Robert McCormick Jr., recorded interview with Windhorst, 1992. Lambert incorrectly states that "the open plan was rejected by the financing institution." Lambert, Oechslin, et al., *Mies in America*, p. 367.

35. For the alternate interior layouts for the 860 building, referred to in the Mies office as "Building No. 2," see *The Mies van der Rohe Archive*, 14:173–88.

36. Caldwell added a dozen sugar maples and assorted hawthorns in a planting plan prepared in 1992.

37. Reproduced in *The Mies van der Rohe Archive*, 14:222. The apartment is misidentified on page 220—it was not on the twenty-sixth floor. Mies's sketch is also reproduced in Lambert, Oechslin, et al., *Mies in America*, p. 369.

38. It was thought that the owners could wash their own windows, so the large upper lights were made to open inward from the top. Even a feeble wind rendered the idea absurd, and the uppers were sealed permanently in the mid-1970s.

39. Remarks by Joseph Fujikawa (as noted by Windhorst) during a panel discussion March 9, 2002, at Chicago's Museum of Contemporary Art, in connection with the traveling exhibition *Mies in America*.

40. Myron Goldsmith, recorded interview with Windhorst, January 6, 1993.

41. Robert McCormick Jr., personal communication with Windhorst, 1991.

42. Robert McCormick Jr. went his own way after 860, and never worked with Greenwald again. He later developed the Borg-Warner Building across from the Art Institute of Chicago.

43. Bruno Conterato recalled: "Whatever Mies said or wanted to try we did. We would never have dreamt of saying, 'Mies, we have so many hours to do this, and we've got to reach a conclusion.' Mies was notorious for not making up his mind, and he had a host of ways to put off a decision." Conterato, interview with Windhorst, 1993. Gene Summers agreed: "[Mies] had no interest in or even the slightest remote thought of efficiency of an office as far as getting a job done. That just didn't enter his mind." Oral History of Gene Summers, p. 24.

44. The living room could not be at the corner.

45. Joseph Fujikawa, personal communication with Windhorst, 1992.

46. Mies, quoted in Lambert, Oechslin, et al., *Mies in America*, p. 512, n. 88.

47. See *The Mies van der Rohe Archive*, vol. 15 (New York: Garland, 1992), p. 527, for a photograph of this model.

48. "Greenwald Dies in Plane Crash," *Architectural Forum* 110 (March 1959): 65–66. See also Civil Aeronautics Board "Aircraft Accident Report," January 10, 1960, SA-339, File No. 1-0038.

49. According to Donald Sickler, who worked on the list of staff to be dismissed, there were nineteen layoffs (personal communication with Windhorst, April 2011). Mies's office was in and out of financial difficulties not only from its early days, when it might be expected, but also throughout the early 1960s. In the early years, Mies ran the office out of his personal finances. Fujikawa recalled that even after several years, Mies "never really figured out that the firm's money was not his own"; at the beginning of each year he would empty the office bank account for himself, creating an annual cash-flow crisis Fujikawa was powerless to stanch. Even with staff salaries at forty dollars a week as late as the early 1950s, a standard six-day workweek, and official time off only for Christmas, the office was barely solvent. Fujikawa, recorded interview with Windhorst, 1993.

50. See Charles Waldheim, ed., *Lafayette Park Detroit* (Munich: Prestel Verlag, 2004).

51. Hilberseimer and Caldwell were shaken by the atomic bombings of World War II. Their schemes for the decentralization of urban districts were much driven by these fears. See Dennis Domer, *Alfred Caldwell: The Life and Work of a Prairie School Landscape Architect* (Baltimore: Johns Hopkins University Press, 1997), pp. 43–44. Domer states that Caldwell, "with the encouragement of Mies and Hilberseimer," rushed to publish a decentralizing scheme in the December 1945 issue of the *Journal of the American Institute of Architects*. Hilberseimer's own essay of 1945, titled "Cities and Defense," is characteristically blunt: "With the advent of the airplane and in connection with the development of atomic weapons, the concentrated city becomes obsolete. . . . Today, security, once provided behind walls, can only be found in the dispersion of cities and industry." (Reprinted in Richard Pommer, David Spaeth, and Kevin Harrington, *In the Shadow of Mies: Ludwig Hilberseimer, Architect, Educator, and Urban Planner* [Chicago: The Art Institute of Chicago, in association with Rizzoli International Publications, Inc., 1988], p. 93.)

52. The McCormick House mullions are W8 × 24, those at 860–880 the slightly lighter W8 × 21 (*The Mies van der Rohe Archive*, 14:476). Structurally, the house's mullions were considered to be load bearing, which accounts for the difference. Kornacker was the structural engineer.

53. Robert McCormick Jr., interview with Windhorst, 1992.

54. See *The Mies van der Rohe Archive*, 14:422ff and 492ff.

55. Oral History of Myron Goldsmith, p. 74; Architecture Department, Art Institute of Chicago.

56. Myron Goldsmith, quoted in *The Mies van der Rohe Archive*, 15:54.

57. Oral History of Myron Goldsmith, pp. 73–74.

CHAPTER TWELVE

1. Crown Hall cost $746,850, according to Peter Carter, *Mies van der Rohe at Work* (New York: Praeger, 1974), p. 110.

2. "The Mecca's End," *Chicago Sun-Times*, December 30, 1951. See also the photo-essay by Wallace Kirkland, "The Mecca, Chicago's Showiest Apartment Has Given Up All but the Ghost," *Life*, November 19, 1951.

3. For more on the Mecca, see Daniel Bluestone, "Chicago's Mecca Flat Blues," *Journal of the Society of Architectural Historians* 57, no. 4 (December 1998).

4. Oral History of Reginald Malcolmson, p. 41; Architecture Department, Art Institute of Chicago.

5. See p. 518, n. 20 in Phyllis Lambert, "Space and Structure," in *Mies in America*, ed. Phyllis Lambert, Werner Oechslin, et al., an exhibition catalog (New York: H. N. Abrams, 2001).

6. Oral History of Reginald Malcolmson, pp. 92–93.

7. Minutes of the IIT Buildings and Grounds Committee, November 25, 1952; University Archives, Paul V. Galvin Library, IIT; cited in Lambert, "Space and Structure," p. 447.

8. Oral History of Gene Summers, p. 58; Architecture Department, Art Institute of Chicago.

9. Mies, interview with Cadbury-Brown (BBC), May 27, 1959.

10. See p. 518, n. 207 of Lambert, "Space and Structure," interview of Joseph Fujikawa by Kevin Harrington. Dirk Lohan, in discussion with the authors May 3, 2011, disputed Fujikawa's claim that the two-foot reduction was driven by glazing parameters; he argued that it was to reduce building cost overall, and that thinner glass was "a by-product of the height reduction."

11. Mies, quoted by Donald Hoffmann, *Kansas City Times*, July 17, 1963.

12. Oral History of Jacques Brownson, p. 131; Architecture Department, Art Institute of Chicago.

13. Ludwig Hilberseimer, *Mies van der Rohe* (Chicago: Paul Theobald, 1956), p. 51.

14. The authors gratefully acknowledge the assistance of structural engineer Koz Sowlat, who at our request analyzed Crown Hall using modern methods.

15. "Notes from a manuscript by Paul Pippin describing his graduate studies at I.I.T. under Mies," 1946/47, unpaginated typescript and longhand; Mies van der Rohe Archive, Museum of Modern Art, New York.

16. Oral History of Myron Goldsmith, p. 47; Architecture Department, Art Institute of Chicago.

17. Edward A. Duckett and Joseph Y. Fujikawa, *Impressions of Mies: An Interview on Mies van der Rohe; His Early Chicago Years 1938-1958* [n.p., 1988], p. 14. The statement "We don't do that here!" appears to be a standard—indeed characteristic—Mies utterance. Witness the report of James Ferris, then a beginning student who worked on models for the 1947 MoMA show: "Ed Duckett ... gave me these model cars and said, 'I want three of these painted black, three white, and three for the Cantor model in gray.' He said, 'Here's the paint. Just let them dry and when they are ready, give me notice and we'll pick them up.' I painted them exactly the way he wanted.... I had one car left over and I thought it was a little dumb that the old stodgy museum wouldn't go for two-tone cars.... I had a little paint so I was painting this one car two-toned and Mies happened by.... He said, 'Vee don't do dot.' I said, 'Oh, I'm sorry, I was just ...' He said, 'Yah, vee don't do dot.' I could never say that this car was left over and I was only fooling around." Oral History of James Ferris, pp. 16–17; Architecture Department, Art Institute of Chicago.

18. Edward Duckett, interview with Windhorst, 1992.

19. The project chronology is in Lambert, "Space and Structure," p. 439. The most detailed account of the competition is Thilo Hilpert's *Mies van der Rohe im Nachkriegsdeutschland—Das Theaterprojekt Mannheim 1953* (Leipzig: E. A. Seeman, 2002). For Crown Hall, see below.

20. Competitors could select from several sites, but this was the most promising, and the one later built on.

21. Mies offered an uncharacteristically detailed design rationale as part of his competition submittal, which also included drawings, model photographs, and the spectacular model itself, which was shipped to Mannheim and remained there. Mies's remarks are reprinted in "A Proposed National Theater for the City of Mannheim," *Architectural Design* 70 (October 1953): 17–19, and were offered simultaneously in German in the Swiss journal *Werk* 10 (1953): 314.

22. The calculation: 516 square meters times two floors versus 25,600 square meters gross area = 4%.

23. Edward Duckett, personal communication with Windhorst, 1993.

24. Oral History of Myron Goldsmith, p. 50. Goldsmith may not have known of Hirche's role or the details of Weber's late entry.

25. See Lambert, "Space and Structure," p. 519, n. 233. Lambert also identifies IIT's president, Henry Heald, as "chairman of the Council of the South Side Planning Board, 1946–52" (p. 326, n. 9).

26. The "first" McCormick Place was completed in 1959 to a design by Shaw, Metz and Associates. Thought to be fireproof because of its steel-and-concrete construction, it was completely destroyed in a 1967 fire.

27. Yujiro Miwa, Henry Kanazawa, and Pao-Chi Chang, "A Convention Hall, A Co-operative Project" (master's thesis, IIT, June 1954). Mies and Frank Kornacker were advisors (cited in Lambert, Oechslin, et al., *Mies in America*, p. 519, n. 238).

28. Gene Summers, working for C. F. Murphy and Associates, designed and realized such a hall in 1971 for McCormick Place in Chicago. The 150-foot spans between columns were structurally rational and programmatically justified—indeed, three further major additions to McCormick Place, totaling over 2 million square feet of exhibition space, have adopted similar spacing.

29. Mies, quoted in Peter Carter, "Mies van der Rohe," *Architectural Design* 31 (March 1961): 116.

Mies's proposition is false, for "they" were not "able to do anything," at least not technically, in the periods in question.

30. Mies, interview with students of the Architectural League of New York, 1951; Mies van der Rohe Archive, Museum of Modern Art, New York.

31. Excepting the design of his own offices.

32. There are qualified exceptions. The Robert H. McCormick Jr. House in Elmhurst, Illinois, was dismantled in 1994 and moved a few blocks, where it was reassembled, with modifications, to serve as a wing of the Elmhurst Art Museum. The steel and much of the interior was saved, but the masonry was abandoned and built anew at the museum's site. In 2010 the so-called Test Cell, a tiny building built into the corner of a surrounding wall at IIT's Boiler Plant, was demolished to make way for a new transit station.

33. The drawings are reproduced in *The Mies van der Rohe Archive*, vol. 14 (New York: Garland, 1992), pp. 241–42 and 273–301. The most developed plan is 4812.309, p. 280 (undated). The alternate scheme is mixed in with sheets for the 109 East Ontario space. None is a working drawing.

34. As reported by Richard Christiansen in the *Chicago Tribune*, December 31, 1989, p. 1.

35. Buck claimed he had donated $50,000 to save the original. Personal communication with Schulze, 2005.

36. Gordon Bunshaft of Skidmore, Owings & Merrill was more critical: "I find Illinois Tech an ugly affair, barren.... I think [it's] partially barren because there was very little money. [Mies] had no choice but to do that. A few of them don't work with all this glass. [Crown Hall] I don't think is anything. It's just a big room." Oral History of Gordon Bunshaft, pp. 137–38; Architecture Department, Art Institute of Chicago.

37. Reproduced in *The Mies van der Rohe Archive*, vol. 12 (New York: Garland, 1992), p. 153, drawing 4903.25.

38. Oral History of Gene Summers, p. 34: "Mies really was not interested in lighting. He knew what he liked and what he didn't, but neither he nor anybody else in the office knew very much about designing lighting."

39. Rettaliata, IIT's second president, served from 1952 to 1973. He held a Ph.D. degree in fluid dynamics from Johns Hopkins University.

40. As Mies's chief academic assistant at the time, Reginald Malcolmson had this view of Rettaliata: "Many people in the architecture school felt Rettaliata didn't understand or care. He didn't even, they thought, want to understand." Oral History of Reginald Malcolmson, p. 83; Architecture Department, Art Institute of Chicago.

41. Donald Sickler identified himself as this "junior architect." Sickler, personal communication with Windhorst, Baltimore, July 29, 2008.

42. Original typescript; box 33, File: "General Office File, I.I.T., General 1949–59, No. 1," Papers of Ludwig Mies van der Rohe, Manuscript Division, Library of Congress.

43. Lora Marx, interview with Schulze, 1980.

44. Oral History of William Hartmann, pp. 129–30; Architecture Department, Art Institute of Chicago.

45. Mies, letter to Gordon Bunshaft, September 2, 1958; box 21, Papers of Ludwig Mies van der Rohe, Manuscript Division, Library of Congress.

46. Oral History of Alfred Caldwell, p. 87; Architecture Department, Art Institute of Chicago.

47. SOM had worked at IIT long before Mies's retirement. The firm designed a dormitory, Gunsaulus Hall, completed in 1949. The building was widely panned, and Mies's office designed the three nearby mid-rise dormitories, in the manner of Promontory, in the early 1950s.

48. Oral History of William Hartmann, p. 132.

49. Phyllis Bronfman Lambert, interview with Schulze, November 11, 1991; quoted in Franz Schulze, *Philip Johnson: Life and Work* (New York: Alfred A. Knopf, 1994), p. 243.

50. Lambert, recorded interview with the authors, Montreal, January 2005.

51. Reginald Malcolmson recalled that as early as 1947, on the occasion of first meeting Mies, he noticed his "arthritis problem." It had progressed severely by the next decade: "[In the middle 50s Mies] was going through . . . a very bad crisis with the arthritis and taking very strong doses of cortisone. I remember one time going to see him, and I went to shake hands with him and he said, 'I'm sorry, I can't. My hand has turned black.'" Oral History of Reginald Malcolmson, pp. 40 and 76.

52. Phyllis Bronfman Lambert, letter to Eve Borsook, December 1, 1954; quoted in "How a Building Gets Built," *Vassar Alumnae*, February 1959, p. 17.

53. Park Avenue between Grand Central Terminal and Ninety-Sixth Street runs above tunneled railroad tracks. At the time Grand Central was built (between 1903 and 1913), the section south of Fifty-Ninth Street was placed underground and electrified. Elimination of steam locomotives transformed this once undesirable section of Park Avenue into prime real estate. The tracks are the reason the grade drops to the east over the Seagram site.

54. Summers reported Mies's pride in the bronze exterior: "Mies and I were approaching the building, which was up only about eight stories. He touched my arm and said '*Ja*, it looks like a good old penny!'" Summers, personal communication with Windhorst, October 2009.

55. One of these clear-span rooms became the famous Four Seasons Restaurant, since 1989 an official New York City "interior landmark," designed by Johnson with furniture by Mies. The transfers carry columns of the bustle, *not* of the 39-story tower.

56. Gene Summers, personal communication with Schulze, March 2, 1981.

57. Philip Johnson, personal communication with Schulze, April 23, 1981.

58. The infill was not marble but a stone called "serpentine," denser than marble and less likely to spall. Summers, personal communication with Windhorst, September 2009.

59. But Summers was not involved in Seagram at the beginning. "I didn't have anything to do with the overall scheme of the building; that was done by the time I arrived [after military service in Korea]. My work really ended up as taking that concept from the model and getting it developed. . . . We had an office that I was more or less in charge of. I say more or less because when I went there David Haid was there, and Ed Duckett. Mies eventually sent them back and I stayed. I had one other person out of the Chicago office, Henry Kanazawa, and the rest of the people were all local New Yorkers, some of whom were from Philip Johnson's office. After a while I ended up being in charge of that." Oral History of Gene Summers, p. 38.

60. Phyllis Bronfman Lambert, interview with the authors, Montreal, January 2005.

61. Gene Summers, personal communication with Schulze, March 2, 1981.

62. Gordon Bunshaft also lobbied the senior Bronfman to spurn the bank's proposal. The bank had approached Bronfman after the building was under construction, and according to Summers, "it became quite an issue." Personal communication with Gene Summers, October 2009.

63. Philip Johnson, personal communication with Schulze, September 23, 1993. Johnson quoted from Robert Stern, ed., *The Philip Johnson Tapes: Interviews by Robert A. M. Stern* (New York: Monacelli Press, in association with the Temple Hoyne Buell Center for the Study of American Architecture, 2008), pp. 149–50.

64. Philip Johnson, quoted in Stern, *The Philip Johnson Tapes*, p. 150.

65. In our interview with Lambert in Montreal in 2005, she recalled a follow-up conversation with Mies: "I asked him the next day, or a few days later, I said, 'Mies, why did you get so angry?' And he said—this is so wonderful—he said, 'It was not right of Philip to criticize Berlage in front of you.' They were all worried about my education."

66. Mies, interview with Dirk Lohan (German-language typescript, Chicago, summer 1968); Mies van der Rohe Archive, Museum of Modern Art, New York.

CHAPTER THIRTEEN

1. Lora Marx, interview with Schulze, September 16, 1980.

2. Seven honorary doctorates were bestowed on him in the 1960s, as well as memberships in professional societies and gold medals from the American Institute of Architects, the Architectural League of New York, the National Institute of Arts and Letters, and the Institute of German Architects. His most prized awards were the highest civilian peacetime decorations of his two countries: the Knight Commander's Cross of the German Order of Merit and the Presidential Medal of Freedom of the United States. Notification of the latter came from President John F. Kennedy four months before his assassination. The medal was presented by President Lyndon Johnson in 1964. Subsequently, Mies was one of the architects considered for the design of the Kennedy Library, the one major commission of his last years that he wanted and did not receive. The commission went to I. M. Pei, though Pei himself said to Mrs. Kennedy that "the job should probably go to Mies as the most prominent of the contenders." But Mrs. Kennedy was not impressed by the seventy-eight-year old Mies: she said he reminded her of "an Egyptian potentate," and "conveyed a sense that he didn't really want the job." Kennedy quotes from Carter Wiseman's *I. M. Pei* (New York: Abram, 1990), pp. 98–99.

3. The City of Chicago bestowed a similar honor on Mies, posthumously in 1986, the year of his centenary, when it renamed North Seneca Street, which Mies's Pearson Street apartment looked out on, Mies van der Rohe Way.

4. "Aus der Wüste in der Städte," *Deutsche Zeitung*, June 6, 1959.

5. Another death affecting Mies in 1959 was that of the structural engineer Frank Kornacker.

6. As a manager, Conterato was an eager understudy. He recalled how Mies would handle a client: "The owner would say 'I don't like this, it bothers me, we should change it.' Mies never argued. He would say '*Ja*, we'll look at it.' Then he would have another meeting, and never bring up that subject. He would have new things, and he would keep going until this guy would either forget about it or give up. Mies knew when to do this. He very rarely had to make a knock-down drag-out battle of anything. And if he did lose, he would simply say, 'We lost that battle, we've got to do the best we can.'" Bruno Conterato, interview with Windhorst, 1993.

7. Oral History of Gene Summers, p. 72; Architecture Department, Art Institute of Chicago.

8. Ibid.

9. Almost fifty years after the fact, Gene Summers offered his own take on how politics intertwined with the preparation and selection of the three concept schemes: "The GSA [General Services Administration of the federal government] was in charge of this project. The project director was an older man who was also very stubborn. He insisted that the buildings go from property line to property line—in other words, no plazas. The real reason for Scheme A [with the open block to the west] was to make Scheme B more plausible. No one anticipated that [Senator Everett McKinley] Dirksen would support Scheme A as strongly as he did. At the time, we were unaware that this building would be named after him. As it worked out, Scheme B was chosen. The old man at GSA was furious, but he couldn't overrule Dirksen." Summers, personal communication with Windhorst, October 2009.

10. Why, then, was bronze used to clad the structural steel of the Seagram Building?

11. Mies had no knowledge of any art program planned for the complex. "It was Carter Manny's idea ... after Mies had died.... All the buildings were finished, and Carter had this idea. They asked me, 'Who do you think?' and I said, 'I think it'd be appropriate for Calder because he was a good friend of Mies's. He liked Calder's work and it had the scale....' I think it's absolutely great, the scarlet red and the black building. I'm sure Mies would have been very happy with it." Oral History of Gene Summers, p. 74.

12. In the *Life* article (pp. 60–69), Mies's few quotations are standard fare: "In our work we don't have a grand idea, a dream, and then try to glue it together.... We just solve problems." "Romanticists don't like my buildings. They say they are cold and rigid. But we do not build for fun. We build for a purpose." "We are not trying to please people. We are driving to the essence of things."

13. Oral History of Gene Summers, p. 50.

14. Gene Summers, "A Letter to Son," *A + U* [Architecture and Urbanism] (January 1981): 182–83.

15. Oral History of Gene Summers, p. 52.

16. Oral History of Gene Summers, p. 59. Mies certainly liked the design. Summers reported the following—perhaps tongue-in-cheek—exchange: "Mies, about Bacardi: 'We'd better get this built soon before Skidmore [Owings & Merrill] copies us.' Summers: 'Mies, we need to worry when they *stop* copying us.'" Summers, personal communication with Windhorst, October 2009.

17. The lower, opaque walls were intended to allow the location of art and sculpture at the interior of the building's perimeter.

18. Oral History of Gene Summers, p. 61.

19. Schaefer's museum was finally realized, in 1997, to a design by Volker Staab Architects of Berlin.

20. Mies, quoted in the documentary film *Mies van der Rohe*, directed by Georgia van der Rohe, sponsored by Knoll International and Zweites Deutsches Fernsehen, Mainz, produced by IFAGE Filmproduktion, Wiesbaden; English version, 1979, German version, 1980.

21. This account of Mies's in-house modeling is drawn from an interview with Dirk Lohan by the authors May 3, 2011; the Oral History of Gene Summers; and an excellent technical summary in *Mies in America*, ed. Phyllis Lambert, Werner Oechslin, et al., an exhibition catalog (New York: H. N. Abrams, 2001), pp. 493–94.

22. Mies, in the documentary film *Mies van der Rohe*.

23. Julius Posener, personal communication with Schulze, June 24, 1982.

24. Gene Summers, personal communication with Schulze, March 2, 1981, and handwritten notes by Summers (by personal communication) titled "McCormick Place," June 1985, 31 pp.

25. Ibid.

26. Ibid. See also the Oral History of Gene Summers, p. 20, where Summers remarks that in the sixteen years he worked in the office, he was praised by Mies only three times.

27. Robert Venturi, *Complexity and Contradiction in Architecture*, Museum of Modern Art Papers on Architecture, no. 1 (New York: Museum of Modern Art, 1966), p. 16. In an article titled "Mies Media," *Journal of Architectural Historians* 66, no. 1 (March 2007), Dietrich Neumann reviews films about Mies. Discussing the film directed by Michael Blackwood, Neumann states (pp. 16–17): "Contemporary critics also have their say—after all, the postmodern movement was still very much alive in 1986—and so we hear ... Robert Venturi poignantly express his regrets over mocking Mies's 'less is more' dictum as 'less is a bore.' '[A]ll architects should kiss the feet of Mies van der Rohe,' he says in perfect seriousness."

28. Philip Johnson, quoted in Franz Schulze, *Philip Johnson: Life and Work* (New York: Alfred A. Knopf, 1994), p. 333.

29. Peter Palumbo, in "Mies van der Rohe Mansion House Square: The Client," *UIA International Architect*, no. 3 (1984): 23.

30. Ibid., p. 24.

31. Stephen Gardiner, "Mies in the London Jungle," *Spectator*, November 1, 1968. Gardiner's article is reprinted in Peter Carter, *Mies van der Rohe at Work* (New York: Praeger, 1974), pp. 182–83. The quotation above is on p. 183.

32. Oral History of Gene Summers, p. 75.

33. Oral History of Joseph Fujikawa, p. 21; Architecture Department, Art Institute of Chicago.

34. Conterato retired as chairman of Lohan Associates in 1991. Lohan's subsequent partners have changed several times; at this writing he heads the firm Lohan Anderson.

CHAPTER FOURTEEN

1. Oral History of Gordon Bunshaft, p. 136; Architecture Department, Art Institute of Chicago.

2. Cited in *Mies in America*, ed. Phyllis Lambert, Werner Oechslin, et al., an exhibition catalog (New York: H. N. Abrams, 2001), p. 571.

3. Oral History of Gene Summers, p. 69; Architecture Department, Art Institute of Chicago.

4. Mies did business in the United States as "Mies van der Rohe—Architect." In Germany he was "Mies van der Rohe—Architekt." In 1969 the firm name was changed to the Office of Mies van der Rohe. See above for details of the name and partnership change.

5. Interview of Mies for the aluminum industry, 1960, New York City, recorded by Peter Associates, p. 63; box 62, Papers of Ludwig Mies van der Rohe, Manuscript Division, Library of Congress.

6. Ibid., p. 21.

7. George Schipporeit, who worked on the Newark buildings in Mies's office, later adapted this idea for his own Lake Point Tower project in Chicago. See appendix A.

8. Joseph Fujikawa, quoted in *The Mies van der Rohe Archive*, vol. 17 (New York: Garland, 1992), p. 324. The recollection was made to George Danforth. The Mies van der Rohe Archive at the Museum of Modern Art, New York, contains the working drawings for the Newark project and for Lafayette Park, and we can compare the curtain wall detail sheets from both projects. Save for one additional detail for Newark and the change of title block, the sheets are *identical*. See *Archive*, 16:656, drawing 6002.71 for Lafayette Park, and 17:412, drawing 5801.40 for Newark.

9. These words, among Mies's most quoted, are from his American Institute of Architects Gold Medal Speech, April 1960, San Francisco; box 61, Ludwig Mies van der Rohe Papers, Manuscript Division, Library of Congress.

> I have been asked many times by students, architects and interested laymen:
> "Where do we go from here?"
> Certainly it is [neither] necessary nor possible to invent a new kind of architecture every Monday morning.
> We are not at the end, but at the beginning of an Epoch;
> An Epoch which will be guided by a new spirit
> Which will be driven by new forces, new technological, sociological and economic forces,
> And which will have new tools and new materials.
> For this reason, we will have a new architecture.

10. Gene Summers, personal communication with Windhorst, September 2009.

11. The truss scheme's upper floor was 128 by 192 feet, or 24,500 square feet, and the long direction filled the site. The building as built has a 14,400-square-foot floor plate, and a large paved plaza.

12. The wood version was also carefully detailed. See the plans in *The Mies van der Rohe Archive*, vol. 18 (New York: Garland, 1992), pp. 167–68.

13. Interview with Mies in John Peter's *The Oral History of Modern Architecture: Interviews with the Greatest Architects of the Twentieth Century* (New York: H. N. Abrams, 1994), p. 172.

14. American codes of the period would typically have required fire-rated exit stairs from the second floor, and these core elements would be expected to handle this requirement. But in Mexico City Mies was not so constrained, and exiting is handled entirely via the pair of architectural stairs in the open well of the interior.

15. *The Mies van der Rohe Archive*, vol. 17 (New York: Garland, 1992), p. 12.

16. Metropolitan Structures was headed by Bernard Weissbourd, Herbert Greenwald's attorney and partner.

17. The reentrant corner detail is on Sheet A-23 of the construction documents, reproduced in *The Mies van der Rohe Archive*, 18:270.

18. There was opposition to an apartment building in this mostly residential area (the site had been occupied by an old mansion), and it was felt that the city would not approve a curtain-wall building in this location. The brick spandrels in the south elevation, which are higher than those on the other three—there is another tall building adjacent—were dictated by the city, ostensibly for reasons of fire safety. Donald Sickler, personal communication with Windhorst, 2008.

19. Ada Louise Huxtable, "Mies: Lessons from the Master," *New York Times*, February 6, 1966, pp. 24–25.

20. The entire Federal Center received a comprehensive exterior renovation ending in 2012.

21. *Regular or Super: A Film by Joseph Hillel and Patrick Demers* (Icarus Films, 2004).

22. The onyx walls at Barcelona and Brno were solid stone. Mies's other stone walls are veneers.

23. The Verseidag Factory, Mies's largest realized European building, is an exception, though his role as designer was limited due to the building's standardized type.

CHAPTER FIFTEEN

1. According to Lora Marx, Mies had cataracts. Though he never lost his sight completely, it became quite limited. "I would sit at one end of his black couch, he at the other. 'Do you recognize me?' Answer, 'No.'" Lora Marx, interview with Schulze, June 17, 1980.

2. Lora recalled that Mies tried to design sunglasses during one of their stays in Tucson. "He sent his driver everywhere to find sunglasses for comparison purposes. He wanted to make the 'perfect pair'—in one piece." Ibid.

3. Summers reported that "he was very interested in astronomy and the whole idea of [the Big Bang,] how the world started." Ibid., p. 16. Marx agreed: "Whenever anyone didn't know what to give him as a gift, they would give him a book, especially a book about the universe." Lora Marx, interview with Schulze, June 17, 1980.

4. Lora Marx, interview with Schulze, June 17, 1980.

5. The UIC collection contains about six hundred volumes. It does not constitute Mies's complete American library, however. Dirk Lohan retains approximately one hundred volumes, many of which are fine or rare editions, and some of which were gifts to Mies.

6. Oral History of Gene Summers, p. 16.

7. Reginald Malcolmson, "A Paradox of Humility and Superstar," *Inland Architect* (May 1977): 16.

8. Joseph Fujikawa, in Edward A. Duckett and Joseph Y. Fujikawa, *Impressions of Mies: An Interview on Mies van der Rohe; His Early Chicago Years 1938-1958* [n.p., 1988], p. 6.

9. Cited in Helmut Reuter and Birgit Schulte, eds., *Mies and Modern Living* (Ostfildern, Germany: Hatje Cantz, 2008), p. 206, and p. 207, n. 51. The Reich material *did* end up in the Mies van der Rohe Archive at the Museum of Modern Art, New York.

10. Vivian Endicott Barnett, "The Architect as Collector," in *Mies in America*, ed. Phyllis Lambert, Werner Oechslin, et al., an exhibition catalog (New York: H. N. Abrams, 2001), p. 93.

11. "Notes from a manuscript by Paul Pippin describing his graduate studies at I.I.T. under Mies," 1946/47, unpaginated typescript and longhand; Mies van der Rohe Archive, Museum of Modern Art, New York.

12. Oral History of Gene Summers, p. 67.

13. Oral History of Paul Schweickher, p. 116; Architecture Department, Art Institute of Chicago.

14. The remainder of the collection warrants comment. In 1941, after Mies had lent Kandinsky's *Winter II* of 1911 to an exhibition at Nierendorf's New York gallery, the dealer exchanged it for another canvas by the same painter, *Herbstlandschaft* (*Autumn Landscape*), completed the same day, January 31, 1911. In 1948 Mies bought from Valentin a *papier collé* cubist still life, *Bouteille et Verre* (*Bottle and Glass*), by Georges Braque.

15. Barnett, "The Architect as Collector," p. 116.

16. Mies's art collection was appraised shortly after his death. On December 19, 1969, an "appraisal in the estate of Mies van der Rohe" was filed in the Circuit Court of Cook County, Illinois, by Matthew J. Danaher, clerk of the Circuit Court, Probate Division:

> Works of Art (Paintings and Collages) appraised (and signed) by Irving S. Tarrant:
> [Total appraised value:] $151,600.
> Oil on canvas: "Bust of a Woman in Colors" (known also as "Buste de Femme II") by Pablo Picasso, executed March 27, 1956: $45,000
> Oil on canvas: "Bewegliche zu Starrem" ("From the Movable to the Static"), by Paul Klee, executed 1932: $22,000
> Oil on canvas: "Umfangen" ("The Embrace"), by Paul Klee, executed circa 1932: $25,000
> Oil on rough hemp: "Die Frucht" ("The Fruit"), by Paul Klee, executed 1932: $35,000
> Oil on canvas: "Reclining Nude, with Mask," by Max Beckmann, executed 1934: $20,000
> Collage: "Black Collage" (1928) by Kurt Schwitters: $1,500
> Collage: "The A Book" (1942) by Kurt Schwitters: $1,000
> Collage: "Cottage" (1946) by Kurt Schwitters: $900
> Collage: "Alma Gassert" (1921) by Kurt Schwitters: $1,200

Without reflecting in detail on the current value of the above—surely into the several millions of dollars—the most dubious of Tarrant's appraisals is that of the Beckmann nude, unquestionably a major work by a major painter. In addition, Tarrant included among "butler's pantry and kitchen" items a lithograph by well-known Chicago artist Misch Kohn, *Little Herald*, certainly worth more than $35.

17. For a fuller treatment of Mies as an art collector, including images of most of his collection, see Barnett, "The Architect as Art Collector." We rely on some of Barnett's research in the paragraphs above.

18. As of 2012, the Art Institute of Chicago had conducted 89 architect oral histories over twenty-eight years. Mies's influence is reflected in the fact that 78 of the 89 architects discuss Mies in their recorded remarks.

19. For Joseph Fujikawa, however, "seldom" was not "never": "Well, he had his moments. He could flare up. If he didn't like something we had done ... he'd blow up. After all, he was only a human being." Oral History of Joseph Fujikawa, p. 22; Architecture Department, Art Institute of Chicago.

20. Tim Samuelson, in *This American Life*, Ira Glass video, 2006.

21. Tim Samuelson, personal communication with Schulze, 2007.

22. "Mies van der Rohe's New Buildings," *Architectural Forum* (November 1952): 94.

23. Oral History of Bruce Graham, p. 18; Architecture Department, Art Institute of Chicago. Graham: "I saw him speak once ... in German, and he was a blabbermouth then."

24. Dirk Lohan, interview with the authors, May 3, 2011. Mies was aware of the difficulty of clear expression in *any* language. He told the following joke to the architect Paul Schweikher: "Ach," he said, "I once asked Rudolph Schwarz why he didn't learn English. Schwarz said, 'As a born German, I have enough trouble speaking German.'" Oral History of Paul Schweikher, pp. 182–83.

25. Joseph Fujikawa, in Duckett and Fujikawa, *Impressions of Mies*, pp. 20–21.

26. Oral History of Reginald Malcolmson, pp. 49–50; Architecture Department, Art Institute of Chicago.

27. Oral History of Werner Buch, p. 5; Architecture Department, Art Institute of Chicago.

28. Peter Roesch, personal communication with Schulze, October 2008.

29. Oral History of James Hammond, p. 15; Architecture Department, Art Institute of Chicago.

30. Oral History of Gene Summers, pp. 12–13.

31. Interview with Gene Summers by Gunny Harboe, September 20, 2000, in S. R. Crown Hall: Historic Structure[s] Report, prepared by the McClier Corporation for Illinois Institute of Technology, October 24, 2000 (unpublished typescript with figures and drawings). Copy in Galvin Resource Center, College of Architecture, IIT.

32. Duckett and Fujikawa, in *Impressions of Mies*, p. 33.

33. Oral History of Reginald Malcolmson, p. 49.

34. Ibid., p. 94.

35. Fujikawa, in Duckett and Fujikawa, *Impressions of Mies*, p. 12.

36. Robert McCormick Jr., recorded interview with Windhorst, 1992.

37. William C. Murphy, interview with the authors, October 13, 2005.

38. Peter Roesch, personal communication with Schulze, October 2008.

39. Lora Marx, interview with Schulze, September 23, 1980.

40. Oral History of Ambrose Richardson, 1990, p. 58; Architecture Department, Art Institute of Chicago.

41. Oral History of Reginald Malcolmson, p. 81.

42. His favorite gin late in life was Seagram's, for obvious reasons. His standard martini was a "Gibson," in which a pickled onion served as the garnish.

43. Lora Marx, interview with Schulze, September 23, 1980.

44. "Another thing he liked was Steinhägers, which is a Bremen drink. It's sort of like very powerful plain liquor. You drink it with a beer chaser." Oral History of Gordon Bunshaft, p. 135; Architecture Department, Art Institute of Chicago.

45. Malcolmson, "A Paradox of Humility and Superstar," 16–19.

46. Written in longhand, with each remark dated. We print here only a selection. Original given to Schulze during a series of interviews in 1980–81.

47. Lora Marx, interview with Schulze, September 16, 1980.

48. Lora Marx, interview with Schulze, June 17, 1980.

49. Ibid.

50. Dr. George Allen, personal communication with Schulze, December 1984.

51. Indeed, within sight of another grave with connections far more personal to Mies. One of the stones a few hundred feet away is marked "Edith Brooks Farnsworth, Nov. 17 1903 — Dec. 5 1977." Since it is part of the Brooks family plot (103 E and F), and Edith is interred next to her brother, mother, and father, there is no reason to suspect that she was party to a posthumous reconciliation with her old antagonist. The authors are grateful to Algis Novickas for pointing out the location of Farnsworth's grave.

52. James Johnson Sweeney, eulogy at Mies memorial service, Crown Hall, IIT, October 25, 1969; Mies van der Rohe Archive, Museum of Modern Art, New York. Sweeney's remarks are reprinted in Peter Carter's *Mies van der Rohe at Work* (New York: Praeger, 1974), pp. 183–84.

53. Interview (1955) with Mies in John Peter's *The Oral History of Modern Architecture: Interviews with the Greatest Architects of the Twentieth Century* (New York: H. N. Abrams, 1994), p. 173.

54. Fritz Neumeyer, *The Artless Word: Mies van der Rohe on the Building Art*, trans. Mark Jarzombek (German edition, 1986; Cambridge, MA: MIT Press, 1991), p. 299.

55. Ibid., p. 324.

APPENDIX A

1. Mies wanted Goldsmith to return to the office, and in his own way tried to woo him back. Through Joseph Fujikawa, Mies made laconic pleas: "I want you to know that we are waiting for you," for example, in a letter dated August 22, 1956 (box 29, Papers of Ludwig Mies van der Rohe, Manuscript Division, Library of Congress). Fujikawa told Goldsmith that Mies "still wanted to explore new things," and that he needed Goldsmith to do so. Gene Summers, in his Oral History (p. 20; Architecture Department, Art Institute of Chicago), described Mies's view of Goldsmith: "Certainly Goldsmith was a person that he admired, there's no doubt about that."

2. Oral History of Myron Goldsmith, p. 87; Architecture Department, Art Institute of Chicago. Fujikawa had a similar take on Mies's methodology: "In problem solving, Mies always took the approach of not jumping to a solution or an answer immediately. That would disturb him tremendously, because he'd say, 'What have I forgotten?' So his approach in problem solving, which we used so much, was to say, 'What else is possible? Regardless of how bad you think it might be, put it on paper.' He said 'We'll put them all down. If you have six possibilities, put them all down. If you have ten, put them down. Whatever you think is possible, try it.' If you had an idea, all he'd say was, 'Try it.' You know, he gave you that freedom. Then by a process of elimination, we'd line them all up and say, 'This one is better than that one because . . .' so that one goes out. Pretty soon you might end up, hopefully, with one or two good possibilities, and then he would say, 'Well, let's take it another step and see which is better, this one or this one.' . . . That was his whole process of working on design problems in architecture." Oral History of Joseph Fujikawa, p. 13; Architecture Department, Art Institute of Chicago.

3. Myron Goldsmith, recorded interview with Windhorst, January 15, 1994.

4. Lora Marx and Mies visited Kitt Peak to see Goldsmith's telescope. The date of this trip has not been determined. Lora Marx, interview with Schulze, 1980.

5. From Allan Temko's introduction to *Myron Goldsmith: Buildings and Concepts*, ed. Werner Blaser (Basel: Birkhäuser Verlag, 1986), p. 7. "Ronchamp" is the chapel of Notre Dame du Haut, Ronchamp, France, designed by Le Corbusier.

6. Oral History of Natalie De Blois, p. 85; Architecture Department, Art Institute of Chicago.

7. A tower's shape and aspect ratio were also critical variables.

8. Myron Goldsmith, interview with Windhorst, 1993.

9. Oral History of Bruce Graham, p. 152; Architecture Department, Art Institute of Chicago.

10. Setbacks would have been the conventional solution. Graham would use them for the even taller Sears Tower in Chicago, completed to his design in 1974.

11. Efforts to prevent oil-canning (waviness in flat metal sheets) of the cladding were a failure. SOM specified a magnetic stainless steel (standard stainless is nonmagnetic) that was critical to a process in which the column cladding was to be shop fabricated. The cladding was designed to have a backup of concrete a few inches thick. The stainless was first laid out on a large, absolutely flat magnetic plate, which was intended to keep the cladding flat while the concrete was poured and cured. But the break forming of the cladding corners introduced large internal stresses in the plate, which the concrete could not resist.

12. There has been lively disagreement about design credit for the Civic Center as between SOM and C. F. Murphy. The most reliable reporting can be found in the Oral History of Carter Manny, pp. 250–53 (Architecture Department, Art Institute of Chicago), where he concludes—we believe authoritatively—that despite early input from SOM, the building is Brownson's design.

13. Brownson's unpublished Master of Science in Architecture thesis, dated June 1954, is titled "A Steel and Glass House." A copy is in the Graham Resource Center of IIT's College of Architecture. In common with other theses under Mies or Hilberseimer, the text is, rhetorically, pure Mies. Brownson concludes his twelve-page project description as follows: "The possibilities of this concept of building are infinite. The refinement and development necessary in any building era will come from hard work, character, and a clear understanding of the problems and forces shaping our times."

14. Mies's American students were prolific designers of their own Mies-inspired houses. The list includes Daniel Brenner, Alfred Caldwell, Bruno Conterato, Joseph Fujikawa, David Haid, James Hammond, Gerald Horn, David Hovey, Carter Manny, Edward Olencki, H. P. Rockwell, George Schipporeit, Paul Thomas, Y. C. Wong, and Paul Zorr.

15. Oswald W. Grube, Peter C. Pran, and Franz Schulze, *100 Years of Architecture in Chicago: Continuity of Structure and Form; Exhibited at the Museum of Contemporary Art, Chicago*, an exhibition catalog (Chicago: Follett, 1977), p. 58.

16. Cor-Ten had been used, famously, for Eero Saarinen's John Deere headquarters in Moline, Illinois, only two years before. The Daley Center was its largest building application to that date.

17. Among SOM's leadership in the 1950s and '60s, William Hartmann enjoyed a personal triumph when he persuaded Pablo Picasso to produce a maquette that was the basis of the monumental sculpture unveiled in 1967 in the plaza in front of the Civic Center.

18. Oral History of Jacques Brownson, p. 191; Architecture Department, Art Institute of Chicago. Joseph Fujikawa, in his Oral History, p. 21, confirms Mies's reaction: "Jack Brownson . . . designed it, but Mies said, 'I couldn't do it better myself,' which is a real compliment to Jack."

19. Oral History of Jacques Brownson, p. 191.

20. Gene Summers and Werner Blaser, *Gene Summers Art/Architecture* (Basel: Birkhäuser Verlag, 2003), p. 16.

21. See Oral History of Gene Summers, p. 76ff., for a full account of this transition.

22. Summers's building covers one-third more area than the original, and has twice the space under roof.

23. Beginning with the cover story of the October 1969 issue of *Architectural Record*.

24. George Schipporeit, interview with Windhorst, 2007.

APPENDIX B

1. Drexler was in error; there are no Mies-designed mullions at Promontory.

2. Arthur Drexler, personal communication with Schulze, 1981.

3. "A Prototype of the New German Architecture," *Arts and Decoration* (April 1911): 272.

4. Cited in Fritz Neumeyer, *The Artless Word: Mies van der Rohe on the Building Art*, trans. Mark Jarzombek (German edition, 1986; Cambridge, MA: MIT Press, 1991), p. 76. Westheim's article is "Mies van der Rohe: Entwicklung eines Architekten," *Das Kunstblatt* 11, no. 2 (1927): 55–62; the quotation is from page 56 of the original German.

5. Blaser worked on his monograph in editorial collaboration with the architect and with the assistance of Mies's staff, members of which made new drawings of Mies's European work, ostensibly with Mies's oversight. Wolf Tegethoff, among others, has noted inaccuracies in some of these new drawings (see Tegethoff's discussion of Blaser's 1964 drawings of the Brick Country House in *Mies van der Rohe: The Villas and Country Houses* [New York: Museum of Modern Art, 1985], pp. 42–44). Blaser portrayed Mies as a structural expressionist *par excellence*, but to a fault ignored other key aspects of Mies's art.

6. Lewis Mumford, *The Highway and the City: Essays* (New York: Harcourt, Brace and World, 1963), p. 167.

7. David Watkin, *Morality and Architecture* (Oxford: Clarendon Press, 1977), p. 37.

8. Charles Jencks, *Modern Movements in Architecture* (London: Penguin, 1985), p. 95.

9. Martin Filler, "Mies and the Mastodon," *New Republic*, August 6, 2001. Online at www.tnr.com/print/articles/mies-and-the-mastodon, p. 4.

10. Ibid., p. 7.

11. Martin Filler, *Makers of Modern Architecture: From Frank Lloyd Wright to Frank Gehry* (New York: New York Review of Books, 2007), p. 68.

Bibliographic Afterword

The most important way to study Mies—a method he would surely have endorsed—is to examine his buildings. Except for some of the early work, almost all are extant. To understand them, however, context is essential; we offer here a shortlist of the literature on Mies that we regard as the most important thus far published:

Philip C. Johnson. *Mies van der Rohe*. Museum of Modern Art, New York, 1947. Second edition 1953, third edition 1975. The first serious study of Mies's career in any language.

Ludwig Hilberseimer. *Mies van der Rohe*. Paul Theobald, Chicago, 1956. The first book to probe Mies's expressive objectives in detail, written by a professional colleague and personal friend intimately close to Mies, in Germany and Chicago, for over thirty years.

Ludwig Glaeser. *Ludwig Mies van der Rohe: Furniture and Furniture Drawings from the Design Collection and the Mies van der Rohe Archive*. The Museum of Modern Art, New York, 1977. The most authoritative examination of Mies's furniture.

Wolf Tegethoff. *Mies van der Rohe: Die Villen und Landhausprojekte*. R. Bacht, Essen, Germany, 1981. English translation: Mies van der Rohe: The Villas and Country Houses. Museum of Modern Art, New York, 1985. Exhaustive, precise and elegant, Tegethoff's book, which covers 1923 to 1950, is arguably the finest single work of Miesian scholarship.

Fritz Neumeyer. *Mies van der Rohe: Das kunstlose Wort; Gedanken zur Baukunst*. Siedler Verlag, Berlin, 1986. English translation: The Artless Word: Mies van der Rohe on the Building Art. MIT Press, Cambridge, Massachusetts, 1991. Neumeyer offers a full-scale interpretive history of the philosophical background of the architect's thought, and reprints and comments on nearly all of Mies's writings, from handwritten notes to published statements.

Terence Riley and Barry Bergdoll, editors. *Mies in Berlin*, an exhibition catalog with essays by Lampugnani, Mertins, Tegethoff, Neumeyer, Maruhn, Lepik, Miller, Bletter, and Cohen. Museum of Modern Art, New York, 2001. This is the most comprehensive (and sumptuously produced) coverage thus far of Mies's career in Germany. The essays vary in quality, but each is informative and trustworthy, and some masterly.

Phyllis Lambert, editor. *Mies in America*. A huge and lavishly illustrated exhibition catalog with essays by Oechslin, Barnett, McAtee, Lambert, Mertins, Whiting, Hays, Eisenman, and Koolhaas. Harry N. Abrams, New York, 2001.

Index

Page numbers in italics indicate captions.